The Courts, Social Science, and School Desegregation

The Courts, Social Science, and School Desegregation

Edited by
Betsy Levin and Willis D. Hawley

Transaction Books
New Brunswick, New Jersey

Library of Congress Catalog Number: 76-3217.
ISBN: 0-87855-150-6.
Printed in the United States of America.

Library of Congress Cataloging in Publication Data
Main entry under title:

The Courts, social science, and school desegregation.
Originally appeared in Law and contemporary problems, v. 39, no. 1-2, 1975.
1. Segregation in Education—Law and legislation—United States—Addresses, essays, lectures.
2. School integration—United States—Addresses, essays, lectures. I. Levin, Betsy. II. Hawley, Willis D. III. Law and contemporary problems.
KF4155.A2C63 344l.73'0798 76-3217
ISBN 0-87855-150-6

CONTENTS

THE LEGAL BACKDROP

NEIGHBORHOOD SCHOOLS AND BUSING

EFFECTS OF SCHOOL DESEGREGATION: WHAT SOCIAL SCIENCE RESEARCH DOES AND DOESN'T TELL US

SOME PRACTICAL PROBLEMS IN DESEGREGATION AND SOME ALTERNATIVES

REFLECTION

FOREWORD

Since *Brown v. Board of Education*[1] was decided in 1954, social science research findings have continued to play a role in school desegregation litigation. The legal issue in *Brown* seemed simple: whether segregated schooling solely on the basis of race, pursuant to state laws requiring—or at least permitting—such segregation, denies minority children the equal protection of the laws[2] even though the segregated public schools are equal in terms of physical facilities, resources, and other tangible factors.[3] But efforts to implement the decision and to extend it to school segregation in the North have revealed not a single issue, but many diverse and complex underlying issues.[4] As the legal issues have become more complex, sociologists, psychologists, economists, demographers, educators, and other social scientists have been making more frequent court appearances as expert witnesses, often introducing ambiguous and contradictory research findings, making it difficult to apply such evidence to the resolution of these issues.

At some point in the early 1960s, school desegregation began to be defended or justified by scholars and others on a very narrow basis—that deseg-

1. 347 U.S. 483 (1954).

2. "No state shall . . . deny to any person within its jurisdiction the equal protection of the laws." U.S. CONST. amend. XIV, §1.

3. 347 U.S. at 492-93.

4. Some illustrative examples of the kinds of issues which the courts confront today are the following: whether the actions of school officials that *result* in segregation in jurisdictions where, unlike the South, there were no state laws requiring segregated schooling, are in violation of the fourteenth amendment; whether the actions of other governmental agencies that result in segregation—such as the adoption of exclusionary zoning policies and the location and construction of public housing projects in certain areas and not in others—is a violation; whether segregation resulting solely from residential patterns imposes an affirmative duty upon school officials to redress the racial imbalance; whether busing to overcome racial imbalance is a valid constitutional tool and, if so, what are the limits to the use of that remedy; whether the usual equitable remedial powers of the district court are limited by the extent of the violation, even if such limits mean a pro forma decree which will have no effect on the segregated schooling of the inner cities; whether school officials, once the system has been desegregated, are responsible for the racial imbalance that occurs through natural shifts in residential patterns; whether minorities who, given a truly free choice between a segregated, community controlled school and integrated schools, may constitutionally choose the former; whether the use of otherwise educationally valid tools—such as ability grouping, tracking, special classes for the handicapped—are constitutionally permissible if the effect is segregated classrooms even though the school building is integrated.

regation would improve the achievement test scores of black students. The argument is as follows: minority segregated schools are inherently inferior (little was said about the harm to whites of attending segregated schools)[5] and as a result, minority children were being held back both educationally and economically.

If blacks were given an "equal educational opportunity"—*i.e.*, by assigning black students to a desegregated school—the achievement gap between white and black students would be eliminated as would, ultimately, the gap in educational and economic attainment between white and black adults. This "myth"—that equal educational opportunity would resolve all the social and economic ills of the nation,[6] as well as bring about racial justice—collided sharply with the social science research of the late 1960's and early 1970's, and disillusionment set in.

The *Coleman Report*,[7] published in 1966, indicated that the major factor affecting pupil performance was the home environment, and that differences in school resources explained very little of the differences in pupil performance. In the early 1970's, the writings of such academics as Arthur Jensen and Richard Herrnstein on the effect of race or class, environment, and IQ on educational outcomes[8] were widely disseminated. They concluded from their analysis of the data that the gap in IQ between blacks and whites explained most of the gap in achievement scores, and that environment played only a small role. Finally, Christopher Jencks' book on the effects of family and schooling,[9] which argued that schooling has little effect on a student's life chances, further undermined confidence that racial justice could be secured through desegregation of the schools. The simplistic faith that merely reassigning bodies to different schools would bring about equality was shattered, with a profoundly unsettling effect not only on education, but on the law.

There are a number of questions about the relationships between social science and the judicial response to school segregation for which there are now no ready answers. What are the legal issues confronting courts today, and which of these issues rely in part on, or can be illumined by, social science research? On which issues is there agreement among social scientists—and on which, disagreement—as to the research findings and the conclusions to be

---

5. *See Hearings on Equality of Educational Opportunity Before the Senate Select Comm. on Equal Educational Opportunity,* 91st Cong., 2d Sess., pt. 1a, at 73 (1970); Hart v. Community School Bd., 383 F. Supp. 699, 740 (E.D.N.Y. 1974).

6. The preamble of the Elementary and Secondary Education Act of 1965, Act of Apr. 11, 1965, Pub. L. No. 89-10, 79 Stat. 27, and the Presidential message accompanying the bill when it was introduced, 1 U.S. CODE CONG. & ADM. NEWS 1448-50 (1965), clearly reflect this belief.

7. J. COLEMAN, EQUAL EDUCATIONAL OPPORTUNITY (1966).

8. *See* Jensen, *How Much Can We Boost IQ and Scholastic Achievement*, 39 HARV. ED. REV. 1 (Winter 1969); R. HERRNSTEIN, I.Q. IN THE MERITOCRACY (1973).

9. C. JENCKS, INEQUALITY: A REASSESSMENT OF THE EFFECT OF FAMILY AND SCHOOLING IN AMERICA (1972).

drawn from those findings? What further research is needed before valid conclusions can be drawn? And broader, more normative questions can also be asked: what role *should* social science play in school desegregation litigation and is the adversary process the appropriate way of dealing with controversial social science issues? Since few judges or lawyers are familiar with the language and methodology of social science, a real possibility exists that substantial misinterpretation and overstatement will accompany the increasing use of social science evidence in the courts. Overgeneralizations—both in the courtroom and in the current debate over desegregation among academics and among the public at large—have been made on the basis of data from small, local studies, perhaps unique as to the circumstances in that particular community; many of these studies were also based on data collected only during the first transitional year of desegregation. It is particularly important that attorneys understand the nature of social science evidence *and its limitations*, as upon them falls the duty of making it understandable to the courts. To quote Judge J. Skelly Wright in a case involving economists as expert witnesses on behalf of both of the parties in the litigation:[10]

> [L]awyers . . . [have] a basic responsibility . . . to put the hard core statistical demonstrations into language which serious and concerned laymen could, with effort, understand.

Given the significance of the subject, it seemed especially appropriate, during the twentieth anniversary of the *Brown* decision, to bring together a number of the nation's leading social scientists and lawyers who are currently engaged in school desegregation litigation or in research on various aspects of school desegregation to explore questions such as these. Consequently, in August 1974, a Conference was convened in South Carolina, its objective being

---

10. The full quotation from Judge Wright's opinion in *Hobson v. Hansen,* reads as follows:
[T]he unfortunate if inevitable tendency has been to lose sight of the disadvantaged young students on whose behalf this suit was first brought in an overgrown garden of numbers and charts and jargon like "standard deviation of the variable," statistical "significance," and "Pearson product moment correlations." The reports by the experts—one noted economist plus assistants for each side—are less helpful than they might have been for the simple reason that they do not begin from a common data base, disagree over crucial statistical assumptions, and reach different conclusions. Having hired their respective experts, the lawyers in this case had a basic responsibility, which they have not completely met, to put the hard core statistical demonstrations into language which serious and concerned laymen could, with effort, understand. Moreover, the studies by both experts are tainted by a vice well known in the statistical trade—data shopping and scanning to reach a preconceived result; and the court has had to reject parts of both reports as unreliable because biased. Lest like a latter day version of Jarndyce v. Jarndyce this litigation itself should consume the capital of the children in whose behalf it was brought, the court has been forced back to its own common sense approach to a problem which, though admittedly complex, has certainly been made more obscure than was necessary. The conclusion I reach is based upon burden of proof, and upon straightforward moral and constitutional arithmetic.
Hobson v. Hansen, 327 F. Supp. 844, 859 (D.D.C. 1971).

the clarification of how social science research has been used—and possibly misused—in school desegregation litigation.

The Conference attempted to identify (1) what existing social science research tells us about the conditions, if any, that maximize the probability that various objectives of school desegregation can be obtained; (2) what are the current social, psychological, and educational consequences of school desegregation; and (3) which directions might future litigation and research on school desegregation take. The debate over the effects of desegregation and the use of busing as a tool to implement the command of *Brown* has tended to obscure the fact that there is substantial agreement on certain aspects regarding the educational effect of desegregation. The objective of the Conference was to highlight this agreement as well as to explore the areas of disagreement and uncertainty, and the nature—both substantive and methodological—of the research needed to respond to questions for which at present there are no adequate empirical answers.

While few of us are without our preferences with respect to the desirability of desegregation, the Conference was not intended to advocate or support any particular course of action or set of policies. Nor was the Conference to be another forum in which to debate *Brown* and footnote eleven, or even to debate whether segregation is harmful per se. Rather, given the Supreme Court's command that school districts desegregate *now*[11] and the increasing involvement of lower courts in drawing school desegregation plans, the focus was on determining the most effective way to make school desegregation work, what social science tells us in this regard, and when is it appropriate—or inappropriate—for courts to intervene in what may appear to be educational policy.

The Conference participants, listed on page 427, were selected after asking dozens of scholars and policy makers to identify the outstanding social scientists and lawyers dealing with issues related to school desegregation. Naturally, not everyone agreed on every name, but the degree of consensus that emerged was remarkable. Working sessions were devoted to the following topics: Effects of School Desegregation on Achievement and Life Chances, Effects of School Desegregation on Personality and Attitudes, Factors in Securing School Desegregation, Integration Within the School and the Classroom, Interdistrict Remedies After *Milliken v. Bradley*, and The Relevance of Social Science Research in Preparing School Desegregation Plans. Each session began with prepared presentations that had been solicited in advance, and was followed by intense and extensive discussion periods.

This symposium issue is the product of that Conference. In order to put the symposium's articles in context, Frank T. Read has traced the judicial evolution of the law of school desegregation from *Brown* to *Milliken*. Professor Read's

---

11. *See* Carter v. West Feliciana Parish School Bd., 396 U.S. 290 (1970); Alexander v. Holmes County Bd. of Educ., 396 U.S. 19 (1969); Green v. County School Bd., 391 U.S. 430 (1968).

article is followed by an article by Betsy Levin and Philip Moise that attempts to set out the legal issues with which courts are concerned today in dealing with school desegregation cases and the extent to which social science has been brought to bear on the resolution of these issues.

In addition to articles from lawyers and social scientists, "comments" were solicited from several of the federal judges who frequently have before them seemingly intractable school desegregation cases. J. Braxton Craven, United States Circuit Judge on the Court of Appeals for the Fourth Circuit and author of that court's opinion in *Bradley v. School Board of City of Richmond*,[12] and James B. McMillan, United States District Judge for the District Court of the Western District of North Carolina and author of the opinion in *Swann v. Charlotte-Mecklenburg Board of Education*,[13] have joined John Minor Wisdom, United States Circuit Judge on the Court of Appeals for the Fifth Circuit, in presenting their views regarding the role that social science plays in the judicial decision-making process. Judge Wisdom's article was originally presented as the keynote address marking the opening of the Conference and it sets the tone for what is to follow.

The relationship of residential segregation—and the use of a neighborhood schools policy—to school segregation is analyzed by Reynolds Farley, followed by Owen M. Fiss's exploration of the most explosive issue in school desegregation today—the use of busing to counteract the results of residential segregation, and the degree to which its social costs ought to be weighed against the constitutional injury it purports to remedy.

Social scientists frequently assert that "facts" must be separated from "value judgments," implying that social science is objective, "scientific" truth. Henry M. Levin argues that this is not true, the problem being that the researcher himself, and certainly those outside the discipline—lawyers and judges particularly—fail to see the bias inherent in his selection of what to study, the way in which he develops his hypotheses, and in his analysis of the data and inclusion or exclusion of various factors. Others, such as Elizabeth G. Cohen, reiterate this view.

Several articles attempt to answer the questions raised at the Conference about the extent to which existing social science research can identify the social, psychological, and educational consequences of desegregation. Meyer Weinberg reviews the impact of desegregation on achievement, Elizabeth Cohen on racial attitudes, and Edgar G. Epps on aspirations, self-concepts, and other aspects of personality.

Gary Orfield's article distinguishes between desegregation that comes from merely reassigning students to different schools and effective integration. He suggests that the latter is a much longer process than the courts, the federal

12. 462 F.2d 1058 (4th Cir. 1972), *aff'd by an equally divided Court*, 412 U.S. 92 (1973).

13. 311 F. Supp. 265 (W.D.N.C.), *rev'd in part*, 431 F.2d 138 (4th Cir. 1970), *district court opinion reinstated*, 402 U.S. 1 (1971).

government, and social scientists have seemed to assume, and that its success depends on the presence of certain factors within the schools, such as the attitudes and abilities of principals and the adaptation of the curriculum to meet the needs of the changing student body. He suggests that, used creatively, the process of desegregation can lead to significant educational reforms that will have a positive effect on *all* children.

In view of the increasing political barriers to complete integration, and the fact that many blacks—particularly those in the inner cities in the North—are still waiting for *Brown*'s promise of equal educational opportunity to be fulfilled, Derrick A. Bell explores some alternatives to integration that he suggests can also bring about equal educational opportunity.

It is important to note that it is not only the extent to which social science has become intertwined with the legal issues of school desegregation that needs to be reassessed, but also the extent to which the courts—especially the federal district courts—are involved in school desegregation and even educational policy issues. Mark G. Yudof provides this reassessment of the role of courts in the context of suspension and expulsion decisions. Other such areas in which courts have become involved are tracking and ability grouping policies,[14] whether or not to "mainstream" mentally handicapped children,[15] and the provision of bilingual educational programs as part of the relief in school desegregation cases affecting Hispano-Americans.[16]

In the concluding article, Willis D. Hawley and Ray C. Rist outline the conditions that seem to affect the probability that various goals of desegregation might be attained. In the process, they highlight some of the significant questions to which further social science research should be addressed.

While the Conference and preparation of the articles for this symposium issue of *Law and Contemporary Problems* were supported by a grant from the Ford Foundation, none of the views expressed herein is necessarily endorsed by the Foundation.

The editors hope that the earnest effort to communicate within and across disciplines has resulted in a symposium that will be of interest not only to scholars of diverse disciplines but will also be a useful resource for the practitioners—the judges, attorneys, educators, legislators and other policy makers—who are currently struggling with the difficult issues involved in school desegregation.

BETSY LEVIN
WILLIS D. HAWLEY

---

14. *See, e.g.*, Hobson v. Hansen, 269 F. Supp. 401 (D.D.C. 1967), *aff'd sub nom.* Smuck v. Hansen, 408 F.2d 175 (D.C. Cir. 1969).

15. *See, e.g.*, Mills v. Board of Educ., 388 F. Supp. 866 (D.D.C. 1972).

16. *See, e.g.*, Serna v. Portales Municipal Schools, 351 F. Supp. 1279 (D.N.M. 1973), *aff'd*, 499 F.2d 1147 (10th Cir. 1974).

JUDICIAL EVOLUTION OF THE LAW OF SCHOOL INTEGRATION SINCE *BROWN V. BOARD OF EDUCATION**

FRANK T. READ†

INTRODUCTION

The frenetic pace and extent of change in race relations in the past twenty years has dimmed the memory of what it was to be a Negro citizen in the South in 1954. All public schools were segregated; public accommodations were segregated; only a minute percentage of registered voters were black; and black public office holders were virtually non-existent. Black families had less than one-half the median incomes of white families, and illiteracy rates were appallingly high. The black American in the South was a second class citizen. Furthermore, it appeared that he was destined to remain locked in that status by a myriad of state-imposed Jim Crow laws deliberately designed to perpetuate the segregation of the races and thus the disparity between black and white citizens.

Then, on May 17, 1954—"Black Monday" to segregationists—the United States Supreme Court decided *Brown v. Board of Education (Brown I)*,[1] unanimously holding that segregation of white and black children in state public schools, solely on the basis of race and pursuant to statutes permitting or requiring such segregation, denied to black children the equal protection of the laws guaranteed by the fourteenth amendment.[2] The *Brown* decision rocked the South, secured the fame (or infamy, in the opinion of some) of the Warren Court, and propelled the nation into the modern era of its on-going revolution in race relations.

This article will survey the evolution of public school desegregation law in the federal courts since *Brown I*. While the article is in many respects not only incomplete but also oversimplified, it should provide the reader with at

---

* This survey article is a severely truncated summary of portions of a study sponsored by the Ford Foundation under a grant (Grant No. 720-0093) to Duke University. The full study, entitled *Let Them Be Judged: The Judicial Integration of the Deep South*, is a review of the history of public school integration activity in the federal courts in the Fifth Circuit states of Alabama, Florida, Georgia, Louisiana, Mississippi, and Texas. As of the date of this publication, it is anticipated that the full study will be released in book form within twelve to eighteen months, co-authored by Professor Frank T. Read, formerly of the Duke University School of Law and Associate Professor Lucy McGough of the Emory University School of Law.

† Dean, University of Tulsa College of Law; Professor of Law, Duke University (1968-1974).

1. Brown v. Board of Educ., 347 U.S. 483 (1954).

2. "No State shall . . . deny to any person within its jurisdiction the equal protection of the laws." U.S. CONST. amend. XIV, § 1.

least the minimally sufficient legal backdrop necessary for an appreciation of the more substantive works that follow in this symposium issue.

I

The Two *Brown* Decisions: A Clarion Call

The decision in *Brown I* had been foreshadowed by several Supreme Court decisions involving institutions of higher education. These cases were bound by the dictates of *Plessy v. Ferguson,*[3] the 1896 case which declared constitutional a Louisiana statute requiring "separate but equal" public facilities for blacks and whites. However, these higher education cases established the principle that in determining whether the facilities were equal, a court could also consider whether *intangible* educational benefits were equally provided to both races. The litany of doom played for segregation at the college and professional school level by such cases as *Missouri* ex rel. *Gaines v. Canada,*[4] *Sipuel v. Board of Regents of the University of Oklahoma,*[5] and *Sweatt v. Painter*[6] should have been a warning that the apartheid structure of public school education in the South, so carefully nurtured since the Civil War, could not long survive further legal scrutiny.

A. *Brown I*: What Did the Supreme Court Actually Hold?

Four separate cases from the states of Kansas, South Carolina, Virginia, and Delaware were consolidated for argument in *Brown I.* In each of the four cases the plaintiff black children sought the aid of the federal courts in obtaining admission to the public schools of their community on a non-segregated basis. In each case, except the Delaware case, a three-judge district court had refused their requests on the basis of the "separate but equal" doctrine of *Plessy v. Ferguson.* On direct appeal to the Supreme Court, Chief Justice Warren, speaking for a unanimous Court, phrased the legal issue to be decided: "Does segregation of children in public schools solely on the basis of race, even though the physical facilities and other 'tangible' factors may be equal, deprive the children of the minority group of equal educational opportunities?"[7] The Court answered that question in the affirma-

3. 163 U.S. 537 (1896).

4. 305 U.S. 337 (1938) (holding that a Missouri law providing tuition grants to its Negro residents for a legal education out-of-state did not satisfy the state's obligation to provide equivalent educational opportunity).

5. 332 U.S. 631 (1948) (holding that a Negro applicant had to be admitted to the University of Oklahoma School of Law even though the state legislature had ordered the establishment of a separate law school within the state for Negroes).

6. 339 U.S. 629 (1949) (holding that a separate law school established in Texas for Negroes did not satisfy the "separate but equal" requirement of *Plessy v. Ferguson,* and that a Negro applicant was therefore entitled to admission to the University of Texas Law School).

7. 347 U.S. at 493.

tive. In a much quoted paragraph, the Supreme Court interpreted the equal protection clause of the fourteenth amendment as flatly prohibiting state-imposed segregation of the races in the public schools: "We conclude that in the field of public education the doctrine of 'separate but equal' has no place. Separate educational facilities are inherently unequal."[8]

In holding that the equal protection clause prohibited state-imposed segregation of the races in public schools, the Supreme Court took judicial notice of the fact that separation of Negro children, solely because of their race, "generates a feeling of inferiority as to their status in the community that may affect their hearts and minds in a way unlikely ever to be undone."[9] In its now-famous footnote eleven, the *Brown I* opinion cited the findings of several prominent social scientists, including Kenneth B. Clark and Gunnar Myrdal, as "modern authority" which "amply supported" the finding that segregation was damaging to black children.[10] That footnote constituted a source of irritation for many jurists and fueled the segregationists' fires ignited by the Supreme Court's new ruling; they erroneously read footnote eleven as an essential underpinning to the Court's holding. In fact, the opinion in *Brown I* is, at its essence, a straight-forward legal interpretation of the equal protection clause, recognizing that state-required segregation by race is an invidious classification, and for that reason unconstitutional. *Brown I* is supportable without citation to the works of the footnote eleven social scientists.[11]

Having decided that the states must provide educational opportunities to all on equal terms, the Supreme Court then faced the immense problem of implementing its decision. Proceeding cautiously, the Court ordered the parties to prepare for a reargument of the case at the next term, and, at that reargument, to focus their attention on the problem of implementation.

B. *Brown II*

On May 31, 1955 (one full year after *Brown I*), *Brown II*, the implementation decision, was handed down—again by a unanimous Court.[12] Sensing the enormous impact of their decision in *Brown I*, the Supreme Court Justices

---

8. 347 U.S. at 495.
9. 347 U.S. at 494.
10. 347 U.S. at 494-95 n.11.
11. See the discussion by Judge John Minor Wisdom in United States v. Jefferson County Bd. of Educ., 372 F.2d 836, 871 n.75 (5th Cir. 1966), and Comment, *HEW Guidelines Constitutionally Require School Boards to Affirmatively Abolish the Existing Effects of De Jure Segregation*, 21 RUTGERS L. REV. 753, 759-63 (1967). *See also* T. EMERSON, D. HABER, & N. DORSEN, POLITICAL AND CIVIL RIGHTS 1625-29 (3d ed. 1967); Fiss, *Racial Imbalance in the Public Schools: The Constitutional Concepts*, 78 HARV. L. REV. 564, 590-98 (1965); Kaplan, *Segregation Litigation and the Schools—Part I: The New Rochelle Experience*, 58 NW. U.L. REV. 1, 21 (1963); Pollak, *Racial Discrimination and Judicial Integrity: A Reply to Professor Wechsler*, 108 U. PA. L. REV. 1 (1959); Wechsler, *Toward Neutral Principles of Constitutional Law*, 73 HARV. L. REV. 1 (1959).
12. Brown v. Board of Educ., 349 U.S. 294 (1955).

proceeded gingerly in *Brown II*. Put simply, in *Brown II* the Court remanded the combined cases of *Brown I* to the federal district courts wherein the cases had originated to take steps consistent with the opinion in *Brown I*. The Supreme Court made several noteworthy points, however, to guide its lower federal courts:

1. Local school authorities have the primary responsibility for implementation.[13]
2. The function of the federal court is to decide whether a local school board's response constitutes good faith implementation.[14]
3. The district court is to be guided by equitable principles "characterized by practical flexibility" in shaping remedies, with the pointed reminder that the principle of equal educational opportunity espoused in *Brown I* is not to yield simply because of disagreement with that principle.[15]
4. Although the district court should take into account the practical problems of implementation, the local school authorities must make a "prompt and reasonable start," and thereafter the court should insure that desegregation proceeds "with all deliberate speed."[16]

In retrospect the Supreme Court's heavy reliance on local school authorities and federal district court judges seems to have been misplaced; and this misplaced confidence exerted enormous influence on the course of desegregation, especially in the early years following *Brown II*.

II

Implementation of the *Brown I* Mandate

A discussion of the implementation of the *Brown I* mandate by the federal courts in the twenty years that have passed since that landmark holding can perhaps best be divided into four historical periods. The first period covers the time frame between *Brown II* in 1955 and the James Meredith affair in 1963. It is characterized by a series of pitched judicial battles over token desegregation. The second period, covering the years between 1963 and 1967, is typified by the struggles of the lower federal courts, without Supreme Court guidance, to evolve desegregation standards and to break down entrenched local resistance. The third period, from 1968 through 1972, is the period of judicial revolution in the Deep South; federal courts, stung by Supreme Court impatience, issued decrees mandating massive

13. *Id.* at 299.
14. *Id.*
15. 349 U.S. at 300.
16. 349 U.S. at 300-01.

integration. The fourth period, from the Supreme Court's holding in *Swann v. Charlotte-Mecklenburg Board of Education*[17] in 1971 to date, is characterized by confusion over the future of integration, attempts to move integration activity from the South to the ghettos and barrios of the East and West, and litigation over a host of second-generation integration problems. Each of the four great integration periods will be discussed in order.

A. The Muted Response to *Brown I*: 1955-1963

1. *The Public*

While there was an intense, immediate reaction to *Brown I* among white southerners and America's black population, the rest of the nation looked on from the sidelines, more concerned about other matters. America was emerging from the aftermath of the police action in Korea; the Army-McCarthy hearings were getting under way; and the disastrous French experience in Indochina was grinding to an end in the ruins of Dien Bien Phu.

To black Americans, *Brown v. Board of Education* signaled the start of a rising tide of hope. It fueled the spirit of a civil rights movement that was to reach its zenith in the early and mid-sixties. To white southerners the decision on Black Monday was received by most with deep resentment or bitter anger, by some with quiet resignation, and by very few with rejoicing. Most southern editorial writers vowed an eternal fight to preserve the southern way of life and prevent the mongrelization of the races. Segregationist organizations flourished: moribund Ku Klux Klan Klaverns gained new life and White Citizens' Councils mushroomed. Opposition leaders were encouraged by strong statements of southern Congressmen vowing to fight to the finish for segregation,[18] and by the deafening silence from the White House, where President Eisenhower refused to make any public comment on the Supreme Court decision and was rumored to be personally opposed to school integration. Although there were some faint indications that the

17. 402 U.S. 1 (1971).

18. On March 12, 1956, ninety-six southern Congressmen issued the "Southern Manifesto." It denounced the school desegregation decisions as a "clear abuse of judicial power [which] climaxes a trend in the Federal judiciary undertaking to legislate in derogation of the authority of Congress and to encroach upon the reserved rights of the states and the people." R. SARRATT, THE ORDEAL OF DESEGREGATION 41 (1966). This much heralded pro-segregation white paper did more than simply champion the doctrine of interposition and "states rights" defenses; psychologically, it lent the patina of moral rectitude to resistance. The signatories, including almost all elected representatives in the southern states, pledged to use "all lawful means" to maintain segregation and "commended those states which have declared their intention to resist." J. PELTASON, FIFTY-EIGHT LONELY MEN 41-42 (1961). In the more colorful vernacular of the southern politician "down home," Georgia's Congressman Jack Flynt termed the Supreme Court's desegregation mandate "a hydraheaded, five-fanged, cloven-hooved, and fork-tailed combination of polecat, dog, and rattlesnake." 47 NEWSWEEK, Feb. 6, 1956, at 25-26.

South might acquiesce in the *Brown* decision,[19] months passed without any noticeable progress in implementation.

Parallel with the growth of overt white resistance was the gradual, but perceptible, change in Negro attitudes from passivity to organization to activism. The success of concerted Negro economic action, which began in Montgomery, Alabama, one December afternoon in 1955 with the refusal of Mrs. Rosa Parks to take the accustomed seat in the back of the bus,[20] was contagious and quickly spread to the younger generation of southern Negroes. The Negro sit-in movement began quite innocuously in Greensboro, North Carolina, in February, 1960, when four black freshmen at a state Negro college requested and were refused service at a dime-store lunch counter.[21] However, despite the growth and viability of the civil rights movement, if implementation of school integration was to occur, it was clear that it would have to be accomplished through the federal judiciary, the weakest of the three governmental branches, since Congress was controlled by southern committee chairmen and paralyzed by threats of southern filibusters, while the President remained silently aloof.

2. *The Courts*

The federal courts in the South, staffed for the most part with native white southerners, were encamped after 1954 in a no-man's land; the litigants in desegregation cases were rarely satisfied by these courts' decisions, no matter what was ordered. For the Negroes, the crucial word in the *Brown* mandate was "speed," while the southern school boards accentuated "deliberate." Furthermore, federal district judges began their quest for desegregation with very little guidance from the Supreme Court (and, for the most part, with little stomach for the battles ahead). Although the second *Brown* decision in 1955 listed specific factors of adjustment which were to be considered by local school boards, the only direction given reviewing federal courts was the nebulous observation that these cases "call for the exercise of the traditional attributes of equity power."[22] The pace of desegregation was apparently to be determined on a case-by-case basis by striking a balance between individual and community interests. The United States Supreme Court did not speak again in amplification of this cryptic mandate until four

---

19. The day after the decision, the Greensboro, North Carolina, Board of Education publicly pledged that it would obey the law. *See* Greensboro Daily News, May 19, 1954, at 1, col. 7.

20. 47 Newsweek, Mar. 5, 1956, at 24; R. Sarratt, *supra* note 18, at 323. Under the leadership of young Martin Luther King, Jr., an estimated 95 per cent of the Negroes in Montgomery honored the boycott and quit riding the buses. As approximately 65 per cent of the transit company's patrons were Negro passengers, fares had to be raised from 10 cents to 15 cents in an effort to stave off economic ruin. 47 Newsweek, Mar. 5, 1956, at 24-25.

21. R. Sarratt, *supra* note 18, at 327.

22. 349 U.S. at 305.

years later,[23] and thereafter it only rarely intervened in the evolution of desegregation litigation.

The most important early decision after *Brown II* occurred in one of the original five school segregation cases remanded to a federal district court for implementation. That case was *Briggs v. Elliott*.[24] There a three-judge federal district court in South Carolina very narrowly interpreted the *Brown II* decision:[25]

> [I]t is important that we point out exactly what the Supreme Court has decided and what it has not decided in this case. It has not decided that the federal courts are to take over or regulate the public schools of the states. It has not decided that the states must mix persons of different races in the schools or must require them to attend schools or must deprive them of the right of choosing the schools they attend. What it has decided, and all that it has decided, is that a state may not deny to any person on account of race the right to attend any school that it maintains. . . . Nothing in the Constitution or in the decision of the Supreme Court takes away from the people freedom to choose the schools they attend. *The Constitution, in other words, does not require integration. It merely forbids discrimination.*

The *Briggs* case was a major stumbling block to the development of desegregation law after *Brown II* until it was finally repudiated in 1966 in light of the subsequent evolution of desegregation implementation.[26] The two most famous sentences of *Briggs* (the italicized portion in the quotation above) became known as the "*Briggs v. Elliott* dictum" and were shortened even further to the shibboleth "desegregation not integration." Most federal court judges were convinced, in the early years following *Brown II*, that the two words—"integration" and "desegregation"—were in fact descriptive of two concepts that could be differentiated. Unfortunately the *Briggs* decision, including its famous dictum, was not appealed and, therefore, the Supreme Court was not afforded the opportunity of either approving or disapproving the *Briggs* interpretation of its holding in *Brown II*.

3. *Delays and Obstruction*

Hampered by adoption of the *Briggs* interpretation of *Brown II* and faced in many areas of the South with massive resistance to even the idea of token desegregation, the federal courts accomplished little in the way of integration in the South in the early years after 1955. While significant desegrega-

---

23. Cooper v. Aaron, 358 U.S. 1 (1958).

24. 132 F. Supp. 776 (E.D.S.C. 1955) (three-judge court).

25. *Id.* at 777 (emphasis added).

26. The Fifth Circuit, for example, adopted the *Briggs* rationale in Avery v. Wichita Falls Independent School Dist., 241 F.2d 230, 233-34 (5th Cir. 1957). It was not until 1965 that it rescinded its approval of *Briggs* in Singleton v. Jackson Municipal Separate School Dist., 348 F.2d 729 (5th Cir. 1965). *Briggs* was finally destroyed in the carefully reasoned opinion of Judge John Minor Wisdom in United States v. Jefferson County Bd. of Educ., 372 F.2d 836 (5th Cir. 1966).

tion did occur voluntarily or with a minimum of resistance in some border states, in the eleven states of the Confederacy school integration cases became mired in delaying tactics and obstructionism at the federal district court level.

The incredibly difficult and complex legal battles that developed provided the incentive for the courts to devise and refine equitable remedies to adequately cope with the ingenuity of die-hard segregationists. The use of the temporary restraining order, the injunction pending appeal, and the ultimate threat of contempt citations became much-used tools in the struggle to realize the promise of *Brown I*.

The State of Texas best typifies the various reactions to *Brown II* in the early years after 1955. There was voluntary desegregation in much of West Texas,[27] organized opposition groups in East Texas that attempted to rally public support to block desegregation,[28] bitterly contested litigation and court ordered desegregation in Dallas[29] and Houston,[30] and mob violence in Mansfield, Texas.[31]

In stark contrast to the grudging, though peaceful, acceptance of the inevitable progress of desegregation in Dallas and Houston stands the record in New Orleans. The New Orleans litigation is, complete unto itself, an encyclopedia of every tactic of resistance ever employed by all other states combined. Over the relatively short span of time between 1952 and 1962, that one case consumed thousands of hours of lawyers' and judges' time: it required forty-one separate judicial decisions involving ultimately the energies of every Fifth Circuit judge, two district court judges, and the consideration of the United States Supreme Court on eleven separate decisions.[32] By the end of the decade, backed by the Fifth Circuit and in the face

27. At least sixty Texas school boards (primarily in West Texas where the Negro population was low) voluntarily decided to open with biracial classes at the beginning of the school term in the fall of 1955. SOUTHERN SCHOOL NEWS, Sept. 1955, at 9.

28. For example, in a referendum taken during the Democratic primary elections of July, 1956, Texas voters indicated by a margin of 3.5 to 1 that they favored continued segregation of public schools. SOUTHERN SCHOOL NEWS, Aug. 1956, at 14.

29. The Dallas litigation was a wearying process that involved six years, twelve court hearings, and the energies of eighteen different judges, including the members of the Supreme Court in their consideration of the writ of certiorari, and yet managed to achieve only token desegregation. The full chain of decisions in the Dallas litigation is as follows: Bell v. Rippy, 133 F. Supp. 811 (N.D. Tex. 1955), *rev'd sub nom.* Brown v. Rippy, 233 F.2d 796 (5th Cir.), *cert. denied,* 352 U.S. 878 (1956); Bell v. Rippy, 146 F. Supp. 485 (N.D. Tex. 1956), *rev'd sub nom.* Borders v. Rippy, 247 F.2d 268 (5th Cir. 1957); Dallas Independent School Dist. v. Edgar, 255 F.2d 455 (5th Cir. 1958); Boson v. Rippy, 275 F.2d 850 (5th Cir. 1960); Boson v. Rippy, 285 F.2d 43 (5th Cir. 1960).

30. The Houston litigation, adroitly handled behind the scenes by Federal Judge Ben C. Connally, surfaced only once in the reported decisions; but even *token* desegregation was not accomplished until 1961.

31. For a description of the difficulties in Mansfield, see J. PELTASON, *supra* note 18, at 144-46.

32. Following is a complete list of reported decisions in *Bush v. Orleans Parish School Bd.*, from its inception through 1962: 138 F. Supp. 336 (E.D. La.) (three-judge court), *motion for leave to file petition for writ of mandamus denied,* 351 U.S. 948 (1956); 138 F. Supp. 337 (E.D. La.

of attacks from all flanks, Federal District Judges J. Skelly Wright and Herbert Christenberry had invalidated a total of forty-four statutes enacted by the Louisiana legislature; had cited and convicted two state officials for contempt of court; and had issued injunctions forbidding the continued flouting of their orders against a state court, all state executives, and the entire membership of the Louisiana legislature. By 1963, both the federal district court in New Orleans and to a lesser extent the United States Court of Appeals for the Fifth Circuit had triumphed in their legal struggle with the State of Louisiana, though some may wonder if it were not a hollow victory. When measured by the pitifully few black children actually integrated, the battle hardly seems worth the price, but before integration could commence in earnest, token desegregation had first to be achieved.[33]

The New Orleans strife is significant not only because the federal courts fully manifested their flexibility, resiliency, and enduring vitality in crisis, but also because the course of action to be taken by other states of the Deep South hung in the balance. Southerners bent on opposition watched with flagging hopes as, one by one, Louisiana legislative strategems were nullified by the courts. Most importantly, however, it tested the strength of the linchpin of the Constitution: the supremacy of federal law. In the final outcome, the federal courts survived and the Supreme Court's mandate was enforced in Louisiana.

4. *Catalysts for Action*

Two important events of this period firmed the resolve of the federal courts and nudged them into the second period of desegregation adjudication: the attempt by Governor Faubus of Arkansas in 1957 to block the token desegregation of Central High School in Little Rock, Arkansas; and the matriculation of James Meredith to the University of Mississippi in 1962. In the mind of every southern federal judge those events etched an indelible impression of the absolute intransigence of some state authorities and the necessity to rely, however reluctantly, on the ultimate might of the executive branch of the federal government to enforce their mandates.

1956), *aff'd*, 242 F.2d 156 (5th Cir. 1957), *cert. denied*, 354 U.S. 921 (1957); 252 F.2d 253 (5th Cir.), *cert. denied*, 356 U.S. 969 (1958); 163 F. Supp. 701 (E.D. La. 1958), *aff'd*, 268 F.2d 78 (5th Cir. 1959); 187 F. Supp. 42 (E.D. La.) (three-judge court), *motion for stay denied*, 364 U.S. 803 (1960), *aff'd*, 365 U.S. 569 (1961); 188 F. Supp. 916 (E.D. La.) (three-judge court), *motion for stay denied*, 364 U.S. 500 (1960), *aff'd*, 365 U.S. 569 (1961); 190 F. Supp. 861 (E.D. La. 1960) (three-judge court), *aff'd*, 366 U.S. 212 (1961); 191 F. Supp. 871 (E.D. La.) (three-judge court), *aff'd sub nom.* Denny v. Bush 367 U.S. 908 (1961); 194 F. Supp. 182 (E.D. La.) (three-judge court), *aff'd sub nom.* Tugwell v. Bush 367 U.S. 907 (1961); *aff'd sub nom.* Gremillion v. United States, 368 U.S. 11 (1961); 204 F. Supp. 568 (E.D. La. 1962); 205 F. Supp. 893 (E.D. La. 1962), *aff'd in part and rev'd in part*, 308 F.2d 491 (5th Cir. 1962).

Although the Supreme Court consistently affirmed decisions of its lower federal courts in the Fifth Circuit, it never issued a full written opinion during the course of the litigation.

33. For a concise, well-written summary of the political history of New Orleans, see M. INGER, POLITICS AND REALITY IN AN AMERICAN CITY: THE NEW ORLEANS SCHOOL CRISIS OF 1960, at 9-16 (1969).

The sad history of the Little Rock crisis is chronicled in the Supreme Court's opinion in *Cooper v. Aaron.*[34] Federal troops and federalized National Guardsmen were assigned to Central High School for the entire school year to protect eight Negro students from "repeated incidents of . . . violence."[35] The Supreme Court Justices cut short their summer recess to hear the case. In perhaps the only opinion ever to be signed personally by all nine members, the Court unequivocally announced to the nation and, perhaps more importantly, to the inferior federal judges in the South, that opposition to the *Brown* mandate, however intense or violent, would not be allowed to stay implementation of the constitutional rights of black children to equal educational opportunities.

The efforts of the United States Court of Appeals for the Fifth Circuit to enforce the enrollment of James Meredith at the University of Mississippi jolted that court from its traditionally reflective appellate role and ultimately required the use of federal troops to put down the most serious federal-state confrontation since the bombardment of Fort Sumter one hundred years earlier.[36] In retrospect, the trauma of Ole Miss seems to have stiffened the resolve of many federal judges to adopt harsh new measures to carry out their *Brown II* marching orders, and propelled the federal courts in the South to search for new methods of implementation and for uniformity in their own decisions.

B. The Search for Standards: 1963-1967

1. *Climate*

The kaleidoscope of events in 1963 provides the setting for the beginning of the second period of public school integration. This was the penultimate year of the civil rights movement. With the abatement of the Cold War, Americans were treated to a daily news fare of triumph and tragedy on the domestic civil rights scene. Across the South black and white citizens or-

34. 358 U.S. 1 (1958).

35. *Id.* at 12-13.

36. For more complete accounts of James Meredith's fight to enter the University of Mississippi, see R. Barrett, Integration at Ole Miss (1965); W. Lord, The Past That Would Not Die (1965); J. Meredith, Three Years in Mississippi (1966); Silver, *Mississippi: The Closed Society,* 30 J. So. Hist. 3 (1964). *See also* V. Navasky, Kennedy Justice (1971); Leonard, Harris, & Wren, *How a Secret Deal Prevented a Massacre at Ole Miss,* 26 Look, Dec. 31, 1962, at 18.

Before federal force finally prevailed in the showdown at Oxford between Mississippi Governor Ross Barnett and President John F. Kennedy, terrible damage had been done to property, to human life, and to the reputation of the University. Two men were dead: Paul Guihard, a French newspaperman representing Agence France-Presse, who was shot in the back, and Ray Gunter, an Oxford workman, who was shot in the forehead while watching the riots. At least 160 marshalls were injured, 38 per cent of those sent to Ole Miss. W. Lord, *supra* at 231. Sixteen of the Mississippi National Guardsmen first led into the riot scene were injured. No one can be sure of the extent of injuries among rioters, but they were much less extensive —a cold indication of where the balance of force lay. Federal forces took over 200 prisoners, only 24 of whom were Ole Miss students. No convictions resulted from the rioting.

ganized, marched, sang, and sat-in. The Student Non-Violent Coordinating Committee (SNCC) initiated its first direct action voter registration drive in Selma, Alabama. President Kennedy sent a voting rights act to Congress; Congress did not respond. Using school children as marchers under the leadership of Reverend Fred Shuttlesworth, the Southern Christian Leadership Conference (SCLC) organized demonstrations in Birmingham, America's most segregated city; Police Commissioner Eugene "Bull" Conner's police over-reacted.[37] President Kennedy sponsored new civil rights legislation desegregating public accommodations, giving expanded powers to the Attorney General to initiate school integration, and setting stringent standards of nondiscrimination in federally financed or assisted programs. Again, Congress did not respond. Governor George Wallace stood in the schoolhouse door to block the enrollment of Vivian Malone to the University of Alabama. He closed the Tuskegee High School to prevent public school integration. Four little girls were killed in the bombing of a Birmingham church, and two Negro boys were shot in the violent aftermath. Medgar Evers was assassinated at his home in Jackson, Mississippi. Race rioting began at Cambridge, Maryland, and Danville, Virginia. The Department of Justice reported that during the ten-week period after the Birmingham demonstrations in 1963, over 186 cities in the South underwent 758 demonstrations[38] resulting in almost 5,000 arrests.[39]

While marked by stark tragedy, 1963 was also the year of the most compelling moment of the civil rights movement: The March on Washington. On one sweltering August day, 1,512 chartered buses and 40 special trains brought over 200,000 civil rights "pilgrims" to the nation's Capitol.[40] "[A]n unprecedented and unpredictable confluence of black leaders, white liberals, movie stars, bishops and tens upon tens of thousands of ordinary citizens [came] to the Capitol to bear peaceful witness to the black American's petition for something called Freedom—Now. It may have been the most romantic single event of twentieth-century America."[41]

2. *The Recalcitrant Bench*

Spurred by the quickening pace of the civil rights movement and the passage of the Civil Rights Act of 1964,[42] new plaintiffs embarked on the

---

37. *See* A. WASKOW, FROM RACE RIOT TO SIT IN 234 (1966).
38. F. POWLEDGE, BLACK POWER, WHITE RESISTANCE 79 (1967).
39. P. BERGMAN, THE CHRONOLOGICAL HISTORY OF THE NEGRO IN AMERICA 579 (1969).
40. 82 NEWSWEEK, Sept. 10, 1973, at 24.
41. *Id.*
42. Title IV of the Act required the Commissioner of Education of the Department of Health, Education, and Welfare (HEW) to render technical assistance to local school boards in their preparation of school desegregation plans. 42 U.S.C. § 2000c-2 (1970). Title IV also authorized the Attorney General to bring desegregation suits on behalf of complainants unable to sue on their own behalf. *Id.* § 2000c-6. Title VI of that same Act proscribed discrimination in any program or activity receiving federal financial assistance, under threat of loss of

choppy seas of desegregation litigation, with new case filings increasing almost geometrically. The greatest burden came to rest on the United States Court of Appeals for the Fifth Circuit. Finding its appellate calendar clogged with school appeals, it granted priority treatment to school cases and accelerated experimentation with new and expanding forms of extraordinary equitable relief. Despite their efforts, the Fifth Circuit judges found that—unlike the normal appeals case where the appellate decision is generally accepted as final—school cases were never finished. The same case would return again and again, exacting an enormous toll in judicial time and patience. Each time a case came back inevitably greater integration was demanded or new mechanisms of delay had to be struck down.

The most disheartening aspect of the school cases was the refusal of many federal district judges to enforce the law at the local level without constant supervision. Cajoling, scolding, complimenting, and preemptorily reversing unevenly performing federal district judges frequently unraveled the patience of the appeals court and stretched the ingenuity of its judges to the breaking point. There were disappointingly few district judges courageous enough to mandate compliance with *Brown II.*[43] Most federal district judges could be classified as passive; they were either unsympathetic, unresponsive, timid, or fearful of community reaction and had to be pushed into taking each step designed to increase the pace of integration.[44] *Brown II* did

funding. *Id.* § 2000d. When combined with the Elementary and Secondary Education Act of 1965, 20 U.S.C. §§ 236 *et seq.*, 241 *et seq.*, 331 *et seq.*, 821 *et seq.* (1970), which greatly increased the amount of federal money available for the nation's public schools—particularly schools in low income areas such as the Deep South—Title VI of the Civil Rights Act of 1964 provided federal officials with both a powerful club and a tempting carrot. With one hand they could offer generous amounts of federal aid to recalcitrant school districts and with the other they could demand that desegregation efforts begin at the risk of the district losing all of those new-found dollars.

43. Two such courageous judges, Frank M. Johnson of Alabama and Bryan Simpson of Florida, were vilified, cursed, and threatened for their stern insistence on enforcing the Supreme Court's mandate in *Brown.* As to Judge Johnson, see 89 TIME, May 12, 1967, at 72-74, 77-78; 86 TIME, Aug. 13, 1965, at 15A; 85 TIME, Mar. 19, 1965, at 25; 83 TIME, Feb. 21, 1964, at 76. Regarding Judge Simpson's efforts in Florida, see SOUTHERN JUSTICE 193-213 (2d ed. L. Friedman 1966).

44. Federal District Judge Frank M. Scarlett of Georgia is a prime example of an obstructionist federal district judge bent on frustrating the *Brown* mandate. His persistent efforts to thwart Negro plaintiffs in school cases in Savannah, Augusta, and Brunswick effectively blocked integration in the Southern District of Georgia long past the time when most other school districts in the Fifth Circuit had begun obeying court-approved integration plans. Seizing on the Supreme Court's citation in footnote 11 of the works of social scientists to support its thesis that segregation was injurious to black children, Judge Scarlett allowed white intervenors to introduce "similar evidence" to disprove the Court's thesis. *See* Stell v. Savannah-Chatham County Bd. of Educ., 220 F. Supp. 667, 668-76 (S.D. Ga. 1963). Judge Scarlett then held that new evidence adduced in his court had proved that Negro children were inherently inferior and therefore segregation did not violate the equal protection clause of the fourteenth amendment. The Fifth Circuit, on appeal, sternly reversed Judge Scarlett's holding with the following rebuke: "We reiterate that no inferior federal court may refrain from acting as required by [the decision in *Brown I*] even if such a court should conclude that the Supreme Court erred either as to its facts or as to the law." 333 F.2d 55, 61 (5th Cir. 1964).

not envision the primary enforcement role as resting on the federal appellate courts—but that is precisely where it landed in most cases.

The United States Supreme Court was not helpful in those middle years. Other than urging its inferior federal courts in the South to move more rapidly—with sharp reminders that the time the courts were to allow for transition from segregated to desegregated schools was decreasing with the passage of years since *Brown*[45]—the Supreme Court did not attempt to give advice on the mechanics of the desegregation process.

3. *Stirrings*

Left adrift by the Supreme Court and faced with the prospect of having to decide each case on its individual facts, the Fifth Circuit began to develop uniform enforcement standards which, it was hoped, would shift the burden of implementation back to the district courts. In 1964 four major cases (involving Birmingham and Mobile, Alabama, and Savannah, Brunswick, and Albany, Georgia) ordered previously approved grade-a-year plans rapidly stepped up.[46] Desegregation was started in the first and second grades and also in the twelfth, in order that no student would graduate without a desegregated education. The cases, while stressing that no inflexible standard was intended, did indicate the importance of uniformity.[47]

In addition to speeding up the grade-a-year plans, the Fifth Circuit moved away from "transfer plans" which had required black students to brave a complex procedural morass to initiate their own transfer to white schools. The Supreme Court's decision in *Shuttlesworth*,[48] approving on its face the Alabama Pupil Placement Act, had acted to retard significant levels of desegregation for years. Finally, it became clear that the sole purpose of such statutes was to frustrate desegregation. Thereafter their application was enjoined. Pupil assignment plans were replaced by freedom-of-choice plans, thereby theoretically[49] allowing every pupil to attend a school based solely on personal choice and the physical capacity of the school. In addition

45. *See, e.g.*, Goss v. Board of Educ., 373 U.S. 683 (1963); Watson v. City of Memphis, 373 U.S. 526 (1963).

46. Gaines v. Dougherty County Bd. of Educ., 334 F.2d 983 (5th Cir. 1964); Stell v. Savannah-Chatham County Bd. of Educ., 333 F.2d 55 (5th Cir. 1964); Davis v. Board of School Comm'rs, 333 F.2d 53 (5th Cir. 1964); Armstrong v. Board of Educ., 333 F.2d 47 (5th Cir. 1964).

47. The 1965 case of Lockett v. Board of Educ., 342 F.2d 225 (5th Cir. 1965), is evidence of the court's desperate push for uniform standards. A target date for the desegregation of all grades was set at September, 1968. That date was picked up and applied to later cases as well. *See* Price v. Denison Independent School Dist., 348 F.2d 1010 (5th Cir. 1965). Note that the court leaves open whether it will use September of 1967 or "as in our recent Court decisions, [September of 1968]." *Id.* at 1014.

48. Shuttlesworth v. Birmingham Bd. of Educ., 358 U.S. 101, *aff'g* 162 F. Supp. 372 (N.D. Ala. 1958).

49. Countless subterfuges to prevent unfettered free choice prevented any significant amount of desegregation under such plans. HEW guidelines approved later by the Fifth Circuit in the *Singleton* and *Jefferson* cases, discussed *infra*, were an attempt to apply rigorous standards to guarantee the workability of freedom-of-choice.

to approving freedom-of-choice plans in the period between 1964 and 1966, the Fifth Circuit also began to require contemporaneous abolition of dual attendance zones—separate school attendance zones for black and white children to which they were initially assigned. The general impatience of the Fifth Circuit is succinctly summarized by Judge Griffin B. Bell's terse statement that "the rule has become: the later the start, the shorter the time allowed for transition."[50]

4. Singleton *and* Jefferson

The groping of the federal courts of appeals for uniform standards that could be utilized in all school cases culminated in four famous Fifth Circuit cases decided between 1965 and 1967: *Singleton v. Jackson Municipal Separate School District (Singleton I*[51] and *Singleton II*[52]*)* and *United States v. Jefferson County Board of Education (Jefferson I*[53] and *Jefferson II*[54]). Those cases mark the most important doctrinal change in interpretation of the equal protection clause, as applied to public education, since *Brown* itself. They mark the end of the middle turbulent years of school desegregation and presage the era of massive integration. Their importance cannot be overemphasized. The *Singleton* and *Jefferson* decisions did not just bring state policy into line with national policy, as indicated by Judge John Minor Wisdom, the architect of the four decisions. Rather they created *new* policy by reinterpreting settled school desegregation law.

Singleton I and *II* and *Jefferson I* and *II* were the logical result of the Fifth Circuit's mounting frustration with tokenism and delay by school boards and federal district courts in the name of "deliberate speed." Each successive opinion from the court of appeals had brought only more appeals, more questions, and more litigation. In the urgent search for uniform standards which would remove the court of appeals from day-to-day supervision of district court decrees, the Fifth Circuit began to consider the "guidelines" established by the HEW Office of Education pursuant to the provisions of section 2000d of the Civil Rights Act of 1964,[55] as perhaps the answer to its problems in fully implementing the *Brown* mandate. The "guidelines" included minimum standards for use in determining whether a local school board's desegregation plan would qualify that local school board for federal financial assistance.[56] Could these administrative "guidelines" be adopted as uniform legal standards?

---

50. Lockett v. Board of Educ., 342 F.2d 225, 228 (5th Cir. 1965).
51. 348 F.2d 729 (5th Cir. 1965).
52. 355 F.2d 855 (5th Cir. 1966).
53. 372 F.2d 836 (5th Cir. 1966).
54. 380 F.2d 385 (5th Cir. 1967).
55. 42 U.S.C. § 2000d-1 (1970). *See* United States v. Jefferson County Bd. of Educ., 372 F.2d 836, 856 (5th Cir. 1966).
56. *See* note 42 *supra*.

The momentum toward the key *Jefferson I* holding was forecast by Judge Wisdom's opinion in *Singleton I*,[57] decided on June 22, 1965. The case began with the following explicit warning: "The time has come for footdragging public school boards to move with celerity toward desegregation . . . ."[58] Judge Wisdom stated that the Fifth Circuit would "attach great weight" to the HEW guidelines.[59] While recognizing that HEW and the judiciary have different functions, Judge Wisdom asserted that all three branches of government were united by a common objective: the elimination of segregated education. It was important that there be a "close correlation . . . between the judiciary's standards . . . and the executive department's standards in administering [the] policy [on desegregation]."[60] Judge Wisdom stated that HEW was better equipped than the courts to weigh alleged administrative difficulties in various desegregation plans, and warned that judicial requirements in desegregation cases should not be "less burdensome than HEW guides" lest school boards flood the courts with desegregation questions in order to avoid HEW's more rigorous guidelines.[61] The court then ordered the local board in *Singleton I* to "be guided" in the preparation of the details of its plan by the new HEW guidelines.[62]

In an extremely important footnote, Judge Wisdom provided the philosophic underpinnings for his favorable recommendation of HEW guidelines to local school boards. He frontally attacked the venerable *Briggs v. Elliott* dictum, the first such attack in a Fifth Circuit opinion, as inconsistent with *Brown I* and *II*:[63]

> In retrospect, the second Brown opinion clearly imposes on public school authorities the duty to provide an integrated school system. Judge Parker's well-known dictum ("The Constitution, in other words, does not require integration. It merely forbids discrimination".) in Briggs v. Elliott . . . should be laid to rest. It is inconsistent with Brown and the later development of decisional and statutory law in the area of civil rights.

Brown v. Board of Education, he reasoned, implied an affirmative interpretation of the fourteenth amendment, positively requiring a state to pro-

57. Singleton v. Jackson Municipal Separate School Dist., 348 F.2d 729 (5th Cir. 1965). *Singleton I* and *II* and *Jefferson I* were all decided by three-judge panels, with Judge Wisdom the author of all three opinions.

58. *Id.* at 729.

59. 348 F.2d at 731.

60. *Id.*

61. *See* note 77 *infra*.

62. 348 F.2d at 731.

63. 348 F.2d at 730 n.5. Judge Wisdom's footnote observation that the *Briggs v. Elliott* dictum "should be laid to rest" provoked a storm of internal controversy among his brothers on the court. An impressive string of cases, all tracing back to *Briggs*, had interpreted the equal protection clause application to school cases as essentially negative. Those cases focused on the "proscriptive" effect of the second sentence of the fourteenth amendment: "No State shall . . . deny to any person . . . the equal protection of the laws." The negative *Briggs* interpretation of *Brown I* said that decision merely forbade states from mandatorily segregating public schools and at most required that artificial legal barriers to desegregation be removed.

vide unitary school systems that were not racially identifiable. He read *Brown I* and *II* as breathing new life into the three Civil War amendments to the Constitution: the thirteenth, fourteenth, and fifteenth amendments.[64] Judge Wisdom placed emphasis on the first positive sentence of the fourteenth amendment that "All persons born . . . in the United States . . . are citizens." He read the thirteenth amendment as not only abolishing slavery but "all badges and indicia of slavery" and he viewed segregated education as an indicium of slavery and racial inferiority. States that had erected legal impediments to full citizenship by creating "badges of slavery," that is, segregated schools, did not satisfy their obligations by removing segregationist laws. It was not enough to retreat to a neutral corner and place on individual Negro citizens the full burden of initiating desegregation. The states that had segregated Negroes in the first place had the primary responsibility for desegregating them.[65]

Seven months after *Singleton I*, *Singleton II*[66] was announced. Although the case had become snarled in extremely complex procedural problems, Wisdom brushed aside the "tangled web" and judged that the only pertinent matter was the "judicial approval of a lawful and effective desegregation plan for schools in Jackson, Mississippi."[67] In noting the weaknesses of freedom-of-choice plans,[68] he again pointed out that the court attached "great weight"[69] to the HEW guidelines and attempted to add teeth to freedom-of-choice plans.[70] Continuing, Wisdom at last held that the *Briggs v. Elliott* dictum could not bar the right of any Negro child to transfer to a white school.[71]

64. *See* Comment, *supra* note 11, at 761.

65. Later, in *Jefferson I*, Judge Wisdom expanded his argument to attack "the popular myth," that *Brown I* fundamentally rested on sociological studies that asserted that segregation caused psychological harm to Negro children. Rather, Judge Wisdom argued that the *Brown* holdings were directly premised on the mandatory language of the fourteenth amendment which prohibited unreasonable classification by a state of its citizens. States which had classified school children by race had not only a duty to *proscribe* past segregation laws, but they also had an affirmative duty to *prescribe* an integrated education for all their children where race was not a factor. *See id.* at 760-61.

66. Singleton v. Jackson Municipal Separate School Dist., 355 F.2d 865 (5th Cir. 1966).

67. *Id.* at 868.

68. 355 F.2d at 871.

69. 355 F.2d at 869.

70. To assuage rising criticism over his *Singleton I* comments about HEW's guidelines, he made it clear that "we do not abdicate our judicial responsibility for determining whether a school desegregation plan violates federally guaranteed rights." *Id.*

71. The Constitution forbids unconstitutional state action in the form of segregated facilities, including segregated public schools. . . . The school children in still-segregated grades in Negro schools are there by assignment based on their race. . . . They have an absolute right, as individuals, to transfer to schools from which they were excluded because of their race.

> This has been the law since Brown v. Board of Education, 1954 . . . . Misunderstanding of this principle is perhaps due to the popularity of an over-simplified dictum that the constitution [sic] "does not require integration," [citing *Briggs v. Elliott*]. But there should be no misunderstanding now as to the right of any child in a segregated

United States v. Jefferson County Board of Education (Jefferson I)[72] is, with *Brown v. Board of Education, Green v. County School Board,*[73] and *Swann v. Charlotte-Mecklenburg Board of Education,*[74] one of the four most important school desegregation cases yet decided. Consolidating seven cases from Alabama and Louisiana, where not one of the school districts involved had made a start toward desegregation until 1965, eleven years after *Brown,* the opinion has had enormous impact on both the law and the pace of desegregation. An understanding of *Jefferson I* is necessary for an appreciation of: (1) how the federal courts turned the corner from token desegregation to massive integration, and (2) how the de jure/de facto distinction became imbedded in desegregation law.[75]

Judge Wisdom's *Jefferson I* opinion is divided into seven parts. In the preamble section he sadly noted that in the years since *Brown,* the Negro child's ". . . 'personal and present' right to equal educational opportunities with white children in a racially nondiscriminatory public school system . . . has been 'of such stuff as dreams are made on.' "[76] The new standards by which courts were to judge the constitutionality of school board desegregation plans were explained:[77]

> *The only school desegregation plan that meets constitutional standards is one that works.* By helping public schools to meet that test, by assisting the courts in their independent evaluation of school desegregation plans, and by accelerating the progress but simplifying the process of desegregation the HEW Guidelines offer new hope to Negro school children long denied their constitutional rights. A national effort, bringing together Congress, the executive, and the judiciary may be able to make meaningful the right of Negro children to equal educational opportunities. *The courts acting alone have failed.*

After the preamble of his opinion indicating that the HEW guidelines were being mandated circuit-wide, Judge Wisdom—having urged in *Singleton II*

> class to transfer to a formerly all "white" class, regardless of the slow pace of systematic desegregation by classes.

355 F.2d at 869-70. *See also* United States v. Jefferson County Bd. of Educ., 372 F.2d 836, 847 n.5 (5th Cir. 1966).

72. 372 F.2d 836 (5th Cir. 1966).

73. 391 U.S. 430 (1968).

74. 402 U.S. 1 (1971).

75. *Jefferson I* is particularly important to the most recent period of judicial activity because it provided the philosophical underpinnings for the de jure/de facto distinction which has perplexed and confounded scholar and layman alike. That distinction is discussed later. *See* text at pp. 24-25 *infra*.

76. 372 F.2d at 845.

77. 372 F.2d at 847. Judge Wisdom emphasized that the new HEW standards were substantially the same as those that had evolved in the difficult middle years from the court's own cases. 372 F.2d at 848. By mandating the standards as new *minimum* constitutional requirements for racial integration, the Fifth Circuit attempted to block school boards from seeking court orders that were less rigorous. The issuance of HEW's new guidelines had already caused a number of recalcitrant school boards, "that had not moved an inch toward desegregation," to seek weak court orders so that the Commissioner of Education would not cut off their federal funding. Judge Wisdom noted:

that school boards "grasp the nettle" and begin real desegregation—stated: "We grasp the nettle."[78] He then plunged into the seven parts of his opinion, justifying his abrupt departure from past precedent, both as to the pace and method of desegregation, with the comment that " '[n]o army is stronger than an idea whose time has come.' "[79]

Space and time do not permit a section-by-section analysis of *Jefferson I.*[80]

> The following statement appeared in the Shreveport Journal for July 1, 1965: "The local school boards prefer a court order over the voluntary plan because HEW regulations governing the voluntary plans or compliance agreements demand complete desegregation of the entire system, including students, faculty, staff, lunch workers, bus drivers, and administrators, whereas the court-ordered plans can be more or less negotiated with the judge."

372 F.2d at 859 n.49. This was not news to the court.

78. 372 F.2d at 849.

79. *Id.* Judge Wisdom was quoting a statement made famous by Senator Everett Dirksen on May 19, 1964, at a press conference concerning passage of the Civil Rights Act of 1964, but more properly attributable to Victor Hugo.

80. The importance of Titles IV and VI of the Civil Rights Act of 1964 was discussed in Part I of the opinion. Judge Wisdom asserted that a new national policy had emerged from the 1964 Civil Rights Act: *"The national policy is plain: formerly de jure segregated public school systems based on dual attendance zones must shift to unitary, nonracial systems—with or without federal funds."* 372 F.2d at 850.

Part II of Judge Wisdom's opinion reviewed in detail the slow pace of desegregation, 372 F.2d at 853-56, and issued a call for a change in both the speed and manner of desegregation in the Deep South. 372 F.2d at 856-61. Part II also dealt at length with the burden placed on the federal courts by school litigation; it is clear that Judge Wisdom viewed the new HEW guidelines as a way of getting the courts out of the endless business of administering local school desegregation plans.

Finally, Judge Wisdom noted that "the lack of uniform standards has retarded the development of local responsibility for the administration of schools without regard to race or color." 372 F.2d at 860. But relief was not to come. The *Jefferson* decree was not self-executing; over 100 school boards were already under court orders not as rigorous as the HEW guidelines. The plaintiffs in those cases, therefore, had to gear up to reopen all of those cases—causing more litigation. *See* Comment, *The Courts, HEW, and Southern School Desegregation,* 77 YALE L.J. 321, 338 (1967). Furthermore, as soon as HEW finally seemed ready for a vigorous push toward desegregation, Richard Nixon was elected President. The federal judiciary then began to sense that its newly found HEW and Justice Department allies were beginning to falter.

Part III of *Jefferson I* is a brillant and scholarly excursion into the meaning of the *Brown* mandate, the Civil War amendments to the Constitution, and evolving school case law. Part III is also the burying ground for the *Briggs v. Elliott* dictum. *See* notes 63 & 71 *supra* and accompanying text. The strength of the Wisdom assault on *Briggs* is seen in the following compelling passages:

> The central vice in a formerly de jure segregated public school system is apartheid by dual zoning: in the past by law, the use of one set of attendance zones for white children and another for Negro children, and the compulsory initial assignment of a Negro to the Negro school in his zone. Dual zoning persists in the continuing operation of Negro schools identified as Negro, historically and because the faculty and students are Negroes. Acceptance of an individual's application for transfer, therefore, may satisfy that particular individual; it will not satisfy the class. The class is all Negro children in a school district attending, by definition, inherently unequal schools and wearing the badge of slavery separation displays. Relief to the class requires school boards to desegregate the school from which a transferee comes as well as the school to which he goes. It requires conversion of the dual zones into a single system. Faculties, facilities, and activities as well as student bodies must be integrated.

The opinion, however, is well worth reading, and it will stand as a monument to the innovative leadership of Judge Wisdom. His concluding paragraph portended brighter days for Negro plaintiffs throughout the South:[81]

> Now after twelve years of snail's pace progress toward school desegregation, courts are entering a new era. The question to be resolved in each case is: How far have formerly de jure segregated schools progressed in performing their affirmative constitutional duty to furnish equal edu-

---

> No matter what view is taken of the rationale in *Brown I*, *Brown II* envisaged the remedy following the wrong, the state's correcting its discrimination against Negroes as a class through separate schools, by initiating and operating a unitary integrated school system. The gradual transition the Supreme Court authorized was to allow the states time to solve the administrative problems inherent in that change-over. *No delay would have been necessary if the right at issue in* Brown *had been only the right of individual Negro plaintiffs to admission to a white school. Moreover, the delay of one year in deciding* Brown II *and the gradual remedy* Brown II *fashioned can be justified only on the ground that the "personal and present" right of the individual plaintiffs must yield to the overriding right of Negroes as a class to a completely integrated public education.*
>
> . . . .
>
> The position we take in these consolidated cases is that *the only adequate redress for a previously overt system-wide policy of segregation directed against Negroes as a collective entity is a system-wide policy of integration.*

372 F.2d at 867-69 (emphasis in original).

Judge Wisdom carefully restricted his opinion to de jure segregation—fully aware that *Jefferson I* would be reconsidered by the entire Fifth Circuit sitting en banc because of its sweeping changes—to persuade other members of his court to adopt his view. He recognized the strength in the argument that the states within the Fifth Circuit in particular had an obligation to affirmatively correct the vestiges of a segregated school system that had been imposed by law. Thus the issue of the applicability of the fourteenth amendment to de facto segregation, caused by housing patterns in urban areas and typical of the kind of segregation existing in the North and West, was not reached in *Jefferson I.* Ironically, therefore, while destroying one distinction (integration/desegregation) that had plagued the progress of integration for years, Judge Wisdom in distinguishing between de facto and de jure segregation helped foster another distinction that would be used to justify different treatment for the South and North. And it is that distinction which still retards integration in the North.

Part IV of the *Jefferson I* opinion was devoted to demonstrating that a specific provision in the Civil Rights Act prohibiting assignment of children to schools "to overcome racial imbalance," 372 F.2d at 878, was meant to apply to de facto, but not to de jure, segregation—further entrenching the new distinction. Judge Wisdom also interpreted the Civil Rights Act not to prohibit teacher desegregation. He said: "As long as a school has a Negro faculty it will always have a Negro student body." 372 F.2d at 883.

Part V of the *Jefferson I* opinion upheld the HEW guidelines' use of percentages as legitimate goals by which the efficiency of desegregation plans could be evaluated.

Part VI of the opinion discussed at length the serious shortcomings present in most freedom-of-choice plans. It then proceeded to detail the elements necessary to make a free choice plan work. The discussion focused on such items as speed of desegregation, mandatory annual free choice, notice, transfers, services, facilities, activities, programs, school equalization, scheduled compliance reports, and desegregation of faculty and staff.

Part VII of the opinion attached a detailed decree to be entered with respect to each of the school boards consolidated before the court in *Jefferson I.* The court then indicated that "the provisions of the decree are intended, as far as possible, to apply uniformly throughout this circuit in cases involving plans based on free choice of schools." 372 F.2d at 894. Then Judge Wisdom pointedly added: "As the Constitution dictates, the proof of the pudding is in the eating: the proof of a school board's compliance with constitutional standards is the result—the performance." *Id.*

81. 372 F.2d at 896.

> cational opportunities to all public school children? The clock has ticked the last tick for tokenism and delay in the name of "deliberate speed".

The reaction to *Jefferson I* was immediate and intense. Praised by most legal commentators in the North,[82] it was roundly condemned by politicians, school boards, some federal judges, and most of the white populace in the South.

The second installment of *Jefferson (Jefferson II)* came shortly.[83] Because of the revolutionary nature of the opinion, an en banc rehearing was granted, requiring all twelve judges of the Fifth Circuit to sit on the rehearing. The per curiam opinion of the court, published March 29, 1967, adopted as its own the full opinion in *Jefferson I.*[84] However, the *Jefferson II* per curiam opinion seemed to go even further than *Jefferson I* in one important respect: Not only were the currently issued HEW guidelines mandated for circuit-wide use, but district courts were also told to give "great weight" to future guidelines, "when such guidelines are applicable to this circuit and are within lawful limits."[85]

Three of the twelve Fifth Circuit judges—Gewin, Bell, and Godbold—vigorously dissented; Judge Coleman wrote a concurring opinion. Judge Gewin, joined by Judge Bell was particularly disturbed by the de jure/de facto distinction. "[T]he opinion and the decree are couched in divisive terms and proceed to dichotomize the union of states into two separate and distinct parts."[86] He could not understand how the Constitution could apply differently in different parts of the country. He eloquently protested:[87]

82. *See, e.g.,* Comment, *supra* note 80, at 364-65; Comment, *supra* note 11, at 777. *But cf.* Comment, *Freedom of Choice in the South: A Constitutional Perspective,* 28 LA. L. REV. 455, 468 (1968).

83. United States v. Jefferson County Bd. of Educ., 380 F.2d 385 (5th Cir. 1967).

84. The Fifth Circuit per curiam opinion succinctly summarized the *Jefferson I* holding:

> Freedom of choice is not a goal in itself. It is a means to an end. A schoolchild has no inalienable right to choose his school. A freedom of choice plan is but one of the tools available to school officials *at this stage* of the process of converting the dual system of separate schools for Negroes and whites into a unitary system. The governmental objective of this conversion is—educational opportunities on equal terms to all. The criterion for determining the validity of a provision in a school desegregation plan is whether the provision is reasonably related to accomplishing this objective.

380 F.2d at 390.

85. *Id.* However, the per curiam opinion expressly reserved decision on whether the HEW guidelines were applicable to de facto situations.

86. 380 F.2d at 397.

87. 380 F.2d at 397-98. Judge Gewin continued:

> Although espousing the cause of uniformity and asserting there must not be one law for Athens and another for Rome, the opinion does not follow that thesis or principle. One of the chief difficulties which I encounter with the opinion is that it concludes that the Constitution means one thing in 17 states of the nation and something else in the remaining states. This is done by a rather ingenious though illogical distinction between the terms of de facto segregation and de jure segregation. While the opinion recognizes the evils common to both types, it relies heavily on background facts to justify the conclusion that the evil will be corrected in one area of the nation and not in the other. In my view the Constitution cannot be bent and twisted in such a man-

> The Negro children in Cleveland, Chicago, Los Angeles, Boston, New York, or any other area of the nation which the opinion classifies under de facto segregation, would receive little comfort from the assertion that the racial make-up of their school system does not violate their constitutional rights because they were born into a de facto society, while the exact same racial make-up of the school system in the seventeen Southern and border states violates the constitutional rights of their counterparts, or even their blood brothers, because they were born into a de jure society. All children everywhere in the nation are protected by the Constitution, and treatment which violates their constitutional rights in one area of the country, also violates such constitutional rights in another area. . . . Due process and equal protection will not tolerate a lower standard, and surely not a double standard. The problem is a national one.

After joining in Judge Gewin's dissent, Judge Bell wrote a dissent of his own, in which Judge Gewin joined. He agreed that the goal of *Brown* was a unitary system but did not agree with the "compulsory integration" language contained in *Jefferson I.* Calling Judge Wisdom's mandate of HEW guidelines on all school systems "new fuel in a field where the old fire has not been brought under control,"[88] Judge Bell argued for a freedom-of-choice plan superimposed on a strict neighborhood school zoning practice. He also argued that the new legal test of an integration plan—"one that works"—was unconstitutionally vague, that the de jure/de facto doctrine was unfair, and that the overruling of the *Briggs v. Elliott* dictum was unjustifiable.

Judge Coleman, in a separate opinion, worried about how "not [to] wreak irreparable injury upon public schools while executing the sentence of death against compulsory segregation."[89] Judge Coleman agreed with Judge Gewin that *Briggs v. Elliott* had been decided correctly and that all areas of the country should be treated the same.

In a separate dissent Judge Godbold expressed fear that the percentages suggested in the guidelines would become fixed requirements of mandatory mixing. And he was convinced that the Constitution did not require race-mixing if it was against the wishes of all concerned.[90]

> ner as to justify or support such an incongruous result. The very subject matter under consideration tends to nullify the assertion that the constitutional prohibition against segregation should be applied in 17 states and not in the rest of the nation.

380 F.2d at 398.

Judge Gewin then took strong issue with Judge Wisdom's conclusion that the 1964 Civil Rights Act provision that prohibited school assignment solely for the purpose of racial balancing applied only to de facto and not to de jure situations. Judge Gewin was further deeply disturbed that the *Jefferson I* opinion called for race-mixing even if against the express wishes of all parties involved:

> There must be a mixing of the races according to majority philosophy even if such mixing can only be achieved under the lash of compulsion. . . . Accordingly, while professing to vouchsafe freedom and liberty to Negro children, they have destroyed the freedom and liberty of all students, Negro and white alike.

380 F.2d at 404-05.

88. 380 F.2d at 412.

89. 380 F.2d at 417.

90. The collision is head-on between individual freedom and paternalistic authoritarian-

Finally, it must be noted that less than a year after *Jefferson II* mandated uniform HEW guidelines on all federal district courts in the Fifth Circuit, the Supreme Court changed the ground rules for school cases in *Green v. County School Board,*[91] and displaced much of the Fifth Circuit's work. However, the per curiam, concurring, and dissenting opinions in *Jefferson II* raised fundamental issues which were not to be decided for another four years or have never been decided: whether racial quotas are mandated by *Brown*; whether the de jure/de facto distinction is meaningless, or even harmful; and whether freedom of choice, where the choice is actually free, is a constitutionally protected civil right. The *Jefferson II* decision aptly demonstrated that some of the most puzzling school desegregation issues today—like still waters—run deep.

C. Massive Integration: 1968-1972

1. *The* Green *Case: Freedom-of-Choice's Death Sentence*

In the early years after *Brown II* the Supreme Court had appeared content to observe from the sidelines as the lower federal courts in the South evolved methods of desegregation under *Brown II's* "all deliberate speed" standard. During the sixties, however, the Supreme Court grew increasingly impatient with the slow pace of desegregation in the South, and there were signals that it would soon reexamine the "deliberate speed" language of *Brown II.* Finally, on May 27, 1968, the Supreme Court acted, through its decision in *Green v. County School Board.*[92] That case initiated a major new emphasis on immediate integration and marked the end of freedom-of-choice plans as a judicially sanctioned method of desegregation.

The *Green* case involved New Kent County, a small rural county in Eastern Virginia with little residential segregation and a student population divided almost equally between blacks and whites. There were only two schools in the entire system: the school on the east side of the county for whites and the school on the west side for blacks. There were no attendance zones. White students were bused to the white school; black students were bused to the black school. Since 1965, the system had operated under a court-imposed freedom-of-choice plan, but under that plan *no* white students had ever chosen to attend the Negro school and only 15 per cent of the county's Negro pupils had enrolled in the formerly all-white school. A unanimous Supreme Court, speaking through Justice Brennan, found that "[t]he pattern

---

> ism. No more invidious discrimination, or improper government objective, can be imagined than national power setting aside the valid exercise of choice by members of a class in the name of the constitutional objective for which the choice was granted to the class in the first place.

380 F.2d at 424.

91. 391 U.S. 430 (1968).

92. *Id.*

of separate 'white' and 'Negro' schools in the New Kent County school system established under compulsion of state laws is precisely the pattern of segregation to which *Brown I* and *Brown II* were particularly addressed, and which *Brown I* declared unconstitutionally denied Negro school children equal protection of the laws."[93] The Court noted that during the first years after *Brown II* the principal focus of federal courts had been to require local school boards to provide a desegregated education for those few Negro children "courageous enough to break with tradition."[94] However, token desegregation was only the beginning step in the process toward unitary nonracial education. *Brown* had charged school authorities with "the *affirmative duty* to take whatever steps might be necessary to convert to a unitary system in which racial discrimination would be eliminated *root and branch.*"[95] Moreover, such steps could not be taken tomorrow or the day after tomorrow: "The burden on a school board today is to come forward with a plan that promises realistically to work, and promises realistically to work *now*."[96] The standard, therefore, was effectiveness. Applying this standard to the facts of the case, the Court held: " 'Freedom of choice' is not a sacred talisman; it is only a means to a constitutionally required end—the abolition of the system of segregation and its effects. If the means prove effective, it is acceptable, but if it fails to undo segregation, other means must be used to achieve this end."[97] Thus, where freedom-of-choice offers *real* promise of achieving a unitary nonracial system there might be no objection to allowing it to be proved in action. But where, as in New Kent County, a freedom-of-choice plan offered no reasonable hope of achieving a unitary system, it was not acceptable. New Kent County had an obligation to use other "reasonably available" methods of desegregation that would be effective.[98]

Close scrutiny of *Green* indicates that the freedom-of-choice plan there was held ineffective essentially because it produced integration of only fifteen per cent of the Negro students into the all-white school. After *Green,* therefore, federal courts naturally focused their attention on the percentage of

93. 391 U.S. at 435.

94. 391 U.S. at 436.

95. 391 U.S. at 437-38 (emphasis added).

96. 391 U.S. at 439.

97. 391 U.S. at 440, *quoting* Bowman v. County School Bd., 382 F.2d 326, 333 (4th Cir. 1967) (Sobeloff, J., concurring). Judge Sobeloff, in drafting that well-known paragraph, borrowed heavily from Judge Wisdom's per curiam en banc opinion in *Jefferson II. See* 380 F.2d at 390.

98. 391 U.S. at 442. Two other school cases decided by the Supreme Court the same day as *Green* reemphasized the obligation of school boards to move forward with integration plans that promised "realistically to work now." A freedom-of-choice plan in Arkansas, similar to the New Kent County plan, was held ineffective, Raney v. Board of Educ., 391 U.S. 443 (1968), and a "free-transfer plan" in Jackson, Tennessee was also held ineffective. Monroe v. Board of Comm'rs, 391 U.S. 450 (1968). Under the free transfer plan, school zones were set up but any child not content with his assigned zone could transfer to another school. All white children residing in Negro school zones in Jackson had transferred to the nearest white school and only a very few Negro children in white zones stayed in white schools.

race-mixing achieved. That statistic became the prime indicator of whether a desegregation plan promised "realistically to work *now*." Therefore, the efforts of the Fifth Circuit in *Singleton* and *Jefferson*, as far as the applicability of HEW guidelines to freedom-of-choice plans was concerned, had a very short life indeed. After *Green*, it became clear to the Fifth Circuit that it had not freed itself from school cases as hoped; it was back in the school business under far more imperative requirements.

A new wave of litigation testing the continued viability of freedom-of-choice plans followed the *Green* decision. The Supreme Court had not defined what it meant when it said that a plan had to "work," nor had the term "unitary school district" been defined with particularity.[99] Any ambiguity that could be found which could conceivably justify further litigation and delay was exploited. Desegregation litigation activity realized new heights as the courts—vigorously pushing desegregation under the *Green* mandate—sought innovative new ways to force school districts to come forward with plans that promised "realistically to work *now*." More and more, attention was focused on the percentage of integration that would result if a particular school board plan were approved.[100]

2. Alexander v. Holmes County Board of Education *and* Carter v. West Feliciana Parish

On October 29, 1969, the Supreme Court issued a peremptory order in the case of *Alexander v. Holmes County Board of Education*, reversing a three-month delay in desegregation and ordering *immediate* action.[101]

---

99. Lower federal courts did receive some enlightenment from the Supreme Court in United States v. Montgomery County Bd. of Educ., 395 U.S. 225 (1969), as to one of the factors necessary in the establishment of a unitary school district: faculty desegregation. In that case the Supreme Court reviewed a desegregation order of Judge Frank Johnson affecting Montgomery County, Alabama. He had held, *inter alia*, that the faculty *of each school* in the district should reflect the racial composition of the district faculty as a whole. Carr v. Montgomery County Bd. of Educ., 289 F. Supp. 647, 654-55 (M.D. Ala. 1968). Judge Gewin, in a cautious opinion joined by District Judge Elliott, reversed Judge Johnson's order as to the required faculty ratio, holding that such a "quota" system was too explicit. 400 F.2d 1 (5th Cir. 1968). The Supreme Court reversed Judge Gewin's opinion and reinstated the district judge's faculty desegregation order in toto. 395 U.S. at 235-36. Thereafter, as far as faculty integration was concerned, it was clear that the Supreme Court approved of absolute racial balancing of a faculty as a valid desegregation step. The Fifth Circuit, chastened by its reversal, began mandating Judge Johnson-type faculty ratio desegregation orders throughout the circuit.

100. Chief Judge Brown, dissenting from the Fifth Circuit's refusal to rehear en banc Judge Gewin's reversal of Judge Johnson in Montgomery County Bd. of Educ. v. Carr, 400 F.2d 1 (5th Cir. 1968), stated succinctly what was to become the overriding concern of the circuit: "The result is in figures." Montgomery County Bd. of Educ. v. Carr, 402 F.2d 782, 786 (5th Cir. 1968).

101. 396 U.S. 19 (1969). Implementation of *Green* infuriated segregationists across the South. For the first time real integration of the public schools—as opposed to token desegregation—appeared as a distinct probability. Encouraged by lukewarm statements on civil rights by Richard Nixon during the presidential election of 1968, southern politicians prepared a last-ditch fight against integration by addressing their protests directly to the highest levels of the new administration. It is reported that to accommodate Senator Stennis of Mississippi, then

While *Alexander* was pending before the Supreme Court, the Fifth Circuit consolidated sixteen major school cases for en banc hearings under the already famous name of *Singleton v. Jackson Municipal Separate School District (Singleton III).*[102] *Alexander* was handed down by the Supreme Court during the en banc arguments. Despite its desire to implement *Alexander* without delay, the Fifth Circuit judges could not believe that the Supreme Court intended for them to issue orders that required the relocation of hundreds of thousands of school children in the middle of an on-going school year. The circuit therefore, in *Singleton III,* decided to divide the integration into a two-step process. Part one of the process required desegregation of faculties, facilities, activities, staff, and transportation no later than February 1, 1970; part two permitted postponement of massive integration of student bodies until the beginning of the new school year in September of 1970.[103]

NAACP lawyers immediately appealed the *Singleton III* holding to the Supreme Court, which again preemptorily reversed the Fifth Circuit, stating that the court had "misconstrued" the holding in *Alexander.*[104] The Fifth Circuit—which had been the most diligent court in America in desegregating public school facilities—was wrist-slapped for delaying massive student desegregation for a short four month period to avoid disruption in the midst of an on-going school year.[105]

Immediate massive desegregation orders had to be issued—in mid-school term—for all school boards in active litigation in the Fifth Circuit area. Legal questions were to be postponed for consideration until *after* institution of unitary school systems.[106] Thereafter, the Fifth Circuit adopted

---

leading a floor fight on deployment of the ABM missle system, President Nixon brought pressure on Secretary Finch to delay the pending desegregation orders in Mississippi. *See* L. PANETTA & P. GALL, BRING US TOGETHER (1971). In any event, Secretary Finch wrote Chief Judge John R. Brown a letter requesting a delay in those counties, stating that implementation of the court orders would produce "chaos, confusion and a catastrophic educational setback" to the children involved. *Id.* at 255. Relying on the Finch letter, the Fifth Circuit approved the requested delay. The NAACP Legal Defense and Education Fund attorneys for the first time broke publicly with the Justice Department and appealed the delay holding to the Supreme Court in *Alexander v. Holmes County Bd. of Educ.*

102. 419 F.2d 1211 (5th Cir. 1969).

103. *Id.* at 1217.

104. Carter v. West Feliciana Parish School Bd., 396 U.S. 290, 291 (1970).

105. Because of the preemptory nature of the Supreme Court's reversal of the Fifth Circuit, Justices Harlan and White concurred separately in *Carter.* It was their view that, while desegregation was to commence immediately and unitary systems were to be immediately established *prior* to appeal of legal issues rather than awaiting appeal, the Fifth Circuit could follow a rule of thumb that their orders were to be implemented in approximately an eight-week time period. 396 U.S. at 293. Justices Black, Douglas, Brennan, and Marshall filed a short statement that the eight-week rule of thumb suggested by Justices Harlan and White was itself a retreat from *Alexander. Id.*. A short memorandum opinion of Chief Justice Burger and Justice Stewart indicated that they would not preemptorily reverse the judges of the Fifth Circuit because that court was more familiar with the facts of the individual cases than was the Supreme Court. 396 U.S. at 294.

106. It was in this context that Chief Judge John R. Brown of the Fifth Circuit and members of his court came to a tacit agreement that no further en banc hearings would be held and

the practice of issuing opinion-orders and urgently sought innovative ideas to handle the new crisis in school desegregation.[107] While enormous progress had been made in desegregation in the Deep South between *Green* and *Carter,* it was the *Carter* reversal that precipitated another quantum leap in school desegregation activity. This frantic pace of school integration continued[108] until the Supreme Court took *Swann v. Charlotte-Mecklenburg Board of Education* on certiorari in June of 1970.

In retrospect, although *Green v. County School Board* marked the first doctrinal shift since *Brown,* the wheels of practical progress in desegregation were set in motion by *Alexander* and *Carter.* Until those two summary reversals unceremoniously sent the cases back to the Fifth Circuit, desegregation had at best been a process marked only by tokenism in the Deep South. But within the short time period during 1970 and 1971, the public schools of the Deep South were substantially integrated—despite wavering by the Departments of Justice and HEW—by court orders based almost exclusively on integration statistics.[109] After the Supreme Court's reversals of the Fifth Circuit in *Alexander* and *Carter,* the long-awaited revolution had arrived. Massive integration came to the public schools of the Deep South.

---

opinion writing by three-judge panels would be avoided where possible. John Brown preached over and over to his judges, "All that can be said about school cases had been said; there is no point in writing further words." Interview with the Hon. John R. Brown, Chief Judge of the United States Court of Appeals for the Fifth Circuit, in Houston, Texas, Aug. 3, 1972.

107. For example, to expedite its school cases, the Fifth Circuit pioneered in developing new procedures to handle its docket: it established new screening and summary procedures that brought its calendar current but also provoked a storm of controversy among lawyers in the circuit. *See* Haworth, *Screening and Summary Procedures in the United States Court of Appeals,* 1973 WASH. U.L.Q. 257.

108. Under the procedures adopted by the Fifth Circuit Judicial Council on December 2, 1969, enormous progress in real integration of the public schools of the South was achieved. From that date to September 24, 1970, the Fifth Circuit handed down 109 opinion orders involving 89 separate school districts. Some of those school districts had two or three separate appeals in that same time period. It must be remembered that the burden of school cases on the judges of the Fifth Circuit was in addition to their regular case load. An example of the intransigence of recalcitrant school boards finally coming into head-on conflict with a determined Fifth Circuit can be seen in the Hinds-Alexander-Holmes County, Mississippi cases. The standing panel of Judges Bell, Thornberry, and Morgan may have set a judicial record that will never be topped. Those three judges handled an additional 57 opinion orders in those Mississippi cases alone (this is in addition to the 109 figure above). Therefore, the grand total for the Fifth Circuit from December 2, 1969 to September 24, 1970, was 166 opinion orders in school cases. Perhaps no court in history has responded with such alacrity and such monumental effort to a preemptory reversal. All of the opinion orders handled by the Fifth Circuit were on an expedited basis. The next closest circuit in school assignment case load was the Fourth Circuit which had 18 school cases during the same time period, only 3 of which were handled on an expedited basis. The above figures on the December 2, 1969 to September 24, 1970 time period were obtained from a letter of September 24, 1970, from Judge John R. Brown to Chief Justice Warren Burger.

109. It is interesting to note that the Fifth Circuit carefully avoided using loaded terms, such as "busing" and "racial balancing," while at the same time requiring extensive transportation and issuing reversals primarily on figures showing an insufficient amount of race-mixing in local schools.

D. *Swann* and the Uncertain Future of School Integration: 1972 to Date

1. Swann v. Charlotte-Mecklenburg Board of Education

On June 29, 1970, the Supreme Court granted certiorari to a case which directly raised—for the first time—questions about the "how" of the massive desegregation preemptorily ordered in *Alexander* and *Carter*.[110] Should courts order racial balancing? Is widespread busing permissible? In *Swann*, Federal District Judge James McMillan of Charlotte, North Carolina, had used a racial-balancing concept in formulating a desegregation plan which required widespread busing in metropolitan Charlotte and surrounding Mecklenburg County.[111] The Fourth Circuit had reversed the busing portion of Judge McMillan's plan as being overly harsh.[112] When the Supreme Court decided to review Judge McMillan's case, waves of anticipation and dread spread throughout the lower federal court system in the South.

Chief Judge John R. Brown of the Fifth Circuit reacted with alacrity. In the only press release he has ever issued, the Chief Judge indicated that the Fifth Circuit would freeze all but the most essential desegregation activity in the circuit until it had received instructions from the Supreme Court in *Swann.* The great integration revolution sweeping the South since *Carter* was suddenly halted in place as the federal courts waited for a definitive statement from the Supreme Court.

The Supreme Court took nine suspense-filled months to issue its opinion —an unconscionably long delay for the same Court which had, in *Alexander* and *Carter,* ordered preemptory reversals of the Fifth Circuit for three and four-month delays. On April 20, 1971, the long wait ended.[113] The opinion satisfied no one, dismayed almost all parties involved in the desegregation struggle, and seemed to raise more questions than it answered. Certiorari had been granted to review two important issues raised by Supreme Court desegregation mandates: "the duties of school authorities and the scope of powers of federal courts. . . ."[114] The Court's unanimous holding in an opinion by Chief Justice Burger was stated as applying, however, *only* to school systems with a background of de jure segregation (school systems that prior to *Brown I* had been mandatorily segregated by law).[115]

---

110. Swann v. Charlotte-Mecklenburg Bd. of Educ., 399 U.S. 926 (1970).

111. 311 F. Supp. 265, 268 (W.D.N.C.), *rev'd in part,* 431 F.2d 138 (4th Cir. 1970), *district court opinion reinstated,* 402 U.S. 1 (1971).

112. Swann v. Charlotte-Mecklenburg Bd. of Educ., 431 F.2d 128, 147 (4th Cir. 1970).

113. Swann v. Charlotte-Mecklenburg Bd. of Educ., 402 U.S. 1 (1971).

114. *Id.* at 5.

115. This case and those argued with it arose in states having a long history of maintaining two sets of schools in a single school system deliberately operated to carry out a governmental policy to separate pupils in schools solely on the basis of race. That was what *Brown v. Board of Education* was all about. These cases present us with the problem of defining in more precise terms than heretofore the scope of the duty of school

The Chief Justice examined the facts of the *Swann* dispute: The Charlotte-Mecklenburg school system—the forty-third largest in the nation—included the city of Charlotte, North Carolina and all of surrounding Mecklenburg County, an area of 550 square miles. The 107 schools served 84,000 pupils, 71 per cent of whom were white, and 29 per cent black. Two-thirds of those black students attended just 21 schools which were either totally or more than 99 per cent Negro (as of June, 1969).[116] After the Supreme Court's decision in *Green,* but before *Alexander* and *Carter,* Judge McMillan had held "numerous hearings and received voluminous evidence,"[117] and had ordered the school board to come forward with a plan for both faculty and student desegregation. The school board, after vigiorous prodding, came forth with only a partially completed plan. In light of the board's failure to comply with the court's mandate, Judge McMillan had appointed Dr. John Finger, an expert in educational administration, to prepare a desegregation plan for the court. The "Finger plan," as finally presented, was extremely controversial in the method by which it dealt with the desegregation of junior and senior high schools, and it aroused heated local debate. On February 5, 1970, after the Supreme Court's decision to accelerate desegregation in *Alexander* and *Carter,* Judge McMillan had adopted the board plan as modified by Dr. Finger's plan for the junior and senior high schools.[118] The final plan had required that as many schools as practicable reflect the 71/29 per cent white/black ratio then existing in the district as a whole. To achieve this balance, the approved plan required extensive busing in the secondary schools and employed the technique of pairing and grouping elementary schools. Fearing that the pairing and grouping of elementary schools would place an unreasonable burden on the board and the system's pupils, the Fourth Circuit Court of Appeals had remanded the district court's decision for reconsideration.[119]

After reviewing the facts, Chief Justice Burger emphasized that the Supreme Court would not retreat from the established principle that state-imposed racial segregation in public schools denied equal protection of the laws. He reaffirmed *Brown I* and *Brown II* and pointedly reminded school authorities that they carried the primary responsibility for desegregation. The Chief Justice further stated that federal courts were to act only after school boards had defaulted, and when forced to intervene, the courts were to be guided by equitable principles.[120] As to the Supreme Court's role in

authorities and district courts in implementing *Brown I* and the mandate to eliminate dual systems and establish unitary systems at once.

402 U.S. at 5-6.

116. 402 U.S. at 7.

117. *Id.*

118. 311 F. Supp. at 266-67.

119. 431 F.2d at 147.

120. 402 U.S. at 15-16.

desegregation, Chief Justice Burger stated: "The problems encountered by the district courts and courts of appeals make plain that [the Court] should now try to amplify guidelines, however incomplete and imperfect, for the assistance of school authorities and courts."[121]

The Court identified the touchstone for its guidelines: "The objective today remains to eliminate from the public schools all vestiges of state-imposed segregation."[122] The task of the district court was to balance individual and collective interests and to develop a remedy that repaired the denial of constitutional rights. The power of school boards in desegregation matters was plenary, while the power of federal courts was limited to correcting constitutional violations where they existed.[123]

The Court then proceeded to define "with more particularity"[124] the elements of an acceptable school desegregation plan. School authorities were only required to eliminate existing invidious racial distinctions. In addition to student assignment plans, existing policy and practices with regard to faculty, staff, transportation, extracurricular activities, and facilities were important indicia of a segregated system.[125] School authorities had an immediate and nondelegable duty to eliminate invidious racial distinctions in *all* of those areas. The Court only briefly discussed desegregation of transportation, staff, and activities; implementation of a desegregation plan in those areas was ostensibly simple. The Supreme Court also recognized that school construction and abandonment policies should not be allowed to "perpetuate or re-establish [a] dual system."[126]

The Supreme Court then gingerly broached the central issue: the problem of student assignment. Again specifically confining its attention to situations involving a prior history of de jure segregation,[127] the Court turned

121. 402 U.S. at 14.

122. 402 U.S. at 15.

123. The Chief Justice quickly disposed of objections to busing based on Title IV of the Civil Rights Act of 1964, 42 U.S.C. § 2000c (1970). He pointed out that language in the Civil Rights Act, purporting to prohibit busing to overcome racial imbalance, "was enacted not to limit but to define the role of the Federal Government in the implementation of the *Brown I* decision." 402 U.S. at 16. Chief Justice Burger said that courts retained all of their existing powers to enforce the equal protection clause of the fourteenth amendment. Furthermore, the legislative history of that section in Title IV indicated that Congress had been concerned only with de facto segregation and not de jure segregation. 402 U.S. at 17-18.

124. 402 U.S. at 18.

125. *Id. See* Green v. County School Bd., 391 U.S. 430 (1968).

126. 402 U.S. at 21.

127. We do not reach in this case the question whether a showing that school segregation is a consequence of other types of state action, without any discriminatory action by the school authorities, is a constitutional violation requiring remedial action by a school desegregation decree. This case does not present the question and we therefore do not decide it.

Our objective in dealing with the issues presented by these cases is to see that school authorities exclude no pupil of a racial minority from any school, directly or indirectly, on account of race; it does not and cannot embrace all the problems of racial prejudice, even when those problems contribute to disproportionate racial concen-

its attention to the explosive question of the appropriateness of racial balancing. The Court held that racial balancing was *not* required by the Constitution:[128]

> If we were to read the holding of the District Court to require, as a matter of substantive constitutional right, any particular degree of racial balance or mixing, that approach would be disapproved and we would be obliged to reverse. The constitutional command to desegregate schools does not mean that every school in every community must always reflect the racial composition of the school system as a whole.

However, almost immediately, the high Court qualified that holding:[129]

> We see . . . that the use made [by Judge McMillan] of mathematical ratios was no more than a starting point in the process of shaping a remedy, rather than an inflexible requirement. . . . As we said in *Green,* a school authority's remedial plan or a district court's remedial decree is to be judged by its effectiveness. Awareness of the racial composition of the whole school system is likely to be a useful *starting point* in shaping a remedy to correct past constitutional violations. In sum, the *very limited use* made of mathematical ratios was within the equitable remedial discretion of the District Court.

Did this mean that every school must reflect the district-wide black/white ratio? The Court held that there was a *presumption* against one-race schools, but it refused to hold that the existence of one-race schools constituted a per se violation of the Constitution.[130]

The Supreme Court then authorized as a valid remedy the altering of attendance zones. The following weapons were within the arsenal of the lower federal courts: "gerrymandering of school districts . . . [and] pairing, 'clustering,' or 'grouping' of schools with attendance assignments made deliberately to accomplish the transfer of Negro students out of formerly segregated Negro schools and the transfer of white students to formerly all-Negro schools."[131]

The last issue that the Court faced was the most troubling, at least from a political standpoint: the busing issue. The Court specifically approved busing as a remedial tool for desegregation.[132] It pointed out that bus transportation

---

trations in some schools.
402 U.S. at 23.

128. 402 U.S. at 24.

129. 402 U.S. at 25 (emphasis added).

130. [T]he existence of some small number of one-race, or virtually one-race, schools within a district is not in and of itself the mark of a system that still practices segregation by law. . . . The court should scrutinize such schools, and the burden upon the school authorities will be to satisfy the court that their racial composition is not the result of present or past discriminatory action on their part.
402 U.S. at 26.

131. 402 U.S. at 27. The Court continued:
All things being equal, with no history of discrimination, it might well be desirable to assign pupils to schools nearest their homes. But all things are not equal in a system that has been deliberately constructed and maintained to enforce racial segregation.
402 U.S. at 28.

132. 402 U.S. at 29.

had been an "integral part of the public education system for years, and was perhaps the single most important factor in the transition from the one-room schoolhouse to the consolidated school."[133] The Court noted that in Charlotte, where there had been impassioned protests against busing, the school board had bused children for years to maintain a dual system of education.[134] Judge McMillan's busing order in Charlotte was reasonable, although there might be limits beyond which busing orders would become unreasonable.[135]

The Court held, in summary, that the district court's order was not unreasonable but was both feasible and workable.[136] Then, in a strange conclusion to an already perplexing holding, the Court seemed to indicate that there was a way out of school desegregation problems:[137]

> At some point, these school authorities and others like them should have achieved full compliance with this Court's decision in *Brown I.* The systems would then be "unitary" in the sense required by our decisions in *Green* and *Alexander.*
>
> . . . Neither school authorities nor district courts are constitutionally required to make year-by-year adjustments of the racial composition of student bodies once the affirmative duty to desegregate has been accomplished

---

133. *Id.*

134. 402 U.S. at 29-30.

135. An objection to transportation of students may have validity when the time or distance of travel is so great as to either risk the health of the children or significantly impinge on the educational process. District courts must weigh the soundness of any transportation plan. . . . It hardly needs stating that the limits on time of travel will vary with many factors, but probably with none more than the age of the students. 402 U.S. at 30-31.

136. 402 U.S. at 31.

137. 402 U.S. at 31-32. Three companion school desegregation cases were decided by the Supreme Court the same day as *Swann.* In another Fifth Circuit case, Davis v. Board of School Comm'rs, 402 U.S. 33 (1971), the Supreme Court reversed the Fifth Circuit for failing to achieve a sufficient amount of desegregation in Mobile County, Alabama. The Fifth Circuit had approved a desegregation order that did not require the busing of students across a major highway which divided Mobile into district zones. Davis v. Board of School Comm'rs, 430 F.2d 883 (5th Cir.), *modified*, 430 F.2d 889 (5th Cir. 1970). The Supreme Court's reversal implicitly indicated that the Fifth Circuit should have ordered more busing to achieve a greater degree of desegregation. The *Davis* case, when read with *Swann*, gave proponents of busing substantial authority to insist that this remedy had been judicially endorsed. Both decisions added fire to the busing controversy that dominated the 1972 presidential primaries.

In a third case, McDaniel v. Barresi, 402 U.S. 39 (1971), the Supreme Court reversed a foolish Georgia Supreme Court holding, Barresi v. Browne, 226 Ga. 456, 175 S.E.2d 649 (1970), that a desegregation plan violated equal protection because it treated students differently because of their race. The Supreme Court tartly commented that in compliance with its duty to convert to a unitary system, the local board of education of Clarke County, Georgia had properly taken race into account in fixing attendance lines in order to achieve desegregation mandated by *Brown I* and *II.*

In a fourth case, North Carolina State Bd. of Educ. v. Swann, 402 U.S. 43 (1971), the Supreme Court held unconstitutional North Carolina's antibusing law, which had attempted to forbid assignment or transportation of any student on the basis of race or for the purpose of creating a racial balance. The Court held that the North Carolina statute was an attempt to prevent implementation of desegregation plans required by the fourteenth amendment and was thus unconstitutional.

and racial discrimination through official action is eliminated from the system.

Swann was to be the last of a long line of unanimous decisions by the Supreme Court in the school integration area. The decision was not innovative; it restated much of the development of prior desegregation law. The pressing question of whether the Constitution applied in the de facto segregated ghettos of the North and the West was not answered. Precise guidelines on the permissible extent of busing were avoided. While racial balancing was not constitutionally required, it was a permissible "starting point"—thus obscuring rather than solving that volatile issue. Lastly, the opinion tantalized the lower courts by indicating that they could get out of the school business once school systems were unitary, without defining when or how that would be determined.

Swann was an opinion for all litigants. It provided language readily adaptable to the position of almost any party in a desegregation battle. And the decision added to the woes of the over-burdened lower federal courts by stimulating further controversy in an area already saturated with litigation.[138] The long-awaited decree from Mount Olympus was instead an ambiguous, two-sided Delphic pronouncement raising crucial issues which have yet to be decided.

2. *Desegregation Outside the South*: *Denver and Detroit*

Notwithstanding the Fifth Circuit's innovative work in bringing Mexican-American children under the protective cloak of *Brown* and *Swann,*[139] and in casting aside the increasingly meaningless distinction between de facto and de jure segregation,[140] the focus of attention after *Swann* shifted away from the South and came to rest on the ghettos and barrios in the North and West. Denver and Detroit, while only two of the scores of northern cities brought to task under the banner of *Brown,* were to become the centerpieces for the Supreme Court's next, and most recent decisions with nationwide impact. Both cases raised the issue of the district court's power to mandate desegregation in areas within or without a city where no de jure segregation had been proved. In Denver the plaintiffs succeeded; in Detroit

138. The most common reaction of lower federal judges was frustration and confusion. In the Fifth Circuit where activity had been held up nine months awaiting a definitive decision there was not only confusion but lingering bitterness. Now composed of fifteen members, the Fifth Circuit found itself divided as to the meaning of *Swann*. Unable to give any more direction to its lower courts than the vague generalities of *Swann*, the Fifth Circuit continued its practice of reversing lower courts primarily on statistics showing insufficient racial mixing, simply appending to its opinion orders the cryptic comment that the reversal was "in light of *Swann v. Charlotte-Mecklenburg Board of Education.*" Many federal district court judges who had been hopeful of receiving comprehensive guidance became bitter not only toward the Supreme Court but also toward the Fifth Circuit.

139. *See* Cisneros v. Corpus Christi Independent School Dist., 467 F.2d (5th Cir. 1972).

140. *See id.;* United States v. Texas Educ. Agency, 467 F.2d 848 (5th Cir. 1972).

they failed, establishing the first major retreat by the Supreme Court in the desegregation area in the twenty years since *Brown.*

a. Denver

Since *Brown II* in 1955, desegregation had been exclusively a southern problem. Unsympathetic to a region that had compelled the separation of the races in public schools by force of law, the rest of the nation ignored the existence of de facto segregated schools in the ghettos of most of its large cities. However, after the Supreme Court in *Green* articulated the right of every child to obtain an integrated education and placed the duty on school boards to come forward with plans that promised realistically to integrate the public schools, most prescient observers realized that a decision day for the North and West could not long be postponed. The day arrived for Denver, Colorado, on June 21, 1973, when the Supreme Court issued its opinon in *Keyes v. School District No. 1.*[141]

In early 1969, the Denver School Board had adopted three resolutions designed to desegregate the schools in the predominantly black Park Hill area of their city. After a local election which produced a school board majority opposed to the three integration resolutions, the plan was scrapped. At that point, Negro plaintiffs filed suit. Initially the plaintiffs in *Keyes* had sought a limited goal; they sued only to desegregate the schools in Park Hill. However, upon achieving success in that endeavor,[142] they expanded their suit to secure desegregation of all of the schools in the Denver school district. The federal district court, however, denied further relief,[143] holding that the fact of deliberate segregation in Park Hill by past school board action—which the court considered to have been proven—did not prove that the school board had followed a similar segregated school policy for the *rest* of Denver where the segregated pattern was of de facto origin.[144] The district court held that the plaintiffs had failed to prove de jure segregation for the other areas of Denver—particularly the core city that they sought to desegregate. The Tenth Circuit affirmed the decision.[145]

141. 413 U.S. 189 (1973).
142. 303 F. Supp. 279 (D. Colo. 1969).
143. 313 F. Supp. 61, 69 (D. Colo. 1970).
144. 313 F. Supp. at 73.
145. Denver was to some extent a tri-ethnic community. The district court did treat "Hispano" students as a separate minority group; but the lack of a finding of de jure segregation in the rest of Denver was held sufficient to block relief as to both blacks and "Hispanos." 313 F. Supp. at 69-75. In an unusual gesture, the district court did find that the core city schools were inferior to other schools; and on the theory that the *Brown I* and *II* holdings applied only to de jure segregation and were not applicable to the core city's de facto segregation, the court breathed new life into *Plessy v. Ferguson's* separate but equal doctrine by ordering that substantially equal facilities be provided to core city students. *Id.* at 77-84. The Tenth Circuit affirmed the holding denying relief based on the de jure/de facto distinction, but reversed the district court's order requiring that better facilities be provided the center city schools. 445 F.2d 990 (10th Cir. 1971).

When certiorari was granted in *Keyes*,[146] most observers believed that the Supreme Court would grapple with the de jure/de facto distinction, provide more explicit guidelines on the extent to which busing could be employed as a remedy, and formulate policy on whether district-wide remedies were required when only portions of a district had been de jure segregated. In fact, the Supreme Court in *Keyes* resolved only one of those issues, the last.

Justice Brennan authored the majority opinion in *Keyes*. Chief Justice Burger concurred in the result; Justice Powell filed a lengthy, but compelling, opinion, concurring in part and dissenting in part; and Justice Rehnquist dissented. Justice White, who is from Denver, did not participate.

Justice Brennan's opinion began by distinguishing *Keyes* from earlier decisions such as *Swann* or *Green*: "[The Denver school] system has never been operated under a constitutional or statutory provision that mandated or permitted racial segregation in public education."[147] However, the black and Hispano plaintiffs alleged that the local school board had effectively segregated the district by manipulating attendance zones, by selecting school sites which would separate the races, and by superimposing a neighborhood school policy on existing residential segregation.[148] The Supreme Court found that the plaintiffs had successfully established that the school board engaged in de jure segregative acts in the Park Hills area of Denver. The school board argued, however, that a finding of state-imposed segregation in only one part of a district—even a substantial part—could not support a finding that the entire district was a dual, segregated system.

Justice Brennan, in response to the school board's argument, stated simply: "We do not agree. We have never suggested that plaintiffs in school desegregation cases must bear the burden of proving the elements of de jure segregation as to each and every school or each and every student within the school system."[149] Rather, Justice Brennan asserted, "common sense" led to the conclusion that where systematic segregation had been practiced in one part of the district, it had also been practiced in all other parts of the same district. The logic was inescapable: if a black school is maintained in one part of the district, neighboring schools would necessarily have a higher ratio of white students than they would have otherwise, and vice versa. The Court concluded by stating that "common sense dictates that racially inspired school board actions have an impact beyond the particular schools that are the subject of these actions."[150] On remand the district court in Denver was

146. 404 U.S. 1036 (1972).

147. 413 U.S. at 191.

148. *Id.*

149. 413 U.S. at 200.

150. 413 U.S. at 203. The Court judicially noticed various school board actions whose effects spread into other parts of the districts:

> First, it is obvious that a practice of concentrating Negroes in certain schools by structuring attendance zones or designating "feeder" schools on the basis of race has the

ordered to determine whether the de jure segregation in the Park Hill area did in fact have a reciprocal effect on the racial composition of other schools in the district. If it did, desegregation could be ordered for the entire district.

Justice Brennan presented the plaintiffs with an alternative route to proving that de jure segregation infected the entire district. The school board had argued that the plaintiffs must prove all of the elements of de jure segregation for the core city schools before the Court could grant a district-wide remedy; that is, the plaintiffs must prove "a current condition of segregation resulting from intentional state action directed . . . to the core city schools."[151] The fact that the core city schools were segregated could not be denied, but the plaintiffs had not shown any actual segregative *intent* on the part of the school board regarding those schools. Such a showing was not necessary, Justice Brennan concluded. Rather, when the plaintiffs were able to show that de jure segregation was practiced in one part of the district—in this case, the Park Hill area—segregative intent with respect to other parts of the same district could be *inferred.*[152] Such burden shifting was not "new or novel," the majority opinion continued, but was "merely a question of policy and fairness based on experience in . . . different situations."[153] And the

---

> reciprocal effect of keeping other nearby schools predominantly white. Similarly, the practice of building a school—such as the Barrett Elementary School in this case—to a certain size and in a certain location, "with conscious knowledge that it would be a segregated school," . . . has a substantial reciprocal effect on the racial composition of other nearby schools. So also, the use of mobile classrooms, the drafting of student transfer policies, the transportation of students, and the assignment of faculty and staff, on racially identifiable bases, have the clear effect of earmarking schools according to their racial composition, and this, in turn, together with the elements of student assignment and school construction, may have a profound reciprocal effect on the racial composition of residential neighborhoods within a metropolitan area, thereby causing further racial concentration within the schools.

413 U.S. at 201-02.

Interestingly, while the Court did not reject the de jure/de facto distinction, it cited as authority a case which did, United States v. Texas Educ. Agency, 467 F.2d 848 (5th Cir. 1972): "Infection at one school infects all schools. To take the most simple example, in a two school system, all blacks at one school means all or almost all whites at the other." *Id.* at 888.

Justice Brennan also quoted a passage from *Swann* which may be picked up by litigants who hope to prove that school boards themselves had been responsible for much of the residential segregation in the nation's cities:

> They [school authorities] must decide questions of location and capacity in light of population growth, finances, land values, site availability, through an almost endless list of factors to be considered. The result of this will be a decision which, when combined with one technique or another of student assignment, will determine the racial composition of the student body in each school in the system. Over the long run, the consequences of the choices will be far reaching. People gravitate toward school facilities, just as schools are located in response to the needs of people. The location of schools may thus influence the patterns of residential development of a metropolitan area and have important impact on composition of inner-city neighborhoods.

413 U.S. at 202.

151. 413 U.S. at 205-06.
152. 413 U.S. at 208.
153. 413 U.S. at 209, *quoting* 9 J. WIGMORE, EVIDENCE § 2486, at 275 (3d ed. 1940).

experience with desegregation warranted requiring local school authorities to explain "actions or conditions which appear to be racially motivated."[154] What was the nature of the school board's burden? The board must produce evidence sufficient to show that "segregative intent was not among the factors that motivated their actions" with respect to the core city schools.[155]

The plaintiffs, in summary, had two choices: (1) they could show that the board's segregative actions with respect to the Park Hill area reciprocally affected the racial composition of other schools in the district, including the core city schools; or (2) they could merely show intentionally segregative school board actions in a "meaningful portion" of the school district and the existence of segregation in other parts of the district, in which case the burden of proof would then shift to the school board. In defense the school board must show either (1) that their segregative actions in Park Hill did not "infect" the rest of the district; or (2) that, in fact, "segregative intent was not among the factors that motivated their actions" in the rest of the district. In either case, after the *Keyes* decision, plaintiffs were much closer to solving the problem of chronic center city school segregation in northern cities. Moreover, although the Court maintained the de jure/de facto distinction, it extended the concept of de jure segregation to a point where it was distinguishable from de facto segregation only by requiring an additional "showing of intent to segregate."[156] After *Keyes* it appeared that plaintiffs across the nation could more easily show that a myriad of governmental actions, both related and unrelated to education, were the actual cause of racial imbalance in their schools.

However, cracks in the previous unanimity of the Supreme Court in school desegregation cases were evident in the Denver case. Justice Powell, in an opinion concurring in part and dissenting in part, first attacked the majority's perpetuation of the de jure/de facto rationale and then worried about the disruptive effects of busing as a remedy, urging that the divisive tool of transportation be used sparingly.[157] Justice Douglas, who had joined the majority opinion, also filed a separate opinion agreeing with Justice Powell's condemnation of the continuation of the de jure/de facto distinction, em-

---

154. 413 U.S. at 209.

155. 413 U.S. at 210. The Court rejected

> any suggestion that remoteness in time has any relevance to the issue of intent. If the actions of school authorities were to any degree motivated by segregative intent and the segregation resulting from those actions continues to exist, the fact of remoteness in time certainly does not make those actions any less "intentional."

413 U.S. at 210-11.

156. The Court stated: "We emphasize that the differentiating factor between *de jure* segregation and so-called *de facto* segregation to which we referred in *Swann* is *purpose* or *intent* to segregate." 413 U.S. at 208. A close reading of *Keys* reveals, however, that the "*purpose* or *intent* to segregate" need not be shown by proof of actual and specific declarations of segregative intent, but may be *inferred* from the various actions of the school board.

157. 413 U.S. at 217-53.

phasizing the futility of requiring that lower federal courts seek out evidence of school board "intent" before protecting constitutional rights.[158] In a dissent that seemed to hark back to the discarded *Briggs v. Elliott* distinction between desegregation and integration, Justice Rehnquist urged that a remedy was warranted only in those particular schools in Denver where de jure segregation had been proven.[159]

b. Detroit

The other recent, crucial school desegregation case outside the South involved the Detroit metropolitan area school districts. That Detroit decision, *Milliken v. Bradley,*[160] had been awaited with trepidation by most metropolitan area school boards of the North and West. However, when it was finally released on July 25, 1974, it caused rejoicing by those who opposed massive integration in large metropolitan areas and drew an anguished response from civil rights advocates.

The case arose after a plan for voluntary integration, adopted by the Detroit City School Board, was barred from implementation by a law passed by the Michigan legislature in 1970, Act 48.[161] Detroit school children and their parents subsequently went to federal court, seeking to enjoin enforcement of the new Michigan law and to implement the school board's voluntary integration plan. The district court, the late Judge Stephen J. Roth sitting, denied the request for a preliminary injunction,[162] but on appeal, the Sixth Circuit declared the state law null and void.[163] Then a complex series of legal events occurred. The district court ordered immediate implementation of a temporary plan.[164] Again, there was an appeal, but the Sixth Circuit upheld the decision and ordered the district court to proceed immediately to the merits of the case.[165]

Detroit did not have a history of statutory segregation. There was, however, a long history of public and private discrimination that, combined with other factors, had produced residential segregation. Detroit's neighborhood schools mirrored this residential racial imbalance. The plaintiffs in *Milliken* claimed, as had their counterparts in Denver, that imposition of school attendance zones over the existing segregated residential pattern had produced a dual school system. They cited the school board's policy in school construction, its approval of optional attendance zones, and other factors to urge that Detroit's school system was a de jure segregated system subject

158. 413 U.S. at 214-17.
159. 413 U.S. at 254-65.
160. 418 U.S. 717 (1974).
161. MICH. COMP. LAWS ANN. § 388.182 (Supp. 1974).
162. *See* 338 F. Supp. 582, 584 (E.D. Mich. 1971) (referring to the court's prior unreported opinion).
163. 433 F.2d 897 (6th Cir. 1970).
164. 338 F. Supp. at 584.
165. 438 F.2d 945, 947 (6th Cir. 1971).

to constitutional attack. Judge Roth agreed and found for the plaintiffs.[166] But instead of restricting his remedy to the Detroit city schools, Judge Roth found that heavy black concentrations doomed any intradistrict integration plan and ordered integration of the entire metropolitan area, holding that "[s]chool district lines are simply matters of political convenience and may not be used to deny constitutional rights."[167] Judge Roth ordered fifty-three suburban school districts in three counties surrounding the city to be joined with Detroit in order to accomplish an effective conversion to a unitary system.[168] The desegregation plan was based on fifteen clusters, each containing part of the Detroit system and two or more suburban districts.[169]

With visions of mass busing into and out of Detroit's violence-ridden ghettos, the defendants appealed immediately. The Sixth Circuit Court of Appeals, sitting en banc, held, however, that it was "within the equity powers of the District Court" to order an interdistrict remedy, even though the district court had received no evidence of de jure segregation in the suburban districts:[170]

> [A]ny less comprehensive . . . plan would result in an all black school system immediately surrounded by practically all white suburban school systems, with an overwhelmingly white majority population in the total metropolitan area.
>
> . . . .
>
> . . . [T]he only feasible desegregation plan involves the crossing of the boundary lines between the Detroit School District and adjacent or nearby school districts for the limited purpose of providing an effective desegregation plan.[171]

Again the case was appealed, this time to the Supreme Court. On the last day of the 1973 term, after months of waiting, the Court handed down a five-to-four decision,[172] reversing the court of appeals and deciding that an interdistrict, metropolitan remedial order—at least in this case—was an unjustified expansion of the remedial power of the district court.[173]

Chief Justice Burger attempted to make it clear that the result in *Milliken* did not signal an abrogation of the principles of *Brown I.* He stated that the case involved only an interpretation of *Brown II,* simply clarifying the reach of the equity powers of the district courts in the area of school desegregation.

---

166. 338 F. Supp. at 592-94.

167. Judge Roth's March 28, 1972 determination that Detroit-only desegregation plans were unacceptable is unpublished.

168. 345 F. Supp. 914 (E.D. Mich. 1972).

169. 418 U.S. at 733.

170. 484 F.2d 215, 250 (6th Cir. 1973).

171. 484 F.2d at 245-49.

172. 418 U.S. 717 (1974).

173. A definitive decision regarding the scope of metropolitan remedies was rendered necessary because of the Supreme Court's failure to resolve that issue in the Richmond case, Bradley v. School Bd. 338 F. Supp. 67 (E.D. Va.), *rev'd,* 462 F.2d 1058 (4th Cir. 1972), *aff'd by an equally divided Court,* 412 U.S. 92 (1973).

He then cited the *Swann* opinion as authority[174] for the "basic principle" that "the nature of the violation determines the scope of the remedy."[175]

Before proceeding to the application of this standard, the Court felt it necessary to deal with the district court's order, ignoring established school district lines as "simply matters of political convenience."[176] "[T]he notion that school district lines may be casually ignored or treated as a mere administrative convenience is contrary to the history of public education in our country."[177]

Chief Justice Burger stressed that "local control" is a deeply rooted American tradition and, that "local autonomy has long been thought essential both to the maintenance of community concern and support for public schools and to the quality of the educational process."[178] He indicated that earlier language to the same effect in *Rodriguez*[179]—the school finance case—was more than just an idle rumination.

What, then, would justify a district court order ignoring school district lines? The answer to that question is the heart of the Supreme Court's decision in *Milliken*: the delineation of the remedial powers of the district court. After repeating the "controlling principle" that "the scope of the remedy is determined by the nature and extent of the constitutional violation," the Court stated:[180]

> Before the boundaries of separate and autonomous school districts may be set aside by consolidating the separate units for remedial purposes or by imposing a cross-district remedy, it must first be shown that there has been a constitutional violation within one district that produces a significant segregative effect in another district. Specifically, it must be shown that racially discriminatory acts of the state or local school districts, or of a single school district have been a substantial cause of interdistrict segregation. . . . In such circumstances an interdistrict remedy would be appropriate to eliminate the interdistrict segregation directly caused by the constitutional violation. Conversely, without an interdistrict violation and interdistrict effect, there is no constitutional wrong calling for an interdistrict remedy.

Under the facts of the Detroit case, the majority opinion thus held there could be no interdistrict remedy. The district court had not received evidence on segregation in the suburban districts and there was no evidence to show that the segregation in the Detroit city schools had been caused by actions originating outside of the district.[181] While brief and to the point, the significance of the majority opinion in *Milliken* can hardly be minimized. The black children of Detroit's core city were locked, constitutionally, into an

174. 402 U.S. at 15-16.
175. 418 U.S. at 738.
176. 418 U.S. at 739.
177. 418 U.S. at 741.
178. 418 U.S. at 741-42.
179. San Antonio Independent School Dist. v. Rodriguez, 411 U.S. 1, 50 (1973).
180. 418 U.S. at 744-45.
181. 418 U.S. at 745.

increasingly black, de jure segregated school district, with no real hope of escape into the better financed, predominantly white schools of the affluent suburbs.[182]

The *Milliken* holding split the Supreme Court badly; four of the Warren Court justices—Douglas, Brennan, White, and Marshall—dissented and Justice Stewart, the other Warren Court member, in a concurring opinion, attempted to narrowly confine the Detroit holding to its facts.[183] Justice White, joined by Justices Douglas, Brennan, and Marshall, argued in his dissenting opinion that the State of Michigan was responsible for the segregative acts of the Detroit school district, that the plan of Judge Roth was administratively feasible, that only a multidistrict plan was likely to provide any effective integration, and that the outlying Detroit school districts were subdivisions of the State of Michigan whose boundaries could be ignored in devising a plan to rectify constitutional violations.[184]

In a separate dissent, Justice Douglas argued that *Milliken,* read with *San Antonio Independent School District v. Rodriquez*[185]—which basically held that poorer school districts had to "pay their own way"[186]—meant that not only would core city black children be left in segregated schools but also that they would be left in inferior schools: "So far as equal protection is concerned we are now in a dramatic retreat from the 7-to-1 decision in 1896 [*Plessy v. Ferguson*] that blacks could be segregated in public facilities, provided they received equal treatment."[187]

In addition, Justices Douglas, Brennan, and White joined Justice Marshall, who had been counsel for the plaintiffs before the Supreme Court in *Brown I* and *II,* in a strongly worded dissent. It began:[188]

> After 20 years of small, often difficult steps toward that great end, the Court today takes a giant step backwards. Notwithstanding a record showing widespread and pervasive racial segregation in the educational system provided by the State of Michigan for children in Detroit, this Court holds that the District Court was powerless to require the State to remedy its constitutional violation in any meaningful fashion. Ironically purporting to base its result on the principle that the scope of the remedy in a desegregation case should be determined by the nature and the extent of the constitutional violation, the Court's answer is to provide no remedy at all for the violation proved in this case, thereby guaranteeing that Negro children in Detroit will receive the same separate and inherently unequal education in the future as they have been unconstitutionally afforded in the past.

---

182. The decision may not be surprising, however, when viewed against the backdrop of *Keyes,* the Denver case, indicating the difficulties faced by plaintiffs in obtaining district-wide remedy when they have only proven the existence of segregative intent in part of the district. *See* note 150 *supra* and accompanying text.

183. 418 U.S. at 753-57.

184. 418 U.S. at 762, 767-81.

185. 411 U.S. 1 (1973).

186. 418 U.S. at 760.

187. 418 U.S. at 761.

188. 418 U.S. at 782.

Justice Marshall emphasized that restricting the remedy in the *Milliken* case to the Detroit city schools would not result in desegregation of those schools.[189] He argued that the State of Michigan, not just the Detroit school district, was responsible for the segregation in Detroit's schools, and therefore school district lines drawn by the state should not block an effective remedy.[190] Justice Marshall gloomily concluded:[191]

> Today's holding, I fear, is more a reflection of a perceived public mood that we have gone far enough in enforcing the Constitution's guarantee of equal justice than it is the product of neutral principles of law. In the short run, it may seem to be the easier course to allow our great metropolitan areas to be divided up each into two cities—one white, the other black—but it is a course, I predict, our people will ultimately regret.

Conclusion

The federal judiciary's desegregation efforts in the South are now largely complete. Appeals from district court school desegregation orders have dropped dramatically and most whites appear to have accepted the integration of their public schools, albeit reluctantly. Contemporary accounts indicate that there are very few differences now in race relations between such towns as Jackson, Mississippi, and Dayton, Ohio, except that, because of massive desegregation orders, Jackson's schools are probably now more integrated than Dayton's.[192] The school litigation that continues to trouble the federal courts in the South is confined primarily to methods of implementing existing desegregation orders in the region's large metropolitan areas. Most rural school districts, on the other hand, have ended their litigation, only reporting back periodically to district courts.

Controversy still rages over methods of implementing desegregation, however. Massive busing, particularly in large urban areas, provokes as much acrimony in the North as it ever did in the South. The major difference between the South and other regions may be that in the South the back of resistance has been broken, while elsewhere—because of the lack of federal judicial activity attributable in large part to the de jure/de facto distinction—resistance is still strong and unbowed. The recent violence in Pontiac, Michigan and Boston, Massachusetts is but the tip of the iceberg.

Moreover, following the recent Detroit case, *Milliken v. Bradley,* the out-

189. 418 U.S. at 783-84.

190. 418 U.S. at 786, 790-98.

191. 418 U.S. at 814-15.

192. Justice Powell, concurring in Keyes v. School Dist. No. 1, 413 U.S. 189 (1973), states for example:

> According to the 1971 Department of Health, Education, and Welfare (HEW) estimate, 43.9% of Negro pupils attended majority white schools in the South as opposed to only 27.8% who attended such schools in the North and West. Fifty-seven percent of all Negro pupils in the North and West attend schools with over 80% minority population as opposed to 32.2% who do so in the South.

Id. at 218 n.3.

look for the North and West is not bright for further desegregation efforts. Although it was carefully limited to its facts, *Milliken* nevertheless may become an effective deterrent to integration of northern ghettos and western barrios—just at a time when it appeared that the school integration effort was moving from the South to the rest of the nation.[193] Only time and further Supreme Court rulings will tell if *Milliken* is to mark the end of the second era of reconstruction, just as the Compromise of 1877 marked the end of the first reconstruction period. However, the parallels do seem striking.

What have been the results of the twenty-year effort to desegregate the public schools? Have the changes been worth the costs? Has there been a lasting transformation in the social fabric of southern life? Have educational opportunities for minorities actually been equalized? Has federal judicial desegregation of the public schools of the South been but a great experiment destined for eventual failure? It is too early to answer any such questions definitively. And the answers are becoming more elusive—and perhaps illusory—since the fragmentation of the civil rights movement in the late sixties. While some black groups—notably the NAACP—have continued to support integration efforts and have urged massive, metropolitan busing plans, others are now voicing many of the same complaints as whites about public school problems.[194] Negro parent groups have opposed busing their children out of neighborhood schools to achieve integration, complaining bitterly that the burden of busing has been one-sided, falling primarily on black children.[195] Other local black groups have supported neighborhood schools in order to maintain black control over all-black schools.[196]

Perhaps the *Milliken* holding is a simple recognition that the problem of providing equal educational opportunities to all defies a legal solution based solely on a race theory of equal protection. As long as "blackness" and poverty are inescapably linked, and as long as minority plaintiffs cannot themselves agree on the proper remedy, perhaps the twenty-year effort to implement the promise of *Brown* has, in fact, reached its logical conclusion. The problems of school segregation in the cities may be so intractible that one tool—the constitutional command of equal educational opportunity for all races articulated in *Brown*—cannot and should not be expected to solve alone the problem of segregated education. Until new tools are found and implemented—a negative income tax or experimentation with John Rawls' theories of distributive justice[197] or some other, yet unborn,

---

193. *But cf.* Newburg Area Council v. Board of Educ. of Jefferson County, 510 F.2d 1358 (6th Cir. 1974) (consolidated with Haycraft v. Board of Educ. of Louisville).

194. *See* Read, *The Southern Negro Fights for Quality Education,* N.Y. Times, Oct. 13, 1969, at 52, col. 4.

195. *See, e.g.*, Norwalk CORE v. Norwalk Bd. of Educ., 423 F.2d 121 (2d Cir. 1970).

196. *See* Oliver v. Donovan, 293 F. Supp. 958 (E.D.N.Y. 1968). *See also* CONFRONTATION AT OCEAN HILL-BROWNSVILLE (M. Berube & M. Gittell eds. 1969).

197. *See* J. RAWLS, A THEORY OF JUSTICE (1971). It is possible that, while the equal protection

idea—it is at least arguable that the limits have been reached in using the Constitution alone as a means for attaining school desegregation.

---

clause of the fourteenth amendment may have been pushed as far as it will go in providing equal educational opportunity to black children as such, new and more neutral equal protection theories will develop based on economics and the problem of the poor generally—rather than being based on race alone.

SCHOOL DESEGREGATION LITIGATION IN THE SEVENTIES AND THE USE OF SOCIAL SCIENCE EVIDENCE: AN ANNOTATED GUIDE

BETSY LEVIN* AND PHILIP MOISE†

INTRODUCTION

A. The Use of Social Science Research in Litigation

Courts on occasion refer to sources outside the trial record to establish "constitutional facts."[1] This is not a new practice, nor a practice that began with *Brown v. Board of Education*,[2] nor even a practice that is confined to school desegregation litigation.[3] Justice Harlan's use of medical and social science data in *Lochner v. New York*[4] in 1905 marks one of the earliest attempts to introduce non-legal material.[5] This was shortly followed by *Muller v. Oregon*, a case involv-

* Associate Professor of Law, Duke University.

† J.D., Duke University, 1974; member of the North Carolina bar; presently on active duty with the United States Army, Judge Advocate General's Corps, Fort Sheridan, Illinois.

Several memoranda by attorneys who have been or are litigating these issues, or who are close students of such litigation, were prepared for the Conference on The Courts, Social Science, and School Desegregation, held in August 1974 in South Carolina. The memoranda presented various views of the issues courts presently face in school desegregation litigation. This article has drawn on the insights provided in those memoranda, although the authors bear the final responsibility for the interpretations and conclusions in this article.

The contributors, whom the authors gratefully acknowledge, were Derrick A. Bell, Jr., Professor of Law, Harvard University; Norman J. Chachkin, Staff Attorney, NAACP Legal Defense and Educational Fund, Inc.; J. Harold Flannery, Director, Lawyers' Committee for Civil Rights under Law; Owen M. Fiss, Professor of Law, Yale University; Harold Horowitz, Professor of Law, University of California at Los Angeles; Sanford Jay Rosen, Legal Director, and Carlos Alcala, Interim Director of Educational Litigation, Mexican-American Legal Defense and Educational Fund; and William L. Taylor, Director, The Center for National Policy Review.

1. For the difference between adjudicative facts and legislative or constitutional facts see 2 K. DAVIS, ADMINISTRATIVE LAW TREATISE § 15.03 (1958). *See also* Hart & McNaughton, *Evidence and Inference in the Law*, 87 DAEDALUS 41 (1958).
2. 347 U.S. 483 (1954).
3. Some have suggested that the Supreme Court's use of social science as evidence in *Brown* was an unprecedented innovation, thus explaining the fierce debate over the propriety of using such evidence in a legal opinion. *See, e.g.*, P. ROSEN, THE SUPREME COURT AND SOCIAL SCIENCE 169-70 (1972). Perhaps, however, the outcry that was raised was due to the fact that the case was not a relatively non-controversial one of low visibility (*e.g.*, an antitrust case involving the introduction of extensive economic data), but a case capable of overturning the social structure of the South, based on segregation and racism.
4. 198 U.S. 45 (1905).
5. *See* P. BREST, PROCESS OF CONSTITUTIONAL DECISION MAKING 938-39 (1975).

ing a maximum hour law for women, in which Louis Brandeis filed a 113-page brief in support of the law's constitutionality, drawing upon such sources as surveys, government statistics, factory reports, and the opinions of doctors, employers, and employees.[6] The so-called "Brandeis Brief" was cited with approval by the Court.[7] Since then, the courts have frequently resorted to nonlegal research to support legal conclusions. Trademark and antitrust litigation, for example, have been areas long dominated by empirical social science evidence. Empirical social science data and research also have been cited in cases involving the death penalty,[8] six-man juries,[9] legal insanity rules,[10] and the use of test scores and education credentials for employment.[11] Social science data

6. Brief on behalf of the people, prepared by Louis D. Brandeis and Josephine Goldmark, Muller v. Oregon, 208 U.S. 412 (1908).

7. 208 U.S. at 419-20 n. 1. Professor Paul Freund would distinguish the "Brandeis Brief" from the use of psychological and sociological research in *Brown* on the ground that the Brandeis Brief was used to *support* legislation—and thus was in line with the usual presumption of constitutionality. In *Brown*, however, extra-legal evidence was used to attack legislation. P. FREUND, THE SUPREME COURT OF THE UNITED STATES 152 (1961).

8. Furman v. Georgia, 408 U.S. 238 (1972).

9. In Williams v. Florida, 399 U.S. 78 (1970), Justice White, writing for the majority, noted that "[w]hat few experiments have occurred . . . indicate that there is no discernible difference between the results reached by the two different-sized [6-man and 12-man] juries," *id.* at 101, citing six sources which were not based on empirical research by social scientists but on the experience of lawyers and judges in reduced jury jurisdictions. Justice White continued in Williams: "In short, neither currently available evidence nor theory suggests that the 12-man jury is necessarily more advantageous to the defendant than a jury composed of fewer members." *Id.* at 101-02. As an example of "theory," the Justice cited H. KALVEN & H. ZEISEL, THE AMERICAN JURY 462-63, 488-89 (1966) for the proposition that "jurors in the minority on the first ballot are likely to be influenced by the proportional size of the majority aligned against them." 399 U.S. at 101 n. 49. Justice White concluded that:

> If a defendant needs initially to persuade four jurors that the State has not met its burden of proof in order to escape ultimate conviction by a 12-man jury, he arguably escapes by initially persuading half that number in a six-man jury; random reduction, within limits, of the absolute number of the jury would not affect the outcome.

399 U.S. at 102 n. 49.

It is of interest to note that one of the authors of the study cited by Justice White has since written with regard to use of this data from *The American Jury*: "It is only fair to point out that the findings were quite different" from the way in which they were stated by Justice White. Zeisel, . . . *And Then There Were None: The Diminution of the Federal Jury*, 38 U. CHI. L. REV. 710, 719 (1971). Zeisel noted that the study suggested that for a juror to hold out against a majority, it was necessary for him to have a companion. Thus although the odds are the same at five to one or ten to two, at ten to two the dissenters will hold out a much higher percentage of the time than if one juror is alone at five to one. *Id.* at 719-20.

10. In Durham v. United States, 214 F.2d 862 (D.C. Cir. 1954), the D.C. Court of Appeals relied in part upon articles on legal insanity by psychiatrists and other medico-legal writers, *id.* at 870-74, in deciding that the traditional *M'Naghten* rule for determining the availability of the defense of insanity in a criminal case (defendant presumed sane unless suffering from a disease of the mind such that he did not know the difference between right and wrong) should be abandoned for a new rule: whether or not the "unlawful act was the product of mental disease or mental defect." 214 F.2d at 875. The court recently reconsidered the *Durham* rule governing the insanity defense and replaced it with the test given in § 4.01 of the American Law Institute's *Model Penal Code*. United States v. Brawner, 471 F.2d 969, 973 (D.C. Cir. 1972).

11. In Griggs v. Duke Power Co., 401 U.S. 424 (1971), the Court relied in part on a study by the Equal Employment Opportunity Commission showing that 58 per cent of white applicants passed a battery of intelligence tests including that used by Duke Power Company, while only 6 per

and research findings were even brought to bear on the racial area before *Brown*. The Supreme Court struck down state court enforcement of racially restrictive covenants in 1948.[12] While it is not apparent in the Supreme Court's opinion, sociological material was introduced at every stage—from the initial trial through the argument before the Supreme Court.[13] In a case concerning the refusal of the University of Texas Law School to admit blacks,[14] anthropological evidence of the relationship between intelligence and race was introduced at the trial.[15]

In a substantial number of these cases, judges unfamiliar with the methodology of social science research have attempted unsuccessfully to assimilate complex data which were equivocal and ambiguous. Ambiguity has led to misunderstanding, and often to misinterpretation and misuse of the research introduced into evidence.[16] Courts have disagreed as to the weight to be assigned social science research findings,[17] just as social scientists themselves have

---

cent of black applicants passed. *Id.* at 430 n. 6. The Supreme Court held that these data established a prima facie case of discriminatory employment criteria, thereby shifting the burden to the Company to show that its requirements were significantly related to a successful job performance, a burden which the Company was unable to meet on the basis of the evidence introduced. *Id.* at 431. Similarly, in Douglas v. Hampton, 512 F.2d 976 (D.C. Cir. 1975), two studies were used to establish a prima facie case of the racially disproportionate impact of the Federal Service Entrance Examination (FSEE). *Id.* at 982-83. These studies showed that the passing rate on the FSEE for those having attended predominantly black colleges was between 12.4 per cent and 8.6 per cent, while for those having attended predominantly white colleges it was between 60.2 per cent and 42.1 per cent. *Id.* at 982.

12. Shelley v. Kraemer, 334 U.S. 1 (1948).

13. Kohn, *Social Psychological Data, Legislative Fact, and Constitutional Law*, 29 Geo. Wash. L. Rev. 136, 137 (1960).

14. Sweatt v. Painter, 339 U.S. 629 (1950).

15. Kohn, *supra* note 13, at 140.

16. *See, e.g.*, Levin, *Education, Life Chances and the Courts: The Role of Social Science Evidence*, 39 Law & Contemp. Prob. no. 2, at 217 (1975); Rosenblum, *A Place for Social Science Along the Judiciary's Constitutional Law Frontier*, 66 Nw. U.L. Rev. 455, 460-61 (1971).

17. In the capital punishment decision, Furman v. Georgia, 408 U.S. 238 (1972), Justice Douglas, concurring, cited Koeninger, *Capital Punishment in Texas, 1924-1968*, 15 Crime & Delinquency 132 (1969) and H. Bedau, The Death Penalty in America 474 (1967) for statistics showing that blacks were executed more frequently than whites. 408 U.S. at 250 n. 15. Justice Marshall, also concurring, cited T. Sellins, The Death Penalty, A Report for the Model Penal Code Project of the American Law Institute (1959) as showing that murders do not increase when capital punishment is banned or decrease in areas that impose the death penalty, 408 U.S. at 348-50, and, citing other studies, argued that "[i]n light of the massive amount of evidence before us, I see no alternative but to conclude that capital punishment cannot be justified on the basis of its deterrent effect." 408 U.S. at 354. Concurring also, Justice Stewart—relying upon H. Bedau, *supra*—purported to show that the evidence of the deterrent effect of the death penalty is so inconclusive that it is insufficient to support the conclusion that the death penalty is not justified. 408 U.S. at 307-08. Justice Powell, dissenting, also drew upon these studies to show the contradictory nature of the evidence of both the deterrent effect of the death penalty and the possible discrimination involved in its imposition. 408 U.S. at 434-50, 454-56.

The only justice to directly controvert the assertion that the death penalty is imposed arbitrarily was Chief Justice Burger, who stated in his dissent that the assertion had "no empirical basis." 408 U.S. at 389, citing for support of the contrary proposition, Note, *A Study of the California Penalty Jury in First-Degree-Murder Cases*, 21 Stan. L. Rev. 1297 (1969) and H. Kalven & H. Zeisel, *supra* note 9. *See also* Maxwell v. Bishop, 398 F.2d 138 (8th Cir. 1968), *vacated and remanded on other grounds*, 398 U.S. 262 (1970).

differed as to the scientific validity of the same studies. The net result of this attempted union of law and social science understandably has been unsatisfactory for jurists and social scientists alike. Mutual distrust has often been the result, and valuable insights have been lost or denied as judges and juries have sought to separate hard fact from educated speculation.

It is not the purpose of this article to explore the host of problems which presently prevent the effective application of social science research to the judicial process. There are numerous articles which deal with those problems.[18] It is enough for our purposes that courts have considered and will continue to consider social science evidence in an attempt to discern the factual and legal truth of school desegregation questions. This article surveys the legal issues presently confronting courts as they decide school desegregation cases, and the extent to which social science research has been brought to bear on those issues.

B. Social Science and the Footnote Eleven Debate

When *Brown* was decided, there was considerable debate concerning the extent to which the Supreme Court's opinion rested upon the social science evidence cited in footnote eleven of the *Brown* opinion,[19] rather than upon principles of law.[20] The strongest voice to challenge the import of footnote eleven was that of Edmond Cahn:[21]

> I would not have the constitutional rights of Negroes—or of other Americans—rest on any such flimsy foundation as some of the scientific demonstrations in these records . . . . [S]ince the behavioral sciences are so very young, imprecise, and changeful, their findings have an uncertain expectancy of life. Today's sanguine asseveration may be cancelled by tomorrow's new revelation—or new technical fad.

---

18. *See, e.g.*, Rosenblum, *supra* note 16; Hazard, *Limitations on the Uses of Behavioral Science in the Law*, 19 CASE W. RES. L. REV. 71 (1967); Lochner, *Some Limits on the Application of Social Science Research in the Legal Process*, 1973 LAW & SOCIAL ORDER 815.

19. Brown v. Board of Educ., 347 U.S. 483, 494-95 n. 11 (1954).

20. *See, e.g.*, C. SWISHER, THE SUPREME COURT IN MODERN ROLE 158-62 (1954); W. WORKMAN, THE CASE FOR THE SOUTH, 26, 30, 197 (1960); Greenberg, *Social Scientists Take the Stand: A Review and Appraisal of Their Testimony in Litigation*, 54 MICH. L. REV. 953 (1956); Sutherland, *The American Judiciary and Racial Desegregation*, 20 MODERN L. REV. 201 (1957); Cahn, *Jurisprudence*, 30 N.Y.U.L. REV. 150 (1955); Clark, *The Desegregation Cases: Criticism of the Social Scientist's Role*, 5 VILL. L. REV. 224 (1959); Black, *The Lawfulness of the Segregation Decisions*, 69 YALE L.J. 421 (1960).

21. Cahn, *supra* note 20, at 157, 167. *See also* Cahn, *Jurisprudence*, 31 N.Y.U.L. REV. 182 (1956). Professor Kalven has noted that:

> His [Professor Cahn's] fear was that scientific fact having been tendered on the issue, the merits would be thought to stand or fall with it, so that a shift tomorrow in the fashions of science would force a shift in the conclusions about segregation.

Professor Kalven, however, found that fear

> unfounded not because the scientific fact might not change, but because it has become clear that neither we nor the Court rested our conviction as to the evils of racial segregation on the scientific proof. That judgment had deeper and perhaps less rational sources.

Kalven, *The Quest for the Middle Range: Empirical Inquiry and Legal Policy*, in LAW IN A CHANGING AMERICA 56, 66 (G. Hazard ed. 1968).

Some lower courts did attempt to do what Professor Cahn had feared. A federal district court in Georgia believed that the question presented in *Brown*—whether segregation of children in public schools is harmful—was a question of fact rather than of law. The judge therefore permitted evidence, much of which was developed after 1954, to be introduced in an attempt to show that[22]

> the separation of Negro and white children in the public schools was not determined solely by race or color but rather upon racial traits of educational significance as to which racial identity was only a convenient index. . . . [and that the] differences in specific capabilities, learning progress rates, mental maturity, and capacity for education in general . . . as well as differences in physical, psychical and behavioral traits . . . were . . . of such magnitude as to make it impossible for Negro and white children of the same chronological age to be effectively educated in the same classrooms.

The court found, on the basis of the evidence submitted, that both white and black students would be seriously injured by integration and that[23]

> [w]hatever psychological injury may be sustained by a Negro child out of his sense of rejection by white children is increased rather than abated by forced intermixture, and this increase is in direct proportion to the number and extent of his contacts with white children.

The Fifth Circuit, however, peremptorily reversed the district court,[24] and this problem rarely surfaced again in such blatant form.[25]

---

22. Stell v. Savannah-Chatham County Bd. of Educ., 220 F. Supp. 667, 668 (S.D. Ga. 1963).
23. 220 F. Supp. at 684.
24. 333 F.2d 55 (5th Cir.), *cert. denied*, 379 U.S. 933 (1964).

> [N]o inferior federal court may refrain from acting as required by [*Brown v. Board of Educ.*] even if such a court should conclude that the Supreme Court erred either as to its facts or as to the law. . . . We do not read the major premise of the decision of the Supreme Court . . . as being limited to the facts of the cases there presented. We read it as proscribing segregation in the public education process on the stated ground that separate but equal schools for the races were inherently unequal. This being our interpretation of the teaching of that decision, it follows that it would be entirely inappropriate for it to be rejected or obviated by this court.

Id. at 61.

25. *But see* Evers v. Jackson Municipal Separate School Dist., 232 F. Supp. 241 (S.D. Miss. 1964), which permitted evidence to be introduced to show that separate schools were not injurious, but instead were advantageous to pupils of both races. *Id.* at 244-50. Such testimony included that of seven "distinguished" scientists as "to the existence of such differences between the two groups to constitute a rational basis for separate schooling"—differences between the races in IQ and in cranial capacity and brain size. *Id.* at 246-47. Evidence was also introduced that the "mixing" of the races in the same school is injurious. *Id.* at 245. Although District Judge Mize expressed the opinion that this evidence "cr[ies] out for a reappraised and complete reconsideration of the findings and conclusion of the United States Supreme Court in the Brown decision," he nevertheless granted the plaintiff's prayer for an injunction, feeling bound by the Fifth Circuit's prior holding in *Stell v. Savannah-Chatham County Bd. of Educ. Id.* at 255.

Judge Wisdom, speaking for the Fifth Circuit on appeal, stated that "[t]hese cases tax the patience of the Court." 357 F.2d 653, 654 (5th Cir.), *cert. denied*, 384 U.S. 961 (1966). In firmly rejecting any further attempts "to overturn Brown on a factual showing," Judge Wisdom declared that the inherent inequality of segregated schools was now a *legal* principle no longer open to question. *Id.*

Since *Brown*, the courts have continued to refer to social science research in segregation cases, although more frequently in regard to questions concerning the nature and extent of the remedies to be applied, rather than whether segregation is a constitutional violation per se. As the legal questions of school desegregation have become more and more complex (compared to the relatively clear and simple issue presented in *Brown*), social science research has become less certain and more debatable—or at least it seems so to many lawyers and judges.[26]

The increasing lack of unanimity on the Court may be a reflection of the growing complexity of the issues. *Swann v. Charlotte-Mecklenburg Board of Education*[27] marked the end of the unbroken line of unanimous Supreme Court decisions in school desegregation which began with *Brown*. The cracks in the wall of unanimity first appeared in two cases which followed *Swann* by only a little over a year—after eighteen years of unanimity in school desegregation cases. Chief Justice Burger dissented in *Wright v. Council of the City of Emporia*,[28] joined by Justices Blackmun, Powell, and Rehnquist. The same four concurred only in the result in *United States v. Scotland Neck City Board of Education*.[29]

The crack widened into a sizable fissure with *Keyes v. School District No. 1* (the Denver case).[30] Justice Brennan wrote the majority opinion; the Chief Justice concurred in the result. Justice Douglas joined the opinion of the Court, but in a separate opinion reprimanded the majority for continuing the de facto-de jure distinction by requiring the plaintiff to produce evidence of the "intent" of school authorities.[31] Justice Powell wrote an opinion concurring in part and dissenting in part. Justice Rehnquist dissented. Justice White did not participate. Finally, with *Milliken v. Bradley* (the Detroit case),[32] the unanimous front ruptured completely—Chief Justice Burger writing for a majority which included Justices Rehnquist, Powell, Stewart, and Blackmun; Justice Stewart filed a separate concurring opinion; Justice White dissented, joined by Justices Douglas, Brennan, and Marshall; another dissent by Marshall was joined by the other three dissenters; and Justice Douglas filed a separate dissent.

In attempting to identify the principal issues, it is useful to treat them as clustered around two separate and distinct categories, although in *Milliken v.*

---

26. *Cf.* Justice Powell's comments in the *Rodriguez* case:

> [T]his case . . . involves the most persistent and difficult questions of educational policy, another area in which *this Court's lack of specialized knowledge and experience counsels against premature interference* . . . . On even the most basic questions in this area the scholars and educational experts are divided. Indeed, one of the major sources of controversy concerns the extent to which there is a demonstrable correlation between educational expenditures and the quality of education . . . .

San Antonio Independent School Dist. v. Rodriguez, 411 U.S. 1, 42-43 (1973) (emphasis added).

27. 402 U.S. 1 (1971).
28. 407 U.S. 451 (1972).
29. 407 U.S. 484 (1972).
30. 413 U.S. 189 (1973).
31. 413 U.S. at 214-16.
32. 418 U.S. 717 (1974).

Bradley, the Supreme Court seems to have merged the two so that there may no longer be as clear a line between them as before. Thus, there are a number of issues comprising the first category establishing the *violation*; *i.e.*, whether a violation of the equal protection clause of the fourteenth amendment has occurred, giving rise to the duty to desegregate the school system. The second category includes issues concerned with *remedy*; *i.e.*, once it has been determined that the equal protection clause has been violated, what are the permissible remedies which courts can order? This article will examine these two questions and the context in which they arise in today's school desegregation cases, as well as the kinds of social science evidence which the courts draw upon in answering these questions.

I
Developments in the Law of School Desegregation From Brown to Swann: A Brief Review[33]

In 1954, four separate cases—from Kansas, South Carolina, Virginia, and Delaware[34]—were consolidated for argument in the Supreme Court. The Court framed the issue before it as being whether "segregation of children in public schools solely on the basis of race, even though the physical facilities and other 'tangible' factors may be equal, deprive[s] the children of the minority group of equal educational opportunities."[35] The Court then held that the fourteenth amendment forbids such state-imposed segregation of races in public schools: "[I]n the field of public education the doctrine of 'separate but equal' has no place. Separate educational facilities are inherently unequal."[36]

The Court approved the finding of the Kansas district court which stated:[37]

> Segregation of white and colored children in public schools has a detrimental effect upon the colored children. The impact is greater when it has the sanction of the law; for the policy of separating the races is usually interpreted as denoting the inferiority of the negro group. A sense of inferiority affects the motivation of a child to learn. Segregation with the sanction of law, therefore, has a tendency to [retard] the educational and mental development of negro

---

33. The tortuous process of the development of school desegregation law is traced in Read, *Judicial Evolution of the Law of School Integration Since* Brown v. Board of Education, 39 Law & Contemp. Prob. no. 1, at 7 (1975).

34. Brown v. Board of Educ. of Topeka, 98 F. Supp. 797 (D. Kan. 1951); Briggs v. Elliott, 103 F. Supp. 920 (E.D.S.C. 1952); Davis v. County School Bd., 103 F. Supp. 337 (E.D. Va. 1952); Gebhart v. Belton, 33 Del. Ch. 144, 91 A.2d 137 (1952).

35. Brown v. Board of Educ., 347 U.S. 483, 493 (1954).

36. 347 U.S. at 495.

37. 347 U.S. at 494. The Court went further and suggested that "[a]ny language in *Plessy v. Ferguson* contrary to this finding is rejected." *Id.* at 494-95. In *Plessy*, it will be recalled, Justice Brown noted that

> the underlying fallacy of the plaintiff's argument consist[s] in the assumption that the enforced separation of the two races stamps the colored race with a badge of inferiority. If this be so, it is not by reason of anything in the act, but solely because the colored race chooses to put that construction upon it.

163 U.S. 537, 551 (1896).

> children and to deprive them of some of the benefits they would receive in a racial[ly] integrated school system.

This finding, suggested the majority, was "amply supported by modern authority," which was named in the now famous footnote eleven of the opinion.

The cases were set down for further argument on the question of appropriate relief. *Brown II*[38] was decided the following year and the cases were remanded with the following directions regarding the extent of the equitable remedial powers of lower courts:[39]

> In fashioning and effectuating the decrees, the courts will be guided by equitable principles. Traditionally, equity has been characterized by a practical flexibility in shaping its remedies [footnote omitted] and by a facility for adjusting and reconciling public and private needs. [Footnote omitted.] These cases call for the exercise of these traditional attributes of equity power. At stake is the personal interest of the plaintiffs in admission to public schools as soon as practicable on a nondiscriminatory basis. To effectuate this interest may call for elimination of a variety of obstacles in making the transition . . . . Courts of equity may properly take into account the public interest in the elimination of such obstacles in a systematic and effective manner. But it should go without saying that the vitality of these constitutional principles cannot be allowed to yield simply because of disagreement with them.

The Court said the objective must be "to effectuate a transition to a *racially non-discriminatory school system*." (Emphasis added.)[40]

For almost twenty years following the *Brown* decision, the problem of establishing a constitutional violation rarely presented itself since subsequent cases arose almost exclusively in southern states in which segregation had been constitutionally or statutorily mandated.[41] This twenty-year struggle to implement *Brown* in the South was, in large part, only a struggle with the question of remedying admitted state-imposed segregation. In the few cases which arose outside of the South, some courts found only de facto segregation and hence no state action requiring desegregation,[42] while others reached the opposite result. No non-southern case, however, reached the Supreme Court until *Keyes* (the Denver case) in 1973.

---

38. Brown v. Board of Educ., 349 U.S. 294 (1955).

39. *Id.* at 300.

40. 349 U.S. at 301.

41. A few courts expressed the belief that since the constitutional rights of minorities depended on the extent of harm that allegedly stemmed from segregation, a showing of the opposite—that there was no harm—meant that there was no right to be violated. See for example the *Stell v. Savannah-Chatham County Bd. of Educ.* situation at notes 22-24 *supra* and accompanying text.

42. Some early lower court cases in which litigants unsuccessfully sought to establish an affirmative right to desegregation without regard to the cause of the existing pattern of segregated schools are Deal v. Cincinnati, 369 F.2d 55 (6th Cir. 1966); Bell v. School City of Gary, 324 F.2d 209 (7th Cir. 1963). In *Deal*, the plaintiffs had argued that black children would be harmed by attending a racially imbalanced school. The Sixth Circuit, however, held that "[a] finding of educational or other harm is not essential to strike down enforced segregation." *Id.* at 59. The court went on to say, however, that "a showing of harm alone is not enough to invoke the remedial powers of the law." *Id.*

A brief review of the kinds of segregatory plans[43] which were adopted by states in the early years of litigation—purportedly to remedy segregation—provides some insights into some of the issues with which courts are grappling today.

(1) *Pupil Placement Laws*. Under pupil placement laws, students were initially assigned to the schools maintained for their race. Requests for transfers were then considered on an individual basis, in light of various "non-racial" factors. In Alabama, the law set forth the following factors, among others, which a board of education should consider in granting or denying a request to transfer:[44]

> the psychological qualification of the pupil for the type of teaching and associations involved, . . . the psychological effect upon the pupil of attendance at a particular school; the possibility or threat of friction or disorder among pupils or others; the possibility of breaches of the peace or ill-will or economic retaliation within the community; . . . the maintenance or severance of established social and psychological relationships with other pupils and with teachers . . . .

It is obvious that it would be very difficult, under such a law, to bring about any significant amount of desegregation.[45] At first courts sustained these kinds of laws, which were constitutional on their face, on the assumption that they were being constitutionally applied.[46] Finally, however, the courts began to hold that since the initial assignment was on the basis of race, such measures were unconstitutional.[47]

(2) *Freedom-of-choice Plans*. School authorities began to replace pupil assignment plans with freedom-of-choice plans. Most of these plans required every pupil to exercise a choice at the beginning of each school year, thus eliminating the automatic initial assignment of pupils to the schools of their race *unless* a transfer were requested. A pupil's choice could only be denied on the basis of overcrowding. However, "freedom-of-choice" plans did not work either.[48] In 1968, with *Green v. County School Board*,[49] the Court finally announced that it would no longer permit freedom-of-choice plans where the

---

43. *See* Read, *supra* note 33, for a much more detailed and comprehensive discussion of the kinds of measures to which the states resorted in attempting to demonstrate that they had moved to a "racially nondiscriminatory school system."

44. Ala. Code tits. 52-56, § 61(4) (1960).

45. Note, *The Federal Courts and Integration of Southern Schools: Troubled Status of the Pupil Placement Acts*, 62 Colum. L. Rev. 1448, 1452-53 (1962).

46. *See, e.g.*, Carson v. Warlick, 238 F.2d 724 (4th Cir. 1956), *cert. denied*, 353 U.S. 910 (1957); Shuttlesworth v. Birmingham Bd. of Educ., 162 F. Supp. 372 (N.D. Ala. 1958), *aff'd on limited grounds*, 358 U.S. 101 (1958).

47. *See, e.g.*, Bush v. Orleans Parish School Bd., 308 F.2d 491 (1962); Northcross v. Board of Educ., 302 F.2d 818 (6th Cir.), *cert. denied*, 370 U.S. 944 (1962).

48. United States v. Jefferson County Bd. of Educ., 372 F.2d 836, 888-94 (5th Cir. 1966), *aff'd on rehearing en banc*, 380 F.2d 385 (5th Cir.), *cert. denied*, 389 U.S. 840 (1967); United States Commission on Civil Rights, Survey of School Desegregation in the Southern and Border States 1965-66, at 51 (1966).

49. 391 U.S. 430 (1968).

"freedom" was illusory, and where it produced only token desegregation.[50] However, it left open the question of what the freedom-of-choice plans it might permit would resemble.[51]

(3) "*All Deliberate Speed Plans*." These included grade-a-year plans and other proposals which brought about—at best—token desegregation. In 1969, the Court, in a short per curiam opinion, made clear that boards of education would no longer be allowed to desegregate "with all deliberate speed."[52]

II
THE CONSTITUTIONAL VIOLATION

Having ordered massive *immediate* desegregation,[53] the unanswered questions that remained were: by what means and up to what limits? What is in the arsenal of equitable remedies which federal judges can draw upon? Are there limits to the use of certain remedies and if so, what are they? The case in which the Supreme Court attempted to come to grips with some of these questions is the now famous *Swann v. Charlotte-Mecklenburg County Board of Education*,[54] decided in 1971.

A. District-wide De Jure Segregation

Until *Keyes v. School District No. 1* (the Denver case)[55] the Supreme Court had only dealt with cases from school districts in which segregation had been

50. New Kent County School Board had made no steps to desegregate until 1965 when it adopted its freedom-of-choice plan. Only 15 per cent of the black students and none of the white students had changed schools under the plan. *Id.* at 441-42.

51.
> We do not hold that "freedom of choice" can have no place in [a desegregation] plan. We do not hold that a "freedom-of-choice" plan might of itself be unconstitutional . . . . Although the general experience under "freedom of choice" to date has been such as to indicate its ineffectiveness as a tool of desegregation, [footnote omitted] there may well be instances in which it can serve as an effective device. Where it offers real promise of aiding a desegregation program to effectuate conversion of a state-imposed dual system to a unitary, nonracial system there might be no objection to allowing such a device to prove itself in operation. On the other hand, if there are reasonably available other ways, such for illustration as zoning, promising speedier and more effective conversion to a unitary, nonracial school system, "freedom of choice" must be held unacceptable.

391 U.S. at 439, 440-41.

52. Alexander v. Holmes County Bd. of Educ., 396 U.S. 19 (1969).

> [T]he Court of Appeals should have denied all motions for additional time because continued operation of segregated schools under a standard of allowing "all deliberate speed" for desegregation is *no longer constitutionally permissible*.

Id. at 20 (emphasis added). *See also* Carter v. West Feliciana Parish School Bd., 396 U.S. 290 (1970).

53. In Professor Read's view, while "enormous progress" had been made between *Green* and *Carter*, "it was the *Carter* reversal that precipitated another quantum leap in school desegregation activity." Read, *supra* note 33, at 32. In *Carter*, the Fifth Circuit had permitted a delay in implementing court-ordered desegregation plans while cases were being appealed. The Supreme Court summarily reversed, causing a shift from token desegregation to massive affirmative integration. *Id.*

54. 402 U.S. 1 (1971). *Swann*'s approach to the question of appropriate remedies is discussed in the text at pp. 81-88 *infra*.

55. 413 U.S. 189 (1973).

required (or at least permitted) by law. *Swann* is representative of the category of cases in which there was an admitted past history of district-wide de jure segregation. The Court found that the Charlotte-Mecklenburg school board had not yet completely disestablished its dual school system and converted it to the "unitary, nonracial system of public education" dictated by *Green*.[56] The school board had argued that the segregated pattern of school attendance was not due to deliberate assignment by race on the part of school officials but rather to the nature of residential patterns. In other words, the board argued, since there was no longer a statute requiring segregated schools and no deliberate acts on the part of school officials to segregate the schools, there was no constitutional violation to be remedied. The schools were segregated, but only fortuitously, as a result of the use of neighborhood attendance zones in a school district in which the neighborhoods were highly segregated.

The Court seemed to agree with the school authorities that there was no discrimination practiced by the school district in its present method of assigning pupils. Nevertheless, the Court presumed that there was a causal connection between the school district's *admitted* past discrimination and the present pattern of segregated schools. This meant that in a system formerly segregated by law, the plaintiff could invoke a presumption that the current segregated patterns were "vestiges" of past state-imposed segregation.[57] Among the factors the courts would look to is whether *past* discriminatory conduct of the school board might have contributed to the creation and maintenance of segregated residential patterns which, when coupled with the *present* use of geographic proximity as a basis for assignment, would produce segregated patterns of student attendance.[58] For example, prior decisions of the school board regarding location and size of schools might explain why assigning students to schools nearest their homes would result in racially homogeneous schools: a new school is constructed to be of such a size that it can serve only a racially homogeneous area or is so situated that it is the closest school to students of only one race.[59]

---

56. 391 U.S. at 436.

57. 402 U.S. at 26.

58. 402 U.S. at 28.

59. *Id.* The *Swann* opinion clearly implies that the location of school facilities can contribute to the development of a pattern of residential segregation as well as the reverse.

> People gravitate toward school facilities, just as schools are located in response to the needs of people. The location of schools may thus influence the patterns of residential development of a metropolitan area and have important impact on composition of inner-city neighborhoods. . . . It may well promote segregated residential patterns which, when combined with "neighborhood zoning," further lock the school system into the mold of separation of the races.

402 U.S. at 20-21.

In a later case—the first school desegregation case outside of the South to be decided by the Supreme Court—the Court referred to the "reciprocal effect" on the racial composition of residential neighborhoods caused by school assignment and other policies which "earmark" schools according to their racial composition. Keyes v. School Dist. No. 1, 413 U.S. 189, 201-02 (1973). For example, in Denver, a small school was constructed in the midst of other elementary schools attended predominantly by blacks, all of which were located in the predominantly black section of

The Court even indicated that plaintiffs could establish a prima facie case of a violation of the equal protection clause without evidence of student assignment policies or of neighborhood residential patterns of segregation when[60]

> it is possible to identify a "white school" or a "Negro school" simply by reference to the racial composition of teachers and staff, the quality of school buildings and equipment or the organization of sports activities . . . .

Thus, what the Court was saying is that in a school district where there is a past history of de jure segregation, it is the *effect* of decisions made by school officials that is important, and not whether those decisions were made with *intent* to maintain segregation.[61]

The Court also indicated, however, that at some point in time the relationship between a system's past segregative acts and present segregation may become so attenuated as to be incapable of supporting a finding of de jure segregation warranting judicial intervention.[62] Consequently, the Court raised, by implication, the question of how long a period of supervision by the courts will be required before they determine whether a dual system has been dismantled. Precisely what a defendant school board must show to overcome the presumption that the segregated pattern is still a "vestige" of previous state-imposed segregation, however, remains unanswered.

Does the Constitution impose on school boards the duty of retarding district-wide resegregation? Resegregation can be caused by changes in residential patterns as a function of "white flight" whether due to "natural mobility" or private bias (*e.g.*, discrimination in the sale, rental or financing of housing in the private market) or to policies and practices of governmental agencies in locating housing, highways and other public facilities, and in developing and maintaining exclusionary land use practices.[63] Are such changes in residential

---

the city. This new school was then used to accommodate the overflow from the nearby black schools, and, although a predominantly-white elementary school just eight blocks away was also overcrowded, no white students were transferred to the newly built school. For the facts of this situation, see 445 F.2d 990, 1000 (10th Cir. 1971) (same case, lower court opinion).

60. 402 U.S. at 18.

61. "Thus we have focused upon the effect—not the purpose or motivation of a school board's action . . . ." Wright v. Council of City of Emporia, 407 U.S. 451, 462 (1972).

62. 402 U.S. at 31-32. The Court's restatement of the original proposition is in *Keyes*, 413 U.S. at 211.

63. In Hart v. Community School Bd., 383 F. Supp. 699 (E.D.N.Y. 1974), a federal district court took cognizance of the fact that other governmental agencies were responsible, at least in part, for segregated residential patterns. *Id.* at 758. The court ordered city, state, and federal housing authorities to provide a joint plan for reducing the racial imbalance in the affected neighborhood. *Id.* at 757. The court suggested that such a plan might include "refertilization" of the area with new white families who would contribute to stabilization; acceleration of housing construction in various parts of the area; and modification of renting and construction patterns to encourage substantial members of white and middle class families with children to move into buildings constructed with the aid of public funds. The police commissioner was ordered to present a plan for adequate protection of children in the vicinity of the school; the Metropolitan Transit Authority was ordered to assist in the planning of adequate transportation to and from the school; and the Commissioner of Recreation was ordered to become involved in planning for the use of the public parks by school children. *Id.* at 757-58. The judge initially joined as additional parties

patterns which are not the result of actions taken by school authorities nevertheless their responsibility to correct through school assignment policies once the school authorities have implemented the desegregation plan and disestablished the heretofore dual school system?

The *Swann* opinion could be read to imply that a school board has *no* obligation to prevent or retard resegregation once it has "cured" the last vestiges of de jure segregation and established itself as a unitary system. Yet notwithstanding the establishment of a unitary system, there would still be certain factors within the control of school officials that could affect resegregation: the overall quality of the educational offering, curriculum content and enrichment; extracurricular activities; improvement of older facilities; and, in particular, preparation of teachers, students, and the community for the process of desegregation.[64] This suggests that a school board might at least be required to refrain from those administrative decisions which would precipitate or accelerate resegregation.

B. Segregative Actions of School Officials in a Part of the District

As the first non-southern school desegregation case to come before the Supreme Court, the Denver case[65] led to the articulation of the issues involved in a school system that had never been segregated pursuant to state statutory or constitutional provisions. There the Court found that certain actions on the part of school authorities amounted to de jure segregation.[66] However, the significance of *Keyes* lies in the manner in which it addressed the fact that while schools throughout Denver were segregated, the segregative actions in this case occurred in only part of the school system.[67] Nevertheless, the Court found district-wide remedies appropriate.

What was needed to find that the pattern of segregation was a result of the school board's unlawful actions? The difference between de facto and de jure segregation was first clearly articulated by Judge Wisdom of the Fifth Circuit in 1966.[68] In *Swann*,[69] the Supreme Court noted that there was a difference

all government agencies whose programs and policies might have an impact on the stability of a desegregation plan, but later abandoned this approach, noting that "the decretal tool is poorly designed for restructuring an entire community." 383 F. Supp. 769, 775 (E.D.N.Y. 1974), *aff'd*, 512 F.2d 37 (2d Cir. 1975).

64. *See* Orfield, *How to Make Desegregation Work: The Adaptation of Schools to Their Newly Integrated Student Bodies*, 39 Law & Contemp. Prob. no. 2, at 314 (1975).

65. Keyes v. School Dist. No. 1, 413 U.S. 189 (1973).

66. *Id.* at 207-08.

67. The Denver School Board was found to have followed a deliberately segregative policy only with respect to schools in the northeastern section of the city, attended by 37.7 per cent of Denver's total black school population. *Id.* at 199. By contrast, de jure segregation was system-wide in *Swann*.

68. United States v. Jefferson County Bd. of Educ., 372 F.2d 836, 878-79 n. 92 (5th Cir. 1966). *See also* Bell v. School City of Gary, 324 F.2d 209 (7th Cir. 1963), *cert. denied*, 377 U.S. 924 (1964). There is a well-developed body of legal writing on de facto segregation; *see, e.g.*, Goodman, *De Facto School Segregation: A Constitutional and Empirical Analysis*, 60 Cal. L. Rev. 275 (1972); Fiss, *Racial Imbalance in the Public Schools: The Constitutional Concepts*, 78 Harv. L. Rev. 564 (1965); Wright, *Public School Desegregation: Legal Remedies for De Facto Segregation*, 70 N.Y.U.L. Rev. 285 (1965).

69. 402 U.S. at 17-18. There, in the context of Title IV of the Civil Rights Act of 1964, the

between de jure and de facto segregation, but it was not until the Denver case, in 1973, that the Court actually spelled out the distinction: " [T]he differentiating factor between de jure segregation and so-called de facto segregation . . . is *purpose* or *intent* to segregate."[70] Thus the plaintiffs "must prove not only that segregated schooling exists but also that it was brought about or maintained by intentional state action."[71] Among the factors which were relied upon as indicators of "purpose" or "intent" to segregate were:

(1) deliberate segregative acts of pupil assignment to schools located in a non-white residential area of the city of Denver;
(2) racial assignment of faculty and staff;
(3) locating a school "with *conscious knowledge* that it would be a segregated school;" (emphasis added)[72] and
(4) adopting policies which "have the clear *effect* of earmarking schools according to their racial composition . . . . (emphasis added).[73]

These indicators were found only in a part of the district rather than system-wide. The Court held, however, that if these intentional segregative acts occurred in a "meaningful portion" of the school district, it in some way tainted the entire district sufficiently to trigger a district-wide remedy.[74] The Court suggested two somewhat related grounds for reaching this conclusion.[75] First, the Court noted that putting all blacks in one school on the basis of racially drawn attendance zones would necessarily keep other nearby schools all white, even though the white students were assigned on the basis of geographic proximity rather than race.[76] Also past decisions with respect to the location and size of one school could have affected the racial composition of nearby schools: if

---

Court indicated that "de facto segregation" means the existence of racial imbalance in the schools "but with no showing that [the racial imbalance] was brought about by discriminatory action of state authorities." *Id.* at 18.

70. 413 U.S. at 208. Several of the justices took sharp issue with this distinction. Justice Douglas contended that *all* school desegregation is a result of state action, and must therefore be struck down as in violation of the Constitution. 413 U.S. at 215. Justice Powell argued that it is discriminatory to presume continued segregative intent (twenty years after *Brown*) in the South and not apply the presumption of segregative intent to segregated school districts in the North. If there is segregation, no matter how caused, the burden should be on the school district to show that the system is actually a unitary, nondiscriminatory system. 413 U.S. at 224.

71. 413 U.S. at 198.

72. 413 U.S. at 201-02 (quoting from district court opinion, 303 F. Supp. at 285).

73. 413 U.S. at 202.

74. Justice Rehnquist rejected the majority's "meaningful portion" test. In his view, *only* in a system where total segregation has been required by statute can a district-wide remedy be imposed. 413 U.S. at 255. In the absence of such a statute, Justice Rehnquist would seem to require a factual determination on a school-by-school basis as to whether particular minority students were denied equal protection of the law, thus placing a heavy burden of proof on the plaintiffs rather than on the defendant school system. 413 U.S. at 256, 263.

75. *See* Fiss, *School Desegregation: The Uncertain Path of the Law*, 4 PHILOSOPHY & PUB. AFFAIRS 3, 22-25 (1974).

76. The Court stated:

> [I]t is obvious that a practice of concentrating Negroes in certain schools by structuring attendance zones or designing "feeder" schools on the basis of race has the reciprocal effect of keeping other nearby schools predominantly white.

413 U.S. at 201 & n. 12.

the board decided that a new school should be a black school in a black area and it is sized to serve only the students in that area, other nearby schools would be white even without deliberately assigning students on the basis of race.[77]

The Denver Court also returned to the theory suggested in *Swann*—that there can be a linkage between *past* discrimination on the part of school authorities and the *present* pattern of residential segregation by race.[78] It found that the various segregatory policies used by Denver school authorities tended to "earmark" schools as black or white,[79]

> and this, in turn, together with the elements of student assignment and school construction, may have a profound reciprocal effect on the racial composition of residential neighborhoods within a metropolitan area, thereby causing further racial concentration within the schools.

Thus one basis for holding that there was sufficient system-wide de jure desegregation to justify imposing a system-wide remedy was the *presumption* that deliberate segregative policies in a "meaningful" or "substantial" part of the school system taken in the past had a reciprocal effect on the remainder of the system.

The second, somewhat related ground was:[80]

> that a finding of intentionally segregative school board actions in a meaningful portion of a school system . . . creates a presumption that other segregated schooling within the system is not adventitious. It establishes . . . a prima facie case of unlawful segregative design on the part of school authorities, and shifts to those authorities the burden of proving that other segregated schools within the system are not also the result of intentionally segregative actions.

Thus, to summarize, the Denver case established the following allocation of the burden of proof for those cases in which segregation has never been mandated by state constitutional or statutory provisions: the *plaintiff* must first establish that there were (1) intentional segregative acts on the part of school authorities, and (2) that such intentional segregative acts were in a "meaningful" or "substantial" portion of the school system. This establishes a prima facie case that the entire system is unlawfully segregated—therefore requiring a district-wide remedy—either on the presumption that intentional acts in a por-

---

77. The Court concluded that:

> [T]he practice of building a school . . . to a certain size and in a certain location, "with conscious knowledge that it would be a segregated school," . . . has a substantial reciprocal effect on the racial composition of other nearby schools.

413 U.S. at 201-02.

78. *See* text accompanying note 58, at p. 60 *supra.* This tends to weaken the rather categorical statement made by Justice Stewart in his concurring opinion in *Milliken v. Bradley* (Detroit) that residential segregation—particularly that due to the increasing concentration of blacks in the central cities—is "caused by unknown and perhaps unknowable factors . . . ." 418 U.S. at 756 n. 2. *See also* Bradley v. School Bd. (Richmond), 462 F.2d 1058, 1066 (4th Cir. 1972), *aff'd by an equally divided Court*, 412 U.S. 92 (1973).

79. 413 U.S. at 202.

80. 413 U.S. at 208.

tion of the school system have had a "profound reciprocal effect" on the rest of the system, or on the presumption that where there are racially imbalanced schools throughout the system, the intentional segregative acts could not have been confined to a sub-area of the district.

The burden of proof at this point shifts to the *school authorities*.[81] They can rebut the prima facie case by disproving any segregative intent with respect to the rest of the school district[82] by showing with sufficient specificity "that segregative intent was *not* among the factors that motivated their actions." (Emphasis added.)[83] However, disproving a negative—*i.e.*, requiring school authorities to "bear the burden of explaining actions or conditions which *appear* to be racially motivated"[84]—is not an easy task. The Court indicated that there may be cases in which the causal connection could be disproved by school authorities by showing that "the geographical structure of, or the natural boundaries within, a school district [have had] the effect of dividing the district into separate, identifiable and unrelated units. . . ."[85] The Court implied, however, that such cases would be rare.[86]

The school district can also "rebut the prima facie case by showing that its *past* segregative acts did not create or contribute to the *current* segregated condition" in the other schools in the district. (Emphasis added.)[87] The Court made it quite clear, however, that mere "remoteness in time has [no] relevance to the issue of intent."[88] On the other hand, the Court reaffirmed the dicta in *Swann*, that there may be "some point in time [when] the relationship between past segregative acts and present segregation may become so attenuated as to be incapable of supporting a finding of de jure segregation warranting judicial intervention."[89] Moreover, where the core city population in a school district has long been predominantly minority, the Court suggested that reliance on a "neighborhood school policy" of pupil assignment could not justify segregated schools where "school authorities have been found to have practiced *de jure* segregation in a meaningful portion of the school system . . . ."[90]

The difference, then, between *Swann* and *Keyes* as to the burden of proof is that in *Swann* a prima facie case of unconstitutional segregative actions was

81. 413 U.S. at 209.

82. 413 U.S. at 210-11.

83. 413 U.S. at 210.

84. 413 U.S. at 209.

85. 413 U.S. at 203.

86. In *Keyes*, a six-lane major highway was *not* considered to be a barrier dividing the district into "separate, identifiable and unrelated units." 413 U.S. at 204-05.

87. 413 U.S. at 211.

88. 413 U.S. at 210.

> If the actions of school authorities were to any degree motivated by segregative intent and the segregation resulting from those actions continues to exist, the fact of remoteness in time certainly does not make those actions any less "intentional."

413 U.S. at 210-11.

89. 413 U.S. at 211 (referring to its opinion in *Swann*, 402 U.S. at 31-32).

90. 413 U.S. at 212.

established by the existence of racially identifiable schools, since the case arose in a jurisdiction formerly segregated by statute. The burden was upon the school board to refute this prima facie case. In *Keyes*, on the other hand, where the school system had never been segregated in accordance with statutory or constitutional provisions, the burden fell initially upon the plaintiff to prove that the school authorities had intentionally and purposefully implemented a system of segregated schools in at least part of the district. Once intent was proven by the plaintiff, the burden shifted to the defendant to prove that the segregative patterns found throughout the district did not emanate from the intentional plan to establish a dual school system in that part of the district where intent had been shown. Thus, the school systems in both *Swann* and *Keyes* were de jure segregated systems, but establishing this fact would be somewhat more difficult for plaintiffs bringing suit in jurisdictions such as Denver where segregation was never required or permitted by law.

In neither *Swann* nor *Keyes* did the Court place any reliance on social science research to support a finding of a constitutional violation. Courts generally have not inquired whether segregation is psychologically or educationally harmful to black and/or white children, nor have they inquired whether desegregation would "benefit" children in terms of improved pupil performance or ability to compete in the marketplace. In *Swann*, the Court reaffirmed the principle of *Brown* that "[s]eparate educational facilities are *inherently* unequal."[91] (Emphasis added.) It would seem, therefore, that although the question of educational harms and benefits may be relevant to the nature and extent of the *remedies* which may be used, it is irrelevant to the determination of a *violation* of the equal protection clause. The only social science evidence usually introduced in such suits is extensive empirical evidence concerning residential segregation patterns and other demographic trends.

C. Segregated Pattern Resulting From Actions of School Authorities Without Apparent Segregative Intent

The Supreme Court has not yet been confronted with a case in which a segregated pattern has resulted from actions taken by school officials in all or a portion of a school district, with no apparent segregative purpose or intent as the Court found in the Denver case. In both *Swann* and *Keyes*, the Court attempted to find a linkage between the existence of a segregated pattern of schooling and deliberate assignment on the basis of race. Since in those cases the Court was unable to find that the present pattern of segregated schools resulted from present deliberate segregative acts of school authorities, the Court permitted the plaintiffs to show that such intentional segregative acts were undertaken in the past.[92] The Court, in *Keyes*, further held that the past discriminatory acts of school authorities need only have been in a *portion* of the

91. 402 U.S. at 11.
92. *See* Fiss, *supra* note 75, at 25.

school district rather than system-wide. This approach, however, stops short of saying that racial imbalance *alone* is a violation of the equal protection clause.[93]

What must a plaintiff show to establish a prima facie case of de jure segregation where there has been no history of statutorily imposed segregation? *Keyes* clearly says that plaintiffs must show that the segregated schooling that exists "was brought about *or maintained* by intentional state action."[94] If, however, there is no *direct* evidence of intent (in resolutions or minutes of board meetings, in the assignment of faculty and staff, or even in site selection for the construction of new schools) and the school district simply has a neighborhood schools policy of student assignment superimposed on a segregated residential pattern which itself is not the result of any actions on the part of the school authorities, is this sufficient to establish "segregative intent"? May segregative intent be *inferred* from school board actions which have the *foreseeable effect* of fostering segregation?[95] Have courts engrafted the tort principle—that a person is responsible for the natural consequences of his actions—onto school desegregation cases in order to establish "intent"?[96]

The Second Circuit has taken the position that specific racial motive need not be shown to underlie the actions of school authorities—that intentional action leading *foreseeably* to discrimination, but taken without racial motivation also constitutes de jure segregation.[97] The court did note, however, that the standard by which state action is to be judged "has not been settled authoritatively by the Supreme Court."[98] Thus, until the Supreme Court says otherwise, the standard which the Second Circuit will apply is as follows:[99]

> [A] finding of *de jure* segregation may be based on actions taken, coupled with omissions made, by governmental authorities which have the natural and foreseeable consequence of causing educational segregation.

A federal district court in Michigan, in holding that the board of education in Kalamazoo had followed a purposeful pattern of racial discrimination by intentional acts of commission or omission,[100] applied general principles of tort

93. Professor Fiss suggests, however, that the nature and extent of the remedy in *Keyes*—and indeed, even in *Swann*—"can be explained only if the segregation itself is viewed as the evil and the past discrimination is viewed as the triggering mechanism." *Id.* at 26.

94. 413 U.S. at 198.

95. Note that one of the factors indicating "intent" in the Denver case is the location of schools "with conscious knowledge" that they will be segregated. 413 U.S. at 201-02.

96. *Cf.* Monroe v. Pape, 365 U.S. 167 (1961). In this 1961 decision, the Supreme Court, in delimiting the elements of a civil cause of action under 42 U.S.C. § 1983 (1970) (imposing civil liability upon "[e]very person who, under color of any statute . . . of any State . . . subjects . . . any citizen of the United States . . . to the deprivation of any rights . . . secured by the Constitution . . . ."), refused to include "specific intent" as a necessary element, ruling that § 1983 "should be read against the background of tort liability that makes a man responsible for the natural consequences of his actions." 365 U.S. at 187. *See* Note, *School Desegregation After* Swann: *A Theory of Governmental Responsibility*, 39 U. CHI. L. REV. 421 (1972).

97. Hart v. Community School Bd. of Educ., 512 F.2d 37, 50 (2d Cir. 1975).

98. 512 F.2d at 49.

99. 512 F.2d at 50.

100. Oliver v. Kalamazoo Bd. of Educ., 368 F. Supp. 143 (W.D. Mich. 1973). The court found

law in determining whether there had been a violation: "[I]t is reasonable to infer that people intend the natural and probable consequences of acts knowingly done or knowingly omitted."[101] The Sixth Circuit agreed:[102]

> A presumption of segregative purpose arises when plaintiffs establish that the natural, probable, and foreseeable result of public officials' action or inaction was an increase or perpetuation of public school segregation. The presumption becomes proof unless defendants affirmatively establish that their action or inaction was a consistent and resolute application of racially neutral policies.

Plaintiffs in Grand Rapids, Michigan attempted to argue that if there was reason to believe that school board policies could result in segregated schooling, there was an affirmative duty to change such policies for those which would eliminate racial imbalance.[103] The plaintiffs in that case asserted that[104]

> the school board had sufficient knowledge and forewarning that continued operation of a neighborhood school system would result in imbalanced schools and that this alone was enough to place on [the school board] the affirmative duty to take action to eliminate such imbalance.

The Sixth Circuit noted, however, that[105]

> the phenomenal increase in the black population in Grand Rapids was *not clearly foreseeable* until the imbalances were so advanced that a far-reaching reshuffling would have been required to correct them.

But the implication is that school officials would have been responsible for correcting racial imbalances in the schools had the residential patterns been foreseeable.

One commentator has recently pointed out that the evidence in the Kalamazoo and Grand Rapids cases was quite similar, yet one district court found that there was a purposeful pattern of racial discrimination and the other court found none.[106] The Sixth Circuit upheld *both* cases. The Sixth Circuit, in its opinion in the Grand Rapids case, indicated that the fact that the Kalamazoo School Board had rescinded a desegregation plan after candidates

---

the *failure* to develop or implement

> any policy designed to positively confront the problem of racial isolation in the Kalamazoo public schools . . . was itself a deliberate decision to forego [the] opportunity to correct the existing segregated conditions and itself was an unconstitutional denial of equal protection of the laws.

Id. at 178-79.

101. 368 F. Supp. at 161.

102. Oliver v. Michigan State Bd. of Educ., 508 F.2d 178, 181-82 (6th Cir. 1974). *Accord*, Morgan v. Kerrigan, 509 F.2d 580, 588-89 (1st Cir. 1974); Cisneros v. Corpus Christi Independent School Dist., 467 F.2d 142, 149 (5th Cir. 1972), *cert. denied*, 413 U.S. 920 (1973); United States v. Texas Educ. Agency, 467 F.2d 848, 863 (5th Cir. 1972). *But see* Johnson v. San Francisco Unified School Dist., 500 F.2d 349, 351-52 (9th Cir. 1974); Soria v. Oxnard School Dist., 488 F.2d 579, 585, 588 (9th Cir. 1973), *cert. denied*, 416 U.S. 951 (1974).

103. Higgins v. Board of Educ., 508 F.2d 779 (6th Cir. 1974).

104. *Id.* at 789-90.

105. *Id.* at 790.

106. Marshall, *The Standard of Intent: Two Recent Michigan Cases*, 4 J. LAW & ED. 227 (1975).

opposed to desegregation were elected to the board, distinguished Kalamazoo from Grand Rapids.[107] This suggests that the Sixth Circuit might require more specific actions indicating segregative intent than the Second Circuit.

D. Segregation Not Attributable to School Board Policies: The De Facto Dilemma

Both the district and the circuit courts in the Denver case found de jure segregation in only a portion of the school district. The separation of the races in the rest of the school district was treated as de facto segregation.[108] Thus the Supreme Court could have used that case as a vehicle for determining whether the equal protection clause imposes upon the school board an affirmative duty to correct de facto segregation or racial imbalance in the schools that results solely from segregated residential patterns. Instead the Supreme Court found de jure segregation in a part of the district and extrapolated that to the entire system. Thus the Supreme Court has yet to review a case of "pure" racial imbalance or de facto segregation.[109] Nevertheless, with the *Keyes* case, desegregation could no longer be said to be exclusively a southern problem—de jure, in other words, means state actions and policies of various kinds which result in segregated schools, not just compelled separation by statute or constitution. A purely de facto segregated school district, then, would be one in which there was neither a history of statutorily-imposed segregation nor intentional segregative acts on the part of school officials. The racial imbalance in the schools is fortuitous, attributed solely to a neighborhood schools policy superimposed on a pattern of residential segregation.[110]

Some commentators and even some courts have suggested that neighborhood schooling coupled with *private* discrimination should, without more, be sufficient to establish a violation of the equal protection clause.[111] One commentator states the argument as follows:[112]

> Residence in the ghetto, and thus membership in the class disadvantaged by the neighborhood [school] assignment policy, is often the immediate conse-

107. 508 F.2d at 791.

108. 313 F. Supp. 51, 83 (D. Colo. 1970), *aff'd*, 445 F.2d 990 (10th Cir. 1971).

109. The next major desegregation case to come before the Court was Milliken v. Bradley, 418 U.S. 717 (1974). There the Court upheld the district court's finding that the racial imbalance within Detroit was clearly de jure.

110. The *Keyes* majority noted that the case had not presented the Court with an "occasion to consider . . . whether a 'neighborhood school policy' of itself will justify racial ethnic concentrations in the absence of a finding that school authorities have committed acts constituting *de jure* segregation." 413 U.S. at 212.

111. *See, e.g.*, United States v. Texas Educ. Agency, 467 F.2d 848, 863-64 n. 22 (5th Cir. 1972) (emphasis added):

> Whether *or not* the residential isolation of whites, blacks, and Mexican-Americans in Austin is . . . the result of state action, the acts of the school authorities in taking official action, including assigning students . . . and drawing zone lines, on the basis of these segregated housing patterns were violative of the fourteenth amendment.

112. Goodman, *supra* note 68, at 320.

> quence of racially discriminatory practices in the housing market. Where race directly determines place-of-residence, grouping students in school by place-of-residence becomes, in effect, racial classification once-removed. It amplifies the consequences of private discrimination; it lengthens the discriminator's arm, giving him a veto over admission to the neighborhood public school.

It has also been suggested that in such a case the Court could look to actions of other governmental agencies which may have contributed to the pattern of residential segregation in order to find that the pattern of segregated schooling constitutes de jure segregation. The question of the effect of such actions was expressly reserved for future decision in *Swann*;[113] likewise, in the Denver case the opinion was confined to actions by the school board alone.[114] If the actions of other government officials are alleged to have caused the patterns of residential segregation, should they be parties to the school desegregation suit?[115] If not, must the school board bear the burden of proving that there was no segregative intent on the part of these *other* governmental agencies or that past segregative acts by these other agencies did not contribute to the present pattern of segregated public schools?

Assuming that plaintiffs could prove that intentional actions by other governmental agencies *had* caused residential segregation, what then is the duty of the school board? Could the Court hold the school board responsible for desegregation of the schools because the racial imbalance could have been reasonably prevented and the board had failed to adopt a "reasonably feasible" alternative which would have reduced the imbalance? In other words, does the fourteenth amendment require affirmative action by the school board to prevent or reduce racial imbalance regardless of the cause?

It is unclear whether the Court would find that school authorities had an affirmative duty to correct de facto racial imbalance in view of the Court's attempt in the Denver case to articulate the distinction between de jure and de facto school segregation: "the differentiating factor between *de jure* segregation and so-called *de facto* segregation to which we referred in *Swann* is *purpose* or *intent* to segregate."[116] The necessary implication is that this distinction must be of constitutional significance.

State courts and lower federal courts have rushed to apply the de facto/de

---

113. 402 U.S. at 23.

114. 413 U.S. at 191.

115. In Hart v. Community School Bd., 383 F. Supp. 699 (E.D.N.Y. 1974), the school board impleaded city, state, and federal housing and urban development agencies on the theory that they had fostered residential segregation which resulted in school segregation. *But see* United States v. Texas Educ. Agency, 467 F.2d 848, 864 n. 22 (5th Cir. 1972) to the effect that the school authorities might still be liable for the segregated schools: "When the segregated housing patterns are the result of 'state action' [and the school board uses a neighborhood schools policy of student assignment], we are faced with *double* discrimination."

The court in *Hart* required the other non-school agencies to participate in the relief; however, the claims of the school board against these other governmental agencies were later recommended dismissed. 512 F.2d 37, 56 (2d Cir. 1975).

116. 413 U.S. at 208.

jure distinction articulated in *Keyes*. In Los Angeles, a trial court ruling in favor of plaintiffs in a school desegregation case which has been in the courts for twelve years was reversed by a California court of appeals.[117] Five years earlier in that case, the trial judge, after a nine month trial, found that the school district, in selecting school sites and in using neighborhood school assignments coupled with restrictive transfer policies, had promoted segregated schooling. The appellate court, however, was unable to find anything in the school district's acts or omissions which demonstrated "purpose or intent" to segregate. The most that the record of the trial proceedings would establish, the appellate court maintained, was inaction rather than actions which were intentionally segregative.[118]

If a case involving a purely de facto segregated school system came before the Supreme Court, would it be found constitutional per se or can there ever be an affirmative constitutional duty upon the school board to lessen racial imbalance? Obviously, for an affirmative duty to arise, it would have to be shown that de facto segregation is a violation of the equal protection clause. Conceivably, to find that the constitutional rights of black students are being impinged, the de facto racial imbalance would have to be shown to be educationally or psychologically harmful. Thus while proof of harm is *not* relevant in a de jure situation—unless *Brown* is to be relitigated,[119] the Supreme Court's articulation of the dichotomy between de jure and de facto segregation suggests that an affirmative duty to overcome *pure* de facto segregation[120] might have to be based on a showing that de facto segregation inflicted the same educational harm as the statutorily-imposed segregation outlawed in *Brown*.

A district court in New York recently has come to such a conclusion, relying on social science data to support its finding of "harm" from non-state-imposed segregation.[121] Similarly, the district court in the Denver case, although con-

117. Crawford v. Board of Educ., _____ Cal. App. 3d _____, 120 Cal. Rptr. 334 (1975).

118. *Id.* at 338.

119. *See* Stell v. Savannah-Chatham County Bd. of Educ., 333 F.2d 55, 61 (5th Cir.), *cert. denied*, 379 U.S. 933 (1964).

120. If pure de facto segregation is defined as that arising *solely* from residential segregation that is attributable neither to policies of school authorities nor of other governmental agencies, the number of city school districts found to be de facto segregated should be very few—if indeed one exists at all.

121. Hart v. Community School Bd., 383 F. Supp. 699, 728-37 (E.D.N.Y. 1974). Among the studies cited were the U.S. Civil Rights Commission's Report, *Racial Isolation in the Public Schools*, the National Advisory Commission's Report on Civil Disorders, and the Fleischmann Commission's Report on the Quality, Cost, and Financing of Elementary and Secondary Education in New York State. *Id.*

It should be noted, however, that the district judge first concluded that racially segregated schools violate the equal protection clause absent statutory compulsion and even absent a finding of "unlawful segregative design." 383 F. Supp. at 739. According to Judge Weinstein, that conclusion is supported by "reason and authority," including Blocker v. Board of Educ., 226 F. Supp. 208 (E.D.N.Y. 1964) (where the finding that 100 per cent of the district's black students attended a disproportionately small school with only one per cent of the district's white students—coupled with a rigid no-transfer policy—constituted "state-imposed" segregation); Fiss, *Racial Imbalance in the Public Schools: The Constitutional Concepts*, 78 HARV. L. REV. 564 (1965); Fiss, *The Charlotte-*

cluding that there was no duty to desegregate the core because there was no finding of district-wide de jure segregation,[122] nevertheless found that "an equal educational opportunity [was] not being provided at the subject segregated schools within the District . . . ."[123] The *only* remedy for that situation was desegregation of the minority-race schools.[124] In arriving at this conclusion, the court relied on testimony that a racially integrated setting is critically important to improving the quality of educational opportunity. Among those who testified were James Coleman (author of the *Coleman Report*), Neil Sullivan (then Commissioner of the Massachusetts State Board of Education and previously Superintendent of the Berkeley School District when that system desegregated), and Robert O'Reilly (then assistant director of research and evaluation for the New York State Department of Education).[125]

The judiciary—and others[126]—have not wholly embraced the argument that, *regardless* of the method of pupil assignment used, segregation stigmatizes blacks and deprives them of an educational opportunity equal to that which could be assured by contact with middle class white students. The courts' reluctance is probably due to the uncertainty surrounding the question of whether a segregated pattern of schooling *itself* means inferior education for blacks; this uncertainty persists not in spite of, but because of, the present state of social science research. A number of black parents and community groups are also beginning to question whether continued efforts to desegregate public schools is the most effective strategy available for improving the quality of education for their children.[127]

Mecklenburg Case—Its Significance for Northern School Desegregation, 38 U. Chi. L. Rev. 697 (1971); and Goodman, *supra* note 68. 383 F. Supp. at 728-35.

122. Keyes v. School Dist. No. 1, 313 F. Supp. 61, 73-77 (D. Colo. 1970).

123. 313 F. Supp. at 83.

124. 313 F. Supp. 90, 96. The Tenth Circuit reversed the district court on this point, noting that equal educational opportunity constitutionally requires only that the state refrain from intentionally segregating by race. 445 F.2d 990, 1004-06 (10th Cir. 1971).

125. 313 F. Supp. at 94-97. Professor Coleman had testified that a school fails to provide equal educational opportunity when its student body is drawn largely from lower socioeconomic groups. *See* Yudof, *Equal Educational Opportunity and the Courts*, 51 Tex. L. Rev. 411, 442-43 (1973) for an excellent analysis of this aspect of the *Keyes* decision. Professor Yudof suggests that the court's conclusion—based on the lower achievement scores of blacks—that they must be brought into contact "with classroom associates who can contribute to the learning process," 313 F. Supp. at 96-97, is faulty inasmuch as Professor Coleman speaks to socioeconomic integration and not racial integration. Professor Yudof also notes that resting the case for desegregation on improved achievement scores could serve to undercut reform if at some future date it were shown that socioeconomic or racial integration failed to raise test scores. Yudof, *supra* at 443. *Cf.* Cahn, *supra* note 20.

126. *See, e.g.*, Bell, *Waiting on the Promise of* Brown, 39 Law & Contemp. Prob. no. 2, at 341 (1975).

127. *Id.*; Comment, *Alternative Schools for Minority Students: The Constitution, the Civil Rights Act and the Berkeley Experiment*, 61 Calif. L. Rev. 858 (1973). See also comments by Rev. Ralph Abernathy and other black community leaders in Cose, *Dr. King's Protest Rose from Desegregation Conflict*, The Chapel Hill Newspaper, June 13, 1975, § A, at 6. *See* Yudof, *supra* note 125, at 471. *But cf.* Hart v. Community School Bd., 383 F. Supp. 699, 742.(E.D.N.Y. 1974), in which the court rejected the argument that self-imposed segregation in public schools was desirable or constitutional. The

If, in the Denver case, David Armor,[128] Barbara Sizemore,[129] Roy Innis,[130] or Ronald Edmonds[131] had testified instead of Coleman,[132] Sullivan, and O'Reilly, would (or should) the result have been different? In other words, does an affirmative duty to correct de facto racial imbalance arise only when the evidence shows that "equal educational opportunity" can *only* be guaranteed to minority children by desegregation? The district court in the Detroit case raised the question whether educational theory and research—"from the Coleman report to its many reanalyses"—on the effects of desegregation on pupil achievement versus increased resource inputs, could "form the basis for requiring judicial intervention and relief in the absence of a finding of de jure segregation . . . ."[133] Judge Roth noted, however, that such evidence is totally beside the point when school segregation is caused in substantial part by governmental action.[134]

Several cases where courts have found school segregation to be de facto rather than de jure suggest that, under certain circumstances, a school district is nonetheless legally obligated to correct racial imbalance. In *People v. San Diego Unified School District*,[135] the principle was stated as follows:[136]

> [S]chool authorities in California have a constitutional duty to "take steps, insofar as reasonably feasible, to alleviate racial imbalance in schools *regardless of its cause" where the imbalance denies the minority group equal educational opportunities* . . . . The action of school authorities in maintaining *de facto* racially imbalanced public schools is not a denial of equal protection of the law unless the imbalance denies the minority group equal educational opportunities. . . . In each case seeking relief from such imbalance the court must determine whether the imbalance is of such a degree [that] it affects the educational opportunities of the minority group; whether, under the circumstances, the minority group, in fact, is denied equal educational opportunities; and whether available steps to alleviate the imbalance are reasonably feasible in light of the degree of the imbalance and the practical necessities of governmental operation.

---

judge relied on several articles opposed to self-segregation: Allen, *The Politics of Urban Education*, in BLACK MANIFESTO FOR EDUCATION 47 (J. Haskins ed. 1973); Clark, *Issues in Urban Education*, in BLACK MANIFESTO FOR EDUCATION 74 (J. Haskins ed. 1973); W.E.B. DUBOIS, THE CRISIS WRITINGS (1972). *See also* studies cited by the district judge on the harmful effects of segregation, *supra* note 121.

128. Armor, *The Evidence on Busing*, 28 PUB. INTEREST 90 (Summer 1972).

129. Sizemore, *Is There a Case for Separate Schools?*, 53 PHI DELTA KAPPAN 281 (1972); Sizemore, *Education for Liberation*, 81 SCHOOL REV. 389 (1973).

130. Rising Black Clamor for Black Separatism, U.S. News & World Report, Sept. 21, 1970, at 82.

131. Edmonds, *Judicial Assumptions on the Value of Integrated Education for Blacks*, in D. BELL, RACE, RACISM AND AMERICAN LAW 592 (1973).

132. While Dr. James S. Coleman has testified in numerous school desegregation suits as to the beneficial effects of racial, and particularly, class integration, and the *Coleman Report* has been cited in countless more cases in support of desegregation, he has recently cast doubt on the merits of court-ordered desegregation. J. Coleman, Recent Trends in School Integration, Apr. 2, 1975 (paper presented at American Educational Research Association).

133. Bradley v. Milliken, 345 F. Supp. 914, 921-22 n. 1 (E.D. Mich. 1972).

134. *Id.*

135. 19 Cal. App. 3d 252, 96 Cal. Rptr. 658 (1971), *cert. denied*, 405 U.S. 1016 (1972).

136. *Id.* at 265-66, 96 Cal Rptr. at 666.

E. Language Exclusion: A Constitutional Violation?

A somewhat different problem to be considered with those cases concerning constitutional violations rather than remedies is the "functional exclusion" from education of ethnic minorities whose native language is not English. There are several million such school-age children. Of these, at least three million have so little proficiency in English that they cannot benefit from regular classes.[137] The failure of the San Francisco school system to overcome the language deficiencies of some of its students was challenged in a recent law suit. That case involved 2,856 Chinese-American students who were compelled to attend schools where subjects were taught only in English—a language they could not understand. The plaintiffs claimed that the school authorities had denied those students an equal educational opportunity in contravention to the equal protection clause. The Ninth Circuit held that in the absence of a finding of past or present de jure segregation or of other state actions contributing to the English language deficiencies suffered by the Chinese-American students, these claims could not be upheld.[138] The court found that[139]

> [e]very student brings to the starting line of his educational career different advantages and disadvantages caused in part by social, economic and cultural background, created and continued completely apart from any contribution by the school system. That some of these may be impediments which can be overcome [by compensatory education] does not amount to a 'denial' . . . of educational opportunity within the meaning of the Fourteenth Amendment should the [school authorities] fail to give them special attention, this even though they are characteristic of a particular ethnic group.

The court also expressed the view that even if a violation of the fourteenth amendment were found, the judiciary should play only a very limited role in shaping the ultimate educational remedy.[140]

> [T]he determination of what special educational difficulties faced by some students . . . will be afforded extraordinary curative action, and the intensity of the measures to be taken, is a complex decision, calling for significant amounts of executive and legislative expertise and non-judicial value judgments. . . . The courts should not be called upon to make pedagogic judgments.

The Supreme Court reversed, but only on the ground that school officials had violated § 601 of the Civil Rights Act of 1964,[141] which forbids the denial to any person, on the basis of race, color or national origin, of the benefits of any program receiving federal financial assistance.[142] The Court also cited

---

137. *Hearings on H.R. 9840 and H.R. 10224 Before the General Subcomm. on Education of the House Comm. on Education and Labor*, 90th Cong., 1st Sess. 7 (1967).

138. Lau v. Nichols, 483 F.2d 791 (9th Cir. 1973), *rev'd on other grounds*, 414 U.S. 563 (1974).

139. *Id.* at 797.

140. 483 F.2d at 799 & n. 17.

141. 42 U.S.C. § 2000d (1970).

142. 414 U.S. at 566-69.

HEW guidelines promulgated under the Civil Rights Act[143] which provide specifically that[144]

> [w]here inability to speak and understand the English language excludes national origin-minority children from effective participation in the educational program offered by a school district the district must take affirmative steps to rectify the language deficiency in order to open its instructional program to these students.

The Court reserved judgment on the equal protection argument,[145] however, apparently leaving intact the legal conclusion of the court of appeals that there was no *constitutional* right to bilingual education. Also, since the Supreme Court ordered nothing more specific than "appropriate relief,"[146] presumably the Ninth Circuit will adhere to its original policy and accordingly limit its role in fashioning a remedy.

In *Serna v. Portales Municipal Schools*,[147] the district court held that the school authorities' failure to establish a meaningful bilingual educational program *in itself* constituted a denial of equal education to Chicano students, and a violation of the equal protection clause.[148] The finding of inequality was based on the results of IQ and language expression tests administered to first and fifth grade students and the testimony of an educational psychologist that language difficulties accounted for 80 per cent of the achievement difference between Anglo and Chicano children.[149]

In arriving at its legal conclusion that the school authorities had a duty to administer bilingual education, the district court rejected the defendants' argument that the language deficiencies were not the result of any state action.[150] The Tenth Circuit, on appeal, affirmed the holding of the district court,[151] but sidestepped the equal protection issue by holding that the Supreme Court's decision in *Lau v. Nichols*[152] controlled and that the Portales school system was in violation of § 601 of the 1964 Civil Rights Act.[153]

Of little legal consequence, but of tremendous practical import is the recent consent decree in *Aspira of New York, Inc. v. Board of Education*,[154] in which the defendants acknowledged the rights of the plaintiff children under the 1964 Civil Rights Act, citing *Lau v. Nichols*, and agreed to implement a bilingual-

143. 414 U.S. at 567.
144. 35 Fed. Reg. 11595 (1970).
145. 414 U.S. at 566.
146. 414 U.S. at 569.
147. 351 F. Supp. 1279 (D.N.M. 1972), *aff'd on different grounds*, 499 F.2d 1147 (10th Cir. 1974).
148. 351 F. Supp. at 1282.
149. 351 F. Supp. at 1281-82.
150. 351 F. Supp. at 1282-83. Note the contrast with the Ninth Circuit's opinion in *Lau v. Nichols*, *supra* note 138 and accompanying text.
151. 499 F.2d 1147 (10th Cir. 1974).
152. 414 U.S. 563 (1974).
153. See statute and regulation at notes 141 & 144 and accompanying text *supra*.
154. Consent Decree (S.D.N.Y. Aug. 29, 1974).

bicultural program of education for "all New York City public school children whose English language deficiency prevents them from effectively participating in the learning process and who can more effectively participate in Spanish."[155] If the *Aspira* consent decree is any indication of the future, it may well be that the *Lau* decision will become the rock upon which bilingual public education is founded even though the constitutional issue was never decided.

These three cases—*Lau v. Nichols*, *Serna* and *Aspira*—indicate that courts may be abandoning the xenophobic "melting pot" view of America, in which ethnic minorities must become assimilated to white Anglo-Saxon values, language and culture. The thrust of these cases is away from the idea many school administrators have had that the language barrier was a problem which the student had to overcome, and toward the idea that the schools must adapt to meet the differing needs of their pupils.

F. The Segregation of Hispano-Americans: Proving the Violation

Most of the case law of school desegregation was spawned by the unconstitutional discrimination against blacks in the deep South or the southern border states. Understandably, therefore, most of the cases referred to in this article measure the treatment and experience of blacks in public education vis-à-vis whites. It must be understood, however, that the benefits of the equal protection clause are guaranteed to *all* identifiable racial or ethnic minorities. The largest identifiable minority, other than blacks, who have asserted their rights under the fourteenth amendment are Hispano-Americans.[156] The segregation of Hispano-Americans by school district and by schools within districts has been well documented.[157] Nevertheless, only a small percentage of desegregation cases have involved such students, and most of these are in the Southwest. Many of the problems confronting Hispano-Americans in their attempts to litigate equal educational opportunity are quite similar to those raised in the context of segregated schooling for blacks, but there are also certain very important differences both as to determining the constitutional violation and as to special remedies.[158]

---

155. *Id.* at 4.

156. Hispano-Americans are the second largest minority group in the public schools, constituting about 5 per cent of the total population in the nation. U.S. Commission on Civil Rights, Mexican American Education Study, Report I: Ethnic Isolation of Mexican Americans in the Public Schools of the Southwest (1971). The term Hispano-American is used to cover both Mexican-Americans and Puerto Ricans. Cubans and other Latin Americans are also included in the term Hispano-American but most of the litigation covers the first two groups. Seventy per cent of the Hispano-Americans, almost all of whom are Mexican-American, attend school in five southwestern states. *Id.* at 59. Another minority currently seeking equal educational opportunity is the Native American, but since Indian education litigation presents some unique factors, discrimination against Native American students will not be dealt with in this article.

157. U.S. Commission on Civil Rights, *supra* note 156.

158. The remedies sought by Hispano-Americans are discussed in the text at pp. 114-20 *infra*.

1. *Are Hispano-Americans an Especially Protected Minority?*

The first question, in determining whether the isolation of Hispano-Americans is a violation of the equal protection clause, is whether they are a minority which should be legally treated in the same manner as blacks. The first case to hold that *Brown* applies to Hispano-Americans as well as blacks was *Cisneros v. Corpus Christi Independent School District*.[159] *Cisneros* found that the Mexican-American students in Corpus Christi were segregated[160] and that "placing Negroes and Mexican-Americans in the same school does not achieve a unitary system as contemplated by law."[161]

In the Denver case the district court also found that Hispano-Americans constituted an identifiable ethnic minority entitled to the benefits of the equal protection clause but, because of their different ethnic origins, would not "lump [Negroes and Hispanos] into a single minority category" in order to determine the segregated character of a school.[162] The Tenth Circuit approved this classification.[163]

The Supreme Court held, however, that "the District Court erred in separating Negroes and Hispanos for purposes of defining a segregated school."[164] The *Keyes* majority noted that[165]

> though of different origins, Negroes and Hispanos in Denver suffer identical discrimination in treatment when compared with the treatment afforded Anglo students. In that circumstance we think [plaintiffs] are entitled to have schools with a combined predominance of Negroes and Hispanos included in the category of "segregated" schools.

In support for its holding, the Court cited a report published by the United States Commission on Civil Rights which found that in certain areas of the Southwest, Hispanos suffer from the same educational inequities as blacks.[166]

The cases following *Keyes* have treated Hispano discrimination in the same manner as discrimination against blacks and, in tri-ethnic areas as in the Denver case, the degree of segregation in any given school will depend in a great many cases on the ratio of whites to the *combined number* of identifiable minority in that school.

---

159. 324 F. Supp. 599, 604-06 (1970). *See* Note, *Project Report: De Jure Segregation of Chicanos in Texas Schools*, 7 HARV. CIV. RIGHTS-CIV. LIB. L. REV. 307, 349 (1972).

160. 324 F. Supp. at 608.

161. 324 F. Supp. at 616.

162. Keyes v. School Dist. No. 1, 313 F. Supp. 61, 69 (D. Colo. 1970).

163. 445 F.2d 990, 1006 (10th Cir. 1971).

164. 413 U.S. 189, 197 (1973).

165. 413 U.S. at 198.

166. 413 U.S. at 197 n. 8. To support its finding that "Hispanos constitute an identifiable class for purposes of the Fourteenth Amendment," the Court cited Hernandez v. Texas, 347 U.S. 475 (1954), a case which dealt with the exclusion of Hispano-Americans from jury service in Texas in which the Court required that the plaintiff factually establish that the racial group existed within the community in order to qualify for special fourteenth amendment protection. 347 U.S. at 478. Once that fact was established, the group was given the same protection afforded to Negroes in Strauder v. West Virginia, 100 U.S. 303 (1880).

2. *Proof of Violation*

In *Swann*, the Court indicated that a prima facie case of unlawful segregation is established if it can be shown that there is segregation in fact and that the formerly dual school system has not yet been disestablished, the pattern of segregated schooling being presumed to be a "vestige" of the previously unlawful, state-imposed segregation. The burden is then shifted to the state to show that the system is now completely unitary and that the segregation that exists is not a "vestige" of the unlawful dual system, but arose fortuitously (through shifting residential patterns) after the system had become unitary.

However, in cases involving Hispanos, the lower federal courts seem to be applying the standard enunciated in the Denver case which places a heavier burden upon the plaintiff attempting to make a prima facie case of unlawful segregation. In *Keyes*, a finding of unlawful segregation was based upon proof of the school board's *intentional* segregative acts in a substantial ("meaningful") portion of the school district. The Hispanic plaintiff, then, in order to make a prima facie case of unlawful segregation, must show that segregated schools exist in fact and that their existence is attributable to some intentional action on the part of school authorities or other state officials. The use of the *Keyes* standard where there was *no* history of statutorily-imposed segregation is due to the fact that many of the states which required the segregation of blacks and whites—either by statutory or constitutional provisions or both—did not have a similar statutory history toward Hispanos.[167] Nevertheless, courts have found a

167. For example, Tex. Const. art. 7, § 7 (1876) required that "[s]eparate schools shall be provided for the white and colored children, and impartial provision shall be made for both." Similarly, in 1905—as part of a bill aimed at improving the public school system—the legislature provided that "[w]hite and colored children shall not be taught in the same schools . . . . The terms 'colored race' and 'colored children' as used in the preceding articles, and elsewhere in this title, include all persons of mixed blood descended from negro ancestry." Ch. 124, §§ 93 & 96, [1905] Gen. Laws of Texas 263. Both this proviso and art. 7, § 7 of the Constitution were repealed at the 1969 legislative session.

In 1930 when Mexican-Americans first challenged separate schools in Texas, the Texas Court of Civil Appeals mentioned cursorily that the Mexican race was one of the several white races and ruled that they could not be segregated solely because they were Mexicans. It was not discriminatory, however, to assign all first through third grade Mexican children to separate schools if, in the opinion of local school authorities, it was in their best interests in order to remedy their language difficulties. Independent School Dist. v. Salvatierra, 33 S.W. 2d 790, 795 (Tex. Civ. App. 1930), *appealed dismissed and cert. denied*, 284 U.S. 580 (1931). It is interesting to note that while the *Salvatierra* court permitted separate Mexican schools in order to remedy language handicaps, Texas statutes proscribed the remedial use of Spanish by teachers. Indeed, until quite recently, a teacher who used Spanish to teach Mexican-American children—except in an approved language curriculum—risked criminal conviction:

> [E]very teacher . . . employed in the public free schools of this state shall use the English language exclusively in the conduct of the work of the schools, and all recitations and exercises of the school shall be conducted in the English language, and the trustees shall not prescribe any texts for elementary grades not printed in the English language . . . . Any teacher . . . failing to comply with this provision of the law shall be deemed guilty of a misdemeanor and upon conviction thereof in proper court shall be subject to fine of not less than Twenty-five Dollars ($25.00) and not more than One Hundred Dollars ($100.00), cancellation of certificate, . . . or both fine and cancellation of certificate . . . .

Ch. 80, §§ 1-2, [1918] Gen. Laws of Texas 170.

history of de jure segregation toward Hispano-Americans based on the acts and policies of school officials.

In *United States v. Texas Education Agency*,[168] a case arising in Austin, the Fifth Circuit found intentional segregative action on the part of the school district—particularly in the choice of school site locations, construction of schools, drawing of attendance zones, student assignment and transfer policies, and faculty and staff assignments.[169] Thus de jure segregation against Hispanos was found despite the absence of a previous statutory requirement. The court stated that discrimination in this case was "no different from any other school desegregation case."[170] Similarly, in *Cisneros v. Corpus Christi Independent School District*,[171] the court found de jure segregation, noting that the[172]

> de jure nature of the existing pattern of segregation within the Corpus Christi Independent School District has as its basis state action of a non-statutory variety—that is, the school board's active pursuit of policies that not only do nothing to counteract the effect of existing patterns of residential segregation in view of viable alternatives of significant integrative value, but, in fact, increase and exacerbate the district's racial and ethnic imbalance. There has been a history of official school board acts which have had such a segregative effect.

Thus, once the necessary intentional segregative actions are found—coupled with the high concentration of Hispanos in certain schools and the low percentage of Hispano teachers in relation to the Hispano percentage of the total student population—a prima facie case of unlawful segregation is established. There are cases, however, in which the Denver case principles are applied to reach a finding of *no* de jure segregation. In *Zamora v. New Braunfels Independent School District*,[173] plaintiffs failed to establish that the actions of school authorities were taken with segregative intent. The court held that the existing segregation was "*de facto* and strictly the result of shifting residential patterns within the community."[174] Since there was no constitutional violation, there could be no relief.

In a school desegregation case in California, the district court initially treated the case as one of de facto segregation but held that the mere existence of the segregated elementary schools was a denial of equal protection of the laws and that the school board had an affirmative duty to eliminate the racial imbalance.[175] The Ninth Circuit remanded the case for a finding of whether or not the school board had intentionally pursued a policy of racial segregation.[176] The circuit court stated that it is not until a finding of intentional segregation

---

168. 467 F.2d 848 (5th Cir. 1972).
169. *Id.* at 864-66.
170. 467 F.2d at 873.
171. 324 F. Supp. 599 (S.D. Tex. 1970).
172. *Id.* at 620 n. 58.
173. 362 F. Supp. 552 (W.D. Tex. 1973).
174. *Id.* at 559.
175. Soria v. Oxnard School Dist. Bd. of Trustees, 328 F. Supp. 155, 159 (C.D. Cal. 1971).
176. 488 F.2d 579 (9th Cir. 1973). On remand the district court did find intentional segregative actions on the part of the board, 386 F. Supp. 539 (C.D. Cal. 1974).

has been made that the affirmative duty of the school board to convert the system to a "unitary" one attaches.[177]

There are cases, however, which seem to have adopted a more lenient standard for establishing a prima facie case than that set forth in the Denver case. In *Serna v. Portales Municipal Schools*[178] the district court did not require a showing of past, intentional segregative acts. Reliance instead was placed on the long-standing educational policy of the school district which failed to take into consideration the specific needs of Spanish-speaking students. The only proof required was the establishment of the existence of a substantial number of Hispano children and the nonexistence of a special curriculum tailored to their needs. The court focused in particular on the district's failure to provide a bilingual educational program. The Tenth Circuit affirmed but on statutory rather than on constitutional grounds.[179]

To sum up, the few cases dealing with the isolation of Hispano-Americans indicate that proof of a violation of the equal protection clause based on the existence of predominantly minority schools requires a showing of de jure segregation attributable to the action of school officials. The same analysis is used for cases of Hispano segregation as is used in cases involving discrimination against blacks except that, since Hispanos do not always have the "benefit" of a previous state statute requiring segregation, intent or purpose to segregate must be read into those actions of school authorities which result in segregated schools. However, the *Serna* case may represent a new approach under which Hispanos will be exempted from having to show past and present intentional segregative actions.

III
Remedial Limits

Except in the case of "pure" de facto segregation, the rules for establishing a constitutional violation are relatively clear and non-controversial. The real concern today is not whether, in a de jure segregated school district, the constitutional rights of black children are being violated. Rather, the primary controversy—once the constitutional violation has been found—is over remedies, *i.e.*, to what extent desegregation will be required, and by which means such desegregation is to be achieved.

A. Background

Local school authorities have the primary responsibility for insuring desegregation. In judging whether local authorities have met that responsibility, and in fashioning remedial decrees where they have not, the federal courts are to

177. 488 F.2d at 585.
178. 351 F. Supp. 1279 (D.N.M. 1972), *aff'd on other grounds*, 489 F.2d 1147 (10th Cir. 1974).
179. 499 F.2d 1147 (10th Cir. 1974).

be guided by traditional principles of equity.[180] The objective to be achieved is "the elimination of . . . deliberately maintained dual school systems with certain schools for Negro pupils and others for white pupils."[181] The local school authorities and the courts must strive to "eliminate . . . all vestiges of state-imposed segregation,"[182] and "achieve the greatest possible degree of actual desegregation, taking into account the practicalities of the situation."[183]

> Once a right and a violation have been shown, the scope of a district court's equitable powers to remedy past wrongs is broad, for breadth and flexibility are inherent in equitable remedies.[184]

And finally, "[t]he remedy . . . may be administratively awkward, inconvenient, and even bizarre in some situations and may impose burdens on some . . . ."[185]

B. Intra-District Remedies

The most detailed discussion of the various equitable remedies available to a federal district court is found in *Swann*. There the Court endorsed a range of possible steps that a lower court could require a school district to take once an equal protection violation had been established; the Court also clearly indicated that the use of these remedial steps is limited, depending upon the circumstances.

The major permissible remedies discussed in *Swann* can be clustered around four somewhat overlapping subject areas: (1) racial balance;[186] (2) one-race schools;[187] (3) altering of attendance zones and pairing, clustering, or grouping of schools;[188] and (4) transportation of students from one part of the district to schools in another part—*i.e.*, busing.[189] Minority to majority transfer plans may also be used *if* they are effective in achieving a non-racial, unitary school system.[190]

---

180. Brown v. Board of Educ. (Brown II), 349 U.S. 294, 300 (1955). "Traditionally, equity has been characterized by a practical flexibility in shaping its remedies [footnote omitted] and by a facility for adjusting and reconciling public and private needs." *Id. But see* Milliken v. Bradley, 418 U.S. 717 (1974), holding in effect that a federal court's remedial powers stop at the school district line or "[T]he scope of the remedy is determined by the nature and the extent of the constitutional violation." *Id.* at 744.

181. *Id.* at 737.

182. Swann v. Charlotte-Mecklenburg Bd. of Educ., 402 U.S. at 15.

183. Davis v. Board of School Comm'rs, 402 U.S. 33, 37 (1971). Desegregation must extend not only to student assignment policies, but also to the hiring, firing, and treatment of faculty and staff; the quality of the physical plant; the use of transportation to and from school; and the organization of extra-curricular activities. Swann v. Charlotte-Mecklenburg Bd. of Educ., 402 U.S. at 18-19.

184. 402 U.S. at 15.

185. 402 U.S. at 28.

186. 402 U.S. at 22-25.

187. 402 U.S. at 25-27.

188. 402 U.S. at 27-29.

189. 402 U.S. at 29-30.

190. 402 U.S. at 26-27.

1. *Racial Balance*

Swann raised the question of the degree to which racial balance can be required in formulating a remedy; that is, to what extent must the proportions of each race in a school correspond to the proportions of each race in the system as a whole? The Court held that the use of mathematical ratios as part of a plan to facilitate the disestablishment of a dual school system is permissible, but in and of itself, racial balance is not required by the Constitution:[191]

> The constitutional command to desegregate schools does not mean that every school in every community must always reflect the racial composition of the school system as a whole . . . [although] the use . . . of mathematical ratios [and] . . . [a]wareness of the racial composition of the whole school system is likely to be a useful starting point in shaping a remedy . . . .

2. *One-race Schools*

In placing limitations on the use of ratios to achieve racial balance, the Court also indicated that the existence of one-race schools is not constitutionally invalid per se. However, the burden in a previously de jure segregated school system is on the school officials to justify that assignments to these schools are non-discriminatory.[192]

> [I]t should be clear that the existence of some small number of one-race, or virtually one-race, schools within a district is not in and of itself the mark of a system that still practices segregation by law. . . . Where the school authority's proposed plan . . . contemplates the continued existence of some schools that are all or predominantly of one race, they have the burden of showing that such school assignments are genuinely nondiscriminatory.

If the one-race school is a relict of a previous policy of racial assignment and the school board has subsequently adopted a neighborhood-schools policy, presumably—according to language in *Swann* regarding the elimination of all "vestiges of state-imposed segregation"—the Court would find assignment to that school discriminatory.

3. *Altering Attendance Zones*

With regard to the pairing of schools and altering of attendance zones, *Swann* indicated that a racially-neutral student assignment plan—such as a neighborhood school plan or a freedom-of-choice plan—is not acceptable if it is ineffective in reducing racial imbalance in a previously de jure segregated school system.[193] When would a neighborhood school assignment policy be

---

191. 402 U.S. at 24, 25; Milliken v. Bradley, 418 U.S. at 740-41 & n. 19. The Court said in *Swann*:

> If we were to read the holding of the District Court to require, as a matter of substantive constitutional right, any particular degree of racial balance or mixing, that approach would be disapproved and we would be obliged to reverse.

402 U.S. at 24.

192. 402 U.S. at 26.

193. 402 U.S. at 28. *Accord*, Wright v. Council of the City of Emporia, 407 U.S. 451, 460 (1972); Green v. County School Bd., 391 U.S. 430, 440 (1968).

permissible? Some members of the Supreme Court seem to place a high priority on neighborhood schools. Chief Justice Burger indicated in *Swann* that such a policy might be preferable, under certain circumstances, to any other policy of assignment:[194]

> All things being equal, with no history of discrimination, it might well be desirable to assign pupils to schools nearest their homes. But all things are not equal in a system that has been deliberately constructed and maintained to enforce racial segregation.

Justice Powell, concurring in part and dissenting in part in *Keyes*, strongly advocated neighborhood schools and sought to curb the use of busing solely for purposes of maximizing racial balance if it would impact too heavily on neighborhood schooling.[195]

In *Ellis v. Board of Public Instruction*,[196] the Fifth Circuit delineated the elements of a legal neighborhood school plan: each student must be assigned to attend the school nearest his or her home, limited only by the capacity of the school, and then to the next nearest school, without variance or exception and without regard to whether the school was formerly black or white.[197] The plan, however, must result in desegregation as measured by the six indicia first outlined in *Green*: desegregation of student bodies, faculty, staff, transportation, extracurricular activities, and facilities.[198] On the basis of this holding, Chief District Judge Frank Johnson later approved the Montgomery school board's proposal for a neighborhood elementary school plan which left one-third of the thirty-three elementary schools with over 80 per cent black enrollment[199]—meaning that 55 per cent of black elementary school students were still enrolled in predominantly black schools. Judge Johnson based his decision on three grounds: (1) "every black student at some point in his school career will be exposed to complete desegregation"[200] since in grades 7-12 the system would be completely desegregated; (2) "the *system* as a whole will be desegregated";[201] and (3) there is educational "value in having elementary children attend schools near their homes,"[202] although he cited no empirical or other evidence to support this statement. He concluded that "[i]f a neighborhood elementary school system can be effected without a sacrifice of constitutional standards, then such a plan should be adopted."[203]

---

194. 402 U.S. at 28.

195. 413 U.S. at 246-52. Also see discussion at note 204 *infra*.

196. 423 F.2d 203 (5th Cir. 1970).

197. 423 F.2d at 207-08.

198. 423 F.2d at 208.

199. Carr v. Montgomery County Bd. of Educ., 377 F. Supp. 1123, 1135-38, 1144 (M.D. Ala. 1974), *aff'd per curiam*, 511 F.2d 1374 (5th Cir. 1975).

200. Quoting Judge Wisdom in Hightower v. West, 430 F.2d 552, 555 (5th Cir. 1970).

201. 377 F. Supp. at 1138.

202. *Id.*

203. *Id.*

4. *Busing*

The most controversial aspect of school desegregation is busing—the transportation of students from one part of the district to a school in another part of the district to achieve desegregation. The Supreme Court in *Swann* approved busing as a tool to be used in disestablishing a dual school system, although it indicated that there are limits to the use of the remedy. While suggesting such limits, however, the Court declined to provide any specific guidelines for future cases, saying only that busing could be used where "feasible," but its use was to be limited by considerations of times and distances which would "either risk the health of the children or significantly impinge on the educational process."[204]

Without explicit guidance from the Supreme Court, lower courts in the post-*Swann* period have taken different approaches with regard to the extent of busing that will be permitted. A federal district court in Memphis—where total desegregation could have been accomplished by a plan involving bus rides of up to 60 minutes—accepted a plan which left some 25,000 black students in 25 all-black schools, but which reduced the average bus ride to 38 minutes with no ride more than 45 minutes.[205] All of this was done without much apparent help from the social or medical sciences in determining whether 60 minutes risks children's health or "significantly impinge[s] on the educational process."[206]

---

204. 402 U.S. at 29-31. In the Denver case Justice Powell took a strong position against the use of large-scale busing as a constitutional remedy, particularly with regard to elementary school children:

> [T]he legitimate community interests in neighborhood school systems [should] be accorded far greater respect. In the balancing of interests so appropriate to a fair and just equitable decree, transportation orders should be applied with special caution to any proposal as disruptive of family life and interests—and ultimately of education itself—as extensive transportation of elementary-age children solely for desegregation purposes. As a minimum, this Court should not require school boards to engage in the unnecessary transportation away from their neighborhoods of elementary-age children. [Footnote omitted.] It is at this age level that neighborhood education performs its most vital role. It is with respect to children of tender years that the greatest concern exists for their physical and psychological health. It is also here, at the elementary school, that the rights of parents and children are most sharply implicated.

205. Plans I and III, as presented to the district court, would have placed 97 per cent of all students in desegregated units, 48,000 children would have been bused, and a majority of those (75 per cent or 80 per cent) would have a bus ride of 31 to 45 minutes each way. Of those bused, 9,700 students would have a 46 to 60 minute ride each way, and most of these would be elementary school students. Plan II, which the court adopted, leaves 25 all-black or predominantly black units (19 elementary schools, 4 junior high schools, and 2 high schools), 83 per cent of the students will attend school in desegregated units, 38,000 children will be bused, and 44 per cent of these will have a 31 to 45 minutes bus ride each way, with no ride being over 45 minutes. Northcross v. Board of Educ., 489 F.2d 15, 16-17 (1973).

206. *See* Northcross v. Board of Educ., 341 F. Supp. 583 (W.D. Tenn. 1972), *aff'd*, 489 F.2d 15 (5th Cir.), *cert. denied*, 416 U.S. 962 (1973). On first appeal, the circuit court upheld the district court's finding that more busing was impractical during that school year, 466 F.2d 890, 895 (6th Cir. 1972). However, the court recognized that further desegregation was necessary and directed the district court to prepare a timetable for the system's future desegregation. *Id*. In rejecting the

In *Thompson v. School Board*,[207] the Fourth Circuit Court of Appeals upheld an order by the district court that a desegregation plan which would have involved bus rides of up to two and one-half hours of travel time a day for first and second graders was not "feasible."[208] The defense introduced the expert testimony of a pediatrician concerning the possible harmful effects of busing on young children which the plaintiffs left uncontroverted.[209]

The use of intradistrict busing has also been limited by Congress under the 1974 Education Amendments.[210] This education package prohibits a federal court from ordering busing to remedy de jure segregation unless the court first makes a finding that all alternative remedies are inadequate.[211] And when

---

defendant's social science evidence as to the ill effects of busing, the circuit court expressly questioned the applicability of the Armor busing study to that case, finding its conclusions to be "inapplicable to the Southern school pattern." 466 F.2d at 894 & n. 4

On remand, the district court, in an unpublished memorandum, approved a final desegregation plan involving the busing of 38,000 pupils, with no rides over 45 minutes long, even though this plan left untouched by the order two all-black high schools, four all-black junior high schools and 19 all or predominantly black elementary schools. 489 F.2d at 16-17. The Sixth Circuit affirmed the district court's consideration of the "practicalities" involved in busing, and quoted with approval from the memorandum decision:

> The lesser degree of desegregation in [the plan adopted] is based primarily upon four factors pertaining to effectiveness, feasibility and pedagogical soundness. Those factors are time and distance traveled on buses, cost of transportation, preservation of desegregation already accomplished, and adaptability.

489 F.2d at 17. Although it had previously rejected the defendant's social science evidence that busing itself was undesirable, the Sixth Circuit apparently approved of the use of such evidence in determining how much busing to use, noting that "[t]he one psychological expert was of the opinion that a shortening of the times and distances of transportation would inure to the benefit of many school children, especially the younger ones." *Id.*

207. 498 F.2d 195 (4th Cir. 1974).

208. *Id.* at 196-97. The district court's finding does not seem unreasonable and the ruling may have been prompted by tactical errors on the plaintiffs' part. Their expert witness was unfamiliar with the local situation in Newport News, and testified that the time and distance to be traveled had not entered into his considerations when preparing the plaintiff's desegregation plan. 363 F. Supp. 458, 461-62 (E.D. Va. 1973).

209. The pediatrician had testified that young children would be "physically and psychologically affected by compulsory bus transportation for long periods of time . . . ." 363 F. Supp. at 460. This decision was upheld on appeal, 498 F.2d at 197. Judge Winter, in his dissenting opinion, found reliance on the pediatrician's testimony inappropriate:

> I record my suspicion of the basis on which the district court approved retention of a dual system for grades 1 and 2. It relied heavily on the testimony of . . . a pediatrician, to the effect that the health of students in kindergarten and the first and second grades would be adversely affected if they were not permitted to attend neighborhood schools. But as I read the testimony . . . it was . . . that the effect of transportation on the physical and mental health of a child depends upon whether he is transported to a school "of his choice or his parents' choice." If the child is unhappy, i.e., not transported to a school of his choice or his parents' choice, "then it follows from there, as the night does the day, that you're just going to have a poor situation." Acceptance of [the pediatrician's] thesis, it seems to me, would be to require application of the equal protection clause to depend upon a plebiscite by parents. . . .

498 F.2d at 198-99.

210. Equal Educational Opportunity Act of 1974, 20 U.S.C.A. §§ 1701-58 (Cum. Supp. 1975).

211. Notwithstanding any other provision of law, . . . no court of the United States shall order the implementation of any plan to remedy a finding of de jure segregation which involves the transportation of students, unless the court first finds that all alternative

busing is used, the amendments provide that no student should be bused beyond the school next closest to his home,[212] *unless* the courts determine that more extensive busing is necessary to ensure the protection of constitutionally guaranteed civil rights.[213] This important proviso seems to leave intact the

---

remedies are inadequate.

20 U.S.C.A. § 1755 (Cum. Supp. 1975).

The alternative remedies, which appear to require their application seriatim, are as follows:

In formulating a remedy for a denial of equal educational opportunity or a denial of the equal protection of the laws, which may involve directly or indirectly the transportation of students, a court, department, or agency of the United States shall consider and make specific findings on the efficacy in correcting such denial of the following remedies and shall require implementation of the *first of the remedies set out below, or of the first combination thereof which would remedy such denial*:

(a) assigning students to the schools closest to their places of residence which provide the appropriate grade level and type of education for such students, taking into account school capacities and natural physical barriers;

(b) assigning students to the schools closest to their places of residence which provide the appropriate grade level and type of education for such students, taking into account only school capacities;

(c) permitting students to transfer from a school in which a majority of the students are of their race, color, or national origin to a school in which a minority of the students are of their race, color, or national origin;

(d) the creation or revision of attendance zones or grade structures without requiring transportation beyond that described in section 1714 of this title;

(e) the construction of new schools or the closing of inferior schools;

(f) the construction or establishment of magnet schools; or

(g) the development and implementation of any other plan which is educationally sound and administratively feasible, subject to the provisions of section 1714 and 1715 of this title.

20 U.S.C.A. § 1713 (Cum. Supp. 1975) (emphasis added).

212. (a) No court, department, or agency of the United States shall, pursuant to section 1713 of this title, order the implementation of a plan that would require the transportation of any student to a school other than the school closest or next closest to his place of residence which provides the appropriate grade level and type of education for such student.

(b) No court, department or agency of the United States shall require directly or indirectly the transportation of any student if such transportation poses a risk to the health of such student or constitutes a significant impingement on the educational progress with respect to such student.

(c) When a court of competent jurisdiction determines that a school system is desegregated, or that it meets the constitutional requirements, or that it is a unitary system, or that it has no vestiges of a dual system, and thereafter residential shifts in population occur which result in school population changes in any school within such a desegregated school system, no educational agency because of such shifts shall be required by any court, department, or agency of the United States to formulate, or implement any new desegregation plan, or modify or implement any modification of the court approved desegregation plan, which would require transportation of students to compensate wholly or in part for such shifts in school population so occurring.

20 U.S.C.A. § 1714 (Cum. Supp. 1975).

213. Any court order requiring, directly or indirectly, the transportation of students for the purpose of remedying a denial of the equal protection of the laws may, to the extent of such transportation, be terminated if the court finds the defendant educational agency has satisfied the requirements of the fifth or fourteenth amendments to the Constitution, whichever is applicable, and will continue to be in compliance with the requirements thereof. . . . No additional order requiring such educational agency to transport students for such purpose shall be entered unless such agency is found not to have satisfied the

remedial powers of the federal courts already judicially defined in cases such as *Green* and *Swann*. The law also allows parents and educational agencies to seek to reopen a busing order but—using language from the *Swann* decision—only if the time or distance traveled is so great as to endanger the health of the student or impinge on the educational process.[214]

The courts may well take a restrictive view of congressional efforts to impose limits on school desegregation. In *Darville v. Dade County School Board*,[215] the plaintiffs challenged the authority of the school district to continue to use pupil assignment and transportation plans "to ensure the continued existence of the unitary system."[216] Plaintiffs alleged that the following provisions of the Education Amendments of 1972 were violated by the actions of the school board:[217]

> No provision of this Act shall be construed to require the assignment or transportation of students or teachers in order to overcome racial imbalance.
>
> No court or official of the United States shall be empowered to issue any order seeking to achieve a racial balance in any school by requiring the transportation of pupils or students from one school to another or one school district to another in order to achieve such racial balance, or otherwise enlarge the existing power of the court to ensure compliance with constitutional standards shall apply to all public school pupils and to every public school system, public school and public school board . . . .[218]

The court noted that school boards are vested with broad discretion in pupil assignments and that there is nothing in the above-quoted amendments which would restrict the actions of public school boards as nothing in either of the amendments applies to voluntary action by local school boards. Moreover, § 1656 can only be read as applying to federal officials and agencies.[219]

5. *Summary of Permissible Intradistrict Remedial Tools*

To summarize, the constitutional objective of the courts is "to eliminate from the public schools all vestiges of state-imposed segregation."[220] To achieve

---

> requirements of the fifth or fourteenth amendments to the Constitution, whichever is applicable.

20 U.S.C.A. § 1718 (Cum. Supp. 1975).

214. > A parent . . . of a child . . . transported to a public school in accordance with a court order, or an educational agency subject to a court order or a desegregation plan under Title VI of the Civil Rights Act of 1964 in effect on [the date of the enactment of this section] and intended to end segregation of students on the basis of race, color, or national origin, may seek to reopen or intervene in the further implementation of such court order . . . if the time or distance of travel is so great as to risk the health of the student or significantly impinge on his or her educational process.

20 U.S.C. § 1717 (Cum. Supp. 1975).

215. 497 F.2d 1002 (5th Cir. 1974).

216. *Id.* at 1003.

217. 20 U.S.C.A. § 1651-56 (1974).

218. 20 U.S.C.A. § 1956 (1974).

219. 497 F.2d at 1004-05.

220. Swann v. Charlotte-Mecklenberg Bd. of Educ., 402 U.S. at 15.

this objective, *Swann* says that an "[a]wareness of the racial composition of the whole school system is likely to be a useful starting point in shaping a remedy to correct past constitutional violations";[221] thus, "the very limited use . . . of mathematical ratios [is] within the equitable remedial discretion of the District Court."[222] Nevertheless, "[t]he constitutional command to desegregate schools does not mean that every school in every community must always reflect the racial composition of the school system as a whole."[223] While there is a presumption against "one-race" schools, it can be overcome if school authorities can show that the racial composition of "some small number of one-race, or virtually one-race, schools" is "not the result of present or past discriminatory action" on the part of school officials.[224] The pairing or clustering of schools, the altering of attendance zones, and majority-minority transfer plans also are permissible remedial tools to achieve the objective. Busing is a permissible tool as well, but it is limited by time and distance according to the age of the students involved.

C. Black Backlash and White Flight

1. *Black Opposition*

There is another important issue in the remedial area: what recourse is there when a specific remedy disproportionately burdens minorities? This issue has arisen in two overlapping contexts: where there is "one-way" busing (only minority students are bused out of their neighborhoods to attend schools in white neighborhoods) and where a formerly all-black school is closed but white schools are not. The first issue was raised in *Norwalk CORE v. Norwalk Board of Education*, which held that one-way busing was within the discretion of the school board absent a finding of either de jure segregation or a lack of good faith on the part of the board.[225]

In some of the more recent decisions, courts have been readier to acknowledge the problem of imposing a disproportionate burden on minorities in any desegregation plan, but in most of these cases—after the court has made the token statement that the burdens of desegregation can not be imposed on only one group—the result is the same. In *Hart v. Community School Board*,[226] for example, the district judge's amended order called for the school in question to be turned into a "magnet" school in order to attract more whites.[227] The plaintiffs objected, in part because substantially more minority students (1050) than

221. *Id.* at 25.
222. *Id.*
223. 402 U.S. at 24.
224. 402 U.S. at 26.
225. 298 F. Supp. 213, 224-26 (D. Conn. 1969), *aff'd*, 423 F.2d 122 (2d Cir. 1970). *Accord*, Moss v. Stamford Bd. of Educ., 356 F. Supp. 675 (D. Conn. 1973).
226. 512 F.2d 37 (2d Cir. 1975).
227. 383 F. Supp. 769, 770-74 (E.D.N.Y. 1974).

white students (650) were to be bused.[228] The Second Circuit held, however, that[229]

> the "burden" of busing cast upon minority students is only a "somewhat heavier burden" . . . . A "somewhat heavier burden" has to fall somewhere, either on white or minority students as a class.

In *Higgins v. Board of Education*,[230] the plaintiffs alleged that the Grand Rapids school board's affirmative desegregation plan was illegal in providing for "one-way" busing from the central city (where blacks were concentrated) to the peripheral areas—because the school board thought that any other plan would result in white flight to the suburbs.[231] The Sixth Circuit, while recognizing that the "burdens and inconveniences of integration should not be placed discriminatorily" stated that[232]

> the authority of school officials to formulate plans for achieving an improved racial balance should not be as restrictive in the case of a school system which has not been found to have engaged in purposeful segregation as for a system which has practiced de jure segregation.

With regard to the "white flight" justification of the school board, the circuit court emphasized that there was a[233]

> valid distinction between using the defense of white flight as a smokescreen to avoid integration and realistically considering and dealing with the practical problems involved in making voluntary efforts to achieve integration.

Despite the often expressed concern over busing particularly young children, courts have not seen fit to regard plans which call for busing only *black* children in the earliest years as being a disproportionate burden on one race. In Nashville, the school board devised a plan which called for busing black students in grades one to four to outlying schools while white students were not bused unless they were in grades five and six.[234] The circuit court approved, stating that "We do not believe . . . that we can appropriately hold the District Judge abused his discretion . . . ."[235] Similarly, the Fourth Circuit considered acceptable a plan whereby black students in grades three through five were to be bused out of their neighborhoods to attend schools in white neighborhoods, while white students in grades six and seven were bused to formerly black schools.[236] The plaintiffs had argued that "such assignments placed an undue and discriminatory burden on black students" inasmuch as[237]

---

228. 512 F.2d at 53.
229. *Id.*
230. 508 F.2d 779 (6th Cir. 1974).
231. *Id.* at 793.
232. *Id.*
233. 508 F.2d at 794.
234. Kelley v. Metropolitan County Bd. of Educ., 463 F.2d 732 (6th Cir.), *cert. denied*, 409 U.S. 1001 (1972).
235. 463 F.2d at 746.
236. Thompson v. School Bd., 465 F.2d 83, 84 (4th Cir. 1972), *cert. denied*, 413 U.S. 920 (1973).
237. 465 F.2d at 84-85.

> the white school child would attend for his first five school years a school formerly identified as a white school and located in a white neighborhood, whereas the black child would be in a school located in a black neighborhood only in his first two grades and in his 6th and 7th grades.

The courts have also held that it is permissible to close formerly all-black schools if the closing is not based on "racial considerations."[238] But what set of facts leads to the conclusion that the closing was due to non-racial reasons? For example, the closing of five formerly black schools in Jacksonville, Florida, was approved on these grounds: all were deteriorated; one was surrounded by a slaughter house, a polluted creek, and a city incinerator; and in three other schools the "[i]ncidences of vandalism and intrusion [were so frequent and serious] that teachers and children [were] locked in their rooms for safety."[239]

It is clear, however, that there is a heavy burden on the school board to show that the closing of formerly black schools is not for racial reasons. With regard to the desegregation of Austin schools, the district court ordered two all-black schools to be closed. The Fifth Circuit found "the closing of two all-black schools and the transfer of the students from those schools to other schools in the system . . . unacceptable . . . where there was no showing that these schools were closed for non-racial reasons" and where a similarly situated white school was not closed.[240] The fact that the possibility of white flight "was the real reason for the closing of the two schools" was *not* a legitimate justification.[241]

In *Arvizu v. Waco Independent School District*, the Fifth Circuit went even further.[242] The school board had given reasons for the closing of minority schools—the facilities were outmoded, they operated at under capacity or the capacity was so limited that the costs of operation were prohibitive, and the physical plant was too small.[243] The court held, however, that the board must do more than give "facially legitimate" justifications. It "must adduce evidence sufficient to support" the conclusion that "their actions were not in fact motivated by racial reasons"[244] sufficient to support the conclusion. The district court, on remand, was to re-examine the justifications for closing the minority schools "in light of the characteristics of the schools permitted to remain in operation . . . and . . . the timing of the proposed school closings . . . ."[245]

---

238. Ellis v. Board of Pub. Instruction, 465 F.2d 878, 880 (5th Cir. 1972), *cert. denied*, 410 U.S. 966 (1973); Lee v. Macon County Bd. of Educ., 448 F.2d 746, 753-54 (5th Cir. 1971); Mims v. Duval County School Bd., 447 F.2d 1330, 1331-32 (5th Cir. 1971); Carr v. Montgomery County Bd. of Educ., 429 F.2d 382, 385 (5th Cir. 1970).

239. Mims v. Duval County School Bd., 447 F.2d at 1332-33. Several of these schools have now reopened. Letter from Norman Chachkin, Staff Attorney, NAACP Legal Defense and Educational Fund, Inc., to the senior author, November 1974, on file at *Law and Contemporary Problems* office.

240. United States v. Texas Educ. Agency, 467 F.2d 848, 871-72 (5th Cir. 1972).

241. 467 F.2d at 872.

242. 495 F.2d 499 (5th Cir. 1974).

243. *Id.* at 505.

244. *Id.*

245. 495 F.2d at 506.

Of what relevance is minority opposition—to the extent that it exists—to desegregation?[246] There have been only a few cases so far even to acknowledge the existence of this possibility. In *Hart v. Community School Board*, the district court noted that some commentators have "urged that self-imposed segregation in the public schools is desirable and therefore constitutional,"[247] citing, among others, Mosteller and Moynihan's review and reanalysis of the *Coleman Report* findings.[248] Responding to this argument, the District Judge noted that[249]

> [t]his position would have to be rejected even were there basis in fact for the proposition that segregated schools improved the education of black students—a proposition belied by data available to date.

Judge Weick of the Sixth Circuit, dissenting in *Mapp v. Board of Education*,[250] took a different position. He opposed the court-ordered integration through busing as resulting "in the violation of the constitutional rights of innocent black children and white children,"[251] primarily the right of freedom of association. In support of this, he stated that "[m]any black people [oppose] forced bussing of their children," citing statements made at the National Black Political Convention held in Gary, Indiana in 1972[252] to the effect that mandatory busing is racist and preserves a black minority structure.

As part of its Experimental Schools program, funded by HEW, the Berkeley school system recently experimented with optional schools offering alternative educational environments for black and Chicano students—schools whose enrollments, although not expressly limited to these minority students, were racially exclusive by choice. The debate over the constitutionality of such schools fostering voluntary segregation seems to pit the *Brown* decision and the fourteenth amendment against the first amendment's freedom of association. Is there a point at which *Brown's* demand for integration becomes satisfied so that resegregation *by choice* becomes constitutionally permissible?[253] Inasmuch

---

246. *See, e.g.*, Bell, *supra* note 126; Epps, *Assimilation, Pluralism, and Separation*, in AMERICAN EDUCATION IN RETHINKING EDUCATIONAL EQUALITY 49 (A. Kopan and H. Walberg eds. 1974); Sizemore, *Is There a Case for Separate Schools?*, *supra* note 129.

247. 383 F. Supp. 699, 742 (E.D.N.Y. 1974).

248. ON EQUALITY OF EDUCATIONAL OPPORTUNITY (F. Mosteller & D. Moynihan eds. 1972). Judge Weinstein also cited Robinson, *Preparation for Life: The Black Classroom*, in BLACK MANIFESTO FOR EDUCATION 3 (J. Haskins ed. 1973) and R. CRARY & L. PETRONE, FOUNDATION OF MODERN EDUCATION (1971).

249. 383 F. Supp. at 742. The court later notes that "the evidence supports neither the argument that desegregated public school education is not helpful to the minorities, nor that it adversely affects whites," 383 F. Supp. at 744, further noting, however, that "much of the current research replies to precise policy based questions with the ambiguity of a Delphic oracle . . . ." *Id.*

250. 477 F.2d 851 (6th Cir.), *cert. denied*, 414 U.S. 1022 (1973).

251. 477 F.2d at 856.

252. 477 F.2d at 856 n. 4.

253. *See* Comment, *Alternative Schools for Minority Students: The Constitution, the Civil Rights Act and the Berkeley Experiment*, 61 CALIF. L. REV. 858 (1973). *Cf.* Comment, *Separate Black Facilities on Campus: A Legal and Practical Evaluation*, 7 COLUM. J.L. & SOCIAL PROB. 107 (1971).

It should be noted that Berkeley had become a fully unitary, integrated system and that the two

as the Court in *Green* said that freedom-of-choice plans are not unconstitutional per se,[254] the Berkeley situation—where the system is unitary and where any minority student may choose to remain in an integrated school in the system—may be the appropriate one for a freedom-of-choice pupil assignment plan.

Somewhat related to these examples is the so-called "Atlanta Compromise." The Atlanta school system had an enrollment that was 70 per cent white and 30 per cent black at the time the first desegregation suit was filed in 1958.[255] By 1973, the enrollment was 79 per cent black and 21 per cent white.[256] Some (but not all) of the plaintiffs who filed the original desegregation suit, seeing that the school system was rapidly resegregating and believing that further efforts to integrate the few remaining white students would be futile, opted instead for an agreement with the school board for the allocation of more administrative positions to blacks—including a black superintendent. The district court approved the plan in *Calhoun v. Cook*[257] with some modifications, noting that it satisfied "the overwhelming majority of the plaintiff class" and the plan was "fair, adequate, and reasonable."[258] The plan left 59,000 black students—about 60 per cent of the school system—in schools 90 per cent black.[259] Enough students were transferred to ensure that there were no schools 90 per cent white.[260] The Fifth Circuit remanded the cases, however, for further findings, saying that the adoption of the compromise was improper since the facts as to the compromise agreement were in dispute.[261]

In an earlier phase of this case, the district court had noted that in view of demographic patterns within Atlanta, the only device which could effect racial balance in each school (70 per cent black to 30 per cent white pupil enrollment) was mass busing. However, the court found that the time and distances involved would make it impractical. The court had considered the possibility of

---

schools—Black House and Casa de la Raza—served a very small proportion of the total number of minority students enrolled in the district. Black House served a student body of 75 high school students, while over 1400 blacks attended integrated high schools in Berkeley. Casa de la Raza served 125 Chicano students of a total of 427.

Under pressure from HEW, the Berkeley public school system withdrew its support for these two schools. HEW's Office of Civil Rights eventually accepted a plan whereby students would be permitted to spend 20 per cent of their school time attending Black House or Casa de la Raza. Black House, however, closed down and has never been revived. Casa de la Raza did submit a skeletal plan to the Berkeley school district last fall, but was told there were no more funds from HEW for the Experimental Schools Program. Communication from David L. Kirp, Associate Professor, Graduate School of Public Policy and Lecturer, School of Law, University of California at Berkeley, and consultant to the Berkeley School System, June 19, 1975.

254. *See* note 51 *supra* and accompanying text.

255. Calhoun v. Cook, 332 F. Supp. 804, 805 (N.D. Ga. 1971). *See also* Bell, *supra* note 126.

256. Calhoun v. Cook, 362 F. Supp. 1249, 1251 (N.D. Ga. 1973).

257. 362 F. Supp. at 1249.

258. 362 F. Supp. at 1252.

259. *Id.*

260. Atlanta Constitution, April 5, 1973, § A, at 1, col. 1.

261. 487 F.2d 680, 682 (5th Cir. 1973). Following remand, the district court issued an unreported opinion which is now on appeal. The case is now in its seventeenth year.

requiring the transportation of black students from the center of the city to the white periphery, but noted, without further explanation, that such a move would be "opposed by a large group of blacks except on a voluntary basis . . . ."[262] Therefore, the remedy of "mass" busing was rejected.

2. *White Flight*

One potential limit to consider in shaping a desegregation remedy is the phenomenon of "white flight." Should a desegregation plan take into account the "tipping point" beyond which "white flight" accelerates precipitously? If a court order seemed likely to induce "white flight" from the community or from the public school system to such a degree that desegregation would become impossible, is it constitutionally permissible to substitute a lesser remedy?

The question of the effect of a court order on "white flight," or vice versa, has arisen several times in the Fourth Circuit. In *Beckett v. School Board*,[263] the district court approved an interim "desegregation" plan consisting only of a limited freedom-of-choice option in the elementary schools. The court took the position that[264]

> [a]ny attempt to radically desegregate schools of Norfolk lying readily adjacent to [predominantly white] Virginia Beach will lead to white-flight, a fact that is certainly not desirable from the stand-point of *sound educational principles*. . . .

In this respect the court relied on a number of social science research studies,[265] quoting at length from that of Professor Pettigrew regarding the advantages of retaining a white majority in schools:[266]

> Negroes in predominantly white classrooms score higher on the average, but those Negroes in classrooms with less than one-half whites do no better than those in all Negro classrooms.

The Fourth Circuit subsequently reversed the decision without specifically addressing itself to the "white flight" issue.[267] In *Brunson v. Board of Trustees*,[268] however, the Fourth Circuit did confront the issue directly. In separate opinions by Judges Craven and Sobeloff, the relevance of such testimony as that of

---

262. 332 F. Supp. at 807-08. The court does not indicate how it obtained the opinion of "a large group of blacks."

263. 302 F. Supp. 18 (E.D. Va. 1969), *rev'd sub nom.* Brewer v. School Bd., 434 F.2d 408 (4th Cir.), *cert. denied* 399 U.S. 929 (1970).

264. 302 F. Supp. at 30 (emphasis added).

265. 302 F. Supp. at 29-30 n. 15.

266. 302 F. Supp. at 30. The Norfolk School Board had followed Professor Pettigrew's "principles" and drew its zones so that each integrated school would have a 60 to 70 per cent white majority. To do this, however, the Board had to leave 19 all-black elementary schools untouched. Approximately 76 per cent of the black elementary students would continue to attend these schools. 434 F.2d 408, 410-11 (4th Cir. 1970).

267. 434 F.2d 408 (4th Cir.), *cert. denied*, 399 U.S. 929 (1970). In reversing, the circuit court indicated that it did not need to discuss the sociological data because where "[w]hite schools remain predominantly white . . . black schools remain black," there is a violation requiring an appropriate remedy. The "quota" was "the antithesis of a racially unitary system." *Id.* at 411.

268. 429 F.2d 820 (4th Cir. 1970).

Professor Pettigrew was hotly debated. Judge Craven's position was that in view of the *serious* threat of white flight—and, indeed, substantial white flight had already taken place—"some degree of moderation in selecting a remedy" was needed.[269] Professor Pettigrew's testimony in *Brewer v. Norfolk City School Board* that the optimum ratio was 30 per cent black to 70 per cent white was cited with favor by Judge Craven.[270]

---

269. *Id.* at 822. Judge Craven noted that in 1969, when there were 2,408 black students and 256 white students enrolled in the schools of Clarendon County, S.C., 110 white students "fled the public school system in favor of a parochial private school," and 100 more applied for admission for the following fall. *Id.* Judge Craven stated that:

> judges in fashioning remedies cannot successfully ignore reality. . . . [S]ome degree of moderation in selecting a remedy is more likely to accomplish the desired result, a unitary, non-racial public school system, than is unyielding fidelity to the arithmetic of race. . . .
>
> The threat of flight from the public school system ordinarily should not be allowed to influence the selection of the plan or its judicial approval. It is relevant here only because the whites constitute such a small minority. . . .
>
> . . . [A] practical approach to the problem would . . . greatly diminish the temptation to flee the system. . . .

429 F.2d at 821-22.

Judge Sobeloff, in a separate concurring opinion, responded:

> The dissenters agree that the Board's freedom of choice plan is deficient, but they consider the remedy too strong. As they point out, we are threatened in this case with an exodus of white students that tends to convert the court-ordered integration into an exercise in futility. . . .
>
> It would . . . astonish the *Brown* court to learn that 16 years later . . . it was seriously being contended that desegregation might not be required insofar as it threatened to impair majority white situations. . . .
>
> . . . .
>
> "White Flight" is one expression of resistance to integration, but the Supreme Court has held over and over that courts must not permit community hostility to intrude on the application of constitutional principles. . . . [D]issidents who threaten to leave the system may not be enticed to stay by the promise of an unconstitutional though palatable plan. . . . [T]he road to integration is served neither by covert capitulation nor by overt compromise . . . . The purported restriction of the thesis to extreme white minority-white flight situations is really no limitation at all. Rather it offers a premium for community resistance. More to be feared than white flight in Clarendon County would be any judicial countenancing of the suggestion that abandoning or qualifying a desegregation program is a legally acceptable way to discourage flight. . . .

429 F.2d at 824, 827. *See also* Craven, *The Impact of Social Science Evidence on the Judge: A Personal Comment*, 39 LAW & CONTEMP. PROB. no. 1, at 150, 154-55 (1975).

270. 429 F.2d at 821 n. 1.

R. CRAIN & C. ROSSELL, EVALUATING SCHOOL DESEGREGATION PLANS STATISTICALLY 18 (1973) proffer a similar thesis:

> (1) That blacks benefit from attending schools which are over 50% white, but there is no additional benefit as the % white increases beyond 70%.
> (2) That whites benefit from interracial contact and a school must be at least 5% black to provide these benefits.
> (3) Social and Political constraints make it inadvisable to bring black students into all-white schools in excess of 30% of the enrollment . . . [although] *no educational research* which demonstrates that a 70% white school is superior to a 50% white school.

A number of districts have developed desegregation plans providing for a 70 to 30 per cent white-black mix, leaving behind in all-black schools what Professor Gordon Foster has referred to as "surplus" blacks. He notes that this has become known as the "warehousing" technique, because the remaining all-black schools are often warehouse-like structures in the middle of the ghetto. G. Foster, November 9, 1974 (paper prepared for conference sponsored by United States Com-

> The federal courts, when plunged into sociology and educational theory, are into something they know very little about. Dr. Thomas F. Pettigrew of Harvard University, who has a respectable social-psychology pedigree and who is a recognized expert in school integration, testified at great length about integration and desegregation in Brewer v. Norfolk City School Board. . . .
>
> Dr. Pettigrew . . . testified that "there does seem to be some optimum level for the achievement of both white and black children that drops after 35 or 40 [percent black students in the school is surpassed]." Dr. Pettigrew has concluded that little advantage is gained for children of either race, and some harm may result, from placing children in a school where they are in a distinct racial minority. . . .

Judge Sobeloff responded by saying that "short shrift" should be given to Dr. Pettigrew's testimony.[271]

> [The] central proposition [of Pettigrew's thesis] is that the value of a school depends on the characteristics of a majority of its students and superiority is related to whiteness, inferiority to blackness. Although the theory is couched in terms of "socio-economic class" and the necessity for the creation of a "middle-class milieu," nevertheless, at bottom, it rests on the generalization that, educationally speaking, white pupils are somehow better or more desirable than black pupils. This premise leads to the next proposition, that association with white pupils helps the blacks and so long as whites predominate does not harm the white children. But once the number of whites approaches minority, then association with the inferior black children hurts the whites and, because there are not enough of the superior whites to go around, does not appreciably help the blacks.
>
> . . . .
>
> The inventors and proponents of this theory grossly misapprehend the philosophical basis for desegregation. It is not founded upon the concept that white children are a precious resource which should be fairly apportioned. It is not, as Pettigrew suggests, because black children will be improved by association with their betters. . . . [S]chool segregation is forbidden simply because its perpetuation is a living insult to the black children and immeasurably taints the education they receive. This is the precise lesson of *Brown*. Were a court to adopt the Pettigrew rationale it would do explicitly what compulsory segregation laws did implicitly.

In *United States v. Board of School Commissioners*, the district court has noted that in Indianapolis, a city where the majority of the black population was already confined to the inner city, "white flight" would become accelerated and irreversible when the percentage of black pupils in a particular school ap-

---

mission on Civil Rights, Washington, D.C.). *See, e.g.*, Northcross v. Board of Educ., 489 F.2d 15 (6th Cir. 1973), *cert. denied*, 416 U.S. 962 (1974).

271. 429 F.2d 820, 824, 826 (4th Cir. 1970). Judge Sobeloff suggests that the Pettigrew plan is just as invidious when considered from the class rather than the racial aspect:

> [E]ven apart from its racial aspect, the Pettigrew plan would be constitutionally illegitimate. . . . The goal of social class segregation is scarcely more defensible than that of racial segregation . . . . Viewing the matter on a policy level, a country as sadly riven as ours stands in no need of additional polarizing projects. From a constitutional standpoint, a program of apartheid according to social class is as impermissible as avowed racial separation—and as repugnant to the Equal Protection Clause. Our constitution does not permit the insulation of whites from blacks, rich from poor, high class from low class.

429 F.2d at 826.

proached 40 per cent, thus leaving a nearly all-black school system.[272] The court—citing the situation in Atlanta as an example—cautioned that a school board, by implementing a desegregation plan that failed to take this "tipping factor" into account, could become indirectly responsible for pushing the racial balance past the "tipping point," resulting in the rapid resegregation of the schools.[273] However, on appeal, the Seventh Circuit responded that "[s]o-called 'white flight' is not an acceptable reason for failing to dismantle a dual school system."[274]

In *Calhoun v. Cook*, the district court noted the precipitous speed of the "tipping process."[275]

> The white students remaining are concentrated at the extreme northern and southern ends of the district, while the vast middle is a broad belt of industry and high-density solid black housing. The line between these areas is steadily creeping towards the ends, with increased black housing and diminished white housing. Since 1961, [the school board] has annually achieved substantial temporary integration by the establishment or construction of "line schools." However, 34 of those schools have gone from all-white to 90% or more black during the period. This "tipping process" is so rapid that it sometimes occurs by the time a facility deliberately located to increase integration can be completed and occupied. Seldom does it last longer than two years. . . .

Thus, according to the court, wholesale busing was "unworkable."

The court observed that "Atlanta now stands on the brink of becoming an all-black city. A fruit-basket turnover through busing to create a 30% white-70% black uniformity throughout the system would unquestionably cause such a result in a few months time."[276]

The question of whether and when there is a tipping point has been raised most often in connection with racial discrimination in housing. Most of the literature indicates that the tipping point will vary—from as low as 6 per cent to

---

272. United States v. Board of School Comm'rs, 332 F. Supp. 655, 676-77 (S.D. Ind. 1971), *aff'd*, 474 F.2d 81 (7th Cir.), *cert. denied*, 413 U.S. 920 (1973). District Court Judge Dillin noted in his opinion only that evidence in the case as to the existence of a "tipping point" of 40 per cent black pupils was "undisputed." 332 F. Supp. at 676. Judge Dillin again addressed himself to "tipping," citing evidence showing that in the Indianapolis schools, white flight had become problematical as the percentage of black pupils reached 25-30 per cent. 368 F. Supp. 1191, 1197-99 (S.D. Ind. 1973). It was partially this concern with the possibility of resegregation that led the district court to include the Greater Indianapolis area in its remedy. On appeal, the Seventh Circuit reversed that part of the district court's decision relating to a metropolitan remedy beyond the boundaries of the county in which Indianapolis is located, and vacated and remanded that part of the remedy that ran to the county boundaries for further findings. 503 F.2d 68 (7th Cir. 1974). *See also* the textual discussion at p. 110 *infra*.

273. 332 F. Supp. at 677.

274. 503 F.2d 68, 80 (7th Cir. 1974). *Cf.* Monroe v. Board of Comm'rs, 391 U.S. 450 (1968), involving a "free transfer" option—defended by the school board on the ground that it would prevent "white flight." The Court found that the plan acted to resegregate the system and, in striking down the free transfer option plan, responded to the "white flight" argument by quoting from *Brown* II: "[I]t should go without saying that the vitality of these constitutional principles cannot be allowed to yield simply because of disagreement with them." *Id.* at 459.

275. 332 F. Supp. 804, 806 (N.D. Ga. 1971).

276. 332 F. Supp. at 808.

as high as 50 per cent, depending upon many factors, including the "intensity of prejudicial feeling in the community."[277] The use of the "tipping point" as the upper limit for a "benign" quota system has been proposed on occasion —the justification being that minorities would benefit in that their feelings of rejection, prompted by their living in separation from the rest of the community, would be eliminated.[278]

The Supreme Court, in *Wright v. Council of the City of Emporia*,[279] recognized the phenomenon of "white flight," but not in the context of minimizing the impact of a desegregation plan by compromising it in an effort to retain whites who might flee if there were total desegregation. Instead, the Court *prohibited* a city from withdrawing from an existing county school district when the combined system was still under a federal court order to desegregate. The dual school system which had been found to violate the constitution was the single city-county unit and therefore it was proper to treat it as a single unit for the purpose of dismantling that system.[280] The possibility of "white flight" from the county system to the proposed city school system was one of the factors the Court felt "would actually impede the process of dismantling the existing dual system."[281] And in *United States v. Scotland Neck City Board of Education*, the Supreme Court reiterated its stand that "while [white flight] may be cause for deep concern to the [school boards], it cannot . . . be accepted as a reason for achieving anything less than complete uprooting of the dual public school

277. *See, e.g.*, Mulvihill, *Problems in the Management of Public Housing*, 35 TEMP. L.Q. 163, 175-78 (1962) (6 to 50 per cent depending upon "the intensity of prejudicial feeling in the community, the extent of private housing to which white tenants can escape and the racial composition of the neighborhood"); LeBlanc, *Race, Housing, and the Government*, 26 VAND. L. REV. 487, 502-04 (1973) (tipping point 40 per cent); Note, *Racial Discrimination in Housing*, 107 U. PA. L. REV. 515, 538-39 (1959) (6 to 50 per cent depending upon differing opinions of "guestimators" and the fact that individual tipping points will vary among housing projects).

As to school desegregation and tipping points, see R. Wegmann, Neighborhoods and Schools in Racial Transition, April 1, 1975 (paper presented at American Educational Research Association, Washington, D.C.). Wegmann, a sociologist, states that desegregating any urban school system where the total black enrollment runs much above 30 per cent will be futile because of "tipping"—white families move out when blacks in the neighborhood school reach some point between 30 and 50 per cent of the student population.

See also, J. Coleman, Trends in Racial Segregation in Schools, 1968-73, April 2, 1975 (paper presented at American Educational Research Association, Washington, D.C.). Professor Coleman argues for more research into white reaction and other indirect effects of desegregation in order to develop alternative strategies. He notes that in refusing to recognize white flight, the courts in the long run will be responsible for separating whites and blacks even more than at present. But see the statement by state Superior Court Judge Max F. Deutz of California that the "tipping" in Inglewood—a suburb of Los Angeles whose enrollment had gone from 60 per cent European American to 80 per cent minority—had begun before his integration order, issued five years ago: "Some people say the plan caused it, and it might have been a factor, but certainly not the predominant factor." N.Y. Times, May 11, 1975, § 1, at 26, col. 1.

278. Mulvihill, *supra* note 277, at 177.

279. 407 U.S. 451 (1972). *See also* United States v. Scotland Neck City Bd. of Educ., 407 U.S. 484 (1972); Monroe v. Board of Comm'rs, 391 U.S. 450, 459 (1968).

280. 407 U.S. at 459-60.

281. 407 U.S. at 466.

system."[282] Although this language has been picked up by the circuits as indicating that white flight cannot under any circumstances be a consideration in formulating a remedy,[283] the Supreme Court has not yet addressed itself to this issue in any broad sense.

D. Metropolitan Area Remedies

When, if ever, may school district lines be disregarded in devising remedies to disestablish an unconstitutional dual school system? Metropolitan areas in which the central city loses total population to the suburban ring while the minority population within the central city increases, are becoming more and more the typical situation. The proportion of minority *students* in the central city school district is increasing even more rapidly than the total minority population. Thus, the "growing core of Negro schools [is] surrounded by a receding ring of white schools."[284] As the proportion of blacks in the central cities increases, it becomes more and more futile to order a desegregation plan which is confined to the city limits inasmuch as there is or will be no one left with whom to integrate.[285] Thus a number of school desegregation suits have sought a metropolitan area remedy.

There are three types of cross-district or interdistrict organizational arrangements which have come before the courts. One involves the formation of a single "super district" by consolidating contiguous districts in the metropolitan area—the remedy proposed by the district court in *Bradley v. School Board*, the Richmond case.[286] The second involves redistricting the metropolitan area into new units which facilitate the reduction of racial imbalance—represented by what the district court and the Sixth Circuit attempted to do in *Milliken v. Bradley*, the Detroit case.[287] Finally, what may be yet another type is represented by the proposed merger of the city of Louisville and its suburban county.[288]

---

282. 407 U.S. 484, 491 (1972).

283. United States v. Board of School Comm'rs, 503 F.2d 68, 80 (7th Cir. 1974).

284. Milliken v. Bradley, 418 U.S. 717, 799 (1974) (Marshall, J., dissenting).

285. Judge Deutz of the Los Angeles Superior Court has recently permitted a five-year old desegregation busing plan for Inglewood to be discarded because "As a practical matter we are now busing black children from predominantly black schools to other predominantly black schools." N.Y. Times, May 11, 1975, § 1, at 26, col. 1.

286. 338 F. Supp. 67 (E.D. Va.), *rev'd*, 462 F.2d 1058 (4th Cir. 1972), *aff'd by an equally divided Court*, 412 U.S. 92 (1973). The remedy sought here would have joined two counties (Henrico and Chesterfield) with the City of Richmond. District Judge Merhige adopted Richmond's metropolitan plan, prepared under the direction of Dr. Thomas Little, Associate Superintendent of the Richmond City Schools, 338 F. Supp. at 186, which provided for a single school board of no more than nine members or less than six to preside over the three-county "super district." *Id.* at 245. For administrative purposes, however, the consolidated system was to be divided into six sub-units. Administration and curriculum decisions would be delegated to the subdivision heads. *Id.* at 191.

287. 345 F. Supp. 914 (E.D. Mich. 1972), *aff'd*, 484 F.2d 215 (6th Cir. 1973), *rev'd*, 418 U.S. 717 (1974). In this case, 53 school districts or parts of school districts were to be joined with sections of the Detroit school district so as to form fifteen new "clusters." 345 F. Supp. at 928-29.

288. Newburg Area Council, Inc. v. Board of Educ., 489 F.2d 925 (6th Cir. 1973), *vacated and*

1. *"Super Districts"*

Under what circumstances may one of the above interdistrict arrangements be ordered? In formulating a desegregation plan for Richmond, the district court was concerned with maintaining a "viable racial mix"[289] in the schools, and therefore desired a plan that would not accelerate white flight from the largely (over 70 per cent) black Richmond schools to the predominantly (over 90 per cent) white schools in the two neighboring counties.[290] The district court concluded that these circumstances justified the joinder of the two outlying counties in its desegregation decree, without requiring proof either that the county boundaries had been drawn with intent to segregate or that the counties had acted in such a way so as to render them responsible for the city's segregation.[291]

The Fourth Circuit, however, reversed the decision, holding that the district court could not consolidate school districts without proof that the actions of authorities in the outlying counties were taken with segregative intent and effect.[292] There was no proof that "the [outlying] counties were . . . keeping blacks in Richmond schools while allowing whites to flee . . . ."[293]

The Fourth Circuit admitted evidence of housing discrimination as relevant to the case, but required greater evidence of complicity among the three units—for the purpose of keeping blacks in Richmond and out of the suburbs—before it would find such discrimination sufficiently related to schools as to support a finding of a *unified* three-county violation of the fourteenth amendment.[294] Thus the circuit court appears to accept the finding that all three units had participated in massive housing segregation, yet each unit was seen to have segregated independently of the other two for the general purpose of racial discrimination and not for the specific purpose of discrimination against Richmond blacks to keep them in Richmond schools. The court went on, however, to say that[295]

> the root causes of the concentration of blacks in the inner cities of America are simply not known . . . . [Any action] the counties may seem to have taken to keep blacks out is slight indeed compared to the myriad reasons, economic, political and social, for the concentration of blacks in Richmond and does not support the conclusion that it has been invidious state action which has resulted in the racial composition of the three school districts. . . .

The court, in taking the position that "economic, political and social" reasons can explain the concentration of blacks in Richmond, was flying in the

---

remanded, 418 U.S. 918 (1974), *on remand*, 510 F.2d 1358 (6th Cir. 1974), *cert. denied*, 95 S. Ct. 1658 (1975).

289. 338 F. Supp. at 184.
290. 338 F. Supp. at 184-86.
291. 338 F. Supp. at 100.
292. 462 F.2d 1058, 1069 (4th Cir. 1972).
293. 462 F.2d at 1065.
294. 462 F.2d at 1065-66.
295. 462 F.2d at 1066.

face of much of the evidence in the record with regard to the widespread existence of racial residential discrimination.[296] For example, Dr. Karl Taeuber, professor of sociology at the University of Wisconsin, testified that his analysis of the census data led him to conclude that about 85 per cent of the pervasive segregation extant in metropolitan areas, including Richmond, was caused by publicly and privately enforced racial discrimination rather than low income.[297] Martin Sloane, then acting deputy staff director of the U.S. Civil Rights Commission, with broad experience in federal housing policies, testified that much of the urban and, consequently, public school segregation, could be attributed to federal housing policies, *e.g.*, FHA insurance or racially-restricted developments.[298] The testimony of the executive directors of the Richmond Redevelopment and Housing Authority and of the Richmond Regional Planning District Commission supported Mr. Sloane's testimony.[299] Yet, to the Fourth Circuit, this type of evidence was deemed insufficient to establish the requisite intentional segregative actions by other governmental agencies. The circuit court noted that[300]

> [w]hatever the basic causes [of the concentration of blacks in the inner city] it has not been school assignments, and school assignments cannot reverse the trend. That there has been housing discrimination in all three units is deplorable, but a school case, like a vehicle, can carry only a limited amount of baggage.

And whatever may have been the situation in the past with regard to *school* desegregation, the three districts were now seen as operating unitary school systems.[301]

The circuit court further noted that the county boundaries had not changed significantly for over one hundred years and stated that this history was not to be ignored.[302] Since the majority saw no constitutional violation (treating each of the three systems separately and finding each unitary), clearly the district court could not override the "states' near plenary power over its political subdivisions."[303] On appeal to the Supreme Court,[304] Justice Powell did not participate in the case and the remaining justices divided evenly. This 4-4 stalemate meant that the Fourth Circuit's decision was allowed to stand.

2. *Redistricting the Metropolitan Area*

The first interdistrict case actually to be decided by the Supreme Court was *Milliken v. Bradley* (the Detroit case).[305] This case was the first instance in which

296. 338 F. Supp. at 212-29.
297. 338 F. Supp. at 213.
298. 338 F. Supp. at 217-18.
299. 338 F. Supp. at 220, 221.
300. 462 F.2d at 1066.
301. 462 F.2d at 1065.
302. 462 F.2d at 1064, 1066.
303. 462 F.2d at 1068.
304. 412 U.S. 92 (1973).
305. 418 U.S. 717 (1974). Actually, the Supreme Court had had before it as early as 1972 a

the Supreme Court *reversed* a lower court order which, after having found unconstitutional segregation, had sought to bring about greater integration.[306] The Court gave its endorsement to the position taken by the Fourth Circuit in the Richmond case—that plaintiffs would have to prove, before interdistrict remedies could be ordered, that actions were taken with deliberate segregative intent by the outlying, predominantly white districts, and that these actions had an effect on the segregation within the city.[307]

a. The Finding of De Jure Segregation

It should be noted that the situation involved in the Detroit case is somewhat different from that involved in the Richmond case. In the latter case, the Fourth Circuit found that each of the three school districts involved in the proposed interdistrict remedy had previously dismantled their former dual systems and were operating unitary systems.[308] In the Detroit case, the district court found that the Detroit School District was de jure segregated,[309] and this aspect of the case was not questioned by the Supreme Court.[310]

The district court's holding with respect to de jure segregation was based on its finding that Detroit school officials had engaged in de jure acts of discrimination, including the drawing of attendance zones to minimize integration and the maintenance of optional attendance zones, the busing of black pupils beyond closer white schools with available space, and the selection of sites for

---

desegregation case in which an interdistrict remedy was sought. In Spencer v. Kugler, 326 F. Supp. 1235 (D.N.J. 1971), *aff'd mem.*, 404 U.S. 1027 (1972), which arose in New Jersey, the plaintiffs alleged that segregation of the school system was attributable to New Jersey statutes which made school district boundaries coterminous with municipal boundaries. 326 F. Supp. at 1240-41. The three-judge district court, however, found this coterminality was "reasonable" in light of the municipal taxing authority. 326 F. Supp. at 1241. The system was unitary and any racial imbalance within a local school district resulted from an imbalance in the population of that district. *Id.* at 1243. The court also pointed to the fact that the Supreme Court, in *Swann*, had distinguished

> between those states which have a history of dual school systems and a separation of the races continued through the use of "freedom-of-choice" and "geographical zoning" plans which create the illusion of conforming to the law, and those wherein so-called "de-facto" segregation results from housing patterns and conventional drawing of school district zones.

326 F. Supp. at 1242.

The Supreme Court summarily affirmed without oral argument, 404 U.S. 1027 (1972), with Justice Douglas dissenting on the ground that redistricting of school districts, by analogy to the reapportionment cases, should be an available remedy where there is racial imbalance—citing Reynolds v. Sims, 377 U.S. 533 (1964).

306. As noted in note 78 *supra*, the Supreme Court split evenly on the *Richmond* case, thus letting the Fourth Circuit decision stand.

307. 418 U.S. at 744-45.

308. Bradley v. School Bd., 462 F.2d 1058, 1065 (4th Cir. 1972), *aff'd by an equally divided Court*, 412 U.S. 92 (1973).

309. Bradley v. Milliken, 338 F. Supp. 582, 592 (E.D. Mich.), *supplemented by* 345 F. Supp. 914 (E.D. Mich. 1971), *aff'd*, 484 F.2d 215 (6th Cir. 1973), *rev'd*, 418 U.S. 717 (1974).

310. The Supreme Court opinion merely noted that the findings of the district court as to de jure segregation appeared correct. 418 U.S. at 738 n. 18. Thus, in the Detroit case—the second northern case to come before the Supreme Court—the Court was unanimous in finding intradistrict discrimination. This is a clear indication that as far as intradistrict discrimination is concerned, the Detroit decision has done nothing to undermine *Swann* or *Keyes*.

school buildings.[311] The district court also found state involvement in actions which maintained segregation in the Detroit school system, looking to a number of factors, including the pattern of residential segregation:[312]

> Governmental actions and inaction at all levels, federal, state and local, have combined, with those of private organizations, such as loaning institutions and real estate associations and brokerage firms, to establish and maintain the pattern of residential segregation throughout the Detroit metropolitan area.

The court then found that "[t]he State and its agencies, in addition to their general responsibility for the supervision of public education, have acted directly to control and maintain the pattern of segregation in the Detroit schools."[313] To support this finding the court noted that:[314]

(1) state transportation services were lesser in quality and quantity in Detroit than in white suburbs, thus limiting pupils' choices to attend other schools.
(2) "other financial limitations, such as those on bonding and the working of the state aid formula" perpetuated segregated schools.[315]
(3) the passage of Act 48 acted to "impede, delay and minimize racial integration."[316]

As to this last factor, the Detroit Board of Education had adopted a plan on April 7, 1970 which provided for changes in some of the high school attendance zones, designed to effect a more balanced ratio of black and white students at the senior high school level.[317] Following the adoption of the plan, the Michigan legislature enacted a statute which provided that the Detroit plan be suspended and that a neighborhood school policy be instituted.[318] The Sixth Circuit had previously held this section of the act unconstitutional.[319] The Sixth Circuit concluded twenty-one pages of discussion of the evidence supporting the district court's findings of constitutional violations by noting that[320]

> [t]his record contains a substantial volume of testimony concerning local and State action and policies which helped produce residential segregation in Detroit and in the metropolitan area of Detroit. In affirming the District Judge's findings of constitutional violations by the Detroit Board of Education and by the State defendants resulting in segregated schools in Detroit, we have not

311. 338 F. Supp. at 592.
312. 338 F. Supp. at 587.
313. 338 F. Supp. at 589.
314. *Id.*
315. *Id.*
316. *Id.*
317. *See* testimony of Dr. Norman Drachler, Superintendent of the Detroit Public Schools, quoted in Bradley v. Milliken, 433 F.2d 897, 898-99 (6th Cir. 1970).
318. No. 48, § 12, [1970] Mich. Public Acts 139-40. The antithesis of local control would seem to be the state legislature telling the local district how to assign its pupils. *See* discussion in the text at pp. 111-14 *infra.*
319. Bradley v. Milliken, 433 F.2d 897, 902 (6th Cir. 1970).
320. 484 F.2d 215, 242 (6th Cir. 1973).

> relied at all upon testimony pertaining to segregated housing except as school construction programs helped cause or maintain such segregation.

The circuit court found that "[t]he discriminatory practices on the part of the Detroit School Board and the State of Michigan revealed by this record are significant, pervasive and *causally related* to the substantial amount of segregation found in the Detroit School System by the District Judge."[321]

b. The Metropolitan-wide Remedy

After the first Detroit decision, in which the district judge found de jure segregation to exist, the court issued a directive to city and state defendants to submit desegregation plans, both Detroit-only (to be submitted by the city) and metropolitan (to be submitted by the state).[322] When the plans were presented, the district judge rejected all three Detroit-only plans, noting that "relief of segregation in the public schools of the City of Detroit cannot be accomplished within the corporate geographical limits of the city."[323] Thus the district court's finding that the *state* was involved in maintaining segregation in Detroit's schools coupled with the fact that any Detroit-only plan would lead very shortly to an all-black Detroit School District, led the judge to the conclusion that only a metropolitan remedy would be appropriate.[324] The Sixth Circuit agreed.[325] But the Supreme Court found that there was no evidence that the acts of suburban school districts had brought about the segregation in the Detroit School District,[326] and therefore reversed. Thus an *inter*district violation is necessary before an interdistrict remedy can be ordered.[327] Chief Justice Burger articulated the principle as follows: "the scope of the remedy is determined by the nature and extent of the constitutional violation."[328]

The basic standards which are to govern the use of cross-district remedies are as follows:[329]

> Before the boundaries of separate and autonomous school districts may be set aside by consolidating the separate units for remedial purposes or by imposing a cross-district remedy, it must first be shown that there has been a constitutional violation within one district that produces a significant segregative effect in another district. *Specifically it must be shown that racially discriminatory acts of the state or local school districts, or of a single school district have been a substantial cause of*

321. *Id.* at 241 (emphasis added).

322. Unreported directive (E.D. Mich. Oct. 4, 1974), discussed at 345 F. Supp. 914, 916, 920-21. *See also* 484 F.2d 215, 218, 220-21; 418 U.S. 717, at 729-33.

323. Unreported findings of fact and conclusions of law (E.D. Mich. Mar. 28, 1972), quoted at 484 F.2d at 244.

324. *Id.*, quoted at 484 F.2d at 243-44.

325. 484 F.2d 215, 249 (6th Cir. 1973).

326. 418 U.S. 717, 752 (1974). In fact, the district court had explicitly stated that it had not even considered any evidence as to the actions of the suburban school districts. 345 F. Supp. 914, 920 (E.D. Mich. 1971).

327. 418 U.S. at 752.

328. 418 U.S. at 744.

329. 418 U.S. at 744-45, 749 (emphasis added).

> *inter-district segregation*. . . . [W]ithout an inter-district violation and inter-district effect, there is no constitutional wrong calling for an inter-district remedy.
>
> . . . Where the schools of only one district have been affected, there is no constitutional power in the courts to decree relief balancing the racial composition of that district's schools with those of the surrounding districts.

The Court left the door only slightly ajar on interdistrict remedies:[330]

> [A]n interdistrict remedy might be in order where the racially discriminatory acts of one or more school districts *caused* racial segregation in an adjacent district, or where district lines have been deliberately drawn on the basis of race.

There was evidence that a predominantly black suburb, which had no high school, sent its high school age students to schools in Detroit—with the "tacit" approval of the State Board of Education—because the nearby white suburbs refused to accept these students.[331] While this would appear to come within the above guidelines, the Court said that this was only an "isolated instance" which could not justify a broad metropolitan-wide remedy.[332] The Court thus found that evidence of state involvement, such as the discriminatory provision of transportation costs, state legislation rescinding a voluntary desegregation plan drawn up by the Detroit school board, cooperation with Detroit officials in school construction policies which fostered segregation, and approval of the busing of black suburban students to Detroit schools was insufficient for a metropolitan-wide remedy.

There would seem to be no established principle of constitutional law requiring the Court to reject the notion that the state, which draws the boundary lines, has no responsibility for the segregated pattern of housing and schooling. Nor is there settled constitutional law which dictates that there is no affirmative duty to correct interdistrict segregation. But it seems clear that to the *Milliken* majority, a "unitary" system can be an all-black system contained within its state-created borders. The Court noted that it has only been in the context of a single "geographic and administrative school system" serving both white and black students that the terms "unitary," "dual," and "racially identifiable" schools have had meaning.[333] But nothing in those earlier cases suggested that a stricter test or standard would be required to cross district lines than to cross attendance zones or neighborhoods. The Court failed to explain why the standard articulated in *Davis*[334] had to be restricted to the boundaries of a school district:[335]

> Having once found a violation, the district judge . . . should make every effort to achieve the greatest possible degree of actual desegregation, taking into

---

330. 418 U.S. at 745 (emphasis added).

331. 418 U.S. at 749-50. *See also* 484 F.2d 215, 231 (6th Cir. 1973).

332. 418 U.S. at 450.

333. 418 U.S. at 746.

334. Davis v. Board of School Comm'rs, 402 U.S. 33 (1971). *Davis* was the companion case to *Swann*.

335. *Id.* at 37.

> account the practicalities of the situation. A district court may and should consider the use of all available techniques . . . . The measure of any desegregation plan is its effectiveness.

Nor does the Court explain why remedies which could be "administratively awkward, inconvenient and even bizarre" within a district, could not run past the district line.[336] In Justice White's view, the Court had[337] "fashion[ed] out of whole cloth an arbitrary rule that remedies for constitutional violations occurring in a single Michigan school district must stop at the school district line."

Neither the majority nor Justice Stewart in his concurring opinion explained why the standards used in the Denver case for determining the violation and its remedy did not apply in Detroit. In the Denver case, the Court presumed that de jure segregation in one area spread to or infected other contiguous areas, shifting the burden to the defendants to prove it did *not*.[338] Using the same approach in the Detroit case, the finding of de jure segregation in a "meaningful portion" of the metropolitan area (the central city) should trigger a presumption either that there is a reciprocal segregative effect in the suburbs or that (State) school authorities have engaged in intentional segregative actions throughout the metropolitan area.[339]

In the Detroit case, however, the burden was upon the *plaintiffs* to prove that de jure acts of (a significant number?) of suburbs have had a segregative effect on Detroit, or that the state drew district boundary lines to contain Detroit.[340] But not only the burden of proof had shifted. As has already been noted, in the Denver case the remedy was not limited to that part of the district where the past segregative acts were shown to have occurred; a *district-wide* remedy—"all-out desegregation"[341]—was triggered.

The remedy and the violation thus appear to have become entangled in the Detroit case, and are no longer separate concepts. The Court seems to be adopting a "culpability" theory; that is, there is no interdistrict violation unless the suburban districts engaged in deliberate segregative acts affecting the degree of segregation in Detroit or the state was involved in deliberately containing Detroit's blacks above and beyond just being responsible for acts of its agent—the Detroit School Board—or even for maintaining existing boundaries where the natural and foreseeable consequence was the isolation of blacks in Detroit.[342]

Pursuing the "culpability" theory a little further, however, it becomes evident that the Court believed that since the suburban white residents and their

---

336. Swann v. Charlotte-Mecklenburg Bd. of Educ., 402 U.S. 1, 28 (1971).

337. 418 U.S. at 768 (White, J., dissenting).

338. 413 U.S. 189, 201-03, 208-12 (1973). *Cf.* United States v. Texas Educ. Agency, 467 F.2d 848, 888 (5th Cir. 1972) (Wisdom, J., dissenting). ("Infection at one school infects all schools.")

339. *See* notes 74-80 and accompanying text at pp. 63-64 *supra*.

340. 418 U.S. at 746.

341. Keyes v. School Dist. No. 1, 413 U.S. 189, 214 (1973).

342. *See* text at pp. 66-69 *supra*.

children were not "guilty" or responsible for the "growing core of Negro schools," they should not be "punished" by forcing them to become part of the remedy. This does not explain, however, why white parents and their children are any more deserving of "punishment" because they live in Denver or in Charlotte rather than in the suburbs of those cities. The approach taken by the Court[343] in this case may serve to increase white flight from the cities by indicating that the suburbs will be a "safe haven" for those who otherwise would be caught up in a desegregation decree. Although having previously prevented a new school district from forming "where its effect would be to impede the process of dismantling a dual system" by encouraging white flight,[344] the Court has now ensured that white flight will proceed even more rapidly from Detroit than heretofore has been the case.

c. Proving Racial Containment

After the Detroit case, what must plaintiffs be able to demonstrate for a metropolitan area remedy? It is not sufficient that de jure segregation exists in one district and that no effective plan for desegregation could be devised without going beyond the borders of that district. It is not sufficient to show that for certain purposes, the metropolitan area should be treated as a unit. It is not sufficient to show that there is a de jure violation in only one other district in the metropolitan area as that would only be an "isolated instance." It may not even be sufficient to show de jure segregation in several districts as it appears that plaintiffs will have to show that segregation in one district *resulted from* discriminatory actions by officials in other—the suburban—school districts or by state education officials.

If plaintiffs cannot readily show that the actions of state or suburban *school* officials contributed to the segregation of the schools within the central city, can plaintiffs establish a prima facie case for interdistrict relief by proving segregative actions by *other* governmental agencies? In other words, if plaintiffs could show that governmental policies in housing and zoning, employment, and welfare in one district produced a significant segregative effect in another district, would this justify an interdistrict remedy?

The majority opinion in the Detroit case seems to suggest that suburban districts could be included in a court-ordered desegregation plan only if *school* officials have been responsible for the de jure segregation in Detroit. If that is true, plaintiffs have an almost impossible burden. In a footnote, however, the majority notes that since the circuit court expressly noted that its decision did not rest on any of the testimony with regard to segregated housing, "the case

343. Justice Stewart, in his concurring opinion, expressed somewhat the same view—that the proposed remedial decree approved by the Sixth Circuit would "include schools and school children in many other school districts that have presumptively been administered in complete accord with the Constitution." 418 U.S. at 755.

344. Wright v. Council of the City of Emporia, 407 U.S. 451, 470 (1972).

does not present any question concerning possible state housing violations."[345] Thus the door may be open to future plaintiffs to show that "the State, along with private persons, [has] caused, in part, the housing patterns of the . . . metropolitan area which, in turn, produced . . . [segregated] neighborhoods . . . ."[346]

For the majority, then, there was no need to examine the trial record to determine whether governmental policies in housing acted to contain blacks in Detroit. Justice Stewart, however, did examine the record, and found that it did not show that "the racial composition of the Detroit school population or that residential patterns within Detroit and in the surrounding areas were in any significant measure caused by governmental activity . . . ."[347] But it is clear that, to Justice Stewart, proof of such actions by other governmental agencies would, in certain circumstances permit an interdistrict remedy:[348]

> Were it to be shown, for example, that state officials had contributed to the separation of the races . . . by purposeful, racially discriminatory use of state housing or zoning laws, then a decree calling for transfer of pupils across district lines or for restructuring of district lines might well be appropriate.

Justice Stewart asserts that in the Detroit case, no evidence was introduced concerning the actions of suburban school districts other than that they had a much larger proportion of white students than did Detroit. This alone was not, in his view, sufficient to justify an interdistrict remedy. The plaintiffs must show "that such disparity was imposed, fostered, or encouraged by the state or its political subdivisions . . . ."[349] Thus, in Justice Stewart's view, there was no evidence of a constitutional violation (outside of Detroit) and Justice Marshall, in his dissent, was incorrect in saying that black children in Detroit had been confined by (external) intentional acts of segregation.[350]

> [S]egregative acts within the city alone cannot be presumed to have produced—and no factual showing was made that they did produce—an increase in the number of Negro students in the *city as a whole*. It is this essential fact of a predominantly Negro school population in Detroit—caused by unknown and perhaps unknowable factors such as in-migration, birth rates, economic changes, or cumulative acts of private racial fears—that accounts for the "growing core of Negro schools," a "core" that has grown to include virtually the entire city. The Constitution simply does not allow federal courts to attempt to change that situation unless and until it is shown that the State, or its political subdivisions, have contributed to cause the situation to exist.

The problem is that Justice Stewart does not make very clear what evidence of other governmental activities would be sufficient. In the Richmond case, plaintiffs had presented extensive evidence of governmental actions which had

345. 418 U.S. at 728 n. 7.
346. *Id.*
347. 418 U.S. at 756 n. 2 (Stewart, J., concurring).
348. 418 U.S. at 755.
349. *Id.*
350. 418 U.S. at 756 n. 2. *But see* 418 U.S. at 799 n. 19 (Marshall, J., dissenting).

contributed to the "growing core of Negro schools,"[351] yet it seems probable that Justice Stewart was one of the four votes against the plaintiffs in that case.[352] Moreover, a respectable number of social scientists would not agree that the causes of the "growing core of Negro schools" are "unknown and perhaps unknowable." They could readily point out factors which explain the demographic patterns which give rise to a "growing core of Negro schools."[353]

3. *City-County Consolidations*

The most significant case to deal with interdistrict remedies to date, in view of the fact that it was decided *after* the Supreme Court decision in the Detroit case is *Newburg Area Council v. Board of Education*.[354] Indeed, the initial decision in that case was appealed to the Supreme Court just as the Detroit case was being decided.[355] Rather than overturn the Louisville decision at that time, the Supreme Court remanded it to the Sixth Circuit, asking it to reconsider the case in light of *Milliken v. Bradley*.[356] The Sixth Circuit *did* reconsider the case and concluded that the problem in *Milliken* had been that the remedy "was broader than the constitutional violation."[357] By contrast, in the Louisville case—where the city school district has a pupil population that is 50 per cent black and Jefferson County (in which Louisville is located) has a pupil population only 4 per cent black—"the situation presented is that of two districts in

351. Bradley v. School Bd., 338 F. Supp. 67, 84-100 (E.D. Va. 1972); Taylor, *The Supreme Court and Urban Reality: A Tactical Analysis of* Milliken v. Bradley, 21 WAYNE L. REV. 751, 765-69 (1975).

352. The decision was affirmed by an equally divided Court, Justice Powell not participating, 412 U.S. 92 (1973). The four votes *for* plaintiffs were probably the same four who dissented in the Detroit case.

353. *See, e.g.*, NATIONAL COMM. AGAINST DISCRIMINATION IN HOUSING AND THE URBAN LAND INSTITUTE, FAIR HOUSING AND EXCLUSIONARY LAND USE (1974); U.S. COMMISSION ON CIVIL RIGHTS, EQUAL OPPORTUNITY IN SUBURBIA (1974); M. Sloan, *Milliken v. Bradley* and Residential Segregation, October 22, 1974 (paper available from National Comm. Against Discrimination in Housing); Farley, *Residential Segregation and Its Implications for School Integration*, 39 LAW & CONTEMP. PROB. no. 1, at 164 (1975); Pettigrew, *A Sociological View of the Post-*Bradley *Era*, 21 WAYNE L. REV. 813 (1975); Taylor, *supra* note 351.

Professor Karl Taeuber, who testified as an expert witness in *Milliken v. Bradley*, has reviewed the causes of residential segregation in a recent article. Taeuber, *Demographic Perspectives on Housing and School Segregation*, 21 WAYNE L. REV. 833, 836-41 (1975). He concludes the discussion by noting that "the prime cause of residential segregation by race has been discrimination, both public and private." Taeuber, *supra* at 840. In the same issue, Professor Farley, after a review of the available data, reaches similar conclusions. Farley, *Population Trends and School Segregation in the Detroit Metropolitan Area*, 21 WAYNE L. REV. 867, 882-89 (1975). Professor Farley examines the question of the absence of blacks from the Detroit suburbs, and finds that "[o]pening the suburbs of Detroit to blacks is not a problem of opening them to low or middle income families; rather it is very specifically a question of opening them to blacks." Farley, *supra* at 884-85.

354. 510 F.2d 1358 (6th Cir. 1974), *cert. denied*, 95 S.Ct. 1658 (1975).

355. 489 F.2d 925 (6th Cir. 1973), *vacated*, 418 U.S. 918 (1974).

356. 418 U.S. 918 (1974).

357. 510 F.2d at 1361.

358. *Id.* Note the culpability or "guilt" language. *See* text accompanying note 342, at p. 105 *supra.*

the same county of the state being equally guilty in failing to eliminate all vestiges of segregation . . . ."[358] Also, the cross-district effect was present: [S]chool district lines in Kentucky have been ignored in the past for the purpose of aiding and implementing continued segregation. Such disregarding of school district lines continues to have an effect on racial imbalance in the county's schools . . . ."[359] Thus, on remand of the case to the district court, the circuit court noted that the desegregation order could, if needed, include an interdistrict remedy.[360]

A second decision since the Detroit case has also found sufficient distinguishing factors to permit an interdistrict remedy. In *United States v. Missouri*,[361] the plaintiffs were seeking the annexation of two districts—one of which was all black—by a third district to create a new district out of the three. The district court found sufficient evidence to show that there was[362]

> an arrangement of school districts which has caused substantial segregation and which is both a vestige of the previously imposed dual school system and a continuing effect of racially discriminatory state actions on the part of the defendants in this case.

The other two districts were "responsible for the maintenance of [the all black district] as a segregated district."[363] The court found the opposition of the electorate to reorganizing the districts in 1949 to be grounded in racial considerations.[364]

> This is an instance where the failure to act or resistance for discriminatory reasons to actions tending to correct segregation amounted to a constitutional wrong.

The final factor differentiating the Detroit case from the Missouri case was that in the latter, "only three districts, not fifty-two districts, are involved."[365]

---

359. 510 F.2d at 1360. For example, for a considerable period, Jefferson County had no black high school and had sent its black students to a black high school in Louisville.

360. 510 F.2d at 1361. The case was appealed to the Supreme Court once again, but the petition for certiorari was denied, 95 S.Ct. 1658 (1975). For district court's order see 8 ED. DAILY, Aug. 5, 1975, at 1.

361. 388 F. Supp. 1058 (E.D. Mo. 1975).

362. 388 F. Supp. at 1059.

363. 388 F. Supp. at 1060.

364. *Id.*

365. *Id.* It is interesting to note that the district court in this case was more aware than most courts of the disproportionate burden that tends to fall on black students in any desegregation order. *See* text at pp. 88-90 *supra*.

> The primary burden of desegregation under the Revised Plan unavoidably falls on black students because of the educational necessity, recognized by all the parties, of terminating the present use of three school facilities located in the Kinloch [all-black] School District. In order to minimize this burden as much as possible, the following steps shall be taken:
>
> (1) Kinloch Elementary [formerly all-black] shall be assigned lower elementary grades instead of grades five and six.
>
> . . . .
>
> (4) School authorities shall take steps to insure that black students transferred to formerly white schools are made to feel a part of such schools. To this end, considera-

Finally, the Indianapolis case[366] also indicates that city-county consolidations may be easier to accomplish than the other two metropolitan arrangements previously discussed. The Seventh Circuit affirmed the district court's findings that state officials had "promoted segregation and inhibited desegregation"[367] within the Indianapolis School District, thus placing upon the state as well as the school district an affirmative duty to desegregate *within* the boundaries of Indianapolis.[368]

The district court had sought to impose a metropolitan area remedy—to include all of Marion County (the county in which Indianapolis is situated), as well as two school districts beyond the county line. Relying upon the Supreme Court's opinion in the Detroit case, the circuit court *reversed* the district court's opinion with regard to the areas beyond Marion County.[369] The court did *not* reverse, but vacated and remanded for further findings, that part of the district court's remedy which included school districts within the county boundaries.[370]

There may well be unique circumstances in the Indianapolis case which could trigger a finding of deliberate segregative intent and effect on the part of the county as well as the city and thus support a city-county consolidation. In 1971, the Uni-Gov Act was passed which consolidated the governments of Indianapolis and Marion County into one metropolitan governmental unit.[371] However, the Act specifically excepted from such consolidation "any [preexisting] school corporation, all or a part of which is in the consolidated city or county."[372] This meant that, in addition to Indianapolis, there were "eight township school systems operating independently within the purportedly unified City . . . ."[373] On remand, the circuit court asked the district court to determine whether "the establishment of the Uni-Gov boundaries without a like reestablishment of [the Indianapolis school district] boundaries warrants an inter-district remedy within Uni-Gov in accordance with *Milliken*."[374]

There are still a few metropolitan area suits pending. At least two of these could be resolved by a city-county consolidation and thus appear to have a better chance of success than a Detroit-type of case. And in one of these

> tion should be given to renaming such schools, changing school colors, etc., and the preservation of Kinloch High School trophies and awards. Non-discriminatory regulation and procedures shall be developed concerning disciplinary measures.

388 F. Supp. at 1061-62.

366. United States v. Board of School Comm'rs, 368 F. Supp. 1191 (S.D. Ind. 1973), *aff'd in part and rev'd in part*, 503 F.2d 68 (7th Cir. 1974), *cert. denied*, 95 S.Ct. 1655 (1975).

367. 503 F.2d at 80.

368. *Id.*

369. *Id.*

370. 503 F.2d at 86.

371. IND. CODE 18-4-1-1 to 18-4-15-2 (1971).

372. IND. CODE 18-4-3-14 (1971).

373. United States v. Board of School Comm'rs, 332 F. Supp. 655, 676 (S.D. Ind. 1971), *aff'd*, 477 F.2d 81 (7th Cir. 1972), *cert. denied*, 413 U.S. 920 (1973).

374. 503 F.2d at 86. The district court, then, ordered cross busing. 8 ED. DAILY, Aug. 7, 1975, at 1.

pending suits[375]—involving Wilmington, Delaware and its predominantly white suburban county—there is evidence that a state statute adopted in 1968, reorganizing and consolidating all school districts with the *exception* of the city of Wilmington,[376] with its over 80 per cent black student enrollment, acted to "contain" minority students within the boundaries of the city.[377] Another potential metropolitan-area suit is *Armour v. Nix*,[378] involving Atlanta and its predominantly white suburban county. In one of its (many) *Calhoun v. Cook* decisions, the district court raised the question of consolidation of the Atlanta school system with the Fulton County system.[379]

> In terms of efficiency, taxes, and quality education, such consolidations normally produce long-range improvements. In terms of the current problem such consolidation might well produce partial, even though not perfect, solutions. . . .

The court of appeals, at various phases of the *Calhoun* case, has also expressed its interest in a consideration of a metropolitan solution.[380]

4. *Local Control: The Making of a Myth*

What considerations might militate against the granting of relief as drastic as desegregation across district lines even if interdistrict intentional segregative acts can be proved? Is the interest in "local control" of schools a relevant factor? In several recent cases, the Supreme Court has begun to acknowledge that local control or local autonomy in public education is a very substantial interest: first, in the school financing case—*San Antonio Independent School District v. Rodriguez*[381]—and now in the Detroit case.[382] In an earlier opinion, Justice Stewart, speaking for the Court, had said that "[d]irect control over decisions vitally affecting the education of one's children is a need that is strongly felt in our society . . . .[383] In his dissent in that same opinion, Chief Justice Burger agreed, stating that local control was of "*overriding* importance,"[384] and he continued this line of thought in his majority opinion in *Milliken v. Bradley*:[385]

---

375. Evans v. Buchanan, 379 F. Supp. 1218 (D. Del. 1974).

376. Ch. 292, § 6, [1967] Del. Laws 979.

377. After the Detroit decision was handed down, the three-judge district court in Delaware ruled that the statute was unconstitutional in its exclusion of the Wilmington school district. The court found the statute to be an "interdistrict violation" that "played a significant part in maintaining the racial identifiability of Wilmington and the suburban New Castle County school districts." ______F. Supp. ______, ______ (D. Del. Mar. 23, 1975). *See* discussion in Taylor, *supra* note 351, at 759-60.

378. Armour v. Nix, Civil No. 16708 (N.D. Ga. June 7, 1972).

379. 332 F. Supp. 804, 809 (N.D. Ga. 1971).

380. 451 F.2d 583 (5th Cir. 1971); 487 F.2d 680, 684 (5th Cir. 1973).

381. 411 U.S. 1, 49-50 (1973).

382. 418 U.S. 717, 741-42 (1974).

383. Wright v. Council of the City of Emporia, 407 U.S. 451, 469 (1973).

384. *Id.* at 478 (emphasis added). "Local control is not only vital to continued public support of the schools, but is of overriding importance from an educational standpoint as well." This statement was subsequently quoted with approval by the majority in *Rodriguez*, 411 U.S. at 49.

385. 418 U.S. at 741-42 (emphasis added).

> Boundary lines may be bridged where there has been a constitutional violation calling for interdistrict relief, but the notion that school district lines may be casually ignored or treated as a mere administrative convenience is contrary to the history of public education in our country. *No single tradition in public education is more deeply rooted than local control over the operation of schools*; local autonomy has long been thought essential both to the maintenance of community concern and support for public schools and to quality of the educational process.

Perhaps the most outstanding feature of these repeated statements sanctifying local control is the dearth of authority cited by way of support.

In the Detroit case,[386] the Sixth Circuit devoted three and one-quarter pages to a review of the evidence of state control over education in Michigan:[387]

> As held by the District Court, it is well established under the Constitution and laws of Michigan that the public school system is a State function and that local school districts are instrumentalities of the State created for administrative convenience.

The circuit court cited constitutional and statutory provisions and Michigan Supreme Court interpretations in support of this statement,[388] and concluded that[389]

> the record [has] establish[ed] that the State has committed de jure acts of segregation and that the State controls the instrumentalities whose action is necessary to remedy the harmful effects of the State acts.

The Supreme Court ignored this treatment, stating only that Michigan, "in common with most States, provides for a large measure of local control,"[390] and citing statutes giving the local school district the power to determine "the day-to-day affairs of the school district . . . ."[391] Justice Douglas vigorously dissented from this view: "[e]ducation in Michigan is a state project with very little completely local control . . . . [T]he school districts by state law are agencies of the State."[392]

Michigan does provide a large measure of local control, yet it has been held repeatedly that a school district is merely a subordinate arm of the state agency.

---

386. Bradley v. Milliken, 484 F.2d 215, 245-49 (6th Cir. 1973), *rev'd*, 418 U.S. 717 (1974).

387. 484 F.2d at 246.

388. *E.g.*, *id.*, citing Child Welfare Soc'y v. Kennedy School Dist., 220 Mich. 290, 296, 189 N.W. 1002, 1004 (1922):

> The Legislature has entire control over the schools of the state subject only to the provisions above referred to. The division of the territory of the state into districts, the conduct of the school, the qualifications of teachers, the subjects to be taught therein, are all within its control.

389. 484 F.2d at 249.

390. 418 U.S. 717, 742 (1974).

391. *Id.* at 742 n. 20.

392. 418 U.S. at 758-59. *See also id.* at 770 (White, J., dissenting); *id.* at 786, 793-97 (Marshall, J., dissenting).

A school district has no inherent power, only power expressly delegated or necessarily implied. Under Michigan law, as is true of most states,[393] the state legislature can consolidate, merge, or eliminate school districts at will, regardless of the local district's opposition to such moves.[394]

A recent study of ten states and the degree to which there was state control over local education decision-making in the areas of curricular requirements, budgetary and taxing restrictions, regulations affecting personnel, and district formation, dissolution, annexation and consolidation, showed that state statutes and regulations sharply limited the degree of local district autonomy in the majority of the ten states studied.[395] Michigan was found to rank fifth in the degree of state-level controls on local district decision making;[396] in the area of district formation and consolidation, however, Michigan was grouped with those states which have the strongest degree of state-level control.[397] Such research casts significant doubt on the Court's developing theory of "local control" as a barrier to otherwise valid remedies for violations of the equal protection clause.

The Court's concern for preserving "local control," as with its concern regarding the administrative and financing (including the validity of long-term bonds) problems presented by consolidating 54 school districts,[398] arguably

---

393. The standard education law textbooks indicate how much of this power is located in the state rather than in the local school district. *See, e.g.*, E. REUTTER & R. HAMILTON, THE LAW OF PUBLIC EDUCATION 61, 108 (1970).

> School districts are governmental agencies of the state created by the state as instrumentalities through which the legislature carries out the state constitutional mandate to provide for a system of public education. At any time the legislature may abolish all local school units and redistrict the state irrespective of the boundaries of the old districts. Unless the constitution of the state requires it, it is not necessary to procure the consent of the inhabitants of the territory as a condition to redistricting. Indeed, even though local inhabitants have voted against a boundary alteration, the legislature can still proceed to effect the consolidation of districts.
>
> . . . .
>
> The powers of local boards, since they are granted by the legislature, may be changed at any time. . . . When in doubt, the courts, under common law, are inclined to find against an implied power. There are no inherent powers in school boards.

This textbook uses a Michigan case, Attorney General *ex rel.* Kies v. Lowrey, 199 U.S. 233 (1905), to illustrate the subchapter entitled "Power of State Legislature to Change District Boundaries." E. REUTTER & R. HAMILTON, *supra* at 86.

See also M. SORGEN, P. DUFFY, W. KAPLIN, & E. MARGOLIN, STATE, SCHOOL, AND FAMILY ch. 2, at 10 (1973).

394. "[T]he State has wide-ranging powers to consolidate and merge school districts, even without the consent of the districts themselves or of the local citizenry." 418 U.S. at 796 (Marshall, J., dissenting). As Justice Marshall points out, *id.*, there has been a substantial effort in the sixties —largely initiated at the state level—to consolidate, annex, and merge school districts. Between 1964 and 1972, the number of school districts dropped from 1,438 to 608. Some of these mergers were state-mandated; others were stimulated by fiscal incentives provided by the state legislature. *See* MICH. COMP. LAWS ANN. §§ 340.401-.415, 340.431-.449 (1967).

395. B. LEVIN & M. COHEN, LEVELS OF STATE AID RELATED TO STATE RESTRICTIONS ON LOCAL SCHOOL DISTRICT DECISION-MAKING (1973).

396. *Id.* at 18, Table 3.

397. *Id.* at 17, Table 2.

398. 418 U.S. at 743.

would not be relevant had the Court determined that there was an interdistrict violation of the fourteenth amendment. The majority notes that[399]

> School district lines and the present laws with respect to local control are not sacrosanct and if they conflict with the Fourteenth Amendment federal courts have a duty to prescribe appropriate remedies.

This suggests, again, that the Court has entangled questions of remedy with questions of constitutional violation.

E. Special Remedies in Cases Involving Hispano-Americans

School desegregation law, as it has developed, in large measure has benefitted Hispano-Americans. Having evolved in the context of the segregation of blacks in the states of the deep South, however, it is not always completely transferable from one group of litigants to the other. School desegregation litigation, by and large, seeks to win for black pupils the right to be treated as others are. For many Hispano-Americans, this seems to be too narrow a focus and a potentially self-defeating objective in view of the desire to retain their language and culture. Does the legal system have the capacity to explore alternatives and broaden the range of issues? And in so doing, what social science evidence can aid in such an endeavor?

Clearly much of the relief sought by the two minority groups is the same. As do blacks, Hispano-Americans seek desegregation of school faculties, staffs, and student populations. And as do blacks, Hispano-Americans seek to challenge the disproportionate assignment of Hispano-American students to classes for the Educable Mentally Retarded (EMR), and their over-representation in "low ability" classes in elementary schools and in noncollege-bound tracks in junior and senior high schools.[400]

But Hispano-Americans also seek special programs—not generally sought by black litigants—which are designed to enhance the educational process. Since much of the learning deficiencies found in Hispano children are attributable to language and culture differences, questions of remedy therefore include—but by no means are limited to—whether and when bilingual-bicultural education can be required.

The difficulty of devising remedies to meet the demands of litigants with somewhat differing needs is most apparent in tri-ethnic school districts. This

---

399. 418 U.S. at 744.

> [W]hatever difficulties [in managing a desegregation plan which includes suburban districts] there might be, they are surmountable; for the Court itself concedes that had there been sufficient evidence of an interdistrict violation, the District Court could have fashioned a single remedy for the districts implicated rather than a different remedy for each district in which the violation had occurred or had an impact.

418 U.S. at 769-70 (White, J., dissenting).

400. Ability grouping and the assignment to classes for the educable mentally retarded (EMR) are discussed in the text at pp. 120-29 *infra*.

problem was dealt with in the Denver case—where the student enrollment in the elementary schools in the fall of 1973 was 17.6 per cent black, 27 per cent Spanish surnamed, and 54.1 per cent Anglo[401]—by adopting a separate remedial plan for Mexican-American students. Following the Supreme Court's remand,[402] the district court heard testimony on various proposed desegregation plans. The Congress of Hispanic Educators, which intervened in the suit, put forward a separate remedial plan which would establish a bilingual-bicultural educational program for Hispano-Americans. The plan was prepared by an educator, Dr. Jose Cárdenas, and was said to be designed to resolve the incompatibilities faced by Spanish-speaking school children who are "expected not only to learn a language with which they are unfamiliar, but also to acquire normal basic learning skills which are taught through the medium of that unfamiliar language."[403] Such a program, it was argued, should include:[404]

(1) development of the child's knowledge of English,
(2) instruction in any substantive subject in the child's native language,
(3) promulgation of minimum educational standards,
(4) distribution of appropriate materials,
(5) recruitment of bilingual educators, and
(6) establishment of pilot schools.

As the district court viewed the Cárdenas plan, it[405]

> recommend[ed] adjustments in the Denver educational system . . . which . . . will make that system more compatible to the minority child's economic circumstances, his cultural and language orientation, his high degree of mobility, and his perceptions of himself and the world around him. Dr. Cárdenas' plan is at heart based on the conviction that minority youngsters often fail or perform poorly in the typical American school system today, because the school the child attends, whether integrated or segregated, is largely an alien world to him, where classes, including the most basic of skills, are taught in a language which the child often does not comprehend or lacks facility in, where he is asked to relate to experiences which have no relevance to him outside the schools, and where he is often taught to regard negatively his own background, culture and personal abilities.

The court found[406]

> the Cárdenas or bilingual-bicultural approach to the education of [Mexican-Americans to be] a very sensible method and to the extent that it can be useful to building bridges between the Spanish and Anglo cultures, it is to be fully utilized.

A number of other courts have also considered bilingual-bicultural approaches as part of the relief in desegregation cases involving Hispano-

401. Keyes v. School Dist. No. 1, 380 F. Supp. 673, 674 (D. Colo. 1974).
402. 413 U.S. 189 (1973).
403. 380 F. Supp. at 695.
404. Brief for Congress of Hispanic Educators as Plaintiff-Intervenor, Keyes v. School Dist. No. 1, Civil Nos. 74-1349 to 50 (10th Cir. June 25, 1974).
405. 380 F. Supp. at 694-95.
406. 380 F. Supp. at 692.

Americans. In *United States v. Texas Education Agency*,[407] the district court, having concluded that bilingual education was the only means of achieving "true integration as opposed to mere desegregation,"[408] ordered a comprehensive bilingual and bicultural educational program to be instituted, covering not only standard classroom instruction, but also professional staff treatment, assignment, and development; student assignment and classroom organization; parent and community involvement; special education; and extra-curricular activities.[409]

In *Serna v. Portales Municipal Schools*,[410] the predominantly Hispano school in that district was already operating a bilingual-bicultural program; however, such a program was not available at the other elementary schools in the district even though these schools were attended by a number of Hispano children. The district court required the establishment of a bilingual-bicultural program at *all* elementary schools in the district as well as the hiring of more Spanish-speaking teachers.[411] The Tenth Circuit[412] followed *Lau v. Nichols*[413] in finding a *statutory* violation of the students' Title VI rights rather than a constitutional violation,[414] but the result was the same. In discussing the question of relief, the circuit court stated:[415]

> The evidence shows unequivocally that appellants had failed to provide appellees with a meaningful education. . . . [T]he trial court had a duty to fashion a program which would provide adequate relief for Spanish surnamed children. . . . Under Title VI of the Civil Rights Act of 1964 appellees have a right to bilingual education. . . . [T]he trial court under its inherent equitable power, can properly fashion a bilingual-bicultural program which will assure that Spanish surnamed children receive a meaningful education.

The court thus indicated that under certain circumstances it is not an unwarranted intrusion for the federal district court, using its equitable powers, to choose among educational programs.

Another illustration of a situation in which a mechanical application to Hispano-Americans of desegregation law developed in the context of southern blacks is inappropriate is that of assignment of minority teachers. Under the

---

407. 342 F. Supp. 24 (E.D. Tex. 1971), *rev'd on other grounds*, 467 F.2d 848 (5th Cir. 1972).

408. *Id.* at 28.

409. *Id.* at 29-38. In reversing the district court, the Fifth Circuit, while "congratulating" the school district's plan for its bilingual programs, cautioned that "[t]hese techniques . . . may not be used as a substitute for adequate desegregation." 467 F.2d 848, 873 (5th Cir. 1972). *See also* Arvizu v. Waco Independent School Dist., 373 F. Supp. 1264 (W.D. Tex. 1973), *aff'd in part, rev'd as to other issues*, 495 F.2d 499 (5th Cir. 1974). There the court ordered a bilingual-bicultural program to be developed with the assistance of "available Mexican-American educational consultants." *Id.* at 1280. *Cf.* Aspira v. Board of Educ., Consent Decree (S.D.N.Y. Aug. 29, 1974).

410. 351 F. Supp. 1279 (D.N.M. 1971), *aff'd on other grounds*, 499 F.2d 1147 (10th Cir. 1974).

411. *Id.* at 1282-83.

412. 499 F.2d 1147 (10th Cir. 1974).

413. 414 U.S. 563 (1974).

414. 499 F.2d at 1152-53.

415. 499 F.2d at 1154.

principle of the *Singleton* ratio,[416] minority teachers are to be distributed throughout the system so that the staff of each school reflects the proportion of minority teachers in the system as a whole. The difficulty with applying this to Hispano-American teachers is that, compared to blacks, there are relatively few trained in teaching. Thus assigning minority teachers so that there is an even distribution throughout a given school district is an inadequate remedy as far as Hispano-American desegregation law suits are concerned. Judge Wisdom, in *United States v. Texas Education Agency*,[417] recognizing this, concluded that the school district should strive for parity hiring rather than distribution of an unrepresentative number of Mexican-American teachers throughout the school district.[418]

In the Denver case, the district court judge also rejected the *Singleton* ratio as an appropriate desegregation remedy for Mexican-Americans due to the fact that while Mexican-Americans comprised 26 per cent of the elementary school population they comprised less than 4 per cent of the teaching staff.[419] The district judge extended Judge Wisdom's logic to require the immediate implementation of an affirmative action plan with goals and a timetable for hiring minority teachers.[420] And the *Serna* court went even further, adding that a good faith effort to recruit Spanish-speaking teachers would not be enough if that effort were unsuccessful.[421]

Substantial numbers of Hispano-American students are excluded from effective participation in the educational process because of language and cultural characteristics. In a study of school districts in the Southwest, undertaken by the United States Commission on Civil Rights, 16 per cent of the Mexican-American students repeated the first grade while only 6 per cent of the Anglo

---

416. Faculty and staff are to be assigned to schools

> so that the ratio of Negro to white teachers in each school, and the ratio of other staff in each, are substantially the same as each such ratio is to the teachers and other staff, respectively, in the entire school system.

Singleton v. Jackson Municipal Separate School Dist., 419 F.2d 1211, 1218 (5th Cir.), *rev'd on other grounds per curiam sub nom.* Carter v. West Feliciana School Bd., 396 U.S. 290 (1970). *See also* United States v. Montgomery County Bd. of Educ., 395 U.S. 225, 235-36 (1969).

417. 467 F.2d 848 (5th Cir. 1972).

418.
> Rigid adherence to . . . [the *Singleton* ratio] principle would be inequitable in this case . . . since there are so few Mexican-American teachers, 3 percent of the total faculty as against a Mexican-American school population of 20 percent.
>
> When the figures speak so eloquently, *a prima facie* case of discrimination is established. . . . The school board therefore should attempt to employ more Mexican-American teachers with the goal of attaining a ratio of Mexican-American teachers within the faculty that reflects more truly the ratio of Mexican-American students to the total population. . . . A showing of a good faith effort to find sufficient qualified Mexican-American teachers to achieve an equitable ratio, will rebut any inference of discrimination. . . .

Id. at 873. *See also* Cisneros v. Corpus Christi Independent School Dist., 467 F.2d 142, 152 (5th Cir. 1972), *cert. denied*, 413 U.S. 920 (1973).

419. Keyes v. School Dist. No. 1, 380 F. Supp. 673, at 674, 680, 688 (D. Colo. 1974).

420. 380 F. Supp. at 688.

421. 351 F. Supp. 1279, 1283, *aff'd on other grounds*, 499 F.2d 1147 (10th Cir. 1974).

students and 8.9 per cent of the black students had to repeat this grade.[422] In Texas, *80* per cent of the Mexican-American children who enter the first grade are not promoted.[423]

Until recently, many states added impediments to the child's ability to learn rather than facilitating their removal. The language barrier was looked upon as the child's burden which he had to overcome, rather than as the school's responsibility.[424] Most states no longer have laws prohibiting foreign languages from being used in schools.[425] Nevertheless a substantial number of school districts in the Southwest still have an official written policy of prohibiting the use of Spanish either on the school grounds or in the classroom. And there is some evidence that children are still subject to corporal punishment, to daily fines, or to suspension and expulsion for using Spanish in violation of this policy.[426] Until recently, Texas made it a crime for a teacher to speak Spanish in the course of ordinary school activities.[427] As late as 1970, a Mexican-American teacher in that state was indicted for conducting a high school history class in Spanish, although the case was subsequently dismissed.[428] One state still provides criminal penalties for violation of the requirement that English be the exclusive language of instruction.[429]

Today, however, many states have adopted laws *permitting* bilingual instruction,[430] and two states have laws *requiring* bilingual instruction where there are a certain number of students whose native tongue is not English.[431] And, as previously noted, there are now a number of judicial decisions in which

422. U.S. Commission on Civil Rights, Mexican American Education Study, Report II: Toward Quality Education for Mexican Americans 35 (1971).

423. T. Anderson & M. Boyer, Bilingual Schooling in the United States 108 (1970).

424. *Cf.* note 139 and accompanying text at p. 74 *supra*.

425. However, eight states still require English as the *exclusive* language of instruction in schools. Ark. Stat. Ann. § 80-1605 (1960); Idaho Code § 33-1601 (1963); Ky. Rev. Stat. Ann. § 158.080 (Supp. 1972); Minn. Stat. Ann. § 126.07 (1960); Mont. Rev. Codes Ann. § 75-7503 to 7504 (1971); Neb. Const. art. 1, § 27; Okla. Const. art. 1, § 5; Okla. Stat. tit. 70, § 11-102 (Supp. 1972); Wis. Stat. Ann. § 40.46(1) (1966).

426. U.S. Commission on Civil Rights, Mexican American Education Study, Report III: Toward Quality Education for Mexican Americans (1971).

427. *See* Ch. 80, [1918] Tex. Gen. Laws, 4th Called Sess. 170 (repealed 1971); text at note 161 *supra*.

428. U.S. Commission on Civil Rights, *supra* note 426, at 15.

429. Ark. Stat. Ann. § 80-1605 (1960). Three other states only very recently amended similar laws with criminal penalties. Ch. 166, [1923] Conn. Pub. Acts. 3591, *as amended* Conn. Gen. Stat. Ann. § 10.17 (Supp. 1975); ch. 198, [1919] Iowa Acts 219, *as amended* ch. 1168, § 6, [1974] Iowa Acts 540; ch. 138, §§ 265-66, [1931] S.D. Laws 175-76, *as amended* S.D. Compiled Laws Ann. 13-33-11 (Supp. 1974).

430. *E.g.*, Ariz. Rev. Stat. Ann. §§ 15-202, 15-1097 to 1099 (Supp. 1974); Cal. Educ. Code §§ 71, 5766-69, 6457, 13273.5 (West 1975); Colo. Rev. Stat. Ann. § 22-1-103 (1973); Conn. Gen. Stat. Ann. § 10.17 (Supp. 1975); Ill. Rev. Stat. ch. 122 §§ 10-22.28a, 34-18.2 (Supp. 1975); Kan. Stat. Ann. § 62-1101 (1972); Me. Rev. Stat. Ann. tit. 20, § 102(16) (Supp. 1974); N.M. Stat. Ann. §§ 77-23-1 to 7 (Supp. 1973); N.Y. Educ. Law § 3204(2a) (McKinney 1970); Ore. Rev. Stat. § 336.074-.079 (1973); Pa. Stat. Ann. tit. 24, § 15-1511 (Supp. 1974); Tex. Educ. Code Ann. § 11.11 (1972).

431. Alaska Stat. § 14.08.160 (Cum. Supp. 1974); Mass. Gen. Laws Ann. ch. 71A (Supp. 1974).

bilingual education has been found to be at least a statutory[432] if not a constitutional right.[433]

Many school districts currently offer Spanish speaking students either segregated bilingual education or integration without bilingual education.[434] Neither of these "Hobson's Choice" alternatives are acceptable to many Hispano-Americans. The district court in *United States v. Texas* recognized the problem of seemingly conflicting objectives:[435]

> [There is] . . . the need . . . for special educational consideration to be given to the Mexican-American students in assisting them in adjusting to those parts of their new school environment which present a cultural and linguistic shock. Equally clear, however, is the need to avoid the creation of a stigma of inferiority akin to the "badges and indicia of slavery" . . . . To avoid this result the Anglo-American students too must be called upon to adjust to their Mexican-American classmates, and to learn to understand and appreciate their different linguistic and cultural attributes.

In the Denver case, however, the district court recognized a desire not to be desegregated if that meant giving up bilingual education.[436] In one of the schools, a pilot bilingual-bicultural program was already underway. The court noted that some "representatives of the Mexican-American community"[437] asked that the school *not* be desegregated during the period the program was developing. The court therefore held that "desegregation is not in its best interests."[438]

Theoretically, bilingual-bicultural education and integration are not incompatible. Federal regulations under the Bilingual Education Act require school districts to make good faith efforts to integrate their federally funded bilingual programs.[439] By and large, however, they are neither integrated nor truly

432. Serna v. Portales Municipal Schools, 499 F.2d 1147, 1153-54 (10th Cir. 1974); Lau v. Nichols, 414 U.S. 563, 566-69 (1974).

433. For legal arguments on behalf of a constitutional right to bilingual education, see Note, *The Constitutional Right of Bilingual Children to an Equal Educational Opportunity*, 47 S. CALIF. L. REV. 943 (1974).

434. Cárdenas, *Bilingual Education, Segregation, and a Third Alternative*, 1975 INEQUALITY IN ED. no. 19, at 20.

435. 342 F. Supp. 24, 28 (E.D. Tex. 1971), *aff'd*, 466 F.2d 518 (5th Cir. 1972). The court, therefore, ordered the creation of a unitary school system in which "neither English nor Spanish is presented as a more valued language . . . ." *Id.* at 30. The court also ordered the implementation of a "bilingual-bicultural instructional program which utilizes the child's language system (English, Spanish, or a blend of both) as the medium of instruction as proficiency in one or more additional language systems is developed." *Id.* at 31.

436. Keyes v. School Dist. No. 1, 380 F. Supp. 673, 692 (D. Colo. 1974).

437. *Id.*

438. *Id.*

439. 20 U.S.C.A. § 880b et seq. (1975).

> A program assisted under this Part shall include such provisions as are necessary to prevent the separation of children by language or ethnic background in any activity included in such programs, unless the applicant demonstrates that such separation for a *portion* of the school day for specific language learning activities is essential to the achievement of the purpose of this part.

40 Fed. Reg. 26517-18 (1975) (emphasis added).

bilingual; rather, the English as a Second Language (ESL) program is what is usually provided. Such programs rely exclusively on the use of the English language; the child is compelled to learn a new language and at the same time to learn course material in the new language. Thus Hispano-American children, not surprisingly, fall behind Anglo children in such substantive curricular areas as math, geography, history, etc.

The principal use of social science in cases involving Hispano students has been through the introduction of expert witnesses—educators or psychologists—who portray the incompatibility between the characteristics of the non-Anglo-Saxon child and the characteristics of the white, middle class educational program being offered. Studies have also been cited which show that large numbers of Hispano students—through the use of IQ or other standardized intelligence and achievement tests that tend to measure the students' ability to read and understand English rather than their actual intelligence —have been improperly assigned to classes for the educable mentally retarded (EMR) or low track or ability groupings.[440]

In sum, that Hispano-Americans may require, as part of any desegregation decree, special remedies not sought by black litigants is a principle gradually being developed by the courts. Coupled with this is the growing recognition of, at the least, a *statutory* right to bilingual education and of the inappropriateness of using tests based on English language skills to determine a child's placement in special classes or tracks.

IV
Second Generation Problems

A school system may in some respects remain segregated even after a court-ordered desegregation plan has been fully implemented. Through various practices such as ability grouping and the selective use of disciplinary measures, minority children may continue to receive different and apparently unequal treatment. These practices may bring about resegregation of the school system in frustration of the court-ordered plan. Do these practices, even when they are educationally valid and racially neutral, violate the fourteenth amendment? If so, to what extent may inexpert judges intervene in the educational process to fashion an appropriate remedy to protect the rights and interests of minority children? And when the courts do intervene, what social science evidence may they turn to for guidance?

A. Tracking and Ability Grouping

One of the most frequently used practices responsible for bringing about resegregation is the use of tracking or ability grouping following the adoption of a desegregation plan. The courts have been fairly consistent in holding that

440. These cases are discussed in the text at pp. 126-27 *infra*.

when a formerly dual, segregated school system is in the process of being or has just recently been dismantled, pupil assignment by standardized achievement or IQ test scores is prohibited when the intended and actual result is the perpetuation of the dual system. This is so whether the continuing segregation exists within the system as a whole,[441] within individual schools,[442] or even within individual classrooms.[443]

> Ability groupings or the so-called "track method" may have academic justification and may be an educational rather than a constitutional issue, but the track system or "ability grouping" is suspect when it first begins to flourish on the eve of or during a desegregation suit.[444]

Apart from the blatant, racially-motivated misuse of such measures, is racially-neutral ability grouping a valid educational practice? It has been argued, in behalf of ability grouping, that the teacher can adjust his or her teaching methods and materials and reach most, if not all, of the students in a given classroom. In a heterogeneous classroom, on the other hand, the teacher would have to aim for the average range of ability, and thus would lose both those students significantly below and those above the average, as the material would either be too difficult or insufficiently challenging. Where the class has a narrower range of ability, the teacher should have more time for individualized, personal instruction.

In addition to improved student achievement, it has been argued that ability grouping promotes self-esteem. The child who does not have to compete with children who are significantly brighter or duller than he, can develop a healthy self-image as he works with children at his own level.[445]

While there is substantial social science research on these issues, the research is so contradictory that it cannot be said with any sense of conviction whether ability grouping does or does not lead to increased achievement and improved self-esteem in children.[446] Some have termed ability grouping a sys-

---

441. *See, e.g.*, Lemon v. Bossier Parish School Bd., 444 F.2d 1400 (5th Cir. 1971); United States v. Sunflower County School Dist., 430 F.2d 839, 841 (5th Cir.), *cert. denied*, 398 U.S. 951 (1970); Singleton v. Jackson Municipal Separate School Dist., 419 F.2d 1211, 1219 (5th Cir. 1969), *rev'd and remanded in part on other grounds sub nom.* Carter v. West Feliciana Parish School Bd., 396 U.S. 290 (1970).

442. *See, e.g.*, Moses v. Washington Parish School Bd., 456 F.2d 1285 (5th Cir.), *cert. denied*, 409 U.S. 1013 (1972).

443. *See, e.g.*, Acree v. County Bd. of Educ., 458 F.2d 486, 488 n. 3 (5th Cir.), *cert. denied*, 409 U.S. 1006 (1972).

444. Singleton v. Anson County Bd. of Educ., Civil No. 2259 (W.D.N.C. July 3, 1967).

445. Goldberg & Passow, *The Effects of Ability Grouping in the Elementary Schools*, in GROUPING IN THE ELEMENTARY SCHOOLS 22-23 (A. Morgenstern ed. 1966). The arguments that have been made, both for and against ability grouping, are summarized in NATIONAL EDUCATION ASSOCIATION, ABILITY GROUPING 8-10 (Research Summary No. 53, 1968).

446. *See, e.g.*, Esposito, *Homogeneous and Heterogeneous Ability Grouping: Principal Findings and Implications for Evaluating and Designing More Effective Educational Environments*, 43 REV. ED. RES. 163, 167-68 (1973); Goodlad, *Classroom Organization*, in ENCYCLOPEDIA OF EDUCATIONAL RESEARCH 221 (C. Harris ed. 1960); Passow, *The Maze of Research on Ability Grouping*, 26 ED. FORUM 281 (1962).

A brief review of two relatively large-scale studies illustrates the differing results obtainable:

tem of "maximizing stigma and minimizing exposure."[447] Even if social science research more clearly indicated that ability grouping *is* a valid educational practice, is its continued use constitutionally permissible when the result, in a system otherwise adjudged to be unitary, is a clear separation of the races?[448] Does *Brown* require racial balance in spite of educationally valid reasons for separation? May segregative intent be inferred from tracking and ability group-

---

The first of these studies was begun in 1956 in New York City: approximately 3,000 fifth grade students were separated into five ability levels on the basis of IQ tests. The children were followed through the end of the sixth grade. The researchers reported that the effects of ability grouping on academic achievement were minimal at best. Goldberg & Passow, *supra* note 445, at 31. In fact, in not a single instance could the size of a child's "achievement increment" be attributed to his status at the beginning of the school year. *Id.* at 33. Student achievement was correlated, not with a child's previously measured achievement, but with whether or not the particular teacher was interested in the particular subject being taught, regardless of the range of student ability in that subject. Moreover, the greatest academic gains for all students were attained in classrooms with the broadest range of abilities. *Id.* at 31-39. The more heterogeneous the classroom, the more *all* the children learned; and what they learned best was what the teacher liked best and consequently taught best.

Goldberg and Passow also found that teachers did not adjust their teaching methods and materials to the level of their students in homogeneous classes. The only adjustments that were ever made were in the lower ability classrooms, where teachers taught less of certain subjects than in the classrooms where brighter children were also present. *Id.* at 32. The result was that the children in the lower ability homogeneous classes learned less than pupils of comparable ability who were placed in heterogeneous classes, especially in the areas of science and vocabulary. Thus "slower" children made greater academic gains when they were placed in heterogeneous classrooms and were exposed to the teaching aimed at the brighter children. *Id.* at 35.

Of the three non-academic variables studied (self-attitude, social perceptions, and interest of pupils), only self-attitudes were sensitive to ability grouping. *Id.* at 34. Ability grouping raised the self-image of the slower children (who were no longer forced to compete with the brightest children) and lowered the high self-ratings of the brightest children (who no longer stood out academically).

The second large-scale study—of 4,000 students in two homogeneous socioeconomic school districts in Utah—conducted in the mid-1960's, reached somewhat different conclusions. W. Borg, Ability Grouping in the Public Schools: A Field Study (1966). The superior students achieved greater academic gains when grouped homogeneously, although their study skills improved in the heterogeneous environment. There were some similarities with the New York study, however: the self-concept of the academic high achievers declined as a result of placement in homogeneous classes. For the slow students, achievement increased significantly and consistently when the students were in heterogeneous groups. Again as in the New York study, these students showed a gain in self-concept and self-esteem when grouped homogeneously. *Id.* at 91.

447. M. McClung, Ability Grouping: The Practice of Maximizing Stigma and Minimizing Exposure in Public Schools, April 19, 1972 (mimeo on file at Harvard Center for Law & Education).

448. The courts have thus far not reached this question. *See, e.g.*, Singleton v. Jackson Municipal Separate School Dist., 419 F.2d 1211 (5th Cir. 1970). "We pretermit a discussion of the validity per se of a [tracking or ability grouping] plan based on testing except to hold that testing cannot be employed in any event until unitary [*i.e.*, desegregated] school systems have been established." *Id.* at 1219. Lemon v. Bossier Parish School Bd., 444 F.2d 1400 (5th Cir. 1971). "We decline once again . . . the invitation to rule on the validity of testing [to determine ability groupings] per se." *Id.* at 1401.

Hobson v. Hansen, 269 F. Supp. 401 (D.D.C. 1967), *aff'd sub nom.* Smuck v. Hobson, 408 F.2d 175 (D.C. Cir. 1969) comes closest to finding the use of tracking a constitutional violation per se.

The best and by far the most comprehensive discussion of tracking and ability grouping—covering the social science research and methodology as well as current legal doctrine—is Kirp, *Schools as Sorters: The Constitutional and Policy Implications of Student Classification*, 121 U. Pa. L. Rev. 705 (1973).

ing practices which result in segregation in all or part of a school system? Who should bear the evidentiary burden? Might such practices which result in segregation require state authorities to bear the burden of showing that such actions are not racially motivated?[449] Should plaintiffs be required to show that there are educationally feasible alternatives to ability grouping? Or should the burden be shifted to the school authorities to show that there is no other way of educating children effectively?

In *Hobson v. Hansen*[450] the court held that a system of tracking which places minority students in lower levels of standard curricula is unconstitutional when it inhibits movement between tracks, thereby rendering the initial assignment to a lower track a permanent assignment. In theory, the track system was established to enable the school system to provide compensatory and remedial education for students in the lowest tracks in order to help those students move into higher tracks. In practice, however, such education was woefully lacking.[451] When coupled with the court's discussion of the serious harm caused by segregation, however it is brought about,[452] these findings suggest that the *Hobson* court might have abolished the tracking system even without the showing that the classifying tests were biased.[453] The court did not reach this precise issue, however, leaving it open for future litigation.

On appeal, the circuit court expressly refused to "plunge into a sea of . . . difficult issues of educational policy" such as the appropriate balance between the "practical need" to group students by ability and the need to ensure equal educational opportunity to every student; the extent to which verbal skills tests can be used without adversely affecting the minority student's educational advancement, and the extent to which verbal tests must be adjusted to reflect available indicators of ability not dependent on verbal skills.[454] The circuit court, therefore, interpreted Judge Wright's decree as abolishing the particular tracking system in existence in the District of Columbia school system at the time of the trial rather than abolishing all forms of ability grouping or tracking in the future.[455]

Attorneys in student classification cases face a number of practical difficulties: what patterns should they look for in order to determine whether grouping, tracking, streaming, or some form of instructional separation is being practiced; what are the weaknesses of each program; what are the available alternative teaching methods—with less of a segregative effect—which can readily be adapted to a particular school district? The sharp and unresolved

449. *Cf.* Keyes v. School Dist. No. 1, 413 U.S. 189, 209-10 (1973); Swann v. Charlotte-Mecklenburg Bd. of Educ., 402 U.S. 1, 18, 26 (1971).

450. 269 F. Supp. 401 (D.D.C. 1967), *aff'd sub nom.* Smuck v. Hobson, 408 F.2d 175 (D.C. Cir. 1969).

451. 269 F. Supp. at 469-70.

452. 269 F. Supp. at 503-06.

453. *See* discussion at notes 431 & 432 *supra* and accompanying text.

454. 408 F.2d at 188.

455. 408 F.2d at 189-90.

controversy over heterogeneous versus homogeneous grouping makes it difficult if not impossible for courts to adjudicate issues surrounding the use of these practices; moreover, given the present state of the art, the feasibility of educational alternatives cannot even be shown.[456]

B. Use of Tests

When ability grouping or tracking is practiced, the decisions as to which children are to be placed in which track are usually based on IQ or standardized achievement test scores, sometimes accompanied by the recommendations of teachers. Several law suits have challenged the tests themselves as being culturally biased, claiming that such tests lead to the misclassification of minority students. The use of untrained school officials in interpreting the tests has also been challenged.[457]

In *Hobson v. Hansen*,[458] the court abolished the tracking system used in the public schools of the District of Columbia which assigned students to a particular curriculum track on the basis of standardized ability test scores. Relying on extensive social science evidence regarding the testing of disadvantaged children,[459] the court found that the tests used were biased against black and other low-income students:[460]

> When standard aptitude tests are given to low income Negro children, or disadvantaged children, . . . the tests are less precise and less accurate—so much so that test scores become practically meaningless. Because of the impoverished circumstances that characterize the disadvantaged child, it is virtually impossible to tell whether the test score reflects lack of ability—or simply lack of opportunity. Moreover, the probability that test scores of the Negro child or the disadvantaged child will be depressed because of somewhat unique psychological influences further compounds the risk of inaccuracy.

---

456. *See* Orfield, *supra* note 64, at 327-28.

457. In Stewart v. Phillips, Civil No. 70-1199-F (D. Mass. Feb. 8, 1971), plaintiffs (black and poor students placed in special classes) asserted that the tests are "biased—standardized to a white, middle class norm" and that the single score "fail[s] to distinguish among a wide range of learning disabilities—emotional, perceptual, linguistic, and cultural." CENTER FOR LAW AND EDUCATION, CLASSIFICATION MATERIALS 283 (rev. ed. 1973) [hereinafter cited as CLASSIFICATION MATERIALS]. Plaintiffs also claimed that "[m]any of the school psychologists administering and interpreting the tests are . . . unqualified." *Id.*

458. 269 F. Supp. 401 (D.D.C. 1967), *aff'd sub nom.* Smuck v. Hobson, 408 F.2d 175 (D.C. Cir. 1969).

459. 269 F. Supp. at 479-88. In support, Judge Wright cited the Lorton Study, N. BURKE & A. SIMONS, A MEASURE OF THE EDUCATIONAL ACHIEVEMENT OF A GROUP OF INCARCERATED CULTURALLY DISADVANTAGED AND EDUCATIONALLY DEPRIVED DROPOUTS (1965), in which results of one of the standard verbal IQ tests were compared to the results of a non-verbal IQ test. The results from the latter test were, on average, 29 points higher. 269 F. Supp. at 485-87 & n. 136. The judge also cited, without discussion, a number of other social science writings on testing disadvantaged children, such as AMERICAN COUNCIL ON EDUCATION, TESTING PROBLEMS IN PERSPECTIVE (A. Anastasi ed. 1967); K. EELS, INTELLIGENCE AND CULTURAL DIFFERENCES (1951); F. RIESSMAN, THE CULTURALLY DEPRIVED CHILD (1962); P. SEXTON, EDUCATION AND INCOME (1961); Deutsch & Brown, *Social Influences in Negro-White Intelligence Differences*, 20 J. SOCIAL ISSUES 24 (1964); and D. GOSLIN, CRITICISM OF STANDARDIZED TESTS AND TESTING (1967). 269 F. Supp. at 479-80 n. 130.

460. 269 F. Supp. at 485.

One difficulty with the *Hobson* decision is that by abolishing the use of standardized tests without suggesting guidelines for procedures which would be constitutional, the court has left the school system without anything to fall back on.[461] There is some doubt as to whether "culture-free" tests can be developed which would fill the gap.[462]

Although the district court in *Hobson* concluded that there had been de jure segregative practices on the part of the school authorities,[463] it blurred the distinction between de jure and de facto segregation,[464] suggesting that the *Hobson* case might be applicable to tracking situations where there has been no showing of de jure segregation.

A number of recent cases have challenged the use of tests to assign minority students to classes for the educable mentally retarded (EMR). The plaintiffs in such suits have alleged that the use of culturally biased tests has resulted in the misassignment of "normal" students to EMR classes.[465] In one recent misclassification case, the use of IQ tests was successfully attacked even though not even *inferred* segregative intent was shown. In *Larry P. v. Riles*,[466] a federal district court enjoined the San Francisco Unified School District from assigning black students to classes for the educable mentally retarded (EMR) on the basis of IQ tests, when the result was a disproportionate number of black students in such classes.[467] Plaintiffs were required to show (1) that a significant racial imbalance existed in the EMR classes, and (2) that the primary determinant of the assignment to an EMR class was the child's IQ test score. After these two things were shown, the burden of proof shifted to defendants to justify the use of the IQ tests. The defendants did not dispute the plaintiffs' evidence that the tests were culturally biased (*e.g.*, when black psychologists administered the same IQ test with slight modifications to take into account the students' cultural background, the test scores were significantly higher). They merely argued that the tests were not the cause of the racial imbalance in the EMR classes, or, in the alternative, the tests, although racially biased, were rationally related to a valid state purpose.[468] The plaintiffs, however, introduced evidence of alternative methods of determining assignment to EMR classes used by other school systems, which minimized reliance on IQ tests.[469] Thus the defendants failed to meet their burden of proof.

Larry P. v. Riles, however, was only a nominal victory for the plaintiffs. The

---

461. *See* Note, Hobson v. Hansen: *Judicial Supervision of the Color-Blind School Board*, 81 HARV. L. REV. 1511, 1521 (1968).

462. Charters, *Social Class and Intelligence Tests*, in SCHOOL CHILDREN IN THE URBAN SLUMS 75 (J. Roberts ed. 1967).

463. 269 F. Supp. at 515.

464. 269 F. Supp. at 508 & 515.

465. *See, e.g.*, Stewart v. Phillips, Civil No. 70-1199-F (D. Mass. Feb. 8, 1971).

466. 343 F. Supp. 1306 (N.D. Cal. 1972).

467. *Id.* at 1314-15.

468. 343 F. Supp. at 1313.

469. 343 F. Supp. at 1313-14.

court refused to order the immediate testing of all black students then in EMR classes; refused to order affirmative action to compensate black students who had been wrongfully placed in EMR classes in the past; and refused to order the hiring of minority group psychologists and consultants for the administration of tests to minority students, and evaluation of the test scores.[470] The court was also extremely wary of, and refused to grant plaintiffs' request for an EMR class-quota system (whereby the percentage of black students could exceed the percentage of black students in the school district as a whole by no more than fifteen per cent), because[471]

> it [would leave] fulfillment of the needs of retarded black students at the mercy of white parents who may decline to consent to placement of their own retarded children in EMR classes and thereby reduce the number of retarded black children who may be placed in them.

And the battle continues. The Portsmouth, Virginia School Board is currently under legal attack in the Federal District Court for the Eastern District of Virginia because of its use of IQ tests for placement of children in special classes and in schools for the mentally retarded. The plaintiffs claim that black students have been misclassified and wrongly assigned to such classes. The plaintiffs are not seeking to abolish all IQ testing, but only those tests which do not take into account the socioeconomic background of the students being tested. In addition, plaintiffs are seeking testing which assesses "sensitivity, vocational, technical and mechanical skills, styles of analysis and the ability to express one's self through oral, non-verbal or graphic means."[472] Testifying for the plaintiffs was Dr. Jonas Chenault, an educational psychologist at the University of Michigan.

Defendants, on the other hand, stressed the importance of the IQ tests in determining which students need special help, and expressed concern that the Supreme Court might abolish the use of IQ tests altogether. The school board also strongly objected to the plaintiffs' allusion to a recent study which allegedly showed that while white students who score below 70 on the IQ tests are generally retarded, blacks who score below 70 are not necessarily retarded.[473]

A number of similar cases which have been brought have been settled. Stipulations in some of these cases acknowledge that large groups of Spanish-speaking children have been inappropriately placed in EMR classes after being tested in English. Perhaps the most significant of these is *Diana v. State Board of Education*[474] which undoubtedly influenced the California legislature's substantial revision of the testing and classification procedures for EMR classes then in

470. 343 F. Supp. at 1314.

471. 343 F. Supp. at 1315.

472. Washington Post, April 19, 1974, § D, at 1, col. 1. The case was filed in the Federal District court for the Eastern District of Virginia.

473. *Id.*

474. Civil No. C-70-37-RFR (N.D. Cal. Jun. 18, 1973). *See* CLASSIFICATION MATERIALS 199-207, 224-29, 429.

use by the California school system.[475] The plaintiffs in that case brought a class action challenging the use of IQ tests to place Mexican-American children in EMR classes,[476] alleging that the nine named children were not mentally retarded; rather, their low test scores resulted from their unfamiliarity with the English language. Each of the nine named plaintiffs was retested, and the children were allowed to answer either in English or in Spanish. All performed significantly better, averaging, as a group, a fifteen point increase in IQ. Seven scored higher than the maximum score used for assigning children to EMR classes. Less than a month after the suit was filed, a stipulation order was entered requiring that children be tested in their primary language and interpreters be used in the absence of a bilingual examiner; that Mexican-American and other foreign language children then in educable mentally retarded classes in the county be retested and reevaluated; that assistance be provided to misplaced children to enable them to readjust to regular classes; and that the state develop and standardize an IQ test on a Mexican-American population living in California.[477]

---

475. CAL. EDUC. CODE § 6902.06 (West Supp. 1972). The Director of the Office of Civil Rights of the Department of Health, Education and Welfare, issued a departmental memorandum noting that schools were not to assign students whose predominant language was other than English to EMR classes on the basis of tests which measured English language skills. 35 Fed. Reg. 11, 595 (1970). Subsequently, OCR cited twenty-eight districts in the Southwest for noncompliance with Title VI; of these, fourteen assigned Mexican-American students to EMR classes on the basis of criteria measuring English language skills. U.S. COMMISSION ON CIVIL RIGHTS, MEXICAN AMERICAN EDUCATION STUDY, REPORT VI: TOWARD QUALITY EDUCATION FOR MEXICAN AMERICANS 58-59 1974).

476. The IQ test used by the school system, which was challenged by the plaintiffs was the verbal Stanford-Binet test, which was standardized in 1937 on 3,184 white native-born Americans and has never been restandardized. Plaintiffs asserted that the cultural bias of the test was self-evident when such questions are asked as "Why is it better to pay bills by check than by cash?" (Plaintiffs point out that this is a difficult question for a child whose parents have never had a bank account) and "Who wrote Romeo and Juliet?" The vocabulary section includes the words "umbrella," and not "sombrero," and "chattel," not "slave." The children are also asked to identify such items as "C.O.D." and "hieroglyphic." *Id.* at 202.

477. The stipulation order also required the California State Department of Education to maintain data on the racial and ethnic composition of all EMR classes in each school district; if there is a higher proportion of racial or ethnic children in the EMR classes than their proportion in the district as a whole, the school district will be required to explain the difference.

One commentator notes that as a result of *Diana* and the new California law, *supra* note 475, thousands of children have been returned to regular classes. The commentator notes, however, that the needs of these children are not being adequately provided for:

> [A] closer look at the situation presents a dismal picture. Children being returned to the regular classes are provided little of the necessary additional support, enrichment, and remedial services which will redress the effects of their prior educational experiences and permit them to function at the level of other students in the regular classes. Apparently, they are not expected to do well, and many will not. It seems certain that the blame for their failure will be placed on the children, rather than on a system that will not modify itself and its resources to meet their particular needs.

Cohen & DeYoung, *The Role of Litigation in the Improvement of Programming for the Handicapped*, in THE FIRST REVIEW OF SPECIAL EDUCATION 270 (L. Mann & D. Sabatino eds. 1973).

See also Guadalupe Organization, Inc. v. Tempe Elementary School Dist., Civil No. 71-435 (D. Ariz. May 9, 1972). The complaint in that case states that Spanish-surnamed children comprised 67.5 per cent of the enrollment in EMR classes and 46.34 per cent of the enrollment in classes for

If legal rights in fact do accrue to minority children who have been wrongly assigned to a lower track or an EMR class on the basis of such tests, what remedies are available? Reassignment to a higher track or into "mainstream" classes? Compensatory education? Monetary damages for a diminished future earning capacity?[478]

Assuming, however, that the tests used to identify mentally retarded students are racially neutral, culturally fair, and educationally valid, should the tests or the assignment to special classes on the basis of those tests be open to legal challenge if the *result* is a disproportionate number of minority children being placed in special classes or schools for the educable mentally retarded? Social science has not yet resolved the question of whether it is educationally wiser to remove educable mentally retarded students from the "mainstream" of education by placement either in special classes or schools or to keep these students in regular classrooms while providing supplemental supportive training both in and out of class. It has been argued that such "mainstreaming" would reduce any stigma attached to placement in special education, as well as prevent the psychological and educational harm arising from misclassification, but there are equally valid educational arguments for separating such children from the others.[479] In view of the uncertainty as to which educational proce-

---

trainable mentally handicapped, although they comprised only 17.78 per cent of the total student population. This case was also terminated by a stipulated settlement.

Covarrubius v. San Diego Unified School Dist., Civil No. 70-394-5 (S.D. Cal. Aug. 21, 1972), also resulted in a settlement agreement. The plaintiffs in that case not only asked for injunctive relief against the continued use of the tests as devices for student assignment—enjoining defendants from administering tests to students who may do poorly on them because of their cultural background and enjoining defendants from placing any child in a special education class before age 10—but also for $400,000 in punitive damages for the period they had spent in mentally retarded classes because of mislabeling. As a result of the settlement agreement, no punitive damages were awarded.

In Ruiz v. State Bd. of Educ., Civil No. 218294 (Super. Ct., Sacramento County, filed Dec. 16, 1971), plaintiffs sought an injunction to prevent the defendants from administering and recording in the plaintiffs' permanent cumulative school records the results of group intelligence tests, which California law requires be given to all sixth and twelfth grade students. The complaint alleges that the tests are designed with reference to middle-class white cultural norms and have no validity in measuring plaintiffs' ability. Despite this, the scores are placed in the permanent records and "are relied upon by teachers, counselors, and school administrators to develop low ability expectations for them and to track, teach, place, evaluate and encourage them accordingly." CLASSIFICATION MATERIALS 289.

478. *Cf.* Peter Doe v. San Francisco Unified School Dist., Civil No. 653-312 (Super. Ct., San Francisco County, filed Nov. 20, 1972). Plaintiff, an 18-year old high school graduate, filed an action seeking general and punitive damages of one million dollars from the school authorities on the ground that he could neither read nor write above fifth-grade level despite having received his high school diploma and despite the school system's repeated reassurances to his mother that he was progressing at a normal grade-level rate.

479. *Compare* Dunn, *Special Education for the Mentally Retarded—Is Much of It Justifiable?*, 35 EXCEPTIONAL CHILDREN 5 (1968) *with* MacMillan, *Special Education for the Mildly Retarded: Servant or Savant?*, 2 FOCUS ON EXCEPTIONAL CHILDREN no. 9, at 1 (1971). A summary of some of the arguments for and against special classes for the retarded is provided in Fink & Glass, *Contemporary Issues in the Education of the Behaviorally Disordered*, in THE FIRST REVIEW OF SPECIAL EDUCATION 137 (L. Mann & D. Sabatino eds. 1973).

dure is more appropriate, should courts intervene? It is at least arguable that once a court has determined that the tests being administered are racially neutral and otherwise valid, and that there are procedural and substantive safeguards to circumscribe the classification process to avoid even unintentional misclassification, there is no basis for a court to intervene further. The difficulty courts face here is in developing remedies that will cure the civil rights violations without interferring with *legitimate* educational judgments about the need to group children by ability.

C. Student Discipline

There is a growing body of evidence indicating that within "integrated" schools and school systems a disproportionate number of black students are suspended, expelled, or otherwise disciplined.[480] This systematic exclusion is now being attacked in the federal courts. In *Hawkins v. Coleman*,[481] it was found that blacks in the Dallas school system were systematically suspended more frequently, endured longer suspensions, and were also subjected to corporal punishment much more often than whites—particularly in schools where whites were a majority.[482] The Dallas superintendent testified that this was attributable to "institutional racism."[483] Testimony from a psychologist indicated that black students would become "more frustrated as the institution continue[d] to refuse to respond to their needs and ambitions" and that "[t]his frustration [would] be reflected either in increased passivity or increased hostility," the latter, of course, resulting in increased "suspendable behavior."[484]

As with ability grouping practices, it is not clear in this area when actions are taken for valid educational reasons and when a court should intervene to protect the rights of minority students. If the actions are taken without intent to discriminate and with adequate procedural safeguards, but the result is a disproportionate number of minority children being disciplined, the same question must be asked: is it appropriate for courts to intervene?[485] And if it is appropriate, what remedies can the courts fashion which will safeguard the rights of minority students, yet leave school officials unfettered to pursue legitimate disciplinary goals? The case law on these points at present is, at best, rudimentary. In the coming years, these "second generation" problems will undoubtedly be a principal focus of attention.

---

480. *See generally* CHILDREN'S DEFENSE FUND, CHILDREN OUT OF SCHOOL IN AMERICA (1974); *Hearings on Equal Educational Opportunity Before the Select Senate Comm. on Equal Educational Opportunity*, 91st Cong., 2d Sess., pt. 3-B, at 1311 (1970).

481. 376 F. Supp. 1330 (N.D. Tex. 1974).

482. *Id.* at 1333-35. *See generally* Yudof, *Suspension and Expulsion of Black Students From the Public Schools: Academic Capital Punishment and the Constitution*, 39 LAW & CONTEMP. PROB. no. 2, at 374 (1975).

483. 376 F. Supp. at 1336.

484. *Id.*

485. *See* Yudof, *supra* note 482, for an excellent discussion of the complexity of the problem of black exclusion from public schools.

Summary and Conclusion

A summary of the development of school desegregation law—spanning the nineteen year period from *Brown* to *Keyes*—reveals the following principles for court-ordered school desegregation:

1) Immediate desegregation is required; delays will no longer be tolerated.[486]
2) All-out desegregation must be accomplished and segregation eliminated "root and branch."[487]
3) In designing a desegregation plan for a formerly dual school system, federal district courts have broad equitable remedial powers—whatever tools are necessary; "[o]nce a right and a violation have been shown, the scope of a district court's equitable powers to remedy past wrongs is broad, for breadth and flexibility are inherent in equitable remedies."[488]
4) Remedies "may be administratively awkward, inconvenient, and even bizarre in some situations . . .";[489] thus noncontiguous and noncompact attendance zones—even zones which "may be on opposite ends of the city"—can be drawn by the district court.[490]
5) There are limits on the extent to which some remedial measures can be used:
   a) Racial balance—there is no substantive constitutional right to racial balance in and of itself,[491] but as a remedy for an already determined constitutional violation, mathematical ratios may be used as a "starting point."[492]
   b) Busing—may be used where feasible, limited only "when the time or distance of travel is so great as to either risk the health of the children or significantly impinge on the educational process."[493]
6) In an area where no prior statutory or constitutional provision has compelled segregation, de jure actions of school officials (*e.g.*, manipulating attendance zones or selection of sites for new school construction) in one part of the district (albeit a "meaningful" part) leads to the presumption that the "infection" has pervaded the entire district or that de jure actions must have occurred throughout the district.[494] The de facto/de jure distinction is still alive.[495] However, it is probable that plaintiffs can with relative ease prove intentional segregative acts on the

---

486. Alexander v. Holmes County Bd. of Educ., 396 U.S. 19, 20 (1969). *See also* Carter v. West Feliciana Parish School Bd., 396 U.S. 290 (1970).
487. Green v. County School Bd., 391 U.S. 430, 437-38 (1968).
488. Swann v. Charlotte-Mecklenburg Bd. of Educ., 402 U.S. 1, 15 (1971).
489. 402 U.S. at 28.
490. 402 U.S. at 27.
491. 402 U.S. at 24.
492. 402 U.S. at 25.
493. 402 U.S. at 30-31.
494. Keyes v. School Dist. No. 1, 413 U.S. 189, 208-09 (1973).
495. 413 U.S. at 208.

part of school officials or actions "which have the natural and foreseeable consequences of causing educational segregation,"[496] of a school district. This coupled with the presumptions that are triggered by such a finding,[497] suggest that Justice Powell's demand—that there be a "uniform national rule"[498] for school segregation—would very likely be met.

Thus in the nineteenth year after the *Brown* decision, it seemed clear that de jure segregation could be found in school districts outside of the South; that the burden of proof, once a prima facie case was made by plaintiffs, would be on the defendant school system to prove either that the pattern of segregated schools was *not* a "vestige" of a formerly dual state-imposed system[499] or was *not* the result of racially motivated actions of school officials[500] and that there were no limits on the equitable remedial powers of federal district courts in providing for all-out desegregation other than those noted above with regard to busing and racial imbalance. There was little indication that the remedial measures which a court could impose could run only to the school district line.

But some cracks had begun to appear in the unanimous front heretofore presented by the Court, as indicated in various concurring and dissenting opinions:

1) "Local control," it was suggested, was desirable and of "overriding importance from an educational standpoint" and weighed heavily against any remedial measure which would interfere with the independence of already defined separate school districts.[501]
2) Deviations in racial balance percentages should not prevent a school system from withdrawing from a larger unit and setting itself up as a separate district to provide "quality education."[502]
3) "In the balancing of interests," busing should be curtailed when it is at the expense of a neighborhood schools policy.[503]
4) Racial gerrymandering of attendance zones or other deliberate segregative actions in a part of the school district is a constitutional violation only as to the minorities within that zone; unless factual inquiry reveals that invidious discrimination has taken place in every zone, the district as a whole can not be treated as a "dual" school system requiring a district-wide remedy.[504]

Twenty years after *Brown*, *Milliken v. Bradley*—the Detroit case—was

496. Hart v. Community School Bd. of Educ., 512 F.2d 37, 50 (2d Cir. 1975).
497. *See* notes 74-80 accompanying text at pp. 63-64 *supra*.
498. 413 U.S. at 232.
499. Swann v. Charlotte-Mecklenburg Bd. of Educ., 402 U.S. at 15.
500. Keyes v. School Dist. No. 1, 413 U.S. at 208.
501. Wright v. City of Emporia, 407 U.S. 451 (1972) (Burger, C.J., dissenting).
502. *See* 407 U.S. at 478-82 (Burger, C.J., dissenting).
503. Keyes v. School Dist. No. 1, 413 U.S. at 189, 251-52 (1973) (Powell, J., concurring in part and dissenting in part).
504. 413 U.S. at 256-58 (Rehnquist, J., dissenting).

decided.[505] The immediate reaction among many was that this was the end of the line. The burden of proof was shifted from the defendants to the plaintiffs to prove the actions of suburban school officials or of state education officials were racially motivated *and* had a segregative effect on the central city district. But the decision need not necessarily be seen—as Justice Marshall suggests—as "a giant step backwards."[506] The door was left slightly ajar to permit proof of intentional actions of state or suburban non-school governmental agencies to establish or maintain residential segregation.[507] Moreover, the admission by the majority that the segregation in Detroit was clearly de jure indicates that school desegregation litigation can continue unabated in the North and West as long as relief is sought on an intra-district basis. There seems to be no withdrawal from *Swann* and *Keyes*.

What function has social science research served in the foregoing legal development and of what relevance will it be in future litigation? First, social science research since *Brown* has not generally been used by the courts to ascertain some degree of "harm" as a predicate to a constitutional violation, although to some extent demographic and other studies have been used to determine whether segregation is attributable to actions of school officials, other officials, or is fortuitous.

There are at least three significant areas in which social science research has been and can be useful to courts. The first area is that left open by the Detroit decision—proof of racial containment in the central city schools by actions of suburban or state agencies. Clearly demographers, sociologists, political scientists and others can aid in determining the factors leading to the "growing core of Negro schools" in the central city, surrounded by nearly all white suburban school districts.

The second area is that of the desegregation plan itself—social scientists and social science data can be and are used to help the court translate from desegregation as simply a "body count" to effective integration. The development of a separate remedial plan for Hispano-Americans in *Keyes* to reflect the unique bilingual-bicultural needs is such an example.[508] Thus, educators, psychologists, sociologists and others are useful in tailoring remedies to the particular needs of litigants.

The third area concerns the problem of resegregation within the school or classroom even though the school *system* is unitary. Social science data have frequently been drawn upon to show the misclassification, as mentally retarded, of a disproportionate number of minority children and the inappropriateness of the tests used in the classification process. Social science also

---

505. 418 U.S. 717 (1974).

506. 418 U.S. at 782 (Marshall, J., dissenting).

507. Clearly Justice Stewart's concurring opinion seeks this kind of evidence, *see* 418 U.S. at 790-808, but the majority may also be receptive to such evidence. *See* 418 U.S. at 48-52.

508. *See* 413 U.S. at 195-98.

suggests, however, that in the absence of clear racial motive, it may not be appropriate for courts to intervene in various educational policy questions such as ability grouping and tracking, the "mainstreaming" or separation of children who are mentally retarded, and the use of disciplinary measures. The courts more appropriately should intervene only to determine whether otherwise valid educational policies actually are used to resegregate and to ensure that minimal due process requirements are met.

To conclude, the legal issues in the field of public school desegregation have become considerably more complex since the focus shifted away from the southern states to the rest of the country. The question of whether the constitution has been violated now involves a search for unobtrusive and racially benign actions which *might* have contributed—directly and indirectly—to the perpetuation of a dual school system. Once a violation has been established, an even more perplexing question becomes how can segregation effectively and fairly be remedied. This increasing complexity requires and will continue to require that courts work from a more solid foundation of fact than ever before in deciding questions of law. Judges will find it increasingly necessary to consider and rely on the testimony of demographers, educators, psychologists, sociologists, and political scientists simply in order to fully understand the nature of the legal issues that are being presented and the likely impact various remedies will have. It is this legal development which places increasing importance on the research of social scientists.

As was stated in the introduction, this article has not attempted to outline the agenda for cooperation between the law and the social sciences. But in delineating the complex unresolved issues in the law of public school desegregation, we recognize the vast potential of social science research as a valuable evidentiary means to realize the promise of *Brown*. The quality of constitutional justice will be enhanced as social scientists and jurists strive to discover and understand the "unknown and perhaps unknowable."

RANDOM REMARKS ON THE ROLE OF SOCIAL SCIENCES IN THE JUDICIAL DECISION-MAKING PROCESS IN SCHOOL DESEGREGATION CASES

JOHN MINOR WISDOM*

INTRODUCTION

It is an honor to open this timely conference. I hope that the participants, each a distinguished authority in the social sciences and school desegregation litigation, will treat with tolerance my random remarks—old hat to many—on the role of social sciences in the judicial decision-making process in school desegregation cases. The conference is timely because the twentieth anniversary of *Brown v. Board of Education*[1] is a logical point at which to assess the relationship between school desegregation and the enhancement of the life chances of members of minority groups.

I have an old-fashioned fondness for Jhering, Erhlich, and Pound[2] who thought of law as a means to the end of protecting social interests by the authority of the state. These are the early socio-legal thinkers whose spirits hover over this conference. Perhaps *Brown* and its progeny may be rationalized in accord with their thinking without doing violence to Wechsler's doctrine of neutral principles.[3]

I

The conference is especially timely for another reason. It comes less than a month after the Supreme Court's five-to-four decision in the Detroit case, *Milliken v. Bradley*,[4] prohibiting busing across school district lines, absent proof that the school lines were drawn in a racially discriminatory manner or that state action caused interdistrict segregation.

Judges must be wary of their words, especially in discussing recent Supreme Court decisions. An important decision breeds litigation. Judges have to avoid the appearance as well as the fact of prejudging issues in cases, perhaps

---

* Judge, United States Court of Appeals for the Fifth Circuit. This article is an edited version of the keynote speech given on August 18, 1974 at the opening of a conference on *The Courts, Social Science, and School Desegregation* held at Hilton Head Island, S.C., August 18-21, 1974.

1. 347 U.S. 483 (1954).
2. See especially, R. JHERING, LAW AS A MEANS TO AN END (I. Husik transl. 1924); E. EHRLICH, FUNDAMENTAL PRINCIPLES OF THE SOCIOLOGY OF LAW (W. Moll transl. 1936); Pound, *A Survey of Social Interests*, 57 HARV. L. REV. 1 (1943); R. POUND, 3 JURISPRUDENCE, pt. 4 (1959).
3. Wechsler, *Toward Neutral Principles of Constitutional Law*, 73 HARV. L. REV. 1 (1959).
4. 418 U.S. 717 (1974).

yet unborn, but generated by a decision such as *Milliken v. Bradley.* I cannot say that this decision now allows the South to bring in de facto segregation, northern style, to school systems, once they are judicially declared unitary. I can safely say, however, based on the Supreme Court's opinion and the briefs in the *Milliken* case, that social science research appears to have had no effect on the final decision-making process in this case, but may have had a great deal to do with the lower courts' decisions approving interdistrict busing for the Detroit metropolitan area. There was expert testimony by educators, one of whom is attending this conference.[5] Some of the lawyers in *Milliken v. Bradley*[6] and in other important school desegregation cases are also here. They have often relied on social scientists as witnesses.

The district court first found, after evidentiary hearings, that the Detroit District School Board had drawn attendance zones, chosen school sites, and taken other action having the "natural, probable, and actual effect" of promoting segregation.[7] After later hearings, the court held that the only effective relief from de facto segregation in Detroit would be to treat the urban and suburban school districts as related parts of one metropolitan area. Any remedy limited to Detroit proper would increase segregation and the flight to the suburbs.[8] As we all know, of course, in many matters having nothing to do with school desegregation, the trend is toward a city and its satellites pooling their interests, voluntarily and by statute.

When the Detroit case reached the Sixth Circuit, that court, sitting en banc, in a lengthy, carefully considered opinion, affirmed the district court's decision.[9] Judge Weick, dissenting, objected strongly:[10] "The District Court was motivated in its decision by social considerations." The district court had said: "We must bear in mind that the task we are called upon to perform is a social one, which society has been unable to accomplish. In reality, our courts are called upon, in these school cases, to attain a social goal, through the educational system, by using law as a lever."[11] This statement of the trial

---

5. Gordon Foster, Professor of Education and Director of the Florida School Desegregation Consulting Center, University of Miami.

6. Norman Chachkin, NAACP Legal Defense and Education Fund, Inc., and Nathaniel R. Jones, NAACP General Counsel.

7. Bradley v. Milliken, 338 F. Supp. 582, 587-89 (E.D. Mich. 1971), *aff'd*, 484 F.2d 215 (6th Cir. 1973), *rev'd*, 418 U.S. 717 (1974).

8. *See* Bradley v. Milliken, 484 F.2d 215, 242-45 (6th Cir. 1973) (quoting the unreported district court opinion). The district court designated as the "desegregation area" a region comprising fifty-four of eighty-six districts in three counties including and adjoining Detroit, see 345 F. Supp. at 918, 922-37. The districts were further divided into clusters for desegregation. *See* 345 F. Supp. at 928-29.

9. Bradley v. Milliken, 484 F.2d 215 (6th Cir. 1973). The court of appeals, however, vacated the district court's order and remanded the case because of the trial court's failure to join the suburban school districts as necessary parties. *Id.* at 251-52.

10. *Id.* at 260.

11. 484 F.2d at 260-61, quoting a statement made at the pretrial conference by the district court.

judge, Judge Roth, could have been made by Jhering or Erhlich, and quoted with approval by Roscoe Pound. "This is incredible!" said Judge Weick. Judges "should [not] assume to act as legislators, for which they are neither fitted nor qualified. It is enough for judges to perform their judicial function and to abide by the separation of powers doctrine provided by our Constitution."[12] It is interesting to note, however, that Judge Weick quoted[13] from the Taeubers' influential study, *Negroes in Cities*,[14] and cited an article by Karl Taeuber in *Scientific American*.[15]

The Supreme Court's decision in *Milliken v. Bradley* carefully avoids any reference to social considerations. The Court decided, as a matter of law, that "absent an interdistrict violation, there is no basis for an interdistrict remedy. . . ."[16] But let us suppose that to bolster its conclusion and to show its general knowledge of the subject the Supreme Court had added one footnote, say footnote 11,[17] citing Coleman, Pettigrew, Armor, Jencks, Moynihan, Jensen,[18] and other authorities for the propositions that the achievement increment of black children who are bused to obtain racial balance is not increased significantly enough to overcome the educational disadvantage of the children

---

12. 484 F.2d at 261.
13. 484 F.2d at 260.
14. K. Taeuber & A. Taeuber, Negroes in Cities (1965).
15. Taeuber, *Residential Segregation*, 213 Scientific American 12 (August 1965).
16. 418 U.S. 717, 752 (1974).
17. In *Brown v. Board of Educ.* the Court stated that segregation in the public schools had a detrimental effect upon the Negro children. "Whatever may have been the extent of psychological knowledge at the time of *Plessy v. Ferguson*, this finding is amply supported by modern authority." 347 U.S. at 494. Footnote eleven reads:

> K.B. Clark, Effect of Prejudice and Discrimination on Personality Development (Mid-century White House Conference on Children and Youth, 1950); Witmer and Kotinsky, Personality in the Making (1952), c. VI; Deutscher and Chein, The Psychological Effects of Enforced Segregation: A Survey of Social Science Opinion, 26 J. Psychol. 259 (1948); Chein, What Are the Psychological Effects of Segregation Under Conditions of Equal Facilities?, 3 Int. J. Opinion and Attitude Res. 229 (1949); Brameld, Educational Costs in Discrimination and National Welfare (MacIver, ed., 1949), 44-48; Frazier, the Negro in the United States (1949), 674-81. And see generally Myrdal, An American Dilemma (1974).

18. James S. Coleman is the principal author of *Equality of Educational Opportunity*, also called the *Coleman Report*, prepared for the Department of Health, Education, and Welfare in 1966. Thomas F. Pettigrew is the principal consultant to the 1967 U.S. Commission on Civil Rights report, *Racial Isolation in the Public Schools*, and the author of *Racially Separate or Together?* which begins with the statement, "[t]his book has grown out of my deep conviction that genuine racial integration can and must be achieved in the United States." Their views differ from those of David J. Armor and Christopher Jencks on the causes for blacks falling behind whites on achievement tests. See, for example, Armor, *The Evidence on Busing*, in The Great School Bus Controversy 81 (N. Mills ed. 1973); C. Jencks, Inequality (1972). Frederick Mosteller and Daniel Moynihan reanalyzed the *Coleman Report* data in *On Equality of Educational Opportunity*. Arthur Jensen's views may perhaps best be seen in Jensen, *How Much Can We Boost IQ and Scholastic Achievement?*, 39 Harv. Ed. Rev. 1 (1969). There is a vast amount of solid research on school desegregation, much of it by participants in this conference. But there is little agreement on methodology or conclusions, even when the data relied on are the same as, for example, that in the *Coleman Report* or *Racial Isolation in the Public Schools*.

from low socioeconomic backgrounds; that the feeling of control over one's destiny has a stronger relationship to achievement than all the school factors together; that the equal protection clause may require affirmative action to integrate the schools, but integration cannot be equated with equal educational opportunity. Or, since, to put it mildly, it is difficult to find a common denominator of the conclusions of these social scientists, and others that might be cited, the footnote may have started, "See generally . . . ."[19] Would the decision have been said to have been based on sociology rather than law?

In any event, the Detroit case was decided opportunely for this conference. Perhaps some of the participants attending the conference may be able to peer down the road and tell us the social consequences of that decision. What *will* be its impact on the trend toward metropolitan-wide solutions to the financing and delivery of public services,[20] or on the preservation of the inner core of cities—their historic areas, for example? What effect will it have on urban and suburban schools, on the socioeconomic gap between the races, on the educational and psychological effects of accelerated isolation of the races? A fruitful source of sociological inquiry will be to determine what data may justify an interdistrict remedy which the majority in *Milliken v. Bradley* permits when there is segregation traceable to interdistrict constitutional violations. Justice Stewart, in his concurring opinion, emphasized that interdistrict busing might be "proper, or even necessary, in other factual situations" than that presented in *Milliken v. Bradley*.[21]

II

Sociology has always played a part in the decision-making process, although frequently it comes in wearing a mask. Sometimes the mask is public policy or the interests of justice, sometimes judicial notice or common knowledge, sometimes legislative or constitutional facts. In these instances the judge, perhaps unwittingly, may be functioning as a sociologist without benefit of witnesses and solid empirical data and perhaps is treating the litigants unfairly.[22]

---

19. The reference in *Brown* to Gunnar Myrdal's *An American Dilemma* stated: "And see generally . . . ." In the hierarchy of citations "and see generally" ranks as the lowliest citation of authority. It has not so been ranked, however, by the uninformed critics of *Brown v. Board of Educ.*

20. *See, e.g.*, the Minnesota plan for the seven county Twin Cities area, contested in Village of Burnsville v. Onischuk, 301 Minn. _____, 222 N.W. 2d 523 (1974), *appeal filed*, 43 U.S.L.W. 3443 (U.S. Dec. 9, 1974) (No. 74-718).

21. 418 U.S. at 755.

22. Under the guise of judicial note [footnote omitted] some courts have conducted independent researches on their own in order to learn social facts not so notorious and indisputable as to be capable of true judicial notice. [Footnote omitted.] They have not usually obtained the information from the primary sources, but rather have had resort to libraries, [footnote omitted] experts, [footnote omitted] government agencies, [footnote omitted] or even employees of an agency which is a party to the case. The greatest

In *Brown I* Chief Justice Warren, speaking for a unanimous court, said:[23]

> To separate [Negro school children] from others of similar age and qualifications solely because of their race generates a feeling of inferiority as to their status in the community that may affect their hearts and minds in a way unlikely ever to be undone.

For Dr. Kenneth B. Clark, who testified in several of the school cases as to his own important studies and organized the social science evidence for the plaintiffs in *Brown I*, the role of the social scientists was crucial in supplying evidence that segregation itself meant inequality.[24]

For Professor Edmond Cahn, one of our great legal philosophers, Chief Justice Warren's statement was a truism, "a fact of common knowledge (e.g. that a fire burns, that a cold causes snuffles . . .)."[25] For him, "[s]egregation does involve stigma; the community knows it does."[26] Dr. Clark's studies were limited in that they did not isolate the effect of segregated schooling from non-school factors such as the effect of a disadvantaged socioeconomic status or of family background. I tend to agree with Edmond Cahn. I too should hate to think that the constitutional right of Negroes *not* to be segregated in education or in any other segment of American life rested on the social science evidence brought forth in *Brown*.

Many leaders in the massive resistance to *Brown* ignored or did not know that Chief Justice Warren's statement had its counterpart in *Plessy v. Ferguson*,[27] the 1896 case that sanctioned Jim Crow laws under the "separate but equal" doctrine. In *Plessy*, the author of the opinion, whose name, significantly, was Brown, observed:[28]

> We consider the underlying fallacy of the plaintiff's argument to consist in the assumption that the enforced separation of the two races stamps the colored race with a badge of inferiority. If this be so, it is not by reason of anything found in the act, but solely because the colored race chooses to put that construction upon it.

---

objection to such practice is the disregard of the parties to the litigation, who are given no opportunity to be heard. [Footnote omitted.]

Note, *Social and Economic Facts–Appraisal of Suggested Techniques for Presenting Them to the Courts*, 61 HARV. L. REV. 692, 697 (1948). *See also* Wyzanski, *A Trial Judge's Freedom and Responsibility*, 65 HARV. L. REV. 1281, 1295-96 (1952).

23. 347 U.S. at 494.

24. Clark, *The Desegregation Cases: Criticism of the Social Scientist's Role*, 5 VILL. L. REV. 224-26 (1959).

25. Cahn, *Jurisprudence*, 30 N.Y.U.L. REV. 150, 161 (1955).

26. *Id.* at 158. *See* Black, *The Lawfulness of the Segregation Decisions*, 69 YALE L.J. 421, 424-26 (1960), in which Professor Charles Black wrote that it is a "canard" to say that "principal reliance was placed on the formally 'scientific' authorities, which are relegated to a footnote and treated as merely corroboratory of common sense." *Id.* at 430 n. 25. *See also* Pollak, *Racial Discrimination and Judicial Integrity: A Reply to Professor Wechsler*, 108 U. PA. L. REV. 1, 26-30 (1959).

27. 163 U.S. 537 (1896). Barton Bernstein, for one, says: "[S]ociological and psychological theories controlled the court's [sic] decision" in *Plessy*. Bernstein, Plessy v. Ferguson: *Conservative Sociological Jurisprudence*, 48 J. NEGRO HIST. 196, 198 (1963).

28. 163 U.S. at 551.

This is no less a sociological statement than Chief Justice Warren's language in *Brown*.

The road is not smooth for the use of social science evidence in the courts. Testimony of experts for the plaintiffs forces the defendants to come forward with experts. If the trial is prolonged and played up in the communications media, the public impression is that the court is elevating sociology at the expense of law. And trial judges, who have less insulation than appellate judges, are sensitive to public opinion. There are not many Frank Johnsons, Bryan Simpsons, Herbert Christenberrys, and Skelly Wrights. All judges have cut their eyeteeth on the theory that they fill in only the tiniest of interstices between existing rules, and a Holmes or a Cardozo does not come along every day to distinguish between the expansible and the non-expansible interstices.[29] Judge Weick's observation in *Milliken* represents the point of view most lawyers and laymen share: judges should stay within the judicial function; social considerations are for legislators.[30]

Segregationists, to a man, criticized the Supreme Court's holding in *Brown* as one that was based on sociology rather than law, as if the two must be antithetical rather than closely related or complementary. For many uninformed people, even now, Gunnar Myrdal was the chief authority the Court relied upon, although his was only one of several names in a footnote. Even James Reston, writing for the *New York Times*, subtitled his article on the case, "Court Founded Its Segregation Ruling on Hearts and Minds Rather than Laws."[31] On this point many advocates of integration were willing to agree with Reston. They regarded the resort to social science testimony as a new approach to school desegregation, and they were proud of the ability and trial strategy of the plaintiffs' lawyers.

As everyone knows, the Supreme Court held in *Brown I* that "separate but equal . . . educational facilities are inherently unequal."[32] And, "even though the physical facilities and other 'tangible' factors may be equal," segregation "deprive[s] the children of the minority group of equal educational opportunities."[33]

There are certain aspects of the opinion that diminish the importance many persons attach to the sociological proof of harm caused by segregated schooling. The Supreme Court, in its opinion, did not refer to the testimony of Dr. Kenneth Clark, who testified in the three cases consolidated with *Brown v. Board of Education*, and to other witnesses, although more than forty social

29. Justice Holmes, dissenting in Southern Pacific Co. v. Jensen, 244 U.S. 205, 221 (1917), said: "Mr. Justice Cardozo used 'this flashing epigram' in developing his own theory that 'in every department of the law . . . the social value of a rule has become a test of growing power and importance.' " B. CARDOZO, THE NATURE OF THE JUDICIAL PROCESS 27 (1921).

30. Bradley v. Milliken, 484 F.2d 215, 261 (6th Cir. 1973) (dissenting opinion).

31. Reston, *A Sociological Decision*, N.Y. Times, May 18, 1954, at 14, col. 4.

32. 347 U.S. at 495.

33. 347 U.S. at 493.

scientists and educators testified in four of the five school desegregation cases[34] that filled four volumes of the record. The Court did not refer to a lengthy statement, filed as an appendix to the plaintiffs' briefs, signed by thirty-two sociologists, anthropologists, psychologists, and psychiatrists.[35] Moreover, the Court did not, in terms, overrule *Plessy v. Ferguson*. That case is yet to be specifically overruled. Justice Douglas still cites it as viable authority[36] and has pointed out that *Milliken v. Bradley* is a retreat from *Plessy v. Ferguson.*[37]

The transcript of the oral argument before the Supreme Court in the first round of the segregation cases shows that the plaintiffs' lawyers[38] stressed the inherent vice of racial classification rather than the harmful lack of equal educational opportunity.[39] Mr. Robert Carter, now Judge, in the first argument in *Brown* in 1952, contended that under the plaintiffs' theory, "[the Supreme Court does] not have to reach the [sociological] findings, because we maintain that this is an unconstitutional classification."[40] Mr., now Justice, Marshall, arguing a companion case during reargument in 1953, asserted: "[Y]ou cannot separate people or denote that one is to go here and one is to go there even if the facilities are absolutely equal."[41] Also in the reargument, Mr., now Judge, Robinson argued that the purpose of the fourteenth amendment was

---

34. The cases referred to were *Brown v. Board of Educ.*, on appeal from the Kansas federal district court, *Briggs v. Elliott*, on appeal from a federal district court in South Carolina, *Davis v. County School Bd.*, on appeal from a federal district court in Virginia, *Gebhart v. Belton*, on *cert.* to the Supreme Court of Delaware, and *Bolling v. Sharpe*, on *cert.* to the Court of Appeals for the District of Columbia. The first four cases were argued separately but resulted in a consolidated opinion, Brown v. Board of Educ., 347 U.S. 483 (1954). The latter case resulted in the opinion in Bolling v. Sharpe, 347 U.S. 497 (1954). Together the cases are often referred to as the Segregation Cases.

35. *The Effects of Segregation and the Consequences of Desegregation: A Social Science Statement*, reprinted in 37 MINN. L. REV. 427 (1953) (appendix to appellants' briefs in *Brown v. Board of Educ.*, *Davis v. County School Bd.*, and *Briggs v. Elliott*, argued together before the Supreme Court and for which the Court issued a consolidated opinion, 347 U.S. 483 (1954)).

36. "But Plessy v. Ferguson has not yet been overruled on its mandate that separate facilities be equal." Gomperts v. Chase, 404 U.S. 1237, 1240 (1971). Again, dissenting in Spencer v. Kugler, 404 U.S. 1027, 1031 (1972), Justice Douglas, wrote: "But there can be *de facto* segregation without the State's being implicated in the creation of the dual system and it is in such situations that *Plessy's* mandate that separate facilities be equal has continuing force." Gayle v. Browder, 352 U.S. 903 (1956), *aff'g per curiam* 142 F. Supp. 707 (M.D. Ala. 1956), however, may be read as silently overruling *Plessy v. Ferguson*.

37. Dissenting opinion, Milliken v. Bradley, 418 U.S. at 759.

38. Three of the better known attorneys who represented the plaintiffs are Thurgood Marshall, now on the Supreme Court; Spottswood Robinson, now on the Court of Appeals for the District of Columbia; and Robert L. Carter, former General Counsel of the NAACP and now District Judge in the Southern District of New York.

39. Kaplan, *Segregation Litigation and the Schools—Part II: The General Northern Problem*, 58 NW. U.L. REV. 157, 173 (1963). Carter has concluded that the principal impact of *Brown* has been its encouragement of the idea among blacks that equality may be demanded as a right, not petitioned for as a favor. *See* Carter, *The Warren Court and Desegregation*, 67 MICH. L. REV. 237, 246-48 (1968).

40. 21 U.S.L.W. 3161, 3163 (Dec. 16, 1952).

41. 22 U.S.L.W. 3157, 3159 (Dec. 15, 1953).

to prevent the imposition of "governmentally cast distinctions, predicated upon race."[42]

Those who have studied *Plessy v. Ferguson* in depth will see a similarity between this argument and that of Albion W. Tourgée, attorney for Plessy, whose words inspired the first Justice Harlan. Tourgée said,[43]

> Why not require all colored people to walk on one side of the street and whites on the other. One side of the street may be just as good as the other . . . . The question is not as to the equality of the privileges enjoyed, but the right of the State to label one citizen as white and another as colored in the common enjoyment of a public highway.

Tourgée declared, in words Justice Harlan paraphrased: "There is no caste here. . . . Justice is pictured blind and her daughter, The Law, ought at least to be color-blind."[44]

Within a short time after the segregation cases, the Court, in a number of per curiam opinions simply citing *Brown*, struck down segregation on public golf courses,[45] on beaches,[46] in parks,[47] in seating in public facilities,[48] in athletic contests,[49] and in other situations where there was separation by racial classification, although there was no sociological evidence of harm, and no possibility of harm except from the stigma inherent in racial segregation.

These cases suggest that the Court itself interprets *Brown* as resting on the principle that forced separation of the races is an invidious classification violative of the equal protection clause. In this respect, it is significant that in *Brown* the Court relied on *Sweatt v. Painter*[50] and *McLaurin v. Oklahoma State Regents*,[51] two decisions which were concerned with segregated higher education. The Court noted that it had, in those cases, resorted to "intangible considerations" which were "incapable of objective measurement."[52] These considerations did away with the necessity of relying on social science testimony which, if leaned on heavily, might create the impression that the Court was legislating social goals into the law. I think, therefore, that while Professor Cahn may have overstated the ineffectiveness of the sociological evidence in *Brown*, that evidence played only a minor role in the decision.[53]

Whatever effect the Court gave to the social science testimony, unarticu-

42. 22 U.S.L.W. at 3157.
43. Brief for the Plaintiff in Error at 29, Plessy v. Ferguson, 163 U.S. 537 (1896).
44. Brief for the Plaintiff in Error at 19, Plessy v. Ferguson, 163 U.S. 537 (1896).
45. Holmes v. Atlanta, 350 U.S. 879 (1955).
46. Mayor & City Council of Baltimore City v. Dawson, 350 U.S. 877 (1955).
47. New Orleans City Park Improvement Ass'n v. Detiege, 358 U.S. 54 (1958).
48. Johnson v. Virginia, 373 U.S. 61 (1963); Schiro v. Bynum, 375 U.S. 395 (1964).
49. State Athletic Comm'n v. Dorsey, 359 U.S. 533 (1959).
50. 399 U.S. 629 (1950).
51. 339 U.S. 637 (1950).
52. 347 U.S. at 493.
53. *But see* Fiss, *Racial Imbalance in the Public Schools: The Constitutional Concepts*, 78 HARV. L. REV. 564, 590-94 (1965).

lated in the opinion, *Brown* was the product of irresistible social and political forces—"an idea whose time had come."[54] But the opinion broke no new ground in judicial methodology. The Court rested its decision on the content of the fourteenth amendment in the context of the time, confident that it was interpreting the Constitution as a living document for all times. Had there been no social data in the record, no footnote eleven, Chief Justice Warren, backed by all the Court, would still have been able (1) to start with the premise, as he did, that "we cannot turn the clock back," but "must consider public education in the light of its full development and its present place in American life";[55] (2) to argue in a traditional judicial manner, as he did, by analogy from *Sweatt* and *McLaurin*, that "intangible considerations" apply with "added force to children in grade and high school";[56] and (3) to conclude that "separate but equal" is "inherently unequal."[57] The social science evidence was the kind of support a court likes to find in a record to lend factual and scientific aura to a result sustainable by other, perhaps purely abstract and sometimes formalistically legal, considerations, but dictated by the moral necessity of changing social attitudes.

Paradoxically, I believe that the reaction of many vocal critics of *Brown* who characterized the decision as based on sociology, rather than law, has had a healthy effect on the use of social science research in the decisional process. Courts, since *Muller v. Oregon*, have respected the "Brandeis-type" brief supporting socially-oriented legislation.[58] In *Muller*, however, and in similar cases, as Professor Paul Freund has pointed out,[59] the data was used to *sustain* social legislation and might be considered legislative or constitutional facts of which a legislature might be presumed to have knowledge. In and after *Brown*, this type of extra-legal evidence has been used to attack legislation. The criticism of *Brown* focused the attention of judges and lawyers on the propriety and value of empirical data and social studies at both the trial and appellate levels. Statistics became more important to courts. "[F]igures speak and when they do, Courts listen . . . ," Chief Judge John Brown of the Fifth Circuit Court of Appeals has written.[60]

What seemed at first to be antagonism between social science and law has now developed into a love match. What began in the field of education spread to many other fields. In case after case the Fifth Circuit, among other courts,

54. "There is no army greater than an idea whose time has come" is a statement made famous by Senator Everett Dirksen on May 19, 1964, at a press conference concerning passage of the Civil Rights Act of 1964, but Victor Hugo said it first.

55. 347 U.S. at 492.

56. 347 U.S. at 493-94.

57. 347 U.S. at 495.

58. Muller v. Oregon, 208 U.S. 412 (1908).

59. Freund, *Review of Facts in Constitutional Cases*, in SUPREME COURT AND SUPREME LAW 47, 49-50 (E. Cahn ed. 1954); P. FREUND, ON UNDERSTANDING THE SUPREME COURT 88-90 (1949).

60. Brooks v. Beto, 366 F.2d 1, 9 (5th Cir. 1966), *cert. denied*, 386 U.S. 975 (1967).

has relied on studies developed by social scientists and other scientists to show pollution, unlawful exclusion of blacks from the jury system, employment discrimination, arbitrary or discriminatory use of the death penalty, discrimination against women, the need for reapportionment, and the cure for malapportionment of various public bodies. Throughout the country, educational centers in various universities have prepared desegregation plans at the request of school boards and district judges.

III

Since *Brown*, in school cases involving de jure segregation, findings of fact are no longer needed to establish a substantive constitutional violation. This is the value of the de jure/de facto dichotomy—*if it has a value.* But fact findings are still needed in devising a remedy in de jure cases.

In de facto segregation cases, Professor Fiss has pointed out that "a principle requiring equality of educational opportunity must be abstracted from the equal protection clause. . . ."[61] In applying this principle, the court must make "the empirical judgment whether the opportunity afforded Negro children is significantly and systematically inferior to that afforded others."[62] This inequality may be apparent on its face. When it is not, a court is required to probe beyond the nominal level to determine whether this factual inequality exists. A court must make another judgment, "whether there is an adequate justification for any existing substantial difference in educational opportunity."[63]

Ten years ago, advocates of segregation asked the courts to make such a judgment. In *Stell v. Savannah-Chatham County Board of Education*,[64] a de jure case arising in Georgia, parents of white children intervened. They sought to justify racial segregation on the ground that social science research had demonstrated that it would be educationally harmful to black children from disadvantaged environments to be forced into competition with white children. Their proof rested on the testimony and studies of several social scientists, some of whom one would have to acknowledge as legally qualified to testify.[65] Counsel for the black plaintiffs was Mrs., now Judge, Constance Baker Motley,[66] who had ably represented James Meredith in desegregating the University of Mississippi. She objected to the social science testimony as irrelevant, in light of the *Brown* case. District Judge Scarlett, who had a long record of re-

61. Fiss, *supra* note 53, at 588.
62. *Id.*
63. Fiss, *supra* note 53, at 589.
64. 220 F. Supp. 667 (S.D. Ga. 1963), *rev'd*, 333 F.2d 55 (5th Cir. 1963), *cert. denied*, 379 U.S. 933 (1964).
65. For example, Dr. Henry Garrett had been the head of the Department of Psychology at Columbia University and had taught there for more than thirty years.
66. Constance Baker Motley is now U.S. District Judge in the Southern District of New York.

versals by the Fifth Circuit in civil rights cases, held that "[t]he factual nature of the finding of injury through segregation in Brown opened the door" to the intervenors' proof.[67] On the basis of the "scientific" evidence, he found that Negro children tested well below white children in various tests and that there was "no evidence whatsoever . . . to show that racial integration of the schools could reduce these differences"; the differences are "attributable in large part to hereditary factors."[68] He added: "Whatever psychological injury may be sustained by a Negro child . . . is increased rather than abated by forced intermixture . . . ."[69] Accordingly, Judge Scarlett dismissed the plaintiffs' suit to desegregate Savannah schools. The Fifth Circuit did not permit Judge Scarlett to stand *Brown* on its head. Our court peremptorily reversed the decision and reprimanded him for abuse of his discretionary powers.[70]

It is interesting that in the Detroit case,[71] the trial judge, Judge Roth, permitted the suburban school boards to take the deposition of Dr. David Armor who earlier had written, based on his studies of various busing "experiences," that "busing is *not* an effective policy instrument for raising the achievement of black students or for increasing interracial harmony."[72] Judge Roth later refused to receive it in evidence on the ground that it was irrelevant; it represented "a new rationale for a return to the discredited 'separate but equal' policy."[73] Indeed, he excluded all evidence on the questionable value of crossdistrict busing. As noted earlier, in the Sixth Circuit

---

67. 220 F. Supp. at 678.

68. 220 F. Supp. at 683.

69. 220 F. Supp. at 684.

70. 333 F.2d 55 (5th Cir. 1963), *cert. denied*, 379 U.S. 933 (1964). In a case similar to *Stell*, District Court Judge Mize in Evers v. Jackson Municipal Separate School Dist., 232 F. Supp. 241 (S.D. Miss. 1964), found from "uncontradicted" testimony by seven "distinguished scientists" that:

> The evidence was conclusive to the effect that the cranial capacity and brain size of the average Negro is approximately ten per cent less than that of the average white person of similar age and size, and that brain size is correlated with intelligence.

Id. at 247. He also concluded from other evidence

> that white and Negro pupils of public school age have substantially different educational aptitudes and learning patterns which are innate in character and do not arise out of economic or social circumstance and which cannot therefore be changed or overcome by intermixed schooling . . . .

Id. at 248. He thus concluded that segregation of races was the only reasonable classification by the state and that *Brown* need not be followed under either *res judicata* or *stare decisis*. However, Judge Mize struck down the segregation employed on grounds that it was bound by prior Fifth Circuit holdings.

> Although it is contrary to the facts and the law applicable thereto, this Court feels that it is required to enter an order making permanent the temporary injunction heretofore entered herein . . . .

Id. at 255.

71. Milliken v. Bradley, 418 U.S. 717 (1974), *rev'g* 484 F.2d 215 (6th Cir. 1973), *aff'g* 345 F. Supp. 914 (E.D. Mich. 1972), and 338 F. Supp. 582 (E.D. Mich. 1971).

72. Armor, *The Evidence on Busing*, 28 PUB. INTEREST 90, 115 (Summer 1972) (emphasis in original).

73. Bradley v. Milliken, 345 F. Supp. 914, 921 (E.D. Mich. 1972).

Court of Appeals, Judge Weick in his dissent, without citing *Stell*, concluded, as had Judge Scarlett in *Stell*, that sociological opinions and evidence should have been admitted because the Supreme Court had rested its decision in *Brown* on sociological data.[74]

At this stage in school desegregation, when the nature of the remedy is important and district courts have broad latitude in using their equitable powers, social science is certain to play an important part in the decisional process.

In 1971, in *Swann v. Charlotte-Mecklenburg Board of Education*,[75] the Supreme Court dealt with de jure segregation in the Charlotte, North Carolina school system. The mandate in all such cases is to dismantle the dual school system lock, stock, and barrel. But the question of *how* to dismantle is the door through which social science research enters. Racially neutral plans may not be sufficient. Affirmative remedial action is required: for example, in the appropriate site selection of new schools, pairing and grouping of noncontiguous school districts, faculty ratios, and greater representation of blacks at the administrative level. However, the most obvious and effective remedy is busing of students. This is the remedy that has worked in the South, certainly in the non-metropolitan areas.

In *Swann* the Supreme Court unequivocally approved busing as a tool of school desegregation—subject to certain conditions. The conditions are unspecific: "the time of distance of travel [must not be] so great as to either risk the health of the children or significantly impinge on the educational process."[76] This is an invitation, if not an advice, to parents and to school boards to produce social scientists as witnesses. It will then be the duty of the trial judge to weigh their testimony and to make findings showing the correlation between the proposed busing and (1) "the health of children to be bused" and (2) the extent to which busing may "impinge on the educational process." If such a case reaches the level of the courts of appeals and the Supreme Court, the appellate court must decide whether the evidence is sufficient to support the trial judge's finding. I expect white parents to come forth some day with social scientists producing data perhaps in the form of testimony and studies by David Armor or Christopher Jencks showing that busing raises the achievement level so slightly that it is not worth the trauma in individual cases or the friction it causes in the community; that the socioeconomic background of a child is a more significant factor in achievement tests than attending a desegregated school, but that this factor is inextricably bound with residential patterns, difficult if not impossible to break; that school achievement tests bear only a slight relation to economic achievement or life chances

74. Bradley v. Milliken, 484 F.2d 215, 265 (6th Cir. 1973).
75. 402 U.S. 1 (1971).
76. 402 U.S. at 30-31.

after children have finished their schooling. That kind of sociological evidence, if we may call it evidence, was in Dr. Armor's excluded deposition in the Detroit case. The courts of appeals and the Supreme Court have not ruled on the relevancy of such testimony under *Swann*. In the Fourth Circuit, however, Judge Sobeloff, in a special concurring opinion in *Brunson*,[77] gave it short shrift as a return, under another name, to the doctrine of the inherent inferiority of blacks as against whites. If such testimony based on social studies is admissible under the *Swann* proviso, proponents of busing will have to come forward with countervailing social science evidence.

Keyes v. School District No. 1[78] arose in a more difficult context for the minorities seeking desegregation. In Denver there is a tri-ethnic population; for decades blacks and Hispanos[79] were concentrated in the central core of the city. But there had never been de jure segregation in Denver in the sense that schools had been segregated by statute, as they had been in the South. The district court found, however, that in one residential section there had been acts of de jure segregation stemming from deliberate, intentional segregative policies on the part of school officials—as demonstrated by a policy of concentrating blacks in black schools, by new school construction, and by boundary changes for school zones.[80] Racial separation in the school system as a whole, however, was not attributable to de jure segregation. The court held that "an equal educational opportunity is not being provided at the . . . segregated [minority] schools . . . ,"[81] and therefore ordered those schools desegregated. The district court relied on the testimony, among others, of Dr. James D. Coleman, author of the *Coleman Report*, Dr. Neil Sullivan, Commissioner of Massachusetts State Board of Education, and Dr. Robert O'Reilly, Assistant Director of Research at New York State Department of Education.

The Supreme Court held, first, that the illegal acts forming the basis of the de jure finding had *reciprocal effects* throughout the system and therefore called for a *system-wide remedy*; and that the de jure finding as to part of the system raised a presumption that racial imbalance elsewhere was due to a policy of segregation which shifted the burden of proof to the school district.

The Court adopted a limited definition of de jure segregation: "the differentiating factor between *de jure* segregation and so-called de facto segregation . . . is *purpose* or *intent* to segregate."[82] In a *Swann*-type case it would relate to the substantive constitutional violation as well as to remedy. Social scientists would have to study and testify on the purpose and natural effect

---

77. Brunson v. Board of Trustees of School Dist. No. 1, 429 F.2d 820, 823, 826 (4th Cir. 1970) (separate concurring opinion).

78. 413 U.S. 189 (1973).

79. Hispanos is the term used by Justice Brennan writing for the Court in *Keyes*.

80. *See* 313 F. Supp. 61, 64-69 (D. Colo. 1970), *aff'd in part and rev'd in part*, 445 F.2d 990 (10th Cir. 1971), *modified and remanded*, 413 U.S. 189 (1973).

81. 313 F. Supp. at 83.

82. 413 U.S. at 208 (emphasis by the Court).

of residential segregation, site selection of schools, "feeder" schools, tracking, and other factors from which an "intention" to segregate blacks and Hispanos could be inferred.[83] Then, if busing is employed as a remedy, the requirements of the *Swann* proviso will have to be met, without crossing school district lines.

In *Keyes,* the Court remanded the case for findings, and on remand the trial court found that the policies and practices of the school board established de jure segregation by the creation of a dual school system.[84]

IV

The Fifth Circuit includes the states of Florida, Texas, Georgia, Louisiana, Alabama, and Mississippi. I have served on that court since July 1957. I remember that in 1960, six years after *Brown*, the admission of three little Negro girls to one class in one white school in New Orleans was regarded as a great stride forward. I remember when transfers under the fraudulent pupil placement law and grade-a-year plans were considered radical.[85] When I see Tulane play the University of Mississippi in a football game with black players on each team, I think of the riots and violence that took place when James Meredith became the first black to attend the University of Mississippi. Only a few months ago, James Meredith won the Democratic nomination for Congress in his district. Today, five of Alabama's six best basketball players are black. Recently Governor George Wallace appointed a black to his cabinet. Spectacular turn-arounds do indeed show that blacks have come a long way since 1954. And I am proud that our court, among other federal courts, has contributed to recognition of the civil rights of minorities.

Nevertheless, I have a nagging feeling that it is not how far the blacks have come that is important, but how far they still have to go. It is particularly disturbing to see a white school become a desegregated school, then a black school; to see the black population in New Orleans and Atlanta public schools increase in ten years from 37 per cent to nearly 80 per cent—to 83 per cent in the seventh, eighth, and ninth grades. It is even more disturbing to know that a large number of the 20 per cent of the students who are white have a socioeconomic background similar to that of the 80 per cent. The effect is to es-

83. *See* 413 U.S. at 211-12.

84. *See* Keyes v. School Dist. No. 1, 368 F. Supp. 207, 209-10 (D. Colo. 1973).

85. The Supreme Court in Shuttlesworth v. Birmingham Bd. of Educ., 258 U.S. 101, *aff'g* 162 F. Supp. 372 (N.D. Ala. 1958), gave its approval to the use of pupil placement laws as a desegregation device. Such laws allowed (black) students to apply to transfer from their segregated schools to schools of the opposite race (white schools) in their district. All too frequently, however, a further barrier was superimposed on the pupil placement system, that being the grade-a-year limitation so that only one grade of students could request transfer the first year of the program and one additional grade each succeeding year. The combined programs effectively retarded significant integration for years. When it finally became clear that their purpose and effect was to frustrate integration, their application was enjoined. *See also* Read, *Judicial Evolution of the Law of School Integration Since* Brown v. Board of Education, 39 LAW & CONTEMP. PROB. no. 1, at 7, 19 nn. 48 & 49 (1975).

tablish an inelastic caste system. The affluent whites have sent their children to private schools. Most of the middle class whites, association with whom would produce a social class climate favorable to blacks in schools, have fled to the suburbs or sent their children to private schools. Apparently, too, the blacks accepted in private schools come from upper and middle class Negro families. The Detroit case will unquestionably increase the social stratification. Blacks, Hispanos, and disadvantaged whites will remain in the inner core of decaying cities, trapped in a vicious circle that, like all circles, has no definable beginning or end, but does have describable parts: inferior schools, poor housing, and low socioeconomic status. I can understand, therefore, the disillusionment black nationalists have with the progress and effectiveness of school desegregation. I can understand how separation of the races, if it means local control by blacks for blacks, may generate not the feeling of inferiority which the Supreme Court found in *Brown*, but a feeling of pride and respect—if the quality of education can be raised and economic opportunity increased. I do not approve of separatism under the guise of decentralization, or under any guise, but I think that I understand its motivation. Blacks suffer from a special stigma not carried by other deprived groups. It is what Professor Charles Black refers to as "walled-off inferiority";[86] a legacy of three centuries of slavery and segregation, one that was legitimized in *Dred Scott.*[87]

I have received some enlightenment but very little comfort from the social science studies I have read. Perhaps, as Dean Frank T. Read has said, "One tool—the constitutional command of equal educational opportunity for all races articulated in *Brown*—cannot and should not be expected to solve alone the problem of segregated education."[88] He is right, of course. Judges should profit from other disciplines. In a sense, a judicial decision represents social science in action. Judges should acquire more knowledge of the social sciences to enable them to fulfil their policy-making function of using law as a means to the ends of serving society wisely and to its good.

Still, I have a deep conviction that the moral philosophy underlying the principle of equality established in the Second American Constitution that arose from the ashes of the Civil War is the primary source of hope for civilized racial relations in an integrated society.[89] I cannot extract this hope from

86. Black, *The Lawfulness of the Segregation Decisions*, 69 YALE L.J. 421, 427 (1960).

87. Scott v. Sandford, 60 U.S. (19 How.) 393 (1857).

88. Read, *supra* note 85, at 48.

89. The task the appellate courts are really engaged in is deciding what the law should be. But, at least in some cases, appellate judges may view a decision as one which ought to be based on moral or ethical imperatives. The point is that in these circumstances social science research may have relatively little to add. For example, the impression one gathers after reading *Brown v. Board of Education* is that the social science evidence on the effects of racially segregated schools made little difference to the case's outcome. Even if the social science evidence had been considerably more open to the question than it was, the Court would likely have concluded that confining children of different races to separate schools violated the

my limited exposure to social science studies of the relationship between segregation and public education.

---

fourteenth amendment's equal protection clause because it was "morally wrong," if for no other reason.

Lochner, *Some Limits on the Application of Social Science Research in the Legal Process*, 1973 LAW & SOCIAL ORDER 815, 838-39.

THE IMPACT OF SOCIAL SCIENCE EVIDENCE ON THE JUDGE: A PERSONAL COMMENT

J. BRAXTON CRAVEN, JR.*

We all do it: even the best of us overread opinions. From the first weeks of law school, iterated and reiterated through our professional lives, we have heard and understood that the opinion of an appellate court is to be read in its own fact context; but we remember a ringing phrase longer than we remember its factual setting. And so we respond to the opinion author's exhortation and hyperbole. Who can forget "neither black schools nor white schools, just schools,"[1] or "the obligation of every school district is to terminate dual school systems at once and to operate now and hereafter only unitary schools,"[2] or "[f]urther delays will not be tolerated in this circuit."[3] But how many of us remember that the first phrase was written in a rural fact setting presenting none of the insoluble integration problems encountered in the cities, and that the second and third were directed toward recalcitrant school boards that had stubbornly set their face against compliance with new constitutional doctrine? The author of such inspirational rubric is sometimes astonished at overcompliance by those who read it out of context.

John Mull never tired of telling me in my first ten years of law practice to "salt down the facts."[4] Facts are the premises of a syllogism to invoke a legal doctrine. I once knew another distinguished lawyer whose respect for the facts was so great that he commonly drew the judgment he sought before drafting his complaint to make sure he pleaded enough facts. Implicit in the Supreme Court's doctrine of "constitutional facts"[5] is its recognition that it can write law all day long to no avail unless its abstractions can be brought to bear upon the conduct of human affairs.

---

* Judge, United States Court of Appeals for the Fourth Circuit. [Judge Craven is the author of Bradley v. School Bd. of City of Richmond, 462 F.2d 1058 (4th Cir. 1972), *aff'd by an equally divided Court*, 412 U.S. 92 (1973). Editors' Note.]

1. Green v. County School Bd., 391 U.S. 430, 442 (1968).
2. Alexander v. Holmes County Bd. of Educ., 396 U.S. 19, 20 (1969).
3. Nesbit v. Statesville City Bd. of Educ., 418 F.2d 1040, 1042 (4th Cir. 1969).
4. The late John M. Mull, Esquire, of Morganton, North Carolina, was forty-four years my senior and my law partner.
5. Legislative facts are those which the court uses to develop law or policy. 2 K. DAVIS, ADMINISTRATIVE LAW TREATISE § 15.03 (1958). Constitutional facts are legislative facts that bear on the constitutionality of governmental practices. P. BREST, PROCESS OF CONSTITUTIONAL DECISION-MAKING (1974). For an example of a case turning on constitutional facts, see Furman v. Georgia, 408 U.S. 238 (1972).

A facetious complaint among lawyers is that they sometimes have trouble identifying the case they tried below as the one being described in the appellate opinion. That this is even partly true illustrates what everyone knows: that judges much more often disagree on the facts or the proper inferences to be drawn from the facts than on the law.

To give a simplistic answer to a difficult question: the role that the social sciences ought to play in the judicial decision-making process is, of course, the same as the role of any other science, whether medical, electronic, or atomic. In short, all sources of human information and knowledge properly contribute to the determination of the facts.

From *Lochner v. New York*[6] to *Roe v. Wade*[7] and *Doe v. Bolton*,[8] there has seemingly been little change in the doctrine of substantive due process. But the facts have changed, or if they have not changed, the Court's awareness of the facts has changed—which is to the same effect. From *Nebbia v. New York*[9] until the present, the Court has become increasingly suspicious of its own expertise in economics and increasingly assured of its own competence in the social science areas. And so there has been less and less protection of contract and property interests and more and more protection of personal liberty, including the discernment of rights that are not apparent on the face of the Constitution.[10] The Brandeis brief was an innovation in *Muller v. Oregon*,[11] but is now standard operating procedure in equal employment, ecology, and major school desegregation cases. The problem is not whether to use the social sciences, or whether it is proper to do so, but how to persuade the courts of the truth of the ultimate facts asserted. Courts are comfortable with evidentiary facts—how fast the car was being driven—and are uncomfortable with conclusory facts—what caused the tire to blow out. One of the few reasons for wanting to retain trial by jury in civil cases is that difficult questions such as negligence can be left to the jury. Aided by the failure to sustain the burden of proof standard, there is no question too hard for the jury to answer. It is not surprising, therefore, that the courts are uneasy in the presence of the ultimate facts or conclusions of the social sciences because we have many times consumed large quantities of social science—from *Dred Scott*[12] to *Lochner*[13]—only to have to regurgitate it.

---

6. 198 U.S. 45 (1905).
7. 410 U.S. 113 (1973).
8. 410 U.S. 179 (1973).
9. 291 U.S. 502 (1934).
10. *See, e.g.*, Griswold v. Connecticut, 381 U.S. 479 (1965).
11. 208 U.S. 412 (1908). Louis Brandeis filed a 113-page brief supporting Oregon's maximum hour law for women, drawing upon foreign, federal, and state studies concerning women's reactions to contemporary working conditions. The views of American, French, and German doctors were cited by Brandeis as evidence that women could not tolerate the same working hours as did men. Brief for Defendant in Error, Muller v. Oregon, *id.*
12. Scott v. Sandford, 60 U.S. (19 How.) 393 (1854).
13. Lochner v. New York, 198 U.S. 45 (1905).

In the year 1856, William A. Smith, Doctor of Divinity and President of Randolph Macon College, entered in the office of the clerk of the district court for the middle district of Tennessee, a copy of his lectures that had been delivered to the classes in moral science at Randolph Macon College for many years. The lectures were entitled *The Philosophy and Practice of Slavery* and were published by Stephenson & Owen, Nashville, Tennessee, in 1857, the same year that *Scott v. Sandford*[14] was decided by the United States Supreme Court. I should think that Dr. Smith would have cheerfully admitted to being a social scientist, and a distinguished one at that. The burden of his message to his contemporaries, as stated in the first chapter, is that domestic slavery is not sinful and that slavery, per se, is right; "or that the great abstract principle of slavery is right, because it is a fundamental principle of the social state; and that domestic slavery, as an institution, is fully justified by the condition and circumstances (essential and relative) of the African race in this country, and therefore equally right."[15]

Chief Justice Taney's opinion does not mention Dr. Smith's book, but it is easy to suppose that he may have read it or others like it. In deciding whether Dred Scott was a citizen and entitled to bring a diversity of citizenship action in a federal court, the Chief Justice displayed great interest in "the state of public opinion in relation to that unfortunate race, which prevailed in the civilized and enlightened portions of the world at the time . . . when the Constitution of the United States was framed and adopted."[16] The factual context within which the Court decided the case was, with respect to the status of the Negro, stated to be as follows:[17]

> They had for more than a century before been regarded as beings of an inferior order, and altogether unfit to associate with the white race, either in social or political relations; and so far inferior, that they had no rights which the white man was bound to respect; and that the negro might justly and lawfully be reduced to slavery for his benefit. He was bought and sold, and treated as an ordinary article of merchandise and traffic, whenever a profit could be made by it. This opinion was at that time fixed and universal in the civilized portion of the white race. It was regarded as an axiom in morals as well as in politics, which no one thought of disputing, or supposed to be open to dispute; and men in every grade and position in society daily and habitually acted upon it in their private pursuits, as well as in matters of public concern, without doubting for a moment the correctness of this opinion.

Some forty years later Mr. Justice Brown concluded that the fourteenth amendment "could not have been intended to abolish distinctions based upon color."[18] Writing for the Court in *Plessy v. Ferguson*,[19] he depended heavily

---

14. 60 U.S. (19 How.) 393 (1854).
15. W. Smith, The Philosophy and Practice of Slavery 11-12 (1857).
16. 60 U.S. (19 How.) at 407.
17. *Id.*
18. Plessy v. Ferguson, 163 U.S. 537, 544 (1896).
19. *Id.*

upon consensus of public opinion with respect to race relations. He nailed down apartheid for his time by reference to the established usages, customs, and traditions of the people.[20] Rather happily he concluded that "if one race be inferior to the other socially, the Constitution of the United States cannot put them upon the same plane."[21] Dr. Smith would have agreed.

But by 1954 the Court was no longer reading Dr. Smith nor was it impressed by "the extent of psychological knowledge at the time of *Plessy v. Ferguson*."[22] In *Brown v. Board of Education*,[23] Chief Justice Warren and members of his Court may have reached a new high in judicial intellectual honesty. Gone is Mr. Justice Brown's sophistry that if enforced separation of the races "stamps the colored race with a badge of inferiority" it "is solely because the colored race chooses to put that construction upon it."[24] Supported only by a compilation of psychological and sociological studies of the status of the Negro in America, the Court flatly concluded that "separate educational facilities are inherently unequal."[25] The decision was not addressed to lawyers but to the people. Although startling at the time, the decision now rests upon a bedrock of public opinion that school assignments and other legal distinctions based upon race are denigrating to the minority ethnic group and are simply unfair. After twenty years of more or less successful attempts to implement *Brown*, I think it can be said that there is a general consensus that enforced separation of any race or group from the mainstream of society stigmatizes those against whom such coercive laws are directed. Beyond that there is little agreement and much uncertainty.

Many an inferior court, overreading *Green v. County School Board of New Kent County*,[26] *Davis v. Board of School Commissioners of Mobile County*,[27] and *Swann v. Charlotte-Mecklenburg Board of Education*,[28] thought that the Court's dogma mandated racial balance[29] despite occasional cryptic disclaimers.[30] What the

---

20. 163 U.S. at 550.
21. 163 U.S. at 552.
22. Brown v. Board of Educ., 347 U.S. 483, 494 (1954).
23. *Id.*
24. Plessy v. Ferguson, 163 U.S. at 551.
25. 347 U.S. at 495.
26. 391 U.S. 430 (1968).
27. 402 U.S. 33 (1971).
28. 402 U.S. 1 (1971).
29. *See, e.g.*, Bradley v. School Bd. of City of Richmond, 325 F. Supp. 828 (E.D. Va. 1971). In *Bradley*, the district court approved the adoption of a Richmond metropolitan school plan where 97 per cent of the black students in the metropolitan area (the three jurisdictions included in the metropolitan area being the City of Richmond, Chesterfield County, and Henrico County) would attend schools with racial compositions in the range of 20-40 per cent black. The Fourth Circuit reversed on the grounds that where each of the districts had achieved unitary school systems, it was not within the district court's authority to order the consolidation of three separate political subdivisions of the Commonwealth of Virginia. 462 F.2d 1058, 1069 (4th Cir. 1972), *aff'd by an equally divided Court*, 412 U.S. 92 (1973).
30. In *Swann*, the district court ordered the school system to establish a 71 to 29 per cent ratio of whites to blacks in the city's schools. On appeal the Supreme Court clarified its position on racial

Court *said* in *Swann* seemed to some not nearly so important as what it *did* in *Davis*.[31] One did not have to be stupid to have thought in 1970 that every class in every grade in every school in every zone within a given district must be integrated, and that integration meant the maximum possible amount of desegregation or mixing of the races. There was a time when members of my court were so concerned with the attainment of mixing that we even considered minimizing the apparent danger of white flight. I debated the question with my late dear friend, Judge Sobeloff, in *Brunson v. Board of Trustees of School District No. 1*,[32] and until *Milliken v. Bradley*[33] was decided on July 25, 1974, I would have thought it a standoff. *Brunson* got us into sociology over our heads. After acknowledging my own ignorance of sociology and educational theory, I quoted Dr. Thomas F. Pettigrew of Harvard University that the optimum mix was 30 per cent black to 70 per cent white.[34] The same sociological input must have influenced Judge McMillan in *Swann*, for he suggested that it would be desirable if the school board assigned students on the basis of a 71/29 ratio of white to black students.[35]

In September, 1969, there were 2,408 black students and 256 white stu-

---

balance. "[T]he use made of mathematical ratios was no more than a starting point in the process of shaping, rather than an inflexible requirement." 402 U.S. at 25. "If we were to read the holding of the district court to require, as a matter of substantive constitutional right, any particular degree of racial balance or mixing, that approach would be disapproved and we would be obliged to reverse. The constitutional command to desegregate schools does not mean that every school in every community must always reflect the racial composition of the school system as a whole." 402 U.S. at 24.

31. The Fifth Circuit, in *Davis*, approved a desegregation plan which used a major north-south highway as a dividing line between two school zones. On the east side of the highway lived 94 per cent of the metropolitan area's Negro students. About 88 per cent of the students on the west side of the highway were white. The Supreme Court reversed and remanded on the basis that every effort to achieve the greatest possible degree of desegregation must be explored, including the possibility of the use of bus transportation and split zoning. While not attacking the racial imbalance itself, the Court did imply that a major highway was not to be a barrier to desegregation. *See* Davis v. Commissioners of Mobile County, 402 U.S. 33 (1971).

32. 429 F.2d 820 (4th Cir. 1970). Because of the small number of whites in Clarendon County, South Carolina, it was feared that unyielding compliance to arithmetical formulas to achieve racial balance would drive whites to the parochial schools. "It will be ironic, and contrary to the spirit of Brown v. Board of Education of Topeka, [citations omitted] if the result of the application of the *Brown* constitutional principle in this case is simply to accomplish an all-black school system." 429 F.2d at 822 (Craven, Haynsworth & Bryan, JJ., concurring & dissenting).

On the other hand, while "white flight" was a factor which Judge Sobeloff regretted, he would not attempt to overcome it by a less stringent application of the arithmetic of racial balance. "[T]he road to integration is served neither by covert capitulation, nor by overt compromise, such as adoption of a schedule of 'optimal mixing.'" 429 F.2d at 827 (Sobeloff, J., concurring).

33. 418 U.S. 717 (1974).

34. 429 F.2d at 821.

35. 311 F. Supp. 265, 268 (W.D.N.C. 1970), referring to an earlier opinion in the same case, 300 F. Supp. 1358, 1372 (W.D.N.C. 1969). The earlier opinion indicated that Judge McMillan relied not only on the testimony of experts for this "racial mix" but also on "inferences from the Coleman Report that although mixing a few whites and a heavy majority of blacks retards the whole group, nevertheless mixing a *substantial majority of whites* and a few blacks helps the blacks to advance without retarding the whites." 300 F. Supp. at 1372.

dents enrolled in School District No. 1 of Clarendon County, South Carolina.[36] Only one white pupil enrolled for the 1973-74 session;[37] thus my fears about white flight have been realized. If the silence of the majority and the dissent of Mr. Justice Marshall in *Milliken* means that white flight can never be a relevant factor in considering the appropriate remedy for dismantling a dual school system,[38] then Judge Sobeloff wins. But he would not be happy to know that the schools of Clarendon County are all black (save one) nor to envision with Mr. Justice Marshall the specter of all-black schools in Detroit. Certainly it would seem that Mr. Justice Marshall correctly concludes that ". . . what desegregation of the public schools is all about" is ". . . to insure that Negro and white children in fact go to school together."[39] And it still seems to me that some is better than none.

Over the past eight years I have observed on my monthly visits to Richmond that it has increasingly become a black city. I said as much in *Bradley v. School Board of City of Richmond*.[40] And I added that "the root causes of concentration of blacks in the inner cities of America are simply not known."[41] Perhaps I should have added "by judges." It is true that Dr. Karl Taeuber, a professor of sociology at the University of Wisconsin, cast most of the blame for the concentration of blacks in Richmond on discriminatory housing policies.[42] But even he admitted that perhaps 15 per cent of existing segregation is attributable to income differentials, and he seemed to attach some weight to what he called "attachments to a particular neighborhood" and "an observable tendency for blacks who can afford better housing not to make, for various reasons, the long jump to a suburban homesite, but rather to move to a peripheral transitional area."[43] The testimony of other social scientists—Dr. Thomas Pettigrew, Dr. Martin E. Sloane, and Dr. Jeanne C. Biggar—were not so precise.[44] I share the belief of the experts that housing segregation policy

36. 429 F.2d at 820.

37. Counsel for the school board, at my request, obtained this information concerning Clarendon School District No. 1 from the state superintendent of education. Letter from D.W. Robinson, Robinson & Pope, Columbia, South Carolina, to the author, Aug. 16, 1974.

38. 418 U.S. 717 (1974).

39. *Id.* at 802.

40. 462 F.2d 1058, 1066 (4th Cir. 1972), *aff'd by an equally divided Court*, 412 U.S. 92 (1973).

41. *Id.*

42. Bradley v. School Bd. of City of Richmond, 338 F. Supp. 67, 212 (E.D. Va. 1972).

43. 338 F. Supp. at 214. *See* Farley, *Residential Segregation and Its Implications for School Integration*, 39 LAW & CONTEMP. PROB. no. 1, at 164 (1975). Professor Reynolds Farley analyzes studies of data collected by Karl and Alma Taeuber and the U.S. Census Bureau. The studies indicate that racial segregation is a far greater factor than its economic counterpart as a determinant of residential segregation patterns. Farley notes that even those blacks who can afford to move to the suburbs are highly segregated from whites in those outlying areas. Other studies indicate that the vast majority of blacks prefer integrated neighborhoods and schools. *Id.* at 174-77, 190. Citing discriminatory housing policies (an "institutional web of discrimination") as the prime factor, Farley concludes that economic factors do not fully explain neighborhood racial segregation patterns. *Id.* at 191.

44. 338 F. Supp. at 214-15.

has been an important factor in the creation of the ghetto pattern in the American cities. But I am unwilling to jump to the conclusion that it was the only factor or even the dominant one. If it is so perfectly clear that restrictive racial covenants and discriminatory housing policies created the ghetto, whether in New York or Boston or Richmond, why is it that years after *Shelley v. Kraemer*[45] and reported changes in such policies, the ghettos remain virtually intact?

Powell v. Texas[46] is a good example of an idea whose time has not yet come. Everyone now knows something about alcoholism, and there is emerging a consensus of opinion that we ought not to put drunks in jail so long as they do not harm other persons. Even so, the Court was uneasy with the "findings of fact" below:[47]

> (1) That chronic alcoholism is a disease which destroys the afflicted person's will power to resist the constant, excessive consumption of alcohol.
> (2) That a chronic alcoholic does not appear in public by his own volition but under a compulsion symptomatic of the disease of chronic alcoholism.
> (3) That Leroy Powell, defendant herein, is a chronic alcoholic who is afflicted with the disease of chronic alcoholism.

The majority was unwilling to use these "findings" as the basis for a constitutional holding that "a person may not be punished if the condition essential to constitute the defined crime is part of the pattern of his disease and is occasioned by a compulsion symptomatic of the disease."[48] Mr. Justice Marshall, writing for a plurality of the Court, thought that the Court had too little knowledge to support the announcement of an important and wide-ranging new constitutional principle.[49]

Just as a raconteur will seldom let the facts interfere with a good story, judges seem to have seldom allowed sociology to interfere with a good theory—until the time of the new idea has come. Sometimes it is a long time coming; but when it arrives, it is then woven into the constitutional fabric.

45. 334 U.S. 1 (1948).
46. 392 U.S. 514 (1968).
47. *Id.* at 521.
48. *Id.*
49. *Id.* at 536-37.

SOCIAL SCIENCE AND THE DISTRICT COURT: THE OBSERVATIONS OF A JOURNEYMAN TRIAL JUDGE

JAMES B. MCMILLAN*

Like most trial judges, I find my research usually confined to what is needed to decide a particular question; broad-spectrum analysis of a whole field of controversy—even if there were time to pursue it—is not my forte. This brief paper will therefore reflect only the observations of one journeyman trial judge who for more than six years has lived and worked closely with some touchy school segregation problems.

What is the role of the social sciences in judicial decisions as to school segregation? It is the same as its role in other matters of general public interest; it is part of the facts and a source of enlightenment and should be considered by the court.

Social science, briefly defined, is the study of human society, the interaction of individuals in and with groups, and the welfare of people in society. Like the legal profession, social science has its own ordained high priests, often with M.A. or Ph.D. degrees. They are the experts. "Why," it has been asked, "shouldn't we leave issues with social implications to experts in that field?" It is a fair question. Judges are neither born nor chosen as experts in social problems. Most of us would welcome a change of venue to some never-never land of expert and happy—and popular—decisions.

The trouble is, social science experts disagree, just as stockbrokers, doctors, engineers, and lawyers do. The goals of education, for example, are today in considerable dispute; former Chicago University President Robert M. Hutchins recently remarked: "Since any free society is likely to be engaged in controversy about the kind of society it ought to be, confusion about the kind of education it ought to have seems inevitable."[1]

Somewhere, in a viable society, there must be a place of decision, where public and individual issues can be settled, and where a path can be charted through conflicting testimony and conflicting expert opinion. Americans tend to go to court for these decisions. As a result, many of us, who once thought Bacon was unique and brave when he proclaimed that he had "taken all

---

* Judge, United States District Court, Western District of North Carolina. [Judge McMillan is the author of Swann v. Charlotte-Mecklenburg Bd. of Educ., 300 F. Supp. 1358 (W.D.N.C. 1969). Judge McMillan wishes to make it clear that the footnotes are the work of the editors and are not "the creation of the writer of the text, who can take footnotes or leave them but would far prefer to leave them [out]." Editors' Note.]

1. Hutchins, *The Great Anti-School Campaign*, in THE GREAT IDEAS TODAY 154, 158 (1972).

knowledge to be my province,"[2] now sadly realize that he was just stating the everyday but unattainable duty of every trial judge!

In this land the power of government is wisely, though often vaguely, divided by our Constitution among executive, legislative, and judicial branches. Of those three branches, on a federal level, obviously the legislative branch, which appropriates over 300 billion dollars a year, and the executive, which spends that much and more, are the most powerful—and the most influenced by rankly political considerations. Though bound by the same constitutional restraints and obligations as judges, they often ignore those restraints until brought before a court where a judge has the unpleasant duty of calling those restraints to their attention.

At their worst, courts are simply a third branch of power; they are the places where day after day judges accept the dare to uphold the Constitution, and where issues of lesser moment which cannot be decided elsewhere are resolved. At their best, they are places where litigants get justice—where controversies are decided on the basis of neutral principles of public morality and law.

Courts, however, have no roving commission to seek out and right wrongs; the jurisdiction of federal courts is limited; and they, fortunately, are only authorized to decide a question after it has been presented as a "case or controversy" under a pertinent statutory or constitutional provision.

Courts have no money, no troops, no CIA, and no police force except the limited number of United States marshals. Federal courts in 1974 cost the taxpayers approximately one fourteenth of one per cent of the federal budget (before credit is taken for fines, costs, penalties and other collections by the courts).[3] The other branches of government cost us almost four times as much every day as the courts do in an entire *year*! Courts tend to stay busy and to be overloaded. Federal procedure permits dispatch but invites delay. The numbers of judges and the numbers of supporting personnel are inadequate to provide fast or consistent justice. It could be said that the federal courts today are like the household gods or icons of the ancient nomads; they look good on the tent rail and they speak high moral platitudes, but we keep them in their place and restrict their power so that their less palatable orders can be "more honour'd in the breach than in the observance."[4]

How, then, is it that courts are still listened to in large affairs? It is my own conviction after twelve years of judging spread over more than a quarter of a century that courts are heard and obeyed because they provide a forum where all sides can be heard; because they try to find the truth from a study of facts

2. Bacon, *Letter to Lord Burghle, 1592*, in 1 J. Spedding, The Letters and the Life of Francis Bacon 108, 109 (1890).

3. The Budget of the United States Government, Fiscal Year 1974, at 175-78 (1973).

4. W. Shakespeare, Hamlet, I, iv, 14.

rather than debate about theory; and because they try to do right based upon fundamental principles of fairness, justice, and morality.

This, of course, states an ideal. Not all judges and writers agree with that ideal. Moreover, a trial judge and, to a much lesser extent a circuit court of appeals judge, is often bound by a controlling statute or precedent. Such statutes or precedents must themselves in time stand the test of justice and morality and usually have so stood that test. However, in many—perhaps most—judicial problems there is room to decide more than one way; and debate has raged throughout history over the true foundations of such decisions. Some of the better known theories of judicial decision are pragmatism,[5] likelihood of success,[6] and likelihood of future acceptance.[7] It even has been suggested that courts as a third branch are simply wielding raw power and should admit it. Time does not permit debate with such noted scholars as Judges Craven and Wright and Professors Bickel and Wechsler on the abstract bases of judicial decisions.

Fortunately, it is not necessary to resolve that debate in order to evaluate the role of social science in judicial decision-making; these human factors in a legal problem are not the monopoly of either "conservative" or "liberal" jurists and they must be weighed by those who are attacked as judicial "activists" and by those who call themselves "strict constructionists."

Whether motivated by principle or by pragmatism, a judge worthy of the name must reckon with facts before he decides. Neither principle nor "pragmatism" has any meaning in a vacuum. The pragmatist must know the score before his pragmatic computer can be fed. The principled jurist must know what happened before he knows what principle applies. Neither the tenth amendment nor the fourteenth amendment relates to a particular controversy except in terms of the grubby, everyday facts—the questions as to who did what to whom, and when and where; whether it was done or countenanced by government authority and, if so, which branch; who gains and who loses from it; what constitutional provision or what statute authorizes the case to come to court. Neither the most starry-eyed idealist nor the most hard-core realist can judge what is pragmatic or what is principled until he has dug out and understood the facts necessary to decide the question before him.

School segregation cases are not unique in this regard; and they are not unique in their dependence upon a great deal of principle and controversy and opinion which goes under the name of "social science." How can an intelligent or just decision, pragmatic or principled, be made without weighing considera-

5. ". . . [E]xpediency: What is best for the nation?" Craven, *Paean to Pragmatism*, 50 N.C.L. REV. 977, 981 (1972).

6. Kurland, *Earl Warren, the "Warren Court," and the Warren Myths*, 67 MICH. L. REV. 353 (1968).

7. A. BICKEL, THE SUPREME COURT AND THE IDEA OF PROGRESS 99 (1970). *Compare* Wright, *Professor Bickel, the Scholarly Tradition, and the Supreme Court*, 84 HARV. L. REV. 769 (1971), *with* Wechsler, *Toward Neutral Principles of Constitutional Law*, 73 HARV. L. REV. 1 (1959).

tions of social science in any case involving such well known legal shibboleths as "due process," "equal protection," "public interest," "commerce," "abstention," "legitimate state interest," "cruel and unusual," "reasonable doubt," "bad faith," "political thicket," "fair trial," "free press," "free speech" or "privilege"; and who can forget the volumes of sociology, genetics, economics, and first and fourteenth amendment problems which Justice Holmes once compressed into six words: "Three generations of imbeciles are enough."[8]

Illustrations of the use of data and opinions from the social sciences abound in both recent and early school segregation decisions. *Brown v. Board of Education*[9] may have been "bad" law when read solely against the historical facts that some framers of the Constitution owned slaves, and that segregation had been officially tolerated and enforced for sixty years since *Plessy v. Ferguson.*[10] But though it may have been technically "bad" law when read purely against those precedents, it would be hard to challenge its basic message from the standpoint of strict construction of the Constitution, of equal protection of laws, of morals, of economics, of equity, fairness and justice, of the progress of society as a whole and of its individual members, and of the Judeo-Christian ethic (perhaps not unique, but ours) which professes to treat men as equal in the sight of God regardless of their condition or fortune. Those things were made the law of the land in the decision (principled or pragmatic) in *Brown*; and whether the persuasion came from Gunnar Myrdal or other sources,[11] the Supreme Court was talking sociology[12] which *ought* to have been law when it said: "To separate [children] from others of similar age and qualifications solely because of their race generates a feeling of inferiority as to their status in the community that may affect their hearts and minds in a way unlikely ever to be undone."[13] Quoting a lower court opinion, the Supreme Court continued:[14]

> 'Segregation of white and colored children in public schools has a detrimental effect upon the colored children. The impact is greater when it has the sanction of the law; for the policy of separating the races is usually interpreted as denoting the inferiority of the [N]egro group. A sense of inferiority affects the motivation of a child to learn. Segregation with the sanction of law, therefore, has a tendency to [retard] the educational and mental development of [N]egro children and to deprive them of some of the benefits they would receive in a racial[ly] integrated school system.'
>
> . . . .
>
> We conclude that in the field of public education the doctrine of 'separate but equal' has no place. Separate educational facilities are inherently unequal.

---

8. Buck v. Bell, 274 U.S. 200, 207 (1927).
9. 347 U.S. 483 (1954).
10. 163 U.S. 537 (1896).
11. The *Brown* Court noted that its finding that state-imposed racial segregation has a detrimental effect on minority children was "amply supported by modern authority"—referring in the now-famous footnote to the works of Professor Kenneth B. Clark and Dr. Gunnar Myrdal, among others. 347 U.S. at 494 n. 11. *See* G. Myrdal, An American Dilemma (1944).
12. *But see, e.g.*, Cahn, *Jurisprudence*, 30 N.Y.L. Rev. 150, 159 (1955).
13. 347 U.S. at 494.
14. *Id.*

Plessy v. Ferguson itself created a segregated society by relying upon an erroneous sociological premise—that separate facilities could be equal. *Brown v. Board of Education* corrected and reversed that premise.[15] In *Swann v. Charlotte-Mecklenburg Board of Education*,[16] before reaching any conclusions, the district court went to considerable pains to review thousands of pages of sociological evidence, most of it from official school board and other government files, and found as fact that segregation in Charlotte was caused and required by numerous discriminatory governmental actions.[17]

---

15. *Id.* Even before *Brown*, there were indications that the "separate but equal" principle was being undermined, at least in the area of higher education. *See, e.g.*, Sweatt v. Painter, 339 U.S. 629 (1950).

16. 300 F. Supp. 1358 (W.D.N.C. 1969).

17. *Id.* at 1365-66.

Charlotte (270,000-plus) sits in the center of Mecklenburg County (550 square miles, total population over 335,000). The central city may be likened to an automibile hub cap, the perimeter area to a wheel, and the county area to the rubber tire. . . . Charlotte originally grew along the Southern railroad tracks. Textile mills with mill villages, once almost entirely white, were built. Business and other industry followed the highways and the railroad. The railroad and parallel highways and business and industrial development formed something of a barrier between east and west.

By the end of World War II many Negro families lived in the center of Charlotte . . . . However, the bulk of Charlotte's black population lived west of the railroad . . . and . . . in the northwest part of town. The high priced, almost exclusively white, country was east . . . . Charlotte thus had a very high degree of segregation of housing before the first *Brown* decision.

Among the forces which brought about these concentrations should be listed the original location of industry along and to the west of the southern railroad; the location of Johnson C. Smith University two miles west of Tryon Street; the choice of builders in the early 1900's to go south and east instead of west for high priced dwelling construction; the effect of private action and public law on choice of dwelling sites by black and by white purchasers or renters; real estate zoning which began in 1947; and the economics of the situation which are that Negroes have earned less money and have been less able to buy or rent expensive living quarters.

Local zoning ordinances starting in 1947 generally allow more varied uses in the west than in the east. Few if any areas identified as black have a residential restriction stronger than R-6, which means that a house can be built on a lot as small as 6,000 square feet. Zoning restrictions in other areas go as high as 12,000 and 15,000 square feet per lot. . . . Many black citizens live in areas zoned industrial, which means that the zoning law places no restriction on the use of the land.

. . . .

[C]oncentration of Negroes in the northwest continues. Under the urban renewal program thousands of Negroes were moved out of their shotgun houses in the center of town and have relocated in the low rent areas to the west. This relocation of course involved many ad hoc decisions by individuals and by city, county, state and federal governments. Federal agencies (which hold the strings to large federal purses) reportedly disclaim any responsibility for the direction of the migration; they reportedly say that the selection of urban renewal sites and the relocation of displaced persons are matters of decision ("freedom of choice"?) by local individuals and governments. This may be correct; the clear fact however is that the displacement occurred with heavy federal financing and with active participation by local governments, and it has further concentrated Negroes until 95% or so of the city's Negroes live west of the Tryon—railroad area, or on its immediate eastern fringes.

Onto this migration the 1965 school zone plan with freedom of transfer was superimposed. The Board accurately predicted that black pupils would be moved out of their

It was the view of the district court at that time, and now, that no answer to the question of discrimination could be given without a serious and careful study of that information. It was indeed thought that the data summarized by the court gave a full picture of how urban segregation had come to pass and was still being maintained by the most powerful of human forces—governmental and otherwise. That such is not a unanimous view is illustrated in the Fourth Circuit decision in *Bradley v. School Board of City of Richmond.*[18] Despite the fact that the district court's findings[19] in that case were rather

---

midtown shotgun housing and that white residents would continue to move generally south and east. Schools were built to meet both groups. Black or nearly black schools resulted in the northwest and white or nearly all white schools resulted in the east and southeast. Freedom of students of both races to transfer freely to schools of their own choices has resulted in resegregation of some schools which were temporarily desegregated. The effect of closing the black inner-city schools and allowing free choices has in overall result tended to perpetuate and promote segregation.

18. 462 F.2d 1058 (4th Cir. 1972).

19. 338 F. Supp. 67, 84-92 (E.D. Va. 1972).

Not only do the existing barriers have no relation to natural obstacles or substantial governmental interests, but they are related to strict housing segregation patterns, maintained by public and private enforcement and owing their genesis in substantial part to the manner in which the three school divisions have been operated and expanded. Thus by the maintenance of existing school division lines the State advantages itself of private enforcement of discrimination and prolongs the effects of discriminatory acts of its own agents. . . . The proof here overwhelmingly establishes that the school division lines between Richmond and the counties here coincide with no natural obstacles to speak of and do in fact work to confine blacks on a consistent, wholesale basis within the city, where they reside in segregated neighborhoods. . . .

. . . .

The longer term impact of the [school construction] policy has been the exaggeration of the racial disproportion between the city and the two neighboring counties. This has come about by virtue of the maintenance of school division lines as obstacles to pupil assignment for purposes of desegregation while the area's housing patterns, when its population grew, became increasingly segregated. The continued operation of the schools of each subdivision as racially identifiable facilities moreover necessarily caused each new school and old ones as well to take on the label of a black or white school.

Furthermore, not only has the manner of expansion of the community's school plant been such as to partake of the discrimination inherent in its housing patterns, but also it has played a substantial part in the development of those patterns. In addition, school officials have been abetted in the perpetuation of housing discrimination by other governmental agencies.

. . . .

The interdependency of housing and school segregation is fully established by the record. Schools were planned with an eye to separate racial occupancy and opened as such, with zone and division lines imposed upon segregated housing patterns. . . . Overall, the area's population expanded, and over time black residents, with fewer options so far as housing was concerned, comprised a greater and greater proportion of the city's residents, while the area's whites occupied the suburban counties.

This was not beyond the power of school authorities in each of the areas and in the State's central offices to influence. By maintaining black schools and white schools, perceived as such, to serve particular areas, they turned such force as might have been exerted by school policies to assist in eliminating housing segregation in the opposite direction. Because the area's overall population was expanding, the consequences of the maintenance of segregated school systems were extreme.

. . . .

similar to those made by the district court in *Swann v. Charlotte-Mecklenburg Board of Education*,[20] the Fourth Circuit said: "We think that the root causes of the concentration of blacks in the inner cities of America are simply not known and that the district court could not realistically place on the counties the responsibility for the effect that inner city decay has had on the public schools of Richmond."[21]

Social science weapons are therefore legitimate; they may serve either or both views of a question; their effect depends upon which direction they can be aimed. Whether the judicial inquiry relates to the "track system";[22] to the "open school" (like the three-teacher, eleven-grade school which I first attended); to problems of student discipline;[23] to the language segregation recently condemned in *Lau v. Nichols*;[24] or to any other of the myriad garbs in which discrimination can be clothed, social science can add valuable information and opinion to responsible judging—pragmatic, principled, or otherwise. Social science, therefore, is entitled to a respected place in the halls of justice. The study of people and their problems is a natural prerequisite of the legal decision of problems among people.

The departure of whites, as has occurred in the City, in the face of an increasing black component was predictable, but it was only possible—and only had reason to occur—when other facilities, not identifiable as black, existed within what was in practical terms, for the family seeking a new residence, the same community. . . .

. . . .

In league with the defendant school administrators in perpetuating the dual school system to the extent that entire city and county school divisions have acquired the label of racial identifiability have been governmental agencies controlling the evolution of housing patterns in the area. Segregation in housing patters [sic], once established, perpetuates itself and expands. New residents adhere to established patterns; private realtors adhere to governmentally enforced practices; and the pattern, once set, acquires an impetus of its own. The public housing policy in the area has, by action and inaction of the governmental bodies involved, contributed to school segregation. County policy has excluded low income housing entirely; in the city itself such housing has been barred when it might contribute to housing desegregation, and efforts to place it in mainly white areas in the city or the counties have been abandoned.

Federal policy to perpetuate segregated residential development and the use of racially restrictive convenants have also forced the area's housing into racially defined patterns. It is not decisive that the sources of these forces now no longer promote them; the momentum of discrimination continues.

20. 300 F. Supp. 1358 (W.D.N.C. 1969). *See* note 17 *supra*.

21. 462 F.2d at 1066.

22. Lemon v. Bossier Parish School Bd., 444 F.2d 1400 (5th Cir. 1971); Hobson v. Hansen, 269 F. Supp. 401 (D.D.C. 1967), *aff'd en banc sub nom.* Smuck v. Hobson, 408 F.2d 175 (D.C. Cir. 1969).

23. Goss v. Lopez, 419 U.S. 565 (1975). *See* CHILDREN'S DEFENSE FUND OF THE WASHINGTON RESEARCH PROJECT, INC., CHILDREN OUT OF SCHOOL IN AMERICA (1974).

24. 414 U.S. 563 (1974).

RESIDENTIAL SEGREGATION AND ITS IMPLICATIONS FOR SCHOOL INTEGRATION*

REYNOLDS FARLEY†

INTRODUCTION

If parents desire that their children attend neighborhood schools and if the nation's Constitution requires racially integrated schools, then neighborhoods must be integrated. Residential areas, however, are highly segregated by race; thus public schools are also segregated except in those school districts operating under court orders or under a voluntarily adopted desegregation plan. Because of the segregated character of most neighborhoods, such desegregation plans rely heavily on busing substantial numbers of students to schools outside their neighborhoods.

This article examines the relationship between school segregation and residential segregation. The first section describes the extent of racial residential segregation. The second section examines racial segregation in public schools and its linkage with residential segregation. The impact of school desegregation litigation upon school integration in large school districts is assessed. Finally, the implications of demographic trends for the future are summarized in the concluding pages.

I

RACIAL RESIDENTIAL SEGREGATION

In this article the "index of dissimilarity" will be used as a measure of the extent of residential segregation.[1] The numerical value of the index represents the proportion of either whites or blacks who would have to shift from one area to another to effect complete integration of the residential areas of a city. If a city were completely integrated so that all neighborhoods or subareas had an identical racial composition, the value of the index would be zero. If, on the other hand, residential segregation were so pervasive that all blacks lived in exclusively black areas and all whites in exclusively white neighbor-

* The research for this article was supported by a grant from the Center for Population Research of the National Institutes of Child Health and Human Development, NIH-71-2210, "The Distribution and Differentiation of Population within Metropolitan Areas." The author thanks Karl Taeuber for making available data on public school segregation in 1972.

† Associate Director, Population Studies Center, University of Michigan.

1. The definitive work was written by Karl and Alma Taeuber based on data from the Census of 1960. K. TAEUBER & A. TAEUBER, NEGROES IN CITIES (1965). After reviewing a variety of proposed measures, the Taeubers selected an index which they identified as *delta* or the index of

hoods, the index would assume its maximum value, 100. Thus low values indicate that there is little residential segregation while high values indicate extensive residential segregation. An analysis of the racial composition of residential areas of the nation's largest cities in 1970, shown in Figure 1,[2] indicates that levels of racial residential segregation were quite high. For example, in Dallas, 97 per cent of either the white or the black population would have had to shift their places of residence to produce a completely integrated city; that is, a city in which every block had the same racial composition. Of the fifteen largest cities, San Francisco has the lowest racial residential segregation—75 per cent of either the white or the black population would have to shift their places of residence to bring about complete integration.

When a larger sample of cities, classified by region, was examined, residential segregation was found to be greatest in the South—where the average value of the "index of dissimilarity" was 91.4, somewhat less in the border states (87.3), and lowest in the North (81.4) and West (81.1).[3] None of the 109 cities in the sample had a segregation score under 60 in 1970. Indeed, only 3 cities had scores of less than 70.[4] The racial residential segregation indices used in Figure 1 are based on data from central cities. There is evidence, however, that if the indices were calculated for the entire metropolitan area there would be no significant difference in their values. Blacks appear to be as residentially segregated from whites in the suburbs as in the central cities.[5]

The pervasiveness and magnitude of racial residential segregation is made apparent by comparing it to the extent of residential segregation by income, occupation, or ethnicity. One might expect that families would be segregated by income. In the Chicago urbanized area in 1970, the index of dissimilarity comparing the residential distribution of white families with incomes over $25,000 to that of white families with incomes of $3,000 to $4,000 was 55.[6] Yet the index comparing the residential distribution of all white families with that

---

dissimilarity. It takes as its standard the racial composition of a city or metropolitan area, and then compares the racial composition of subareas—usually city blocks or census tracts—to the racial composition of the entire city or metropolitan area.

In each subarea, i, suppose there are w_i whites and n_i blacks. The entire city or metropolitan area contains W whites and N blacks. The index of dissimilarity is calculated as follows:

$$\frac{1}{2} \Sigma_i \left| \frac{n_i}{N} - \frac{w_i}{W} \right|$$

See id. at 236, app. A.

2. The indexes in Figure 1 were computed from 1970 Census data.

3. The small values of the standard deviations of the indices given in Figure 1 indicate that the residential segregation scores are clustered around the high values.

4. The three cities were Cambridge, Massachusetts, and Camden and East Orange, New Jersey.

5. *See* N. KANTROWITZ, ETHNIC AND RACIAL SEGREGATION IN THE NEW YORK METROPOLIS 19, Table 2.2 (1973); K. TAEUBER & A. TAEUBER, *supra* note 1, at 55-62; Hermalin & Farley, *The Potential for Residential Integration in Cities and Suburbs: Implications for the Busing Controversy*, 38 AM. SOCIOLOGICAL REV. 595, 607, Table 7 (1973).

6. These indexes of dissimilarity were calculated from census tract data.

FIGURE 1

INDEXES OF RACIAL RESIDENTIAL SEGREGATION FOR THE NATION'S LARGEST CITIES, 1970

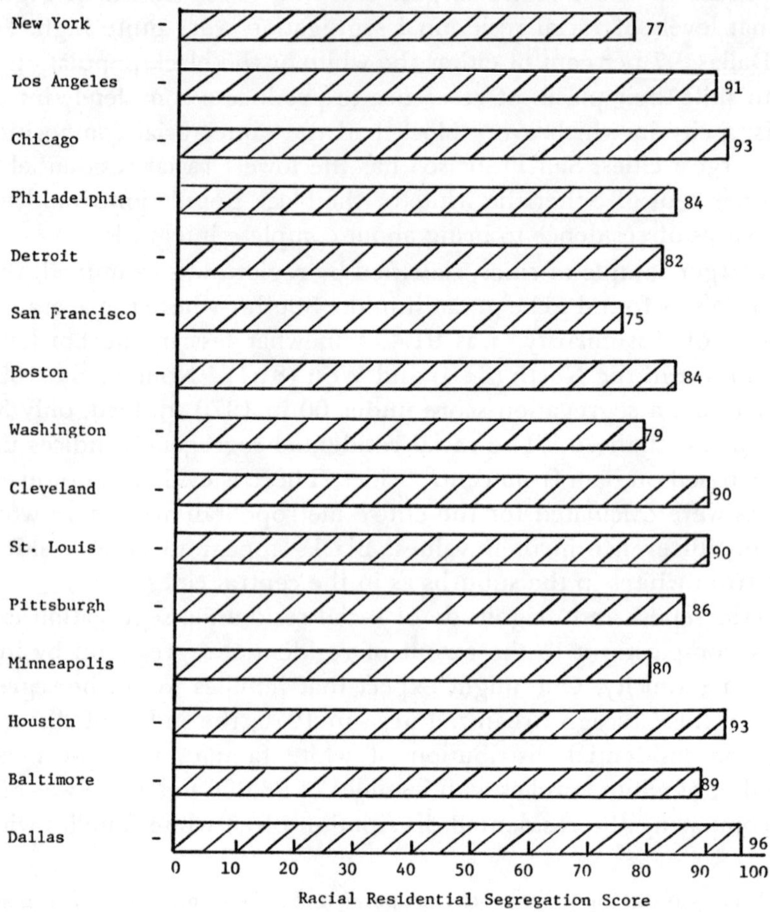

Summary of Racial Residential Segregation Indexes for Cities Classified by Region

	Northern States	Western States	Border States	Southern States
Number of cities	53	10	12	34
Average racial segregation scores	81.4	81.1	87.3	91.4
Standard deviation of segregation scores	6.9	7.1	7.4	2.7

Source: A. SØRENSEN, K. TAEUBER, & L. HOLLINGSWORTH, INDEXES OF RACIAL RESIDENTIAL SEGREGATION FOR 109 CITIES IN THE UNITED STATES, 1940 to 1970, at 7 (Studies in Racial Segregation No. 1, 1974).

of all black families was 93. A comparison of the residential distribution of white families with incomes exceeding $25,000 with that of black families in the same income group in the Chicago urbanized area provides an index of 94.[7] Thus well-to-do whites are much more segregated from affluent black families than they are from poor white families.

Segregation scores for white ethnic groups have also been computed.[8] The index of dissimilarity based on the residential distribution of native whites and of people of Polish stock in the New York area for 1960 was 43.[9] By contrast, the index of dissimilarity based on the distribution of native whites and blacks was 80.[10] Thus racial residential segregation is significantly greater than the residential segregation of socioeconomic or ethnic group.

An analysis of changes in the extent of residential segregation during the period since 1970 cannot be undertaken because of the unavailability of data. Nevertheless, the presumption is that levels of residential segregation have changed little since the 1970 Census. Between 1950 and 1960, only modest declines in racial residential segregation were recorded.[11] Preliminary data for 1970 indicate that this trend toward only slightly lower levels of segregation has continued.[12] Thus, the nation's neighborhoods are almost as segregated now as they were thirty years ago. If present trends persist, schools organized on a neighborhood basis will remain racially segregated indefinitely.

II

THE CHANGING RACIAL COMPOSITION OF URBANIZED AREAS

A. Trends in Residential Patterns

As recently as 1940, four-fifths of the black population lived in the South, and almost two-thirds of those resided in rural areas.[13] However, World War II

---

7. These indexes were computed using census data for 1970 from the Indiana and Illinois portions of the Chicago urbanized area. This area includes 3.4 million residents of Chicago and 2.8 million who lived in the suburban ring. 1 U.S. BUREAU OF THE CENSUS, DEP'T OF COMMERCE, 1970 CENSUS OF POPULATION: CHARACTERISTICS OF THE POPULATION pt. 15, at 60, Table 12 (1973).

8. N. KANTROWITZ, *supra* note 5.

9. *Id.*

10. *Id.*

11. K. TAEUBER & A. TAEUBER, *supra* note 1, at 44, Table 5.

12. A. SØRENSEN, K. TAEUBER, & J. HOLLINGSWORTH, INDEXES OF RACIAL RESIDENTIAL SEGREGATION FOR 109 CITIES IN THE UNITED STATES, 1940-1970, at 7 (Studies in Racial Segregation No. 1, 1974). Changing values of indexes of dissimilarity must be interpreted with caution. With the rapid growth of the black population in central cities, many neighborhoods experience a relatively slow transition from all white to all black. Thus these will be reported as "integrated neighborhoods" for a few years during the transition, and an increase in the number of such transitional neighborhoods will produce a lower index value during these years despite the fact that at the end of the transition residential segregation may be as great as before.

13. D. PRICE, CHANGING CHARACTERISTICS OF THE NEGRO POPULATION 9, 11, Tables I-1 & I-3 (1969).

and the prosperous postwar years saw the movement of blacks away from the rural South and into cities. By 1970, the percentage of all blacks who lived in urbanized areas, 81 per cent, exceeded that for whites, the comparable figure being 72 per cent.[14] At present, the black population outside the South is approximately as large as the black population within the South.[15]

Within urbanized areas, there has been a differential rate of growth of black and white populations. Overall, the share of the nation's white population living within central cities has declined while the proportion of blacks in central cities has risen. The trends for the nation's fifteen largest urbanized areas are shown in Figure 2.[16] In each of the central cities of the fifteen urbanized areas, the black population grew faster than the white. The percentage of blacks in Detroit, for example, increased from 29 to 44 per cent between 1960 and 1970. In Washington, the increase in the percentage of blacks in the same period was from 54 per cent to 71 per cent. In the suburbs, on the other hand, the changes in the percentage of the population that was black were generally small. In eleven of the suburban areas shown in Figure 2, the growth rate of the black population exceeds that of whites, but in four areas—Baltimore, Dallas, Detroit, and Houston—the percentage of blacks in the suburbs actually declined because the growth rate of the white suburban population exceeded that of the black.

It is extraordinarily difficult to generalize about demographic trends in urbanized areas, since there is substantial variety in urban growth patterns.[17] Thus there are significant exceptions to the generalization that white out-migration and black in-migration characterize the nation's large cities and that suburban rings contain few blacks. Nevertheless, the white population of the largest cities reached a peak around 1960 and since then, the increase in the white population has been concentrated in the suburbs. The black population

---

14. 1 U.S. Bureau of the Census, Dep't of Commerce, 1970 Census of Population: Characteristics of the Population, pt. 1, at 279-80, Table 54 (1973). The Census Bureau uses the term "urbanized area" to refer to a large central city and its contiguous densely settled suburban fringe. *See* 1 H. Shryock & J. Siegel, The Methods and Materials of Demography 160-61 (1973). In most areas of the country, municipal, county, and school district boundaries are not coterminous with the boundaries of an urbanized area.

15. 1 U.S. Bureau of the Census, *supra* note 14, at 281, Table 55; U.S. Dep't of Commerce, Current Population Reports: Special Studies 11, Table 2 (Bureau of the Census Series P-23, No. 48, 1974).

16. Figure 2 shows the percentage of the total central city and suburban population for 1960 and 1970 that is black. In the New York, Los Angeles, Chicago, San Francisco, and Minneapolis urbanized areas, the Bureau of the Census designated more than one central city. The data in Figure 2, and in subsequent figures, are derived from the sum of all central cities in an urbanized area.

17. *See* L. Schnore, Class and Race in Cities and Suburbs (1972); Schnore, *Urban Structure and Suburban Selectivity*, 1 Demography 164 (1964); Schnore, *The Socio-Economic Status of Cities and Suburbs*, 28 Am. Sociological Rev. 76 (1963).

has grown both within cities and the suburban rings, although the numerical growth in the black population is much greater in cities.[18]

During the 1960's two new trends in the distribution of the black population in the urbanized areas became evident. First, the black population in suburban areas increased more rapidly. Indeed, during that decade, the rate of growth of the black population in the suburbs was generally greater than that of the white population, although the numerical increase for whites was much greater than for blacks.[19] The suburban rings surrounding New York, Los Angeles, Philadelphia, and Washington now contain large and rapidly expanding black populations. This growth does not necessarily portend residential integration in the suburbs. Many of the suburban areas with substantial black populations are extensions of central city ghettos, while others are black suburban enclaves.[20] Second, the growth rate of the black population in central cities declined during the 1960's. Several large cities which had attracted many blacks in the period of the 1950's experienced a net outmigration of both blacks and whites between 1960 and 1970.[21]

In summary, the patterns of population change in many urbanized areas suggest that opportunities for school integration are minimal. In many cities there has been a substantial out-migration of whites with a concomitant growth of the black population. Even those cities which are experiencing a net outmigration of blacks appear to be losing whites at a higher rate, thus increasing the percentage of the total population that is black. Although the suburban populations of both blacks and whites are now growing, this does not seem likely to result in racially integrated suburbs; rather the patterns of residential segregation typical in central cities appear to be duplicated in the suburban rings.

B. Black Enrollment in Public Schools

Total population figures underrepresent the black pupil population in public schools. The number of black students as a percentage of the total public

---

18. U.S. DEP'T OF COMMERCE, CURRENT POPULATION REPORTS: SPECIAL STUDIES 11, Table 4 (Bureau of the Census Series P-23, No. 48, 1974).

19. *Id.*; André, Schnore, & Sharp, *Black Suburbanization, 1930-70*, 80 AM. J. SOCIOLOGY (forthcoming 1975); Taeuber, *The Changing Distribution of the Population of the United States in the Twentieth Century*, in 5 COMMISSION ON POPULATION GROWTH AND THE AMERICAN FUTURE, POPULATION DISTRIBUTION AND POLICY 83 (S. Mazie ed. 1972).

20. Rose, *The All-Negro Town: Its Evolution and Function*, 55 GEOGRAPHICAL REV. 362 (1965); S. SUTKER & S. S. SUTKER, RACIAL TRANSITION IN THE INNER SUBURBS (1974); Farley, *The Changing Distribution of Negroes within Metropolitan Areas: the Emergence of Black Suburbs*, 75 AM. J. SOCIOLOGY 512 (1970).

21. U.S. BUREAU OF THE CENSUS, DEP'T OF COMMERCE, 1970 CENSUS OF POPULATION AND HOUSING: GENERAL DEMOGRAPHIC TRENDS FOR METROPOLITAN AREAS, 1960 TO 1970—UNITED STATES SUMMARY 62-68, Table 12 (1971). The term "net migration" refers to the total increase or decrease in the population of an area, less the number of persons projected to be added to the area from the natural increase of the population.

FIGURE 2

BLACKS AS A PROPORTION OF THE TOTAL POPULATION OF THE NATION'S LARGEST CENTRAL CITIES AND THEIR SUBURBAN RINGS, 1960 AND 1970

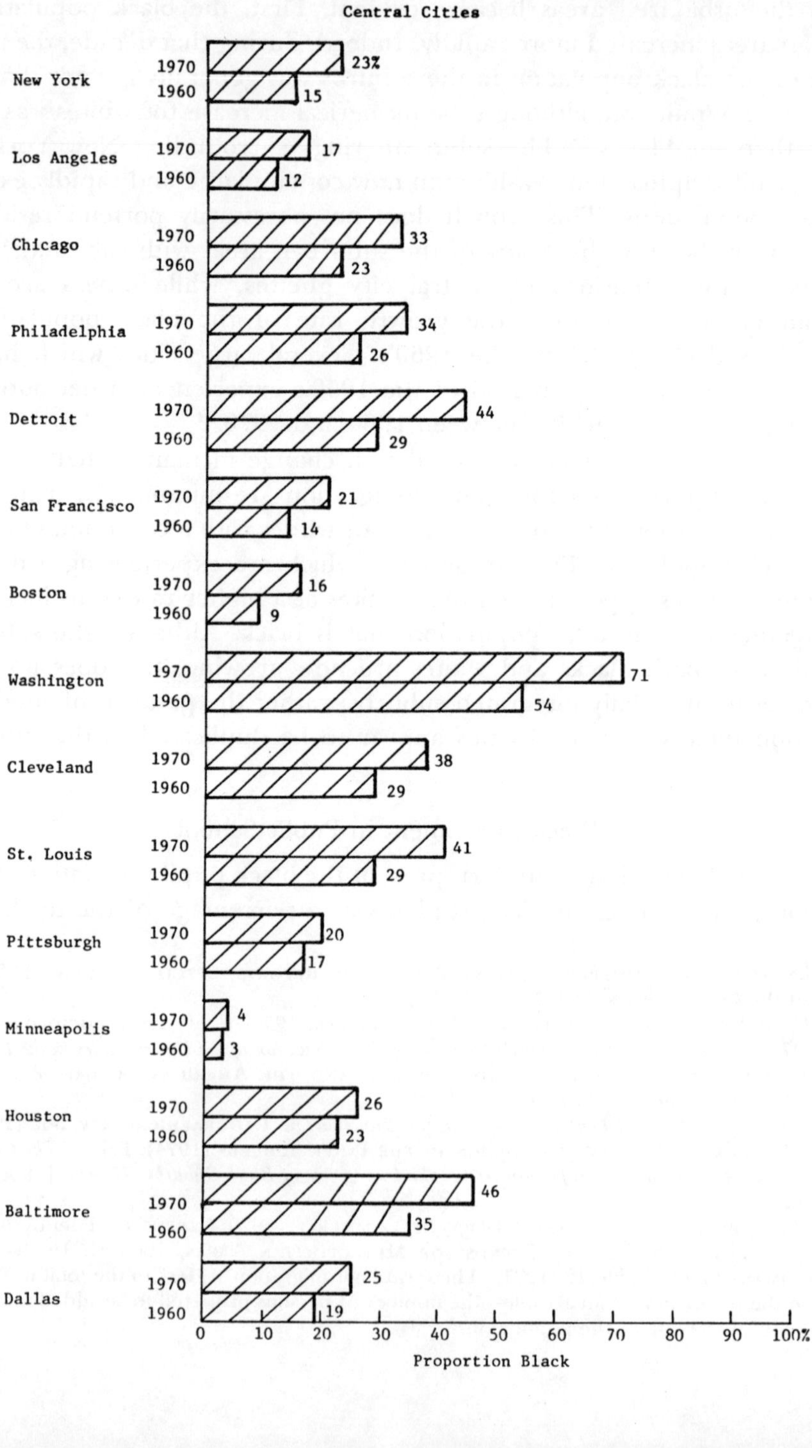

FIGURE 2 (cont.)

BLACKS AS A PROPORTION OF THE TOTAL POPULATION OF THE NATION'S LARGEST CENTRAL CITIES AND THEIR SUBURBAN RINGS, 1960 AND 1970

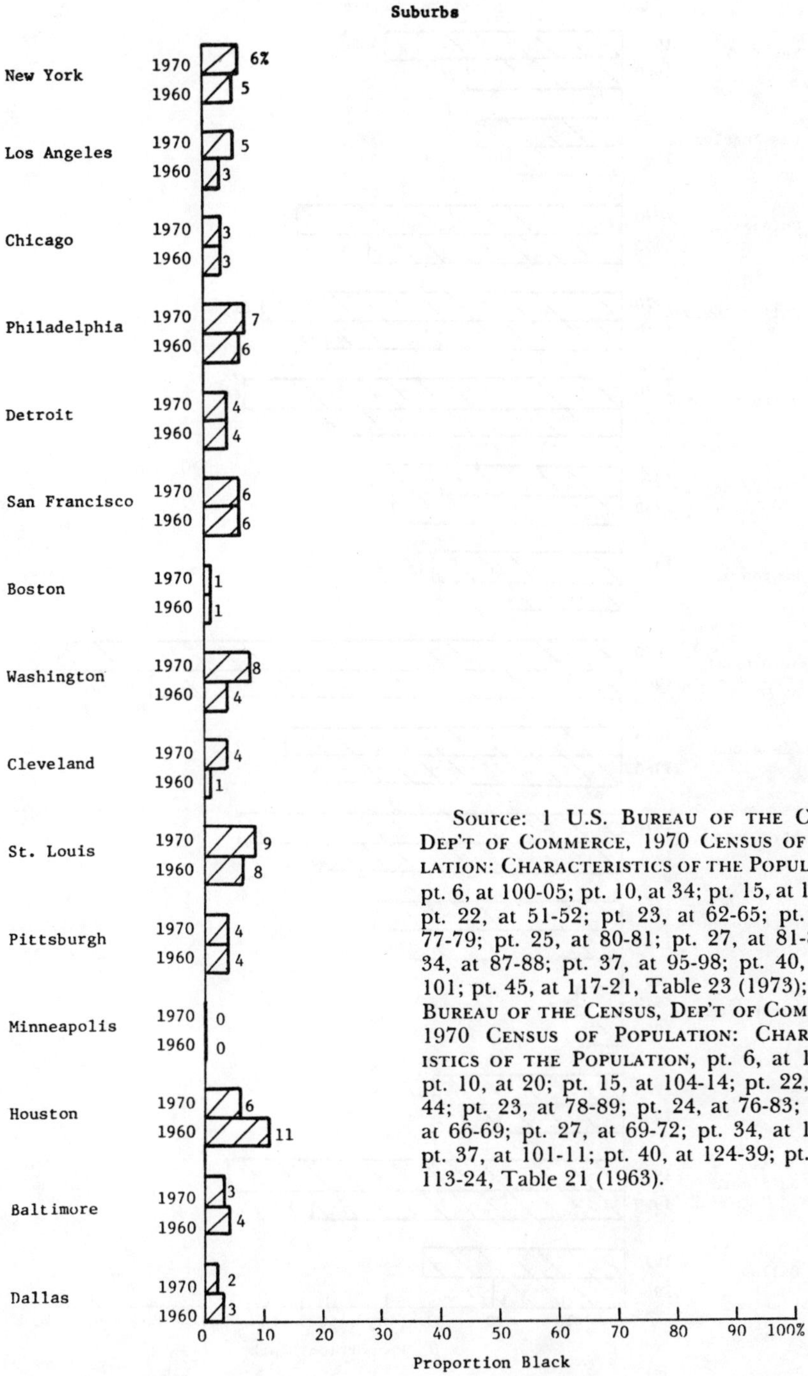

Source: 1 U.S. BUREAU OF THE CENSUS, DEP'T OF COMMERCE, 1970 CENSUS OF POPULATION: CHARACTERISTICS OF THE POPULATION, pt. 6, at 100-05; pt. 10, at 34; pt. 15, at 103-06; pt. 22, at 51-52; pt. 23, at 62-65; pt. 24, at 77-79; pt. 25, at 80-81; pt. 27, at 81-82; pt. 34, at 87-88; pt. 37, at 95-98; pt. 40, at 99-101; pt. 45, at 117-21, Table 23 (1973); 1 U.S. BUREAU OF THE CENSUS, DEP'T OF COMMERCE, 1970 CENSUS OF POPULATION: CHARACTERISTICS OF THE POPULATION, pt. 6, at 127-44; pt. 10, at 20; pt. 15, at 104-14; pt. 22, at 42-44; pt. 23, at 78-89; pt. 24, at 76-83; pt. 25, at 66-69; pt. 27, at 69-72; pt. 34, at 100-10; pt. 37, at 101-11; pt. 40, at 124-39; pt. 45, at 113-24, Table 21 (1963).

FIGURE 3

BLACKS AS A PROPORTION OF TOTAL PUBLIC ELEMENTARY SCHOOL ENROLLMENT IN CENTRAL CITIES AND THEIR SUBURBAN RINGS, 1960 AND 1970

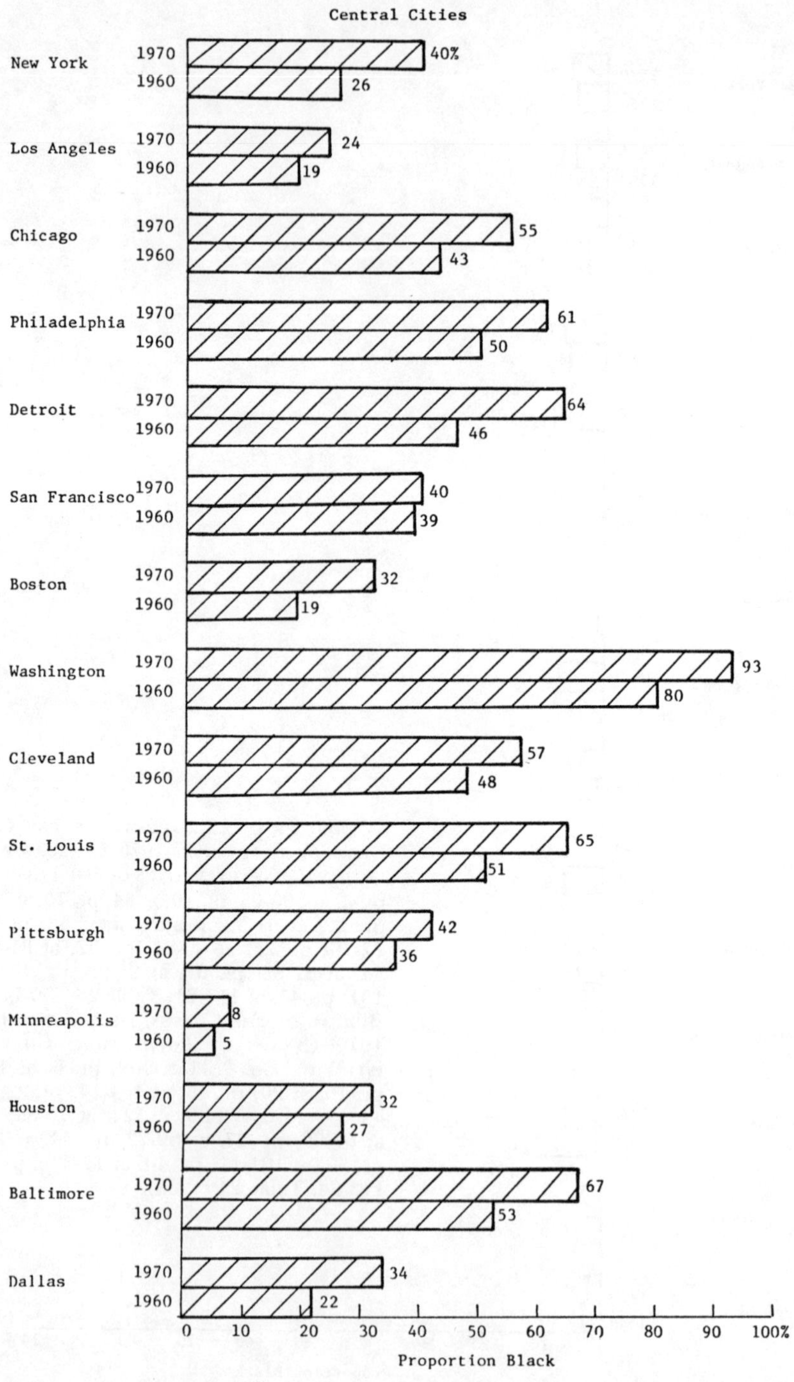

FIGURE 3 (cont.)

BLACKS AS A PROPORTION OF TOTAL PUBLIC ELEMENTARY SCHOOL ENROLLMENT IN CENTRAL CITIES AND THEIR SUBURBAN RINGS, 1960 AND 1970

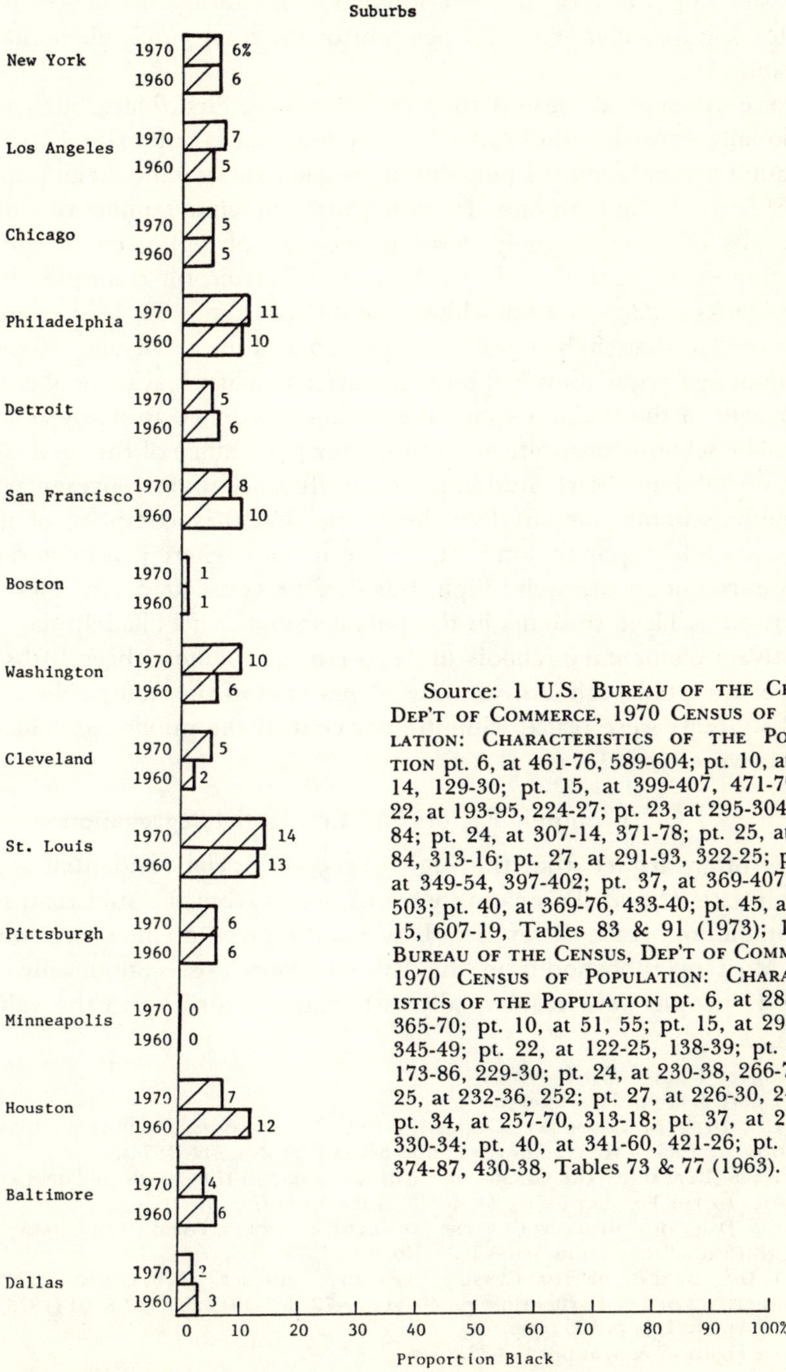

Source: 1 U.S. BUREAU OF THE CENSUS, DEP'T OF COMMERCE, 1970 CENSUS OF POPULATION: CHARACTERISTICS OF THE POPULATION pt. 6, at 461-76, 589-604; pt. 10, at 113-14, 129-30; pt. 15, at 399-407, 471-79; pt. 22, at 193-95, 224-27; pt. 23, at 295-304, 375-84; pt. 24, at 307-14, 371-78; pt. 25, at 281-84, 313-16; pt. 27, at 291-93, 322-25; pt. 34, at 349-54, 397-402; pt. 37, at 369-407, 492-503; pt. 40, at 369-76, 433-40; pt. 45, at 503-15, 607-19, Tables 83 & 91 (1973); 1 U.S. BUREAU OF THE CENSUS, DEP'T OF COMMERCE, 1970 CENSUS OF POPULATION: CHARACTERISTICS OF THE POPULATION pt. 6, at 285-304, 365-70; pt. 10, at 51, 55; pt. 15, at 293-305, 345-49; pt. 22, at 122-25, 138-39; pt. 23, at 173-86, 229-30; pt. 24, at 230-38, 266-70; pt. 25, at 232-36, 252; pt. 27, at 226-30, 246-47; pt. 34, at 257-70, 313-18; pt. 37, at 274-87, 330-34; pt. 40, at 341-60, 421-26; pt. 45, at 374-87, 430-38, Tables 73 & 77 (1963).

elementary school enrollment in the fifteen largest cities for the census years 1960 and 1970, as shown in Figure 3, is considerably higher than the black population as a percentage of the total city population. For example, blacks comprised 33 per cent of the total population of Chicago in 1970;[22] in the same year, black pupils comprised 55 per cent of the total public elementary school population.[23]

There are several reasons for this difference. First, black birth rates have traditionally exceeded those of whites. While blacks comprise 11 per cent of this nation's population, 14 per cent of the elementary school age population is black.[24] Second, the high rate of out-migration of white families of childbearing age results in a considerably lower proportion of white school age children remaining in the central cities. In the city of Detroit, for example, the median age of blacks is 23, while for whites, the median age is 36. Whites account for 77 per cent of that city's population aged 65 and over, but only 46 per cent of the school age population.[25] Third, private and parochial schools enroll about 10 per cent of the nation's elementary school students. In many central cities, non-public schools constitute an even higher percentage of the total elementary school enrollment. Black students are significantly underrepresented in these non-public schools compared to the proportion they comprise of the public elementary school population.[26] In northern cities, where private and parochial school enrollments are quite high, this has the consequence of increasing the proportion of black students in the public schools. In Philadelphia, for example, private elementary schools in 1970 enrolled almost three-fifths as many pupils as the public schools, yet only 11 per cent of the non-public elementary school students were black, while 61 per cent of the public elementary school students were black.[27]

C. Economic Factors and Residential Segregation

It is often argued that the high degree of racial residential segregation found in cities[28] and the near-absence of blacks from the suburban ring[29] are attributable to income differences between the races. Such contentions are not valid. Most neighborhoods in the United States are economically heterogeneous. If people were residentially distributed according to the value of the

22. Figure 2, at pp. 170-71 *supra*.

23. Figure 3, at pp. 172-73 *supra*.

24. U.S. Dep't of Commerce, Current Population Reports: Population Estimates and Projections 2, Table 1 (Bureau of the Census Series P-25, No. 511, 1974).

25. 1 U.S. Bureau of the Census, Dep't of Commerce, 1970 Census of Population: Characteristics of the Population pt. 24, at 100, Table 24 (1973).

26. U.S. Dep't of Commerce, Current Population Reports: Population Characteristics 3, Table 1 (Bureau of the Census Series P-20, No. 261, 1974).

27. 1 U.S. Bureau of the Census, Dep't of Commerce, 1970 Census of Population: Characteristics of the Population, pt. 40, at 371-72, 435-36, Tables 83 & 91 (1973).

28. *See* Figure 1, at p. 166 *supra*.

29. *See* Figures 2 & 3, at pp. 170-73 *supra*.

housing they can afford, instead of according to skin color, levels of residential segregation would be low. Figure 4 indicates the percentage of black families and of white families in an urbanized area that actually lived in the suburban ring in 1970, and the percentage of black families that *would* live in the suburbs if the only factor affecting their residential location were their income. We assume, for instance, that if 40 per cent of white families in the urbanized area with incomes of $8,000 to $10,000 lived in the suburbs, then the same proportion of blacks at that income level would be living in the suburbs. We are assuming that blacks retain their actual incomes but are as well represented in the suburbs as whites at each income level.

FIGURE 4

ACTUAL PROPORTION OF BLACK AND WHITE FAMILIES LIVING IN SUBURBAN RING AND PROPORTION OF BLACK FAMILIES EXPECTED IN SUBURBAN RING ON THE BASIS OF THEIR INCOME, 1970

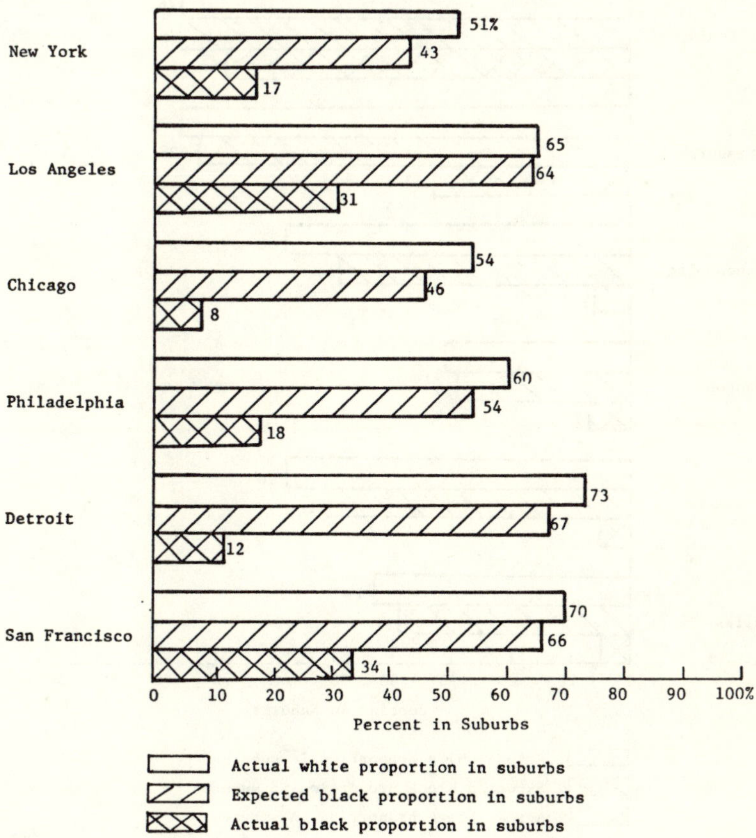

(continued on next page)

FIGURE 4 (cont.)

ACTUAL PROPORTION OF BLACK AND WHITE FAMILIES LIVING IN SUBURBAN RING AND PROPORTION OF BLACK FAMILIES EXPECTED IN SUBURBAN RING ON THE BASIS OF THEIR INCOME, 1970

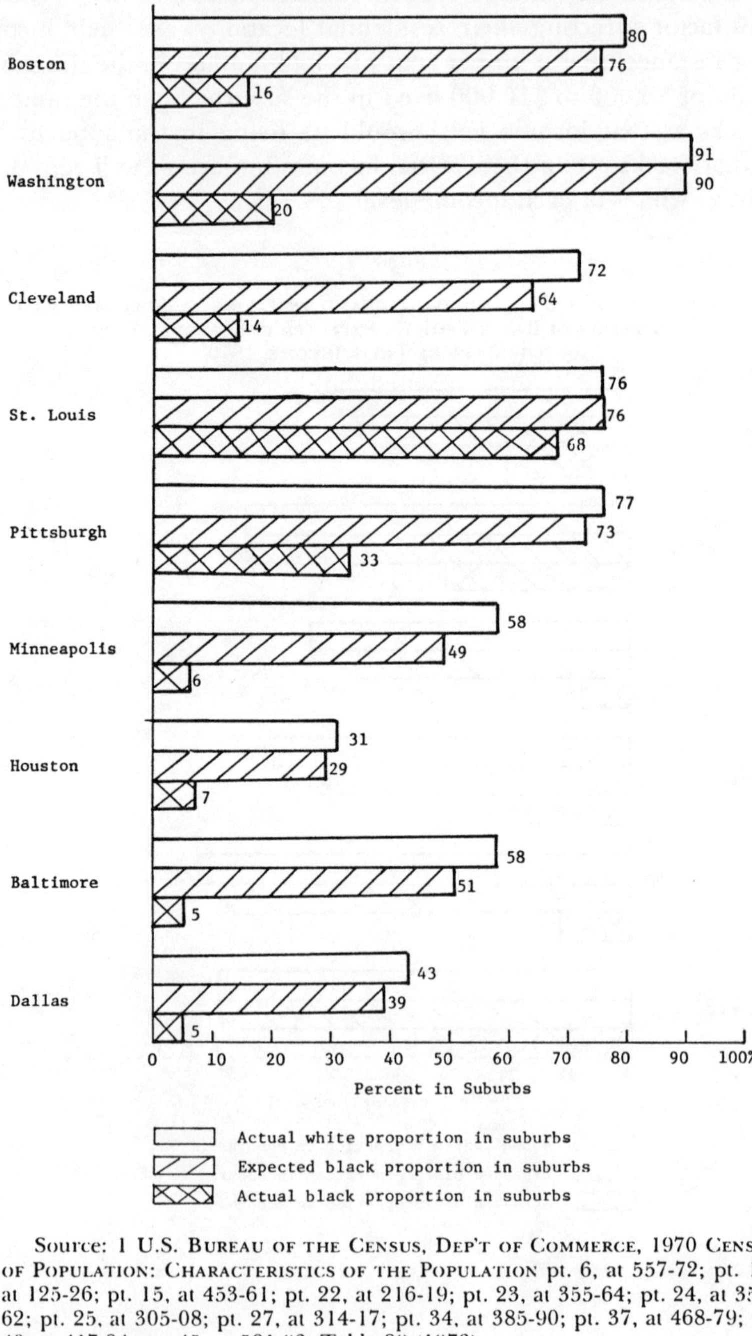

SOURCE: 1 U.S. BUREAU OF THE CENSUS, DEP'T OF COMMERCE, 1970 CENSUS OF POPULATION: CHARACTERISTICS OF THE POPULATION pt. 6, at 557-72; pt. 10, at 125-26; pt. 15, at 453-61; pt. 22, at 216-19; pt. 23, at 355-64; pt. 24, at 355-62; pt. 25, at 305-08; pt. 27, at 314-17; pt. 34, at 385-90; pt. 37, at 468-79; pt. 40, at 417-24; pt. 45, at 581-93, Table 89 (1973).

In most urbanized areas, the racial composition of the suburbs would be greatly altered if blacks occupied housing according to their ability to pay. In 1970, 73 per cent of the Detroit area's white families, but only 12 per cent of the area's black families, actually lived in the suburban ring. If blacks were as well represented in the suburbs at each income level as whites, 67 per cent of the black families—rather than 12 per cent—would be suburban residents.

Other studies which have analyzed the role that economic variables play in the residential segregation of blacks from whites within central cities[30] or in suburban areas[31] also demonstrate that economic factors explain only a small proportion of the residential segregation found in American metropolises.

III

RACIAL SEGREGATION IN PUBLIC ELEMENTARY SCHOOLS

Southern schools were completely segregated by race in 1954. Many northern city schools were also highly segregated because of school board practices and because neighborhoods were segregated by race.[32] For approximately a decade after the Supreme Court's ruling in *Brown v. Board of Education*,[33] private lawsuits on behalf of students in southern districts brought about limited advances in racial integration, particularly in schools in border states.[34]

The Civil Rights Act of 1964[35] gave the Justice Department power to bring school desegregation suits[36] and provided that the Department of Health, Education, and Welfare (HEW) could terminate funds in districts which maintained segregated facilities.[37] The latter provision gained further importance with the passage of the Elementary and Secondary Education Act of 1965,[38] which channeled large amounts of federal funds to southern districts.[39]

Governmental pressures for school desegregation increased after 1965 as HEW issued guidelines[40] and negotiated with many southern districts about

---

30. K. TAEUBER AND A. TAEUBER, *supra* note 1, at 78-95.

31. Hermalin & Farley, *supra* note 5, at 605-08.

32. For evidence concerning school segregation prior to 1967, see 2 U.S. COMMISSION ON CIVIL RIGHTS, RACIAL ISOLATION IN THE PUBLIC SCHOOLS 12-19, Table A-3 (1967).

33. 347 U.S. 483 (1954).

34. *See* G. ORFIELD, THE RECONSTRUCTION OF SOUTHERN EDUCATION 15-32 (1969); J. PELTASON, FIFTY-EIGHT LONELY MEN 114-15 (1961); U.S. BUREAU OF THE CENSUS, DEP'T OF COMMERCE, 1972 STATISTICAL ABSTRACT OF THE UNITED STATES, 118 (1972).

35. 42 U.S.C. § 2000 (1970).

36. *Id.* § 2000c-6.

37. *Id.* § 2000d-1.

38. 20 U.S.C. § 241a *et seq* (1970). *See also* 42 U.S.C. § 2000d-5 (1970).

39. *See* G. ORFIELD, *supra* note 34, at 94.

40. U.S. OFFICE OF EDUCATION, DEP'T OF HEALTH, EDUCATION, & WELFARE, GENERAL STATEMENT OF POLICIES UNDER TITLE VI OF THE CIVIL RIGHTS ACT OF 1964 RESPECTING DESEGREGATION OF ELEMENTARY AND SECONDARY SCHOOLS (1965). The Fifth Circuit Court of Appeals in effect adopted the HEW guidelines as minimum standards in Singleton v. Jackson Municipal Separate School Dist., 348 F.2d 729, 730-31 (5th Cir. 1965) (Singleton I), and Singleton v. Jackson Municipal Separate School Dist., 355 F.2d 865, 869 (5th Cir. 1966) (Singleton II). *See also*

discriminatory practices.[41] Federal courts enunciated new and encompassing integration principles. For example, the 1968 Supreme Court decision in *Green v. County School Board of New Kent County*[42] held that freedom-of-choice integration plans were acceptable only if they actually desegregated schools. In *Alexander v. Holmes County Board of Education*[43] the Supreme Court demanded that school districts terminate dual systems at once and begin immediately to operate unitary systems. The Denver decision, *Keyes v. School District No. 1*,[44] called for school integration in a northern city which did not have the history of state-prescribed de jure segregation common to the southern school districts. The Supreme Court's unanimous decision in the Charlotte, North Carolina case, *Swann v. Charlotte-Mecklenburg Board of Education*,[45] legitimized large-scale busing as an integration device and permitted the use of a "mathematical racial balance reflecting the pupil constituency of the system" as "a starting point in the process of shaping a remedy."[46]

The Civil Rights Act of 1964 also provided for the collection of data concerning the racial composition of students and staff in public schools.[47] These data permit the measurement of trends over time in school segregation. An analysis of large city school districts, 85 in the North and 58 in the South,[48] enrolling 20 per cent of the nation's white public elementary school students in the fall of 1972 and 65 per cent of the black students, was undertaken to determine the extent of intradistrict school segregation.[49]

The index of dissimilarity,[50] used in the first part of this article as a measure of residential segregation, can also be used to measure school segregation.

Read, *Judicial Evolution of the Law of School Integration Since* Brown v. Board of Education, 39 LAW & CONTEMP. PROB. no. 1, at 7, 20 (1975).

41. *See* U.S. OFFICE OF EDUCATION, *supra* note 40, at 87-102, 142-50, 338-39. *See also* Read, *supra* note 40, at 20-22.

42. 391 U.S. 430 (1968).

43. 396 U.S. 19 (1969).

44. 413 U.S. 189 (1973).

45. 402 U.S. 1 (1971).

46. *Id.* at 25, 29.

47. 42 U.S.C. § 2000c-1 (1970); Pub. L. No. 88-352, § 402, 78 Stat. 247 (1964).

48. The 85 northern districts and the 58 southern districts selected for this analysis met the following criteria: (1) The city associated with the school district had a total population of 100,000 or more in 1970. Seventeen cities under 100,000 for which residential segregation scores were available were also included. In most states, city school district boundaries are coterminous with the boundaries of the municipality. In some southern states, however, the city school district is coterminous with the entire county. The Charlotte-Mecklenburg school district, for example, includes both the city of Charlotte and Mecklenburg County, North Carolina. (2) Data concerning school segregation were available for the years 1967, 1970, and 1972. The district of Detroit provided 1966 data rather than 1967 and eight other districts provided 1968 data rather than 1967. (3) At least 3 per cent of the district's public school enrollment was black.

49. *See* U.S. DEP'T OF COMMERCE, CURRENT POPULATION REPORTS: SPECIAL STUDIES (Bureau of the Census Series P-23, No. 48, 1974).

50. This index, used for measuring racial residential segregation, is discussed in note 1 *supra*. When used to measure school segregation, the index of dissimilarity compares the racial composition of individual schools to the racial composition of the entire school district. The numerical

Large values indicate a substantial degree of segregation while low values indicate that the school district is effectively integrated. In 1967, segregation indices for Montgomery, Alabama and Shreveport, Louisiana[51] exceeded 97, indicating the existence of a dual school system in each of those cities.

Several federal judges, having found that a school system is unconstitutionally segregated, have ordered as part of the judicial relief that the individual schools in an unconstitutionally dual system should have approximately the same racial composition as the entire district. In *Swann v. Charlotte-Mecklenburg Board of Education*,[52] the district court mandated that school authorities assign pupils such that each school would approximate the 71 per cent white, 29 per cent black ratio of the district.[53] The integration plan designed for the Louisville area, where about 20 per cent of the student population is black, specified that for the fall of 1974, the proportion of blacks in every school must be between 12 and 30 per cent.[54] If these remedial orders are implemented, the indices of dissimilarity will be low for these school districts.

Indices of dissimilarity measuring racial segregation in the public elementary schools in the fifteen largest cities in the South and Border States and the fifteen largest cities in the North and West[55] are given in Figure 5. In 1967, the southern and border districts had high segregation indices ranging from a low of 76 in Louisville to a high of 97 in Oklahoma City. Schools were somewhat less segregated by race in the North and West, but not significantly so. New York was the only northern district with an index below 60, while San Fran-

---

value of the index represents the proportion of either white students or black students who would have to be shifted from one school to another to effect complete integration of the schools in the district. If a school district were completely integrated so that all schools had the same racial composition, the value of the index would be zero. If, on the other hand, school segregation were so pervasive that all students attend racially homogeneous schools, the index would assume its maximum value, 100. Thus low values indicate that there is little school segregation while high values indicate extensive school segregation.

51. The Shreveport index is derived from data for Caddo Parish rather than being limited to the city itself.

52. 311 F. Supp. 265 (W.D.N.C.), *aff'd in part and vacated and remanded in part*, 431 F.2d 138 (4th Cir.), *dist. ct. order reinstated pending further proceedings*, 399 U.S. 926, *aff'd as to part aff'd by ct. of app. and aff'd dist. ct. order stemming from remand*, 402 U.S. 1 1970).

53. 311 F. Supp. at 267-68. On appeal, the United States Supreme Court approved the use of such racial quotas as "a starting point in the process of shaping a remedy, rather than an inflexible requirement." 402 U.S. at 25. However, the Court went on to say:

> If we were to read the holding of the District Court to require, as a matter of substantive constitutional right, any particular degree of racial balance or mixing, that approach would be disapproved and we would be obliged to reverse. The constitutional command to desegregate schools does not mean that every school in every community must always reflect the racial composition of the school system as a whole.

402 U.S. at 24.

54. 12 INTEGRATED EDUCATION 13 (September-October, 1974).

55. For results of similar studies see Farley & Taeuber, *Racial Segregation in the Public Schools*, 79 AM. J. SOCIOLOGY 888 (1974); Rossell, *Measuring School Desegregation*, in POLITICAL STRATEGIES IN NORTHERN SCHOOL DESEGREGATION 171-182 (D. Kirby, T. Harris, R. Crain, & C. Rossell eds. 1973); Farley, *Racial Integration in the Public Schools, 1967 to 1972: Assessing the Effect of Governmental Policies*, 8 SOCIOLOGICAL FOCUS 1 (1975).

FIGURE 5

INDEXES OF RACIAL SEGREGATION IN PUBLIC ELMENTARY SCHOOLS, 1967, 1970, AND 1972

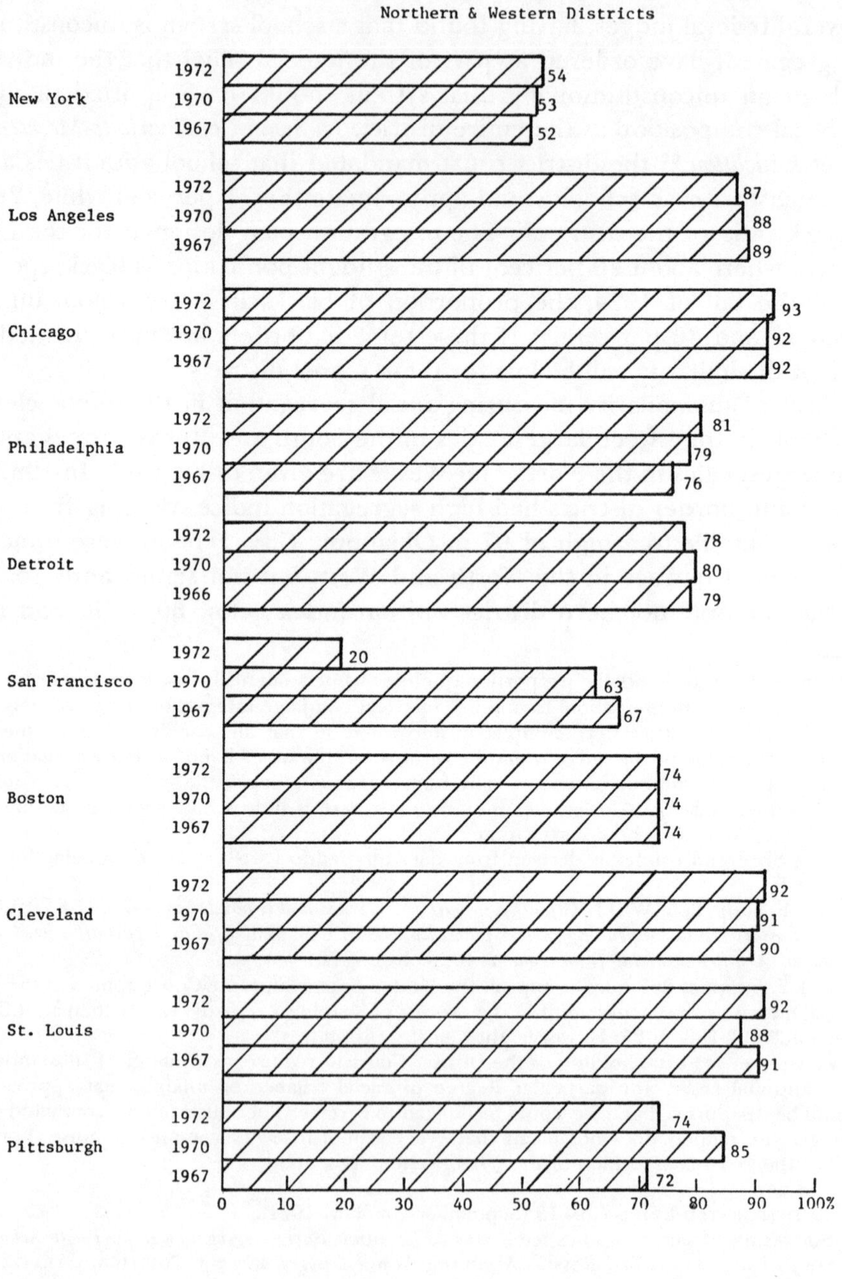

FIGURE 5 (cont.)

INDEXES OF RACIAL SEGREGATION IN PUBLIC ELEMENTARY SCHOOLS, 1967, 1970 AND 1972

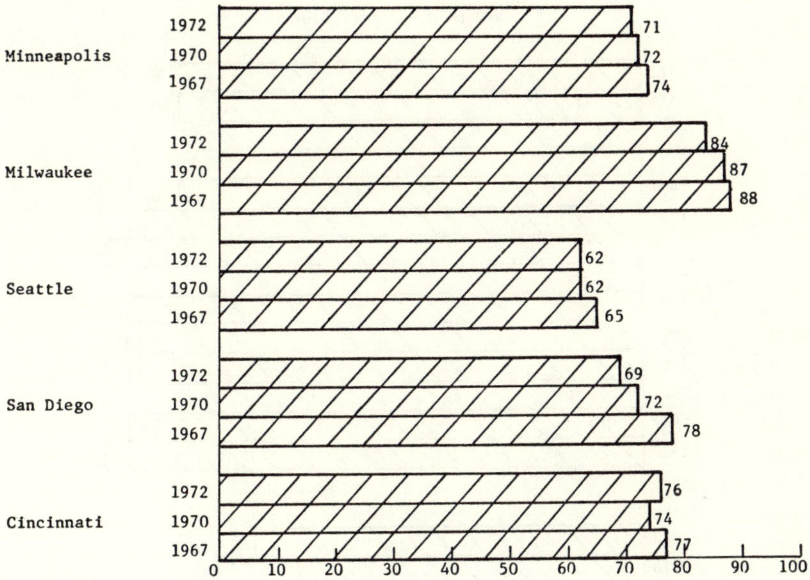

	Northern Districts N=85		
	1967	1970	1972
Student Racial Segregation Indexes			
Mean	68	62	58
Standard Deviation	15	18	20

Source: U.S. NATIONAL CENTER FOR EDUCATIONAL STATISTICS, DIRECTORY: PUBLIC ELEMENTARY AND SECONDARY SCHOOLS IN LARGE DISTRICTS (Fall 1967); U.S. OFFICE FOR CIVIL RIGHTS, DEP'T OF HEALTH, EDUCATION, AND WELFARE, DIRECTORY OF PUBLIC ELEMENTARY AND SECONDARY SCHOOLS IN SELECTED DISTRICTS (Fall 1970); U.S. OFFICE FOR CIVIL RIGHTS, DEP'T OF HEALTH, EDUCATION, AND WELFARE, DIRECTORY OF PUBLIC ELEMENTARY AND SECONDARY SCHOOLS IN SELECTED DISTRICTS (Fall 1972).

(continued on next page)

FIGURE 5 (cont.)

INDEXES OF RACIAL SEGREGATION IN PUBLIC ELEMENTARY SCHOOLS, 1967, 1970, AND 1972

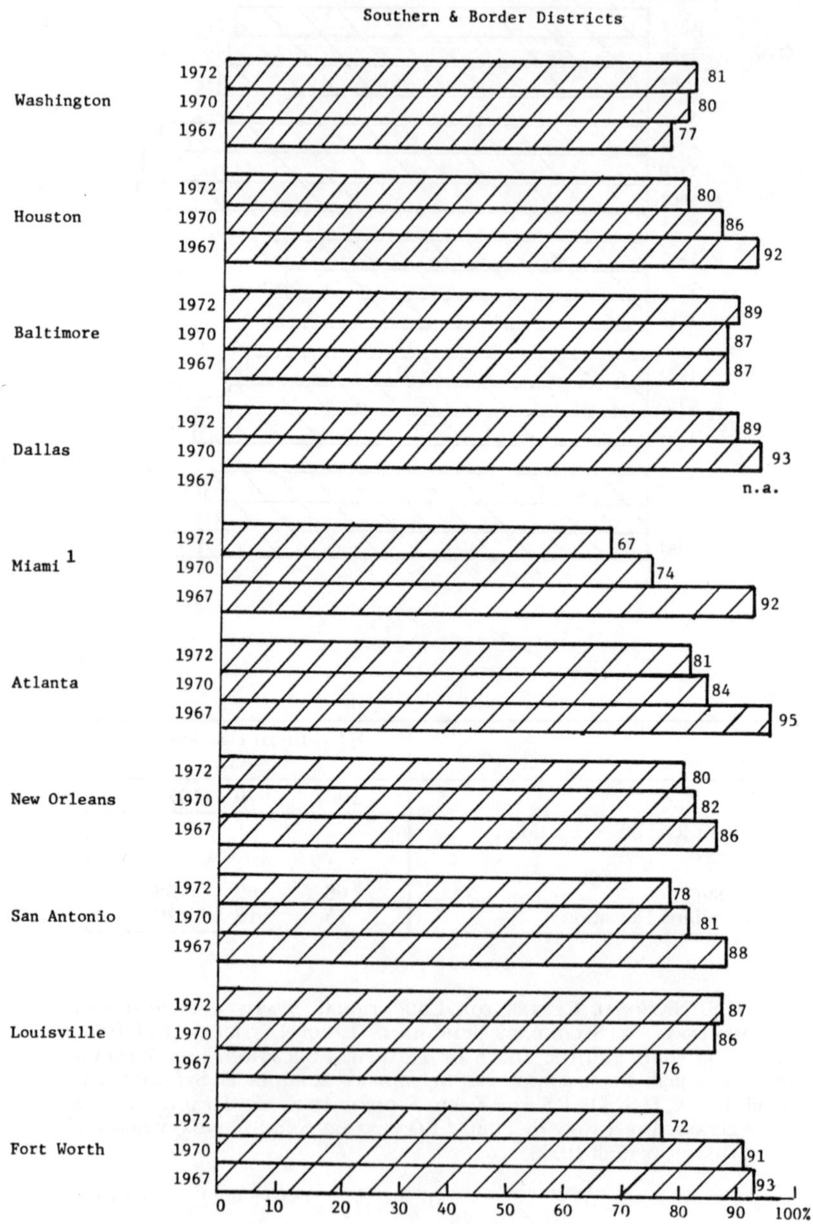

[1]Data for the school districts refer to an entire county.

FIGURE 5 (cont.)

INDEXES OF RACIAL SEGREGATION IN PUBLIC ELEMENTARY SCHOOLS, 1967, 1970, AND 1972

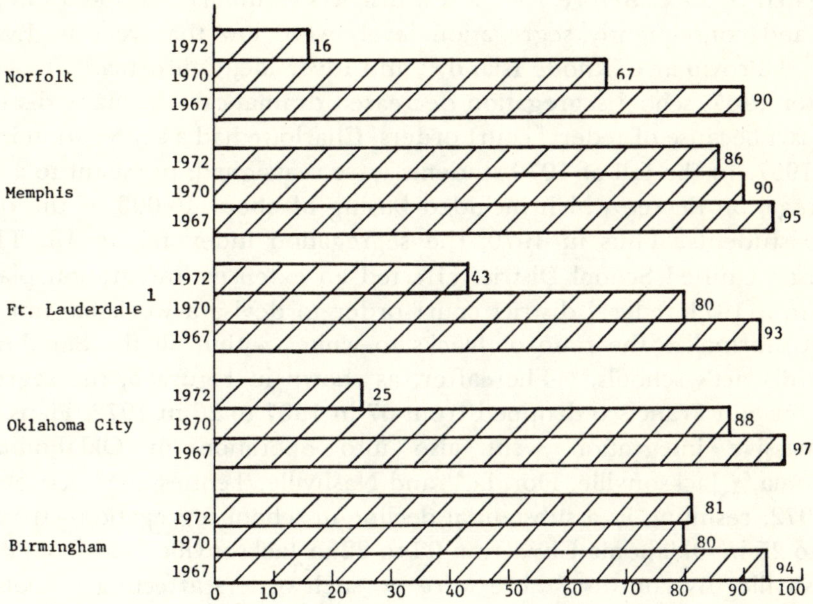

	Southern Districts N=58		
	1967	1970	1972
Student Racial Segregation Indexes			
Mean	86	75	53
Standard Deviation	11	16	26

Source: U.S. NATIONAL CENTER FOR EDUCATIONAL STATISTICS, DIRECTORY: PUBLIC ELEMENTARY AND SECONDARY SCHOOLS IN LARGE DISTRICTS (Fall 1967); U.S. OFFICE FOR CIVIL RIGHTS, DEP'T OF HEALTH, EDUCATION, AND WELFARE, DIRECTORY OF PUBLIC ELEMENTARY AND SECONDARY SCHOOLS IN SELECTED DISTRICTS (Fall 1970); U.S. OFFICE FOR CIVIL RIGHTS, DEP'T OF HEALTH, EDUCATION, AND WELFARE, DIRECTORY OF PUBLIC ELEMENTARY AND SECONDARY SCHOOLS IN SELECTED DISTRICTS (Fall 1972).

cisco and Seattle had indices under 70. The average student segregation indices for the two major regions are shown in Figure 5.

Changes over time in school segregation can be readily summarized. Prior to a major desegregation effort, schools in all these districts were extensively segregated by race. Before 1967 a few districts voluntarily adopted integration plans and consequently segregation levels were low that year in Evanston, Illinois,[56] Providence, Rhode Island,[57] and Riverside, California.[58]

After 1967, school segregation decreased dramatically in many districts, in large part because of federal court orders. Charlotte had a segregation index of 77 in 1967. In the fall of 1970 students were reassigned, pursuant to a federal desegregation decree which included busing of about 46,000 of the district's 80,000 students. Thus in 1970, the segregation index fell to 18. The San Francisco Unified School District effected an extensive integration plan pursuant to a 1971 federal district court order to devise a workable integration plan to normalize the ratio of blacks to whites within all the San Francisco school district's schools.[59] Thereafter, as shown in Figure 5, the segregation index for San Francisco dropped from 67 in 1967 to 20 in 1972. Plans requiring massive integration went also into operation in Oklahoma City, Oklahoma,[60] Jacksonville, Florida,[61] and Nashville, Tennessee,[62] between 1970 and 1972, resulting in a substantial decline in school segregation—from 97 in 1967 to 25 in Oklahoma City, from 92 to 22 in Jacksonville, and from 85 to 37 in Nashville. By contrast, there were no such orders affecting schools in St. Louis, Chicago, Cleveland, or Los Angeles, and, as indicated in Figure 5, the level of school segregation actually increased slightly between 1967 and 1972 in three out of four of these cities. The decrease in the fourth city, Los Angeles, was small—from 89 in 1967 to 87 in 1972.

Although federal courts and—in a few districts—state courts[63] played the dominant role in reducing school segregation, an analysis of data for these 143 districts indicates a general trend toward decreasing segregation in schools, even without court orders. After eliminating those districts involved in large-

---

56. *See* U.S. Commission on Civil Rights, The Diminishing Barrier: A Report on School Desegregation in Nine Communities 16-22 (1972).

57. *See* H. Pfautz, Providence, R.I.: The Politics of School Desegregation (1968) (unpublished manuscript on file with the Dep't of Sociology, Brown University).

58. *See* Hickerson, *Integrated vs. Compensatory Education in Riverside-San Bernardino Schools*, in School Desegregation in the North 116, 123-25 (T. Edwards & F. Wirt eds. 1967).

59. *See* Johnson v. San Francisco Unified School Dist., 339 F. Supp. 1315 (N.D. Cal. 1971). *See also* 3 Race Relations Law Survey 141 (1971).

60. *See* Dowell v. Board of Educ., 465 F.2d 1012 (10th Cir.), *cert. denied*, 409 U.S. 1041 (1972).

61. *See* Mims v. Duval County School Bd., 447 F.2d 1330 (5th Cir. 1971).

62. *See* Kelley v. Metropolitan County Bd. of Educ., 463 F.2d 732 (6th Cir.) *cert. denied*, 409 U.S. 1001 (1972).

63. *See* U.S. Commission on Civil Rights, *supra* note 56, at 23-28 (Harrisburg, Pa.); Fort, *Decision Making in the Sacramento De Facto Segregation Crisis*, in School Desegregation in the North, *supra* note 58, at 77-115 (Sacramento, Cal.).

scale desegregation programs, a pattern of modest declines in segregation levels is evident, the declines being greater in the South than in the North. One study[64] suggests that the pattern in many cities during the 1960's was as follows: demands by black parents for improved or integrated schools, initial rejection of these demands by school boards, followed by stronger demands from blacks and actions by courts no longer willing to tolerate delays in disestablishing dual school systems,[65] and finally school boards and administrators responding by improving some black schools, closing older and inadequate facilities, reorganizing school attendance zones, busing students, or devising open-enrollment plans.[66] These actions help to account for the decrease in student segregation.

The summary data provided in Figure 5 for all 143 school districts indicate that in 1967 southern districts were considerably more segregated, with an index value of 86, than those outside the South, where the index value in 1967 was 68. By 1972, however, the average segregation index was smaller in the South, 53, than in the North and West, where it was 58. In 1967 the standard deviation for segregation scores was low in the South since southern districts all had similar levels of segregation. By contrast, the standard deviation for the South in 1972 was high, 26, indicating wide variations among southern districts in their levels of segregation. Those southern districts operating under court orders had low segregation indices—frequently under 25—while those not under such court orders in 1972—including Dallas, Houston, and Louisville —had indices exceeding 80.

IV

SCHOOL AND RESIDENTIAL SEGREGATION WITHIN DISTRICTS

Outside the South, we would expect a correspondence between a city's racial residential segregation index and its school segregation index since school attendance zones are often drawn on a neighborhood basis. It is more difficult to anticipate the relationship in the South. In 1954, southern schools were segregated regardless of whether or not racial residential segregation was present.[67] By the late 1960's, some of the South's larger, urban school districts

64. *See* Rossell, *supra* note 55.

65. For an excellent analysis of the reaction of the Fifth Circuit Court of Appeals to footdragging by school districts and lower federal courts, see Read, *Judicial Evolution of the Law of School Integration Since* Brown v. Board of Education, *supra* note 40, at 18-20.

66. *See* J. BOLNER & R. SHANLEY, BUSING: THE POLITICAL AND JUDICIAL PROCESS 193-95 (1974); C. WILLIE, RACE MIXING IN THE PUBLIC SCHOOLS ch. 2 (1973); Coleman, *Foreword: Three Phases of School Integration*, in AFFIRMATIVE SCHOOL INTEGRATION 5-6 (R. Hill & M. Feeley eds. 1967).

67. Green v. County School Bd. of New Kent County, 391 U.S. 430, 432 (1968), represents a situation where there is *no* residential segregation (New Kent County being a rural county in Eastern Virginia), but where there was *total* school segregation through 1965.

adopted the neighborhood schools concept[68] prevalent in the urban districts in the North. Others, however, retained dual systems with a slight sprinkling of blacks in the white schools resulting from the use of pupil placement plans[69] or freedom-of-choice plans.[70]

To determine the linkage between school segregation and residential segregation, school segregation indices of 94 cities (the 61 northern and 33 southern cities for which residential information was available) for 1972 were compared to the residential segregation indices for 1970 of the same cities. This analysis, shown in Figure 6,[71] indicates that there is no relationship between the extent of school segregation and residential segregation in the South—cities with high residential segregation scores were no more likely to have large school segregation scores than cities whose neighborhoods were relatively integrated. The slight relationship between school and residential segregation in the South that existed in 1967 has disappeared, undoubtedly because of the activity of federal courts, which have ordered school integration in many cities where blacks and whites are highly segregated by residence. These districts include Asheville, North Carolina,[72] Norfolk[73] and Richmond,[74] Virginia, and Oklahoma City, Oklahoma.[75] At the other extreme, public schools in Baltimore, Dallas, and St. Louis were highly segregated, reflecting their high degree

---

68. Charlotte, for instance, adopted a neighborhood system in the mid 1960's but freely permitted parents to transfer their children. U.S. COMMISSION ON CIVIL RIGHTS, FIVE COMMUNITIES: THEIR SEARCH FOR EQUAL EDUCATION 34 (1972). *Cf.* Swann v. Charlotte-Mecklenburg Bd. of Educ., 306 F. Supp. 1299, 1305 (W.D.N.C. 1967).

69. Pupil placement plans allowed school authorities initially to assign students to the schools maintained for their race. Each application for reassignment to schools of the opposite race was considered in light of various nonracial factors, *e.g.*, availability of staff or transportation, curricula suitable for the individual pupil's abilities and academic preparation, the psychological effect the assignment would have on the pupil, and his morals, conduct, home environment and health. Such plans were declared constitutionally permissible in Shuttlesworth v. Birmingham Bd. of Educ., 358 U.S. 101 (1958), *aff'g* 162 F. Supp. 372 (N.D. Ala. 1958). However, even Circuit Judge Rives, the author of the lower court opinion in *Shuttlesworth* (heard by a three-judge district court), recognized that the law easily could be applied unconstitutionally and that in that event it would be struck down. 162 F. Supp. at 381-82. Later, when it finally became clear that the sole purpose of such plans was to frustrate desegregation, they were enjoined. *See* Read, *supra* note 40, at 19.

70. Freedom-of-choice plans were designed, theoretically, to desegregate by allowing each student to attend the school he personally chose, limited only by the dimensions of the school district, the nature of the school, and the physical capacity of the school. *See* Read, *supra* note 40, at 19. Generally, however, they achieved no sizeable integration, as illustrated by the New Kent County, Virginia school system where a freedom-of-choice plan in effect between 1965 and 1968 resulted in no whites attending the formerly black high school and only 15 per cent of the county's black students enrolling in the formerly all-white high school. This result caused the Supreme Court to strike down freedom-of-choice plans which failed to achieve integration in Green v. County School Bd. of New Kent County, 391 U.S. 430 (1968). *See* Read, *supra* note 40, at 28-29.

71. Farley, *supra* note 55, at Table 4.

72. *See* Allen v. Asheville City Bd. of Educ., 434 F.2d 902 (4th Cir. 1970).

73. *See* Brewer v. School Bd., 397 F.2d 37 (4th Cir. 1968).

74. *See* Bradley v. School Bd. of City of Richmond, 317 F. Supp. 555 (E.D. Va. 1970).

75. *See* Dowell v. Board of Educ., 338 F. Supp. 1256 (W.D. Okla.), *aff'd*, 465 F.2d 1012 (10th Cir.), *cert. denied*, 409 U.S. 1041 (1972).

of residential segregation, since these districts were not operating in 1972 under federal court orders requiring massive integration.[76]

The northern city districts, however, do show a moderate relationship between residential and school segregation. Where neighborhoods are highly segregated, schools tend also to be highly segregated; and the variance in residential segregation accounts for one-sixth of the variance in school segregation. Those school districts where the degree of school segregation is much less than was predicted on the basis of their level of residential segregation are districts which put massive integration plans into operation, curtailing the extent to which the neighborhood school concept of pupil assignment was used. These districts include Berkeley,[77] Evanston,[78] Evansville,[79] Harrisburg,[80] Pasadena,[81] Providence,[82] and San Francisco.[83] Northern districts whose levels of school segregation greatly exceeded what would be predicted from their residential segregation scores include Chicago—a city in which both federal courts and HEW have failed to integrate schools[84]—and Cleveland.

V

CAUSES OF RESIDENTIAL SEGREGATION

At the beginning of this article, it was noted that if parents desired neighborhood schools and if the Constitution requires integrated schools, then neighborhoods must be integrated. It is therefore appropriate to examine the causes of residential segregation and possibilities for change. In his concurring opinion in *Milliken v. Bradley*, Justice Stewart noted that there was a " 'growing core of Negro schools surrounded by a receding ring of white schools in Detroit' " and that this "predominantly Negro school population in Detroit" was

---

76. The residential and school segregation scores for these cities, given in Figures 1 and 5, at p. 166 & pp. 180-83 *supra*, are as follows:

	Residential (1970)	*School* (1972)
Baltimore	89	89
Dallas	96	89
St. Louis	90	92

77. *See* Freudenthal, *Berkeley High Schools Integrate*, in SCHOOL DESEGREGATION IN THE NORTH, *supra* note 58, at 49-64; Hayman, *Berkeley*, in AFFIRMATIVE SCHOOL INTEGRATION 21-31 (R. Hill & M. Feeley eds. 1967).

78. *See* U.S. COMMISSION ON CIVIL RIGHTS, *supra* note 56, at 16-22; Coons, *Evanston*, in AFFIRMATIVE SCHOOL INTEGRATION, *supra* note 77, at 14-20.

79. *See* CENTER FOR NATIONAL POLICY REVIEW, JUSTICE DELAYED & DENIED 99-101 (1974).

80. *See* U.S. COMMISSION ON CIVIL RIGHTS, *supra* note 56, at 23-28.

81. *Cf.* Spangler v. Pasadena City Bd. of Educ., 427 F.2d 1352 (9th Cir. 1970), *cert. denied*, 402 U.S. 943 (1972); Spangler v. Pasadena City Bd. of Educ., 311 F. Supp. 501 (C.D. Cal. 1970).

82. *See* H. Pfautz, *supra* note 57.

83. *See* Johnson v. San Francisco Unified School Dist., 339 F. Supp. 1315 (N.D. Cal. 1971).

84. *See* CENTER FOR NATIONAL POLICY REVIEW, *supra* note 79, at 7-10; G. ORFIELD, *supra* note 34, at ch. 4.

FIGURE 6

SCHOOL SEGREGATION SCORES IN 1972 AND RESIDENTIAL SEGREGATION SCORES IN 1970, SELECTED NORTHERN AND SOUTHERN SCHOOL DISTRICTS

A. Data for the North (N = 61)

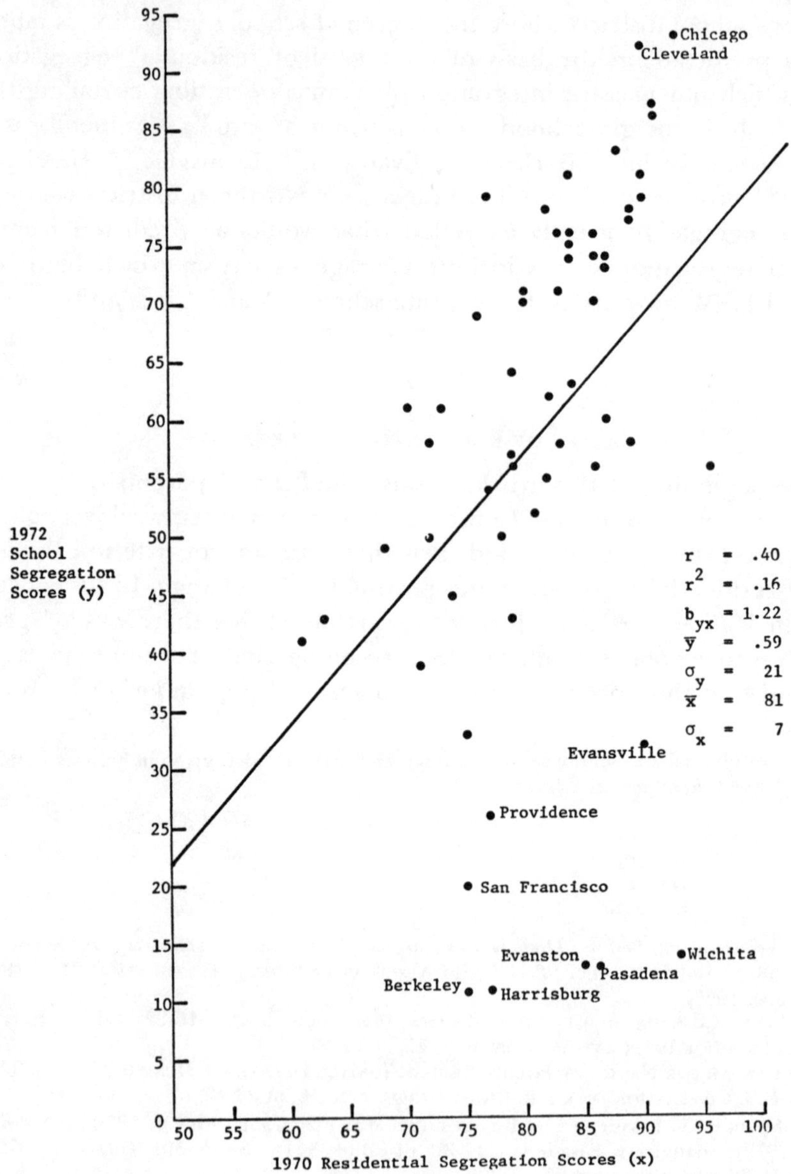

FIGURE 6 (cont.)

SCHOOL SEGREGATION SCORES IN 1972 AND RESIDENTIAL SEGREGATION SCORES IN 1970, SELECTED NORTHERN AND SOUTHERN SCHOOL DISTRICTS

B. Data for the South (N = 33)

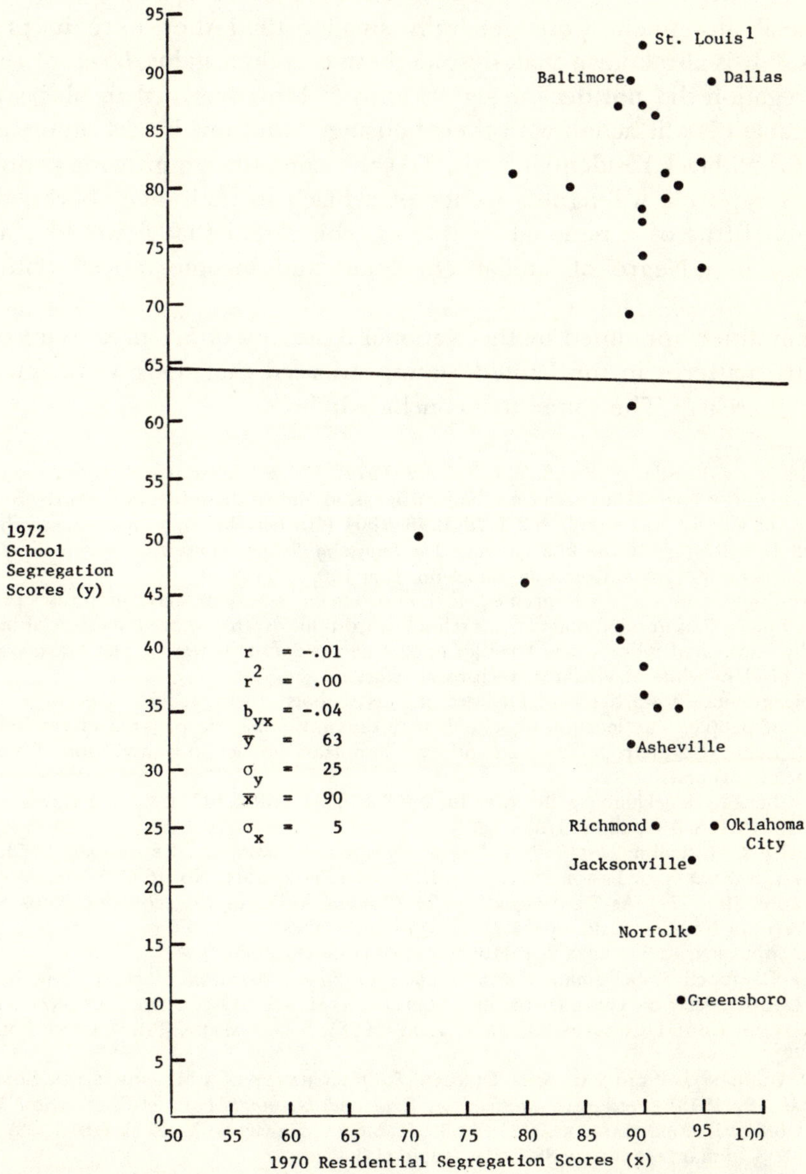

[1]The Bureau of the Census classifies Missouri as a northern state. However, since schools in that state were once segregated by law, it is here treated as a southern state.

Source: Data in Figures 1 and 5.

"caused by unknown and perhaps unknowable factors such as in-migration, birth rates, economic changes, or cumulative acts of private racial fears . . . ."[85]

Many aspects of the trend toward residential segregation are known, however. For example, it is known that blacks made sizable economic gains during the 1960's and that by 1970 racial differences in occupation, income, and educational attainment were generally smaller than they were in previous decades.[86] It is also known that, despite these economic gains, levels of residential segregation did not decline significantly.[87] Moreover, urban blacks report considerable dissatisfaction with their housing,[88] and few blacks report a preference for all black residential areas.[89] At the same time, a growing proportion of whites report a willingness to accept a black in their neighborhood;[90] in 1972, four-fifths of a national sample of whites said that it would make no difference if a Negro of similar education and income moved onto their block.[91]

A committee appointed by the National Academy of Sciences to investigate residential patterns in the United States, observed that there were few stable interracial areas.[92] The committee concluded:[93]

---

85. Milliken v. Bradley, 418 U.S. 717, 756 n.2 (1974). Judge Craven, speaking for the majority in the Richmond metropolitan area case, had earlier used almost these identical words. Bradley v. School Bd. of City of Richmond, 462 F.2d 1058, 1064 (4th Cir. 1972), *aff'd by an equally divided Court*, 412 U.S. 92 (1973). *See also* Craven, *The Impact of Social Science Evidence on the Judge: A Personal Comment*, 39 LAW & CONTEMP. PROB. no. 1, at 150, 155 (1975).

Interestingly, however, the Supreme Court, in two major school desegregation cases preceding *Milliken v. Bradley*, has implied that various school board policies which have the effect of maintaining racially segregated schools may have an impact on residential patterns. The "earmarking" of schools as black or white may have a "reciprocal effect":

> People gravitate toward school facilities, just as schools are located in response to the needs of people. The location of schools may thus influence the patterns of residential development of a metropolitan area and have important impact on composition of inner-city neighborhoods.

Swann v. Charlotte-Mecklenburg Bd. of Educ., 402 U.S. 1, 20-21 (1971). *See also* Keyes v. School Dist. No. 1, 413 U.S. 189, 200 (1973).

86. Farley & Hermalin, *The 1960s: A Decade of Progress for Blacks?*, 9 DEMOGRAPHY 353, 354-65 (1972). *See* U.S. BUREAU OF LABOR STATISTICS, DEP'T OF LABOR, BULL. NO. 1699, BLACK AMERICANS: A CHARTBOOK 39 (1971). As Figure 4, at pp. 75-76 *supra*, indicates, the economic status of blacks does not account for their residential segregation from whites.

87. A. SØRENSEN, K. TAEUBER & J. HOLLINGSWORTH, *supra* note 12.

88. *See* Campbell & Schuman, *Racial Attitudes in Fifteen American Cities*, in THE NATIONAL ADVISORY COMMISSION ON CIVIL DISORDERS, SUPPLEMENTAL STUDIES FOR THE NATIONAL ADVISORY COMMISSION ON CIVIL DISORDERS 23, Table II-m (1968); 3 G. GALLUP, THE GALLUP POLL 2037, 2195 (1972).

89. O. DUNCAN, H. SCHUMAN, & B. DUNCAN, SOCIAL CHANGE IN A METROPOLITAN COMMUNITY 108, Table 48 (1973); Pettigrew, *Attitudes on Race and Housing: A Social-Psychological View*, in SEGREGATION IN RESIDENTIAL AREAS 21, 44-45, Table (A. Hawley & V. Rock eds. 1973). *See also* Campbell & Schuman, *supra* note 88, at 16, Table II-6.

90. O. DUNCAN, H. SCHUMAN, & B. DUNCAN, *supra* note 89, at 99, Table 41.

91. NATIONAL OPINION RESEARCH CENTER, NATIONAL DATA PROGRAM FOR THE SOCIAL SCIENCES 36 (1972).

92. SOCIAL SCIENCE PANEL, NATIONAL ACADEMY OF SCIENCES, FREEDOM OF CHOICE IN HOUSING (1972).

93. *Id.* at 20.

> Today, in many metropolitan areas there are in fact two housing markets, not one. A web of institutional discrimination exists that reduces the "effective" supply, especially for nonwhite minorities. The institutional web, comprised of many interrelated components, ranges from the services of realtors, mortgage lenders, appraisers, and developers; to the laws, government regulations, and administrative and political behavior of government officials; to patterns and practices related to employment, schools, transportation, and community services.

The implications of this institutional web of discrimination have also been apparent to several judges in school integration cases outside of the South.[94] Courts have not, however, solved the problem of how to cut through this web.

CONCLUSION

The analyses undertaken in this article have indicated first, that neighborhoods in the United States are extensively segregated by race and there is no compelling evidence that residential segregation is significantly decreasing. Second, within many—but not all—metropolitan areas, the out-migration of a substantial proportion of white families of childbearing age is responsible in large part for the existence of central cities with large black populations and surrounding suburban rings with primarily white populations. Third, pressures from the federal government for school integration greatly increased during the last decade, significantly reducing the degree to which central city school districts are segregated. Analysis of 143 school districts has indicated that, on the average, the proportion of either black or white students that a district would have to shift to bring about the same racial composition in each of the

---

94. In *Bradley v. Milliken*, Judge Roth pointed out that residential segregation within the city of Detroit and throughout the metropolitan area is "substantial, pervasive and of long standing." 338 F. Supp. 582, 586 (E.D. Mich. 1971), *aff'd*, 484 F.2d 215 (6th Cir. 1973), *rev'd*, 418 U.S. 717 (1974). In attempting to explain this phenomenon, Judge Roth continued:

> While the racially unrestricted choice of black persons and economic factors may have played some part in the development of this pattern of residential segregation, it is, in the main, the result of past and present practices and customs of racial discrimination, both public and private, which have and do restrict the housing opportunities of black people. . . .
>
> Governmental actions and inaction at all levels, federal, state and local, have combined, with those of private organizations, such as loaning institutions and real estate associations and brokerage firms, to establish and to maintain the pattern of residential segregation throughout the Detroit metropolitan area.

338 F. Supp. at 586-87.

Judge Keith, whose order integrated the schools in Pontiac, Michigan, in considering the role of the school board when confronted with the development of a residentially segregated pattern in that city, also touched on these factors:

> A Board of Education simply cannot permit a residential segregated situation to come about and then blithely announce that for a Negro student to gain attendance at a given school all he must do is live within the school's attendance area. To rationalize thusly is to be blinded to the realities of adult life with its prejudices and opposition to integrated housing.

Davis v. School Dist., 309 F. Supp. 734, 742 (E.D. Mich. 1970), *aff'd*, 443 F.2d 573 (6th Cir.), *cert. denied*, 404 U.S. 913 (1971).

schools in that district fell from 75 per cent in 1967 to 56 per cent in 1972. Those districts operating under court order, or which have voluntarily implemented integration plans, have segregation levels which are now dramatically lower than they were a decade ago. Intradistrict integration has proceeded most rapidly in the South, and today, on average, schools in that region are less racially segregated than schools in the North and West.

This article has attempted to address the relationship between residential segregation and school segregation. As the indices of school segregation given in Figures 5 and 6 have shown, schools can be integrated despite the existence of very high levels of residential segregation. However, residential segregation makes school integration more difficult to accomplish, and as the proportion of black students in large school districts increases, it will become necessary to bus more and more children longer distances to achieve integration of the schools.

Furthermore, the growing concentration of blacks in central cities, and the almost exclusively white school populations in the suburban rings, means that further court orders directed only to the central city will have limited impact. Public school enrollments in many of the largest cities are predominantly black and thus complete intradistrict integration in Chicago, Cleveland, Detroit, and Philadelphia would result in integrated schools which would be about three-fifths black; in Atlanta and New Orleans, such desegregated schools would be four-fifths black. The general trend toward out-migration of both whites and blacks and the decline in birth rates mean that both black and white enrollments in central city public schools will decline. The decline, however, will be greater among whites than blacks, meaning that integrated central city schools will enroll fewer and fewer white students.

When cities and their suburban rings are consolidated into single school districts—as is the case with the Miami-Dade County (Florida) school district, the Nashville-Davidson County (Tennessee) school district, and the Charlotte-Mecklenburg (North Carolina) school district—intradistrict integration will not lead to predominatly black central city schools. The recent Supreme Court decision in the case of Detroit and its suburbs suggests, however, that courts may have no power to *compel* such consolidations.[95] Thus the opportunity for achieving integrated schools by combining central city and suburban areas may only occur in the case of voluntary consolidations.

As the data have indicated, court-ordered or voluntary desegregation plans confined to the central city initially have a substantial impact on the degree of school integration, even though residential segregation remains firmly entrenched. However, as long as present demographic trends continue with the pupil population of the many cities becoming increasingly black, implementa-

95. Milliken v. Bradley, 418 U.S. 717 (1974). *See also* Bradley v. School Bd. of City of Richmond, 462 F.2d 1058 (4th Cir. 1972), *aff'd by an equally divided Court*, 412 U.S. 92 (1973). *But see* Newburg Area Council v. Board of Educ. of Jefferson County, 510 F.2d 1358 (6th Cir. 1974) (consolidated with Haycraft v. Board of Educ. of Louisville).

tion of such plans will have limited impact on the extent of school segregation. On the other hand, even if courts were willing to order integration on a metropolitan-wide basis, because of the extensive residential segregation both within the central city and between the city and the suburban ring—for what seem to be all too "knowable" factors of "institutional discrimination"—such integration of the schools could be accomplished only by sacrificing the neighborhood school concept.

THE JURISPRUDENCE OF BUSING

OWEN M. FISS*

School desegregation decrees have become a familiar part of the contemporary judicial landscape, and yet they remain enmeshed in controversy. These decrees have engendered two types of criticism. One is addressed to the merits and asserts that segregation is not sufficiently harmful to warrant the costs of busing. Another type of criticism, and the subject of this article, is institutional. It focuses on the predicate of decision—the judgment that segregation is sufficiently harmful to warrant the remedial costs; it notes the controversial character of that judgment; and it then asserts that a court should not coerce corrective action whenever its decision rests on such an uncertain basis.

This strain of institutional criticism has its roots in the attacks on *Brown v. Board of Education* that claimed that the decision was "sociology, not law," seizing on footnote eleven of that opinion, in which the Court referred to certain social science studies.[1] It is a line of criticism that has gained additional momentum as the nature of the school desegregation problem has changed and as the uncertainty has become more acute. My intent is to evaluate this criticism. As a first step, and in order to locate the sources of uncertainty, I will try to structure a desegregation decision.

I

THE STRUCTURE OF DECISION

A decree imposes a legal obligation to take corrective action. It must be predicated on the proposition (referred to as the underlying proposition) that the practice to be corrected or eliminated is sufficiently harmful that it justifies the consequent costs entailed in complying with the order. Other conditions might also have to be satisfied—for example, the judge must also find that the state is responsible for the harmful practice—but the proposition asserting that the harm is sufficient to justify the remedial costs is the necessary decisional predicate. This is a statement of ideal and expectation: what should be the basis of the decision and what usually is.

The underlying proposition can, in turn, be divided into three components that identify the range of judgments a court must make before relief is granted. First, the judge must identify and assess the harmfulness of the prac-

* Professor of Law, Yale University.

1. *See* 347 U.S. 483, 494 (1954). For an extensive bibliography and useful discussion of the footnote eleven attack, see P. ROSEN, THE SUPREME COURT AND SOCIAL SCIENCE (1972); Goodman, *De Facto School Segregation: A Constitutional and Empirical Analysis*, 60 CALIF. L. REV. 275, 278-83 (1972).

tice to be corrected (the harmfulness component); second, he must identify and assess the remedial costs (the remedial-cost component); and third, he must determine whether the harm is sufficient to justify the remedial costs (the relational component).

These are the judgments that must be made in every injunctive suit, even one based on the Constitution. The Constitution does not restrict the range of judgments. It does not make any of the components superfluous. Rather the Constitution operates within each component. It requires that the harm be of a certain character, it precludes the consideration of certain remedial costs, and it defines the nature of the relationship that must exist between the harm and the costs.

A. The Character of the Harm

Since a school decree seeks to implement the Equal Protection Clause, the target practice must not just be harmful, but particularly harmful to some identifiable class. It is this class-oriented quality of the harm that enables it to be perceived as a form of unequal treatment, and thus a subject of concern under the Equal Protection Clause.

There is some dispute as to which social classes are to be so shielded by the Equal Protection Clause. For example, should the Clause protect such classes as the "poor" or "illegitimate children" from particularly disadvantaging practices? But there is no dispute that wherever the line is drawn, blacks—the class allegedly injured in a desegregation suit—must be included. Both the historical origins of the Equal Protection Clause and the identity of blacks as a discrete class—indeed, as the perpetual underclass—suggest that blacks should be considered the prime beneficiary of that Clause.[2]

B. The Relevance of Remedial Costs

The relevance of remedial costs is often obscured in constitutional litigation. It is commonly asserted that violation of a "constitutional right" must be corrected regardless of the cost. Indeed, vindication-at-any-cost is often thought to be one of the special attributes of a right deemed "constitutional." This conceptualization may be appropriate for a narrow band of constitutional provisions, those that specifically confer a readily discernible right—such as the provision guaranteeing trial by jury—though even then a court may take account of the remedial costs in defining the incidents of the right—such as the number of jurors required[3] or the unanimity requirement.[4] But for constitutional provi-

2. The classic statement of this position is contained in the Slaughter House Cases, 83 U.S. (16 Wall.) 36, 71-72 (1873), and has been repeated on many occasions. *See, e.g.*, Oregon v. Mitchell, 400 U.S. 112, 126-27 (1970); Shelley v. Kraemer, 334 U.S. 1, 23 (1948).

3. *See, e.g.*, Williams v. Florida, 399 U.S. 78 (1970).

4. *See, e.g.*, Apodaca v. Oregon, 406 U.S. 404 (1972); Johnson v. Louisiana, 406 U.S. 356 (1972).

sions like the due process or equal protection clauses the remedial costs are clearly relevant in determining whether there is a violation. With these provisions, the judiciary has considerable latitude in shaping the contours of a "constitutional right"—in determining whether segregation is to be deemed a denial of the equal protection of the laws and whether blacks have a "constitutional right" to have the system integrated. In making that judgment, the court must not only consider the harmfulness of the particular practice being challenged but also whether it is sufficiently harmful to warrant the costs of eliminating it.

Not all costs should be taken into consideration in deciding whether to invalidate a particular practice. A distinction must be made between allowable and non-allowable costs. The paradigmatic instance of an allowable cost would be the time and money consumed in busing. The psychic costs imposed on white racists who wish to keep blacks in a position of subordination would be a paradigmatic instance of a non-allowable cost.[5] A non-allowable cost has two defining features: (a) allowance would, as a practical matter, result in the continued subordination of the racial minority; and (b) the existence and magnitude of these costs are subject to individual control. The recognition of costs that have such qualities would be inconsistent with a central purpose of the Equal Protection Clause, and for that matter would also be inconsistent with the very idea of a constitutional restraint. The restraint would become dependent on the consent of those being restrained. If the psychic costs of the racist, for example, were considered an allowable cost and thus a restraint on remedial efforts, an incentive would be created for the racist to constantly escalate his hostility to blacks, at least until it is sufficient to stop the remedial effort.

The remedial costs of a busing decree, of course, do not categorize themselves as "allowable" and "non-allowable." That task of categorization is for the court, and often it is exceedingly difficult. This is particularly true of the remedial cost of greatest concern to those most interested in preserving the value of community—the disruptive impact of a busing decree on a neighborhood. For the community may be in part defined in terms of racial antipathy, an associational preference that, if it were standing alone, should be deemed non-allowable. In such a situation, the court must try to disaggregate the interests and preferences served by the demand to preserve the integrity of the community, determine which are allowable and which non-allowable, and make an assessment of the role that each one performs—obviously a treacherous task.

The distinction between allowable and non-allowable remedial costs is further blurred by the fact that the latter costs cannot be totally ignored. The frustration of racist associational preferences may, for example, result in temporary boycotts, permanent withdrawal from the public school system, and

5. *See generally* Watson v. City of Memphis, 373 U.S. 526 (1963); Cooper v. Aaron, 358 U.S. 1 (1958); Buchanan v. Warley, 245 U.S. 60 (1917).

violence—activities that limit the capacity of the court to eliminate the practice. Perhaps the most that can be said is that these non-allowable costs have a practical relevance, not a normative one. Non-allowable costs should not bear upon the creation and enforcement of rights and duties, although they may do so out of sheer necessity.

C. The Nature of the Relational Judgment

The judge must consider not only allowable remedial costs but, more importantly, he must conclude that they are justified by the eradication of the harm (the benefit). Two factors make this relational judgment particularly difficult. First, it calls for a comparison between the costs of the harm and those of the remedy even though these costs are not reducible to a single currency. Without a rate of exchange, a judge is faced with an apples-and-orange situation: how does he compare, for example, the dignitary harm of segregation with the costs of a school busing program?[6] Second, there is no clear understanding of the relationship that must exist between the harm and the remedial costs. It is clear that the harm must be "sufficient to justify" the remedial costs; but this concept is notably open-ended and susceptible to several interpretations.

If the harm is greater than the remedial costs, then the decree would seem justified. That would make a "greater-than" relationship a sufficient condition. The troublesome question is whether it is also a necessary condition.[7] Three features of the school desegregation problem lead me to a negative answer: (1) The claim is not merely that the practice is harmful, but that it is particularly harmful to one of our worst-off classes, blacks. (2) The remedial costs are spread generally through society, borne by both the minority and the majority.[8] (3) The decrees are predicated on the Equal Protection Clause whose guarantee seems to have constitutionalized a distributional preference. It prohibits the maximization of total welfare at the expense of the racial minority, or, to put the same point somewhat differently, it requires—in addition to

---

6. An objection to transportation of students may have validity when the time or distance of travel is so great as to either risk the health of the children or significantly impinge on the educational process. District courts must weigh the soundness of any transportation plan . . . . It hardly needs stating that the limits on time of travel will vary with many factors, but probably with none more than the age of the students. The reconciliation of competing values in a desegregation case is, of course, a difficult task with many sensitive facets but fundamentally no more so than remedial measures courts of equity have traditionally employed.

Swann v. Charlotte-Mecklenburg Bd. of Educ., 402 U.S. 1, 30-31 (1971).

7. Although these factors are not quantifiable, assume that the remedial costs were 300. There seems little doubt that a decree would be justified if the harm of the challenged practice were 500. The question posed here is whether the harm *must* be greater than 300 (the amount assigned to the remedial costs) in order for the decree to be justified.

8. The Supreme Court, by generally limiting the remedy to within-district busing, Milliken v. Bradley, 418 U.S. 717 (1974), may have introduced an economic bias into the remedy—its costs fall on those not wealthy enough to move out of the district into the suburbs.

the non-allowance of certain costs—the elimination of practices harmful to a racial minority, even at the expense of the polity as a whole.

For these reasons, the controlling standard should be one that requires not that the harm be greater than the remedial costs, but that the remedial costs not be "excessive"—not out of proportion to the harm.[9] Under this standard of proportionality, the visual image of the structure of the judicial decision is not one of "balancing," but rather one of having the harm—the fact that the challenged practice particularly disadvantages blacks—serve as a triggering mechanism, the impetus for relief, and having the remedial costs serve as the restraining force. The remedial effort is not brought to a halt when the remedial costs become greater than the harm but only when those costs become "excessive."

The judgment as to whether the remedial costs are excessive turns on the quality and quantity of harm, but not exclusively so. A judgment must also be made about alternative remedies. The judge must have some sense of the relationship between the harm and the remedial costs of alternative remedies before he decides whether the remedial costs of a decree he is contemplating are out of proportion to the harm. If an alternative remedy would eliminate the same amount of harm at less cost, then that remedy seems preferable.[10] The court need not choose the remedy that has the best cost-benefit relationship since it may eliminate a smaller portion of the harm. But, on the other hand, the cost-benefit relationship of alternative remedies is not rendered totally irrelevant by the Equal Protection Clause. An enormous saving in remedial costs might be worth a slight decrease in the total amount of harm eliminated.[11]

In making these judgments about alternative remedies, the judge must

---

9. The same general point could be accommodated under a "greater-than" standard if the minority interests were weighted, or if some value equal to the benefit society would receive from the elimination of the harm were either added to the minority-harm side or subtracted from the remedial-cost side. I am not sure that there are any advantages to be gained from these alternatives, and indeed, explicit weighting might have undesirable symbolic consequences.

10. For example, suppose the harm were 100; the remedial costs of one decree (decree A) were 300; but of another one (decree B) were 200. If both eliminate the same 100 harm, obviously B would be preferable. Similarly, if a cash payment of $150 (the gilded-ghetto strategy) truly compensated for the 100 units of harm and if it were less costly than either decree A or B—with no monetary value as yet placed on either decree—then the cash payment would be preferable. Of course, it is doubtful that the remedial costs could be translated into monetary terms, or that money would adequately compensate for the harm.

11. In Carr v. Montgomery County Bd. of Educ., 377 F. Supp. 1123 (M.D. Ala. 1974), *aff'd per curiam*, 511 F.2d 1374 (5th Cir. 1975), District Judge Frank Johnson rejected plaintiff's plea for greater desegregation, citing to "an excessive and unnecessarily heavy administrative burden" that the plan would place on the school system. 377 F. Supp. at 1129. In Northcross v. Board of Educ. of Memphis Schools, 489 F.2d 15 (6th Cir. 1973), *cert. denied*, 414 U.S. 1022 (1974), the additional transportation time required for 100 per cent desegregation led the court to affirm approval of a plan that left nineteen all-black or predominantly black schools, including some that were all-black at the inception of the litigation in 1960. *See also* Goss v. Knoxville Bd. of Educ., 482 F.2d 1044 (6th Cir. 1973), *cert. denied*, 414 U.S. 1171 (1974); Mapp v. Board of Educ., 477 F.2d 851 (6th Cir. 1973), *cert. denied*, 414 U.S. 1022 (1974).

consider alternative decrees. He must consider different types of school decrees (for example, pairing versus rezoning) and perhaps even decrees that seek to eliminate the segregated residential patterns themselves.[12] In addition, the judge might even consider the possibility of relying upon remedies that are within the control of other agencies, such as the state education authority. In such an instance, where the alternative remedy is beyond his control, the judge must speculate both about the efficacy of the alternative remedy and the probability of it being utilized.

II
THE GROWING UNCERTAINTY

The uncertainty that surrounds desegregation decrees is introduced primarily at two points in the judicial decision—in the harmfulness component and the relational component. How harmful is the challenged practice? Is it sufficiently harmful to justify the remedial costs? Twenty years ago those judgments might have been difficult enough. In recent years the difficulty has only grown.

A. The New Harmful Practice

In *Brown* there were two possible candidates for the harmful practice—the assignment of students to schools on the basis of race, and the segregated pattern of student assignment itself. Both phenomena were present in the dual school system. Today, the typical situation is one in which students are assigned not on the basis of race but on the basis of geographic proximity—yet the resulting pattern of student attendance is segregated.[13] Hence there

12. See, for example, Judge Weinstein's initial order in Hart v. Community School Bd. of Brooklyn, 383 F. Supp. 699 (E.D.N.Y.), *appeal dismissed*, 497 F.2d 1027 (2d Cir.), *order amended*, 383 F. Supp. 769 (E.D.N.Y. 1974). In that case, Judge Weinstein ordered that the school be desegregated and referred the matter to a special master. The responsibility for racial segregation was thought to be two-fold:

> [A]ction or inaction by the school board; and action by the housing authorities which greatly increased the proportion of black and Puerto Rican families, particularly as a proportion of families with children in what had been a predominantly white neighborhood. Because of this the court, although finding "liability" solely on the part of the school authorities, considered it appropriate to impose duties on the housing officials as well, and indeed in addition on the Police Commissioner, the Commissioner of Recreation, and the Metropolitan Transit Authority . . . . Housing officials of the city, state, and federal governments were directed to provide a joint plan so designed that . . . the area would be "refertilized with new families."

497 F.2d at 1029-30. Judge Weinstein, however, subsequently amended his order with respect to housing and other non-school authorities, albeit leaving open the possibility of post-judgment orders in this area. 383 F. Supp. at 775.

13. I do not deny the possibility of gerrymandering (assignments purporting to be made on the basis of geographic criteria, but in truth made on the basis of race). Nor do I deny that gerrymandering might exist in many school systems throughout the nation. On the other hand, I do not believe that in any single district in which there is residential segregation will gerrymandering be the cause—in any direct contemporary sense—of the overall demographic school pattern of segregation in that district. In such a situation, gerrymandering usually accounts for the racial composition of the schools along the borders of the residential neighborhoods.

is only one candidate for the harmful practice that is the target of the contemporary school desegregation decree—the segregated pattern of student attendance, not racial assignment.

The courts still talk about racial assignment, but that is not the harmful practice that is the predicate of the corrective obligation. The courts are referring to past racial assignment and by definition that practice is at an end. Admittedly, a contemporary vestige of a harmful practice can be the target of a corrective order and whenever the Supreme Court has affirmed busing decrees it has spoken of segregation as a vestige of past racial assignment.[14] But even if this language were to be taken at face value,[15] and the judge were to deem the segregation of a particular district a vestige of past racial assignment, he must still decide whether that segregation is harmful. If it is not, there is no point in eradicating it. A practice that is itself a vestige of another harmful but earlier practice can indeed get some "help" from that earlier practice—perhaps the later practice need not be as harmful as it might otherwise have to be were it standing alone, and it might not itself have to constitute a form of unequal treatment since the violation of the Equal Protection Clause would be the earlier, sufficiently harmful practice of which it is a vestige. But the present practice that is the target of the decree must to some degree also be regarded as harmful in and of itself in order that the corrective obligation be intelligible.

B. The Sources of Doubt—The Harmfulness Component

A theory can be articulated to explain why segregation is particularly harmful to blacks, and that theory need not be dependent upon a claim that race is the criterion of assignment, or that it is *believed* to be the criterion of assignment. That theory consists of three propositions: (1) Segregation is a badge of inferiority—it stigmatizes blacks. The assertion is that this stigmatization occurs regardless of the method of assignment. Racial assignment would give rise to it, but so would the use of geographic criteria when segregation is the foreseeable and avoidable result. (2) Segregation deprives blacks of valuable contacts with the educationally, socially, and economically dominant group, and thereby perpetuates their subordinate position. (3) Segregation has the inevitable effect of reducing the financial and physical resources available to all-black schools because these schools are attended only by members of the least powerful group.

The question, of course, is whether these assertions are true. We seem to have increasing doubts that they are, and thus we have grown more uncertain in our belief that segregation is harmful. Part of this change may be based on

---

14. *See* Swann v. Charlotte-Mecklenburg Bd. of Educ., 402 U.S. 1, 15 (1971).

15. I have argued elsewhere that this language should not be taken at face value. Fiss, *School Desegregation: The Uncertain Path of the Law*, 4 PHILOSOPHY AND PUB. AFFAIRS 3, 19-26 (1974).

the merits—a systematic review of the evidence reveals that our previous beliefs were mistaken. But I suspect that other, more extraneous factors have been controlling.

First, there is no longer a consensus in the relevant academic professions as to the harmfulness of segregation, and that change may not be attributable primarily to the state of the evidence. As Robert Crain recently stated:[16] twenty years ago there was no respectable social science evidence tending to show that segregation was harmful, and yet social scientists were nearly unanimous in believing that it was. Today there is respectable evidence tending to show that it *is* harmful, but no one in the profession believes it. This phenomenon, Crain speculated, is due to an increasing concern in the profession for methodological perfection, almost for its own sake, and also to the growing disbelief in the possibility of social betterment through government intervention—a disbelief not confined to social scientists nor to the problem of school desegregation.

Second, the escalation of the remedial costs has caused us to scrutinize our beliefs about the harmfulness of the challenged practice with greater care. When the harmful practice was racial assignment, or the segregation caused by racial assignment, the remedial costs were essentially non-allowable. The remedial order—prohibiting the use of race as the basis for assigning pupils to schools—would do no more than frustrate the associational desires served by the use of the racial criterion and require the school board to adopt an alternative, non-racial method of student assignment. But once the perceived harmful practice became segregation attributable to the use of neighborhood school assignment policies, the typical (though by no means the only) remedial order had to be a busing decree. This remedy consumes fiscal resources of the community (including those that otherwise might be spent on education), exposes children to safety hazards, reduces the time available for classes, and loses whatever psychological or emotional advantages might arise from having all the children in a neighborhood attend the school identified with that neighborhood.[17] An awareness of these allowable costs gives rise to some second thoughts about the harmfulness of segregation. We naturally tend to ask whether segregation is *that* harmful, and begin to wonder if it is harmful at all.

Third, there is no longer a consensus in the black community itself that segregation (or to put it more neutrally, that the all-black school) is harmful. Once again this may be traced to factors other than social science evidence. Some blacks have raised their voices against integration because of its conflict with the ideal of self-determination—most concretely embodied in the demand for community-controlled schools, which would leave the segregation of the

16. Statement made at The Courts, Social Science, and School Desegregation Conference, Hilton Head Island, S.C., Aug. 20, 1974, on file at *Law and Contemporary Problems* office.

17. There may be some doubt as to whether these costs to the community are allowable, see text at p. 196, *supra*, and that, too, may be another source of the growing uncertainty.

all-black school intact, albeit within a school district that blacks controlled.[18] Others are concerned with the racist strains inherent in the typical method of achieving integration—one-way busing—by which blacks are bused to the traditional white schools without a reciprocal obligation being imposed on whites.[19] Others are offended by the racist implication of one strand of the theory against segregation—that blacks will learn better when they are in a setting dominated by the more academically advantaged and ambitious whites.[20] And still other members of the black community may be concerned with the diversion of resources inherent in any busing program, and insist that those resources be used for more traditional academic purposes.[21]

Fourth, the increased doubts about the harmfulness of school desegregation can be linked to the proliferation of antidiscrimination remedies in other areas, such as housing and employment. Federal fair housing and employment laws now apply to the private sector, and are being enforced more vigorously than before. These laws enhance residential mobility for blacks, and thus lend credence to the claim that many blacks *choose* to live in all-black neighborhoods.[22] That supposition in turn calls into question some aspects of the traditional theory against segregation. If, for example, the all-black residential pattern

---

18. *See, e.g.*, Brief for CORE as Amicus Curiae, Swann v. Charlotte-Mecklenburg Bd. of Educ., 402 U.S. 1 (1971); Oliver v. Donovan, 293 F. Supp. 958 (E.D.N.Y. 1968) (Ocean Hill-Brownsville); Hamilton, *Race and Education: A Search for Legitimacy*, 38 HARV. ED. REV. 671 (1968); Bell, *School Litigation Strategies for the 1970's: New Phases in the Continuing Quest for Quality Schools*, 1970 WIS. L. REV. 257.

19. *See, e.g.*, Norwalk CORE v. Norwalk Bd. of Educ., 423 F.2d 121 (2d Cir. 1970).

20. *See, e.g.*, the statement made by Roy Innis, Director of the Congress of Racial Equality, that school integration is a "bankrupt, suicidal method . . . based on the false notion that black children are unable to learn unless they are in the same setting as white children." N.Y. Times, Mar. 13, 1972, at 30, col. 4. *Cf.* Brunson v. Board of Trustees of School Dist. No. 1, 429 F.2d 820, 826 (4th Cir. 1970) (concurring opinion), in which Judge Sobeloff rejects the implication that *Brown* stood for the proposition that "association with white pupils helps the blacks," or that "white children are a precious resource which should be fairly apportioned" and that "black children will be improved by association with their betters." *See* note 21 *infra*.

21. Edmonds, *Judicial Assumptions on the Value of Integrated Education for Blacks*, in D. BELL, RACE, RACISM AND AMERICAN LAW (1973).

22. *See also* Craven, *The Impact of Social Science Evidence on the Judge: A Personal Comment,* 39 LAW & CONTEMP. PROB. no. 1, at 150, 155 (1975). *But see* Farley, *Residential Segregation and Its Implications for School Integration*, 39 LAW & CONTEMP. PROB. no. 1, 164, (1975).

Many commentators have argued that the device of zoning has been used to exclude minorities and the poor. *See generally* R. BABCOCK & F. BOSSELMAN, EXCLUSIONARY ZONING: LAND USE REGULATION AND HOUSING IN THE 1970s (1973). *See also* U.S. COMMISSION ON CIVIL RIGHTS, EQUAL OPPORTUNITY IN SUBURBIA (1974); Sager, *Tight Little Islands: Exclusionary Zoning, Equal Protection, and the Indigent*, 21 STAN. L. REV. 767 (1969). In recent years, exclusionary zoning has come under heavy judicial attack. *See, e.g.*, Banks v. Perk, 341 F. Supp. 1175 (N.D. Ohio 1972), *aff'd in part, rev'd in part*, 473 F.2d 910 (6th Cir. 1973); Park View Heights Corp. v. City of Black Jack, 467 F.2d 1208 (8th Cir. 1972); Providence of St. Mary of the Woods v. City of Evanston, 335 F. Supp. 396 (N.D. Ill. 1971); Kennedy Park Homes Ass'n v. City of Lackawanner, 436 F.2d 108 (2d Cir. 1970), *cert. denied*, 401 U.S. 1010 (1971); Southern Burlington Co. NAACP v. Township of Mt. Laurel, ___ N.J. ___, ___ A.2d ___ (1975). All exclusionary land use litigation up to 1974 is summarized in NATIONAL COMMITTEE AGAINST DISCRIMINATION IN HOUSING AND THE URBAN LAND INSTITUTE, FAIR HOUSING & EXCLUSIONARY LAND USE 13-51 (1974).

were truly voluntary, school segregation would not as readily be perceived as a dignitary harm. Similarly, if blacks chose not to move to an integrated district, it would become increasingly difficult to argue that integrated education is preferable. I do not suggest that these housing and employment laws have now made the choice of residence truly voluntary, or that there are not other non-educational reasons for keeping one's residence in all-black neighborhoods. Instead I am suggesting that the increased availability of housing and employment laws, like the black nationalist assertions, have begun to call into question the earlier assumption that the residential patterns are involuntary, and that the all-black area is a ghetto—an assumption that was a basis for our beliefs that school segregation is particularly harmful to blacks.

C. The Sources of Doubt—The Relational Component

Much of the uncertainty has developed in connection with the harmfulness component. But several of the factors that generate uncertainty concerning the harmfulness of segregation have also made the relational judgment more difficult. A second locus of uncertainty has thus been created. Even if one agrees that segregation is harmful, the question must then be faced whether it is "sufficiently" harmful to "justify" the costs of eliminating it.

The increase in the allowable remedial costs has not only caused us to be more careful in judgments about the harmfulness of segregation, but also made the relational judgment more problematic. If there are no allowable remedial costs, then the remedial judgment is straightforward. The relief can be predicated exclusively on the conclusion that the challenged practice is harmful. But the situation changes once the remedial costs become allowable. Then the judge must confront the difficulty of weighing noncomparable factors—the harm and the remedial costs—and of applying the ambiguous proportionality standard. The difficulty is further compounded by the increased availability of employment and housing remedies, alternatives that might be less costly than a busing decree. While these remedies are not likely to achieve the same degree of integration within the same time span, they cannot be totally disregarded. Time may be considered as just another cost in the judicial calculus, and in any event the prospect of instant integration by way of a busing decree may be illusory. Whites have the capacity—constitutionally enhanced by the Supreme Court in *Milliken v. Bradley* and *Pierce v. Society of Sisters*—to insulate themselves from the busing decree by enrolling in private schools[23] or by moving to predominantly white school districts. From this perspective, housing and employment remedies become more com-

---

23. Milliken v. Bradley, 418 U.S. 717 (1974); Pierce v. Society of Sisters, 268 U.S. 510 (1925). *But see* Craven, *supra* note 22, at 155, indicating that "the silence" of the majority in *Milliken*, coupled with Justice Marshall's dissent, may mean "that white flight can never be a relevant factor in considering the appropriate remedy for dismantling a dual school system . . . ."

parable and the choice between them and the busing decree therefore more difficult.

III
The Avoidance Strategy

Although the contemporary context is characterized by a growing doubt as to the harmfulness of segregation and by an increased awareness of both the need to make an explicit relational judgment and the difficulty of that judgment, these factors have not precluded the issuance of desegregation decrees. They have meant, however, that once issued, a significant residue of uncertainty remains. The judge believes the underlying proposition to be true—that the segregation is sufficiently harmful to warrant the remedial costs of busing—but he cannot in good conscience deny the possibility that he may be wrong. Some element of uncertainty is present in every instance of judicial law-making. The argument made by the critics of busing, however, is that in this area of decision the uncertainty is sufficiently "high" to make it inappropriate for a *court*—perceived as a very distinctive social institution—to issue the order.

The initial response to this criticism has not been confrontation, but avoidance. The institutional criticism has not been evaluated; instead, it has uncritically been assumed to be valid, and ways have been sought to make the judgments about the harmfulness of segregation appear more certain. The strategy has been one of deempiricalizing the harmfulness component—of trying to make assertions about the harmfulness of segregation rest on a nonempirical base, divorced from the findings of social scientists. This strategy has taken several forms. One builds on the contemporary consensus that racial assignment to segregate is wrongful and seeks to conceptualize segregation as a "vestige" of past racial assignment.[24] Another has been to postulate a value—such as "universalistic ethic" (making it a good to eliminate barriers among groups)—that is necessarily inconsistent with segregation.[25] I find the avoidance strategy unappealing in either of its guises.

A. The Conceptual Flaws

The avoidance strategy seeks to eliminate uncertainty by freeing the harmfulness judgment from a dependence on the outcomes of social science research. As such, it rests on two questionable premises: (1) uncertainty is exclusively, or at least primarily, introduced by the harmfulness judgment; and (2) the truth of assertions concerning the harmfulness of segregation depend on the outcomes of social science research.

---

24. This is the strategy chosen by the Supreme Court in Swann v. Charlotte-Mecklenburg Bd. of Educ., 402 U.S. 1 (1971), and Keyes v. School Dist. No. 1, 413 U.S. 189 (1973). The doctrinal complexities of these cases are analyzed in detail in the article referred to in Fiss, *supra* note 15.

25. *See* Yudof, *Equal Educational Opportunity and the Courts*, 51 Texas L. Rev. 411, 456-64 (1973).

The first premise, which explains why the avoidance strategy concentrates on the harmfulness component, ignores the large measure of uncertainty introduced by the relational component. Even if segregation can be classified as a vestige of past discrimination or as a wrong because it violates the universalistic ethic, the task of determining whether it is sufficiently harmful to warrant the remedial costs still remains. This determination not only requires an assessment of both the remedial costs and the harm but also a comparison of the two and an application of the vague proportionality standard.

We tended to ignore the relational judgment when the harmful practice was racial assignment—its wrongful quality alone seemed a sufficient basis to grant relief. For that reason, the avoidance effort seeks to construct a theory that would make segregation of the schools as wrongful as assignment to schools on the basis of race. This is done with the hope that the same automatic connection between the harm (or wrong) and the remedy will be created, thereby eliminating the need for the relational judgment. But it won't work. Even if a segregated pattern of school attendance—attributable solely to the assignment of students to schools on the basis of geographic criteria—can be given the same moral status as racial assiignments designed to segregate, the parallelism breaks down on the remedial side. In such a system, which is the typical one today, the remedial costs are likely to be pronounced; that fact makes the relational judgment at once necessary and extremely problematic. De-empiricalizing the harmfulness component can make no contribution toward the elimination of that uncertainty.[26]

The second premise—positing that judgments about the harmfulness of segregation depend on the uncertain outcomes of social science research—is also mistaken. It reflects either a misunderstanding of the epistemological character of the assertions underlying the theory of the harmfulness of segregation or an exaggerated notion of the reach of the social sciences. Admittedly the traditional theory embraces assertions that might be susceptible to methods of social science research. The assertion that integration will improve the achievement and aspiration levels of blacks is such an instance. But the theory also includes assertions that are beyond the reach of social science, and in that sense, nonempirical. An example would be the assertion that, regardless of the method of assignment, segregation is a "living insult to blacks."[27]

---

26. Professor Yudof seems to give the remedial costs a role in the choice of competing ethics, but no role once the universalistic ethic is adopted:

> Because they [the universalistic ethic, and what is conceived to be the competing value, the racial-neutrality principle] both embody a morality "of excellence, of the fullest realizations of human powers," these two principles fall within what Fuller terms the "morality of aspiration" rather than within the "morality of duty." According to Professor Fuller, "[o]n the level of duty, anything like economic calculation is out of place. In a morality of aspiration, it is not only in place, but becomes an integral part of the moral decision itself."

Yudof, *supra* note 25, at 462 n. 266 (citation omitted).

27. "[S]chool desegregation is forbidden simply because its perpetuation is a living insult to . . .

One can speak of an assertion about dignitary harm as being true or false, but its truth or falsehood cannot conclusively be determined on the basis of discrete, observable events and behavior that are the province of social science research. A dignitary harm may have psychological consequences but it is not reducible to those consequences. Nor can the truth of an assertion about dignitary harm conclusively be determined on the basis of a questionnaire addressed to the alleged victims, even assuming a method can be devised for making certain that the responses to the questionnaire are sincere. Such a questionnaire might be illuminating, but not decisive. I say this for two reasons. First, there is no intellectual mechanism for resolving conflicts in responses that would be able to cope with the likely situation of nonunanimity (where some blacks say that they are insulted and others deny it). Secondly, the concept of a dignitary harm has built into it some understanding of what the appropriate or "reasonable" response should be. The statement "I am insulted" is neither a necessary nor sufficient condition for concluding that a particular practice inflicts dignitary harm: even assuming—unrealistically—that this statement is unanimously made by blacks in the face of segregation, it is always possible to claim, in the style of *Plessy v. Ferguson*,[28] that they are oversensitive; and if the contrary statement is unanimously made, it is always possible to claim that they are undersensitive. The "right" degree of sensitivity cannot be fixed in some conclusive manner by averaging prevailing practices. In the final analysis, it is always possible for the judge, as an impartial spectator, to imagine himself in the place of the alleged victim and to ask whether he would be insulted by the challenged practice.

I do not mean to suggest that the theory against segregation should be reduced to the assertion about dignitary harm, or that the assertion is unquestionably true, but only that it is part of the theory and is as much in doubt as the empirical assertions about achievement levels. Hence it is wrong to think, as those attempting to formulate the avoidance strategy do, that the uncertainty surrounding the traditional theory of segregation stems from a dependence on the outcomes of social science research.

B. The Ineffectiveness of the Strategy

The avoidance strategy not only rests on flawed premises but is also ineffective. It does not eliminate the uncertainty introduced by the harmfulness component. I concede that if the avoidance strategy were adopted in either of its

---

black children and immeasurably taints the education they receive." Brunson v. Board of Trustees of School Dist. No. 1, 429 F.2d 820, 823, 826 (4th Cir. 1970) (Sobeloff, J., concurring).

28. We consider the underlying fallacy of the plaintiff's argument to consist in the assumption that the enforced separation of the two classes stamps the colored race with a badge of inferiority. If this be so, it is not by reason of anything found in the act, but solely because the colored race chooses to put that construction upon it.

163 U.S. 537, 551 (1896).

guises there would no longer be a need to rely, even in part, on the outcome of social science research aimed at determining whether segregation is harmful. But uncertainty would still arise in determining whether segregation is harmful or wrongful—whether it is a condition that should be corrected.

The effort to categorize segregation as a vestige of past racial assignment seeks to capitalize on the consensus developed over the last twenty years that racial assignment for segregative purposes is wrong. But empirical uncertainty is introduced by the need to rely on factual assertions purporting to connect the past with the present. The fact that these assertions try to explain the present behavior—residential segregation—of an enormous mass of people on the basis of a school board's past and sometimes near-ancient conduct of assigning students to racially-identifiable schools on the basis of their race, makes the uncertainty acute. Indeed, in order to make the issues triable or capable of ever producing relief, the Supreme Court had to create a set of presumptions in favor of the existence of these linkages and those presumptions, especially when viewed as a set, do not seem supported by natural probabilities.

With the other avoidance strategy, postulating an ethic that is necessarily inconsistent with segregation, the uncertainty is introduced at the outset—the choice of value. The traditional theory against segregation starts with a value that is widely shared and, more important, that has a clear constitutional basis: it is wrong to assign students in a manner which makes inferior the education afforded to blacks. The inquiry then centers on whether the particular practice violates that norm. The universalistic-ethic avoidance technique, however, proceeds differently. It confines the controversy to the initial choice of value, though concededly once the ethic is adopted there is little need for further inquiry.

Stated in its most general and abstract form, the universalistic ethic does have great intuitive appeal. Who can be against eliminating barriers among groups? But that is not the proper level of inquiry. The process of choosing the ethic must be seen in its proper context, and when it is, the choice becomes controversial. (1) Controversy will arise when we attempt to apply the ethic to a particular social problem and to determine, for example, what "barriers" must be eliminated. We then must face such troublesome questions as whether a commitment to the universalistic ethic also entails a commitment to eliminating school segregation that results from and parallels residential segregation. (2) Controversy arises when we realize that the process of ethic adoption is a competitive one. The question is not whether the universalistic ethic is "good" or "appealing," but whether it is more "appealing" or "better" than those ethics that would make us more tolerant of segregation—for example, the community-first ethic, making it desirable to preserve the integrity of communities or neighborhoods, or the libertarian ethic, making any coercion undesirable. (3) Controversy will also arise once we insist upon a constitutional peg for the universalistic ethic. The traditional theory against segregation fits within the contours of the Equal Protection Clause, viewed as a protection against state practices that disadvantage the racial minority. But I doubt whether this is true for the universalistic ethic since, in order to preserve its separate identity, it cannot be reduced to a view about the betterment of the racial minority.

These difficulties inherent in the process of ethic adoption—in deciding whether the universalistic ethic is applicable to school segregation when linked to residential segregation, whether it is superior to competing ethics, and whether it is constitutionally sound—have the effect of reintroducing uncertainty into the harmfulness component. Thus, we remain as uncertain as ever about the harmfulness or wrongfulness of school segregation. Ironically enough, the resolution of our doubts may in part depend on empirical inquiries of a nature similar to the ones this universalistic strategy sought to avoid. As Professor Yudof, author of the strategy, acknowledges:[29]

> The problem of course is that the measure and likelihood of symbolic or real benefits [of competing ethics] are unclear, for the causal relationships are largely unknown. . . . Thus, ignorance of causal relationships, which originally made ethical theories seem so attractive, resurfaces as an impediment to rational choice between competing ethical theories.

C. The Price of Avoidance

Finally one can question the very purpose of any avoidance strategy. To some degree, it may spring from the desire to obtain wider general acceptance of the busing orders. But it remains to be seen why those decrees are entitled to any acceptance beyond that which they can earn on their own terms. Obedience to a decree is not a transcendental value. Once we embark on the questionable mission of camouflaging the grounds for decision in order to enhance the basis for its public acceptance, the possibility of a viable tradition of public accountability is seriously undercut. The strategy will also have a diversionary effect: while obscuring the uncertainty may enhance the acceptability of the decree, it may concurrently make the resolution of that uncertainty more unlikely. Only when the uncertainty is faced in a direct and explicit manner will there be the kind of investment in discussion and research that might—if anything can—either reduce that uncertainty or determine whether this institutional criticism has any validity.

IV
The Institutional Criticism Examined

A distinction should be made between two species of the institutional criticism—one is couched in terms of *preference* and the other in terms of *competence*. The preference issue asks whether the judiciary, as opposed to some

29. Yudof, *supra* note 25, at 463-64.

other government agency[30] such as a legislature or school board, is the *best* institution for making the decision on the merits. The competence issue asks whether the judiciary is *entitled* to issue the decree. The competence critic is willing to assume that the judiciary is the best decisional agency, or for that matter the only one. He argues that, even on such an assumption, the judiciary should refrain from making a decision on the merits.

A. The Preference Issue

The preference for non-judicial institutions might be based on the view that these institutions have superior fact-finding tools and that they thereby have the means of eliminating a greater portion of the uncertainty.[31] I cannot agree. The fact-finding processes of the legislature and school board may be more informal and more tolerant of ex parte presentations than those of a court, but that does not make them superior for the resolution of any of the relevant questions, including the factual ones. Some of the distinguishing features of the judicial process—for example, the right of cross-examination—enhance rather than impede the inquiry into the truthfulness of whatever opinions witnesses might express.[32] Moreover, the concept of relevancy is flexible enough to permit the judicial hearing to be as broad as the legislative inquiry; and with either institution the ultimate decision is to be made by a non-expert. Admittedly, some school boards may develop more familiarity with a desegregation claim over time, but it is difficult to generalize on this score. Many school boards, particularly the elected ones, have constantly shifting memberships. On the other hand, many federal district judges have developed a great familiarity with the school desegregation problems of the particular communities within the judicial district.

---

30. A non-governmental institution, such as the family, might be considered as an alternative decisional agency under a freedom-of-choice system—one in which students are assigned to schools on the basis of their parents' choice. Parents could then judge whether the benefits to be obtained from an integrated education were worth the attendant costs. The difficulty with this decisional system is twofold: (a) It would result in the localization of all remedial costs on the racial minority—which seems inconsistent with the Equal Protection Clause. The only result that realistically could be contemplated is one-way busing—with some blacks choosing to go to white schools, while a substantial proportion remain in all-black schools. A freedom-of-choice system not only permits an informed judgment, but also choices based on prejudice; and even if this freedom were not abused, the same pattern is likely to result. Few would claim that the education of whites would be improved by placement in a predominantly black school. (b) There are likely to be interferences with the choice, thus making the freedom illusory. Some interference may be retaliatory—violence, loss of employment, hostile reception by white teachers and students. Interference may also arise from the system itself: the decisions of some black families may tend to coerce the choice of others, for few enjoy the feeling of isolation.

31. Yudof, *supra* note 25, at 413.

32. Part of the footnote eleven attack stemmed from the judicial reliance on evidence beyond the record, and nothing I have said should be construed as condoning that practice in the busing context. Judicial notice should be kept at a minimum. It should be permitted not simply because a factual assertion can be classified as "legislative," but because of clear and compelling considerations of judicial administration or because the issue is not one that can be illuminated by an evidentiary presentation.

More probably, the preference for non-judicial institutions has an ethical basis: the more uncertain the underlying proposition, the less appropriate it is to impose obligations through the least representative branch. Coercion requires certitude. Decisions of those institutions more directly responsive to the citizenry—such as the legislature or school board—seem more self-imposed, less intrusive, less coercive, and thus are more compatible with a high degree of uncertainty.

Stated in general terms, this argument has great appeal. But it loses some of its force where, as in this case, the benefits of the obligation are to be primarily conferred on a racial minority and the costs imposed on all. There the risk is very high that the decision of the legislature or the school board may not be a conscientious exercise of self-governance, but rather a manifestation of majority self-interest. Once account is taken of that risk, the ethical basis for preferring nonjudicial institutions is substantially weakened, if not destroyed.[33]

Whenever a decision is entrusted to a legislature or any body directly responsible to the citizenry, the risk is high that the outcome will only manifest the interest of the dominant group. It may therefore seem that in raising doubts about the ethical superiority of relying on the legislature or school board, particularly if the board is an elective one, I may also be reflecting doubt—not widely shared—about the superiority of the democratic process in general. But I do not believe so. Society's commitment to the ideal of self governance is not so intense or absolute as to preclude an exception for minority rights. The Equal Protection Clause, primarily a restraint on majoritarian action directed at minorities, is ample evidence of that fact.

The integrity of this claimed exception to our democratic commitment depends on whether the "minority" can be defined so as not to be coextensive with the ordinary loser of the legislative battle. Only then will the exception not eliminate the rule. But I believe that the concept of "minority" can be so defined, and that the racial minority should and would be included in any such definition. The special historical position of the racial minority in this country—two centuries as slaves and a third century as the victims of political,

---

33. That is why it is ethically permissible to construe section 5 of the fourteenth amendment as a one-edged sword:

> [Section] 5 does not grant Congress power to enact "statutes so as in effect to dilute equal protection and due process discussions of this Court." We emphasize that Congress' power under § 5 is limited to adopting measures to enforce the guarantees of the Amendment; § 5 grants Congress no power to restrict, abrogate, or dilute these guarantees. Thus, for example, an enactment authorizing the States to establish racially segregated systems of education would not be—as required by § 5—a measure "to enforce" the Equal Protection Clause since that clause of its own force prohibits such state laws.

Katzenbach v. Morgan, 384 U.S. 641, 651-52 n. 10 (1968). It also explains why little deference should be paid to the legislative judgments reflected in the recent federal anti-busing legislation embodied in Title II of the Equal Education Opportunities Act of 1974, 20 U.S.C.A. 1701 (Supp. 1975). *See generally* Comment, *Interpreting the Anti-Busing Provisions of the Education Amendments of 1972*, 10 HARV. J. LEGIS. 256 (1973); Note, *Nixon Busing Bills and Congressional Power*, 81 YALE L.J. 1542 (1972).

social, educational and economic discrimination—gave it a discrete set of interests and diminished its power in a way that cannot be corrected simply by the extension of the franchise. That is why we needed not just the thirteenth and fifteenth amendments, but also the fourteenth; and that is why, true to the intent of the framers of that amendment, black citizens have long been deemed its prime beneficiaries.

B. The Competence Issue

The claim of institutional competence does not contend that it is better to leave the resolution of this uncertainty to another more appropriate branch of government, but rather that the uncertainty of the underlying proposition makes judicial law-making illegitimate. The desegregation decree cannot properly be called "law." It is called law because it issues from a legal authority, but it is not entitled to that status. It should not be issued by a judge.

Three different types of arguments have been made to support this claim, all of which stem from the uncertainty of the underlying proposition.[34] That uncertainty (1) differentiates the busing decree from the usual decree issued by a court; (2) prevents the obligation emanating from a busing decree from attaining two characteristics deemed essential to a constitutional obligation —timelessness and community-invariance; and (3) creates too much latitude for the individual judge. Implicit in all three arguments is a common conception of law, one which aspires for legal obligations and legal rules the same degree of certainty that marks objective reality; and that is why I use the term "objectivist" to refer to the competence critic.

1. *Departure From the Usual*

The competence critic may allow the prevailing practices to define the appropriate bounds of proper judicial law-making and then assert that the uncertainty of the underlying proposition differentiates the busing order from other judgments or decrees. The normative premise of this argument is obviously troubling—I fail to see why "what is" should determine "what ought to be." But so is the factual premise—namely, that the uncertainty of a busing decree is "unusual."

In the typical case, there may be little doubt about the existence of harm. But there are many exceptions—the tort suit providing recovery for injury to reputation or for a dignitary harm is such an instance. And even where there is no uncertainty about the harm, uncertainty is introduced in the typical case by the need for a relational judgment. The Hand formula in torts (is the cost of avoidance less than the discounted harm?) is such an example.[35] So are the

---

34. Some of the arguments that support the competence criticism also may be used to support the preference position; thus there is some overlap and I hope that my evaluation of an argument in one context will carry over to the next.

35. *See* Conway v. O'Brien, 111 F.2d 611, 612 (2d Cir. 1940), *rev'd on other grounds*, 312 U.S. 192 (1941); United States v. Carroll Towing Co., 159 F.2d 169 (1947).

recent constitutional cases declaring a right to an adversary hearing before the termination of welfare benefits (is the increased procedural protection worth the diminution of substantive benefits?).[36] In these cases, the uncertainty is introduced by the relational component rather than the harmfulness one, but the precise point at which this uncertainty interjects itself does not seem significant. One might argue that there is more uncertainty inherent in the proposition underlying a school decree than in the comparable propositions of these other cases to which I have referred. But without having some way of measuring the amount of uncertainty, it is impossible to give that claim much weight.[37]

2. *Departure From the Ideal*

Alternatively, the objectivist may postulate the proper characteristics of a legal or constitutional obligation, and then express a dissatisfaction with the obligation emanating from a busing decree because it does not incorporate those features. It is not uncertainty itself but the very basis of decision—the underlying proposition—that prevents the attainment of them. Uncertainty is antithetical to the postulated characteristics and arises from that decisional predicate. As the uncertainty becomes more pronounced so do the limitations of that predicate and the unlikelihood of achieving the ideal of the objectivist.

One characteristic postulated by the objectivist is permanence or near-timelessness. The obligation of a busing decree is time bound. It may cease to exist if, as the argument is stated, the latest social science experiment demonstrates that segregation is not harmful or not "that" harmful.[38] A second characteristic postulated by the objectivist is community-invariance. If the obligation is dependent on assessment—at this time and in this place—of the harmfulness of segregation and of the remedial costs, a school board in one community may have an obligation to eliminate the segregation either because, given the general social setting, segregation is particularly harmful, or because,

---

36. *See, e.g.*, Goldberg v. Kelly, 397 U.S. 254 (1970).

37. In this context, a confession of Justice Cardozo seems appropriate:

> I was much troubled in spirit, in my first years upon the bench, to find how trackless was the ocean on which I had embarked. I sought for certainty. I was oppressed and disheartened when I found that the quest for it was futile. I was trying to reach land, the solid land of fixed and settled rules, the paradise of a justice that would declare itself by tokens plainer and more commanding than its pale and glimmering reflections in my own vacillating mind and conscience. . . . As the years have gone by, and as I have reflected more and more upon the nature of the judicial process, I have become reconciled to the uncertainty, because I have grown to see it as inevitable.

B. Cardozo, The Nature of the Judicial Process 166 (1921).

38. This proposition is suggested by Edmund Cahn's well-known comment:

> I would not have the constitutional rights of Negroes—or of other Americans—rest on any such flimsy foundation as some of the scientific demonstrations in these records . . . . [S]ince the behavioral sciences are so very young, imprecise, and changeful, their findings have an uncertain expectancy of life. Today's sanguine asseveration may be cancelled by tomorrow's new revelation—or new technical fad. It is one thing to use the current scien-

given the geographic configurations, it is easier to correct. A school board in another community, on the other hand, may well not have such an obligation.[39]

It is not a sufficient response to the objectivist to produce counter-examples by pointing to existing instances of a legal or constitutional obligation which do not meet the two postulated criteria. The objectivist's answer would be that these counter-examples, like the obligation imposed by a desegregation decree, are not properly "law." Nevertheless the existence of these counter-examples is not without some ethical significance. The objectivist must explain why his notion of law should be applied to the duty to desegregate and not to the counter-examples. Without an explanation, it appears as though a double standard is being applied.

The objectivist might explain that his standard is being applied to busing decrees only as a starting point, and that in time it will be applied to all the counter-examples. The sufficiency of that explanation, of course, depends upon the sincerity of the commitment to apply the standard thoroughly to all other situations where legal or constitutional obligations are predicated on a comparable proposition. Without that commitment, the explanation is wanting. However, with it, the full sweep of the institutional criticism becomes apparent, and that in turn may cause one to recoil. One might accept the objectivist standard if it is to be applied to one corner of the law, the duty to desegregate, but not if it meant a wholesale rejection of commonly acknowledged legal obligations.

Aside from the problem of using a double standard in different areas of the law and of applying the higher standard only to the duty to desegregate, the value preference inherent in the objectivist position should be made explicit: the good to be achieved by confining legal obligations to those that meet the criteria of objectivity is greater than the good to be achieved by imposing a duty to desegregate. This value preference is, of course, not a flaw in the objectivist's position; but the explication of the preference does illustrate what is entailed in accepting that position. It also shows that one can reject the position either by (a) denying that the law-notion desired by the objectivist is good at all, or by (b) claiming that the good to be achieved by the duty to desegregate outweighs the evil that might be involved in imposing a legal obligation that cannot achieve

---

> tific findings, however ephemeral they may be, in order to ascertain whether the legislature has acted reasonably in adopting some scheme of social or economic regulation; deference here is shown not so much to the findings as to the legislature. It would be quite another thing to have our fundamental rights rise, fall, or change along with the latest fashions of psychological literature.

Cahn, *Jurisprudence*, 30 N.Y.U.L. REV. 150, 157-58, 167 (1955). For a general consideration of timelessness value, see Mishkin, *Foreword: The High Court, the Great Writ, and the Due Process of Time and Law*, 79 HARV. L. REV. 56 (1965).

39. This was first suggested in a discussion with Professor Alexander M. Bickel, during which he criticized the approach to de facto school desegregation that I had first articulated in *Racial Imbalance in the Public Schools: The Constitutional Concepts*, 78 HARV. L. REV. 564 (1965). In retrospect, it is not clear to me whether Professor Bickel was making a competence or a preference argument.

the criteria postulated by the objectivist. (A commitment to position (a) also includes a commitment to position (b), but not the other way around.)

Either of these anti-objectivist positions is logically coherent, and I believe that both positions are more attractive than that of the objectivist. This assertion is not predicated on a belief in the overwhelming good to be achieved by desegregation—a belief that I remain dubious about and that would, in any event, only support the second, more limited position. Instead, it is based on the view that the aspirations of the objectivist are ill-founded, that the postulated characteristics are not an ideal. They are not an evil, but neither are they a good. We should not in the least be concerned by our failure to attain them.

I fail to see any value to be served by having timeless legal obligations. Of course, if I have a right today, I would hate for the court to decide tomorrow—having, for example, changed its view about the harmfulness of segregation—that I no longer have that right. But I am objecting to the merits of the decision—the denial of the right—and not the fact that the right was so short lived. If the court is correct in deciding that segregation is not harmful, then the right should cease to exist. Similarly, one can complain if the determination of rights turns on the results of the most recent social science study, such as, for example, a study which measures the impact of segregation on achievement levels. But once again, the objection here is to the basis of the decision—the harmfulness of segregation is denied on the basis of one study which may be methodologically flawed and which, in any event, only measures one possible type of harm. The force of the complaint does not derive from the fact that the right is short-lived.

In this context, the goal of timelessness is not rooted in the norm of consistency nor in the norm of protecting reasonable expectations (the norms underlying the doctrine of stare decisis). By hypothesis, the predicate for change lies in the assessment a judge makes of the harmfulness of segregation or of the remedial costs. That means that the change does not violate the norm of consistency; the case is no longer a like case, and hence need not have the same outcome.

Attention to the predicate of the change also bears on the problem of disappointment. What one is entitled to expect in the future is not the imposition of the obligation to desegregate, but rather that an obligation will be imposed if segregation is deemed sufficiently harmful to warrant the remedial costs. Stare decisis attaches to the rule rather than its applications, and a context where there is little need for predictability, there is no evil in permitting that rule to be stated at a high level of generality or abstractness.

A similar point can be made with the demand that the legal obligation be community-invariant—that a practice held unconstitutional shall be deemed unconstitutional throughout the United States. The ideal of a uniform, nationwide rule follows from the notion of a single constitution for the entire nation. But we must be careful about what has to be uniform. It is not that the percentage of white and black students in each class must be exactly the same, or even that there shall be no all-black schools in the United States. Instead, what is constitutionally mandated is the uniformity of the rule of law. That rule can be stated with a high degree of generality: whenever segregation is deemed sufficiently harmful to warrant the remedial costs, an obligation will be imposed to eliminate it. There may be a natural tendency to gravitate away from such an abstract statement of the rule and to search for a more concrete one; for example, there shall be no all-black schools. But that tendency, regardless of how natural it might be, cannot be rooted in the theory of a "single constitution." The Constitution does not establish the appropriate degree of abstractness. Once severed from its constitutional roots, the community-invariant ideal is thus as unappealing as the alleged ideal of timelessness.

3. *Permitting Excessive Latitude*

Finally, there is the problem of judicial abuse. The objectivist may complain, not about the qualities of the obligation, but about the risk of a judge deciding the case on the basis of his personal bias rather than on the merits. Arguably, this risk arises from two circumstances: (a) the underlying proposition gives the judge great latitude, and (b) the truth value of that proposition is so much in doubt that the controlling institutions—appellate courts or citizen-critics—have no basis for scrutinizing an individual judge's decision—anything he says goes.

I doubt, however, whether we have reached this situation. The truth value of the underlying proposition may be uncertain, but not that uncertain. Moreover, in assessing this objection, it is important to separate, on the one hand, the alleged evil of judicial latitude itself and, on the other hand, our views about the merits of the case. Very often an objection to judicial latitude or discretion springs from a prediction as to how this power will be used, and from an implicit value preference as to what is a right decision. Usually we object to judicial latitude because we fear it might not be exercised in the manner that we deem proper. For example, our views about the permissibility of the pardoning power—to take the most discretionary power—in large part depends on whether we believe it will be used to dispense mercy to the weak or unfortunate or whether it will be used to dispense favors to the politically rich and powerful. The judicial latitude itself is in large part ethically neutral.

One evil can, nevertheless, be tied to judicial latitude or discretion and that is the increased likelihood of a differential decisional pattern that cannot be explained in terms of the governing rule of law. The greater the latitude left to individual judges and the less central the control, the more non-rule-based diversity in outcome is likely to result. The segregation of two communities might be identical in every relevant respect (*i.e.*, in the harm and the remedial costs); yet an obligation to desegregate is imposed in one but not in the other. The only explanation is the difference in the judges.

I readily admit this decisional pattern offends my sense of equal treatment and the idea of a single constitution. But the objectivist not only wants to eliminate this pattern; he also wants to eliminate judicial latitude altogether—either by denying the courts the power to decide the merits at all or by establishing a per se rule. This position is based in part on two premises: (a) a differential decisional pattern flows from the fact that the judiciary has wide latitude, and (b) the pattern cannot easily be eliminated by the ordinary methods of appellate review. I am willing to accept both premises, but still not accept the objectivist conclusion which fails to take sufficient account of the price to be paid by the elimination of judicial latitude. The differential decisional pattern would be avoided, but only at the cost of forcing us to live with an indeterminate number of decisions or outcomes in school cases that are necessarily incorrect.

Suppose, for example, judicial latitude were abolished by establishing a per se rule always requiring the elimination of segregation—that there can be no all-black schools in America. Then the differential pattern would be eliminated, but at the expense of requiring busing in some situations where none should be required. Or suppose that the per se rule that the objectivist wants to establish required the school boards to stop making racial assignments but never required them to eliminate segregation. Once again the differential pattern would be eliminated, but at the expense of withholding relief when it is due.

Recognition of either contingency is a sufficient basis for parting company with the objectivist. But, quite frankly, it is the second contingency that gives me the greatest pause, for two reasons. First, it is the contingency most likely to materialize: such a prophecy is based on the fact that we are dealing with the claim of the racial minority, and that the decisional power is generally in the hands of members of the dominant racial class and thus sensitive to the interests of that class. It is not realistic to expect elites—even judicial ones—to be too counter-majoritarian. Second, the kind of erroneous decision produced under the second contingency—no remedial obligation even when one should be imposed—is no ordinary mistake. It is, by definition, a denial of a constitutional right. The concept of a single national constitution (or the Equal Protection Clause itself) may give a constitutional basis to the value of eliminating the differential decisional pattern. But the desegregation claim is also based on the Constitution and there is no basis for preferring the constitutional value of singleness over the constitutional value of not disadvantaging blacks.

EDUCATION, LIFE CHANCES, AND THE COURTS: THE ROLE OF SOCIAL SCIENCE EVIDENCE

HENRY M. LEVIN*

INTRODUCTION

Public policy attempts to improve the "life chances" of youngsters from low income and minority backgrounds have focused primarily on the schools. "Life chances" is defined as a child's future ability as an adult to participate fully in the social, economic, and political life of society. More narrowly, "life chances" may be considered in terms of such outcomes as ultimate earnings, occupational status, and political efficacy. The crucial role of the school in preparing students for these eventualities has been tacitly assumed. It is no surprise, therefore, that in their quest for greater equality among persons of different races and social class origins, both policy makers and the courts have devoted extensive efforts in an attempt to alter the organization and financing of education.[1]

There are three principal areas of reform to which policy makers and the courts have directed themselves in the last two decades: school desegregation, the provision of additional resources for the education of children from low income families, and reform of state educational finance systems by reducing the reliance upon local property wealth as the determinant of local school expenditures.[2] Each of these reform measures comports with notions of basic fairness and, indeed, could be defended on these grounds alone. But this view of reforms—that they are essential in a "just" society—has been overshadowed by the claim that social science research has shown that the particular educational strategies offered to the courts enhance the life chances of children. Educational reform litigation increasingly relies on social science evidence, as seen in the challenges to school segregation, to the present methods of financing education, and to student classification policies.[3]

This article explores the appropriateness of using social science evidence as a basis for formulating public policy and for deciding law suits in these particu-

---

* Professor, School of Education and Department of Economics, Stanford University.

1. *See generally* D. KIRP & M. YUDOF, EDUCATIONAL POLICY AND THE LAW chs. 4, 6, & 7 (1974).

2. A recent summary of these strategies is contained in STAFF OF SENATE SELECT COMM. ON EQUAL EDUC. OPPORTUNITY, 92D CONG., 2D SESS., REPORT: TOWARD EQUAL EDUCATIONAL OPPORTUNITY (Comm. Print 1972). *See also* J. COONS, W. CLUNE III, & S. SUGARMAN, PRIVATE WEALTH AND PUBLIC EDUCATION (1970); J. OWEN, SCHOOL INEQUALITY AND THE WELFARE STATE (1974); Wise, *School Desegregation: The Court, the Congress, and the President*, 82 SCHOOL REV. 159 (1974).

3. D. KIRP & M. YUDOF, *supra* note 1.

lar areas. In the course of this exploration, four questions have to be addressed: (1) To what degree can social science methodology determine the impact of schooling on such life chance outcomes as income and occupational attainment, separating out other factors influencing life chances such as family background and IQ? (2) To the extent that social science research presents conflicting theories of these relationships, why do some theories receive considerable attention in the policy arena while others do not? (3) What impact does social science evidence have on the evolution of law and public policy with respect to education? (4) Finally, what contribution can the social sciences make to the issues raised in litigation?

I

Effects of Education on Life Chances

How might the social scientist attempt to trace the effects of a particular educational strategy on the life chances of an individual or group of persons? The difficulties inherent in this task can be illustrated by considering the fundamental characteristics of the problem. At the outset, there is a complex multitude of psychological, social, genetic, political, economic, and educational influences that can determine occupational attainments and earnings. The actual effect of education and of a particular educational environment is particularly difficult to trace because the outcomes that we wish to review are very much removed in both time and context from the schooling process. Typically, research in this area is intended to relate the income and occupation of an individual or a group of persons to the schooling which they received many years before and under circumstances very different from their present situations. Also, the educational experiences of an individual are so closely tied to his social class origin and family experiences that it is virtually impossible to isolate the distinct influences of each on life chances.

In addressing this issue, social scientists have two basic approaches at their disposal.[4] The first is the purely experimental approach. In theory, an experiment would select persons who were similar in every respect and assign them to a different quantity and quality of education, and then monitor them over their life-times in order to determine how the differences in educational experiences are translated into differences in life-time experience. Such an experiment would probably require a minimum of thirty years and would have to ensure

4. For the best discussion of the experimental and quasi-experimental approaches in a related context see D. Campbell & J. Stanley, Experimental and Quasi-Experimental Designs for Research (1966). For a more skeptical statement on the ability of social science research to provide "proof" for a theory see Address by D. Campbell, before the Society for the Psychological Study of Social Issues meeting with the American Psychological Association, New Orleans, La., Sept. 1, 1974 (to be published in J. Social Issues). *See also* J. Katz, Experimentation with Human Beings: The Authority of the Investigator, Subject, Professions and State in the Human Experimentation Process (1972).

that the individuals in both the experimental and control groups were treated identically in their pre-adult years, with the exception of schooling. In other words, such factors as genetic background, family environment, community factors, medical care, nutrition, friendships, and so on, would have to be identical in order to draw an accurate inference about the effects of differences in schooling.

For obvious reasons, however, such an exercise is impossible. Not only do we lack the luxury of several decades or a life-time to carry out research for impending policy decisions, but the conditions that we would have to place on the human subjects in order to conduct the experiment could very well raise questions about a violation of their constitutional rights.[5] Even were such an experiment feasible, we would not be able to generalize beyond the actual educational strategies that were utilized and the specific persons or groups of persons that were involved in the experiment. Since there are infinite combinations of both, even a relatively large scale experiment would reveal information about only a limited range of alternatives and population groups. Moreover, in a society such as ours, the relationship of education to one's life chances is likely to change from generation to generation, meaning that the results obtained from a particular experiment might not be applicable to conditions some forty years later when the experiment was finally completed.

Thus, the most powerful investigative tool that science has to offer for an understanding of the relationship between education and life chances is politically and practically infeasible. At best, experimentation can be used to test minor hypotheses that may be related to some later outcome.[6] For example, it may be possible to set up an experiment to determine the effect of teachers' attitudes on student achievement or educational aspirations, assigning students randomly to two different types of teachers, and holding other factors constant for the period of the experiment. Outcomes would be measured by standardized test scores and such elements of educational aspiration as incentive for further schooling. Even with this more limited type of experiment, it is a formidable endeavor to fulfill the *ceteris paribus* conditions. And even more problematical is the relationship of the experimental outcomes to life success. One would have to make the assumption that student test scores and attitudes

---

5. It is very difficult to explain the experimentation in such precise terms that a layman will understand the full implications of the testing and thus be able to provide an effective waiver. Compare the requisite standards for valid consent in the area of medical experimentation and research. *See* Kaimowitz v. Department of Mental Health, Civil No. 73-19 434-AW (Mich. Cir. Ct., July 10, 1973) for a judicial response to the legal and medical issues posed by experimental psychosurgery. In that case, the court determined that the consent must be competent, voluntary, and knowledgeable. *Id.* at 31-32. *See also* Herch & Flower, *Medical and Psychological Experimentation on California Prisoners*, 7 U. CAL. DAVIS L. REV. 351 (1974).

6. A creative attempt at using experimental methodology to ascertain the effects of intervention on racial interactions is found in Cohen & Roper, *Modification of Interracial Interactions Disability: An Application of Status Characteristic Theory*, 37 AM. SOCIOLOGICAL REV. 643 (1972).

are related initially to educational attainment, and ultimately to income and occupational attainment. While the logic of such a relationship may be compelling, any conclusion in this respect is beyond what could be substantiated by results from the experiment just outlined.

An alternative social science strategy that is used when direct experimental research is not feasible is the quasi-experimental approach.[7] This latter strategy represents an attempt to parallel the experimental conditions by using statistical procedures to "correct" for those factors that cannot be controlled experimentally. Sometimes the quasi-experimental approach is termed a "natural" experiment because data are collected from an actual life situation rather than an experimental one. For instance, a researcher who is interested in the effects of schools on life chances might collect historical data for a sample of adult males or females. These data would include the present earnings and occupation of the individuals, information on their parents' class origins, characteristics of the schools that they attended, information on their friends, their work experience, and so on. A statistical model would then be constructed in an attempt to determine the relationship between the educational variables and the occupational and income attainments of the sample being studied.

Quasi-experimental studies attempt statistically to relate all relevant factors that might explain a particular phenomenon. The success of such an approach is dependent upon the ability to identify and measure these factors and to relate them in the statistical analysis in a manner reflecting the true phenomenon. As mentioned previously, however, there are an unlimited number of potential influences on adult outcomes and there are a variety of plausible ways that each can be measured and related to other variables in the analysis. In an area where choices must be made among the myriad of possible variables, measures, and relationships, the complexity and arduous nature of this type of statistical analysis necessarily limits the researcher to a narrow set of alternative formulations. The actual choice of factors to be included in a study, the measures of those that are ultimately selected, and the structure used to relate them is in part determined by the personal predilections of the researcher.[8]

In summary, there are enormous difficulties in determining how a host of genetic, psychological, social, cultural, political, economic, educational, and chance factors determine a person's ultimate life attainments. These difficulties and the complex nature of the problem suggest the inability of social science research to derive answers that can be utilized with any reasonable degree of reliability. Indeed, it is little wonder that opinions on the subject differ as much among social scientists as they do among laymen. Because of the inherent inadequacy of our present tools, there is no social science concensus on the

---

7. *See* D. CAMPBELL & J. STANLEY, *supra* note 4.
8. *See generally* Levin, *The Social Science Objectivity Gap*, 55 SATURDAY REV. no. 46, at 49 (1972).

appropriate educational strategies for improving the life chances of children from low income and minority backgrounds.[9]

II

HYPOTHESES ABOUT SCHOOLING AND ADULT ATTAINMENTS

The fact that social science has not provided a definitive or even a tentatively acceptable analysis of the relation between schooling and adult attainments does not mean that there exist no hypotheses on the subject. To the contrary, there are at least four such theories relating schooling to eventual adult occupation and income. Each of them presumes a relatively different educational approach toward improving the life chances of disadvantaged students.

A. Skills or Cognitive Achievement

Much of the literature on schooling and adult income is dominated by the notion that education produces verbal and mathematical skills as well as other knowledge that translate into higher productivity in the market place and consequently higher earnings. Under this hypothesis, the more cognitive knowledge that children acquire in school, the greater will be their life attainments. Accordingly, the effect of schooling or income is determined by the effect that schooling has on skills and knowledge. Those schools that contributed toward greater gains on achievement tests ostensibly would have the greatest impact on improving the future adult attainments of their pupils. Hence, the appropriate educational strategies would be those that are consistent with increasing the test scores of children from low income backgrounds. The most notable of these approaches is the provision of additional educational resources as exemplified by programs of compensatory education in the elementary and secondary schools[10] and such pre-school programs as Project Head Start.[11] It has also been argued that greater social class and racial integration of schools will have this effect.[12]

---

9. *See* Address by D. Campbell, *supra* note 4.

10. In addition to programs under Title I of the Elementary and Secondary Education Act, 20 U.S.C. § 241 (1970), several states provide funds for compensatory programs. *See, e.g.*, CAL. EDUC. CODE §§ 6499.230-6499.238 (West 1975); WIS. STAT. ANN. §§ 115.90-115.94 (Supp. 1974).

11. Project Head Start, instituted under authority of Title II of the Economic Opportunity Act of 1964, 78 Stat. 516 (1964), *as amended* 42 U.S.C. § 2781 (1970), offers a variety of health, social and educational services to enable pre-school children from deprived families to enter kindergarten or first grade.

12. *See* Coleman, *Toward Open Schools*, 9 PUB. INTEREST 20 (Fall 1967).

B. Noncognitive Characteristics for Work Relations

In contrast to the cognitive achievement hypothesis outlined above, the second thesis views the school as inculcating students with the appropriate behaviors for occupying particular positions in the occupational or organizational hierarchy. Such characteristics as respect for rules, dependability, and internalization of the norms of the workplace have been found to be strong predictors of employee ratings by supervisors and of income levels.[13] The workplace is seen as a hierarchically differentiated organization in which different positions require varying worker characteristics:[14]

> those at the base of the hierarchy requiring a heavy emphasis on obedience and rules and those at the top, where the discretionary scope is considerable, requiring a greater ability to make decisions on the basis of well-internalized norms. This pattern is closely replicated in the social relations of schooling. Note the wide range of choice over curriculum, life style, and allocation of time afforded to college students, compared with the obedience and respect for authority expected in high school.

According to the second hypothesis, while minimal skills are necessary for productivity, most of the discrepancy in occupational attainment and earnings is attributable to noncognitive work traits. Four of these work prerequisites —proper level of subordination, discipline, supremacy of cognitive over affective modes of response, and motivation according to external reward structures—have been identified.[15] Also identified are the ways in which the schools are structured to foster these traits. For example, subordination and proper orientation to authority along hierarchical lines are necessary in virtually all modern work enterprises. Thus, "[a]s the worker relinquishes control over his activities on the job, so the student is first forced to accept, and later comes personally to terms with, his loss of autonomy and initiative to a teacher who acts as a superior authority, dispensing rewards and penalities."[16] Similarly, it is argued that other school practices are related to the requirements of the workplace; students from lower social class origins are being prepared to occupy lower status occupations and those from higher class backgrounds are being socialized to undertake professional and managerial roles.

This hypothesis suggests that the contribution of schooling should be evaluated in terms of its impact on creating productive worker characteristics. Unfortunately, the work hierarchy is so unequal in terms of job requirements, satisfaction, income, and prestige that providing everyone with the "most productive" traits is not likely to increase life chances for everyone. Rather, it

---

13. *See* R. Edwards, Alienation and Inequality: Capitalist Relations of Production in a Bureaucratic Enterprise, July 1972 (unpublished Ph.D. thesis, Department of Economics, Harvard University).

14. Bowles, *Understanding Unequal Economic Opportunity*, 63 AM. ECON. REV. 346, 353 (1973).

15. Gintis, *Education, Technology and the Characteristics of Worker Productivity*, in *Proceedings of the Eighty-Fourth Annual Meeting*, 61 AM. ECON. REV. 266 (1971) [hereinafter cited as Gintis].

16. *Id.* at 274.

would simply redistribute opportunities among the population with some individuals improving their standing and others losing ground in terms of productive adult roles. In contrast with the thesis that everyone's productivity is enhanced by the attainment of greater cognitive skills, it is difficult to argue that productivity for all individuals would rise with the inculcation of higher echelon occupational traits, so long as the number of such positions is rationed by the occupational pyramid. In short, the view that the schools affect the life chances of students by preparing them for particular levels of the work hierarchy suggests that schools perform their function when they differentiate and produce the highly unequal outcomes that correspond to adult roles.[17] The most that could be accomplished by the schools in such a world is that students from disadvantaged backgrounds would have the same chance to be prepared for particular roles as those from advantaged backgrounds, in contrast with the present system which relegates racial minorities and the children of the lower class to corresponding lower class adult roles.

C. Screening and Certification

The third major hypothesis of how education affects earnings and occupational status views the school as an organization whose principal function is to sort and select students. According to this interpretation, the schools carry out a sophisticated process of assessing the cognitive and personal attributes of a student and then assigning him to a particular educational fate. Through testing, ability grouping and tracking, curriculum assignment, grading systems, and stratification by social class among neighborhoods, the schools act as an enormous filter.[18] Students who have the low-level skills and personality characteristics suitable for the lower end of the work hierarchy are placed in slow ability tracks or in inner-city schools that provide them with little incentive for further schooling. In contrast, students with high test scores and with personality attributes that correspond with the upper level of the job hierarchy are encouraged to pursue further education and will be rewarded with the high grades which represent the admission requirement for obtaining superior educational credentials.

The screening and certification hypothesis assumes that the occupational and income attainment process for an individual is determined largely by the amount of schooling he has received, his field of study, and the prestige of the institutions that he attended.[19] Thus, the sorting and selection of each stu-

---

17. *See* Levin, *A Conceptual Framework for Accountability in Education*, 82 SCHOOL REV. 363 (1974).

18. *See* I. BERG, EDUCATION AND JOBS: THE GREAT TRAINING ROBBERY (1970); Hall, *On the Road to Educational Failure: A Lawyer's Guide to Tracking*, 12 INEQUALITY IN ED. 1 (1970); Kirp, *Schools as Sorters: The Constitutional and Policy Implications of Student Classification*, 121 U. PA. L. REV. 705 (1973); Sorgen, *Testing and Tracking in Public Schools*, 24 HASTINGS L.J. 1129 (1973). Use of the term "filter" is adopted from Arrow, *Higher Education as a Filter*, 2 J. PUB. ECON. 193 (1973).

19. *See generally* Bowles, *Unequal Education and the Reproduction of the Social Division of Labor*, in

dent according to his initial and developing characteristics are identified in the job market by an educational credential which is used to establish his place in the occupational structure. Since such credentials are awarded on the basis of "productive" characteristics, employers need only to find out which "certificate" an individual possesses in order to judge his suitability for a particular position.[20] The hypothesis thus suggests that schools do not serve to educate students but instead to select them for their future fates according to characteristics derived from their genetic heritage and non-school environments. It has been further argued that the traits used for selection have little to do with real productivity differences and that persons with higher educational credentials are simply placed in jobs that are ostensibly more productive because of such factors as, for example, greater capital investment per worker.[21]

Presumably, then, the reason that children from lower income and minority backgrounds do more poorly in both schools and later careers is that they are filtered out rather early on the basis of low initial test scores and personality traits deemed inappropriate for further educational selection. Their low educational credentials mean that they will occupy low productivity jobs with little hope of access to the more productive and remunerative ones.[22] The educational policy implications of this hypothesis are not unlike those of the second hypothesis discussed earlier, which is concerned with the noncognitive characteristics or behavior appropriate at various levels. In both instances, the schools tend to reinforce the initial attributes of students; according to the third hypothesis, through selection and certification procedures, and according to the second hypothesis, through selection, differentiated preparation by category of student (especially social class), and certification. The major distinction between the two views of the educational process is that the sorting hypothesis assumes that the school has no educational effect on the student and that the observed differences merely reflect variation in natural endowments and out-of-school influences. The noncognitive socialization theory, on the other hand, assumes that schools do have an effect—that of further reinforcing these initial differences.

Only by eliminating all sorting and selection based on characteristics that coincide solely with race and social class will educational credentials be distributed in a more nearly random manner. Yet, since grades and examination scores are based substantially upon behavior and language styles which in turn are heavily determined by racial and social class backgrounds, drastically dif-

---

SCHOOLING IN A CORPORATE SOCIETY 36 (M. Carnoy ed. 1972); Karabel, *Community Colleges and Social Stratification*, 42 HARV. ED. REV. 521 (1972).

20. *See* Arrow, *supra* note 18; Spence, *Job Market Signaling*, 87 Q.J. ECON. 355 (1973).

21. *See* Thurow, *Education and Economic Equality*, 28 PUB. INTEREST 66 (Summer 1972); I. BERG, *supra* note 18.

22. *See* D. GORDON, THEORIES OF POVERTY AND UNDEREMPLOYMENT (1972). *See also* Harrison, *Education and Underemployment in the Urban Ghetto*, 62 AM. ECON. REV. 796 (1972).

ferent criteria would have to be developed for determining a student's educational success.

D. Reduction of Social Class and Racial Frictions

The final hypothesis considers the attitudes of all students towards racial and social class differences. The premise is that the better all racial and social class groups understand each other, and the greater the number of intergroup contacts, friendships and interactions, the less racial and class conflicts there will be in adult life.[23] The role of the school in this regard is crucial, for racial, cultural, and social class diversity in the educational environment is considered to be a prerequisite to greater justice in the distribution of jobs and earnings among the population. It is assumed that such a policy would have a marked impact on reducing labor market discrimination against racial minorities and members of the lower classes.

The obvious educational strategies that are consistent with this hypothesis are those which lie at the heart of the school desegregation movement. These include greater social class and racial heterogeneity among students and the introduction of a more multi-culturally oriented curriculum. The former action would be accomplished through massive desegregation of schools, thereby increasing the diversity of student populations and of the resultant educational and social interactions. The latter approach, which emphasizes a greater balance among the cultural contributions of different social and racial groups, would be implemented through changes in instructional materials, teacher training, and teacher selection.

III

EMPIRICAL SUPPORT FOR THE HYPOTHESES

According to the conventional image of science, mere application of research methodology to competing hypotheses will reveal which one best describes the world. Thus, through the use of sophisticated empirical research techniques we should be able to distinguish among those approaches worthy of elevation to the level of explanatory theory and those which should be banished

---

23. Contacts that bring knowledge and acquaintance are likely to engender sounder beliefs about minority groups . . . . Prejudice . . . may be removed by equal status contact between majority and minority groups in the pursuit of common goals. The effect is greatly enhanced if this contact is sanctioned by institutional supports (i.e., by law, custom, or local atmosphere), and if it is of a sort that leads to the perception of common interests and common humanity between members of the two groups.

G. ALLPORT, THE NATURE OF PREJUDICE 268, 281 (1954); *see* M. DEUTSCH & M. COLLINS, INTERRACIAL HOUSING: A PSYCHOLOGICAL EVALUATION OF A SOCIAL EXPERIMENT (1951); J. DOLLARD, CASTE AND CLASS IN A SOUTHERN TOWN (1937); G. MYRDAL, AN AMERICAN DILEMMA (1944). *But see* Armor, *The Evidence on Busing*, 28 PUB. INTEREST 90, 102-05 (Summer 1972); Armor, *The Double Double Standard: A Reply*, 30 PUB. INTEREST 119, 127-29 (Winter 1973).

as falsehood. But, as noted previously, the tools of social science are inadequate for this task. The social science evidence that does exist is incomplete, fragmented, and applicable to narrow populations only. It cannot, therefore, be conclusive.[24]

Although each hypothesis can be shown as consistent with some observable facts, the same facts often lend support to more than one of the hypotheses. Table I represents a summary of the evidence in support of the four hypotheses linking education with the life chances of poor and minority students. The educational strategies and the measures of educational outcome that are consistent with each hypothesis are shown in this table. But beyond this, the important concern is whether certain specified educational outcomes have been produced successfully by the corresponding educational strategy. The extent to which the desired educational outcome is linked to such adult attainments as income and occupational status is of substantial concern as well. These aspects are essential to determining the degree to which we can expect a particular educational strategy to produce enhanced income and occupational positions. Accordingly, the summary of the evidence linking the educational strategy to a specified educational output, and the educational output to measures of life attainment is also provided in Table I. It is important to observe that a lack of evidence for the impact of any particular strategy does not mean that the approach is without merit. It simply means that existing research—which may be quite minimal on the subject—has not provided sufficient empirical support for such a strategy.

A. Measures of Educational Outcome

The cognitive skills hypothesis has as its measure of educational outcome standardized test scores. Despite the fact that there are many and diverse measures of the broad range of cognitive skills, the evidence, as indicated below, is remarkably consistent whether IQ tests, achievement tests, reading tests, mathematics tests, or others are used. In order to raise the level of cognitive performance of low income and minority youngsters, the educational strategies usually invoked are the provision of greater resources for compensatory education and racial and socioeconomic integration. The evidence is weak that either of these policies has significant impact on test scores. For example, neither the *Coleman Report*[25] nor subsequent studies, some of which used the data collected for the *Coleman Report*, found that differences in the level of educational resources have any major impact on test scores.[26] An analysis based on the statistical results of a number of these studies has shown that even major increases of those educational resources most related to test

24. *See* Address of D. Campbell, *supra* note 4.
25. J. COLEMAN, EQUALITY OF EDUCATION OPPORTUNITY (1966).
26. *See, e.g.*, C. JENCKS, INEQUALITY 93-95, 255 (1972) [hereinafter cited as JENCKS].

TABLE 1

SUMMARY OF EVIDENCE IN SUPPORT OF FOUR HYPOTHESES LINKING EDUCATION TO LIFE CHANCES OF LOW INCOME AND RACIAL MINORITY STUDENTS

	HYPOTHESES			
	A. Cognitive Skills	B. Noncognitive Work Characteristics	C. Sorting and Selection	D. Reduction of Racial and Class Frictions
Educational Strategy	Compensatory Education & Integration	Compensatory Education & Integration	Changes in Selection Mechanisms	Integration & Multi-Cultural Environment
Measure of Educational Outcome	Test Scores	Values, Attitudes, Behavior	Values, Attitudes, Behavior and Test Scores	Attitudes Towards Self and Other Groups
Evidence of Strategy's Success for Enhancing Educational Outcome for Poor and Racial Minorities	Weak	Weak	Weak	Inconclusive
Evidence Linking Educational Outcome to Income and Occupational Attainment	Consistent Statistical Tie, But Only Nominal Effect	Strong Inferential Evidence, But Little Direct Support	Not Separable From Cognitive and Noncognitive Results	Very Little Direct Evidence

scores would not come close to eliminating the performance gap between white and black students.[27] Evaluations of compensatory education programs carried out under Title I of the Elementary and Secondary Education Act of 1965[28] similarly have been unable to demonstrate any significant relationship between increased resources and improved test scores.[29]

While some studies have suggested that both socioeconomic and racial integration improve the test scores of minority and low-income students,[30] these conclusions have been contested in other evaluations.[31] Thus, neither compensatory education strategies nor those related to desegregation show anything other than a weak relationship to cognitive gains. Even when statistical differences in favor of these strategies are reported, the improvement in cognitive skills is generally marginal.

Assuming that strategies other than compensatory education and racial and class integration could be found which did improve cognitive scores substantially, what would be the impact of such an improvement on income and occupational attainments of poor and minority youngsters? Numerous studies demonstrate a consistent statistical relationship between test scores and these measures of life success.[32] The explanatory significance of this relationship is

---

27. Carnoy, *Is Compensatory Education Possible?*, in SCHOOLING IN A CORPORATE SOCIETY 175 (M. Carnoy ed. 1972).

28. 20 U.S.C. § 241 (1970).

29. *See, e.g.*, M. Wargo, G. Tallmadge, D. Michaels, D. Lipe, & S. Morris, ESEA Title I: A Reanalysis and Synthesis of Evaluation Data From Fiscal Year 1965 Through 1970, March 1972 (unpublished document on file at American Institute for Research, Palo Alto, Cal.); Levin, *Effects of Expenditure Increases on Educational Resource Allocation and Effectiveness*, in SCHOOL FINANCE IN TRANSITION 177 (J. Pincus ed. 1974). A study prepared by the Rand Corporation acknowledges that "[v]irtually without exception, all of the large surveys of the large national compensatory education programs have shown no beneficial results on average." THE RAND CORPORATION, HOW EFFECTIVE IS SCHOOLING? 124-25 (1971). The study, however, is quick to note that "the evaluation reports on which the surveys are based are often poor and research designs suspect." *Id.* at 125. The caveat points to such factors as non-random assignment of children, bias in project selection, "continuation" of the questionable evaluation procedures. *Id.* at 106-07. Consequently, "no . . . assurance is possible . . . that the survey evaluations used in arriving at such a verdict were themselves an accurate description of the real world. . . ." *Id.* at 105.

30. *See* J. COLEMAN, *supra* note 25; U.S. COMMISSION ON CIVIL RIGHTS, RACIAL ISOLATION IN THE PUBLIC SCHOOLS (1967); Pettigrew, Useem, Normand, & Smith, *Busing: A Review of "The Evidence,"* 30 PUB. INTEREST 88 (Winter 1973).

31. *See* Armor, *The Evidence on Busing*, 28 PUB. INTEREST 90 (Summer 1972); Bowles & Levin, *The Determinants of Scholastic Achievement—A Critical Appraisal of Some Recent Evidence*, 3 J. HUMAN RESOURCES 3 (1968); Cohen, Pettigrew, & Riley, *Race and the Outcomes of Schooling*, in ON EQUALITY OF EDUCATIONAL OPPORTUNITY 343 (F. Mosteller & D. Moynihan eds. 1972); Hanushek & Kain, *On the Value of* Equality of Educational Opportunity *as a Guide to Public Policy*, in *id.* at 116; St. John, *Desegregation and Minority Group Performance*, 40 REV. ED. RESEARCH 111 (1970); Smith, *Equality of Educational Opportunity: The Basic Findings Reconsidered*, in ON EQUALITY OF EDUCATIONAL OPPORTUNITY, *supra* at 230.

32. *See, e.g.*, D. DUNCAN, D. FEATHERMAN, & B. DUNCAN, SOCIOECONOMIC BACKGROUND AND ACHIEVEMENT (1972); JENCKS; T. Ribich & J. Murphy, The Economic Returns to Increased Educational Spending, 1974 (to be published in J. HUMAN RESOURCES); P. Wachtel, The Effect of School Quality on Achievement, Attainment Levels and Lifetime Earnings, May 1974 (unpublished paper at the New York University Graduate School of Business Administration); Griliches & Mason,

nonetheless quite weak.[33] At most only about 10 per cent of the differences in income can be explained by test scores, leaving 90 per cent or more to be explained by other factors. Furthermore, relatively large increases in test scores are associated with only modest increases in income. While the apparent effect of test scores on occupational status is somewhat higher, it still only explains—at the most—about 25 per cent of the variance.[34] Differences in test scores, therefore, are not a major factor in explaining why occupational attainments and incomes differ among various cross sections of the population. In summation, the hypothesis that improving the cognitive test scores will raise the adult attainments of children from low income and minority families shows little promise of success because (1) available educational strategies have not demonstrated much success in improving test scores of these students and (2) increases in test scores show only modest effects on adult income and occupations.

B. Evidence on Noncognitive Work Characteristics

In contrast with the numerous studies exploring the relationship between test scores and increased resources or integration, there are few research studies devoted to the other hypotheses. Nonetheless, there have been some attempts to explore the noncognitive worker characteristics thesis. As indicated previously, the measure of educational outcome relating such traits to income and occupation are those values, attitudes, and behaviors which are required for work positions in a hierarchical setting. These include such characteristics as dependability, subordination to authority, respect for rules, and internalization of work norms.[35] Measures of noncognitive work traits have been demonstrated to be related to grades awarded by teachers, more so than are test scores.[36] However, there is apparently no study which has attempted to determine the *degree* to which the worker characteristics of poor and minority students can be altered by compensatory education or integration. Contrariwise, there is a strong presumption that the present approach will resist change because it is functional to the reproduction of the capitalist work hierarchy.[37] Accordingly, the relationship between the educational strategy and the desired educational outcomes must be considered as weak.

Education, Income, and Ability, 80 J. POL. ECON. 574 (1972); Sewell & Hauser, *Causes and Consequences of Higher Education: Models of the Status Attainment Process*, 54 AM. J. AGRIC. ECON. 851 (1972); Taubman & Wales, *Higher Education, Mental Ability, and Screening*, 81 J. POL. ECON. 28 (1973).

33. *See* Bowles & Nelson, *The Inheritance of IQ and the Intergenerational Reproduction of Economic Inequality*, 56 REV. ECON. & STATISTICS 39 (1974).

34. *See generally* O. DUNCAN, D. FEATHERMAN, & B. DUNCAN, *supra* note 32; JENCKS; Bowles & Nelson, *supra* note 33; Griliches & Mason, *supra* note 32; Sewell & Hauser, *supra* note 32.

35. *See, e.g.*, R. Edwards, *supra* note 13; Bowles, *supra* note 14; Bowles & Gintis, *IQ in the U.S. Class Structure*, 3 SOCIAL POLICY 65 (Nov./Dec. 1972, Jan./Feb. 1973); Gintis.

36. *See* Gintis.

37. *See* Bowles, *supra* note 14; Bowles, *supra* note 19.

There is, however, evidence linking noncognitive outcomes to income and occupational attainments. The amount of schooling a person receives is a more powerful determinant of income and occupation than are test scores. For example, three studies using longitudinal data—permitting prior schooling experiences and test scores to be linked to earnings—have found either a nonexistent or a relatively negligible correlation between test scores and earnings. This is in contrast to the rather pronounced impact that the amount of schooling has on ultimate income.[38] Thus it appears that the amount of schooling a person receives has a considerable effect on adult success, independent of the cognitive skills attained from the educational process.

But there is additional evidence supporting the noncognitive work characteristics hypothesis: teachers tend to award higher grades to students who exhibit personality characteristics functional in the work hierarchy.[39] One study of a sample of workers from three different enterprises found that these personality traits or characteristics are related both to supervisors' ratings and to earnings, even after differences in cognitive skills among employees is accounted for.[40] Obviously, much more research is needed in this area, but the view that noncognitive educational outcomes have more important influences on life attainments than cognitive ones has considerable support. Nevertheless, the lack of evidence indicating that educational strategies can alter the distribution of these traits suggests that the policy implications of this hypothesis are minimal.

C. Evidence on Sorting and Selection

The difficulty in evaluating the sorting and selection hypothesis is that there is virtually no reliable way to distinguish its effects from those generated by the cognitive and noncognitive socialization hypotheses. Essentially, the difference between the sorting and selection hypothesis and the other two is that the former assumes that schools do not produce the cognitive and noncognitive traits that are reflected in educational attainments and credentials. Rather, schools simply identify and select students according to those traits which they already possessed or acquired outside of the school setting, and bestow upon them differing educational rewards. Whether schools sort according to already-existing characteristics or actually inculcate these characteristics in students cannot be determined without very intensive studies. Possibly both aspects are prevalent but there is no apparent evidence that permits differentia-

38. *See* T. Ribich & J. Murphy, *supra* note 32; P. Wachtel, *supra* note 32; Sewell & Hauser, *supra* note 32. Even when test scores are included in the analysis, the effect of schooling alone on earnings is not significantly reduced. *See* Bowles, *supra* note 14; Gintis; Griliches & Mason, *supra* note 32.

39. *See* Gintis.

40. *See* R. Edwards, *supra* note 13.

tion between the two.[41] Thus, any evidence tending to support the cognitive and noncognitive socialization hypotheses would certainly be consistent with a sorting and selection hypothesis as well.

D. Evidence on Reduction of Frictions Between Races and Classes

Finally, the hypothesis on reducing racial and social class frictions measures educational outcome by the attitudes of representatives of each group towards themselves (self-image and sense of efficacy), as well as by attitudes that connote an understanding and acceptance of members of other groups. Whether the educational strategies of desegregation and multi-cultural emphasis[42] have long-run effects on attitudes and behavior is questionable. That the evidence in these areas is both controversial and contradictory is reflected in recent debates on the subject.[43] In some instances desegregation of the schools appears to have improved the self-images of racial minorities and racial attitudes of both majority and minority students;[44] in other cases there seem to have been no effects, or even negative ones.[45] One of the basic problems that pervades this research is the questionable reliability and stability of any measure of human attitudes. Given the variable quality of desegregation efforts and multi-cultural educational programs, it is not surprising to find such a divergence of results.

There is at least some empirical evidence supporting the view that socioeconomic integration improves the life chances of low status children. An analysis of data collected for a sample of youngsters then in the ninth grade, supplemented by follow-up information on their subsequent schooling, occupational attainments, and income nine years later, indicates that students who had similar test scores and social class backgrounds as well as educational attainments had higher incomes if they had attended secondary schools with other students from high socioeconomic backgrounds.[46] A particularly interesting aspect of this study was that low status individuals appeared to "gain" more than twice as much income from this effect as did the high status individuals. However, even this finding applies only to the young adults in this particular

---

41. A related question is the degree to which educational credentials reflect differences in productivity as opposed to their role in screening employees for particular occupational positions without regard for productivity. *Compare* Taubman & Wales, *supra* note 32, *with* Layard & Psacharopoulos, *The Screening Hypothesis and the Returns to Education*, 82 J. POL. ECON. 985 (1974).

42. *See* text at p. 226 *supra*.

43. *See* Armor, *supra* note 31; Armor, *supra* note 23; Pettigrew, Useem, Normand, & Smith, *supra* note 30.

44. *See* G. ALLPORT, *supra* note 23; M. DEUTSCH & M. COLLINS, *supra* note 23; J. DOLLARD, *supra* note 23; G. MYRDAL, *supra* note 23. *See also* Epps, *The Impact of School Desegregation on Aspirations, Self-Concepts and Other Aspects of Personality*, 39 LAW & CONTEMP. PROB. no. 2, at 300 (1975) for a review of the research on the impact of desegregation on self-esteem, and Cohen, *The Effects of Desegregation on Race Relations*, 39 LAW & CONTEMP. PROB. no. 2, at 271 (1975) for a review of the research on the impact of desegregation on interracial relations.

45. *See* Armor, *supra* note 23.

46. *See* T. Ribich & J. Murphy, *supra* note 32.

sample. Furthermore, it is not clear why socioeconomic composition per se should lead to higher incomes.

IV

Social Science and the Choice of a Strategy

The difficulty of using social science research to determine how different educational strategies can be used to affect the future life chances of low income and minority students is clear. While virtually all of the four hypotheses discussed above have some support, the results are ambiguous and inconclusive. Advocacy of any particular approach, therefore, is not based so much upon its general acceptance in the scientific community as it is upon the predilections of researchers and policy makers. The fact that they as well as the courts have not been neutral among competing ideas suggests that it is useful to explore the reasons that particular strategies are selected.

At the outset, one may very well ask how social science researchers can commit themselves to a particular hypothesis or approach on the basis of ambiguous, fragmented, and often contradictory findings. The answer, seemingly, is that researchers often have commitments based upon deeply ingrained social experiences that affect their understanding of how society functions. The natural consequence of these experiences encourages the social scientist to accept the evidence which reinforces his own experience and to be skeptical of that which does not.[47] As Polanyi has noted:[48]

> I start by rejecting the ideal of scientific detachment. In the exact sciences, this false ideal is perhaps harmless, for it is in fact disregarded there by scientists. But we shall see that it exercises a destructive influence in biology, psychology and sociology and has falsified our whole outlook far beyond the domain of science.

To a substantial degree the social scientist is himself a product of the very forces he wishes to study. Long before he has received his professional training he is exposed to such phenomena as class, race, family structure, money, prices, religion, industry, politics, work, the messages of the media on all of these subjects, and more. His perspective of the world is largely a cumulative result of his role as a child, student, sibling, husband, consumer, professor, rich man, black, woman, mother, and so on. All of these roles have defined the bound-

---

47. *See generally* P. Berger & T. Luckman, The Social Construction of Reality (1966); T. Kuhn, The Structure of Scientific Revolutions (1962); K. Mannheim, Ideology and Utopia (1936); R. Merton, Social Theory and Social Structure (1949); R. Merton, The Sociology of Science (1973); M. Polanyi, Personal Knowledge (1958); K. Popper, Objective Knowledge: An Evolutionary Approach (1972); Y. Elkana, Rationality and Scientific Change, 1972 (unpublished manuscript at Department of History and Philosophy of Science, Hebrew University, Jerusalem); Y. Elkana, The Theory and Practice of Cross-Cultural Contacts, 1972 (mimeograph at Hebrew University, Jerusalem).

48. M. Polanyi, *supra* note 47, at vii.

aries of experience which in turn mold his social reality.[49] In a more specific sense, the social scientist who studies the effects of schooling on achievement has been socialized to a large degree by his own particular experiences during his education. His knowledge about the determinants of poverty is influenced by his own class origins and experiences. His image of political reality is conditioned by his own interactions with the political system and other institutions that inculcate political attitudes. Interacting with these influences is his professional training which emphasizes particular metaphysical and epistemological frameworks for viewing the world.

Moreover, since researchers are not randomly assigned to studies, the effects of the researcher's commitment and ideology on the interpretation of research findings is not a chance event. To the contrary, there is a self-selection of problems by researchers according to their predilections, as well as the selection by government and other decision makers, based upon the "outlook" of the researcher and the sponsoring agency. Social science investigators choose those problems that interest them and to which they feel they can contribute something of value. Of course, research support is also a prerequisite, but most social science analysts—particularly in the academic setting—have a choice of problems on which to focus. Public policy-oriented research has a substantive or topical component that may or may not be of interest to potential investigators. Such motives as a sincere wish of the individual to improve government decision-making are often strong factors in the choice of problems, but they also coincide with a deep personal involvement in the outcome of the study. That is, the researcher is likely to have relatively strong viewpoints about what proper policy should be in advance of his research.

The agencies that support research are just as likely to select a researcher on the basis of his values as on his "scientific" competence. As Paul Samuelson has remarked:[50]

> The leaders of this world may seem to be led around through the nose by their economic advisers. But who is pulling and who is pushing? And note this: he who picks his doctor from an array of competing doctors is in a real sense his own doctor. The Prince often gets to hear what he wants to hear.

It would be inconceivable to think of the United States Commission on Civil Rights hiring a researcher for his neutrality on the desegregation issue. Indeed, we expect that government decision makers seek out those investigators who are sympathetic to the agency's own orientation.

Obviously, these phenomena dovetail very closely with the use of social science evidence in the courts. Legal proceedings are endeavors in advocacy, each side seeking that "evidence" which will support its own position. There is always some social science evidence on virtually any phenomenon, so one must

---

49. *See* P. BERGER & T. LUCKMAN, *supra* note 47.
50. Samuelson, *Economists and the History of Ideas*, 52 AM. ECON. REV. 1, 17 (1962).

ask what types of evidence are likely to be drawn into the courts. I assert that the social science evidence which courts are likely to receive has the following attributes: (1) It tends to be based upon complex, statistical methodologies that are generally beyond the experience and the competence of the court to question. (2) It directly supports or refutes the matter under consideration. (3) It is based upon a theory which is credible and understandable to the court. (4) And, finally, it implies a remedy that is readily within the court's power and is politically feasible.

The first requirement evolves from the image that the layman has of science. "Good" social science is characterized by large data sets, complicated statistical methodologies, and an aura of technical competence. While the researcher has made many personal judgments with respect to his formulation of the problem—selection of a framework for the analysis, definition and measurement of variables, technique of data analysis and interpretation of results—all will tend to be obscured by what appears to be a strictly technical analysis. The greater the methodological sophistication, the more difficult it is to demystify the analysis and the more tempting it becomes to see "the emperor's new clothes." The bias in favor of sophisticated empirical studies also rules out the consideration of hypotheses that are not conducive to empirical evaluation.

The second requirement suggests that ambiguity in research findings will be shunned. Alternative interpretations of the results can obviously be dangerous to the advocate who uses the evidence to support his client's case. Thus, the social science research that is utilized must unequivocally support the particular objectives of the advocate. This tends to eliminate any opportunity for a thoughtful analysis of all of the competing hypotheses.

The third requirement, that the social science evidence presented to the court be based upon a credible hypothesis, is illustrated by the fact that while social science research in the Marxian tradition may be both extremely sophisticated and unambiguous, the theory upon which it is based may not be acceptable to those heavily indoctrinated with the capitalist viewpoint.

Another example: no evidence has been presented in either the desegregation or the school finance cases that argues in favor of the noncognitive worker characteristics hypothesis as an explanation of the effects of schools on the life attainments of children from low income and racial minority backgrounds.[51] To the educated layman the cognitive skills theory is much more credible than the noncognitive one.

---

51. *But cf.* Serrano v. Priest, Civil No. 938,254 (Cal. Super. Ct., Apr. 10, 1974). In that case, conflicting evidence was introduced on the proper test to be applied in determining the quality of education existing within a school district, defendants urging the "pupil-achievement standard" while the plaintiffs urged a "school-district-offering standard." *Id.* at 52. The controlling dispute did not focus on the relationship between noncognitive theories of education and life attainment, and much of the opinion *was* cast in terms of the skills and cognitive achievement hypothesis. *See,*

Finally, the requirement that the social science evidence presented to the court implies a remedy that is both within the court's remedial powers and is politically feasible, is illustrated, for example, by the fact that given the present institutional framework, it is not possible for the court to interfere with family child-rearing for educational purposes. Yet studies have shown that such interventions will improve the life chances of students from low income families.[52]

In light of these principles it is understandable that the courts and other policy makers have focused primarily on the cognitive skills approach. Firstly, the research in this area, beginning with the *Coleman Report*[53] and the "Racial Isolation" report of The U. S. Commission on Civil Rights the following year,[54] has the aura of being methodologically sophisticated and empirical. Enormous data sets (about 650,000 students and 70,000 teachers comprise the *Coleman Report* data), sophisticated methodologies such as multiple regression analysis, and quantification of educational outcomes as reflected in test scores, create a strong image of valid scientific endeavor. Secondly, these studies purport to show unambiguously that socioeconomic and racial integration as well as certain school resources improve the test scores of low income and minority students. Thirdly, educated men tend to believe that cognitive test scores are important determinants of life chances because they are likely to attribute their own educational and occupational success to their relatively high levels of knowledge and skills rather than to "less rational" factors such as those related to family socioeconomic origins. Cognitive skills are an attractive basis for constructing the meritocracy.[55] Finally, implementation of the desegrega-

---

e.g., *id.* at 89. By holding for the plaintiffs, however, the court accepted the testimony that "Standardized achievement tests . . . are not appropriate for measuring the degree of attainment of many of the educational goals of the State. . . ." They "do not measure for progress in the affective domain—a pupil's personality characteristics, interests and attitudes, interpersonal skills and socialization skills." *Id.* at 91. In concluding that standardized test scores are not determinative of the quality of an educational program, the court also adverted to the parties' stipulation to the following:

> That a child's self-concept can be improved by the educational process; that the educational process can reinforce a child's negative self-concept; that schools can, do, and should, play a role in providing a child with acceptable social values and behavior norms; that schools can, do, and should, play a role in equipping children with what it takes to get along in a technological society; that schools can, do, and should, play a role in making children better future citizens; that many components of a good education are not measured by pupil performance on achievement tests; that many aspects of a student's capabilities and progress are not measured by performance on achievement tests; and that the scope of skills measured by achievement tests is limited.

52. *See, e.g.*, Bowles, *supra* note 14; Bowles, *supra* note 19; Hess, Shipman, & Jackson, *Early Experience and the Socialization of Cognitive Modes in Children*, 36 CHILD DEVELOPMENT 869 (1965); Olim, Hess, & Shipman, *Role of Mothers' Language Styles in Mediating Their Pre-School Children's Cognitive Development*, 75 SCHOOL REV. 414 (1967).

53. *See* J. COLEMAN, *supra* note 25.

54. *See* U.S. COMMISSION ON CIVIL RIGHTS, *supra* note 30.

55. *See* R. HERRNSTEIN, IQ IN THE MERITOCRACY (1973); M. YOUNG, THE RISE OF THE MERITOCRACY (1958); Bowles & Gintis, *supra* note 35.

tion and compensatory education strategies implied by the cognitive hypothesis are within the powers of the courts and educational decision makers.

V

Effects of Social Science Evidence

Thus far, it has been argued that the social sciences cannot produce conclusive results that would support a particular educational strategy for improving the life attainments of students from low income and minority families. Also, it has been asserted that the evidence that does enter the courts or policy arena is considered and utilized on the basis of factors other than its scientific "validity." What are the implications of these assertions for the evolution of public policy and the law?

There are three possible cases. The first is the happy one where the evidence presented is somehow the "best" that is available. In other words, the evidence is based upon the clearest attainable picture of the world and is unequivocally better than that which supports alternative hypotheses on the subject. It is not clear how this would happen but to the degree that it does occur, it can be viewed as advancing the wisdom of the legal system. The second case is a less benevolent one in which the social science evidence, while representing just one among competing views on the subject, nonetheless carries the day. To the degree that the results of the research are erroneous, the use of social science may be harmful.

But in many ways it is the third case that is most interesting. Here social science evidence is used to support both sides of a legal dispute.[56] In educa-

---

56. In Hobson v. Hansen, 327 F. Supp. 844 (D.D.C. 1971), Judge J. Skelly Wright commented on the utilization of expert social science evidence in an adversary proceeding:

> Plaintiffs' motion for an amended decree and for further enforcement has now been argued and reargued via a series of motions and written memoranda for one full year. During this time the unfortunate if inevitable tendency has been to lose sight of the disadvantaged young students on whose behalf this suit was first brought in an overgrown garden of numbers and charts and jargon like "standard deviation of the variable," statistical "significance," and "Pearson product moment correlations." The reports by the experts—one noted economist plus assistants for each side—are less helpful than they might have been for the simple reason that they do not begin from a common data base, disagree over crucial statistical assumptions, and reach different conclusions. Having hired their respective experts, the lawyers in this case had a basic responsibility, which they have not completely met, to put the hard core statistical demonstrations into language which serious and concerned laymen could, with effort, understand. Moreover, the studies by both experts are tainted by a vice well known in the statistical trade—data shopping and scanning to reach a preconceived result; and the court has had to reject parts of both reports as unreliable because biased. Lest like a latter day version of Jarndyce v. Jarndyce this litigation itself should consume the capital of the children in whose behalf it was brought, the court has been forced back to its own common sense approach to a problem which, though admittedly complex, has certainly been made more obscure than was necessary. The conclusion I reach is based upon burden of proof, and upon straightforward moral and constitutional arithmetic.

Id. at 859.

tional finance litigation, the constitutionality of state school finance systems was challenged on the ground that they provided lower quality education for children in low property wealth districts than for those in more affluent districts. The defense relied upon social science research which, they asserted, indicated no relationship between the level of expenditures and the quality of an education program. The defense arguments were buttressed by the *Coleman Report*[57] and other research,[58] tending to show that there was little or no causative effect between educational expenditures and other measures of school quality and student achievement. The plaintiffs countered with witnesses and research that disputed the methodologies and data employed in the studies cited by the defense, and which indicated a correlation between increases in educational resources and improved pupil achievement.[59] In some cases the plaintiffs won the argument;[60] in others, the courts were unpersuaded.[61]

Even where both sides draw upon social science evidence and the court decides between the two competing presentations, there is a possibility that use of such evidence will tend to redefine the issue itself. Presentation of evidence on the relationship between educational expenditures and cognitive achievement implicitly narrows the context within which the effects of unequal expenditure patterns will be considered. While the two sides to this debate disagree on the effect of school resources, both have accepted the view that standardized achievement scores are the appropriate focus for exploring educational outcomes. Since courts and policy makers generally find it easier to understand a point of agreement than of contention, such points of accord have more influence on the assimilation of the policy implications of research than the conclusions of the research itself. Thus, much of the legal debate surrounding the challenge to present methods of financing education does not address the basic unfairness reflected by state arrangements to spend more on the education of children in rich districts than in poor ones. Rather, the prima facie inequities are ignored as the courts are tortured with the convoluted arguments provided by social scientists about whether money makes a difference for "poor kids."[62] It is unfortunate that the issue has now become framed in

---

57. *See* J. COLEMAN, *supra* note 25.

58. *See generally*, JENCKS; ON EQUALITY OF EDUCATIONAL OPPORTUNITY, *supra* note 31.

59. *See, e.g.*, J. GUTHRIE, G. KLEINDORFER, H. LEVIN, & R. STOUT, SCHOOLS AND INEQUALITY (1971); E. HANUSHEK, EDUCATION AND RACE (1972); Bowles & Levin, *supra* note 31; Hanushek & Kain, *supra* note 31.

60. *See, e.g.*, Serrano v. Priest, Civil No. 938,254 (Cal. Super. Ct., Apr. 10, 1974); Robinson v. Cahill, 62 N.J. 473, 303 A.2d 273 (1973).

61. *See, e.g.*, Jensen v. State Bd. of Tax Comm'rs, Civil No. 24,474 (Ind. Cir. Ct., Jan. 15, 1973).

62. It seems inconceivable that prior to the *Coleman Report* a state would defend its arrangements to spend more money for the education of children in wealthy districts than in poor ones by arguing that dollars do not affect educational outcomes. I believe that this assertion would seem incredulous to a court. Common sense suggests that if higher expenditures make a difference for children in wealthy districts, they also make a difference for pupils in poorer districts. At the least, a court should question why a state sanctions such high expenditures in wealthy districts if such

terms of whether additional expenditures for children in poor school districts will raise their test scores.[63]

A second example of the tendency of a tacit consensus among litigants having a greater influence on policy formation than the actual research results, is the controversy over the effects of school desegregation. Until the mid-1960's, the case for racial desegregation was one that was based largely upon the type of society one envisioned.[64] For those who equated a fair society with the absence of racial separation, segregation of schools was contradictory. For those who defined a fair society in other ways, racial isolation in the educational system was of little consequence. The argument was primarily a moral one, dealing with normative visions of the world.[65]

With the advent of the *Coleman Report* and the 1967 Report of the U. S. Commission on Civil Rights, *Racial Isolation in the Public Schools*, a new dimension was added. These studies attempted to demonstrate that segregated school environments retarded the test scores of black children and other students from lower socioeconomic backgrounds. By 1972, serious questions were being raised about the validity of the earlier findings. Reanalysis of the Coleman data did not support the hypothesis that the test scores of black students were a function of the racial composition of the schools.[66] A subsequent analysis of several longitudinal studies of the effects of busing argued that the data do not support the conclusion that racial integration of schools in itself will improve the achievement levels of racial minorities and that there is at least some evidence that harmful changes in attitudes take place.[67]

The results of this study were shocking[68] due to the fact that heretofore there seemingly had been one point of agreement in the social science studies on desegregation—that "[i]ntegrated education will enhance the academic achievement of minority groups, and thereby close (or at least substantially reduce) the achievement gap."[69] Despite the very contradictory literature on school desegregation, the case for desegregation was seen as hinging *primarily* on whether it improves the achievement test scores of minority students.

---

resources are "wasted." *Cf.* Hobson v. Hansen, 327 F. Supp. 844 (1971), where the court stated that the defendants "cannot be allowed in one breath to justify budget requests to the Congress and to the District of Columbia City Council by stressing the connection between longevity and quality teaching, and then in the next breath to disavow any such connection before the court." *Id.* at 855.

63. *See* Carrington, *Financing the American Dream: Equality and School Taxes*, 73 COLUM. L. REV. 1227 (1973).

64. *See generally* Clark, *Social Policy, Power, and Social Science Research*, 43 HARV. ED. REV. 77 (1973).

65. *Compare* Cahn, *Jurisprudence*, 30 N.Y.U.L. REV. 150 (1955), *with* Clark, *The Desegregation Cases: Criticism of the Social Scientists' Role*, 5 VILL. L. REV. 224 (1960).

66. *See* Cohen, Pettigrew, & Riley, *supra* note 31, at 439-50, 356.

67. Armor, *supra* note 31.

68. The critics moved in quickly to question the criteria, statistical procedures, choice of studies reviewed, and other aspects of the Armor analysis. *See* Pettigrew, Useem, Normand, & Smith, *supra* note 30. The reply to this criticism also quickly followed. *See* Armor, *supra* note 23.

69. Armor, *supra* note 23.

Rather than considering what kind of educational policy regarding school racial patterns is consistent with our democratic ideals, the issue seems to be whether or not blacks and other minorities gain a few more points on a vocabulary or reading test. This standard is far removed from the declaration of the Supreme Court of 1954 that the separation of black children "because of their race generates a feeling of inferiority as to their status in the community that may affect their hearts and minds in a way unlikely ever to be undone."[70] At this stage, the issue has thus been cast in terms of the achievement scores of blacks rather than in terms of the larger moral and human dilemmas raised by segregated public institutions. There is little doubt that the research agenda has framed the issue.

CONCLUSION

What is the proper role of social science in charting educational policy for improving the life chances of low income and minority students? The answer to that question is not clear. The question of the relationship between educational influences and actual adult status addresses a very complicated area of social and individual behavior. In particular, little is known about the effects of different school environments on human behavior, about underlying theories of human productivity and its determinants in a particular social setting, about the myriad of other influences that can intervene between the educational strategy and the adult outcomes many years hence, and about the appropriate measurements of even those factors that do seem relevant. Further, the fact that experimentation as an empirical investigating tool is politically and practically infeasible limits severely our ability to uncover the true relationships.

Some observers may react to these conclusions by suggesting the social science evidence in these complicated areas is likely to be so misleading and value-laden that we ought to ignore it.[71] In contrast, some technocrats will argue that the case *against* the ability of social science to validate the relationships between education and life chances has been overstated and that rapid scientific advances in research methodology will even nullify those anomalies which have arisen. Both of these views assume that the social sciences must play a deterministic role in contributing to policy or that they can play no role at all. Yet, it may be the heuristic aspects of social science research which are most useful.

Alice Rivlin has suggested that we acknowledge the development of a "forensic social science," rather than pretending "to be part of the tradition of balanced, objective social science in which the scholar hides (or claims to hide)

---

70. Brown v. Board of Educ., 347 U.S. 483, 494 (1954).

71. In *Rodriguez* Justice Powell noted that in view of the division of opinion among "scholars and educational experts . . . [on] the extent to which there is a demonstrable correlation between educational expenditures and the quality of education," the judiciary should refrain from deciding the issue. 411 U.S. at 42-43. *See also id.* at n.86.

his personal biases, and attempts to present all the evidence on both sides of a set of questions so that the reader may judge for himself."[72] Using the notion of a forensic social science for addressing policy issues,[73]

> scholars or teams of scholars take on the task of writing briefs for or against particular policy positions. They state what the position is and bring together all the evidence that supports their side of the argument, leaving to the brief writers of the other side the job of picking apart the case that has been presented and detailing the counter evidence.

The problem with such an approach is that it assumes that all of the sides will be fairly represented. But adversary proceedings normally are based upon only two conflicting points of view.[74] Moreover, the fact that the epistemology of the social sciences itself limits the analysis to a specific set of hypotheses (particularly ones that have readily identifiable empirical consequences) suggests that the issue might be framed in an erroneous manner. Of course, this type of bias can be avoided by permitting non-social scientists to enter the forum to present their views and argue their evidence. It is not clear what criteria would be used to select such witnesses nor is it obvious how one could determine how many points of view should be permitted. It is also not clear that the courts would attach great weight to "non-scientific" presentations. Finally, the court lacks expertise in selecting among alternative presentations that are grounded in complex statistical procedures and highly technical language.[75] Of course, the court could hire its own experts for examining and interpreting the evidence, but what guarantees the objectivity of the "wise men" who advise the court?[76]

Social science research can best be used to frame the issues and their consequences rather than to obtain conclusive evidence on what is right and what is to be done. This approach requires a recognition that while many aspects of the world cannot be quantified or analyzed in a social science setting, such factors should be considered along with the results of social science research.[77] It is not clear that utilization of social science research in this manner is consistent with an adversary framework. Further, if social science findings increasingly are used to create what appear to be technical issues out of essentially moral dilemmas, this presents a potential social danger. The apparently increasing reliance of the courts on social science evidence suggests that intensive debate on these issues should be given high priority.

---

72. Rivlin, *Forensic Social Science*, 43 HARV. ED. REV. 25 (1973).

73. *Id.*

74. While in most school litigation expert testimony is offered by both parties to the dispute, see, *e.g.*, Serrano v. Priest, Civil No. 938,254 (Cal. Super. Ct., Apr. 10, 1974); in Robinson v. Cahill, 118 N.J. Super. 223, 287 A.2d 187 (1972), only the plaintiffs introduced expert witnesses on the relationship between expenditures and achievement.

75. *See* note 56 *supra*.

76. And even if the court's own expert is "objective," by what criteria, for example, is he to choose between two competing economic theories?

77. *See* Address by D. Campbell, *supra* note 4.

THE RELATIONSHIP BETWEEN SCHOOL DESEGREGATION AND ACADEMIC ACHIEVEMENT: A REVIEW OF THE RESEARCH

MEYER WEINBERG*

> [T]he outcome of any serious research can only be to make two questions grow where one question grew before.
>
> — Thorstein Veblen

INTRODUCTION

Desegregation has become a major factor in American education. The courts have emphatically declared that segregation must end; school boards must take those measures "which promise realistically to convert promptly to a system without a 'white' school and a 'Negro' school, but just schools."[1] The Supreme Court soon made clear what "promptly" meant.[2]

> [C]ontinued operation of segregated schools under a standard of allowing "all deliberate speed" for desegregation is no longer constitutionally permissible. . . . [T]he obligation of every school district is to terminate dual school systems *at once* and to operate *now* and hereafter only unitary schools.

And the Supreme Court, in the *Keyes* case, indicated that these requirements were to extend to those school districts which had never operated "under a constitutional or statutory provision that mandated or permitted racial segregation in public education,"[3] if there was evidence of purposeful segregation practiced by school officials in at least a portion of such districts.

Many have contended that *Brown*[4] did not rest on social science evidence that segregation is psychologically harmful to Negro students,[5] or on the belief

---

* Professor of History, Loop College, City Colleges of Chicago; Lecturer, Northwestern University School of Education; editor of *Integrated Education*.

1. Green v. County School Bd., 391 U.S. 430, 442 (1968).
2. Alexander v. Holmes County Bd. of Educ., 396 U.S. 19, 20 (1969) (emphasis added).
3. Keyes v. School Dist. No. 1, 413 U.S. 189, 191 (1973).
4. Brown v. Board of Educ., 347 U.S. 483 (1954).
5. There has been continuing debate over *Brown*'s footnote eleven and whether the Supreme Court's opinion was based upon the sociological and psychological studies cited therein, whether this citation was merely "make-weight," or whether it was judicial fact-finding to which legal principles were then applied. *See, e.g.*, C. SWISHER, THE SUPREME COURT IN MODERN ROLE 158 (1958); W. WORKMAN, THE CASE FOR THE SOUTH 26, 30, 197 (1960); Clark, *The Social Scientists, the Brown Decision, and Contemporary Confusion*, in ARGUMENT: THE ORAL ARGUMENT BEFORE THE SUPREME COURT IN BROWN v. BOARD OF EDUCATION OF TOPEKA, 1952-55 at xxxi, xxxvi (L. Friedman ed. 1969); Black, *The Lawfulness of the Segregation Decisions*, 69 YALE L.J. 421 (1960); Cahn, *Jurisprudence*, 30 N.Y.U.L. REV. 150 (1955).

that the educational opportunity which the Court ordered states to provide equally without regard to race would lead to improved academic achievement on the part of Negro students. Nevertheless, since *Brown*, social scientists have sought to prove or disprove the linkage between racial and class integration and pupil performance.[6]

This article reviews school desegregation research that has been undertaken in this area, much of it unpublished. A major purpose, then, of this article is to disseminate information concerning these studies more extensively so that researchers and policy makers may build upon them. It is beyond the scope of this article, however, to systematically critique the methodology and approach used by the studies included herein.[7] Having alerted the researcher to the existence of these studies and their general findings and conclusions, it must remain for each interested person to undertake the in-depth, critical analysis necessary to an understanding of the full implications of these studies and the likelihood that the results will be replicated elsewhere. While research on the impact of desegregation on academic achievement has been inadequate,[8] over the last decade research efforts have increased somewhat. But unless support for continuing research is forthcoming from the federal government and foundations, it is questionable whether there will be significant advances beyond what the studies reviewed in this article have shown.

What can social scientists tell us about the effects of school desegregation on academic achievement? The primary focus of school desegregation research to date has been on the cognitive skills (*e.g.*, reading and mathematics) of nonwhites. The greatest number of such studies report positive gains as a result of desegregation, although it is clear that much additional research is needed before the findings can be fully understood and translated into effective policy. This is due in part to the fact that social scientists' understanding of the learning process is not very well developed, so that explaining the causes of improved pupil performance, even when race is not an issue, is a problematic endeavor. Moreover, some problems arise from the research methodology used; some of these problems are discussed in this article.[9]

There are some social science research findings of the effects of desegregation on the academic achievement of nonwhites, however, about which there is a degree of consensus among social scientists:

---

6. *See* Levin, *Education, Life Chances, and The Courts: The Role of Social Science Evidence*, 39 LAW & CONTEMP. PROB. no. 2, at 217 (1975).

7. The most useful analysis in this regard is N. ST. JOHN, SCHOOL DESEGREGATION OUTCOMES FOR CHILDREN (1975).

8. A decade ago, a federal official in charge of desegregation enforcement activities replied to a Congressional inquiry about the relative lack of research on desegregation: "The basic problem is there are very few researchers that want to work on it for some reason, but it is a very real problem." *Hearings on Guidelines for School Desegregation Before the Special Subcomm. on Civil Rights of the House Comm. on the Judiciary*, 89th Cong., 2d Sess. 139 (1966) (testimony of David S. Seeley, then assistant to the U.S. Commissioner of Education, Department of Health, Education, and Welfare).

9. *See also* Levin, *supra* note 6.

1. *Of the dozens of studies of the effects of school desegregation on the achievement of nonwhites, only a very few give any indication that placing nonwhites in desegregated schools might lessen their rate of academic achievement.*
2. *There is virtually no evidence, out of a substantial body of research, that desegregation lowers the achievement levels of whites.*

Thus the available research gives little reason to believe that school desegregation, in most settings, will adversely affect the academic achievement of either white or black students.[10] But will it improve academic performance?

Before attempting to answer this question on the basis of evidence provided by existing research studies, the paramount problem in most of the research should be noted: the difficulty in isolating those factors other than interracial contact that might account for the findings on the effects of desegregation. An important determinant of academic achievement appears to be the home environment. Few studies, however, are able to deal adequately with this factor. Efforts to "control" for the socioeconomic background of children is often used as a surrogate for the student's family situation, but it is not a very precise measure. People from different social classes may have similar attitudes toward education and child rearing. And almost nothing is known about how differences in family attitudes and values relevant to school achievement affect learning *within* socioeconomic groupings. Another very important factor affecting desegregation studies is the student's academic aptitude.

The studies reviewed in this article come to a variety of conclusions about the effects of desegregated schooling on the academic achievement of black students and other minorities. These studies are categorized on the basis of their conclusions as follows:

1. racial mixing is found to result in a general increase in nonwhite student academic achievement;
2. multiracial schooling is found to have a mixed effect on nonwhite student academic achievement;
3. attendance at racially mixed schools has no apparent effect on student academic achievement;
4. desegregation has negative effects on the achievement gains of nonwhite students.

---

10. It is possible—if the theory that student culture and teacher expectations are crucial determinants of learning is a valid one—that when the desegregation process results in placing students in settings dominated by low achievers of whatever race, there will be an overall loss in achievement levels. The effects of such situations on individual students will probably depend on the degree to which the student's family and, in later years, his or her immediate peer group, provide support for learning. *See, e.g.*, Hanushek, *Teacher Characteristics and Gains in Student Achievement Using Micro-Data*, 61 AM. ECON. REV. 280 (1971); St. John & Lewis, *The Influence of School Racial Context on Academic Achievement*, 19 SOCIAL PROBLEMS 68 (1971); Davis, *Busing*, in 2 NATIONAL OPINION RESEARCH CENTER, SOUTHERN SCHOOLS: AN EVALUATION OF THE EFFECTS OF THE EMERGENCY SCHOOL ASSISTANCE PROGRAM AND OF SCHOOL DESEGREGATION 83 (1973) [hereinafter cited as SOUTHERN SCHOOLS]. Robert Crain, study coordinator, however, suggests that Davis's finding may be a function of inadequate controls for the social background of the students. *Id.* at 116 n.10.

This article reviews some of the more important studies representing each of these categories. In addition, attention is given to research on whether busing itself—with or without desegregation as its purpose—affects learning.

I

Studies Showing a Positive Effect of Interracial Schooling on Academic Achievement

One of the most methodologically sophisticated and extensive studies of the effects of school desegregation is the recent evaluation of the Emergency School Assistance Program (ESAP),[11] published late in 1973.[12] The ESAP evaluation found that achievement scores of black male high school students who attended schools receiving federal desegregation aid were one-half grade level higher than their peers in other schools. This was attributed by the researchers to "improvements in the [experimental] schools' racial climate affecting the motivation of these students."[13] Only about half of the between-school variance in achievement was explained by social-class factors. Leadership by principals and teachers was found to be very effective in helping white students accept desegregation.[14]

A similar study[15] of the effect of school and classroom integration on academic achievement was undertaken in the late 1960's by James McPartland, using *Coleman Report* data.[16] This study attempted to answer questions which had arisen in earlier investigations:

1. *Do racial effects on achievement persist even after adjusting for differences in social class?* Racial classroom desegregation was found to have a positive effect on achievement that is, for the most part, independent of family background.

2. *Is there a different racial effect on achievement in desegregated schools as contrasted with desegregated classrooms?* "Regardless of the racial composition of the schools, the average achievement level of Negro students increases with the proportion of their classmates who are white."[17] However, "when classroom racial composition as well as family background differences are held constant, there is no evidence that the percent white enrolled in the school has any appreciable influence on Negro student achievement."[18] And "Negro students

---

11. 20 U.S.C. §§ 1601-1686 (1970).

12. *See* 1-2 Southern Schools.

13. 1 Southern Schools iv.

14. *See* Orfield, *How to Make Desegregation Work: The Adaptation of Schools to Their Newly Integrated Student Bodies*, 39 Law & Contemp. Prob. no. 2, at 314 (1975).

15. *See* J. McPartland, The Relative Influence of School Desegregation and of Classroom Desegregation on the Academic Achievement of Ninth Grade Negro Students, September 1967 (unpublished document on file with the Center for the Study of Social Organization of Schools at Johns Hopkins University). This study utilized achievement test scores derived from 5,075 Negro ninth-graders in New England and Middle Atlantic states.

16. J. Coleman, Equality of Educational Opportunity (1966).

17. J. McPartland, *supra* note 15, at 3.

18. *Id.* at 4. A study of six schools in Tacoma, Washington between 1963 and 1967 at a time

who remain in segregated classes in a 'desegregated' school receive no benefit in terms of their academic growth." Indeed, McPartland found that "segregated classes may be more detrimental for Negro student achievement if they occur in mostly white schools rather than mostly Negro schools."[19]

3. *Are racial effects on achievement simply artifacts of ability grouping procedures?* Matzen, in his San Francisco Bay area study,[20] found that ability grouping accounted for a good deal of what appeared to be racial differentials in achievement. While McPartland also found that school selection processes play a role, it was a distinctly minor one. He concluded, therefore, that the desegregative effect on classroom achievement could not be explained by the schools' selection processes, and that race was an autonomous factor.[21]

Under the auspices of the United States Commission on Civil Rights, McPartland, with Robert York, reanalyzed some of the *Coleman Report*[22] data in an effort to separate the effects of race from that of social class upon achievement scores.[23] The study concluded that "there is a positive association of achievement scores with the racial composition of the classroom, no matter what the racial composition of the school may be."[24] Even when "holding constant the social class of the student and his school—there remains an upward

---

when the percentage of black enrollment city-wide went from 6.6 per cent to 8.9 per cent—where the school was the unit of analysis rather than the classroom—showed little evidence of a racial effect on achievement. J. Laurent, Effects of Race and Racial Balance of School on Academic Performance, 1969 (unpublished doctoral dissertation at University of Oregon). *See also* J. LAURENT, DO PUPIL RACE AND/OR SCHOOL RACIAL BALANCE AFFECT ACADEMIC PERFORMANCE? (1970).

19. *Id.*

20. See discussion at pp. 254-55 *infra*.

21. It should be noted that McPartland's study was cross-sectional, not longitudinal, meaning that it was based on data collected at one point in time. Longitudinal studies are those which include at least two sets of data gathered over a period of time. Usually the data show the changes in a particular characteristic or phenomenon over time. At best, then, McPartland's data suggest relationships in interracial classrooms, irrespective of whether the classroom had ever been anything but interracial.

22. The *Coleman Report* had been released in 1966. With respect to achievement, it made the following findings:

> 1. [A]s the proportion white in a school increases, the achievement of students in each racial group increases.
> 2. [T]his relationship increases as grade in school increases.
> 3. The higher achievement of all racial and ethnic groups in schools with greater proportions of white students is largely, perhaps wholly, related to effects associated with the student body's educational background and aspirations [rather than with better facilities and curriculum].
> 4. [A]verage test performance [for Negroes increases] as the proportion of white classmates increases . . . .
> 5. Those students who first entered desegregated schools in the early grades do generally show slightly higher average scores than the students who first came to desegregated schools in later grades.

J. COLEMAN, *supra* note 16, at 307, 321.

23. *See* 2 U.S. COMMISSION ON CIVIL RIGHTS, RACIAL ISOLATION IN THE PUBLIC SCHOOLS 35 (1967).

24. *Id.* at 38.

trend in average achievement level [of blacks] as the proportion of white classmates increases."[25]

McPartland and York suggest two reasons for the apparent inconsistency between their findings and those of the *Coleman Report* on this point: (1) the statistical techniques used in the earlier study tended to confuse social class and race; and (2) the *Coleman Report*, in the regression analyses, used the school rather than the classroom as the unit of analysis. Yet, the authors stress that "it is in the classroom within the school where the characteristics of the fellow-students have their effects."[26] Negro students in a segregated classroom, for example, do not benefit even if the school as a whole is racially balanced. The research design employed in the *Coleman Report* did not permit this kind of distinction to be made.

Several studies relating higher achievement of black students to attendance at non-segregated schools were completed in 1971 by Nancy St. John.[27] Black ninth-graders in the city of Pittsburgh who had attended non-segregated elementary schools for a large part of their early education showed higher achievement scores in mathematics than black students who had attended segregated schools. She also found that the academic success of these black children was dependent to a significant degree upon social acceptance by white classmates. Thus, concludes St. John, optimistic and skilled guidance by an understanding teacher is crucial in the non-segregated school. St. John came to parallel conclusions following a study in Boston.[28] She and Lewis studied 908 white and black sixth-graders in eighteen different schools, distributed among thirty-six classrooms. A positive association between increased achievement of blacks in arithmetic and the school's percentage of white enrollment was found, with black pupils achieving greater gains if their schools were majority white.[29]

James Fortenberry studied Negro achievement in Oklahoma City, comparing the achievement scores of a sample of eighth and ninth grade Negro students with their sixth grade scores.[30] Some of the children had never attended a desegregated school, and others had attended segregated schools through the sixth grade but were placed in a desegregated school for the seventh and eighth grades. All of the students had had statistically similar achievement test scores in sixth grade. By eighth grade, students in racially mixed classes had significantly improved their performance in arithmetic compared to those in segregated schools, although there was no difference in performance on reading achievement tests. By ninth grade, children in mixed

25. *Id.* at 40.
26. *Id.* at 42.
27. *See* N. St. John, School Integration, Classroom Climate, and Achievement (1971).
28. *See* St. John & Lewis, *supra* note 10.
29. *Id.* at 71.
30. *See* J. Fortenberry, The Achievement of Negro Pupils in Mixed and Non-Mixed Schools, 1959 (unpublished doctoral dissertation at University of Oklahoma).

classes scored higher in arithmetic and language expression achievement tests, while the children in segregated classes scored higher in reading achievement. Fortenberry's overall conclusion was that "in general, Negroes achieve better in mixed than in non-mixed classes."[31]

A study which compared the achievement of black students in racially balanced and imbalanced schools in a city in upstate New York showed no significant differences in achievement by type of school attended. But when students who had attended these schools for two years or longer were examined separately, significantly higher achievement scores were found among children who attended racially balanced schools.[32]

In an ongoing longitudinal study of 316 Negro and 501 white students attending six schools in two cities, one in the West and one in the Midwest, Michael Rosenfeld reported that while Negro students scored lower on the achievement tests administered, "there were tests in the battery and time periods during which Negro and white students grew at the same rates *when initial differences between the two groups were taken into account*."[33]

Robert Frary and Thomas Goolsby studied the effects of compensatory education on black children in segregated and non-segregated settings in Gulfport, Mississippi.[34] Twenty classrooms of first-graders were involved, ten experimental and ten control groups. Children in the experimental classes were assigned at random; they also came from poorer homes than black children in the control group. Children in the non-segregated group gained significantly more than those in segregated classes.[35] Children who had scored low on the Metropolitan Readiness Tests responded especially well to the special instructional measures of the compensatory education program. Indeed, "the achievement scores of the low readiness, integrated Negroes exceed those for either white group in spite of a much lower mental age mean . . . ."[36] Goolsby and Frary warn of the depressive effect on low readiness children of being placed in a segregated classroom. In such settings "very low achievement may become the accepted norm."[37]

Seventy-five Negro fourth, fifth, and sixth grade students in five desegregated schools in Nashville were compared with a like number from three all-

---

31. *Id.* at 44.

32. *See* J. Lockwood, An Examination of Scholastic Achievement, Attitudes and Home Background Factors of Sixth-Grade Negro Students in Balanced and Unbalanced Schools, 1966 (unpublished doctoral dissertation at University of Michigan).

33. M. ROSENFELD, NEGRO AND WHITE DIFFERENCES IN INTELLECTUAL GROWTH 6 (1968) (emphasis added).

34. *See* Frary & Goolsby, *Achievement of Integrated and Segregated Negro and White First Graders in a Southern City*, 8 INTEGRATED ED. 48 (July-Aug. 1970).

35. T. Goolsby & R. Frary, Enhancement of Educational Effect Through Extensive and Intensive Intervention: The Gulfport Project 41, 56, July 1969 (unpublished document on file with the Gulfport Municipal Separate School District, Gulfport, Miss.).

36. *Id.* at 50.

37. *Id.* at 52.

Negro schools.[38] The former, who constituted from 8 to 33 per cent of enrollment in their schools, had attended desegregated schools for up to six years. All children in the sample were from the same neighborhoods. Academic achievement was found to be significantly higher among students attending the desegregated than the segregated schools. Children who entered a desegregated school near the beginning of their school career achieved significantly better than segregated pupils. On the other hand, children who were not desegregated until the fifth or sixth grade achieved less than did Negro children in the segregated schools. However, the significance of this research is difficult to gauge because even though students came from similar neighborhoods, no explicit controls for social class were employed.

A study was conducted of New Rochelle schools after approximately 50 per cent of the enrollment of an all-Negro elementary school was transferred to several predominantly white schools.[39] After one year, achievement tests were administered to all of the Negro transferees. Achievement test score changes for students in grades one through five were found to be statistically insignificant.[40] To determine the effect of social class, average reading scores of both Negro transferees and those who remained in the all-Negro school were compared with those of the white children in the receiving school; the latter were significantly higher, despite the fact that the white students were of the same social class background as the Negro children.[41] An analysis of achievement gains among black kindergarten children showed a statistically significant change after a year of desegregated education. Gains of this group exceeded those of the Negro non-transferees and the whites in the receiving schools. The study suggests that this is evidence of the importance of early intervention. "[E]xposure to favorable learning circumstances at an early enough age can have a salutary and compensatory effect on the educational potential of minority and otherwise deprived children."[42] Unfortunately, no statistical data are presented in the article so that it is not possible to fully assess this research.

A study was undertaken in Richmond, Virginia to determine whether the academic program of black students who graduated from a segregated junior high to a non-segregated senior high school would suffer. The study found no impairment of their academic progress.[43]

A study of 883 eighth-graders in southern schools, some of whom had

38. *See* L. Anderson, The Effects of Desegregation on the Achievement and Personality Patterns of Negro Children, 1966 (unpublished doctoral dissertation at George Peabody College for Teachers, Nashville, Tenn.).

39. *See* Wolman, *Learning Effects of Integration in New Rochelle*, 2 INTEGRATED ED. 30 (Dec. 1964-Jan. 1965).

40. *See id.*

41. *Id.* at 30-31.

42. *Id.* at 31.

43. *See* L. Savage, Academic Achievement of Black Students Transferring from a Segregated Junior High School to an Integrated High School, July 1971 (unpublished master's thesis, at

attended desegregated schools for some time and others who entered such schools only during the year of the study (1970-71), reported that the scores of black students increased significantly in both reading and arithmetic.[44] In terms of grade-equivalents, black students gained .91 and white students 1.07 on the Iowa tests. As is true of so much of this kind of research, the reasons for success in this project were not immediately apparent. The study concludes, however, that "[i]t makes little difference whether academic improvement by the students can be attributed primarily to the desegregation of the races; of primary importance is that under a desegregation plan these schools have been able to provide conditions that facilitated academic improvement for all students."[45]

Several studies of the effects of desegregation on pupil achievement have been undertaken in North Carolina. In one study, student achievement in grades five, seven, and nine in a desegregated school in Chapel Hill were compared with achievement in segregated schools.[46] Negro achievement rose significantly in mathematics at grades five and seven; and for white students, at grade five. Reading scores did not show any significant increase, however. Two separate studies of desegregation in Goldsboro, North Carolina showed significant gains for black students in both reading and mathematics.[47]

A study in New Albany, Indiana was undertaken to determine whether school learning proceeded at comparable rates for Negro and white children when children were not desegregated until they reached junior high school and for Negro students in desegregated schools compared with those in segregated schools[48]—controlling for such variables as socioeconomic status and intelligence. In the first comparison, Negro and white students were matched and their academic achievement over two years was compared, using both achievement tests results and classroom grades. In the second comparison, two groups of Negro students were the subjects: one consisted of children who had attended a segregated school and the other of children who had been

---

Virginia State College). A control group of students who attended a black senior high school was utilized in this study.

A number of studies showing positive achievement gains from desegregation are collected in Pettigrew, Useem, Normand, & Smith, *Busing: A Review of "The Evidence,"* 30 PUB. INTEREST 88 (Winter 1973). A study conducted in Berkeley, California concluded that achievement gains of students were greater from a desegregation program than from a compensatory program. This was true, apparently, even though desegregation was accompanied by a reduction in school services. *Id.* at 98.

44. *See* W. Howell, The Correlates of Change in School Integration with the Academic Achievement of Eighth Grade Students, 1972 (unpublished doctoral dissertation at University of South Carolina).

45. *Id.* at 48.

46. Prichard, *Effects of Desegregation on Student Success in the Chapel Hill City School*, 7 INTEGRATED ED. 33 (Nov.-Dec. 1969).

47. Pettigrew, Useem, Normand, & Smith, *supra* note 43, at 94.

48. *See* I. Samuels, Desegregated Education and Differences in Academic Achievement, 1958 (unpublished doctoral dissertation at Indiana University).

desegregated in junior high school. It was found that after two years of desegregation, the achievement gap between Negro and white students had narrowed significantly. This was attributed directly to desegregation. The study also found that Negro children who attended interracial elementary schools started out in first grade achieving at the same level as did Negro children in the segregated school. By third grade, however, the desegregated Negro children had pulled ahead; this continued into sixth grade. Overall, the study concludes that:[49]

> [T]he longer the association between any particular group of white and Negro students the smaller the differences in academic achievement appear to be . . . and that the Negro students who had been educated in mixed schools achieved as well as and sometimes better than white students in the integrated program.

The achievement scores of sixty-four black children whose all-black school in Tulsa, Oklahoma was closed in 1968, requiring them to be transferred to a non-segregated school, were analyzed. On five of six sub-tests of the Stanford Achievement Test, as well as on IQ tests, the transferred children scored significantly higher than the "control" group—a matched group in an all-black school. While the transferred students earned lower grades than children in the control group, they nevertheless had a more positive attitude toward school than did the control group.[50]

Desegregation of the schools in Riverside, California has been the subject of a number of studies. One significant study investigated the development of cognitive skills during the first year of desegregation. The researcher found that the higher IQ and reading scores in the desegregated sample were accounted for by increases in Anglo scores only.[51] Achievement tended to rise in proportion to the duration of desegregation. With implications for ability grouping, the study further noted that:[52]

> In tallying the results for the primary grades, the writer was impressed several times to find that groups of integrated pupils achieved at different levels according to the level of the children with whom they were grouped. Children with equal or lower IQ's scored higher on the reading tests when they were scattered severally among the classes in the receiving school, rather than clustered together in one or two groups.

Florence Denmark conducted a study in Manhasset, New York which found that social interaction between black and white children improved the verbal ability test scores of the black children.[53] As other researchers have also noted,

---

49. *Id.* at 100.

50. *See* J. Griffin, The Effects of Integration on Academic Aptitude, Classroom Achievement, Self-Concept, and Attitudes Toward the School Environment of a Selected Group of Negro Students in Tulsa, Oklahoma, 1969 (unpublished doctoral dissertation at University of Tulsa).

51. *See* M. Purl, Progress Report No. 4, Oct. 15, 1968 (unpublished document on file with Riverside Unified School District, Riverside, Cal.).

52. *Id.* at 21. *See also* Wicker, *Integration and Innovation*, N.Y. Times, Apr. 2, 1974, at 39, col. 1.

53. *See* Denmark, *The Effect of Integration on Academic Achievement and Self-Concept*, 8 INTEGRATED ED. 34 (May-June 1970).

Denmark found that teachers in desegregated schools did not give full recognition to the extent of the progress the black students had made because of the higher standards these teachers had compared to those of teachers in the segregated environment. Thus, black students might be learning that improved academic performance does not bring increased rewards.

Several studies of school desegregation are of small-scale, *voluntary* programs. One such program is Project Concern, a program involving the placement of inner-city minority children in suburban schools in various areas in Connecticut. Five studies have been made of various components of Project Concern. The academic achievement of minority students attending kindergarten through grade five—a year after the program was initiated—was studied by Bruce Wood, who selected a control group which matched the Project Concern students in WISC-Verbal IQ scores.[54] A summary of Wood's findings shows the following:[55]

> *Grades K-1*: Achievement scores in arithmetic, vocabulary, and verbal IQ increased.
> *Grades 2-3*: Total performance on IQ tests increased significantly.
> *Grades 4-5*: Vocabulary score increased significantly; while gains were not sweeping, the overall direction was clear. The achievement gains of white children in the receiving schools were not affected.

A study of Hartford, Connecticut, two years after the implementation of Project Concern, was undertaken by Aline and Thomas Mahan.[56] Black students in grades K-3 were found to have "significantly different (and higher) scores on measures of mental ability and achievement generally."[57] More significant, however, was the fact that the cognitive functioning of the Negro children improved in general.[58]

> The direction of this impact is toward greater verbal productivity, increased accuracy in the associative and sorting processes, and an enhanced willingness to take a risk in terms of verbal responses to situations . . . . There are indications that there is a tendency toward better understanding of expectations (i.e., better test-taking skill), increased self-discipline, and increased ability to evaluate responses in terms of external standards.

An investigation of the Project Concern experience in suburban Cheshire, Connecticut, undertaken by Marilyn Levy, involved only twenty-five students, probably all from New Haven.[59] No significant changes in average achievement

54. *See* B. Wood, The Effects of Busing Versus Non-Busing on the Intellectual Functioning of Inner City, Disadvantaged Elementary School Children, 1969 (unpublished doctoral dissertation at the University of Massachusetts).
55. *Id.* at 60-66.
56. *See* Mahan & Mahan, *Changes in Cognitive Style: An Analysis of the Impact of White Suburban Schools on Inner City Children*, 8 INTEGRATED ED. 58 (Jan.-Feb. 1970).
57. *Id.* at 60.
58. *Id.*
59. *See* CHESHIRE DEP'T OF EDUCATION, PROJECT CONCERN IN CHESHIRE: A PRELIMINARY REPORT

scores were recorded. On the other hand, over the same twelve month period, the per cent of children scoring above grade-level rose from thirty to fifty-two. The explanation for these varying results is not clear. A study of 196 Project Concern children from Hartford, conducted by Aline Mahan over a two year period, showed more positive results.[60] In the suburban schools, the relationship between social acceptance and achievement was significantly stronger than in the schools of Hartford. Mahan reported that being in a high-achieving classroom helps, even if the school is in the inner city—although the impact is much greater when the school is in the suburbs. A study of 138 New Haven Project Concern children also found greater gains in reading among such children than were found in two comparable groups of students not part of Project Concern.[61]

Three studies have been undertaken in different areas of Florida, two of which show a strong relationship between desegregation and Negro achievement. The third, showing mixed results, is described in the next section of this article.[62] An investigation into the impact of desegregation on black students in Brevard County, Florida[63] showed that while Negro students attending desegregated schools scored lower than their white classmates on five out of six measures of achievement, they scored significantly higher than the Negro students who remained in the segregated high school.[64]

The second study involved students in the fourth, sixth and eighth grades in a northwestern urban county of Florida between 1966 and 1967.[65] After one academic year, black students in desegregated schools had significantly higher achievement scores than a comparable group of students who remained in segregated schools. The test-anxiety level of both groups of black students was similar, however.[66]

An evaluation of a voluntary busing project in Boston, Massachusetts, known as Operation Exodus, was undertaken by James Teele. Teele's sample

---

(1970), in *Hearings on Equality of Educational Opportunity Before the Senate Select Comm. on Equal Educational Opportunity*, 91st Cong., 2d Sess., pt. 1B, at 590 (1970).

60. *See* A. Mahan, Social Factors and the Academic Success of Urban Children, 1969 (unpublished doctoral dissertation at the University of Connecticut).

61. *See* J. Samuels, A Comparison of Projects Representative of Compensatory, Busing, and Non-Compensatory Programs for Inner-City Students, 1971 (unpublished doctoral dissertation at the University of Connecticut). *See also* Samuels, *Busing, Reading, and Self in New Haven*, 10 INTEGRATED ED. 23, 24-28 (Nov.-Dec. 1972).

62. See discussion at pp. 253-60 *infra*.

63. *See* F. Williams, An Analysis of Some Differences Between Negro High School Seniors from a Segregated High School and a Nonsegregated High School in Brevard County, Fla., 1968 (unpublished doctoral dissertation at the University of Florida).

64. *Id.* at 44-53. At the start of the 1964-65 school year, white and Negro students attending segregated high schools took a statewide ninth grade achievement test. In 1965 the white high school was desegregated and a group of Negro students were enrolled in that school. In 1967-68, the same students took the twelfth grade achievement test.

65. *See* T. Starnes, An Analysis of the Academic Achievement of Negro Students in the predominantly White Schools of a Selected Florida County, 1968 (unpublished doctoral dissertation at the University of Southern Mississippi).

66. *Id.* at 26.

consisted of approximately 600 black students with a control group of children who remained in all-black schools.[67] The data suggest that the longer the minority students participated in Operation Exodus, the more likely it became that their reading achievement would improve significantly.[68] Just as important, the black child's feeling of being accepted increased.[69] The two factors of achievement and acceptance seem, according to Teele, also to be closely interrelated, suggesting that "[t]hose planning school integration programs for black children should be at least as concerned with issues and conditions of emotional and social development as they are with issues of cognitive development."[70]

Some studies have found that the beneficial effects of attending non-segregated schools extend beyond in-school academic achievement. Robert Crain found a substantial impact on achievement scores of blacks who attended non-segregated schools, even after allowing for socioeconomic differences.[71] In part, the beneficial outcome resulted from more resources and association with larger numbers of students in higher socioeconomic classes in the non-segregated schools. But in addition, Crain suggests that black students learn what "it means to live in a white man's world,"[72] which stimulates the black child to higher achievement. A further analysis indicated that in addition to improving their academic achievement, black students in a non-segregated setting were more likely to complete high school, attend college, and enter occupations customarily closed to blacks.[73] For northern blacks, attendance at non-segregated schools also was associated with increased level of home ownership, financial responsibility, and job stability. Furthermore, these findings are not the result of higher socioeconomic background. "[S]urprisingly, black students in integrated schools do not come from higher-status families than those in segregated schools."[74]

II
STUDIES SHOWING MIXED EFFECTS OF INTERRACIAL SCHOOLING ON ACADEMIC ACHIEVEMENT

A sizable number of studies of the impact of desegregation on academic achievement have shown mixed and ambiguous results. In part, this can be attributed to inadequacies in the methodology. But part of the ambiguity is also due to the fact that we have no well-developed theory of learning which would permit us to interpret and explain some of the results. This section of

67. *See* J. TEELE, EVALUATING SCHOOL BUSING 11-12 (1973).
68. *Id.* at 74.
69. *Id.* at 76, 117.
70. *Id.* at 119.
71. *See* Crain, *School Integration and the Academic Achievement of Negroes*, 44 SOCIOLOGY OF ED. 1 (1971).
72. *Id.* at 25.
73. *See* R. CRAIN & C. WEISMAN, DISCRIMINATION, PERSONALITY, AND ACHIEVEMENT (1974).
74. *Id.* at 160.

the article describes some of these mixed studies and, where feasible, suggests some of the missing factors which may explain these results.

A major study of the effect of racial composition upon achievement in the San Francisco Bay area, undertaken by Stanley Matzen, analyzed the relationship between the proportion of Negro students in a classroom and the average academic achievement of Negro and non-Negro students.[75] The findings were as follows:

1. *In general, there was a tendency for achievement to vary inversely with the percentage of Negro students in the classroom*. There were some "notable exceptions," however. Of twenty-one fifth grade classrooms, data for five showed exceptional trends. For example, thirty-one students in one classroom were below average in achievement and IQ scores, and had fewer Negroes than the average classroom. Another classroom was considerably above average in IQ score, below average in achievement, and very high in percentage of Negro students. Much of the negative relationship between per cent Negro and Negro achievement may be attributable, according to this study, to the practice of classroom grouping. Relatively few high-achieving Negroes, for example, will be placed in classrooms with high-achieving whites. Thus, the author argues, the result is a more negative relationship between race and achievement than might otherwise be found.

2. *IQ, like achievement, tended to vary inversely with the percentage of Negro students*. The report points out, however, the presence of "numerous exceptions" and characterizes the relationship between the two variables as "far from perfect."[76]

3. *Achievement varied directly with socioeconomic status*. While the entire student sample was heavily lower class, over half the fifth graders achieved above grade level. Only one-third of the seventh graders were above grade level.

4. *When IQ and socioeconomic status were held constant, achievement tended to fall as the percentage of Negroes rose, but the tendency was not strong enough to be of statistical significance*. Thus per cent Negro turned out not to be a depressive factor in itself, but only when combined with low socioeconomic status and low IQ. Yet, the percentage of Negro students in the classroom and achievement scores were differently related in fifth grade than in seventh grade. One possible reason offered in the report is a difference in classroom grouping practices. In the fifth grade, students were much less homogeneously grouped than in seventh grade; therefore, Negro-white differentials were greater in grade five.

75. *See* S. Matzen, The Relationship Between Racial Composition and Scholastic Achievement in Elementary School Classrooms, 1965 (unpublished doctoral dissertation at Stanford University). Eleven hundred students in eleven schools in the San Francisco Bay area were tested. The tests were administered to fifth and seventh grade Negro and Caucasian students in the fall of 1963. Findings were reported in terms of four major relationships: (1) per cent of Negroes in the classroom and achievement; (2) per cent of Negroes and average intellectual ability; (3) average intellectual ability and achievement; and (4) socioeconomic status and achievement.

76. *Id*. at 42.

In grade seven, on the other hand, grouping was quite homogeneous with higher-achieving Negro children being placed in classrooms with higher-achieving white children. Negro-white differences were thus minimized. In other words, in the fifth grade, one was likely to find equal numbers of Negroes and whites in the low-scoring as in the high-scoring classrooms. In the seventh grade, high-scoring whites tended to be in one classroom, and low-scoring Negroes in another one. In the latter case, the negative reaction between per cent Negro and achievement scores was high; in the former case, it was low.

It is quite possible to interpret these findings as indicating that the presence of Negroes must be minimized if achievement is to be maximized. Matzen provides an alternative explanation: that a new variable "E Q" (educational quality) be constructed, which would be comprised of indices of teacher competence and motivation, quality of textbooks and other instructional materials, enrichment-value of the classroom and school environment, and similar determinants—in terms of *school* resources—of how much pupils learn.[77] Matzen hypothesizes that E Q would be found to be negatively correlated with the percentage of Negro students, and positively related to IQ scores, achievement scores, and socioeconomic status.[78] In short, with schools of equal quality, the per cent of Negroes in a classroom might no longer have a negative effect on achievement.

A study of Negro and white pupils in the public schools of Jackson, Michigan was designed to determine the effect of social interaction on achievement.[79] The hypothesis to be tested by the research was that "the measured intelligence of the group of Negro children will be significantly changed as the consequence of school experience which enhances their opportunities for social interaction with the dominant white culture."[80] All children—which included 193 Negroes and 1,061 whites—who entered kindergarten in the fall of 1957 and of 1958 were given standard intelligence tests. The children were then retested in the second grade, during the fall of 1959 and of 1960. The Negro students were treated as an experimental group and the whites as a control.[81] Average IQ scores were as follows:[82]

	1957-1958	1959-1960
Experimental group (Negro)	83.06	89.74
Control group (white)	102.04	103.91

77. *Id.* at 114.

78. *Id.* at 115.

79. *See* W. Katzenmeyer, Social Interaction and Differences in Intelligence Test Performance of Negro and White Elementary School Pupils, 1962 (unpublished doctoral dissertation at Duke University).

80. *Id.* at 9.

81. A more appropriate methodology or research design would have been to match the experimental group with a control group of Negro children.

82. W. Katzenmeyer, *supra* note 79, at 57-58.

The study concluded that the change in IQ of the experimental group could be explained principally by the social interaction between Negro and white children. In Jackson, "the great majority of the Negro population is confined to a small area of the city by economic limitations and by discriminatory policies and pressures in the sale of real estate. . . . Thus, for most Negro children, entry into the racially mixed public school program represents the beginning of a period of increased social contact."[83] Another part of the explanation is the high per pupil expenditure in Jackson schools. Presumably, the Negro child, more deprived to begin with, benefited more from the increase in educational resources.[84] The report concludes that:

> [W]hile the implications of this study point to some of the disadvantages of segregated schools, they suggest that the answer to the equalization of educational opportunities lies only partially in "integration" per se; they suggest that a problem basic to the school lies in guiding and encouraging the assimilative process.

A second Michigan study was of black children in Grand Rapids who were being bused to white schools.[86] Those children who were bused for two years registered significantly higher gains in arithmetic than did students who were bused only one year; and, in turn, the students bused for one year showed significantly higher gains than those who were not bused at all. No reading achievement effect was apparent for either group of bused children.[87]

A three-year program in Evanston, Illinois was evaluated by Jayjia Hsia, who found that, on the whole, achievement of black children did not improve significantly. However, a number of special situations were found to relate to academic growth: fourth grade students who were bused to school gained significantly over those who walked to a new school; fifth grade students who remained in their non-segregated neighborhood school registered higher gains than students transferred to a new school, regardless of whether they walked or were bused there.[88] Comparisons are especially difficult to make in the Evanston study because data on the socioeconomic status of students were not used in the analysis.

First grade minority children from Newark, New Jersey who participated in

---

83. *Id.* at 64.

84. *Id.* at 67.

85. *Id.*

86. *See* W. Scott, A Study of Bused and Non-Bused Children, June 1970 (unpublished document on file with the Grand Rapids Public School System, Grand Rapids, Mich.).

87. *Id.* at 3.

88. *See* J. Hsia, Integration in Evanston, 1967-71: A Longitudinal Evaluation, August 1971 (unpublished document on file with Educational Testing Service, Princeton, N.J.). For a negative evaluation, see Kurtz, *An Independent Assessment of Integration in Evanston, 1967-1971: A Longitudinal Evaluation: A Report on the Educational Consequences of Desegregation in District 65 of Evanston, Ill.*, in *Hearings on School Busing Before Subcomm. No. 5 of the House Comm. on the Judiciary*, 92nd Cong., 2d Sess., pt. 3, at 1436-43 (1972).

a voluntary busing plan to Verona, a suburb of Newark, scored significantly higher on achievement tests than their peers who remained in schools in the inner city. Second-graders, however, failed to register such gains.[89] In neither case are data on family background of bused and non-bused students provided.

The impact of open enrollment on an upper-middle to middle class white K-5 school in New York City was investigated in 1969.[90] Ninety-five black children were bused to a school with a white enrollment of 1,005 students. The evidence indicated that academic achievement levels of both the bused children and the children in the receiving school did not drop as a result of the program; nevertheless, many of the white parents in the area were convinced of the opposite. The teachers in the receiving school also tended to underestimate the performance levels of the black children. The children, however, had little doubt of the value of the new school. In the researcher's interviews with twenty of them, they expressed the following typical evaluations: "We learn more . . . . Most of the time in the other school we do easy phonics, easy math, easy everything. . . . In this school, the teachers know more . . . . We didn't do no work there."[91]

The impact of desegregation on achievement was investigated in a small urban area within the New York City metropolitan area.[92] Black children who had attended a non-segregated school since kindergarten had a markedly more favorable attitude toward school than their white peers. Black and white children of the same IQ level scored comparably well in reading tests, regardless of whether they had attended a non-segregated school since kindergarten or since second grade.[93] One implication of this latter finding is that achievement effects of desegregation may not depend upon the earliest possible but only early attendance in a desegregated school.

The effect of school pairing on achievement has also been studied in New York City.[94] Negro students in the paired schools scored significantly higher on arithmetic achievement tests than did Negro students in a segregated school. No significant differences between the two groups of students showed up in any other achievement measures, however. White children in the paired schools continued to learn at their previous rates.

---

89. Zdep, *Educating Disadvantaged Urban Children in Suburban Schools: An Evaluation*, 1 J. APPLIED SOCIAL PSYCHOLOGY 173, 180 (1971).

90. *See* B. Brooks, A Study of Ninety-Five Children Traveling by Bus to a K-5 School as Part of the Open Enrollment Program in a Large Urban School System, 1969 (unpublished doctoral dissertation at Columbia University).

91. *Id.* at 95-97.

92. *See* M. Moreno, The Effect of Integration on the Aptitude, Achievement, Attitude to School and Class, and Social Acceptance of Negro and White Pupils in a Small Urban School System, 1972 (unpublished doctoral dissertation at Fordham University).

93. *Id.* at 76.

94. *See* I. Slone, The Effects of One School Pairing on Pupil Achievement, Anxieties, and Attitudes, 1968 (unpublished doctoral dissertation at New York University).

During the 1971-72 school year, the elementary schools of Fort Worth were desegregated by federal court order.[95] Black fifth graders who attended newly-desegregated schools were found to have made significantly higher gains in reading and arithmetic than did their peers in predominantly black neighborhood schools. Desegregated black fourth-graders, however, showed no such achievement gains.[96] The achievement record of white students who attended formerly majority-black schools was compared to that of their peers who continued in neighborhood schools; no difference was found.[97] In a separate report on the 1972-73 school year, the same researcher found significantly greater achievement for bused black students than for their peers who remained in majority-black neighborhood schools. In addition, he found this advantage applied not only to fourth-graders but to black children in the third and fifth grades as well.[98]

San Francisco is a multiracial city but it did not desegregate all its elementary schools until 1971—when it did so under court order.[99] Following a year of planning, one area had been desegregated the year prior to the court order. Of the minority students in this area, who had thus experienced one more year of desegregation than minorities in the rest of the school district, blacks and Orientals showed greater gains in math, but Spanish-speaking and Filipino students did worse.[100] On the other hand, Spanish-speaking students from those schools that had been desegregated for the additional year made greater gains in reading. All other minorities from the prior desegregated area, with the exception of the Chinese students (who were unaffected), showed fewer gains in reading than did minority students from other parts of the city. Again, no controls for social class or the previous achievement levels of individual students were apparently employed.

Two studies of "one-way" busing programs were undertaken in Buffalo, New York. The first study found that black students who were bused to a predominantly white school had a much higher rate of academic achievement than did their peers who remained at the all-Negro school.[101] The researchers reported, however, that in classrooms where the racial composition exceeded 30 per cent black, the achievement levels were no higher than those in an

---

95. *See* Flax v. Potts, 464 F.2d 865 (5th Cir. 1972).

96. *See* C. Evans, Short-Term Desegregation Effects: The Academic Achievement of Bused Students, 1971-1972, January 1973 (unpublished document on file with Fort Worth Independent School District, Fort Worth, Tex.).

97. *Id.* at 23.

98. *See* C. Evans, Integration Evaluation 2, August 15, 1973 (on file with Forth Worth Independent School District, Fort Worth, Tex.).

99. Johnson v. San Francisco Unified School Dist., 339 F. Supp. 1315 (N.D. Cal. 1971), *vacated and remanded for further findings*, 500 F.2d 349 (9th Cir. 1974).

100. *See* San Francisco Unified School District, Evaluation of San Francisco Unified School District Desegregation Data from Integration 1971-72, at 36, 38, 56, & 58, October 1972 (unpublished document on file with San Francisco Unified School District, San Francisco, Cal.).

101. *See* R. Banks & M. Di Pasquale, A Study of the Educational Effectiveness of Integration, January 1969 (unpublished document on file with Buffalo Public School System, Buffalo, N.Y.).

all-black classroom. However, insufficient information was supplied—*e.g.*, the socioeconomic status of the white children in predominantly black classrooms—to adequately evaluate this research.

The second study followed the desegregation process in six schools in Monroe County over the period September 1, 1967 to June, 1970 which were involved in a voluntary one-way busing project in which minority students from Buffalo were transported to predominantly white schools in the county.[102] The study found that[103]

> [d]isadvantaged Negro pupils in compensatory and integrated classes for the same time showed similar outcomes in scholastic development. Similar pupils enrolled in segregated classes where no major efforts were directed toward remediation, enrichment, or integration were significantly lower [in academic achievement] than those who had these scholastic experiences.

Also, the earlier that students were enrolled in compensatory or other similar programs, the greater the achievement levels were. Achievement gains were not found to be incompatible with segregation. On the other hand, attendance in enriched classes which were segregated was not as beneficial as either desegregation or compensatory education—*i.e.*, a comprehensive program of remediation. The researcher concluded that educational planners should seek to combine desegregation with compensatory educational programs as the best overall strategy for educational success.

Several evaluations of the desegregation process in Rochester, New York showed that white students in schools to which blacks were reassigned continued to learn at their customary rate.[104] Within the same school, a significant learning advantage accrued to students in integrated rather than in segregated classes. On the other hand, and contrary to findings as to the impact the previous year, integrated classes did not continue to show achievement superiority over segregated classes with a component of compensatory education, a finding similar to that of the Buffalo study.[105] A report the following year reached the same conclusion: that blacks in segregated settings did not have the achievement gains that children in desegregated classrooms had. Whether a black child attended a desegregated school near his own neighborhood, whether he was bused to a desegregated school near his own neighborhood, or whether he was bused to a desegregated school in the suburbs made no difference in his academic achievement gains.[106]

102. *See* O. Bowman, Scholastic Development of Disadvantaged Negro Pupils, 1973 (unpublished doctoral dissertation at State University of New York at Buffalo).

103. *Id.* at 85.

104. *See* H. Goldberg, J. Griffith, R. Green, & O. Bowman, An Interim Report on a Fifteen Point Plan to Reduce Racial Isolation and Provide Quality Integrated Education, July 1969 (unpublished document on file at the Rochester Board of Education, Rochester, N.Y.).

105. O. Bowman, *supra* note 102.

106. Division of Planning and Research of Rochester City School District, A Three Year Longitudinal Study to Assess a Fifteen Point Plan to Reduce Racial Isolation and Provide Quality Integrated Education for Elementary Level Pupils (1970).

In Syracuse, a group of Negro children were bused from a segregated school—Croton Elementary—to a predominantly white school—Edward Smith Elementary School. At the end of the school year, white children at Edward Smith showed their customary achievement gains, but the minority children who were transferred to Edward Smith failed to increase their academic achievement levels any more than the black children who had remained at Croton.[107] In the second program, students bused from another segregated school—Washington Irving—to other, predominantly white schools were compared with non-bused students at Croton. As in the previous case, white children at the receiving school continued to improve at their customary rate in reading. The children from Washington Irving School, however, gained significantly more than the non-bused children at Croton. The thirty bused pupils achieved a mean growth in months double that of the non-bused children.[108]

III

Studies Showing No Positive Effect of Interracial Schooling on Academic Achievement

This section is concerned with those studies which fail to show a positive impact of desegregation on academic achievement. In some cases, the lack of positive impact is due to the fact that the researcher failed to control either for intelligence or socioeconomic status and failed to obtain achievement scores for Negro and white students for the period prior to desegregation. Thus it is not possible to ascertain whether the rate of achievement increased or declined as a result of desegregation. Where desegregation studies have failed to take these factors into account, the results are almost meaningless. The academic achievement of approximately 600 Negro and white high school students in Angleton, Texas—after a year of desegregation—was analyzed by James Bryant.[109] Desegregation was found to have no effect on academic achievement, but the study suffered from all of the defects just noted.

The six-year desegregation experience of Riverside, California has been extensively analyzed by Harold Gerard and his colleagues.[110] While finding that desegregation led to improvements in the capacity of children to gain

---

107. *Hearing Before the U.S. Comm'n on Civil Rights (Rochester, N.Y.)*, at 323-26 (1967).

108. *Id.*

109. *See* J. Bryant, Some Effects of Racial Integration of High School Students on Standardized Achievement Test Scores, Teacher Grades, and Drop-out Rates in Angleton, Texas, 1968 (unpublished doctoral dissertation at University of Houston).

110. The following discussion is based on a series of drafts of separate articles, kindly supplied to the author by Professor Harold B. Gerard. These are to be published as a group in a forthcoming issue of *Journal of Social Issues*, under the editorship of Professor Gerard. Since the published versions of the articles may well differ from the drafts, quotations from these articles have been kept to a minimum.

self-direction, little evidence was found that desegregation resulted in achievement gains in the desegregated schools.[111] As part of this overall investigation of Riverside's desegregation experience, children's speech characteristics were studied. Minority children appeared to exhibit no "language deficit" upon entering school, nor was there any evidence that language development differed between minority and majority groups, although minority children who went through the desegregation experience tended to talk less freely.[112]

Desegregation in the Riverside schools did not stop the growing trend towards a greater disparity in achievement between Anglo and minority children found in most comparisons of the academic progress of minorities with that of whites. Gerard suggested that "the inevitable invidious comparison undoubtedly had deleterious effects on the minority children."[113] He also noted that the relative deterioration occurred in the context of schools which had 80 per cent or more white student enrollment. It was found that minority students still operated somewhat as outsiders in the classrooms, even after a period of over four years. Since the Gerard group felt that "the social climate of the classroom is the most important determinant of the child's success," noninvolvement in "the work structure of the classroom" led to low achievement by minority children.[114] Acceptance by white children was more likely to lead to higher achievement by minority children, especially the more able ones.[115] The Riverside study clearly revealed the power that peer acceptance and teacher attitudes have on the achievement of minority children. Teachers who deprecated the ability of minority children to learn usually saw the children fall behind their Anglo classmates. At the same time, some teachers who were not overtly discriminatory nevertheless were "patronizing." In other words, they at first tended to be "easier" in grading minority children;[116] this did not lead to higher achievement among these children.

Gerard and his colleagues view the Riverside experience as desegregation without integration. They speculate that more sweeping measures of desegregation might have led to other outcomes. They argue that successful desegregation depends more on the creation of beneficial classroom structures than on personality changes in the students.[117]

Mabel Purl, Director of Research for the Riverside schools, has been more concerned with discovering access points for future change than in evaluating the desegregation experience in that school district. She has compiled achievement test results for 529 minority students enrolled in nineteen schools in the

111. *Id.*
112. *Id.*
113. *Id.*
114. *Id.*
115. *Id.*
116. *Id.*
117. *Id.*

first, second, and third grades during 1972-73.[118] During that period, these minority students achieved at or above national norms on the various Cooperative Primary Tests which assess achievement in Listening, Word Analysis, Mathematics, and Reading. There was little difference between Mexican-American and Negro children in test results.

How, in the face of the overall failure of desegregation to generate improvement in achievement, did more than a third of the minority students in the first three grades in Riverside make such achievement gains? The conventional reply to this type of query is to suggest that the high achievers are students who came from families of relatively high socioeconomic status. However, Purl studied the relationship of socioeconomic status to achievement of high-scoring minority students, and while she found the relationship to be significant, there were considerable variations in scores that had little or nothing to do with socioeconomic status.[119] Purl examined the two minorities (Negro and Mexican-American) in four schools and found a negative relationship between socioeconomic status and achievement in several cases. She suggests that her finding "has made competing explanations such as school or teacher level causes more worthy of exploration."[120] This conclusion is consonant with the views of the Gerard group.[121]

The most widely publicized study is that of David Armor who concludes from his analysis of studies of five cities which, by and large, covered a one year period of desegregation: "[n]one of the studies were able to demonstrate conclusively that integration has had an effect on academic achievement as measured by standardized tests."[122] A study of longer-term effects of desegregation upon which he bases many of his conclusions is that of the Riverside, California school system for which there were data over a five year period. However, Purl states that Armor actually added together two studies of the same two and one-half year period and overlooked other significant factors as well.[123]

In a study of students attending kindergarten through grade two in segregated and non-segregated schools in a northern surburban community, desegregation appeared to have no effect on academic achievement.[124] In several

118. This compilation was supplied to the author by Mabel Purl, Director of Research, Riverside Unified School District, Riverside, Cal.

119. *See* M. Purl, The Relationship of SES to Higher Achieving Minority Pupils, July 1974 (unpublished document on file with Riverside Unified School District, Riverside, Cal.).

120. *Id.* at 1.

121. *See* note 110 *supra*.

122. Armor, *The Evidence on Busing*, 28 PUB. INTEREST 90, 99 (Summer 1972). In view of the wide dissemination of the article, there is no need here to describe the studies analyzed by Armor.

123. Orfield, *School Integration and Its Academic Critics*, 5 CIVIL RIGHTS DIG. 2, 8 (Summer 1973). The criticism which has received most attention is that in Pettigrew, Useem, Normand, & Smith, *Busing: A Review of "The Evidence,"* 30 PUB. INTEREST 88 (Winter 1973). Orfield, *supra*, notes that Armor himself has qualified his conclusions about one of the five cities he studied in testimony before a Senate committee, in light of new findings of achievement gains of minority students in the integrated situation compared to the control group.

124. *See* D. Long, Educational Performance in Integrated and Segregated Elementary Schools, 1968 (unpublished doctoral dissertation at Yeshiva University).

respects, however, the population studied by Long was quite different from most others reported in this article. The Negro children were not economically disadvantaged, they scored at least at the level of the national norm for the achievement tests in both the segregated and non-segregated schools, and they "had comparable staffs, facilities, and educational programs."[125] Vane's study in another suburban school district—comparing two groups of seventeen Negro children, matched by IQ score and parent's occupation, over their entire school career—indicated that racial composition had no impact on achievement.[126]

Similarly, a study of Negro children in two Ypsilanti, Michigan schools, one all-Negro and the other a school with 45 per cent Negro students, indicated that there was no statistically significant difference between the two groups in achievement gains.[127] This can not be explained by differences between the two groups of students in socioeconomic background or in IQ scores since they were substantially the same.

Robert Klein, at the University of South Carolina, studied the initial effects of desegregation during an eight month period in three high schools located in a southern metropolis:[128] one recently desegregated, one all-Negro, and the other virtually all-white. Higher scores on mathematics and biology were first registered for Negro children in the desegregated school, but when parental occupation, family size, and parental education were controlled, this superiority disappeared. Klein concluded that "[t]he integrated school setting is neither educationally deleterious nor educationally beneficial for Negro students, at least over an eight-month period."[129] He also observed that "[t]he academic achievement of matched groups of integrated white and Negro students did not differ significantly. . . . The academic achievement of matched groups of segregated Negro students and integrated white students did not differ significantly."[130]

Otis Geiger has also reported on a study in a southern city, undertaken after one year of desegregation. Instead of tracing the progress of individual children, he focused on the effect of racial composition of classes on achievement. He reported that "no significant relations were found between percentage of Negroes in the class and amount of achievement."[131] The results of the

125. *Id.* at 80, 85.

126. Vane, *Relation of Early School Achievement to High School Achievement When Race, Intelligence and Socioeconomic Factors Are Equated*, 3 PSYCHOLOGY IN THE SCHOOLS 124, 128 (1966).

127. *See* N. Radin, A Comparison of the Test Performance of Negro Students Attending All-Negro and Integrated Elementary Schools in One Community, April 15, 1966 (unpublished paper on file with the Ypsilanti Public School District, Ypsilanti, Mich.).

128. *See* R. Klein, A Comparative Study of the Academic Achievement of Negro 10th Grade High School Students Attending Segregated and Recently Integrated Schools in a Metropolitan Area of the South, 1967 (unpublished doctoral dissertation at the University of South Carolina).

129. *Id.* at 49.

130. *Id.*

131. *See* O. Geiger, Effects of Desegregation on Classroom Achievement 27, 1968 (unpublished doctoral dissertation at the University of South Carolina).

study, Geiger observed, "suggest that fears of necessary detrimental effects of desegregation on classroom achievement may not be firmly based."[132] Of course, the results also show that beliefs that desegregation would foster higher achievement are unsupported.[133]

Two studies undertaken in Ann Arbor failed to find a positive gain in reading achievement after one to three years of desegregation. One study, by Frank Aberdeen, found that a single grade experienced an increase in reading achievement along with greater social acceptance from white classmates. Aberdeen concedes, however, that no general conclusion about desegregation and achievement can be derived from his study.[134] His failure to use control groups makes his study even more inconclusive. In a similar study, a control group was used, but the results were the same.[135]

Moorfield found that desegregation had no effect on the achievement scores of minority students in Kansas City, Missouri.[136] Whether or not desegregation has actually occurred is questionable, however. Students from six predominantly Negro schools were bused to twelve receiving schools. One of the receiving schools had a Negro enrollment of 65.8 per cent before busing and 99.3 per cent after busing, while another had 35.8 per cent before and 42.8 per cent after.[137] Out of the total number of minority students bused, one-fifth were bused to these two schools.[138] Achievement data are not reported by individual school.

Elliott and Badal attempted to determine whether the "racial composition of the school make[s] a difference in achievement when scholastic aptitude is controlled."[139] Their subjects were 4,693 fifth-graders. Schools were classified by per cent Negro: 80 per cent and over, 46 to 79 per cent, 11 to 40 per cent, and 10 per cent and less. Every child took an aptitude test (SCAT) and three

---

132. *Id.* at 29.

133. Several other studies have also found no effect on achievement scores after desegregation has occurred. *See, e.g.*, H. Walberg, An Evaluation of an Urban-Suburban School Bussing Program: Student Achievement and Perception of Class Learning Environments 9-10, (1971); E. Clark, Analysis of the Differences Between Pre and Post Test Scores (Change Scores) on Measures of Self-Concept, Academic Aptitude, and Reading Achievement Earned by Sixth Grade Students Attending Segregated and Desegregated Schools, 1971 (unpublished doctoral dissertation at Duke University); R. Marcum, An Exploration of the First-Year Effects of Racial Integration of the Elementary Schools on a Unit School District, 1968 (unpublished doctoral dissertation at the University of Illinois).

134. *See* F. Aberdeen, Adjustment to Desegregation: A Description of Some Differences Among Negro Elementary School Pupils, 1969 (unpublished doctoral dissertation at the University of Michigan).

135. *See* P. Carrigan & F. Aberdeen, Some Early Effects of Compulsory Desegregation on Elementary School Children (1970).

136. *See* T. Moorfield, The Busing of Minority Group Children in a Big City School System, 1967 (unpublished doctoral dissertation at the University of Chicago).

137. *Id.* at 25, Table 2.

138. *Id.* at 22, Table 1.

139. Elliott & Badal, *Achievement and Racial Composition of Schools*, 16 Cal. J. Ed. Research 160 (1965).

achievement tests (STEP). Mathematics achievement scores rose as the per cent Negro enrolled fell. Writing achievement scores also rose for the two (out of six) highest ability levels of children; for the lower ability levels, no significant differences were found. Reading achievement scores seemed altogether unaffected by the racial composition of the school. All in all, concluded Elliott and Badal, racial composition makes no important difference for achievement when scholastic aptitude is controlled.

A study of Richmond, California, undertaken by Alan Wilson, concludes that the "racial composition of the school, while tending to favor Negro students in racially integrated schools, does not have a substantial effect—not nearly so strong as the social-class composition of the school."[140] Wilson also found that the social class composition of the school had more effect on Negro than on white students, although he notes that "[t]here are hardly any Negroes in our sample in predominantly white schools or predominantly upper [social] status schools,"[141] meaning that the Negro sample in the Richmond study was too small to be able to test the relation of social class and race in schools of varying racial composition. It should also be noted that Wilson used the school rather than the classroom as the unit of analysis. Thus if the school system being studied resorts to tracking and ability grouping practices, there may be internal segregation even though the school is said to be desegregated.[142]

Finally, Denmark and Guttentag investigated the effects of non-segregated pre-schooling on the cognitive skills of sixty-three four-year-old Negro children.[143] Four pre-school groups were organized, only one of which was integrated. The researchers concluded that a good, creative, enjoyable learning climate may be more important than the racial composition of the experience.[144]

IV
STUDIES SHOWING A NEGATIVE EFFECT OF INTERRACIAL SCHOOLING ON ACADEMIC ACHIEVEMENT

As noted at the outset, there is little reason to believe that desegregation has negative consequences for nonwhites. To be sure, desegregation—or any other

140. 2 U.S. COMMISSION ON CIVIL RIGHTS, RACIAL ISOLATION IN THE PUBLIC SCHOOLS 186 (1967).

141. *Id.* at 184.

142. It has been pointed out that school systems which maintain classrooms of heterogeneous ability

> tend to record the most encouraging improvements in academic achievement after desegregation. By contrast, systems . . . which increase [the] use of ability grouping after desegregation, have tended to show the most disappointing results.

Pettigrew, *A Sociological View of the Post-*Bradley *Era*, 21 WAYNE L. REV. 813, 821 (1975).

143. *See* Denmark & Guttentag, *Effect of Integrated and Non-Integrated Programs on Cognitive Change in Pre-School Children*, 29 PERCEPTUAL & MOTOR SKILLS 375 (1969).

144. *Id.* at 379.

significant event—will disturb the progress of some children in any large sample. But in this article, the focus has been on the net effects and only two studies of the dozens reviewed herein report that more students than not actually experienced lower rates of achievement as a result of attending a racially mixed rather than a segregated school.

A study of 224 Negro students—drawn from ten predominantly black schools and bused to thirty-two predominantly white schools in Seattle—found that while their attendance records in their new schools improved sharply, their school record as measured by grades suffered: "43 per cent of the total group are doing poorer than they did last year, 41 per cent are doing the same, and 6 per cent are doing better."[145] Because no achievement test scores are reported, however, it is not possible to know whether the absolute achievement of bused children rose or fell—achievement scores and grades are not always highly correlated in desegregated schools.

A Florida study examined changes in achievement between the academic years of 1969-70 and 1970-71 for Dade County elementary school students. Black students in grades two, four, and six, who had remained in a predominantly black school, attained higher levels of achievement than did those who moved to desegregated schools, as did black junior high school students who remained in black schools.[146]

V
Studies Showing the Effect of Busing on Academic Achievement

Because of the emphasis given to busing by both those who see it as the most feasible way to achieve school desegregation and those who view busing as the symbol of attempts to destroy the neighborhood schools concept,[147] it is surprising that the possible educational consequences of busing have received the attention of only a handful of researchers.

By far the most sophisticated and comprehensive study of the effects of busing, involving 450 schools, is that conducted by James A. Davis as part of the *Southern Schools* research of Robert Crain and his associates.[148] The study, which examines the effects of busing on tension in schools, student morale,

---

145. *See* A. Hammond, L. Sawhill, & R. Williams, A Survey of the Adjustment of the Negro Students Who Transferred to Schools Outside Their Neighborhoods During 1963-1964 Under the New Seattle School Board Rulings 48, 1964 (unpublished master's thesis at the University of Washington).

146. *Id.* at 25, 55.

147. Mandatory busing for segregation was a standard practice throughout the South until well into the 1960's. In the early 1970's more students in the South were transported to public school by a motor-powered vehicle (57.5 per cent) than by walking and/or bicycle-riding (42.5 per cent). U.S. Department of Transportation, School Bus Task Force, Pupil Transportation Safety Program Plan (1973).

148. *See* 2 Southern Schools.

race relations, and academic achievement, gave particular attention to the need to control for the social background of students. The study concludes:[149]

> First, there is no evidence that busing per se has any negative consequences. On the contrary, the strongest finding in the set is the association between busing white students and benign levels of tension in the schools.
>
> Second, there is no evidence that attending *one's own* neighborhood school has any effects, positive or negative, on a school's achievement levels or social climate.[150]

In a study of five West Virginia high schools, Straley compared 348 transported with 256 non-transported seniors—without considering the race of the students. Achievement test scores were significantly higher for the non-transported students; the difference was greater for boys than for girls. Academic grades, however, were the same for both transported and non-transported groups. When Straley matched students in both groups by IQ and sex, the differences between female students who were transported and those who were not disappeared, while for male students, the differences narrowed but remained statistically significant. Straley could find no relationship between academic achievement and distance transported,[151] so the differences remain unexplained.

Among the remaining busing studies are the following: Davies, in a study of a school in Volusia County, Florida, analyzed the achievement record of fifty-five pairs of transported and non-transported elementary school students.[152] Non-transported students attained a higher rate of achievement in mathematics but not in other subjects. Another study investigated 240 fourth, fifth, and sixth-graders in an urban area of Oklahoma, half of whom were transported and 98 per cent of whom were Caucasians. In no area of achievement measured by the Iowa tests was there a significant difference between transported and non-transported students.[153] A third study found statistically significant achievement differences in favor of a non-transported group of second-grade students. No difference, however, was found for fourth and sixth grade stu-

149. *Id.* at 118.

150. This should not be taken to mean that the characteristics of the school one attends do not affect achievement. Busing more children from certain types of schools to others may affect achievement, but not because of the bus ride itself or the fact that the school is or is not the closest to the student's home.

151. *See* H. Straley, A Comparative Study of the Academic Achievement and Social Adjustment of Transported and Non-Transported High School Seniors, 1956 (unpublished doctoral dissertation at the University of Virginia).

152. *See* E. Davies, A Comparative Study of the Academic Achievement of Transported and Non-Transported Pupils at Holly Hill Elementary School, Holly Hill, Florida, 1969 (unpublished master's thesis at Stetson University).

153. *See* D. White, The Effects of Public School Transportation upon the Overall School Adjustment of Urban Elementary School Students, 1970 (unpublished doctoral dissertation at the University of Oklahoma). *See also* White, *Effects of Bussing on Urban School Students*, 29 ED. LEADERSHIP 255, 256-57 (1971).

dents in the same study.[154] The fourth study, which compared students who were bused with those who walked to desegregated schools in Evanston, Illinois, found that those bused were more likely to experience larger achievement gains.[155]

In sum, while the existing research is quite limited, attribution of negative educational effects to mandatory student transportation for purposes of desegregation is unwarranted by research evidence thus far available. Those studies which show some negative effects of busing are countered by studies that show no losses in academic performance due to busing. Moreover, even when some negative effects are found, they seem to defy theoretical explanation. This is in part due to the failure adequately to control for the social background of students. It seems likely that bused students come from more rural areas. In the South, this may mean that bused students are poorer while in other areas distance from school may be positively related to family wealth. While it is necessary that more research be done on this inflammatory issue, there seems to be little or no reason to believe that busing children to a newly-desegregated school would have a different impact on students' academic performance than creating a desegregated school by re-drawing attendance boundaries or by pairing of schools.

Conclusion

A review of these studies leads me to conclude that, overall, desegregation does indeed have a positive effect on minority achievement levels. Why and under what circumstances this is so is not yet clear, as the studies differ in too many ways to permit us to draw more specific conclusions: the measures of achievement are not the same from study to study; the extent to which schools are truly integrated is seldom well defined by researchers; and many of the studies do not adequately control for factors other than desegregation—such as socioeconomic status—that might influence academic achievement. And the fact that the processes by which desegregation occurs vary substantially between school districts and between schools also makes comparison difficult. For example, many of these studies involve voluntary desegregation. Obviously, the students of parents who have chosen to bus their children to predominantly white schools may be importantly different from those not bused even though IQ, social class background, and other student characteristics are similar.

All of these qualifications of the findings of available research does not mean the research provides no guidance. As noted at the outset, there seems to be agreement that (1) the achievement levels of white majorities in desegre-

154. Dunlop, Harper, & Hunka, *The Influence of Transporting Children to Centralized Schools upon Achievement and Attendance*, 44 Ed. Administration & Supervision 191, 196 (1958).

155. J. Hsia, *supra* note 88.

gated schools do not decline; (2) the net effect of desegregation on the academic achievement levels of nonwhites, in most studies, is positive and in others is at least neutral (since most of the research has been with blacks, further research will be necessary to determine whether this is true of achievement levels of other minorities as well); and (3) the instrument for obtaining integration—whether through busing, pairing of schools, altering of attendance zones, etc.—has no direct bearing on the achievement of the children involved.

In addition, there appears to be substantial agreement among desegregation researchers that the likelihood that desegregation will lead to gains in achievement of racial minorities is greatest when the following characterize the desegregated schools:

1. a relative absence of interracial hostility among students,
2. teachers and administrators who understand and accept minority students, encouraged and reinforced by aggressive in-service training programs,
3. the majority of students in a given classroom are from middle and/or upper socioeconomic classes,
4. desegregation at the classroom as well as at the school level, particularly in elementary schools,
5. no rigid ability grouping or tracking, particularly in elementary schools,
6. an absence of racial conflict in the community over desegregation, and
7. younger children are involved (though this last conclusion should be considered very tentative).

Some of the apparent positive impact of racial integration on academic achievement that is found in some of the studies is traceable to interclass rather than interracial mixing of students. Of course, since nonwhite children are disproportionately from working class and poor families, racial integration also tends to result in socioeconomic mixing.

Since researchers can study only that which social practice puts before them, many of the effects of desegregation reported in this article are investigations of what is essentially token desegregation rather than of integration; until very recently, this was the only kind available. Tokenism, by its nature, sets all the psychological burdens of desegregation upon the shoulders of the minority child. It also accentuates his or her own awareness of minority status, and may encourage among white students and teachers a certain paternalism toward the minority child which ill-serves both sides of the transaction. Tokenism is thus an unfavorable framework for productive desegregation. Moreover, many of the studies cover only a single year of desegregation. The scale of desegregation in the South has increased considerably since 1969, but little research has been undertaken in the South until the Crain study of 555 southern schools in districts receiving federal funds under the Emergency

School Assistance Program.[156] This data base will be a fruitful source for further research and analysis in the future.

The present generation of Americans has seen the passing of the traditional one-race school. Recent progress in desegregation has brought children together to an unprecedented degree. Under segregation, minority children were not permitted equal opportunities in any meaningful sense. A black-white achievement gap seemed to be a permanent fixture of schools. It appears, however, that more often than not, academic achievement of minority children improves when they learn together as part of a deliberate desegregation process or as a result of non-segregated housing.

---

156. *See* 1-2 SOUTHERN SCHOOLS.

THE EFFECTS OF DESEGREGATION ON RACE RELATIONS

Elizabeth G. Cohen*

Introduction

This article on the effects of desegregation on interracial attitudes and behavior has three major objectives. The first is to show the relationship between implicit social values and social science research and the utility of such research to legal issues surrounding the desegregation question. The second is to distinguish between empirical questions to which the social scientist can provide useful answers and those empirical questions which social scientists cannot answer—such as whether a forty-five minute bus ride is more harmful than a thirty minute bus ride.[1] Finally, this article presents an example of the type of research which might prove useful to school officials, lawyers, and others who are involved in developing desegregation plans.

I

Social Values and Race Relations

In order for a social scientist to answer a lawyer's question regarding the harmful consequences of desegregation, the meaning of the term "harmful" will have to be developed first, by specification of the underlying values to be maximized. If overt physical violence is minimal, yet black children experience persistent name-calling, teasing, and rejection, does this constitute harm? And how much harm has to be done before there is a sufficient basis to question the "costs" of maximizing the value goal of desegregation? The social scientist can aid in the articulation of implicit values and the possible consequences which can result from maximizing one particular value while incurring other social costs.

Also relevant to the problem of court-ordered desegregation is the issue of whether some desegregated schools, through planned social change, are able to achieve that state of interracial behavior in which blacks and whites are able to relate to each other as people rather than as members of racial groups. Such

---

* Professor and Director of the Environment for the Teaching Program, Stanford University School of Education. This article is based in part upon research conducted under Contract No. OEC 9-71-0037 (508) with the National Institute of Education. Additional support was provided by the Stanford School of Education, Stanford Center for Research and Development in Teaching, NIE Contract No. NE-C-00-3-0062. The views expressed herein do not necessarily reflect the position, policy, or endorsement of the National Institute of Education.

1. *See* Swann v. Charlotte-Mecklenburg Bd. of Educ., 402 U.S. 1, 30-31 (1971); Northcross v. Board of Educ. of Memphis City Schools, 489 F.2d 15, 16-17 (6th Cir. 1973), *cert. denied*, 414 U.S. 1022 (1974).

educational planning might then be taken into account in developing desegregation plans in response to a court order.

The implicit value goal of research on the effects of desegregation is a broad concern with social integration. If racial conflict and racial separatism grow too pronounced, researchers apparently feel that their concept of an integrated American society is threatened. In a certain sense, children are being asked to solve the problems of integration which their parents have been unable to handle in society at large. In addition, the school—one of the most conservative institutions in society—is being asked to bear the costs of social change.

A narrower value concern is increasing the opportunity for upward mobility of those minorities residentially segregated—increasing opportunity through contact with the dominant majority. Another value concern is that white children be educated as to the falsity and undesirability of prejudicial and stereotypical thinking to encourage them to behave toward blacks in an egalitarian and non-discriminatory manner. The favorable effect on whites of a desegregation process appears to be a value goal discussed only by social scientists, apparently absent from legal[2] and political considerations. Finally, the issue of interracial interaction and acceptance appears to be related to the question of how integration might improve black academic achievement levels. In order to maximize this goal of black achievement, some argue that black children must associate with achieving white children.[3]

The importance of articulating these implicit value goals is inextricably tied to any evaluation of the available social science literature dealing with the effects of desegregation on race relations. Such research can then be evaluated in terms of its effectiveness in attaining certain goals of the particular researcher—such as the diminution of white prejudice. Alternatively, the research can be evaluated in terms of its relationship to concerns of the legal system—such as reduction of the level of interracial tension and conflict in desegregated schools. However, if the available literature is evaluated from this

---

2. Dr. Kenneth Clark, who was one of the compilers of the social science brief submitted to the Supreme Court in Brown v. Board of Educ., 347 U.S. 483 (1954), has commented on the Supreme Court's failure to consider this issue:

> Ironically, the U.S. Supreme Court, when it handed down its decision in 1954, was in possession of evidence which attempted to pinpoint and to specify the type of damage which was done to white children as a consequence of racially segregated schools in consequence of a racially segregated society.
>
> . . . [The Court] . . . ignore[d] the materials which we presented to it on the damage to white children.

Hearings on Equal Educational Opportunity Before the Senate Select Comm. on Equal Educational Opportunity, 91st Cong., 2d Sess., pt. 1a, at 73 (1970).

One court, quite recently, has noted the harm to whites from a segregated system: "Although the principal victims of a racially segregated education are the minority students, it is no less true that racially segregated schools inflict considerable harm on white students and society generally." Hart v. Community School Bd., 383 F. Supp. 699, 740 (E.D.N.Y. 1974).

3. J. Coleman, Equality of Educational Opportunity 307 (1966); R. Crain & C. Rossell, Evaluating School Desegregation Plans Statistically (1973).

latter point of view, much of it turns out to be irrelevant because the research has been based on other value concerns. For example, researchers who are interested in diminishing white prejudice often use a survey questionnaire methodology designed to measure underlying interracial attitudes and tolerance rather than interracial behavior. Parents, the courts, and policy makers, however, may be much more interested in interracial behavior, *i.e.* whether any interracial contact takes place within the desegregated school and how the groups relate to each other. Unfortunately, the relationship between measures of the extent of prejudice and the likelihood of positive social relationships between the races is little understood. Therefore, the majority of the studies using the survey questionnaire methodology, no matter how well designed or carried out, are not of great utility to lawyers or policy makers interested in interracial behavior.

In addition to analyses of white prejudice, researchers resort to sociometric criteria in order to judge the success of the desegregation process. Thus the subjects of the study would be asked to select class members who are friends or with whom they would enjoy social relationships. Insofar as a choice of social partners is a measure of successful contact between the two social groups, this would seem to be a reasonable questionnaire device. However, insofar as the use of sociometric devices implies that the desired end-state is one of ties of friendship between masses of black and white students, we are using indicators of an outcome which is not only unrealistic but also only weakly related either to the researcher's value goals of social integration or to the court's goals of an orderly desegregation process. The mechanism of desegregation is not intended to create universal love and brotherhood. The goal of the desegregation process is a reasonable degree of social integration and a lack of overt conflict whereby blacks and whites, given an objective important to both, can trust each other and listen to each other sufficiently well to complete the task at hand, whether it be a vocational task, an educational task, or a political task.

It should be kept in mind that the two most important evaluation criteria in considering the usefulness of social science to the courts are pertinence of research findings to underlying value issues under scrutiny in the courts, and the extent to which there is sufficient information upon which to establish a cause-effect relationship between the desegregation process and certain favorable or unfavorable outcomes. In reviewing the social science research on school desegregation, I will attempt to specify the implicit value goals involved. The reader can then evaluate the research in terms of its relevance to particular value issues deemed critical.

II

ASKING SOCIAL SCIENTISTS ANSWERABLE QUESTIONS

Even if social scientists and lawyers were to engage in a dialogue long before cases were actually brought to court, and the value concerns were clearly separated from the purely empirical questions, there would remain a very serious problem. Many of the empirical questions which lawyers ask are not answerable with a sufficient degree of certainty given present theories and methodology. For example, suppose the lawyers were to ask these three significant questions of the social scientist: First, assuming that a major goal is improved social integration of black and white members of American society, will school desegregation improve racial integration? Secondly, how *much* will it improve racial integration? And thirdly, how can the desegregation process be carried out in such a way as to maximize the chances of interracial harmony? This section of the article attempts to describe the criteria used to evaluate whether or not the basic questions being posed are answerable with a satisfactory level of certainty.

Why cannot so central a question as whether school desegregation will improve racial integration be answered? The problem lies in the cause-effect relationship underlying the question. What is being asked is whether a court-ordered change in a school's racial composition will *cause* an improvement in race relations. Science deals with cause and effect by means of general theories which offer an explanation of how causal variables operate to produce specified effects under certain conditions. Clearly, there are no widely accepted general theories which are applicable to this particular question about desegregation and interracial relationships. We cannot even agree how to characterize school desegregation as a variable which might under certain conditions bring about specified effects. In order to work with a concept like "court-ordered desegregation," the social scientist must translate that concept into a different kind of abstraction—it must be conceptualized as a phenomenon for scientific study. But desegregation is a political-legal concept, used in widely differing ways by different courts. And when researchers attempt to locate settings in which to study desegregation, they too differ as to what constitutes "desegregation." Some say a school with 10 per cent black students is "desegregated," others a 30 per cent black student population. This disagreement as to what is an operational definition of desegregation reveals an underlying disagreement about what kind of social science phenomenon court-ordered desegregation represents.

Even if there were agreement on this point, however, there still are problems in isolating the effects of a process of desegregation with any degree of certainty. This is because there is no relevant theory as to *how* the process of desegregation affects interracial attitudes and behavior. Absent an understanding of the cause-effect relationship, researchers do not know what indicators to use or the conditions under which to expect desirable outcomes. As long as social scientists have no theoretical ideas concerning the effects desegregation brings about and no theoretical framework to dictate which variables should be controlled and which indicators of these variables should be utilized, researchers will continue to reach conflicting results: some studies will show beneficial effects of desegregation and others harmful effects.

The major criticism of existing research on race relations has been directed to its methodological flaws. Thus the impression is that if only the investigator had used longitudinal data, following groups of students over time,[4] if only the investigator had used a "matched" control group of segregated students, if only the investigator had controlled variables such as classroom racial balance, staff preparation for desegregation and expectations—then the connection between desegregation and desired effects would have been determined with some certainty.

This article takes a more radical position: the available studies on the effects of desegregation are deficient primarily on theoretical grounds. For instance, there is no way of knowing what changes in social history constitute fundamental changes in the parameters of the process, thus rendering studies done in the 1960's inapplicable in the 1970's. This is not to say that research has nothing to contribute toward an understanding of these social issues. It is possible to ask the social scientist questions that are empirical in nature and answerable. There are two different kinds of answerable questions in an interchange between law and social science on the issue of desegregation. The answerable questions differ from the unanswerable questions in that the former are much more concrete and descriptive, or are oriented to explanation and process rather than to unconditional questions about effects. Questions about desegregation and its possible effects fall between useful case studies that can be done of particular school systems undergoing desegregation and basic studies of the conditions under which specified outcomes become much more probable.

A. Local Decision-Making Studies

There are very few studies in the research literature which examine the incidence of overt physical interracial confrontation or the extent to which there is any interracial contact in different schools in a district under a court-ordered desegregation plan. Such descriptive studies do not involve propositions about cause and effect. It is possible to construct indices of the outcomes which concern the decision makers without having to develop basic theories, ascertaining only that the sampling of observed conflicts or contacts adequately represents the total of such conflicts or contacts. These case studies are essentially historical rather than scientific; they document what has happened in a sample of desegregated schools in a particular city at a particular point in time.

4. Cross-sectional studies are those based on data collected at one point in time. Relationships are static between people or groups or whatever it is that is being studied at that point in time. Longitudinal studies, on the other hand, include at least two sets of data gathered over a period of time. Usually they are the changes in a particular characteristic or phenomenon over time that are studied.

Yet such descriptive studies can prove very useful to decision makers in determining which schools need further expert assistance and resources to enhance the effectiveness of the desegregation process.

These studies do not attempt to determine general outcomes of desegregation. Instead they ask the question: are we experiencing much more interracial conflict in School A as compared to School B? If the results indicate this to be the case, some remedial steps may be taken in School A; and the study may be replicated to ascertain whether the desired improvement has been achieved.

B. Process-Oriented Studies

In contrast to relatively concrete questions which are of prime interest to local decision makers, there are important questions to be answered about the conditions under which interracial contact might be expected to result in desirable interracial attitudes and behavior. These questions become answerable by concentrating on what lawyers, policy makers, and parents agree are desirable outcomes of the desegregation process. If agreement on such desired outcomes can be reached, then questions about which conditions are more likely to achieve these desired outcomes can be answered. This knowledge can then be utilized by lawyers, school officials, and others in formulating desegregation plans. Some of the outcomes of desegregation deemed socially desirable do coincide with other areas of social science. The conditions under which we might expect to produce "equal status behavior" between black and white students—described in greater detail later in this article—is an example.

Jane Mercer has described this kind of useful dialogue succinctly and aptly:[5]

> There are some questions concerning how to achieve those values which can perhaps be answered by applied research. Perhaps we could clarify the difference between the two categories of value questions and empirical scientific questions so that lawyers would not ask social scientists to come up with answers to questions involving value criteria. This would limit us to rather concrete questions: "How do we get from here to there, if we both agree we want to go to there?" Then, in certain circumscribed areas, I think we could say, "Yes, there seem to be ways to get from here to there."

III

Review of Existing Social Science Research

This section analyzes the available social science research literature on the relationship of desegregation to interracial attitudes and behavior. In evaluating the state of the knowledge, the implicit value goals are specified where possible and the relevance of the research to attaining those goals as well as its relevance to attaining values of more direct interest to the courts are discussed.

---

5. Statement made at The Courts, Social Science, and School Desegregation Conference, Hilton Head Island, S.C., Aug. 20, 1974, on file at *Law and Contemporary Problems* office.

Secondly, the problem of using correlational studies to make inferences concerning the effects of desegregation without the benefit of explanatory theories is discussed. Finally, special attention is paid to those studies which indicate social processes essential to achieving desired outcomes in desegregated settings.

A. Early Research on Racial Mixing

In her review of research undertaken between 1937 and 1973 on desegregation and racial prejudice, St. John points out that most studies begin with the assumption that children are racially prejudiced; the researcher seeks to determine whether changes in the school's racial composition will affect that level of prejudice.[6] Pre-1968 research utilizing questions concerning the race of classmates chosen as friends showed a consistent tendency for in-group preference—or intolerance of other races—to increase with age.[7] But studies which focus on the effects of interracial contact among children come to conflicting conclusions. A classic early study found that after a two-week interracial camping experience during which whites still preferred whites as friends, there was a significant drop in the extent to which these preferences were found.[8] By contrast, another study found black children in segregated schools and both black and white children in naturally desegregated schools more prejudiced than whites in segregated schools.[9] Similarly, a study of black and white junior high school children in California before and after integration revealed that white children who had experienced integration were less tolerant of Negroes.[10]

An oft-cited study was undertaken for the United States Commission on Civil Rights.[11] Utilizing data collected by the Equality of Educational Opportunity survey[12] on over 75,000 whites and blacks from grades nine and twelve in the metropolitan Northeast, a preference by students for desegregated schools and friends of other races was found to be positively related to both the number of years students had attended desegregated schools and the present proportion of white students in their classrooms.[13]

It was realized relatively early that whether or not school desegregation would have a positive effect on race relations would depend on a number of

---

6. N. ST. JOHN, SCHOOL DESEGREGATION OUTCOMES FOR CHILDREN 65 (1975).

7. Carithers, *School Desegregation and Racial Cleavage, 1954-1970: A Review of the Literature*, 26 J. SOCIOLOGICAL ISSUES 25, 32-35 (1970).

8. Yarrow, Campbell, & Yarrow, *Acquisition of New Norms: A Study of Racial Desegregation*, 14 J. SOCIOLOGICAL ISSUES 8, 27 (1958).

9. Dentler & Elkind, *Intergroup Attitudes, Academic Performance, and Racial Composition*, in THE URBAN R'S (R. Dentler, B. Mackler, & M. Warshauer eds. 1967).

10. Webster, *The Influence of Interracial Contact on Social Acceptance in a Newly Integrated School*, 52 J. ED. PSYCHOLOGY 292, 295-96 (1961).

11. U.S. COMMISSION ON CIVIL RIGHTS, RACIAL ISOLATION IN THE PUBLIC SCHOOLS (1967).

12. J. COLEMAN, *supra* note 3.

13. *See* U.S. COMMISSION ON CIVIL RIGHTS, *supra* note 11.

factors. The report to the United States Commission on Civil Rights cited such factors as "leadership given by state and local officials, application of the plan to all schools in the community; measures taken to minimize the possibility of racial friction in newly desegregated schools and the desegregation of classes within schools."[14]

Criticism of this earlier literature centered on two main points: the first noted the need for some theoretical concepts such as Gordon Allport had put forth on the necessary conditions for the reduction of prejudice as a consequence of "equal status contact";[15] and the second reflected a growing dissatisfaction with the methodology used in these studies. Some social scientists[16] contend that this research wrongfully assumes that integration is "unsuccessful" if *any* type of interracial contact fails to be associated with reduction in prejudice, maintaining that this is a misreading of Allport's theory which specified that *only if* certain conditions are met will contact result in lessened prejudice.[17] Thus it has been argued that studies of integration should take into account whether or not particular desegregated schools have met these conditions.[18] A study in which the entire literature on intergroup contact was reviewed concluded that changes in ethnic relations do occur following contact, but that if the conditions are unfavorable, intergroup tension and prejudice increase, and if conditions are favorable, there may be a diminution of prejudice.[19] Other criticisms of these early studies can be summarized as follows:

1. The studies are cross-sectional rather than longitudinal, so that one cannot document the hypothesized improvement or deterioration in interracial relations over time.[20]
2. They do not have an appropriate comparison or control group, so there is no way of telling whether or not a group of students not experiencing desegregation would show exactly the same attitudes or change in attitudes.
3. Different studies use different measures of prejudice.
4. Even if there is an attempt to follow a sample over time, the desegregation process may have to take effect over a much longer period of time before favorable effects are shown.
5. Many important variables such as the socioeconomic status of the student, the racial composition of the classroom, or the racial composition of prior schooling are not controlled.

---

14. *Id.* at 154.
15. G. Allport, The Nature of Prejudice 280-81 (1954).
16. *See* Pettigrew, Useem, Normand & Smith, *Busing: A Review of "The Evidence,"* 30 Pub. Interest 88 (Winter 1973).
17. *Id.* at 91-93. *But see* Armor, *The Evidence on Busing*, 28 Pub. Interest 90 (Summer 1972).
18. Pettigrew, Useem, Normand & Smith, *supra* note 16, at 93.
19. Amir, *Contact Hypothesis in Ethnic Relations*, 71 Psychological Bull. 319, 338 (1969).
20. *See* note 4 *supra*.

B. The Research: 1968-1974

A systematic review of the post-1968 research literature was undertaken for this article.[21] There are a number of problems with these more recent studies. First, none of them build upon pre-1968 findings. Despite the suggestions of early studies, the post-1968 research still fails to take into account the steps schools might have taken to bring about integration as opposed to mere desegregation. Only five of the twenty-four studies reviewed took into account interracial contacts within the schools. In other words, some of the desegregated schools studied may have resegregated within the school or even the classroom by means of tracking or ability grouping.[22] Only three studies contain detailed information on staff attitudes and the extent to which the staff was prepared for desegregation. Similarly, only one study provides detailed information on curricular changes in preparation for desegregation. Lastly, only one study gives detailed information on the racial composition of the school staff after desegregation has occurred.

The most disappointing aspect of these studies is the fact that little, if any, thought has been given to the sociopolitical context in which the desegregation process occurs. Only two studies deal solely with non-voluntary desegregation, an issue of paramount importance to court litigation. Eight studies deal with various voluntary programs such as the METCO program in the Boston area.[23] Seven studies contain observations on both voluntary and mandatory situations without any distinction between the two processes of desegregation, and six studies fail even to tell which phenomenon is being studied.

A further difficulty is that none of these studies employ a systematic theoretical framework as an aid in understanding why the desegregation process should have certain consequences or the specification of the *conditions under which* desegregation leads to certain consequences.[24] While eight of the

---

21. A computer search of the Educational Resources Information Center (ERIC) system and of the *Psychology Abstracts* retrieval system located over 500 references to the effects of desegregation on interracial attitudes and behavior. *Sociology Abstracts* was also utilized. Many of the references found through ERIC dealt with practical, educational, and political ways of desegregating schools or were historical and impressionistic case studies of how desegregation was undertaken in a particular city. On the other hand, much of the psycho-social research on the effects of desegregation was concerned with the effects of a change in self-concept or in level of aspirations on black students. Thus, much of this material is irrelevant to the topic under discussion. More pertinent were a number of evaluation studies of the desegregation process in particular cities which included measures of interracial attitudes and behavior.

The methodology was as follows: each research report was described, critically evaluated, and coded as to type of dependent variable studied, study design, number and types of controls used, sampling, non-response problems, and presence or absence of explanatory concepts and theories. In all, 24 studies covering interracial attitudes and behavior were analyzed.

22. *See, e.g.*, Moses v. Washington Parish School Bd., 456 F.2d 1285 (5th Cir. 1972), *cert. denied*, 409 U.S. 1013 (1972).

23. The METCO program, which originated in 1966, is a voluntary busing program which places a relatively small number of black students from Boston in selected white suburban schools.

24. The only possible exception is a study which attempted to test Allport's contact hypothesis.

studies referred to an explanatory concept such as "equal status contact," they failed to integrate it into the study design. A contrast between schools with high amounts of "equal status contact" and those with low amounts should be built into a study of a selected set of schools. Alternatively, an indicator of the concept of "equal status contact" should be introduced in the statistical analysis to see if desired effects of the desegregation process are associated with its presence. Twelve studies do use such relatively concrete explanatory concepts as the presence or absence of teacher leadership. Only seven studies involved measures of interracial behavior, observed or reported. The bulk of the studies, twenty-two of the twenty-four, used survey questionnaire measures of attitudes. Four utilized sociometric criteria of interracial friendship.

Almost all of the studies can be faulted on their basic design. Only four studies are longitudinal, *i.e.*, the same subjects were studied before and after the desegregation process took place. Ten studies attempt to approximate a longitudinal design by taking several cross-sections of the schools being studied at various times during the desegregation process. The principal improvement over pre-1968 research is the inclusion of a control or comparison group of some type in seventeen of the studies.

Controlling certain variables, such as social class, presented many problems. Thirteen of the twenty-four studies have some control for the social class of the *schools* being compared, but only eight studies control the social class of the *individuals* being studied. Issues of race and social class are closely intertwined, and studies of desegregation must try to disentangle the effects of these two major variables.

Although 14 studies utilized more than 500 subjects and 9 used between 100 and 500, only 5 of these studies used random-sampling. The non-response rates on questionnaire items were also severe: seven studies report less than a 25 per cent non-response rate; three report a 25 to 50 per cent non-response rate, while one reports more than a 50 per cent non-response rate. Thirteen of the studies fail even to indicate the extent of the rate of non-responses to questionnaires. The presence of non-response rates is quite serious when one is trying to describe negative attitudes between social groups; for example, one can make a reasonable argument that students who are the most hostile and negative toward others are most likely to fail to respond to questionnaires.

Lewis & St. John, *Contribution of Cross-Racial Friendship to Minority Group Achievement in Desegregated Classrooms*, 37 Sociometry 79 (1974).

Allport's contact hypothesis is as follows:

> Contacts that bring knowledge and acquaintance are likely to engender sounder beliefs about minority groups . . . . Prejudice . . . may be reduced by equal status contact between majority and minority groups in the pursuit of common goals. The effect is greatly enhanced if this contact is sanctioned by institutional supports (i.e., by law, custom, or local atmosphere), and if it is of a sort that leads to the perception of common interests and common humanity between members of the two groups.

Allport, The Nature of Prejudice 268, 281 (1954).

C. Interpretation of the Results

If the findings of these studies are in part attributable to uncontrolled variables or are an artifact of the nature of the population selected for busing programs, or if the observed correlation has no relation to a hypothetical causal process, then the results of these studies cannot be easily summarized. In view of these difficulties, then, can anything be learned from these studies about the extent to which desegregated schools meet conditions for equal status contact; whether desegregation can, under specified conditions, become a setting for interracial interaction which in turn leads to reduced racial prejudice and stereotyping; how students respond to the change in student body composition in newly desegregated schools; whether there are changes as time passes; and finally, whether peer acceptance of blacks leads to improved black achievement?

With regard to the conditions surrounding contact between the races which will decrease prejudices, these desegregation studies represent no advance in knowledge as to a causal theory. Nor is there anything in the research that provides some basis for testing assumptions about the process by which integration can assist black achievement through the medium of peer acceptance.

Though the existing research is inadequate in the ways I have described, this does not mean that it can or should be ignored or undervalued. In the following section, research on the effects of desegregation on race relations is reviewed, with particular attention to work completed since 1968. First, studies relating to the acceptance of desegregation by students—their preferences with respect to interracial contact and racial prejudice—are examined. Second, a review is undertaken of those studies not concerned primarily with interracial acceptance per se, but with the implicit theory held by many social scientists and policy makers: that if blacks are accepted by whites in more achievement-oriented white classrooms, their achievement will improve. Finally, studies which deal explicitly with the conditions that seem to enhance race relations are examined as well as the implications of these findings for strategies of interracial mixing in schools.

1. *Desegregation and Reducing White Prejudice*

Some forty-one studies were examined by St. John with regard to their findings of diminution in prejudice among whites and blacks as measured by tests of attitudes and friendliness.[25] For either race, positive findings are somewhat less common than negative findings, and in many cases there is no effect or the effects are mixed.[26]

> It is also apparent that the direction of findings is as often contradictory as it is consistent for the two races. Sometimes desegregation is reported to have

25. N. ST. JOHN, *supra* note 6.
26. *Id.* at 67-68.

ameliorated the prejudice of whites but intensified that of blacks, sometimes the reverse.[27]

What is more important, St. John breaks these studies down according to various criteria, seeking consistent results within certain subcategories. For example, she asks: are the results consistent within categories if we divide up the schools studies as to whether they represent integrated neighborhood housing patterns, voluntary or mandated desegregation? When the findings of these studies are classified according to the *manner* in which desegregation was accomplished, it appears that whites who deliberately choose desegregated programs may have had favorable attitudes to start with. In general, however, self-selection does not seem to have regularly resulted in more positive findings. "Findings are contradictory regardless of whether desegregation was 'natural,' mandatory or voluntary."[28] Desegregation in the South seems to be associated with negative interracial attitudes by students more often than desegregation in the North.[29] However, it could be that increasing prejudice can be an indication that the community climate, rather than interracial contact, is affecting attitudes.[30]

In a similar manner, studies which are longitudinal in design are compared with those that are cross-sectional, finding that cross-sectional studies without "before and after" measurements indicate attitudinal gains among white children. Longitudinal studies with control groups, however, indicate attitudinal losses.[31] If these studies are categorized as to whether they deal with sociometric or attitudinal indices, equally mixed results are revealed. By taking into account background characteristics of the students involved, St. John finds a number of studies that report difficulties experienced by black females as contrasted to black males in the desegregation process.[32] Too few studies have utilized proper controls on socioeconomic status, but several studies suggest that results for desegregation are more favorable when the socioeconomic backgrounds of the two races are substantially similar.[33] Younger children appear to benefit from desegregation somewhat more than older children.[34]

The studies that have been analyzed for this article appear to yield the same mixed results as the studies reviewed by St. John. Following is a sample of the studies of interracial attitude and acceptance that have been reviewed:

1. A study of the willingness of children to associate with various social

---

27. N. St. John, *supra* note 6, at 68.
28. N. St. John, *supra* note 6, at 76.
29. *Id.*
30. *See* E. Campbell, The Attitude Effects of Educational Desegregation in a Southern Community, 1956 (unpublished doctoral dissertation, Vanderbilt University) referred to in N. St. John, *supra* note 6, at 76.
31. N. St. John, *supra* note 6, at 73.
32. N. St. John, *supra* note 6, at 78, 110.
33. N. St. John, *supra* note 6, at 126.
34. N. St. John, *supra* note 6, at 77.

groups was undertaken in a de facto segregated school, an all-white school, and a nonsegregated school. Whites attending nonsegregated schools were more willing to associate with blacks than whites in segregated schools. Negroes attending nonsegregated schools were also more accepting of whites than Negroes in segregated schools. On a scale of aggression and achievement, white children saw blacks as more aggressive and as non-achievers if they had classroom contact than if they had no classroom contact.[35]

2. A comparison of students from rural white high schools in an all white area of Alabama with an integrated school (6 per cent blacks since 1965), also in Alabama, indicated that white students in the integrated school were significantly more "prejudiced" than whites in the segregated school.[36]
3. A public school in the Atlanta area with only seven black students enrolled was compared with a Catholic parochial school with a black population of 28 per cent. Only 56 out of 101 volunteers completed the questionnaires measuring acceptance or rejection of prejudicial statements about a number of religious, racial, and behavioral out-groups. The analysis indicated that students who attended the integrated school for four years were significantly less prejudiced toward all the out-groups than students in the all-white school. The researchers acknowledge the grave problem of the special selection of white parents who choose to send their children to the integrated inner city school.[37]
4. A sociometric measure and measures of classroom preference for white and black teachers and students, according to the extent to which the racial balance of the classroom in which the child is located reflects the racial composition of the entire school, indicate that the polarization of racial friendship grouping was only slightly less extreme in racially balanced as opposed to unbalanced classes.[38] A study of third graders in racially mixed elementary schools in a large eastern city school district —eliminating slum and upper class schools and schools in which one race comprised less than 25 per cent or more than 75 per cent of the population—showed that race strongly affects choice of friends.
5. In an investigation of the southern response to desegregation, a study was undertaken of two high schools in two rural Georgia counties or-

35. *See* D. Singer, Interracial Attitudes of Negro and White 5th Grade Children in Segregated and Unsegregated Schools, 1966 (unpublished doctoral dissertation, Columbia University).

36. *See* Wade & Wilson, *Relatively Low Prejudice in a Racially Isolated Group*, 28 PSYCHOLOGICAL REP. 871 (1971).

37. *See* Patterson & Smits, *Reactions of Inner-City and Suburban Adolescents to Three Minority Groups*, 80 J. PSYCHOLOGY 127, (1972).

38. *See* Koslin, Koslin, Pargament, & Waxman, *Classroom Racial Balance and Students' Interracial Attitudes*, 45 SOCIOLOGY OF ED. 386 (1972).

dered to desegregate by the fall of 1970.[39] Students were administered questionnaires before the desegregation process began and one year after the process of desegregation was underway. Black and white students were found to differ from each other in their expectations and evaluations of desegregation. Before desegregation, 80 per cent of the whites expected maintenance of racial separation within the desegregated schools. Seventeen per cent of the blacks did not expect that desegregation would really come about, but only 45 per cent expected resegregation within the school if it were to be desegregated. A year after the schools were desegregated, only one-fifth of both races report the existence of interracial contact on a social level. There was a decline in positive evaluations of desegregation among blacks—whereas before desegregation, 44 per cent had believed they would receive a better education in the integrated school; a year after the process of desegregation had begun, only 9 per cent felt that their education had improved. The proportion of black students who felt that desegregation served a useful purpose dropped from 75 per cent to 35 per cent, while there was either no change or only a slight improvement in white evaluations of integration.

6. Another southern study[40] utilized a random sample of blacks and whites from a cross-section of rural and urban secondary schools in western Tennessee, an area highly resistant to racial desegregation. Students attending newly desegregated schools, segregated schools, and schools desegregated for a year or more were compared. The wisdom of including a segregated control group is shown by the researchers' finding that the black students' satisfaction with school, including their perception of "kindness of other pupils," went down in all three kinds of settings over the course of the school year.

In general, studies of integration in northern cities present a very mixed picture with results frequently quite different for white and black students, and for male and female students. A well designed longitudinal study of elementary and secondary classrooms in Kalamazoo, Michigan[41] during a two-way busing desegregation process—with data collected just prior to desegregation and one year later—revealed that the opinions of all students were significantly less positive after desegregation than before on such questionnaire items as "class

---

39. *See* Bullock & Braxton, *The Coming of School Desegregation: A Before and After Study of Black and White Student Perceptions*, 54 SOCIAL SCIENCE Q. 132 (1973).

40. *See* Williams & Venditti, *Effect of Academic Integration on Southern Negro Students' Expressed Satisfaction With School*, 79 J. SOCIAL PSYCHOLOGY 203 (1969); Williams & Venditti, *Effect of Academic Desegregation on Southern White Students' Expressed Satisfaction With School*, 38 J. NEGRO ED. 338 (1969).

41. *See* W. Coats, A Longitudinal Survey of Desegregation in Kalamazoo, Michigan, Sept. 7, 1972 (paper presented at the American Psychological Association Annual Convention, Honolulu, Hawaii).

orderly," "class fun," "teacher likes you," and "liking for school." White secondary students' overall evaluation was not strongly affected as measured by the item concerning friendliness of other students, but they were less likely to report that they were learning a lot. The attitudes of white elementary students showed only one statistically significant change—they saw the students in their class as friendlier.

A study based on questionnaires addressed to graduating high school seniors in Berkeley, California probably involves the longest period of desegregation of any of the studies reviewed here, inasmuch as the school system had been desegregated since the graduating seniors had been in the seventh grade.[42] Questionnaires had been addressed to these students when they were in junior high school when desegregation was initiated. Since the first questionnaire, an increase in reported interracial mixing was noted. Some of this increase appears to be due to cross-sex mixing: black males and white females are reported to date often, but white males and black females are reported as dating infrequently.[43] There are also important class differences associated with interracial mixing; given a more middle class black population, the number of white and Asian friends reported increases. However, among whites, the number of black friends decreases given a more middle class white population. Blacks were more likely to report experiencing aggressive acts than whites; but of the aggressive encounters reported, students saw them as primarily instigated by blacks.

Several evaluations of the effects of Boston's METCO program, involving a voluntary program which buses black children from predominantly black schools in Boston to predominantly white schools in the surrounding suburbs, have been undertaken.[44] In one study, questionnaires were administered to a random sample of white tenth graders in eight high schools which very small numbers of METCO students had attended for a period of from one to three years. Although a majority of white students were found to favor the program, a highly significant variation exists between the schools. In two of the schools only 43 per cent and 55 per cent of the white students felt the program should be continued. This is a low percentage considering the small number of black newcomers and the northern setting of the study. It is important to recognize the profound difference a particular school context can make in accounting for

---

42. *See* OFFICE OF EDUCATION, U.S. DEP'T OF HEALTH, EDUCATION AND WELFARE, FOLLOW-UP STUDY OF STUDENT ATTITUDES TOWARD SCHOOL REORGANIZATION OF THE PUBLIC SCHOOLS IN A NORTHERN CITY, FINAL REPORT (1972). Unfortunately, the study is weakened by a poor response rate—only 44 per cent of the black students returned their questionnaires.

43. Educators working in desegregated northern settings often comment on the frustration and rage at this state of affairs experienced by black female students, but most researchers do not deal with such delicate and important matters.

44. *See* Armor, *supra* note 17; Useem, *White Students and Token Desegregation*, 10 INTEGRATED ED. 46 (1972); H. Walberg, An Evaluation of an Urban-Suburban School Busing Program on Student Achievement and Perception of Class Learning Environments, Feb. 1971 (paper presented at annual meeting of the American Educational Research Association, N.Y.).

different responses to racial mixing. Furthermore, these differences in the METCO study could not be explained by differences in student socioeconomic status, in religion, or prior contact with blacks.[45]

The other two METCO studies both examined data collected on 732 bused children and 352 siblings of these children who stayed behind in their predominantly black schools. Children in both groups were given achievement tests and questionnaires to complete in the fall of the school year in which the program started, and again in the spring. Children in the third through fifth grades who were bused to white suburban schools saw their classes as significantly more satisfying than did their siblings who continued to attend predominantly black schools.[46] However, a questionnaire given to junior and senior high school students showed that the bused students were significantly more likely to favor the ideology of "black power" and black separatism than the control group.[47]

These studies are in no sense comparable with each other. Any difference in "favorability" toward desegregation that is found may be a consequence of one or more of the following factors: different research designs; different questionnaire items; differences in time and place; or differences in the actual phenomena being studied (racial mixture may actually represent several social phenomena). *Within* each of these studies, there are important differences between schools, between male and female students, between races, and between classes. These differences both within and between studies suggest that in order to gain any kind of practical understanding of the consequences of desegregation, the social scientist must avoid undertaking studies of this particular type and focus on local decision-making studies or more theoretically oriented studies.

Case studies of individual cities utilize various indicators of attitude changes. Some assume that the most vital variables for measurement are Negro self-concept or achievement motivation, without stopping to examine the murky issues underlying this particular choice of variables. These studies often neglect questions of considerable concern to parents and others such as: How is the process of desegregation proceeding? Is there interracial friction? Are students supportive of the process?

Only one study dealing directly with the relationship between racial hostility and the desegregation process was found.[48] In this study, black junior and senior high students who were first to desegregate previously all-white schools in the state of Alabama were interviewed. From a list of 500 such students,

45. Useem, *supra* note 44, at 51.
46. *See* H. Walberg, *supra* note 44.
47. Armor, *supra* note 17, at 103.
48. *See* M. Chesler & P. Segal, Characteristics of Negro Students Attending Previously All-White Schools in the Deep South, Sept. 1972 (mimeograph at Institute for Social Research, University of Michigan).

one-half of the names from each community were randomly selected and interviewed during the summer of 1966. In the initial days and weeks of desegregation, 48 per cent of the black respondents felt they encountered considerable resentment and hostility; they were particularly sensitive to "passive resentment communicated to them through hostile stares, efforts at physical avoidance, laughing and teasing behind their backs and general unfriendliness."[49] Fifty-six per cent of the respondents said that their white classmates called them derogatory names such as "nigger," "darkie," and "coon."[50] Behavior of whites toward the respondents was by no means uniform, as 36 per cent of the respondents said that the reactions of whites varied, ranging from friendly to hostile. Seventy-four per cent of the black students interviewed reported that at least some whites acted in a friendly way; in a substantial number of the cases, however, these budding relations seemed to generate more negative responses from white peers: other whites sometimes harassed the white students who were friendly to blacks.[51]

Later in the year, a majority of the black students enrolled in the previously all white schools reported that white students were acting differently toward them than at the beginning. Just over half of the changes were in a positive direction—less fighting, rejection, and isolation. However, of those students reporting change over the year—52 per cent of all such students—only half of these changes were in a positive direction meaning that only one-fourth the total population experienced positive changes. The majority of the students reported contact with whites outside the class, and 75 per cent felt that they had some friends among their white peers.

2. *Improving Black Achievement Through Peer Acceptance*

Interracial relations have not only been of interest because of the value placed on social integration, but they also have been a key link in the argument that integrated schools will improve the achievement levels of black students through their acceptance by high achieving white peers. In an early, highly influential review of evidence as to the effects of desegregation,[52] Katz argued that friendliness on the part of the white majority group might be helpful to incoming black students in two ways: (1) acceptance by the dominant racial group in the classroom might reduce social threat and raise self-confidence, and (2) acceptance by achievement-oriented peers might increase their influence as role models and lead to adoption of their norms.[53]

This reasoning leads to the proposition that academic success of minority

49. *Id.*

50. *Id.*

51. *Id.*

52. Katz, *Review of Evidence Relating to Effects of Desegregation on the Intellectual Performance of Negroes*, 19 AM. PSYCHOLOGIST 381 (1964).

53. *Id.*, at 382-83.

group students in interracial classrooms may be contingent upon their acceptance into the majority group peer structure.[54] A reanalysis of the 1966 *Coleman Report*'s cross-sectional data showed that interracial friendship was a predictor of black achievement only when classrooms were at least half white.[55] The evidence that acceptance is necessary in order for desegregation to have a positive effect on black achievement is slight. Often cited in discussions of this topic is a study which found that peer status is related to achievement in generally all-white classrooms. One can not be sure, however, whether achievement caused popularity or if popularity caused achievement.[56]

In an effort to disentangle the issues of cause and effect, and to determine how black students' achievement is affected by their popularity among white students, an analysis of a sample of racially integrated Boston elementary classrooms was undertaken. The effects of early academic achievement, early school racial composition, and family socioeconomic status were also taken into account. The results indicated that popularity with whites does contribute to improved achievement levels of blacks.[57] Even in this study, however, the researchers cannot rule out the possibility that achievement affects popularity rather than popularity affecting achievement.[58]

If popularity is simply a byproduct of achievement in majority white classrooms, then many black children placed in middle class classrooms where they cannot compete for grades will not benefit by desegregation. Even more important, if the underlying reason for this correlation is the fact that majority white classrooms are achievement-oriented while some majority black classrooms are not because there are too many students who have no hope of success in a traditional, middle class curriculum, then one can argue that changing the curriculum in these all-black classrooms so as to encourage success will improve achievement levels, just as easily as one can argue that desegregation will improve achievement levels of blacks.

This argument concerning the importance of acceptance by white peers has assumptions underlying it which are similar to those expressed in the cultural deficit literature.[59]

> The cultural deficit literature is basically concerned with explaining why it seems that low-income minority groups have not acquired American middle-

---

54. *See* N. St. John & R. Lewis, Children's Interracial Friendships: An Exploration of the Contact Hypothesis, 1973 (unpublished manuscript at the University of Massachusetts).

55. *See* J. McPartland, The Segregated Student in Desegregated Schools: Sources of Influence on Negro Secondary Students (The Johns Hopkins University Center for the Study of Social Organization of Schools Report No. 21, 1968).

56. *See* Schmuck, *Some Relationship of Peer Liking Patterns in the Classroom to Pupil Attitudes and Achievement*, 71 The School Rev. 337 (1963).

57. *See* N. St. John & R. Lewis, *supra* note 54.

58. *See* St. John & Lewis, *Race and Social Structure of the Elementary Classroom* (to be published in Sociology of Educ. in 1975).

59. D. Kirk & S. Goon, Desegregation: An Examination of the Literature, 1972 (unpublished paper at School of Education, Stanford University).

class attitudes, values, and behaviors. The problem, according to that literature, is due to the lack of contact low-income minority group children have with American white middle class children, especially within the schools during their formative years. It is assumed that contact will alleviate the problem. . . . The discrepancy between what middle-class children received as part of their education and that received by low-income children in conjunction with their respective achievement levels seemed to clearly indicate to these authors that one could affect achievement levels by equalizing educational inputs. It is, therefore, assumed that educational inputs would be equalized when there is racial balance.

The failure to recognize the underlying assumption that blacks can only become achievement-oriented by close ties with whites is like the failure to recognize the fears that less educated white parents have concerning busing plans which will send their children back into lower class, black neighborhood schools.[60] The policy maker is unprepared for the deep resistance to desegregation expressed both by some blacks—particularly the younger intelligentsia and the adherents of Black Power ideology—and by less educated whites. Without explicit attention to the underlying value assumptions, reliance upon social science research evidence may have some unfortunate consequences.

3. *Conditions for Desired Interracial Behavior*

Some commentators have urged that schools be examined not so much in terms of racial composition, but in terms of the conditions necessary for "equal status contact."[61] It is argued that some desegregated schools are creating conditions far more closely approximating equal status contact than others and that certain conditions are essential before positive effects can be expected from intergroup contact: equal status, common goals, institutional supports, and a non-competitive atmosphere.[62]

Some integrated schools represent conditions in which, rather than being dissipated, racial stereotypes held by blacks and whites are actually reinforced. In some of these schools, black children's relative lack of academic success is interpreted as due to their inherent inferiority, while the white children's relative academic success is attributed to their superiority. Furthermore, in some of these schools, stereotypes of blacks as hostile and dangerous, and stereotypes of whites as untrustworthy and "always trying to put you down," are reinforced. Physical conflict is not the only consequence of such stereotypes; another con-

60. *See* S. RUBIN, BUSING AND BACKLASH (1972).

61. *See* Pettigrew, Useem, Normand & Smith, *supra* note 16.

62. *Id.* at 91. This argument is based on a much earlier study in which Allport set forth certain conditions for attaining "equal status contact." G. ALLPORT, *supra* note 15.

Some of the problems with Allport's theory are discussed in C. Riordan, The Conditions and Effects of Equal Status Contacts: A Critical Review, 1974 (unpublished paper at Providence College, Providence, R.I.). For example, does "equal status" mean that individuals must be of the same class if they are of different races? Must *all* of Allport's conditions be met before the desired results of intergroup contact are obtained, or is it sufficient if only some of them are met?

sequence can be the failure of black students to make a significant contribution to the interaction, and the tendency of whites to dominate the interaction.

One study provides some remarkable evidence to the effect that such white-dominated interaction can and does take place among interracial groups of children who have attended integrated schools.[63] This study used an experimental criterion of interracial behavior in examining the quality of interracial interaction among children who had experienced desegregation. Twelve four-person biracial groups of third grade boys who had participated in a voluntary desegregation plan were contrasted with twelve biracial groups who attended segregated elementary schools. The groups were given non-academic tasks to perform which demanded that the members work closely together. In both types of groups, whites were more likely to be active at the task than blacks. If anything, the whites who had experienced integration were more likely to dominate the blacks than were the whites who had attended segregated schools.

By contrast, other studies of schools in which interracial contact occurs suggest that favorable social learning does take place and black and white students learn to treat each other as individuals rather than as members of racial categories. Can these studies help to answer the question: what are the conditions under which the second of the two outcomes of interracial behavior will occur, instead of the first, in which racial stereotypes were reinforced?

The knowledge that a school has 20 per cent black students tells us nothing about the critical conditions in that organization favoring one type of social interaction over another. The school must be analyzed in its organizational context as an institution which strongly structures the nature of the contact between the races. Furthermore, the relationships of students of different races within the school must be examined in the context of interracial relationships in society outside the institution of education.

Several studies indicate that the school, as presently structured, does not present many opportunities for interracial interaction. Purely social groupings are likely to be racially segregated.[64] Social segregation of the races is found even in a school where the staff is interracial and there are strong staff commitments and efforts toward true integration.[65] The ordinary classroom does

63. J. Seidner, Effects of Integrated School Experience on Interaction in Small Bi-Racial Groups, 1971 (unpublished doctoral dissertation at the University of Southern California).

64. *See* J. Silverman & M. Shaw, Effects of Sudden Mass School Desegregation on Interracial Interaction and Attitudes in One Southern City, Apr. 1971 (paper presented at the Eastern Psychological Association Annual Meeting in New York, N.Y.); P. Cusick & R. Ayling, Racial Interaction in an Urban, Secondary School, Feb. 1973 (paper presented at American Educational Research Association in New Orleans, La.).

65. *See* M. Lachat, A Description and Comparison of the Attitudes of White High School Seniors Toward Black Americans in Three Suburban High Schools: An All White, a Desegregated, and an Integrated School, 1972 (unpublished doctoral dissertation at Teacher's College, Columbia University).

not utilize much student interaction; classrooms are typically teacher-dominated—especially in secondary schools. These are aspects of "life in classrooms" irrespective of the racial mixture of the class. However, one study has found a significant *decrease*—after a year of desegregation—of student talk, student-initiated talk, and student-to-student verbal interaction.[66] The study also showed an increase in drill and structured instruction after desegregation, suggesting that teachers respond to desegregation by instruction in more traditional and even more teacher-dominated ways, thereby providing even fewer opportunities for interracial interaction than might otherwise have been the case.

A recent study suggests that the differential in socioeconomic status between whites and blacks may be instrumental in preventing equal status interaction.[67] The researchers apply Allport's conditions for reducing prejudice to a sample of interracial classrooms, using an overall classroom measure of interracial acceptance as an indicator of racial prejudice. They state that the ideal classroom test of the contact theory would involve:[68]

> gathering of longitudinal data in order to compare the development of interracial acceptance among groups of children differentiated according to (1) duration of desegregation; (2) majority group/minority group ratio in the classroom; (3) equality of majority/minority group status in regard to family background and academic achievement; and (4) racial attitudes of the classroom teacher and his or her ability to show each pupil respect, attention, and expectation of success, and to stress cooperation in pursuit of common goals rather than competition in pursuit of scarce goals.

A cross-sectional design was used in this study although this was supplemented with early grade records and week-long observations in the classrooms. Thirty-four interracial classrooms in eighteen schools, drawn in a random stratified sample of racially mixed elementary schools, were studied. Utilizing multiple regression (correlational) techniques, the researchers attempted to determine the extent to which each of the following factors contributes to children's interracial friendliness: the degree to which the child's previous schooling was desegregated, present classroom racial composition, the difference between whites and blacks in social class level, the achievement differential between races, and the teacher's behavioral style. Whether or not a child's previous schooling was desegregated and the present classroom racial composition were found not to be important predictors of interracial friendliness once the other factors were held constant. On the other hand, the smaller the white/black differential in class, the greater was the interracial

---

66. W. Coats, A Longitudinal Survey of Desegregation in Kalamazoo, Michigan, Sept. 7, 1972 (paper presented at the American Psychological Association Annual Convention, Honolulu, Hawaii).
67. N. St. John & R. Lewis, *supra* note 54.
68. *Id.* at 80.

friendliness. This factor was the most powerful predictor in the study. It should be noted, however, that it is difficult, if not impossible, to disentangle this class differential from the achievement differential between blacks and whites.[69] In a classroom where there is no great differential among students in socioeconomic status, there is likely to be only a small achievement differential.

In a subsequent analysis of the same data,[70] it was found that, on an individual level, high academic performance contributed significantly to popularity of white and black children among children of both races.

It appears that the organizational context of the school also may have important effects on the quality of interracial relations. A study of attitudes of white high school seniors toward black Americans was undertaken in three suburban high schools.[71] One school was an all-white high school while the other two were racially mixed. The purpose of the study was to distinguish between an integrated setting which seeks to facilitate positive interaction of a racially mixed student body and a desegregated setting not characterized by such practices. In the "integrated" high school, 71 per cent of the white seniors had favorable attitudes toward blacks, while only 37 per cent of the white seniors at the "desegregated" high school had favorable attitudes toward blacks. The all-white school was intermediate in favorability. These two contrasting schools were similar in terms of ethnic groups and socioeconomic levels. The integrated school had a racially balanced staff, a conscious staff commitment to deal with problems of integration, and utilized heterogeneous grouping procedures. The social studies and English departments instituted courses and units relating to the black experience. Teachers expressed a desire to provide classroom encounters that would erase stereotypes and myths. By contrast, the desegregated school had none of these features. The hypothesis to be drawn from this study is that mere desegregation is a necessary but not a sufficient condition for attaining desired goals concerning interracial attitudes and behavior.

An observational study of the social adjustment of both black and white newcomers to a school concluded that more important than the race of the student or his socioeconomic status in determining adjustment and assimilation in the new school was the particular educational environment of the school and the leadership of the principal.[72] Another observational study of an urban high school that had a history of racial discord came to the conclusion that rigid structuring of interaction in the school, designed to prevent further hostility, also had the unwitting function of perpetuating the social distance between the races.[73]

---

69. *Id.*
70. St. John & Lewis, *supra* note 58.
71. M. Lachat, *supra* note 65.
72. C. Willie & J. Beker, Race Mixing in the Public Schools (1973).
73. P. Cusick & R. Ayling, *supra* note 64.

IV

THE UTILITY OF APPLIED RESEARCH WITH A THEORETICAL BASE

This article has examined social science research which began with the existence of desegregation or racial mixing in schools as a starting point and which then tried to disentangle its "effects." In the process of reviewing this research literature, those studies that hypothesize a concept which will explain why desegregation should have different consequences under different sets of conditions have been highlighted. These explanatory theories, although helpful, are not sufficiently developed so that any degree of certainty can be attributed to the cause-effect propositions put forth.

A completely different research strategy has been developed, however, which may prove better at identifying the essential conditions for the desired results of the desegregation process. Thus there is a series of studies which begins with a phenomenon and identifies this phenomenon as an instance of reasonably well-developed sociological theory and moves from laboratory studies to field studies.

A. Interracial Interaction Disability

Since 1968, I have been working with the problem of producing equal status behavior in interracial groups of students working together on tasks. The source of the problem—a phenomenon termed "interracial interaction disability"—was identified in the initial study.[74] White and black male junior high school students were brought together in four-person groups to play a game requiring them to make decisions as a team. A pattern of white domination was observable despite the fact that the players had no basis for expecting special competence in the game from previous knowledge of the task, from knowledge of each other, or from perceived relevance of the task to school performance.

This pattern of white dominance was identified as a consequence of expectations of greater competence for higher status group members; expectations held by both black and white students. These initial expectations were activated by the differential in racial status, resulting in observably different rates of contribution to the task, and ultimately, in differential rates of influence, with the prestige and peer ranking of the groups replicating the status ranking or order of society at large. It is important to note that these children were matched in every respect except race—socioeconomic status, height, attitude toward school—and yet stereotypical expectations were fulfilled and reinforced.

In a study of college students, this same pattern of white dominance in interracial groups was found.[75] The black college students being studied dis-

---

74. Cohen, *Interracial Interaction Disability*, 25 HUMAN RELATIONS 9 (1972).
75. Katz & Benjamin, *Effects of White Authoritarianism in Biracial Work Groups*, 61 J. ABNORMAL &

played marked social inhibition and subordination to their white partners in a cooperative problem-solving situation. Even when subjects were matched as to intelligence and were made to display equal ability on certain group tasks, blacks ranked whites higher on intellectual performance.

My own study was based on the theory of status characteristics and expectation states.[76] Expectations stemming from status characteristics are part of our culture: it is generally believed that men are more competent than women, that adults are more competent than children, and that whites are more competent than blacks. These beliefs may be consciously or unconsciously held, but given certain conditions, they can infect new situations so that the prestige and power order in the new situation resembles the status order in the larger society.

From my initial study of interracial interaction disability, the inference may be drawn that even though blacks and whites might be brought together in a desegregated school in an "equal status" manner, it is still quite possible for the racial difference to act as a strong status differential triggering expectations for whites to do better in a new situation and for blacks to do less well. If this occurs in the school situation, then the racial stereotypes which contribute to these expectations are only reinforced and confirmed by the interracial interaction in the desegregated school.[77] It should be a matter of great concern if the process of desegregation actually does result in reinforcing such stereotypes of racial incompetence.

It is important to note that these expectations are not necessarily consciously held by the participants. It is quite possible for a white person to express racial tolerance in response to an appropriate questionnaire or racial attitude survey, and still hold unconscious racist expectations. This ideologically tolerant individual can behave dominantly and insensitively in the interracial setting. Also, it is important to note that the origin of the problem lies in the beliefs and expectations of *both* blacks and whites. It is not a problem of "lack of assertiveness" of blacks alone, to be treated by compensatory education. Nor is it a problem of bigotry and miseducation of whites alone, to be treated with a seminar in black history or other intellectual multicultural methods.

B. Expectation Training

Having identified the problem as an instance of what is called a "diffuse status characteristic," an application of the theory could produce truly equal status behavior. When a group behaves in an "equal status" manner, one cannot tell from a person's color the amount of influence he will exert on the

---

SOCIAL PSYCHOLOGY 448 (1960); Katz, Goldston, & Benjamin, *Behavior and Productivity in Biracial Work Groups*, 11 HUMAN RELATIONS 123 (1958).

76. *See* Cohen, *supra* note 74. The general theory was developed earlier in Berger, Cohen, & Zelditch, *Status Characteristics and Expectation States*, in SOCIOLOGICAL THEORIES IN PROGRESS 29 (J. Berger ed. 1966).

77. *See* J. Seidner, *supra* note 63.

particular experimental task assigned to the group. "Expectation training" was designed to treat those initial expectations with which blacks and whites enter a new situation.

The black children involved in the experiment came to the laboratory earlier than the white children. They were taught how to build a two-transistor radio and how to teach its construction to someone else. Then the white children were brought in and the interracial groups were shown a videotape of their prospective young black teachers assembling the radio set and explaining its operation. Each black child then taught a white child how to build the radio. Following this experience, a four-person, interracial group was assembled and instructed in the decision-making game used in previous studies. Those groups which were treated with "expectation training," did not show the pattern of white dominance characteristic of untreated groups.[78] Equally important in this experiment was a situation in which the black students were taught how to build the radio, but then taught a black administrator instead of a white peer. These black students received just as much success experience and reinforcement as those who taught white students, but in this part of the experiment, the expectations of the white students went totally untreated. They were brought in just before instructions for the decision-making game were presented. The result was white dominance as much as in the case of wholly untreated groups. This suggests that the problem can not be resolved only by treating expectations of blacks; *the whites must be treated as well.*

In Oakland, during the summer of 1972, I operated the Center for Interracial Cooperation in a junior high school that had been experiencing severe problems of interracial friction.[79] Two contrasting treatments were used to produce equal status interracial behavior. One was a version of "expectation training," with black students trained to teach white students in four different tasks. Instruction was conducted over five weekday mornings. The white students had a different black teacher for each of the four tasks. An alternative treatment involved the same tasks, but learning took place in small interracial groups under the supervision of an interracial teaching team. Teachers and teacher aides on this team saw to it that each child was successful in learning the four tasks and that the classroom was totally non-competitive.

Following these two treatments, we held four weeks of classes in which the children, still separated by the treatment they had experienced, were assigned to sex-segregated interracial classrooms under the supervision of interracial teaching teams. Here they studied a curriculum which did not demand reading and writing, although the tasks were of an intellectual and creative character. Students carried out their instructional tasks in small interracial groups; each

---

78. *See* Cohen & Roper, *Modification of Interracial Interaction Disability: An Application of Status Characteristic Theory*, 37 AM. SOCIOLOGICAL REV. 643 (1973).

79. *See* Cohen, Katz, & Lohman, *Center for Interracial Cooperation: A Field Experiment* (to be published in SOCIOLOGY OF ED. in 1975).

group, rather than the individual, was responsible and accountable for the group product. Even though there was a sharp social class and achievement differential between middle class whites and inner-city blacks in this study group, both races participated actively.

The experimental design provided for evaluation of "intergroup relations" immediately after the initial treatment and once again at the end of six weeks. Equal status behavior was maintained successfully throughout the summer school session both for students who had experienced "expectation training" and for those who had experienced the alternative treatment.

C. Application to the Integrated School

To apply this laboratory work on "equal status experience" to groups of children separated by a wide social gulf, in a school setting where there is competition for scarce rewards and where there are typically large achievement differentials in conventional academic skills, will be extremely difficult. First, even if the children were all of the same race but entered schools with differential skills and aptitudes for the conventional curriculum, a status order based on classroom achievement would emerge which would be just as effective in triggering self-fulfilling prophecies as race. In other words, the achievement status which emerges in competitively structured classrooms is capable of infecting new situations so that those who have low achievement status will expect to do less well on any new task when combined with those students who have a higher achievement status in the classroom. A study of junior high school students revealed that the status ranking in a classroom based on perceived academic ability was capable of affecting interaction and influence on a new group task with no intellectual or academic components.[80] There is also evidence that competition aggravates the effect of diffuse status characteristics such as age or race.[81]

There are several other factors which make the desegregated school a very difficult place in which to produce equal status interaction. Of prime importance is the nature of the conventional curriculum. At the junior high school level, almost every subject requires the student to exhibit reading, writing, or computational skills in order to achieve satisfactory grades. Thus, if students enter a desegregated situation with a lower level of skills, they will be perceived as having little academic ability in almost every class they attend, even where there is no tracking or ability grouping. Analysis of the curriculum content reveals that aside from the overlap from subject to subject of required skills,

---

80. D. Hoffman & E. Cohen, An Exploratory Study to Determine the Effects of Generalized Academic Performance Expectations Upon the Activity and Influence of Students Engaged in a Group Simulation Game, 1972 (paper presented at the American Educational Research Association in Chicago, Ill.).

81. *See* B. Awang Had, Effects of Status and Task Outcome Structures Upon Observable Power and Prestige Order of Small Task-Oriented Groups, 1972 (unpublished doctoral dissertation at Stanford University).

only a very narrow range of mental abilities is dealt with in our public schools—there is a strong emphasis on convergent right-answer thinking and recitation in standard English. Furthermore, from kindergarten through high school, curricula are geared to the socialization practices of the middle class.[82] Another factor which may be of vital importance is the presence of interracial classroom teams of teachers and a school administrative structure which is carefully balanced between black and white throughout its ranks.

The findings from these "equal status" experiments accomplish the following:

1. They suggest why desegregation has not been uniformly accompanied by interracial cooperation and improved black achievement.
2. They explain why, even when the conditions postulated by Allport as necessary for equal status contact exist,[83] one can still anticipate the effects of racism in American society inside the desegregated school.
3. They suggest that expensive and radical changes in the social structure of the school and its curriculum content may be necessary.
4. They provide a way to analyze particular integrated school situations as to the conditions that trigger self-fulfilling prophecies.
5. They provide a rigorous behavioral method of measuring whether interracial behavior at a given interracial school is of the "equal status" variety.
6. They specify the situations to which experimental results are generalizable.

V

INTERRACIAL ATTITUDES AND BEHAVIOR: SOME USEFUL QUESTIONS

This review of the available social science research on the psychosocial effects of desegregation has shown the inutility of such research as support for limiting or expanding the nature of the remedy sought in school desegregation litigation or for a particular desegregation plan. For every study showing certain effects, another study reaching opposite results can be cited. This review of the available social science research literature has revealed that the findings are of such a mixed character that any attempt to use this evidence on the psychosocial effects of desegregation in a court could easily be contradicted by citing another study with opposite results. Furthermore, many of the studies are only of tangential interest to the courts.

I have tried to go beneath these generalizations to determine reasons for this state of affairs. One problem I have discussed is the failure to disentangle value questions from empirical questions. Thus one of the principal difficulties in resorting to studies of the sort reviewed in this article, in those areas where

82. E. Cohen, An Experimental Approach to School Effects, Feb. 1, 1974 (paper presented at the Western Sociology of Education Association in Monterey, Cal.).

83. *See* G. ALLPORT, *supra* note 15.

there will be legal consequences, lies in this failure to separate issues involving value judgments from empirical questions. Many of the implicit value goals of researchers are not relevant to the issues before the courts—for example, the interest of social scientists in the reduction of white prejudice as a goal of integration.

A second problem with the research reviewed here lies in its lack of any theoretical explanation of why desegregation should have any effect, positive or negative, on interracial attitude and behavior. In a scientific sense, the studies reviewed have given very little thought to what kind of a phenomenon desegregation represents; widely differing social settings and contexts are selected for study of the "effects" of desegregation. Equally important is the lack of systematic attention, in the studies reviewed, to the process inside desegregated schools which will lead to attitude change or to desirable or undesirable interracial behavior.

Studies which have looked at outcome variables on a school-by-school basis strongly suggest that different schools under the same desegregation plans may result in very different states of interracial attitudes and behavior among students. In some cases, desegregation may result in self-fulfilling prophecies whereby the pattern of white dominance in society at large is clearly reflected within the schools. In other schools, staff commitment, principal leadership, and deliberate planning for interracial understanding appear to be associated with more favorable outcomes. Certainly, the studies suggest that the conventional school structure does not present many opportunities for interracial interaction. If it is true that there are critical pre-conditions for desegregated schools to achieve favorable interracial behavior, and if the studies of desegregation have no theory by which they can classify schools into those in which the essential conditions are met and those where they are not, the research to date is not likely even to become cumulative as to the effects of desegregation. Furthermore, until there is some idea of the process which accounts for the effect of the antecedent events on the resulting consequences, there is no way to tell which variables it is essential to control. It is always possible to argue that control of another variable would have changed the results. Finally, until a theory is developed sufficiently so that suitable indicators of particular concepts may be inferred, there is no way to decide whether a particular measure is appropriate. In other words, no matter how large the sample, no matter how many statistical controls are employed, and no matter how elaborate the statistical analysis, information about the "effects of desegregation" cannot be obtained with any reasonable level of certainty.

In sum, questions as to the effects of desegregation are essentially unanswerable with the tools of social science. By contrast, some more useful and answerable questions have been posed in this article. Local decision-making studies which contrast the current state of interracial relations in each school experiencing court-ordered desegregation can be useful. Studies of the fears and conflicts in the wake of an order to desegregate can produce the information necessary to make wise decisions as to those schools which will need support, pressure, and attention.

The other type of answerable question advocated here is a question as to the types of conditions under which it is more likely that a valued outcome can be achieved. If the question is phrased in this fashion, there are some outcomes such as equal status behavior between blacks and whites which might be desirable outcomes from desegregation orders and plans.

Applied research, such as that described in this article, would also enable one to determine to what extent integrated schools have approximated the model of those conditions which lead to equal status interaction. It would even permit interracial interaction to be measured in the relatively narrow and specific sense of whether or not there is a pattern of white dominance. If such a measure were utilized, it would undoubtedly reveal that very few programs are producing equal status behavior.[84]

In conclusion, the understanding gained from more theoretically oriented social science research could indirectly become influential upon the law. At the very least, it would become clear that schools, as they are presently constituted, are severely limited in bringing about desired social change. Perhaps courts and other decision makers would come to realize that trying to change the status order of an entire society by a superficial change in the racial composition of an organization which traditionally has reflected faithfully the power and status order in society at large is not an easy thing to do either politically or practically. There is no easy solution to the social integration of children in a society exhibiting segregation throughout its institutions. Yet if the society is willing to make the commitment to particular value goals, there is nothing in this research that says that schools cannot alter in such a way as to become more supportive of desired social change.

---

84. A possible exception might be that desegregated school in which militant race consciousness on the part of blacks would cause them to resist any white influence. It has been shown that this ideological state among blacks is associated with a weakening of the expectations for incompetence held by blacks. R. Newby, The Effect of Racial Consciousness of Black Youth on White Influence in Small Groups, 1974 (unpublished doctoral dissertation at Stanford University).

THE IMPACT OF SCHOOL DESGREGATION ON ASPIRATIONS, SELF-CONCEPTS AND OTHER ASPECTS OF PERSONALITY

Edgar G. Epps*

Introduction

The traditional measure of desegregation—the percentage of blacks in majority-white schools—reduces efforts to assess the effectiveness of desegregation to little more than a body count rather than an examination of the quality of education available to children in the schools. The focus of this article is on the impact of desegregation on certain aspects of personality generally considered to be important outcomes of schooling: aspirations, self-concept, sense of control over the environment, and achievement orientation.

I

Aspirations

Most studies of student occupational and educational aspirations undertaken over the past twenty years have indicated that black students have aspirations equal to or higher than those of white students of similar socioeconomic status.[1] Black students are also somewhat more likely than white students of similar socioeconomic background to want to attend college and they are about equally as likely to expect to attend college as white students of the same class. White students, however, are more likely to have actually submitted college applications and made other concrete preparations for attending college than black students.[2]

What impact has desegregation had on these occupational and educational aspirations? There is little solid research in this area upon which one can rely for an assessment of the impact of desegregation and the results of the studies which do exist are mixed. For example, a study was undertaken in Ann Arbor, Michigan during the first year in which the school system was desegregated. The findings revealed an increase (albeit slight) in black student aspirations.[3]

---

* Marshall Field IV Professor of Urban Education, University of Chicago.

1. M. Rosenberg & R. Simmons, Black and White Self-Esteem: The Urban School Child 107 (1972). When students are asked about the aspirations their parents have for them, the results are quite similar. C. Gordon, Looking Ahead: Self-Conceptions, Race and Family as Determinants of Adolescent Orientation to Achievement 37 (1972).

2. *See* M. Rosenberg & R. Simmons, *supra* note 1.

3. *See* P. Carrigan, School Desegregation via Compulsory Pupil Transfer: Early Effects on Elementary School Children, Final Report (1969).

On the other hand, a recent study of black college freshmen found that those students who attended traditionally black colleges were more likely to aspire to a master's or doctorate degree but less likely to aspire to a degree in one of the professions than their counterparts attending predominantly white institutions.[4] Finally, a study of the METCO experiment in Boston—a voluntary program in which a number of black students from the inner city were bused to predominantly white suburban schools—showed no significant differences in occupational aspirations between those black students participating in the busing program and their siblings who remained in predominantly black schools in the inner city.[5]

In terms of educational attainment, however, a higher proportion of the black students who participated in the METCO program—77 per cent—enrolled in four-year colleges after completing high school[6] than did the control group, and the rate of those remaining in college was slightly higher than the national average.[7]

Similarly, another study found that black students attending northern schools which had been desegregated were less likely to drop out of high school and more likely to enter college than black students attending segregated schools.[8] One must interpret these results cautiously, however. The study also found that those blacks who attended desegregated schools had a higher socioeconomic status than those blacks attending the segregated institutions.[9] It is less evident in other studies, but it can safely be inferred that some parental or student motivational or socioeconomic selection process was involved.

Another aspect of the educational and occupational aspirations—as contrasted with actual years of schooling or high status jobs attained—is raised by the drop-out or "push-out" phenomenon disproportionately experienced by poor and minority students.[10] Even if black students' aspirations are not

---

4. Bayer, *The New Student in Black Colleges,* 81 SCHOOL REV. 415 (1973).

5. Armor, *The Evidence on Busing*, 28 PUB. INTEREST 90, 101 & fig. 5 (Summer 1972). *See also* Pettigrew, Useem, Normand & Smith, *Busing: A Review of "The Evidence,"* 30 PUB. INTEREST 88, 107-08 (Winter 1973).

6. Pettigrew, Useem, Normand & Smith, *supra* note 5, at 110-11. *See also* Armor, *supra* note 5, at 105-06.

7. Pettigrew, Useem, Normand & Smith, *supra* note 5, at 110-11. *But see* Armor, *supra note* 5, at 105, noting that the college drop-out rate of the bused blacks was substantially higher than that of the control group, so that by the end of the sophomore year the percentage of bused blacks still in college was almost the same as that of the control group.

8. *See* 3 J. BACHMAN, YOUTH IN TRANSITION 37-40 (1971). Black adults who had attended school with whites from elementary school through high school attained a greater number of years of schooling than those who had attended only segregated schools or who had been segregated in the elementary grades. Crain, *School Integration and the Academic Achievement of Negroes,* 44 SOCIOLOGY OF ED. 1 (1971).

9. 2 J. BACHMAN, YOUTH IN TRANSITION 40 (1970).

10. Several studies have documented this phenomenon, the most recent and most comprehensive one being CHILDREN'S DEFENSE FUND OF THE WASHINGTON RESEARCH PROJECT, INC.,

dampened by their treatment in desegregated schools, if the effect of desegregation is to reduce the proportions of black students who complete high school, then the net impact of desegregation could be a loss in occupational and educational attainments for blacks. Another barrier to eventual higher occupational and educational attainments faced by minority students is introduced by the use of tracking in the newly desegregated systems. While black student aspirations may remain high in desegregated situations, their chances of fulfilling these aspirations are considerably reduced if they are systematically placed in vocational or general tracks on the basis of culturally biased tests.[11]

No study of black student aspirations has shown that they are substantially lowered by introducing these students into a desegregating system. It seems clear, however, that those systems which desegregate only to resegregate through the use of such devices as tracking[12] or selective use of suspensions and expulsions, will at least diminish the *opportunities* of minority students for higher occupational and educational attainment.

CHILDREN OUT OF SCHOOL IN AMERICA (1974). *See also Hearings on Equal Educational Opportunity Before the Select Senate Comm. on Equal Educational Opportunity*, 91st Cong., 2d Sess., pt. 3-B, at 1311 (1970).

Hawkins v. Coleman, 376 F. Supp. 1330 (N.D. Tex. 1974), a recent case involving the Dallas, Tex. school system, found that black students were systematically suspended more frequently, endured longer suspensions, and were subjected to corporal punishment more often than white students—especially in schools where whites were a majority. *Id.* at 1333-35.

11. *See* Mercer, *I.Q.: The Lethal Label*, 6 PSYCHOLOGY TODAY 44 (Sept. 1972). In dealing with the use of tracking by the District of Columbia school system, which assigned students to a particular track on the basis of standardized achievement test scores, Judge Wright noted that the tests used were biased against black and poor students:

> When standard aptitude tests are given to low income Negro children, or disadvantaged children, the tests are less precise and less accurate—so much so that test scores become practically meaningless. Because of the impoverished circumstances that characterize the disadvantaged child, it is virtually impossible to tell whether the test score reflects lack of ability—or simply lack of opportunity. Moreover, the probability that test scores of the Negro child or the disadvantaged child will be depressed because of somewhat unique psychological influences, further compounds the risk of inaccuracy.

Hobson v. Hansen, 269 F. Supp. 401, 485 (D.D.C. 1967), *aff'd sub nom.* Smuck v. Hobson, 408 F.2d 175 (D.C. Cir. 1969).

In *Hobson*, Judge Wright comments on the rigidity of such a system—referring to the four-track system as a "four-rut system," 269 F. Supp. at 464—and its effect on future occupational and educational attainments:

> [T]he limits on [a lower track student's] academic progress, and ultimately the kind of life work he can hope to attain after graduation, are set by the orientation of the lower curricula. Thus those in the lower tracks are, for the most part, molded for various levels of vocational assignments; those in the upper tracks on the other hand, are given the opportunity to prepare for the higher ranking jobs and, most significantly, for college.

269 F. Supp. at 512.

12. *See, e.g.*, Moses v. Washington Parish School Bd., 456 F.2d 1285 (5th Cir.), *cert. denied*, 409 U.S. 1013 (1972); Lemon v. Bossier Parish School Bd., 444 F.2d 1400 (5th Cir. 1971); United States v. Sunflower County School Bd., 430 F.2d 839 (5th Cir. 1970); United States v. Tunica County School Dist., 421 F.2d 1236 (5th Cir.), *cert. denied*, 398 U.S. 951 (1970).

II

SELF-CONCEPT

It is a widely held assumption that blacks, because of their low status in American society, are likely to exhibit low self-esteem[13] despite the fact that this is not supported by the majority of studies which compare black and white students on various measures of self-concept or self-esteem. The early work of Kenneth and Mamie Clark, in which they found that black children chose white dolls in preference to black dolls, was interpreted as indicating racial self-hatred and a low sense of self-worth.[14] The Clark doll study was an important foundation of one of the "psychological" studies footnoted in *Brown v. Board of Education*,[15] and hence undoubtedly has had a substantial impact on social scientists. Indeed, some social scientists refuse to believe the results of more recent studies and have exerted great effort to explain them away by suggesting that findings of "high self-esteem on the part of Negroes is a defense mechanism against discrimination."[16]

A. The Development of Self-Esteem

How does "self-esteem" develop? And why is it thought by social scientists to be so important? The way society responds to an individual depends upon the degree to which he exhibits the traits—ascribed or achieved—that are valued in that society. Every major social institution, therefore, directly affects the extent to which individuals and groups are held in high or low esteem. Individuals are said to evaluate themselves and others according to the societal value system. Membership in a subordinate class or racial group may result in negative evaluations when there are interactions with members of higher status groups. According to this view, societal institutions are designed to

13. *See* R. CRAIN & E. WEISMAN, DISCRIMINATION, PERSONALITY AND ACHIEVEMENT 71 (1972). Some social scientists have begun to question this assumption. *See, e.g.*, McCarthy & Yancey, *Uncle Tom and Mr. Charlie: Metaphysical Pathos in the Study of Racism and Personal Disorganization*, 76 AM. J. SOCIOLOGY 648 (1971).

14. Clark & Clark, *The Development of Consciousness of Self and the Emergence of Racial Identification in Negro Preschool Children*, 10 J. SOCIAL PSYCHOLOGY 591 (1939). More recent studies have questioned the application of these results to current situations. *See, e.g.*, Datcher, Savage, & Checkosky, *School Type, Grade, Sex and Race of Experimenter as Determinants of the Racial Preference and Awareness in Black and White Children*, 20 J. SOCIAL & BEHAVIORAL SCIENCES no. 1, at 41 (1974); Greenwald & Oppenheim, *Reported Magnitude of Self-Misidentification Among Negro Children—Artifact?* 8 J. PERSONALITY & SOCIAL PSYCHOLOGY 49 (1968).

15. 347 U.S. 483, 494 n.11, 495 (1954). Kenneth Clark, as Social Science Consultant to the legal staff of the NAACP, gave sworn testimony in *Brown* as to both the general findings of the 1939 doll study and his findings when the test was given to some of the black plaintiff children. He found that some of these children showed signs of the same psychological damage attributed in the prior study to the effects of racial segregation and discrimination. *See* Clark, *The Desegregation Cases: Criticism of the Social Scientists' Role*, 5 VILL. L. REV. 224, 229 (1959-60).

16. *See generally* E. MCDILL, E. MEYERS, & L. RIGSBY, SOURCES OF EDUCATIONAL CLIMATES IN HIGH SCHOOLS ch. 10, 16 (1966).

maintain established patterns of dominance and subordination between competing groups, by supporting and encouraging the norms of the dominant group and disparaging those of subordinate groups.[17]

> Fundamental to the idea of social identity . . . are the ascribed role and category designations conferred on the individual at birth, which typically remain with him throughout his lifetime. They may well be viewed as one set of major "structural locators" that serve to position the individual with regard to the major axes of differentiation in his society.[18]

These ascribed categories include sex, social status, racial or national heritage, and religious affiliation. Social judgments are made using an assumed societal norm (usually upper or middle class values) as a yardstick.

It is likely, however, that minority group children who grow up with minimal contacts with the dominant group do not internalize the dominant group's negative evaluations of them. In effect, the family and community mediate societal evaluations for the child. Status within the subordinate group may supersede societal status as a determinant of self-esteem in young children. Thus, for many children, the first personal contact with the negative evaluations of the dominant group may come only when they enter school.

It should not be assumed that disadvantaged or minority children will develop low self-esteem even after entering school, although the research on this aspect seems to be mixed. A study comparing the self-esteem of children attending elementary school in a disadvantaged neighborhood with those attending school in a middle class neighborhood found that "not only did the disadvantaged group indicate positive self-perceptions, it also had higher self-perceptions than the advantaged group."[19] Two other studies also indicate that there is little relationship between self-esteem and socioeconomic status.[20] By contrast, another study reported a significant positive relationship between self-esteem and socioeconomic status.[21]

It would appear that for young children, the relationship of social background to self-concept is in large part a function of the instruments used to measure self-esteem, the conditions under which they are administered, and the social comparisons perceived by the subjects.[22] Studies of self-concept,

---

17. "Every society or group has its standards of excellence, and it is within the framework of these particular standards that self-evaluation occurs." M. ROSENBERG, SOCIETY AND THE ADOLESCENT SELF-IMAGE 14 (1965).

18. Gordon, *Self Conceptions: Configurations of Content*, in THE SELF IN SOCIAL INTERACTION 115, 124 (C. Gordon & K. Gergen eds. 1968).

19. Soares & Soares, *Self-Perceptions of Culturally Disadvantaged Children*, 6 AM. ED. RESEARCH J. 31, 42 (1969).

20. M. ROSENBERG, *supra* note 17, at 40; S. COOPERSMITH, THE ANTECEDENTS OF SELF-ESTEEM 82-84 (1967).

21. Ziller, Hagey, Smith, & Long, *Self-Esteem: A Self-Social Construct*, 33 J. CONSULTING & CLINICAL PSYCHOLOGY 84 (1969).

22. *Cf.* Greenberg, *Comments on Self-Perceptions of Disadvantaged Children*, 7 AM. ED. RESEARCH J. 627 (1970); Long, *Critique of Soares & Soares' "Self-Perceptions of Culturally Disadvantaged*

therefore, should make explicit the social comparison referents. Minority group children will not always rate themselves the way they are rated by whites. Young children have their own groups to which they relate, and are probably not exposed to the negative evaluations of the dominant group.[23]

Achieved characteristics also have an impact on self-esteem. One commentator has explained the relationship between self-esteem and achievement as follows:[24]

> Self esteem concerns the amount of value an individual attributes to various facets of his person and may be said to be affected by the successes and failures he has experienced in satisfying central needs. It may be viewed as a function of the coincidence between an individual's aspirations and his achievement of these aspirations.

Some selectivity is clearly involved in the development of self-esteem. An individual will choose among various types of qualities or characteristics—valuing those characteristics at which he believes he is good and disregarding or undervaluing those characteristics or qualities at which he views himself as being poor.[25]

The maintenance of self-esteem is probably the most important aspect of cognitive balance. The development and maintenance of a general sense of competence is an esssential aspect of positive self-regard. Although the individual may choose from among a number of characteristics in his efforts to maintain self-esteem, not all of the choices or options are positively related to academic achievement. If one of the goals of education is to provide opportunities for each individual to enhance his or her self-esteem and to develop the feeling that he or she is a person worthy of esteem, such a program should provide all children with opportunities for successful acquisition of the skills needed for later educational and occupational attainments. If such opportunities are not provided, the individuals who are labeled as "failures" are likely to seek opportunities for self-enhancement outside the classroom.

One's self-esteem may be based upon such varied characteristics as athletic prowess, dress and physical appearance, attractiveness to the opposite sex, skill at verbal repartee, and skill at fighting, as well as academic achievement. The particular combination of attributes which comprise the basis of "high esteem" will vary from individual to individual. The variation, however, will be systematically related to the values held by others, *e.g.*, parents or friends. Thus, white middle class children are likely to have a larger component of

---

Children," 6 AM. ED. RESEARCH J. 710 (1969); Soares & Soares, *Critique of Soares and Soares' Self-Perceptions of Culturally Disadvantaged Children—A Reply*, 7 AM. ED. RESEARCH J. 631 (1970).

23. *See* Soares & Soares, *supra* note 22.

24. Cohen, *Some Implications of Self-Esteem for Social Influence*, in THE SELF IN SOCIAL INTERACTION 383 (C. Gordon & K. Gergen eds. 1968).

25. *See* Rosenberg, *Psychological Selectivity in Self-Esteem Formation*, in THE SELF IN SOCIAL INTERACTION 339 (C. Gordon & K. Gergen eds. 1968). *See also* R. BROWN, SOCIAL PSYCHOLOGY 651 (1965).

academic status as part of their overall self-esteem than black lower class children.[26] Conversely, black lower class youngsters are likely to place greater value on athletic ability or skill at fighting.

B. The Impact of Desegregation on Self-Concept

The finding that there is a much stronger relationship between school grades and self-esteem among white students than among blacks can be attributed to the fact that, to some extent, the two groups base self-esteem on different attributes. A successfully integrated school, therefore, might be able to resolve such value differences by making it possible for school values and community values to move closely together, thus increasing the value of academic status to minority lower class children. One should be cognizant of the fact that academic self-esteem is more strongly related to school achievement than total self-esteem,[27] when evaluating the impact of desegregation on self-concept. In other words, it is not enough to ask if desegregation has an impact on self-esteem; we must also ask what specific aspects of self-esteem are affected by desegregation, and under what conditions.

A major survey of adult blacks[28] attempted to determine the effects, if any, of attending "integrated" versus segregated schools, and found that blacks born and raised in the North scored higher in self-esteem than those born in the South. Indeed, their scores were equal to those of whites. Although this study found self-esteem not to be related to desegregation,[29] there may be a "self-selection" aspect affecting these results.

As in other areas, the results of research on the impact of desegregation on black self-esteem are mixed.[30] A study of Baltimore City[31] undertaken recently found that in junior high school, black students in predominantly black schools have slightly higher self-esteem than black children in predom-

26. One study has found a much stronger relationship between school grades and self-esteem among white students than among blacks. *See* M. Rosenberg & R. Simmons, *supra* note 1.

27. Epps, *Correlates of Academic Achievement Among Northern and Southern Urban Negro Students*, 25 J. Social Issues no. 3, at 55 (1969).

28. R. Crain & E. Weisman, *supra* note 13, at 74. This survey of 1,651 black men and women aged 21 to 45 living in metropolitan areas in the North, undertaken by the National Opinion Research Center for the U.S. Commission on Civil Rights, used a self-esteem scale which measures the degree to which an individual is willing to assert that he is better than other people.

29. R. Crain & E. Weisman, *supra* note 13, at 85.

30. Where self-concepts of Puerto Ricans and Mexican-Americans have been studied, the results also tend to be mixed. *See, e.g.*, Zirkel & Moses, *Self-Concept and Ethnic Group Membership Among Public School Students*, 8 Am. Ed. Research J. 253, 254 (1971); Anderson & Johnson, *Stability and Change Among Three Generations of Mexican-Americans: Factors Affecting Achievement*, 8 Am. Ed. Research J. 285, 301 (1971); Mercer, Coleman, & Harloe, *Racial/Ethnic Segregation and Desegregation in American Public Education*, in Uses of the Sociology of Education 311-12 (C. Gordon ed. 1974).

31. M. Rosenberg & R. Simmons, *supra* note 1. Interviews were administered to 2,625 randomly selected black and white students in grades three to twelve distributed among 26 schools. The number of elementary school students attending desegregated schools was too small for analysis. The self-esteem measure was a six-item Guttman scale. *See also* M. Rosenberg, Society and the Adolescent Self-Image 303-04 (1965).

inantly white schools. In senior high school, however, the students who remained in segregated schools had substantially higher self-esteem than those attending desegregated schools. The conclusion is that segregation *protects* self-esteem, while the impact of desegregation is to lower self-esteem. This result is in agreement with that reported in the *Coleman Report*,[32] which found that academic self-concept decreases among black students as the per cent of white students in the school increases.[33]

Other studies, however, report no observable differences between the self-esteem of segregated and non-segregated black students,[34] or they report that black students in desegregated schools have self-concepts equal to or higher than those of whites.[35] A study of self-perceptions among recently desegregated students in a small southern city revealed that "[t]here was no evidence that changes in self-perception of black students were any different from the changes in the self-perceptions of whites."[36] Subjects were tested in the fall and in the spring of the first year of desegregation on four aspects of self-image: sociability, independence, hostility, and achievement orientation. Although the extent of the overall change in self-perceptions was the same for both races, there were significant differences between blacks and whites on the four measures, the primary one being that blacks perceived themselves as being significantly more independent and hostile than did whites. Thus, this study concludes that it is not enough to study the question of positive or negative self-image resulting from the desegregation process; rather, the particular characteristics an individual attributes to himself must be examined.

In summarizing the research on self-esteem, several points seem clear. First, there is a body of consistent findings which strongly supports the conclusion that blacks have relatively high self-esteem when compared to whites. Second, the evidence on the impact of desegregation is inconsistent, but seems to warrant the conclusion that desegregation has no effect on black self-esteem, or lowers it only slightly. The majority of the findings suggest that there is little reason to believe that desegregation will do significant damage to black children's images of themselves.

Among the difficulties in this area—which may help explain the varying

---

32. J. COLEMAN, EQUALITY OF EDUCATIONAL OPPORTUNITY (1966).

33. *Id.* at 323-24. *See also* S. Weber, T. Cook, & D. Campbell, The Effect of School Integration on the Academic Self-Concept of Public School Students, 1971 (unpublished paper read at the Midwestern Psychological Association meeting, in Detroit, Mich.) (both black and white students who had been in predominantly black schools in Evanston, Ill. reported to have lower academic self-concept scores after two years in predominantly white schools).

34. *See, e.g.*, F. Aberdeen, Adjustment to Desegregation: A Description of Some Differences among Negro Elementary Pupils, 1969 (unpublished doctoral dissertation at University of Michigan); Knight, White, & Taff, *The Effect of School Desegregation, Sex of Student, and Socioeconomic Status on the Interpersonal Values of Southern Negro Students*, 41 J. NEGRO ED. 4 (1972); Zirkel & Moses, *supra* note 30, at 260.

35. *See, e.g.*, Mercer, Coleman, & Harloe, *supra* note 30.

36. Shaw, *The Self-Image of Black and White Pupils in an Integrated School*, 42 J. PERSONALITY 12, 21 (1974).

results which these studies reach—is the use of different measures of self-concept, the fact that students of different ages are being tested, and the fact that there are considerable differences in demographic characteristics. This frequently makes comparison of the results of various studies practically impossible. The development of greater consensus among researchers on the measurement of self-esteem would make the task of future reviewers less burdensome. A related issue for further research concerns the components or dimensions of self-esteem since there is reason to believe that blacks and whites emphasize different characteristics in their self-evaluations. Finally, the role that reference groups play in self-evaluation should be investigated: the impact of desegregation on self-esteem is probably mediated by the extent to which the child uses his parents, community, same-race peers, or whites as sources of input for developing his self-concept. It is quite probable that across class as well as racial lines, the significance of common general variables (*e.g.*, academic success, athletic ability, physical appearance, and ability to attain and maintain friends) will vary as contributors to the child's overall level of self-esteem. The significance of the three major sources for self-evaluation—the family, the school, and the peer group—also will vary in the extent to which they contribute to the child's overall level of self-esteem.[37]

III
Sense of Environmental Control

The development in the individual of a sense of control over his environment has been the subject of considerable research under such labels as powerlessness, alienation, anomie, personal efficacy, and internal versus external control of reinforcements. Although there are a number of different instruments used to measure an individual's sense of environmental control, they all seem to be concerned with the same general personality dimension: the individual's sense of being able to make things turn out the way he wants. This personality characteristic may be defined as the individual's generalized sense of competency or as the individual's tendency to expect success or failure to be directly related to his own efforts or actions, rather than to external factors over which he has no control.

A study of the relation of an individual's sense of control of the environment to the racial composition of his school was undertaken as part of the *Coleman Report*.[38] High internal control was found to be positively related to school achievement, with white students having higher scores than blacks, and middle class students higher than lower class students. Most importantly, blacks in desegregated schools had higher levels of internal control than blacks in segregated schools.

37. *See* B. Hare, Relationships of Social Background to Dimensions of Self-Concept, 1975 (unpublished doctoral dissertion, University of Chicago).

38. *See* J. Coleman, *supra* note 32, at 320-24.

A study reaching similar results[39] with regard to the relationship between the level of internal control in black children and desegregation, also examined the relationship of various combinations of self-esteem and internal control to achievement and desegregation. Students with a combination of high self-esteem and high internal control were characterized as "Achievers," while those with high self-esteem and low internal control were characterized as "Militants." Students with low self-esteem and high internal control were characterized as "Accepters" and those with both low self-esteem and internal control as "Drifters."[40] Since the study showed that the highest levels of both self-esteem and internal control occur in integrated situations, it would seem that the "Achievers" were more likely to have attended desegregated schools.

Another study has found that the internal control expectancies of disadvantaged preschool children in Head Start classes, when compared with those of middle class children enrolled in private preschools, were significantly lower.[41] But there was little difference in the internal control expectancies between black and white Head Start children. The study concludes that the relatively high external control expectancies of disadvantaged children, black or white, antedate their school experience. Thus, one important question for research in this area concerns the type of school program, teacher behavior, and so forth that will be most effective in enhancing the development of internal control expectancy. Preliminary research suggests that teacher characteristics do have an impact on sense of control of environment and other achievement-related measures.[42] "[C]hild-orientation or interpersonal competence in teachers contributes significantly to reading growth [in black sixth graders] and seems to lead to improved conduct and attendance and belief in teacher's approval. Fairness in teachers contributes to improved conduct and sense of environmental control, as well as to friendliness from white classmates."[43] There may also be some relationship between classroom friendliness of blacks and whites and enhancement of a sense of internal control, although this is not clear from the data. It is important to note, however, that the teacher characteristic

---

39. R. CRAIN & E. WEISMAN, *supra* note 13, at 15. The study actually interviewed adults who were asked to report on their school experiences.

40. R. CRAIN & E. WEISMAN, *supra* note 13, at 80-85. The Crain and Weisman study also indicates that elementary school desegregation, although it has little or no effect on high school performance, is an important predictor of the rate of black college enrollment. The authors of the study urge that this be viewed with caution however, because relationships may have changed as a result of societal changes following the major civil rights developments of the late sixties and early seventies. R. CRAIN & E. WEISMAN, *supra* note 13, at 156-58.

41. Stephens & Delys, *External Control Expectancies Among Disadvantaged Children at Pre-School Age*, 44 CHILD DEVELOPMENT 670 (1973).

42. St. John, *Thirty-Six Teachers: Their Characteristics and Outcomes for Black and White Pupils*, 8 AM. ED. RESEARCH J. 635 (1971).

43. *Id.* at 646.

which had the greatest impact on growth in reading achievement—task orientation or subject competence—was negatively related to the other variables.[44] This suggests that the relationship between improvement in internal control and in achievement scores may not be positive as has commonly been assumed. Indeed, it suggests that, in selecting programs or personnel, choices will have to be made between enhancing internal control and reading achievement.

IV
Other Achievement-Related Characteristics

A. School Anxiety

Anxiety or fear of failure is one characteristic that is thought to have an effect on school achievement. School anxiety or test anxiety is especially relevant in this context. If desegregation has a negative effect on the adjustment of black students to school, it may appear as increased school anxiety. However, this was not the case in a study of recently desegregated children in Ann Arbor, Michigan,[45] wherein the black transfer pupils showed no change, or a decrease, in school-related anxiety following the transfer, even though they scored below white students in the receiving schools. General anxiety, although high in the transfer group, also showed a decline from the pre-transfer level.

By contrast, in a study of recently desegregated elementary schools in four southern California school districts, both black and Mexican-American children manifested significantly higher levels of school anxiety than white children.[46] On a measure of "Status Anxiety"—a measure of students' response to competitive situations, such as being graded and being chosen for team captain or class officer—black children indicated significantly higher levels of anxiety than either the white or the Mexican-American students.[47] This study concludes that the impact that desegregation has upon anxiety appears to depend upon the educational environment provided by the school. This conclusion should be viewed with caution, however, since no comparisons were made with minority students in segregated schools. Thus it cannot be stated with any certainty whether the high anxiety levels of minority students are the result of desegregation or the reaction of these students to schools as institutions. In other words, it is possible that there is a mismatch between the cultural styles of minority students and schools that would result in high levels of anxiety even if they were in racially homogeneous schools.

---

44. *Id.*
45. P. Carrigan, *supra* note 3.
46. Mercer, Coleman, & Harloe, *supra* note 30, at 312. This study involved administering questionnaires to a sample that included 3,479 white children, 2,213 black children, and 1,222 Mexican-American third and sixth grade children. Ratings were also obtained from 972 teachers.
47. Mercer, Coleman, & Harloe, *supra* note 30, at 312-13.

B. Achievement Motivation

An attempt to measure achievement motivation directly revealed that achievement motivation significantly increased for black male students after one year in a desegregated elementary school while the achievement motivation of black females did not change appreciably.[48] It has been argued that the decrease in aspirations that sometimes accompanies desegregation should be viewed as a positive motivational outcome. This is based on the premise, derived from achievement motivation theory, that highly motivated students set realistic, attainable goals rather than lofty but unattainable goals. The reduction in aspiration is thus viewed as a move toward realism, and therefore, higher motivation is inferred. This line of reasoning puts minority students in a "Catch-22" situation: they are considered under-motivated if they have low aspirations, but they are also considered under-motivated if they have high aspirations. The problem with this theory is the possibility that teachers or counselors who have low expectations for minority students would be encouraged to take upon themselves the task of *imposing* realism upon minority students by such administrative devises as tracking.

C. Teacher Attitudes

Turning from student characteristics to the learning environment provided by the school, there is evidence that teachers perceive minority students differently than they perceive white students, that is, more negatively. A study of school desegregation in Goldsboro, North Carolina reported that the way students are treated by teachers is both related to the race and the sex of the students:[49]

(1) White males were by far the most skillful in taking advantage of teacher-interaction and black males were the least skillful of the four sex-race groups.
(2) All students engaged more in interaction with teachers in desegregated schools than in a segregated school. However, this difference may be accounted for by the greater incidence of open classrooms in the desegregated schools.
(3) The black male spends a greater proportion of his time in disciplinary encounters with the teacher than any other sex-race group. This differential was accentuated in segregated schools and was equally true of black teachers as well as white teachers.
(4) Black students were most likely to participate on a par with white students in open classrooms in desegregated schools where the teaching staff was balanced in leadership and competence between black and white teachers.

Other studies report this same phenomenon—that the school environment is less congenial to minority children than to whites. In a study of schools

48. Veroff & Peele, *Initial Effects of Desegregation on the Achievement Motivation of Negro Elementary School Children*, 25 J. SOCIAL ISSUES no. 3, at 71 (1969).

49. R. MAYER, C. KING, G. BORDEN-PATTERSON, & C. MCCULLOUGH, THE IMPACT OF SCHOOL DESEGREGATION IN A SOUTHERN CITY 108 (1974).

in California,[50] teachers rated white children higher on competence and sociability than either Mexican-American or black children. Black children were rated significantly lower than others on obedience, cooperativeness, patience, kindness and ease with which they could be disciplined. Teachers also had higher occupational and educational expectation for white children. The study concludes that the schools in the sample had not yet achieved an integrated educational environment in the affective domain—those processes involving feeling or emotion.[51]

V

Summary and Conclusions

Despite the fact that research results are conflicting in some areas and inadequate in others, a few generalizations can be drawn. First, low occupational and educational aspirations do not seem to be a major problem of black students. While it is not entirely clear whether desegregation depresses black students' aspirations, the aspiration level should not be the major concern. Rather, the major concern should be with attainment. The available evidence suggests that desegregation, where accompanied by congenial race relations and acceptance by white peers and teachers, may enhance educational attainment—but the evidence is far from conclusive. On the other hand, there is little convincing evidence that minority control of their own schools would produce both high aspirations and high attainment. Longitudinal studies of high-achieving minority schools might help resolve some of these questions.

In the area of self-esteem, similar conclusions seem justified. First, there is no reason to believe that blacks suffer from low self-esteem. In fact, it appears that blacks have higher over all self-esteem than whites. There are differences in the way blacks and whites evaluate themselves, which suggests that the components or dimensions of self-esteem are probably more important in the school context than overall self-esteem. Blacks appear to rely less on school achievement than whites in their self-evaluations, peer influences appearing to be more important. At any rate, programs aimed at increasing self-esteem would be misguided unless they focus on school-related or academic self-esteem. Even here, it is probable that the academic values held by classmates would determine whether or not changes in self-evaluation were accompanied by improved achievement. At best, all that can be said is that there is little evidence that desegregation seriously impairs black self-esteem; nor can it be said that desegregation, in itself, enhances self-esteem.

In other areas such as sense of control over one's environment, anxiety, and motivation, there is even less evidence and broad generalizations seem even less warranted. On the basis of the studies reviewed in this article, how-

---

50. Mercer, Coleman, & Harloe, *supra* note 30, at 313-14.
51. Mercer, Coleman, & Harloe, *supra* note 30, at 327.

ever, it does appear that the sense of internal control of black students is enhanced by attending desegregated schools, although it should be noted that these studies are based on cross-sectional data and may not be supported by longitudinal studies with both pre-test and post-test measures.[52] There are indications that enhancing internal control may not lead to improved academic achievement, although it seems more fruitful to look upon internal control as an independent but valuable outcome of schooling in its own right. Nor, on the basis of the studies reviewed, can it be determined with any degree of certainty what impact desegregation has on anxiety or motivation. All one can say is that the evidence seems to point in the negative direction for anxiety and in the positive direction for motivation.

Finally, there is considerable evidence that minority children are finding desegregated schools to be less congenial environments than do their white peers. There is insufficient evidence, however, to determine whether this is attributable to desegregation or whether minority students find segregated schools just as repressive.

My own conclusion is that the focus of future research should be on the learning environment and how it interacts with the characteristics of the individual child. Of necessity, then, small scale, in-depth, longitudinal studies are called for rather than national or even district-wide survey-type studies.

---

52. Cross-sectional studies are those based on data collected at one point in time. Relationships are static between people or groups or whatever it is that is being studied at that point in time. Longitudinal studies, on the other hand, include at least two sets of data gathered over a period of time. Usually they are changes in a particular characteristic or phenomenon over time that are studied.

HOW TO MAKE DESEGREGATION WORK: THE ADAPTATION OF SCHOOLS TO THEIR NEWLY-INTEGRATED STUDENT BODIES

GARY ORFIELD*

INTRODUCTION

After a full generation of effort, most southern school systems are now desegregated, and in a number of northern and western cities the desegregation process is now beginning. The experience has shown very clearly, however, that reassignment of students is only the first step in a long process of building integrated schools. If we really believe that the schools are our most important public institution and that race is our central social problem, the difficulty in bringing about effective integration should not be surprising.

Desegregation, to be termed successful, must have eliminated widely-held racial stereotypes, broadened the cultural values transmitted by the schools, and increased the access of minority children to quality educational programs—the conduit to preferred colleges and jobs. A social revolution of this scale requires extensive adaptations within the internal processes of the school. Since schools are usually stable—often rigid—institutions, these changes are difficult to accomplish. Whenever possible, the initial desegregation plan—whether court-ordered or voluntarily drawn up by school officials—should be designed to facilitate successful adaptation within the schools.

Some of the "second generation" desegregation problems, widely publicized, have generated responses from lawyers, the courts, and civil rights officials in the Department of Health, Education, and Welfare. HEW began to impose requirements for faculty desegregation in its 1966 school desegregation guidelines.[1] Many contemporary desegregation orders include provisions modeled on the *Singleton* case,[2] which required ratios of black to white teachers in every school in a school district to reflect the ratio of black to white teachers in the school district as a whole. There has been litigation dealing with the firing of black teachers following court orders to establish a unitary school system,[3]

---

* Research Associate, Brookings Institution. This work was made possible by the opportunity the author was given to visit desegregated urban schools across the country while serving as Scholar-in-Residence at the United States Commission on Civil Rights, 1972-73. Neither the Commission nor Brookings, of course, are responsible for the author's conclusions.

1. *See* U.S. OFFICE OF EDUCATION, DEP'T OF HEALTH, EDUCATION, & WELFARE, REVISED STATEMENT OF POLICIES FOR SCHOOL DESEGREGATION PLANS UNDER TITLE VI OF THE CIVIL RIGHTS ACT OF 1964 (1966).

2. *See* Singleton v. Jackson Municipal Separate School Dist., 419 F.2d 1211 (5th Cir.), *rev'd in part*, 396 U.S. 290 (1970).

3. *See* Moore v. Board of Educ., 448 F.2d 709 (8th Cir. 1971); North Carolina Teachers Ass'n v. Asheboro City Bd. of Educ., 393 F.2d 736 (4th Cir. 1968); Wall v. Stanly County Bd. of Educ., 378

the use of discriminatory teacher qualification examinations,[4] and other related issues. There has been litigation on the downgrading of minority administrators in desegregated school systems[5] and on attempts to curb the practice of "push-outs" of minority students by the use of discriminatory suspension and expulsion practices.[6] The assignment of disproportionate numbers of minority children to classes for the mentally retarded has been challenged[7] as has the assignment of minority children to segregated lower tracks.[8] Both the courts[9] and HEW[10] have shown increasing concern over the rights of non-English speaking children in desegregation plans, taking steps to provide opportunities for bilingual classes.

All of these issues are important, sometimes extremely important in a given school district, but they reflect an incomplete view of the desegregation process. They deal largely with the problem of who should be in a particular classroom or particular school at a given time, not with what goes on in the classroom. It is assumed that by controlling access, somehow the educational process will work out all right. Indeed, education often seems to be treated as a residual.

This essay is based on the premise that what goes on in the classroom and the nature of the educational leadership of the school are centrally important both to the success of desegregation and to the quality of education offered to all children in the system. Desegregation plans should take into account the educational changes necessary to make desegregation work. Otherwise, seem-

---

F.2d 275 (4th Cir. 1967), *rev'g* 259 F. Supp. 238 (C.D.N.C. 1966); Johnson v. Branch, 364 F.2d 177 (4th Cir. 1966).

4. *See* Baker v. Columbus Municipal Separate School Dist., 329 F. Supp. 706 (N.D. Miss. 1971), *aff'd*, 462 F.2d 1112 (5th Cir. 1972); Armstead v. Starkville Municipal Separate School Dist., 325 F. Supp. 560 (N.D. Miss. 1971), *aff'd*, 461 F.2d 276 (5th Cir. 1972).

5. *See* Singleton v. Jackson Separate School Dist., 419 F.2d 1211 (5th Cir.), *rev'd in part*, 396 U.S. 290 (1970).

6. *See* Hawkins v. Coleman, 376 F. Supp. 1330 (N.D. Tex. 1974). *Cf.* Mills v. Board of Educ., 348 F. Supp. 866 (D.D.C. 1972).

7. *See* Larry P. v. Riles, 343 F. Supp. 1306 (N.D. Cal. 1972); Arvizu v. Waco Independent School Dist., 373 F. Supp. 1264 (W.D. Tex. 1973), *rev'd in part on other grounds*, 495 F.2d 499 (5th Cir. 1974). Consent decrees have been entered in several other cases challenging educationally or linguistically biased testing procedures for placing students in mentally retarded classes. *See, e.g.*, Guadalupe Organization v. Tempe Elementary School Dist., CA 71-435 PHX (D. Ariz. Jan. 9, 1972); Diana v. California Bd. of Educ., C 7037 REP (N.D. Cal. June 18, 1971).

8. *See* Hobson v. Hansen, 269 F. Supp. 401 (D.D.C. 1967) (Wright, J., sitting as District Court Judge), *aff'd sub nom.* Smuck v. Hobson, 408 F.2d 175 (D.C. Cir. 1969); Moses v. Washington Parish School Bd., 330 F. Supp. 1340 (E.D. La. 1971), *aff'd*, 456 F.2d 1285 (5th Cir. 1972). *See also* Lemon v. Bossier Parish School Bd., 444 F.2d 1400 (5th Cir. 1971); United States v. Sunflower County School Dist., 430 F.2d 839 (1970).

9. *See, e.g.*, Arvizu v. Waco Independent School Dist., 373 F. Supp. 1264 (W.D. Tex. 1973), *rev'd in part*, 495 F.2d 499 (5th Cir. 1974); United States v. Texas, 342 F. Supp. 24 (E.D. Tex. 1971), *aff'd*, 466 F.2d 518 (5th Cir. 1972); Johnson v. San Francisco Unified School Dist., 339 F. Supp. 1315, 1322 (N.D. Cal. 1971), *vacated*, 500 F.2d 349 (9th Cir. 1974).

10. For example, note the HEW proposal in United States v. Texas Educ. Agency, 467 U.S. 848, 860-61 (5th Cir. 1972), and the HEW regulation requiring school systems to take remedial steps to rectify language deficiency problems. 35 Fed. Reg. 11595 (1970).

ingly sensible goals can lead to perverse results. Under a court-ordered desegregation plan which rigidly prohibits any sort of tracking or ability grouping, a Puerto Rican high school student from a segregated ghetto school which had provided him with an abysmal mathematical background suddenly could be transferred to a school where the standards had been set by children from a white middle-class and professional neighborhood. If the receiving school complied with the prohibition against tracking and did nothing else to change either teaching methods or grading systems, the minority child who had been transferred to such a school probably would be condemned to failure—in the name of equality. This simple example illustrates the need carefully to analyze the relationship between policies articulated in desegregation plans and the actual processes of education.

Strange as it may seem, social scientists have produced little systematic, carefully controlled research on educational processes within desegregated schools. Most of the existing desegregation research merely measures achievement scores at the beginning and end of the first year of desegregation.[11] And even this simple research effort is often done in a manner which, by aggregating all scores from a given school or a given grade level throughout a school system, obscures possible findings about ways the process facilitates or impedes effective integration.

Probably the best available data are contained in an evaluation of 555 southern schools that were among the last to desegregate and were studied in the early transitional phase of the process.[12] This study found dramatic differences among the schools in the ways in which the desegregation process was handled. There are also a number of interesting smaller studies, including those by participant/observers who spent substantial periods of time in a single school.[13] The analysis presented in this article draws both on these research findings and on interviews conducted by the author in twelve desegregated urban school districts in different parts of the country. Unfortunately, there is very little systematic research on a number of the issues discussed in this article; thus this analysis should be understood more as an effort to point out potentially significant relationships to those who must make decisions based on imperfect knowledge rather than as a presentation of well-established social science findings. At this time, social scientists can perhaps be most useful to litigators and courts by suggesting more accurate conceptualizations of desegregation as a complex long-term process of institutional change than by pretending to have firmly established optimal formulae for easy application.

---

11. *See* Orfield, *School Integration and Its Academic Critics*, 5 Civil Rights Digest 2 (Summer 1973); N. St. John, School Desegregation Outcomes for Children 16-43 (1975).

12. 1-2 National Opinion Research Center, Southern Schools: An Evaluation of the Effects of the Emergency School Assistance Program and of School Desegregation (1973) [hereinafter cited as Southern Schools].

13. See, e.g., studies referred to in notes 17, 28, 53, 54 *infra*.

On the basis of presently available evidence, the following general conclusions about the educational requirements for successful desegregation seem worthy of serious consideration in designing school desegregation plans:

(1) Successful desegregation requires basic adaptations in the teaching methods which prevail in most schools, but teachers find it very difficult to change well-established teaching approaches and expectations.

(2) Principals play a crucial role in the adjustment and adaptation of a school to its altered student body and community setting, both in providing educational leadership and in setting a social climate supporting desegregation.

(3) Desegregation often creates a readiness within schools to "integrate" the curriculum and these changes may well facilitate effective adaptation of the school. School systems, however, must provide for more than superficial training of staff in the development and use of new materials and teaching units. Furthermore, it is often incorrect to assume that minority teachers automatically are qualified to teach minority history or culture.

(4) Desegregation plans should be designed so that the educational programs needed by non-English speaking children are not disrupted; but there is no evidence at present to show that a bilingual program cannot be as effective or more effective in properly planned integrated bilingual schools.

(5) Successful desegregation is achieved most readily with children at the youngest age levels; children who begin their schooling in an integrated setting experience very few of the educational and social complications found among older children coming from previously segregated schools.

(6) The process of change and adaptation of the desegregated school usually takes place over several years; thus the typical approach—embodied in the federal desegregation assistance program[14]—of concentrating special resources in the period immediately before and after the desegregation process begins is probably far less helpful than continuing long-term support for a period of several years.

I

DESEGREGATION AS A CRISIS FOR TEACHERS

Public attention in any school desegregation crisis tends to focus on angry citizens or on the children who are bused to a new school. The public hysteria soon recedes, however, and the students usually adapt fairly rapidly to a new status quo. But the teacher often faces a deeper and more persistent crisis—the

14. Emergency School Aid Act, 20 U.S.C.A. §§ 1601-19 (1974).

professional crisis of realizing, consciously or subconsciously, that he or she doesn't know how to teach effectively children whose background is very different from that of the dominant group, or what had been the dominant group, in the school. Older teachers, who have long taught in middle class neighborhoods in schools which ignored the small numbers of children with serious learning problems, have a particularly traumatic adjustment.

Teachers in "good schools" with strongly motivated, high achieving, generally well-behaved, middle class children often have built their professional identity as good teachers around the successes of their students. In fact, these schools are often rigid, unimaginative institutions that do violence to students who cannot conform to school norms. The majority of these middle class students succeed because there is little the school could do to stop their success, given the enormous advantages they bring from their homes, reinforced through the interaction of the students among themselves. When these "good" teachers are confronted with large numbers of students who do not respond in the school's "typical" way, they must either blame the newcomers or recognize and acknowledge a very serious professional inadequacy. If they blame the students, the desegregation process is severely impaired. If they admit a need to modify their basic educational approach, then the desegregation crisis has presented a rare opportunity for institutional change. Desegregation plans should attempt to facilitate positive adaptations.

The desegregation transition is extremely difficult for such teachers. Although the problem is usually described as one of helping teachers come to terms with their personal prejudices, it often involves the more fundamental problem of helping experienced teachers learn a new way to teach. Many teachers feel severely inadequate. Principals report teachers crying in their offices during the first months, and school district curriculum consultants describe incessant appeals for advice about handling the new situation. The awareness that something is wrong is often widespread. In San Francisco, for example, a survey of teachers during the first year of desegregation found more than 60 per cent of the district's teachers agreeing that "our curriculum needs major revisions if it is to meet the needs of minority children in the integrated classroom."[15] Of those favoring change the largest number mentioned development of techniques to respond to the range of individual needs in the classroom.[16]

An intensive year-long study of three desegregated schools in a California city school district during its fourth year of desegregation underlined some of the difficulties of the adjustment process.[17] The change was particularly hard

---

15. San Francisco Unified School District, Evaluation of San Francisco Unified School District Desegregation/Integration, 1971-72, October 1972, at 164 (unpublished document available from school district offices).

16. *Id.*

17. M. Metz, Authority in the Junior High School: A Case Study, 1971 (unpublished doctoral dissertation, University of California at Berkeley).

on the older teachers in a formerly high status school, called Hamilton in the study, which had served a solidly middle class neighborhood with an exceptionally high average educational level. Neither the teachers nor the principal had had experience with minority children. A number of teachers had been in the school for years:[18]

> They stressed academic material above all else, and they expected punctuality, neatness, and deference to be displayed by the students as a matter of course. . . . These teachers were for the most part used to dealing with middle class children only. Many resented the influx of lower class children with fewer academic skills, less orderly behavior, and less acceptance of adults. The teachers, some of whom had come to Hamilton to get away from such children, often had few methods for coping with this kind of child and low motivation to set about acquiring such methods.

Some of the older teachers were hostile, feeling their "comfortable school invaded by strange children with no respect for their ideas of what a classroom should be like."[19] The major changes in this school came from a growing number of new faculty members who wished to teach in an integrated setting.

A survey of teachers conducted in two rural southern counties and one suburban county showed that the transition was particularly difficult for teachers who developed their teaching styles in white middle class schools. This is especially true of high school teachers, who were more likely to feel that their schools had not made a successful adaptation and that standards had been lowered.[20] One white teacher in four reported that teaching had become less enjoyable.[21] Teachers worried about cultural and communications differences, about how to deal with their own prejudices, and about finding ways to deal with diverse student needs. Forty per cent of the white high school teachers said they had lowered their standards, half of them saying they had modified grading practices to the point where they were "compromising their professional ethics."[22] Forty-four per cent of the white teachers said they would prefer teaching in a less-integrated school, and only about half the whites thought their schools had made adequate adjustments to the new situation.[23]

The black teachers in these three school districts responded very differently. A fifth of them said that they had raised their standards, 93 per cent said teaching was as enjoyable or more enjoyable than it had been before, and three-fourths preferred to continue teaching in integrated schools.[24] These strong positive findings occurred even though the black faculty members were somewhat less optimistic about the success of their particular schools in adapting to the new situation.

---

18. *Id.* at 113, x-10.
19. *Id.* at viii-23.
20. Buxton, Prichard, Bingham, Jackson, & Talps, *Black and White Teachers and Desegregation*, 12 INTEGRATED ED. 19, 20 (Jan.-Apr. 1974) [hereinafter cited as *Teachers and Desegregation*].
21. *Teachers and Desegregation* 21.
22. *Id.*
23. *Teachers and Desegregation* 20.
24. *Teachers and Desegregation* 20-21.

II

THE CENTRAL ROLE OF THE PRINCIPAL

Report after report on desegregated schools mentions the central role the principal plays in determining the school's response to the desegregation crisis. While in normal circumstances the principal's role may be ambiguous, his authority limited, and his job largely routine, when schools are suddenly reconstituted with substantial numbers of new students and faculty members from racial and ethnic groups not previously represented, the principal often becomes an extremely important figure. He must control and manage the early conflicts and tensions, build positive morale, strengthen school-community relationships, and help teachers work out better educational responses.

A 1972 study of principals in Virginia described the typical principal as "untrained for the almost overwhelming new task thrust upon him, lacking the power to do the job properly, seldom consulted by decision makers in the school district."[25] The desegregation process gave principals the role of "change agent." Eighty-six per cent of the Virginia principals included in the study recognized that they were "very important in setting the tone of acceptance of desegregation."[26]

Preliminary findings of research currently under way in New Haven and in the San Francisco Bay area highlight the importance of the principal's role.[27] In both areas, principals have been central to the achievement of major educational adaptations in the schools.

The importance of the principal's role was underlined in a 1973 case study of the desegregation process in four schools in a middle-sized northern city[28] with a population of approximately 250,000. The study concludes:[29]

> [I]t is clear that the most favorable school environment—that which contributed most to good education, racial integration, and pleasant working conditions for the teaching staff—was to be found at the Highland Elementary School. This environment was due . . . [primarily] to the principal's attitude of acceptance and his leadership skill.

Other studies of integrated schools reach the same general conclusions.[30]

---

25. M. TURNAGE, THE PRINCIPAL: CHANGE AGENT IN DESEGREGATION i (1972).
26. M. TURNAGE, *supra* note 25, at 3, 5-6, 19.
27. Comments by James P. Comer on work underway at the Yale Child Study Center and Elizabeth G. Cohen on work in progress at Stanford University, at The Courts, Social Science, and School Desegregation Conference, Hilton Head Island, S.C., Aug. 20, 1974, on file at *Law and Contemporary Problems* office.
28. C. WILLIE, RACE MIXING IN THE PUBLIC SCHOOLS 11-12 (1973).
29. C. WILLIE, *supra* note 28, at 70.
30. *See, e.g.*, Useem, *White Students and Token Desegregation*, 10 INTEGRATED ED. 48 (Sept.-Oct. 1972). Pettigrew, *A Sociological View of the Post-*Bradley *Era*, 21 WAYNE L. REV. 813, 823 (1975). F. Wirt, Contemporary School Turbulence and Administrative Authority 24, October 30-November 1, 1974 (unpublished paper prepared for David W. Minar Memorial Conference on Problems in the Politics and Governance of the Learning Community, Northwestern University).

Within the school organizational structure, there is probably no real substitute for leadership by the principal in adapting the school to its new educational responsibilites:[31]

> Highly specialized supervisors may tend to drive curriculum areas farther apart, not bring them more closely together—unless an overview of the total supervisory service in a school is an operating part of the principal's job. This point cannot be overemphasized; it is the principal whose vantage point enables him to see all of the various aspects of the school program in its totality.
>
> . . . The point we make is that if the elementary school principal does not assume the responsibility for developing and improving curriculum and instruction in his building, no one else will.

Principals may also hamper the desegregation process. A recent survey of the attitudes of principals in three major Texas cities suggests considerable hostility toward the desegregation process.[32] While the low response rate to the survey (47 per cent) dictates that the results be read with a great degree of caution, principals reported considerable resistance to racial change. Two-thirds of the white, all the Chicano, and nearly half the black principals opposed busing.[33] Black principals, however, were two and one-half times more likely to approve of busing of their own children than principals in the other categories.[34] Two-thirds of the black principals, but virtually none of the others believed that the federal government should take a more active role in desegregation.[35] Two-thirds of the white and most Chicano principals were concerned about dating and inter-marriage, and a third of each non-black group thought that "stereotyping black children as lacking ambition causes no harm."[36] A substantial minority of the white and Mexican-American administrators disputed the proposition that "most Negro families are stable and law abiding."[37] About a fourth of the white principals thought that integration would diminish educational quality for white students.[38] Solid majorities of each group agreed that administrators "have much effect on racial issues" and that they needed "more minority training."[39]

The *Southern Schools* report shows that schools with black principals, or white principals who strongly support integration, fare far better in making the process work.[40]

---

31. Curtin & Gilbertson, *The Principal and the Instructional Program*, in THE ELEMENTARY SCHOOL PRINCIPAL IN ACTION 124-25 (L. Bradfield & L. Draft eds. 1970).

32. The three cities are Dallas, Houston, and San Antonio. *See* Stones, *School Administrator Attitudes and Racism*, 11 INTEGRATED ED. 54 (Mar.-Apr. 1973).

33. *Id.* at 57.

34. *Id.*

35. Stones, *supra* note 32, at 58.

36. Stones, *supra* note 32, at 54, 56.

37. Stones, *supra* note 32, at 56.

38. Stones, *supra* note 32, at 57.

39. Stones, *supra* note 32, at 58.

40. Narot, *Teacher Prejudice and Teacher Behavior in Desegregated Schools*, in 2 SOUTHERN SCHOOLS 17, 31.

> If the principal is black, teachers are less prejudiced. (Since, in at least some cases, the principal is free to choose his staff, this may reflect recruitment strategy rather than influence.) Teachers are also perceived as less prejudiced both by other teachers and by students. In addition, when the principal is black, teachers are more positive in their evaluation of desegregation. . . . In general, the more racially liberal the principal, the more liberal are the teachers, and the more favorable the [white] student's perception of them.
>
> . . . [An indication that the principal] has spoken to the faculty about racial issues . . . is an important predictor of black student perceptions of the staff. Principal's race, racial liberalism, and willingness to talk with the teachers in the school are the three largest predictors of black student perceptions of staff attitudes.

As the school's crisis manager, faculty leader, and chief disciplinarian, as well as the school's "contact point" with parents and community, the principal has many ways to express his attitudes and make his views felt. It is hard to conceive how a school could successfully undergo basic and difficult change without at least tacit support from the principal.

If further, more systematic, research sustains the early findings on the importance of the principal in the desegregation process, it will have some obvious implications for desegregation planning. The fact that desegregation in the South has usually been accompanied by decisions shunting black principals aside to other jobs may well mean that southern districts have sacrificed one of their most valuable resources for making desegregation work.[41] The significant growth in the number of minority principals in the border and northern states, on the other hand, should provide real assistance in the desegregation process.

While it is obvious that principals with extraordinary talent and dedication are a great asset to any school system, it is hardly in the power of the courts to expand the supply. What is important, from the standpoint of desegregation planning, is that principals with certain attributes seem to handle the process of transition more effectively. Desegregation plans might include efforts to provide extensive in-service training for principals, and require affirmative recruitment and upward mobility programs. Searching scrutiny of the job-relatedness of certain certification requirements that have tended to screen out otherwise qualified minority administrators should also be undertaken. Understanding and support for the process of bi-racial or multi-ethnic integration should itself become a major job qualification, one that could perhaps be institutionalized through a screening process representing the various affected community groups.

---

41. The dramatic decline in the number of black principals in southern schools after desegregation has been repeatedly documented. *See Hearings on Displacement and Present Status of Black School Prinicpals in Desegregated School Districts Before Senate Select Comm. on Equal Educ. Opportunity*, 92d Cong., 1st Sess. (1971); Freeman, Desegregation, Political Power, and the Employment of Black School Teachers 5, September 1974 (unpublished paper, Harvard Institute of Economic Research); Butler, *Black Educators in Louisiana—A Question of Survival*, 43 J. NEGRO ED. 9, 22-24 (1974); Egerton, *When Desegregation Comes, the Negro Principals Go*, 3 SOUTHERN ED. REP. 8 (Dec. 1967).

III

IN-SERVICE TRAINING

One of the activities school administrators almost universally support and almost never evaluate adequately is in-service training for teachers and staff facing desegregation. Many school districts attempt rapidly to sensitize their staffs to the viewpoints of other groups through human relations training shortly before or after the desegregation process begins. This training is directed primarily to uprooting prejudices. Only after a long period, if ever, does the emphasis shift to curriculum changes.[42]

An evaluation of the impact of a human relations training program in Riverside, California provides some interesting results.[43] The researchers found that the most effective efforts caused attitude changes "*in both directions*."[44] According to the evaluation:[45]

> The graph reveals that the leader who created the most change in a *positive* direction also created the most change in a *negative* direction. In other words, within the group that had the greatest number of "gainers" there was also the greatest number of "losers." Conversely, in the one group that had the least number of "gainers," there were also the least number of "losers." As has been expressed elsewhere, *this is interpreted to mean that a vigorous and open exchange of feelings and emotions may indeed bare the individual's feelings, but that this causes the individual to more strongly adhere to whatever viewpoint he previously held.* If he happens to be, for example, in favor of a greater amount of racial integration and a greater understanding and acceptance of cultural variation, etc., then the individual will travel in *that* direction. Conversely, if an individual seems to be of a mind *not* to change toward that direction, he will, after having expressed his views, form even *more* rigid opinions or be less willing to adopt the feelings which are contrary to his own way of thinking.

While this evaluation in itself is a wholly inadequate base upon which to pass judgment on a great variety of programs in very different circumstances, it at least raises some questions about possible alternative approaches to in-service training. If one concedes that short-term emotional sessions are unlikely to restructure deeply rooted prejudices, the question arises about whether in-service training resources might not be more appropriately applied to conveying needed factual information (about teaching minority history, for example) or to assist in the development of new teaching styles. Such approaches would probably encounter far less resistance, since they fit teachers' notions of "professional" activities and they meet immediate day-to-day classroom needs, particularly if carried out after the desegregation process is under way.

---

42. Interview with Richard Foster, Superintendent of Schools, in Berkeley, Calif., Oct. 27, 1972.

43. T. Carter, E. Casavantes, & C. Fowler, Final Report and Evaluation of the Riverside In-Service Institute, Dec. 1, 1967 (unpublished document available from authors).

44. *Id.* at 9.

45. *Id.*

Another approach might be to concentrate, at least initially, on training of principals. Since the principal's racial attitudes and ability to support curricular experiments appear to play such an important role in the successful adaptation of a desegregated school, this might be a logical focus for intensive use of scarce resources.

Social science research cannot determine what is the most appropriate in-service training for varying circumstances. What social scientists can do is to raise some questions about overly simplistic and possibly counter-productive approaches. If the desegregation process is understood to be one requiring a long-term educational adaptation of schools, then it may well be appropriate to divert some funds from short-term human relations sessions to long-range curriculum development and training in new methods of instruction.

IV

Tracking and Ability Grouping

A. The Difficulties Inherent in Simultaneously Desegregating and Eliminating Tracking

The need for institutional change becomes evident when one considers the educational implications of a movement away from a tracking system at the secondary school level. While it is easy to say that inter-classroom (and sometimes even intra-classroom) segregation can be eliminated by prohibiting the track system, it is important to consider the implications of taking this step without the necessary supporting educational changes. For example, what would be the consequences of suddenly placing newly desegregated Chicano high school seniors in the traditional college-oriented English literature class a teacher has taught in the same way for the past fifteen years? If the teacher offered a full year of Chaucer, Shakespeare, and Milton to a class where there was now a ten-grade range of reading and composition achievement scores, with some children lacking English fluency, some students would be targeted for failure and humiliation. In this situation, many students would probably prefer tracking, and, indeed, tracking might well do less damage to them.

If the teacher is to come to terms with the increased diversity of the student body without resorting to ability grouping, watering down the existing curriculum to the least common denominator, or blaming the children, he or she often must develop a new teaching style employing some form of individualized instruction, helping each student to build on his strengths and overcome his weaknesses. Experience shows that individualized instruction is a feasible alternative for many elementary school teachers and probably for certain secondary level courses. Until we are confident that it will work in high schools generally, I believe we should avoid taking a rigid position in opposition to high school tracking, particularly if there is significant integration within each track. The Department of Health, Education, and Welfare, which has been actively following a policy of ending in-classroom segregation by ability grouping at the elementary level, has not at this time put strong pressure on the high schools to do the same.[46]

The extremely difficult problem of teaching students with a wide range of achievement levels is apparent in responses to a survey of seventh grade teachers in the Presidio Junior High School in San Francisco. One wrote:[47]

> A teacher in Jr. High School faced with a range of reading ability from 2nd grade to 9th or 10th grade—all within one 45 minute period—finds herself frustrated to the utmost. How can she save the below-grade student from suffering more pain—how can she keep him from feeling failure—how can she keep the above average student from boredom?

Another teacher wrote that "ability in class is too widespread,"[48] while a third said that "it takes about three times as much time to cover materials."[49] Teachers in that school responded to the challenge in very different ways. One said that he had to "water down the course to what they can do in class or else they get left behind and then become behavior problems."[50] Another wanted restoration of the track system. Some faculty members, however, sensed the need to respond to changing attitudes and ability spectrums with "a new approach to teaching."[51] One teacher commented that while the furor over busing would die down, "our lack of adequate positive learning programs will cause trouble year after year until we improve considerably."[52]

When the Berkeley school system decided to end tracking in 1968, its leadership recognized the simultaneous need to adopt a new teaching style. "Groupings will be flexible," said Superintendent Neil Sullivan, "and individualized instruction in small groups will be emphasized."[53]

In a detailed case study of an integrated school in White Plains, New York, a teacher and parent-volunteer are reported to have come to similar conclusions:[54]

> How can we teach children of widely varying abilities and skills in one classroom without discouraging the less able and holding back the fast learners? This is a problem that arises in any classroom. . . . In an integrated classroom, however, it is underlined by the racial issue. . . . Children who are

---

46. Interview with Lloyd Henderson, Director, Education Division, HEW Office for Civil Rights, Washington, D.C., Sept. 30, 1974.
47. San Francisco Unified School District, Zone I, Evaluation Report #5, July 1972, at 35 (unpublished document available from school district offices) [hereinafter cited as Evaluation Report #5].
48. Evaluation Report #5, at 37.
49. *Id.*
50. Evaluation Report #5, at 41.
51. Evaluation Report #5, at 42.
52. Evaluation Report #5, at 43.
53. N. SULLIVAN, NOW IS THE TIME: INTEGRATION IN THE BERKELEY SCHOOLS 159 (1969).
54. I. SCHLESINGER & M. D'AMORE, CHILDREN IN THE BALANCE 99-100 (1971).

> made to feel frustration and failure at the academic level and who are forced to attend a class in which they cannot meaningfully participate become bored and begin to look upon themselves as worthless. They will then try to draw attention to themselves by any means they can devise. . . .
>
> The only approach to teaching that makes any sense in human terms, it seems to me, is individualized instruction. This means that we must recognize the fact that every child learns at his own pace and in his own way. In a classroom full of children of the same age group, every student will have mastered different skills to a different degree.

They favor a system diagnosing the particular skills of each student and prescribing carefully defined sequential materials to meet each student's particular needs. The system, when properly implemented, shows the tremendous variation among both minority and majority children and gives each child specific, highly structured tools which can help him meet his needs. This is a drastic departure from the normal system where the rule is: "All should know this, and those who don't are behind."[55]

There is some confirmation for the importance of a change in teaching methods, and the impact of tracking, in very fragmentary data in the *Southern Schools* report. The study included only two schools which relied on individualized approaches, in an effort to minimize the pressures students were feeling from direct competition. In both of these schools the investigator reported "extremely positive racial tension scores," scores "on the far end of the distribution of scores."[56] The authors offered a hypothesis:[57]

> Teaching machines and other individualized forms of instruction allow students to move at their own pace without tracking. There is a definite stigma attached to being in a class for slow readers. Working with an individualized programmed teaching machine lets every student move at his or her own pace with no stigma attached to it.

Tracking, on the other hand, had a "consistently strong negative effect" on the students' attitudes toward integration at the elementary school level.[58] The study also has some evidence that pro-integration attitudes are better developed in non-tracked elementary schools in rural areas than elsewhere.[59]

The study shows a very different picture, however, at the high school level. At this level, where white students possessed extreme stereotypes of black inferiority and had opposed integration, tracking—which lessens racial contact in integrated high schools—seems to have some positive impact in fostering more favorable racial attitudes.[60] While this finding on tracking is only an isolated finding, it does suggest that in certain situations abolition of tracks at the high school level may not be helpful. The practical problems of managing a high

---

55. *Id.* at 101.
56. 1 Southern Schools 124.
57. *Id.*
58. 1 Southern Schools 74.
59. 1 Southern Schools 81.
60. 1 Southern Schools 83, 87.

school class in certain courses where there is no ability grouping can be very formidable. In cases where the students are entering high school classes from segregated schools which have built up both racial stereotypes and achievement gaps, the problems can be even more severe. While I observed substantial efforts to transform elementary schools and some intermediate schools in desegregated districts across the country, most school administrators expressed very little optimism about the possibility of basic change at the high school level.

B. Research on the Effects of Ability Grouping

A recent review of the results of some fifty years of educational research on the effect of ability grouping on children concluded that the research was contradictory, often of low quality, and limited largely to simplistic studies which attempted to measure the impact of ability grouping on test scores without adequate statistical controls on other factors influencing the learning process.[61] The research on achievement levels has been said to be "at best, mixed, inconclusive and indefinite."[62] To the extent that one could say anything, the data suggest some possible gains from ability grouping for the most able students, but "almost uniformly unfavorable evidence" for average and below-average students.[63]

On the more complex issue of the impact of ability grouping on the self-esteem of children, the research was even less adequate and had produced "at least some data to support almost any stand one might take on this issue."[64] The evidence was certainly insufficient to document the widespread belief among educators that low ability children developed more desirable attitudes and self-esteem in classes with narrow ability ranges.[65] Some recent studies suggest that tracking may act to "inflate the self-esteem of children assigned to relatively high ability groups, and to reduce the self-esteem of children assigned to average and low ability groups," but this finding is not firmly established.[66]

The defects of the existing research literature are greatly magnified when one attempts to adapt curriculum and tracking programs designed for a stable, non-integrated school in a typical white, middle class neighborhood structure to accommodate minority students who often come to the new school years behind in achievement levels and find they must confront older faculty members who find it difficult to change the way they teach. This situation presents

61. Eposito, *Homogeneous and Heterogeneous Ability Grouping: Principal Findings and Implications for Evaluating and Designing More Effective Educational Environments*, 43 REV. ED. RESEARCH 163, 167 (1973).
62. *Id.*
63. *Id.*
64. Eposito, *supra* note 61, at 168.
65. *Id.*
66. *Id.*

very special educational challenges and suggests the need to avoid overly simplistic legal principles which might possibly damage minority children.

The complexity of the tracking issue is further heightened, as Edgar Epps points out,[67] if one conceives of the high school not as an institution primarily for cognitive learning, social adaptation, and personal fulfillment, but as an institution for filtering and channeling students to higher education and other career opportunities. Some existing data suggest better college placement for black students who are enrolled in integrated schools.[68] By the same token, it seems extremely likely that enrollment in a college preparatory track is strongly associated with eventual college enrollment, everything else being equal. Lawyers and others involved in the negotiations on remedies should keep in mind the very difficult challenge the process poses, particularly to teachers from middle class white schools. Perhaps a strategy for litigating the tracking issue at the high school level might be built around a requirement of open enrollment for the upper tracks. To the extent possible, school desegregation plans should include in-service training of teachers and provision of teacher aides or trained volunteers to handle the additional burdens of individualized instruction, and retraining of the counseling staff to avoid racial channeling. At the same time, tracking and ability grouping in the elementary grades should be ended. Finally, recruitment and retention of minority teachers should be urged as they seem to be able to adapt to integrated situations more easily.

V

Integrating the Curriculum

In striking contrast to the situation a few years ago, educators now have available a broad array of integrated and black-oriented teaching materials. A major study of American history texts, undertaken in 1972 by a leading critic of the neglect of minority contributions in such texts, concluded:[69]

> The time has come . . . to praise what the American-history textbooks have at this point of time achieved in their treatment of black Americans. . . . Whatever weaknesses and gaps still linger among a very few of the texts of the 1970s, the attention given to the black American experience is many times greater than that given to any other minority group. . . .
>
> . . . Indeed, many of the texts are sold and promoted as texts which tell the story of America in terms of the *peoples* of the nation. . . . Beyond that, however, there are some texts which have achieved to near perfection a fully integrated American-history textbook.

---

67. Statement made at The Courts, Social Science, and School Desegregation Conference, Hilton Head Island, S.C., Aug. 20, 1974, on file at *Law and Contemporary Problems* office.

68. *See, e.g.*, Armor, *The Evidence on Busing*, 28 Pub. Interest 90, 114 (Summer 1972). Armor's critics claim that he actually understated this positive finding in his analysis of Boston area desegregation. A major retrospective study of blacks educated in integrated schools found a positive relationship for college attendance, particularly for those with elementary school integration. Crain, *School Integration and the Academic Achievement of Negroes*, 44 Sociology of Ed. 1, 5-7 (1971).

69. I. Sloan, The Negro in Modern American History Textbooks 4 (4th ed. 1972).

The new texts can be found in urban and integrated school systems across the country—even in conservative areas of the South.

More interesting, perhaps, is the extensive revision of curricular materials now under way in desegregated areas and districts. In 1972, for example, the South Carolina State Department of Education released a guide on *Ethnic Contributions to U.S. History*. The guide, developed by a statewide committee, is based on the premise that all children in the state need a better understanding of black contributions, a need particularly clear now that the schools are desegregated. The committee concluded:[70]

> No history course should leave an individual with a sense of inferiority. . . . Every community and school district must rise above the conditions of mistrust which divide and destroy the fabric of any society. If one group insists on espousing superiority over another, we all lose.

The guide departs dramatically from the orthodox southern treatment of the Reconstruction period, reflecting the perspective of recent revisionist works by black and white scholars. "Negroes led the way," the guide says, "in democratizing state constitutions, guaranteeing equal rights, and developing programs of state-financed education, agricultural experimentation, et cetera."[71]

A program in Jacksonville, Florida reflects another approach. Working with local black college students, the project helped reconstruct the unrecorded history of the community through old scrapbooks, diaries, and oral history to describe the local roots of blacks who later played a national role. Thus to facilitate desegregation, the schools helped to create a black history of the community.

Recognizing that the curriculum materials built around the experiences of blacks in Harlem or Watts might have very little relevance to that of children growing up in an urban southern community with a different cultural tradition, the Duval County school system in Jacksonville, Florida initiated a project of preparing "learning activity packages" based on the history of the local black community.[72]

One of the serious problems for curriculum planners has been the continued lack of good materials for non-black minorities. While publishers have responded to the demands for a more accurate portrayal of the nation's largest minority, they have been much slower to develop materials on Chicano, Puerto Rican, Indian, and other minorities which have contributed to American society. School systems have been forced to improvise. The Minneapolis school system developed materials dealing with Indian tribes which account for a

70. South Carolina State Department of Education, Ethnic Contributions to U.S. History, 1972 (mimeograph curriculum guide prepared by statewide committee in cooperation with the Charleston, S.C. School District).

71. *Id.* at 22.

72. Interview with Delphenia Carter and Benetta Sherard, Duval County Schools Multi-Ethnic Program, Jacksonville, Fla., Dec. 8, 1972.

substantial fraction of the district's minority enrollment.[73] When fifth graders study the westward movement of settlers, for example, they devote considerable attention to the problem of Indian land rights and the ways in which the whites' takeover of the land and establishment of the reservation system destroyed tribal ways of life. In the sixth grade, the history curriculum portrays the historic role of the Chippewa and Sioux peoples. Because of the paucity of good materials on Minnesota Indians, the district commissioned an Indian educator to develop a series of filmstrips and tape cassettes dealing with tribal economies, commonly portrayed stereotypes held by whites, reservation life and schooling, tribal history, and the changes that Indian children face moving from the reservation to the city.

A basic purpose of American public education has been to convey to students a common understanding of our history, our political institutions, and our national purpose. The image conveyed, however, has usually been one of white Americans devising and operating extraordinarily successful political institutions in a society that had solved most of its problems. The rapid change to materials that emphasize diverse contributions to American society, that deal much more openly with the nation's historic failings, and that present a range of views about contemporary controversies represents a very important curricular shift. Unfortunately, there is extremely little research so far that evaluates its impact.

A recent study of 104 third grade students discloses an impact on racial attitudes of the students attributable to the discussion of books which deal with "black feelings, situations, ideas, and the contributions that black Americans have made to cultural, political, and scientific developments in the United States."[74] By testing the seven-year-old children before and after classroom use of six books on the black experience, the research concludes that "reading and discussion of multiethnic social studies materials can influence attitudes toward black Americans in white urban and rural children of early childhood age."[75] Such early exposure, the author suggests, influences the basic "response sets" of the children.[76]

One basic weakness in adopting a multiethnic curriculum is the fact that few teachers, including minority teachers, have any training in these areas. Far too frequently, the task of preparing new teaching units is assigned to teachers lacking adequate academic preparation in the fields.[77] The result is often trivial or misleading material which does not become an integral part of the general

---

73. Interview with Christian Skjervold, II, Project Administrator, Task Force on Ethnic Studies, Minneapolis Public Schools, Minneapolis, Minn., Oct. 19, 1972.

74. Yawkey, *Attitudes Toward Black Americans Held by Rural and Urban White Early Childhood Subjects Based Upon Multi-Ethnic Social Studies Materials*, 42 J. NEGRO ED. 164, 166 (1973).

75. Yawkey, *supra* note 74, at 167.

76. Yawkey, *supra* note 74, at 167-68.

77. The pattern in many school districts receiving federal aid funds has been to assemble a small team of teachers, without special training, who then spend a summer preparing teaching

curriculum. Even when good materials are obtained or developed, faculty members usually are not provided with the professional training they need to use these resources.

In many districts "black studies" or other minority group courses have been a central point of tension and conflict, particularly within high schools during the early part of the desegregation process. This often results from the failure of the formerly white schools to make any move toward curriculum change or even to recognize Black History Week or major ethnic holidays.

The initial stopgap response of many school districts is to set up special elective high school courses for interested minority students while leaving the basic, required courses largely untouched. For the 1970-71 school year, for example, 937 American high schools reported offering such courses, but they enrolled only seven-tenths of one per cent of the national enrollment.[78] The U.S. Civil Rights Commission reported that less than 2.5 per cent of Chicano elementary students and less than one per cent of secondary students in schools of the Southwest were enrolled in special courses in Mexican or Mexican-American history.[79] The courses enrolled few Anglo students, and some administrators reported that these courses are completely segregated.[80]

These separate courses have been widely criticized, and many curriculum planners believe they will eventually be displaced by integrated basic courses. In Miami, for example, Richard White, head of the program development office, recalls how the huge Dade County system "went through the whole sequence."[81] In the beginning, separate black history and literature courses were developed and installed at all high schools and there was strong initial student response. Three or four years later, however, the courses were rapidly being eliminated because not enough students were enrolling to justify the cost of an additional teacher. As a result, the system is now working on building new materials into the general curriculum.

Although there is little social science evidence on the merits of the alternative approaches, enrollment statistics strongly suggest that if the new perspectives are to reach most minority children and more than an insignificant fraction of Anglo children, they must be incorporated into the standard course curricula. Desegregation plans should require a review of the district's curriculum, and opportunities for substantial retraining of teachers in the fields most affected. From the perspective of managing the desegregation crisis, such an enterprise would have the additional advantage of alerting principals to

---

units. The quality varies enormously. Sometimes the units present outdated research findings or speculative judgments as facts.

78. D. GERTLER & L. BARKER, PATTERNS OF COURSE OFFERINGS AND ENROLLMENTS IN PUBLIC SECONDARY SCHOOLS 1970-71, at 12 (1972).

79. U.S. COMMISSION ON CIVIL RIGHTS, MEXICAN AMERICAN EDUCATION STUDY, REPORT VI: TOWARD QUALITY EDUCATION FOR MEXICAN AMERICANS 9 (1974).

80. *Id.*

81. Interview with Richard White in Miami, Fla., Dec. 6, 1972.

some minimum gestures of recognition of the new groups of students in their schools, a problem that has created considerable tension during the first year of desegregation in many high schools.[82]

Properly managed, then, desegregation offers an opportunity not only to revise teaching styles but also to unearth unconscious cultural biases in the curriculum. Desegregation makes an invisible problem suddenly very visible and creates both interest among teachers and a constituency within the student body for change. While courts should not dictate curriculum, a requirement that the district itself set up a fully representative review process and set aside resources for staff development would aid successful desegregation.

VI

Desegregation and Bilingualism

As the school desegregation drive moves from the South into northern and western cities, desegregation plans are being drawn in school districts which have considerably more complex social groupings than are found in the South. A body of law practice, devised to deal with desegregation of English-speaking blacks who share large elements of a common culture, cannot be transported without adaptation into systems where there are a variety of racial and ethnic groups, widely diverse cultures, and large numbers of students whose basic language is not English. When the Supreme Court declared, in the *Keyes* (Denver) case,[83] that "Southwest Hispanos and Negroes have a great many things in common" and that in Denver they "suffer identical discrimination in treatment when compared with the treatment afforded Anglo students," it was surely over-simplifying a complex issue. The resulting district court decision, however, permitted the retention of some segregated bilingual programs for children requiring language training assistance.[84]

The San Francisco school board has recently ordered revision of the city's desegregation plan to prevent the transfer of Chicano students who are now in schools providing bilingual education.[85] The Supreme Court's decision in *Lau v. Nichols*[86] has sustained HEW's power to require school districts to provide special programs for children without a working knowledge of English. But if programs for Spanish-speaking children and other linguistic minorities continue to be operated on a segregated basis, these programs will conflict with the goals of a desegregation plan.

No significant research has yet been undertaken on bilingual-bicultural

---

82. *See, e.g.*, Melton v. Young, 465 F.2d 1332 (6th Cir. 1972); Smith v. St. Tammany Parish School Bd., 448 F.2d 414 (5th Cir. 1971), *aff'g* 316 F. Supp. 1174 (E.D. La. 1970). *See also* Caldwell v. Craighead, 432 F.2d 213 (6th Cir. 1970), *cert. denied*, 402 U.S. 953 (1971).

83. Keyes v. School Dist. No. 1, 413 U.S. 189, 197-98 (1973).

84. Keyes v. School Dist. No. 1, 380 F. Supp. 673, 692 (D. Colo. 1974).

85. San Francisco Chronicle, June 12, 1974, at 6, col. 1.

86. 414 U.S. 563 (1974).

programs or even on the question of whether such programs are the best remedy for children with English language problems. A recent review of the research reports that there are only four studies which were carefully controlled and truly experimental; only one of these was undertaken in the United States.[87] At present, substantial numbers of Spanish-speaking children are achieving at well below grade level. Most of the argument for bilingual and bicultural programs is based on the assumption that education in the child's own language would be more effective than education in English. However, it has been urged that other approaches should be examined:[88]

> Alternative hypotheses as to the failure of the educational process for Spanish-cultured children should also be considered. It may be that better prepared and more sensitive teachers who do not have low expectations and negative stereotyped views of the children they serve may produce results better than or equal to those produced by bilingual/bicultural education progams.

Many of the federally funded bilingual programs operate in segregated schools. If, however, the *Coleman Report's* general finding—that the background of the other children in the classroom affects learning far more than does the quality of the teaching staff[89]—applies to Spanish-speaking children learning English, one would expect more reinforcement for mastery of the new language in a classroom and school with many English-speaking children. The rapid loss of foreign language mastery for English-speaking children who have no regular opportunity to use the new language, except with their teacher, might be replicated for children learning English in a context where all the informal conversation is Spanish. These are questions in urgent need of research. As the federal government channels growing sums into bilingual education,[90] state legislatures enact legislation requiring bilingual education,[91] and the courts begin to be confronted with these questions,[92] the need for reasonably clear information on what works best grows increasingly serious.

Social science findings about the desegregation process can lend support to some common sense principles in dealing with the large numbers of non-black minority students affected when a school system is forced to devise a desegregation plan. It is only rational, for example, not to distribute children needing intensive language training so thinly across a school system that it becomes administratively impossible to offer them the help they need. While distributing minority children on a fixed ratio across a school system may be a sound

---

87. *See* 1 R. CRAIN, DESIGN FOR A NATIONAL LONGITUDINAL STUDY OF SCHOOL DESEGREGATION 71 (1974).

88. *Id.* at 74.

89. J. COLEMAN, EQUALITY OF EDUCATIONAL OPPORTUNITY 302 (1966).

90. *See* Bilingual Education Act, 20 U.S.C. § 880b (1970).

91. *See, e.g.*, MASS. ANN. LAWS ch. 71A, § 2 (Supp. 1974). Many other states have recently enacted statutes authorizing—rather than requiring—bilingual education programs. *See, e.g.*, TEX. EDUC. CODE § 21.109 (Supp. 1974); CAL. EDUC. CODE § 5761.4 (1975).

92. *See, e.g.*, United States v. Texas Educ. Agency, 467 F.2d 848 (5th Cir. 1972).

"starting point" to remedy segregation of blacks, as the Supreme Court held in *Swann*,[93] it is probably a poor remedy for linguistic minorities present in relatively small numbers in the school system and needing special programs which cannot feasibly be offered in all schools because of the cost and the shortage of qualified staff. Secondly, it is a serious mistake to develop desegregation plans which consider Chicano students as "Anglos" and use them to desegregate black schools.[94] One of the few consistent findings in desegregation research is that the educational value of desegregation comes basically from the placement of lower income children in educational settings with more "advantaged" students.[95] The Houston[96] and Miami[97] plans for desegregating black schools by mixing Spanish-speaking children with black children—thus dealing with the issue of the racial identifiability of a school by adding another victimized minority—make no sense educationally.

Desegregation litigation in devising workable remedies (as the Supreme Court recognized in the *Keyes* case), should consider large distinctive ethnic minority groups as separate categories. The major ethnic minorities are distinctive in history, culture, educational background, and aspirations, as well as language. Thus conscious planning built around the special situation of each major group victimized by past segregation is essential. The problem is exacerbated by the continuing shortage of adequate texts for non-black minorities.[98]

VII

Priority for Desegregation at the Earliest Grade Levels

One of the few points of consensus in desegregation studies and in interviews of school officials is that young children experience the least difficulty in adapting to desegregation. This fact is probably because elementary school children have fewer stereotypes, even in the Deep South.[99] In addition, the achievement gap between white and minority students at the elementary school level is much smaller than at the upper grade levels,[100] and some research has suggested that integration at the earliest level can substantially diminish the characteristic year-by-year widening of the achievement gap between white and black children.[101]

---

93. Swann v. Charlotte-Mecklenburg Bd. of Educ., 402 U.S. 1 (1971).

94. *See, e.g.*, Ross v. Eckels, 434 F.2d 1140 (1970).

95. This proposition is supported by the *Coleman Report* (*see* J. Coleman, *supra* note 89, at 320-25), by the extensive reanalysis of the Coleman data contained in On Equality of Educational Opportunity (F. Mosteller & D. Moynihan eds. 1972), and by the analysis of the *Southern Schools* studies, Narot, *The Effects of Integration on Achievement*, in 2 Southern Schools 61, 68.

96. *See* Ross v. Eckels, 434 F.2d 1140 (1970).

97. *See* Pate v. Dade County School Bd., 434 F.2d 1151 (1970).

98. *See* U.S. Commission on Civil Rights, *supra* note 79, at 7-8.

99. *See* 1 Southern Schools 45-47, 79.

100. *See* J. Coleman, *supra* note 89, at 274-75.

101. *See, e.g.*, M. Purl, The Achievement of Pupils in Desegregated Schools, March 1971, at 4 (unpublished document on file with the Riverside Unified School District, Riverside, Calif.).

Pettigrew summarizes the sociological argument for early integration:[102]

> Racial isolation is a cumulative process. Its effects over time on children of both races make subsequent integration increasingly more difficult. Separation leads them to grow apart in interests and values. [The] Coleman [Report] showed that black children who had begun their interracial schooling in the first five grades evinced higher achievement test scores . . . . And specific studies in Hartford, Connecticut, Ann Arbor, Michigan, Newark-Verona, New Jersey, Bridgeport-Westport, Connecticut, and Riverside all show the best achievement gains for those who begin desegregation in kindergarten and the first grade . . . . The Coleman data also indicate that the most positive attitudes toward having interracial classes and blacks as close friends are found among white children who begin their interracial education in the earliest grades. . . .

From the school's perspective, the nature of the subject matter at the elementary level may make elementary school curricula more adaptable to individualized procedures than curricula for upper levels. Primarily concerned with developing student mastery of certain basic skills, the elementary schools deal largely with cumulative bodies of knowledge graded by levels of difficulty. Subjects such as reading, arithmetic, spelling, punctuation, and writing, can be broken down into small segments, often logically related. With properly designed materials and procedures, teachers can handle students operating at very different levels within the same classroom without inordinate difficulty. Primary school teachers tend to be more flexible and less wedded to traditional ways of teaching traditional bodies of knowledge than the subject-matter-oriented teachers in the higher grades.

Desegregation plans that operate on the assumption that children should remain in their neighborhoods for the first grades and then transfer to desegregated schools can find no support in social science research. The information we do possess about the operation of the process strongly argues for making early desegregation a top priority in litigation and planning. This is one of the few clear and unambiguous recommendations that can be made on the basis of the existing research.

VIII

INTEGRATION AS A LONG-TERM PROCESS

The usual focus of attention is on the desegregation "crisis"—the period just prior to desegregation, when plans are being developed, through the actual accomplishment of those plans and after the conflicts within the community or within the student body largely have ended. This is the period when community leaders actively discuss desegregation, when the press covers the process, and when school authorities often receive some special federal[103] and/or local funds to ease the transition. This is also the period when the desegregation process is evaluated by researchers.

---

102. Pettigrew, *supra* note 30, at 822. *See also* 1 SOUTHERN SCHOOLS 53.

103. *See, e.g.*, Emergency School Aid Act, 20 U.S.C.A. §§ 1601-19 (1974).

This "transitional" period is very important. Administrators must deal with frictions and tensions and confusion both within the schools and within the community. During this period, school officials primarily are concerned with the restoration of some semblance of normality. They must deal in an atmosphere where minor fights are seen as serious racial incidents. School officials, in an effort to reduce tensions, provide human relations training for staff members, and try to reassure worried parents. It is a vitally important job to diminish community hostility and maintain morale within the schools. In educational terms, however, this is usually a period of defense of the status quo.

Since the assumption is that when calm has been restored, integration has been accomplished, the attention of the public recedes, and resources provided to assist in the desegregation process are withdrawn. However, the really significant changes may be just beginning. In the schools that I have visited, adaptation to desegregation is almost invariably seen as a process requiring several years, including replacement of some of the personnel. Published case studies often reflect the same conclusion.[104] This suggests the importance of incorporating into desegregation plans a program of several years' duration, designed to help principals and teachers develop educational processes responsive to their new student bodies.

There is virtually no large scale research on this particular issue, so that this section of the article will examine changes in individual schools and present what some involved officials and academic observers think happens as desegregated schools try to move toward successful integration.

Thomas Phillian, a principal in Riverside, California, has been through the process of educational change following the desegregation of two schools.[105] Palm School, a white middle class school, had an older, closely-knit faculty, most of whom were unprepared for desegregation and who worried about a decline in the school's high test scores. Teachers had tended to ignore the small number of white children with serious learning problems. Although the Riverside administrators strongly supported desegregation, the transition at Palm School was difficult and traumatic. Teachers who had been doing the same thing for fifteen or twenty-five years suddenly found they really didn't know what to do. At first, he says, "They just cried a lot."

Phillian began to work for change by scheduling two meetings a week to talk over articles and see films on new educational approaches. Teachers began to visit other schools which were trying new procedures. Even with this intense effort, it took almost a year and a half before the faculty calmed down and the first changes were made. A much longer time was required to change the basic teaching style of the school.

---

104. *See* M. Metz, *supra* note 17.

105. Interview with Thomas Phillian, Principal, Adams Elementary School in Riverside, Calif., Oct. 27, 1972.

After achieving some success at Palm School, Phillian took over the troubled Adams School in the middle of the 1970-71 school year. The student body there included two hostile groups of Chicano students from different parts of town. Guns, knives, and chains were found in the school, and children called it "the prison." At Adams teachers had retained traditional tracks and had segregated classrooms. Phillian told the teachers that they would have to change or quit and closely monitored those he judged inadequate until some left. Openings were filled by enthusiastic newcomers, and the school began to embark on a variety of new approaches. Two years later the faculty was conducting a needs assessment of its community and crystalizing the results into a new set of curriculum goals. The changes had helped the school to move from twentieth to fourth place in the district in reading achievement test scores. One of the side effects of the changes in both schools was to produce far better opportunities for white students with learning problems.

David Tew, principal of the Longfellow School in Riverside, tells a similar story of a long process of transition.[106] Longfellow, with a 52 per cent minority enrollment, was plagued with discipline problems and poor morale. It had a pervasive sense of failure and the lowest test scores in the system. At first, Tew spent many hours dealing with complaints and handling "name-calling, fights, racial epithets, filthy language and vandalism." The teachers had struggled with the problems in a variety of ways: some tried "harsh discipline," others used tracking, and some were trying to find ways to use teacher aides effectively.

Tew, who had been working on a non-graded way to teach reading skills, brought with him a small nucleus of three teachers, including a reading specialist. He asked two of the seventeen existing teachers to leave and explained to the rest what he thought needed to be done in changing teaching methods, telling them they should "feel free to ask for a transfer" if they felt uncomfortable.

After some initial anxiety and some departures, things settled down and only a single teacher requested a transfer during the next six years. The teachers began by carefully analyzing the problems of fifth and sixth graders with reading difficulties. The analysis uncovered "many areas that just were not dealt with." For example, it was found that some of the students still lacked the eye-hand coordination necessary to begin reading. In response, new exercises were built into the physical education curriculum. When the Riverside school system implemented decentralized planning and budgeting, the staff of Longfellow became intensely involved in developing a plan for change. The school won a $10,000 grant from the district to carry out a special three-year program including systematic development of the new reading and math methods.

106. Interview with David Tew, Principal, Longfellow Elementary School in Riverside, Calif., Oct. 27, 1972.

The process of shared planning, Tew believes, pulled the members together behind the new program.

The results of the new philosophy and newly implemented programs were dramatic. In the first year after the new methods had been introduced, the school's achievement scores moved from last in the district to the middle level. The next year, the school was first in the district.[107]

At the South San Jose Elementary School in Jacksonville, Florida, Principal Marie Patterson recalls that before the desegregation process took place, there were teachers who had never seen below-average children in the affluent white school.[108] "We had been," she said, "a little private school in a private community, supported by public funds." Teachers were "fearful that they would not be able to handle the range of abilities." Rapid curriculum change came to this school when parents demanded that the school implement individualized approaches which had been tried out elsewhere in the district. When this was done, a substantial number of the children that had transferred to private schools returned, the number of parents serving as volunteers in the school increased, and the PTA began to raise funds for some necessary equipment.

A school which has successfully been through this long process of adaptation and change often ends up with a program that offers broadened opportunities for *all* children. In Roanoke, Virginia[109] a number of elementary and intermediate schools moved to individualized instruction following desegregation of the school system. Interesting changes took place in surprising areas of the curriculum. The staff found, for example, that their policies of concentrating on arts and crafts and choral music at black schools, and classical music and traditional art instruction at the white high schools, had overlooked strong interests which crossed racial lines in both directions.[110]

Principals in those schools which have responded to desegregation with educational reforms report cycles of early fear, then exploration and planning, and finally change. None think that they have a magic formula or one that is

---

107. A similar story of traumatic initial adjustment, but eventual success—after more than five years—was related by Principal Etta Mae Mosely of the Meadow Park Elementary School in Palm Beach County, Fla., Dec. 4, 1972.

108. Interview with Marie Patterson, Principal of South San Jose Elementary School in Duval County, Fla., Dec. 8, 1972.

109. Interview with Roanoke school system staff members in Roanoke, Va., Oct. 13, 1972. The Virginia State Department of Education, operating in the state that had once led "massive resistance" to token desegregation, acted in the early 1970's to sponsor the development of an integrated curriculum for the VIRGINIA! television series broadcast for state-wide classroom use through the state's instructional television network. Interview with Mary Franklin in Richmond, Va., Sept. 19, 1972. Although this state, in the very recent past, has required the use of the *Cavalier Commonwealth* text, which had portrayed the happy lot of slaves, a prominent black historian is now playing a major role in constructing the course guide.

110. A similar experience occurred in Greenville, S.C., where school officials found that there was considerable white student interest in auto mechanics and other skilled trade courses that had been offered only in the black schools before integration. Interview with Wayman Burton, Principal, Bryson Ninth Grade Center, in Greenville, S.C., Dec. 13, 1972. The comments of a principal in

suitable to all teachers or all schools. Most strongly emphasize the importance of faculty involvement in planning, and no one disputes the fact that the transition takes years.

If real desegregation is a long-term process requiring an analysis of basic educational philosophies and a restructuring of the way classrooms operate, this should be considered at the time that the desegregation plan is developed. It is at this point where there can be some leverage on a school system to support the needed long-term changes. Desegregation plans should provide expert assistance, and, if possible, small budgets to support experiments within individual schools to help work out the necessary adjustments. It is also important for teachers and principals who are deeply confused to have a chance to visit schools where desegregated education is working. School principals usually have very little money for new departures once their obligations for salaries, supplies, and fixed costs are met. Targeting even a few thousand dollars for planning, curriculum development, and needed materials can greatly facilitate change. Unfortunately, most existing federal desegregation aid funds are targeted on the immediate period of transition and withdrawn long before the process has run its course.[111] In too many cases, it has not even begun by the time funds are withdrawn.

CONCLUSION

Desegregation raises new educational problems for schools, but it also presents them with a very rare opportunity. Older school systems, especially the large urban systems, are notoriously resistant to reform. Some tend toward the kind of mindless unchanging bureaucracy described in David Rogers' *110 Livingston Street*[112] and other recent books about central city school systems.[113] Professor Willis Hawley, in his study of organizational rigidity in school systems, attributes much of the system's inability to adapt to changing educational requirements to a rigid centralized bureaucratic structure which strongly reinforces the tendency of schools to perpetuate traditional curricular offerings and teaching methods.[114] School systems, he reports, tend to impose uniformity on everything from the age placement of students, to texts, to the type of

---

Little Rock, Ark., also indicate that by offering a stereotyped curriculum, many white students had been disadvantaged.

> I've been a principal for 20 years in Little Rock, and my job is far more difficult—but far more interesting—than before integration. I think we neglected lower-level youngsters in our all-white schools before, and it took integration to show the need for an expanded curriculum.

J. PEPPLER, LITTLE ROCK 17 YEARS AFTER 10 (1974).

111. *See, e.g.*, Emergency School Aid Act, 20 U.S.C.A. §§ 1601-19 (1974); Civil Rights Act of 1964, Titles IV & V, 42 U.S.C. §§ 2000d & 2000e (1970).

112. D. ROGERS, 110 LIVINGSTON STREET (1968).

113. *See, e.g.*, M. GITTELL, PARTICIPANTS & PARTICIPATION (1967).

114. W. Hawley, Dealing with Organizational Rigidity in Public Schools: A Theoretical Perspective, Fall 1974 (unpublished paper delivered at the 1974 annual meeting of the American Political Science Association).

person selected as a teacher. Their desire for stability and uniformity thus causes resistance to change that may well require several decades for the general adoption of major innovations. Naturally enough, this rigid structure strongly discourages creativity by teachers. Thus, "special opportunities" for change come with crisis situations:[115]

> At critical points in all crises the climate is right for a major innovation. If it is the right proposal for the right time and people, substantial progress can be made in the system. The reason may be that as strain continues, most parties to the strife are anxious for a plausible solution.

The advent of desegregation is such a crisis for many teachers and administrators. It can also be the opportunity for the initiation of very important educational reforms in circumstances where reforms are normally very difficult. To the extent possible, litigants, judges, and planners within school systems should attempt to devise plans which recognize that physical desegregation is only the first step toward social and educational adaptation of the schools. Court should draw on the broad equitable power they possess to remedy segregation by requiring local school officials to prepare a long-term educational plan to make desegregation work educationally and help turn physically desegregated schools into genuinely integrated schools. Even in cases where the local school officials adamantly oppose preparation of the plan for physical desegregation, they should be ordered to devise a supporting program of educational change. The plans should respect the individual school as an important institution faced with a major challenge and should attempt to aid principals and teachers in working out better ways to meet the diverse needs of students within a context of successful integration.

---

115. Outside of the "special opportunities" provided by crisis situations, educational innovations have generally been adopted less frequently in the area where the need for them is most urgent—the ghettos and central city schools—than where they are least needed—the suburbs. One recent study of innovation, for example, concluded that communities with higher economic status, educational levels, and staff exposure to ideas from outside the system were more likely to be receptive to change. Hearn, *The Where, When and How of Trying Innovations*, 53 PHI DELTA KAPPAN 358-61, 374 (1972). The Ford Foundation's evaluation of its educational reform experiments of the 1960's produced a similar finding about the tendency of suburban systems to be far more responsive to new methods, see P. NACHTIGAL, A FOUNDATION GOES TO SCHOOL 18 (1972).

WAITING ON THE PROMISE OF *BROWN*

DERRICK A. BELL, JR.*

Black Parents Equal Educational Opportunity Committee
Delta County, Southland

Dear Friend,

We have always been concerned about good schools for our children. When the Supreme Court said, more than twenty years ago, "it is doubtful that any child may reasonably be expected to succeed in life if he is denied the opportunity of an education," we felt that the Court understood our concern. We placed our faith in the Brown *decision. There have been many changes for the better in the last two decades, but we are still waiting for the promise of* Brown *to be realized in our public schools.*

Several years ago, the black community in Delta County formed the Black Parents Educational Opportunity Committee. This Committee has worked to desegregate our schools in order to obtain the equal educational opportunity to which the Court said our children were entitled. In 1963 the Delta County School Board was taken to court; during the long years of litigation many favorable court rulings were obtained, but most succeeded only in stopping school board action intended to maintain segregated schools.

Delta County, located in a hilly area, is bisected by the scenic, but virtually non-navigable Barrier River, as shown on the enclosed map. In the mid-1940's, when public schools were segregated by law, the county schools were consolidated into one school system. That system, controlled by an all-white board—selected every four years on an at-large basis—serves the children of the roughly 5,000 white and 3,000 black residents of the county. There are approximately 1,000 black and 2,000 white children of public school age eligible to attend the county's two schools, each of which serves grades one through twelve.

The district contains only two schools: Jefferson Davis School, located in Suburbville, a middle-class residential area in the northwestern portion of the county, where most of the white population of the county lives; and Booker T. Bledsoe School, located in Deltaville in the southeastern part of the county, where most of the blacks live—either in Deltaville itself or on small farms in the outlying areas. Black families in the county earn little, but in recent years a few dozen of the more affluent blacks have moved to Suburbville.

In 1968, five years after suit was filed to halt the assignment of all black children to Bledsoe School and all white children to Davis School, the federal court ordered a "freedom of choice" plan for the county. Despite harassment and economic pressures

*Professor of Law, Harvard University.

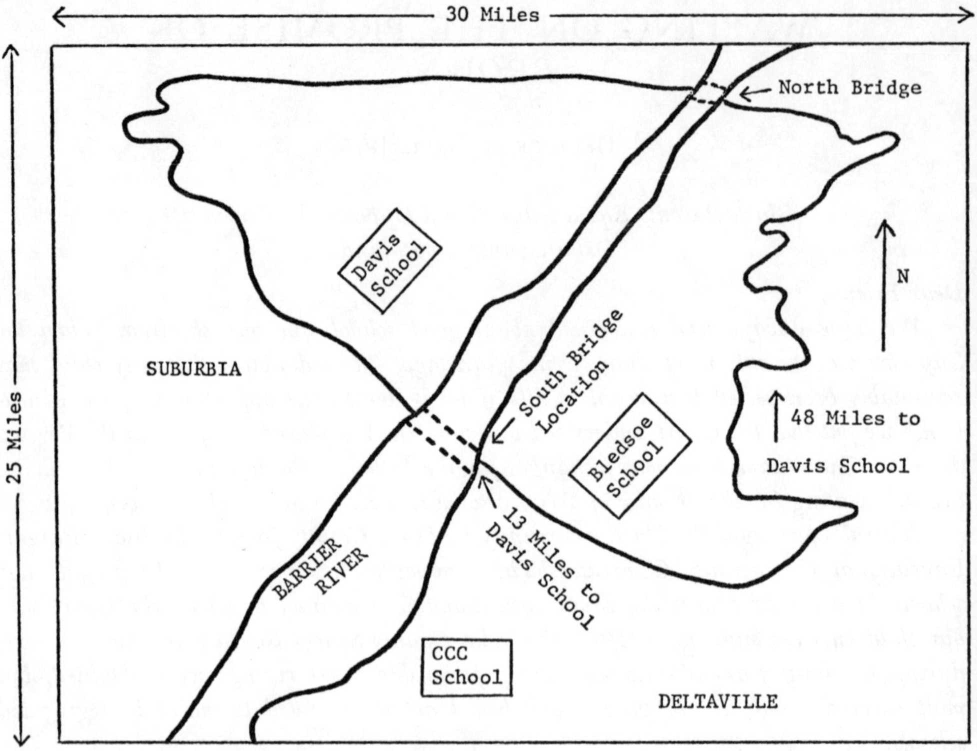

by certain elements of the white community, about 100 black children were enrolled in the Davis School under this plan. In 1972, however, the court ruled that the freedom-of-choice plan was inadequate to disestablish the dual school system and ordered the board to pair the two schools so that Davis would serve all students in grades one through six while Bledsoe would serve all students in grades seven through twelve. Under this "pairing" plan, 1,500 students would be transported across South Bridge each school day.

There was tremendous opposition in the white community to this plan, and the board exhausted all available judicial appeals. In September 1974, on the night before the plan was to go into effect, South Bridge—the only crossing over Barrier River in the proximity of the two schools—was mysteriously blown up. Despite continued requests from the black community, neither state nor federal officials have been able to finance reconstruction of the bridge. Both have concluded that the cost, estimated at ten million dollars, cannot be appropriated before late 1976. Even when funding is obtained, engineers expect that because of construction difficulties, the new bridge will not be completed until 1979.

Destruction of South Bridge did not seriously disrupt business, most of which flows to neighboring counties. But the loss of the bridge has greatly affected the county's school integration plans:

a. When South Bridge was destroyed, the school board petitioned the district court to delay the pairing plan. Attorneys for the plaintiffs countered with the suggestion of implementing the plan using North Bridge, but the school board objected, claiming transportation of students from one side of the county to the other by way of North Bridge would require bus rides averaging three hours per day. (We have verified that, for most children, the ride over rough, hilly roads would total three to four hours.)

The board suggested, and the court approved, an "emergency proximity plan' that assigned each child to the school closest to his or her home. The board is now seeking judicial approval of its emergency plan until South Bridge is replaced. Under the "proximity" plan, as it operated during the 1974-75 school year, there were 1,500 white and 50 black students (all of whom reside in Suburbville) enrolled and attending Davis School. There were 950 black and 500 white students assigned to Bledsoe School.

b. None of the white students assigned to Bledsoe School enrolled. Some white families moved to the west side of Barrier River; the remainder, mostly low-income families, placed their 500 school-age children in the new Deltaville private school, Caucasian Children's Choice (CCC). Enrollment in CCC is limited to the descendants of those residents who attended, or were eligible to attend, Davis School prior to 1954. Some of us would like to desegregate or at least lessen its attractiveness to white parents as a haven from desegregation. As far as we know, it receives no government money or supplies.

c. Booker T. Bledsoe II, the principal of Bledsoe School, is the son of the founder for whom the school was named. He has held this position since the school was built. Dr. Bledsoe is not an effective educator and cares little for the concerns and needs of the black community. He refuses to permit courses or even class discussion of black history, civil rights, or other subjects which he feels will "stir up" the students. More importantly, he resists implementing special teaching techniques needed by many black youngsters who come from culturally different homes. Scholastic achievement scores at Bledsoe School are low and drop-out rates are high. The faculties at both schools have been desegregated by court order, but Dr. Bledsoe has hired teachers—black and white—who reflect his antiquated and conservative approach to teaching.

d. School board members have approached leaders in the black community about a possible "final settlement" of the school question. Their proposal is the following: they will appoint any qualified person the black community designates to replace Dr. Bledsoe, who retires at the end of the current school year. They promise not to limit the new principal in his selection of teachers, curriculum, or teaching techniques and to make extra funds available with which to implement these programs. In return, the black community is to accept the emergency proximity pupil-assignment plan as permanent.

The national civil rights organization which has been handling the school litigation for the plaintiffs since the first suit was filed in 1963, has condemned the plan as an "unconscionable compromise" of school integration goals. I estimate, though, that about half of the black community favors acceptance of this plan, providing it is legal. We are not impressed by the way in which black children are treated at Davis

School and schools in other counties where desegregation has taken place; we increasingly wonder whether further integration efforts will benefit our children. Some of the black residents, however, still favor busing students over North Bridge; others are undecided.

As you can see, we are faced with serious difficulties. We hope you will soon send us your recommendations as to the legally permissible solutions to these problems. We need to hear from you; please do not fail us in this difficult time.

Sincerely yours,
Faith-Ann Courage
Chairperson

Dear Ms. Courage:

The Supreme Court's decision in *Brown v. Board of Education*[1] was less a promise than an opportunity. By withdrawing Constitutional approval of segregated schools, the Court did not guarantee racially integrated schools. Rather, the judicial acknowledgment of the social and psychological harm done black children under the never-realized "separate but *equal* standard," provided black Americans with an opportunity to seek a non-coerced, nonracial foundation on which to structure public school policies. Because the Court denounced official segregation, it followed—or at the time seemed to follow—that the *Brown* decision sanctioned desegregation as *the* remedy to which black children were entitled.

Resistance to school desegregation was so great and some of the methods of evasion so insidiously deceptive that civil rights proponents and, later, courts were forced to measure compliance with desegregation court orders by the extent to which the school system actually interspersed black and white children in the same schools.[2] Somewhere in the struggle to overcome the fierce resistance to desegregation,[3] civil rights lawyers and others, and particularly the courts, began to equate the elimination of the dual school system with the attainment of equal educational opportunity.

Your letter reflects the justifiable fear that these two aims are not the same. Former NAACP General Counsel, now Federal District Judge Robert L. Carter wrote: "[F]ew in the country, black or white, understood in 1954 that racial segregation was merely a symptom, not the disease; that the real

1. 347 U.S. 483 (1954).

2. *See, e.g.*, Read, *Judicial Evolution of the Law of School Integration Since* Brown v. Board of Education, 39 LAW & CONTEMP. PROB. no. 1, at 7 (1975).

3. *See* Fairman, *The Supreme Court, 1955 Term—Foreword: The Attack on the Segregation Cases*, 70 HARV. L. REV. 83 (1956); Knowles, *School Desegregation*, 42 N.C.L. REV. 67 (1963); Meador, *The Constitution and the Assignment of Pupils to Public Schools*, 45 VA. L. REV. 517 (1959); Powe, *The Road to* Swann: *Mobile County Crawls to the Bus*, 51 TEX. L. REV. 505 (1973); Comment, *State Efforts to Circumvent Desegregation: Private Schools, Pupil Placement, and Geographic Segregation*, 54 NW. U.L. REV. 354 (1959).

sickness is that our society in all of its manifestations is geared to the maintenance of white superiority."[4]

Thus, the dilemma you face in Delta County does not result, as some legal scholars would suggest, from analytical inadequacies in the *Brown* opinion,[5] or from the Court's unfortunate failure to require immediate compliance with its mandate.[6] Full implementation of *Brown* remains an uncertain future prospect because of the continuing resistance of many whites who fear that the realization of "equal educational opportunities" for blacks will mean the loss of economic and status benefits that they and their children now enjoy solely on the basis of race.

The essence of the advice contained in this response is that white resistance in Delta County, and elsewhere, may be neutralized by utilizing the right to school desegregation as a valuable lever with which to achieve community-designated educational goals otherwise unavailable to an economically and politically powerless minority. But this leverage should be applied in ways other than, or in addition to, the enrollment of black children in predominantly white schools.

Conditions in Delta County require discussion of the following points: the legal and educational inappropriateness of placing total reliance on immediate integration of the Delta County schools; the considerations involved in accepting the school board's settlement offer; and a reexamination of what the *Brown* decision has meant to blacks, including suggestions on how to restore its waning vigor.

I

TOTAL RELIANCE ON IMMEDIATE INTEGRATION

School desegregation statistics show that the *Brown* decision has done much of what it was intended to do—eliminate the dual school system based on race—and in precisely that area of the country where the Court intended its mandate to have effect—the South.[7] But the impact of *Brown* has been weakened, and its very existence as legal precedent endangered by the effort to apply its holding rigorously and inflexibly in large urban areas of the country, North and South, where public schools today are more racially seg-

---

4. Carter, *The Warren Court and Desegregation*, 67 MICH. L. REV. 237, 247 (1968).

5. Wechsler, *Toward Neutral Principles of Constitutional Law*, 73 HARV. L. REV. 1, 31-34 (1959). *See also Note: Rights Under* Brown *and the Associational Dilemma*, in D. BELL, RACE, RACISM AND AMERICAN LAW 452 (1973).

6. *Compare* the broad, flexible standards of compliance in Brown v. Board of Educ., 349 U.S. 294 (1955), *with* the more precise judicial guidelines set out sixteen years later in Swann v. Charlotte-Mecklenburg Bd. of Educ., 402 U.S. 1 (1971).

7. U.S. COMMISSION ON CIVIL RIGHTS, THE FEDERAL CIVIL RIGHTS ENFORCEMENT EFFORT —1974: A REPORT 49-51 & nn. 116-28 (1975).

regated than they were in 1954,[8] and where the barriers to desegregation, for all practical purposes, are virtually insurmountable.

In Delta County, geographic conditions compounded by community resistance have generated school desegregation problems quite similar to those found in large urban areas of both North and South. This is highly unusual in rural areas where, as the Supreme Court has noted, consolidated school systems implemented by bus transportation have enabled school adjustments "more readily than [in] metropolitan areas with dense and shifting population, numerous schools, congested and complex traffic patterns."[9]

That the rights of black children under the *Brown* decision must encompass more than the entitlement to attend desegregated schools is evidenced by the suggestion in several recent Supreme Court decisions that there are limits to the extent to which school desegregation need be carried out. "No fixed or even substantially fixed guidelines can be established as to how far a court can go, but it must be recognized that there are limits."[10] Even after the demise of the "all deliberate speed" standard as justification for delay,[11] a plan will not necessarily be enforced under any and all circumstances.[12]

For at least the following reasons, it is doubtful that the courts will require implementation of a pairing plan in Delta County before South Bridge is restored:[13]

a. *Busing is a limited remedy* because the majority of white parents do not perceive it as a means of obtaining a better education for their children than

---

8. Staff of Senate Select Comm. on Equal Educ. Opportunity, 92d Cong., 2d Sess., Report: Toward Equal Educational Opportunity 102-04 (Comm. Print 1972). In the period 1968-1971, the percentage of black students in the 11 southern states attending 80 to 100 per cent minority schools was reduced from 78.8 per cent to 32.2 per cent; the change in the remaining states during that time was negligible. *Id.* at 110-11. In many large urban areas, racial isolation increased. "About half the Nation's black students, 3.4 million, are located in the 100 largest school districts." *Id.* at 114. In 1971, 73.4 per cent of them attended 80 to 100 per cent minority schools, and 59 per cent were in 95 to 100 per cent minority schools. *Id.*

9. Swann v. Charlotte-Mecklenburg Bd. of Educ., 402 U.S. 1, 14 (1971).

10. 402 U.S. at 28.

11. Alexander v. Holmes County Bd. of Educ., 396 U.S. 19, 20 (1969).

12. In Milliken v. Bradley, 418 U.S. 717, 744, 745 (1974), despite the fact that the only effective desegregation plan was a metropolitan area plan, the Court held that desegregation stops at the city limits, unless it can be shown that deliberately segregative actions were taken in the surrounding school districts contributing to the segregation of the city's school system or that district lines were deliberately drawn on the basis of race. *But see* Newburg Area Council v. Board of Educ. of Jefferson County, 510 F.2d 1358 (6th Cir. 1974) (consolidated with Haycraft v. Board of Educ. of Louisville). Similarly in *Swann*, the Court indicates that even if busing were the only tool which could produce effective desegregation in a particular school district, it need not be utilized "when the time or distance of travel is so great as to either risk the health of the children or significantly impinge on the educational process." 402 U.S. at 30-31.

13. Milliken v. Bradley, 418 U.S. 717 (1974), eliminated the possibility of federal courts ordering the consolidation of the hypothetical Delta County schools with those in neighboring counties for purposes of desegregation in the absence of proof that "the racially discriminatory acts of one or more school districts caused racial segregation in an adjacent district, or where district lines have been deliberately drawn on the basis of race." 418 U.S. at 745. *Milliken* was followed by the Sixth Circuit which reversed a metropolitan desegregation order

would be possible otherwise. Where school desegregation is not an issue, the school bus has become an accepted and generally welcome component of American public education.[14] But federal courts, aware of the resistance to busing over long distances as a means of effecting an end to segregated schools, have, in effect, legitimized this resistance "when the time or distance of travel is so great as to either risk the health of the children or significantly impinge on the educational process."[15]

Chief Justice Burger has indicated that he personally would stay a school desegregation order involving average daily travel times of three hours.[16] Other members of the Supreme Court have indicated that busing, and integration in general, must be balanced against its disruptive effects on public education and "the rights and interests of children affected by a desegregation program . . . ."[17] And although unlike the Delta County situation, *Swann* involved busing across noncontiguous geographic school attendance zones, the majority of the Court suggested that had there been "no history of discrimination, it might well be desirable to assign pupils nearest their homes."[18]

Lower courts have rejected plans as not "feasible" where pupils would have been required to travel up to 2 1/2 hours a day,[19] where the location

---

in United States v. Board of School Comm'rs of Indianapolis, Ind., 503 F.2d 68 (1974). *Milliken* was distinguished, however, by that same circuit in a case involving the possible consolidation of the city of Louisville and Jefferson County school districts. Newburg Area Council v. Board of Educ. of Jefferson County, 510 F.2d 1358 (6th Cir. 1974) (consolidated with Haycraft v. Board of Educ. of Louisville).

14. NAACP Legal Defense and Educational Fund, *It's Not the Distance, 'It's the Niggers,'* in THE GREAT SCHOOL BUS CONTROVERSY 322 (N. Mills ed. 1973). In 1972 HEW estimated that "43.5% of the total public school enrollment or 18,975,939 pupils are transported to school daily." *Id.* at 324. "The National Highway Traffic Safety Administration reports that the total cost, including capital outlay for pupil transportation for 1971-72 is $1.7 billion." *Id.* Of the 256,000 buses that travel 2.2 billion miles, *id.*, only a small percentage were bused to achieve school desegregation.

Judge Winter, dissenting in Thompson v. School Bd., 498 F.2d 195 (4th Cir. 1973), charged that the district court had relied on expert testimony which measured the effect of busing on children's physical and mental health on "whether he is happy which, in turn, depends upon whether he is transported to a school 'of his choice or his parents' choice.' " *Id.* at 198.

15. Swann v. Charlotte-Mecklenburg Bd. of Educ., 402 U.S. at 30-31 (1971). *See also* Davis v. Board of School Comm'rs of Mobile County, 402 U.S. 33 (1971), requiring "every effort to achieve the greatest possible degree of actual desegregation, taking into account the practicalities of the situation." *Id.* at 37.

16. Winston-Salem/Forsyth Bd. of Educ. v. Scott, 404 U.S. 1221, 1227 n. 1 (1971).

17. Keyes v. School Dist. No. 1, 413 U.S. 189, 247 (1973) (Powell, J., concurring in part and dissenting in part).

18. Swann v. Charlotte-Mecklenburg Bd. of Educ., 402 U.S. at 28. Even so, the plan subsequently approved by the district court in Charlotte required the transportation of 46,667 students. 334 F. Supp. 623, 626-27 (W.D.N.C. 1971).

However, *apropos* the Delta County situation, the Fourth Circuit has rejected a desegregation plan which retained racially identifiable schools because it did not encompass transfer of students across a river which divided the city. Medley v. School Bd. of City of Danville, 482 F.2d 1061 (4th Cir. 1973), *cert. denied*, 418 U.S. 1172 (1974); Gaines v. Dougherty County Bd. of Educ., 465 F.2d 363 (5th Cir. 1972).

19. Thompson v. School Bd., 498 F.2d 195, 196-97 & n. 1 (4th Cir. 1971). It should be

of highways and railroad yards posed serious obstacles to the required transportation,[20] and where the age of students to be bused "lengthy" distances would have a "probable adverse effect upon the physical health and mental processes of the children."[21]

Applying the above standards to Delta County, the court's 1972 pairing plan requiring the use of bus transportation was clearly appropriate when ordered.[22] With the destruction of South Bridge and no more feasible means than North Bridge available for crossing Barrier River, implementation would require bus rides of three to four hours—substantially greater than those in other plans which courts have refused to approve.[23]

b. *Violent opposition to school desegregation* does not constitute a valid basis

---

noted, however, that this finding of infeasibility was based almost entirely on the testimony of a pediatrician, Dr. Hogge, who testified as an expert witness on behalf of defendants and whose testimony was confined to the effect on school children in grades kindergarten through two. The issue relating to grades three through seven was disposed of on entirely different grounds. *Id.*

20. *See* Thompson v. School Bd., 363 F. Supp. 458 (E.D. Va. 1973). *But see* Keyes v. School Dist. No. 1, 413 U.S. 189, 204-05 (1973) (six lane highway not a significant barrier to integration).

21. Thompson v. School Bd., 363 F. Supp. 458, 459 (E.D. Va. 1973).

22. The continued existence of Bledsoe as a "one-race" school does not per se invalidate the Board's proximity plan; it merely

> warrants a presumption against schools that are substantially disproportionate in their racial composition. Where the school authority's proposed plan for conversion from a dual to a unitary system contemplates the continued existence of some schools that are all or predominately of one race, they have the burden of showing that such assignments are genuinely nondiscriminatory.

Swann v. Charlotte-Mecklenburg Board of Educ., 402 U.S. at 26. Arguendo, then, if there is no reasonable means by which Bledsoe can be desegregated, the burden could be assumed to have been met.

23. For limitations on busing notwithstanding the fact that the result substantially reduced potential desegregation see Northcross v. Board of Educ. of Memphis City Schools, 489 F.2d 15 (6th Cir. 1973), *cert. denied*, 416 U.S. 962 (1974); Mapp v. Board of Educ., 477 F.2d 851 (6th Cir. 1973), *cert. denied*, 414 U.S. 1022 (1974); Goss v. Knoxville Bd. of Educ., 482 F.2d 1044 (6th Cir. 1973), *cert. denied*, 414 U.S. 1171 (1974).

In *Northcross* the court had three plans from which to choose. Plans one and three would assure 100 per cent desegregation, but 80 per cent of those bused would ride 31 to 45 minutes each way whiie 20 per cent (mostly elementary school students) would ride 46 to 60 minutes each way. Plan two would only accomplish 83 per cent desegregation, but 100 per cent of those bused would ride 31 to 45 minutes each way. The court was influenced—perhaps decisively —by the "practical considerations set forth in *Swann*" as outlined by the district court. 489 F.2d at 17.

In both *Mapp* and *Goss* the Sixth Circuit Court of Appeals affirmed the decisions of the district court which approved plans requiring no busing: *Mapp*, because of the disruptive effect on the educational program that busing would have and the substantial amounts of capital outlay it would entail; *Goss*, because a unitary system already existed and the busing was proposed in order to improve the racial mix; both, because endemic geographic concentrations of blacks were responsible for the racial patterns of the school population.

In Carr v. Montgomery County Bd. of Educ., 377 F. Supp. 1123 (M.D. Ala. 1974), *aff'd per curiam*, 511 F.2d 1374 (5th Cir. 1975), the Fifth Circuit approved (two-to-one) a plan in which 55 per cent of the black elementary school pupils were enrolled at schools 87 per cent or more black, and nearly 40 per cent of the junior high school students are enrolled in schools 80 per cent or more black. District Judge Frank Johnson rejected plaintiffs' plan for greater desegregation. He found it was designed "for the sole purpose of attaining a strict racial balance

for noncompliance or delay.[24] But where, as in Delta County, violent opposition has rendered implementation very difficult, there appears to be little by way of judicial precedent to justify a desegregation order which would exceed the *Swann* standards for busing, if done in retaliation against the violent acts which made the excessive busing necessary. Violent interference with school desegregation orders violates the federal criminal code;[25] it may also justify civil relief.[26] But future remedies provide little comfort to parents understandably concerned about the immediate danger of having their children transported over long stretches of country roads in a community where fanatics are willing—in order to prevent busing—to destroy bridges with evident impunity. Civil rights policies that limit the scope of *Brown* to rights obtainable only on pain of daily fear of physical harm should no longer be accepted without question by black parents in Delta County, or anywhere else.

c. *New school construction* in a location near North Bridge is an expensive alternative to reconstructing South Bridge—which the school board will not undertake voluntarily and which, because of the great cost involved, courts are not likely to require. School boards have been ordered to select "the construction sites of future schools so that desegregation will be enhanced."[27] The purchase of new buses to enable the transportation of school children has also been required,[28] even in a school system which had never before operated a transportation system and which did not promote a dual system by using buses.[29] And, where the selected site would perpetuate the dual school system,[30] at least one court ordered a halt to new construction until

---

in each elementary school. . . . [T]he plaintiffs' plan would be disruptive to the educational processes and would place an excessive and unnecessarily heavy administrative burden on the school system." 377 F. Supp. at 1129.

24. Cooper v. Aaron, 358 U.S. 1 (1958); *cf.* Brown v. Board of Educ., 349 U.S. 294 (1955) ("the vitality of . . . constitutional principles cannot be allowed to yield simply because of disagreement with them").

The violent measures resorted to in the fictitious Delta County situation appear extreme; however, there are recent reports of law enforcement officials in Boston indicating that an alleged terrorist campaign has been initiated by a group of anti-busing activists who reportedly plotted to destroy five to seven bridges which provide access to South Boston where the blue-collar white community has mounted a continuing protest against school desegregation ordered by federal courts. Boston Evening Globe, Dec. 20, 1974, at 34.

25. 18 U.S.C. § 245 (1970). *See also id.* §§ 241-242; Hayes v. United States, 464 F.2d 1252 (5th Cir. 1972) (denying post-conviction relief to defendants convicted under 18 U.S.C. § 241 for bombing school buses used to transport black students to desegregated schools).

26. *See Note: Private "Self-Help" Efforts by Whites*, in D. BELL, RACE, RACISM AND AMERICAN LAW 318 (1973).

27. Dandridge v. Jefferson Parish School Bd., 332 F. Supp. 590, 594 (E.D. La. 1971), *aff'd*, 456 F.2d 552 (5th Cir. 1972). *See also* Clark v. Board of Educ. of Little Rock School Dist., 449 F.2d 493 (8th Cir. 1971); Trahan v. Lafayette Parish School Bd., 362 F. Supp. 503 (W.D. La. 1973).

28. *See* United States v. Greenwood Municipal Separate School Dist., 460 F.2d 1205 (5th Cir. 1972). *See also* Henry v. Clarksdale Municipal School Dist., 480 F.2d 583 (5th Cir. 1973).

29. *See* Brown v. Board of Educ. of City of Bessemer, 464 F.2d 382 (5th Cir. 1972).

30. *See* United States v. Board of Pub. Instruction of Polk County, 395 F.2d 66 (5th Cir. 1968).

the school board took action to ameliorate the situation. Ordering construction of a new school, even in the unique Delta County situation, would exceed judicial limits for equitable relief in school desegregation cases.[31]

d. *The emergency plan* adopted by the Delta County School Board after the destruction of South Bridge will likely be approved by appellate courts even though the effect of assigning each child to the closest school perpetuates the dual school system. The Supreme Court has suggested that "the effect —not the purpose or motivation of a school board's action" is the crucial determinant in weighing the validity of a school desegregation plan,[32] and, by its decision in *Green v. County School Board*,[33] implicitly endorsed the statement that "[t]he only school desegregation plan that meets constitutional standards is one that works."[34] But, as I've just indicated, no other, more effective desegregation plan can meet the Court's tests of "reasonableness" and "feasibility."[35] The addition of a "freedom-of-choice" provision to the emergency plan might be sought in order to accommodate parents wishing to voluntarily transport their children to Davis School.[36] The school board might even be required to provide buses for these students.[37] Regardless of whether this relief is obtained, the relatively small number of black children who chose Davis School under the pre-1972 plan suggests that no more are likely to do so now that the distances to be traveled are so much greater and the enthusiasm for integration in the black community is greatly diminished.

e. *The private school*, Causasian Children's Choice (CCC), by offering a segregated sanctuary to white families wishing to avoid integrated schools, poses

31. A court might require construction of temporary classrooms at a midway point between the two schools for special integrated classes which all students might attend on a rotating basis perhaps once each week.

32. Wright v. Council of City of Emporia, 407 U.S. 451, 462 (1972).

33. 391 U.S. 430 (1968).

34. United States v. Jefferson County Bd. of Educ., 372 F.2d 836, 847 (5th Cir. 1966), *cert. denied*, 389 U.S. 840 (1967).

35. Swann v. Charlotte-Mecklenburg Bd. of Educ., 402 U.S. at 31. "[A school board is] under an obligation to exercise every reasonable effort to remedy the violation, once it [is] identified . . . ." A plan that is "reasonable, feasible and workable" is within "the scope of [equitable] remedial power," although in defining "the limits on remedial power of courts, . . . [s]ubstance, not semantics, must govern . . . ." 402 U.S. at 24 n.8, 31.

36. In *Green v. County School Board*, the Court struck down the freedom-of-choice plan under which the school district had operated, but in doing so, it did not condemn freedom-of-choice plans per se.

> Where a "freedom of choice" plan offers real promise of achieving a unitary, nonracial system there might be no objection to allowing it to prove itself in operation, but where there are reasonably available other ways, such as zoning, promising speedier and more effective conversion to a unitary school system, "freedom of choice" is not acceptable.

391 U.S. at 439-41.

37. *Swann* indicates, that, in order to be approved, a majority-to-minority "transfer arrangement must grant the transferring student free transportation and space must be made available in the school to which he desires to move." 402 U.S. at 26-27. *Cf.* Northcross v. Board of Educ. of Memphis City Schools, 489 F.2d 18 (6th Cir. 1973) (approving orders requiring the city to provide funds and necessary gasoline needed for court-ordered busing).

a serious obstacle to the elimination of the dual school system in Delta County, and thus is an appropriate target for legal challenge. CCC's discriminatory admissions policy is barely concealed by the ingenuous device of limiting admission to the children of residents who attended or were eligible to attend Davis School at a time prior to 1954 when it was segregated by law.[38]

Private schools, which, as "segregation academies" to which white anti-integrationists escape, making school desegregation efforts futile, are barred from receiving any state aid in the form of tuition grants,[39] tax exemptions,[40] books and other school supplies,[41] school buildings, either by purchase[42] or lease,[43] and even the exclusive use of publicly-owned facilities.[44]

In addition, there is some judicial authority indicating that a post-Civil War federal civil rights law[45] may require admission of black children even to a wholly private school, when their rejection is based solely on race.[46] In order to challenge CCC's policy which now offers shelter for whites who don't wish to send their children to school with blacks, some Delta County black parents may be willing to apply for their children to be admitted. However, litigation to achieve this result is likely to be prolonged, as it affects the whole range of exemptions from civil rights laws that private clubs presently enjoy.[47]

---

38. *Cf.* Guinn v. United States, 238 U.S. 347 (1915); Lane v. Wilson, 307 U.S. 268 (1939).

39. Poindexter v. Louisiana Financial Comm'n, 275 F. Supp. 833 (E.D. La. 1967), *aff'd per curiam*, 389 U.S. 571 (1968); Coffey v. State Educ. Finance Comm'n, 296 F. Supp. 1389 (S.D. Miss. 1969); Griffin v. State Bd. of Educ., 296 F. Supp. 1178 (E.D. Va. 1969); Brown v. South Carolina State Bd. of Educ., 296 F. Supp. 199 (D.S.C. 1968), *aff'd per curiam*, 393 U.S. 222 (1968).

Earlier private school cases are cited in T. EMERSON, D. HABER, & N. DORSEN, POLITICAL AND CIVIL RIGHTS IN THE UNITED STATES, 1280-82 (student ed. 1967).

40. Green v. Connolly, 330 F. Supp. 1150 (D.D.C. 1971), *aff'd sub nom.* Coit v. Green, 404 U.S. 997 (1971); Bob Jones University v. Connally, 472 F.2d 903 (4th Cir. 1973), *aff'd*, 416 U.S. 725 (1974); Crenshaw County Private School Foundation v. Connally, 474 F.2d 1185 (5th Cir. 1973); *cf.* Pitts v. Department of Revenue, 333 F. Supp. 662 (E.D. Wis. 1971) (denying a state tax exemption to a segregated fraternal order).

41. Norwood v. Harrison, 413 U.S. 455 (1973); Graham v. Evangeline Parish School Bd., 484 F.2d 649 (5th Cir. 1973).

42. Wright v. Baker County Bd. of Educ., 501 F.2d 131 (5th Cir. 1972); McNeal v. Tate County School Dist., 460 F.2d 568 (5th Cir. 1972); Wright v. City of Brighton, 441 F.2d 447 (5th Cir. 1971).

43. United States v. Mississippi, 499 F.2d 425 (5th Cir. 1974).

44. Gilmore v. City of Montgomery, 417 U.S. 556 (1974).

45. 42 U.S.C. § 1981 (1970).

> All persons within the jurisdiction of the United States shall have the same right in every State and Territory to make and enforce contracts, to sue, be parties, give evidence, and to the full and equal benefit of all laws and proceedings for the security of persons and property as is enjoyed by white citizens.

Id.

46. *Compare* Gonzales v. Fairfax-Brewster School, Inc., 363 F. Supp. 1200 (E.D. Va. 1973), *with* Riley v. Adirondack Southern School for Girls, 368 F. Supp. 392 (M.D. Fla. 1973) (holding that a private school did not violate 42 U.S.C. § 1981 where a black applicant was denied admission "although race was one of the factors along with age, level of maturity, and family background.")

47. 42 U.S.C. § 2000a(e) (1970) exempts "a private club or other establishment not in

Moreover, litigation intended to send black children to a school like CCC would be difficult to justify on educational grounds. And it could backfire as a tactic with which to undermine private schools: CCC officials might admit the few black children who applied, both as a defense against integration litigation and as a means of obtaining tax-exempt status and other governmental benefits from which they are now excluded.

Rather than risk unintentionally assisting CCC—by having black children apply and thereby test the school's admission policies—it may be tactically wiser, given the limited nature of resources in the black community, to focus efforts on improving Bledsoe School. Without government support or the morale boost of defending against a desegregation suit, CCC may well fail on its own, as do large numbers of private, segregated academies and schools each year. The low income status of the parents who must finance CCC makes failure a good possibility. Indications that Bledsoe is functioning effectively could increase that possibility to a virtual certainty.[48]

II

The Settlement Offer

Assuming the Delta County School Board's emergency plan is upheld until South Bridge is replaced, the immediate question for the black community is whether the *Brown* precedent offers alternative relief for the educationally unsatisfactory conditions in all-black Bledsoe School. An assessment of the availability and value of such relief is necessary in order to determine the relative merit of the settlement plan offered by the board.

If black parents in Delta County share the educational priorities of blacks in other sections of the country, they are less concerned that Bledsoe School remains all-black than that its academic record is poor and that the community it serves is unable to influence basic decisions concerning personnel, curriculum, and teaching philosophy. These are the concerns that have motivated efforts by black parents to improve their children's public schools across the country in recent times, as well as for 150 years before the *Brown* decision.[49]

---

fact open to the public . . . ."

See also Note, *Desegregation of Private Schools: Section 1981 as an Alternative to State Action*, 62 Geo. L.J. 1363 (1974); Note, *Private Schools: A Limitation on Racially Motivated Refusal to Contract*, 11 Houston L. Rev. 691 (1974); Note, *The Desegregation of Private Schools: Is Section 1981 the Answer?*, 48 N.Y.U.L. Rev. 1147 (1973); Comment, Jones v. Alfred H. Mayer Co. *Extended to Private Education:* Gonzales v. Fairfax-Brewster School, Inc., 122 U. Pa. L. Rev. 471 (1973).

48. For reasons more fully discussed in Part III of this article, white opposition to school desegregation is based, in part, on the conviction—strengthened by the over-stated condemnations of integrationists—that black schools are bad schools.

49. Bell, *School Litigation Strategies for the 1970's: New Phases in the Continuing Quest for Quality Schools*, 1970 Wisc. L. Rev. 257, 259-67.

A number of approaches may be considered:

a. *The "separate but equal" doctrine* of *Plessy v. Ferguson*[50] may have been reoriented rather than overruled by *Brown.*[51] The evil of "separate but equal" is less that its promise of equality was never achieved than that, as Judge J. Skelly Wright has observed: "the doctrine itself, imposed by a white society, unconstitutionally stigmatizes Negroes in that society."[52] The demand in *Brown* that school "segregation" be replaced by "integration" may "merely be semantic if the underlying reality of black powerlessness does not change."[53] If *Brown* was intended to renew the nation's languished commitment to blacks made when the fourteenth amendment was adopted, then the separate-but-equal standard may serve as a point of departure in measuring the validity of school policies, particularly in those situations where integration is not feasible.

Justice Douglas implies as much in a case where several factors contributed to the racial isolation of a predominantly black high school.[54] Even if the causes of racial isolation in the schools did not constitute segregation for which the school board could be held responsible under *Brown*, Justice Douglas felt that the problem was not resolved unless the school facilities provided for blacks and whites were equal as required by the *Plessy* doctrine.[55]

In other contexts, some courts have recognized that minority-group children are entitled not only to a desegregated education, but to a school program that is tailored to their educational needs. For example, an educational program tailored to the middle class child from an English-speaking family

---

50. 163 U.S. 537 (1896).

51. In neither *Brown* nor the immediate post-*Brown* decisions is the *Plessy* decision itself expressly overruled.

52. Wright, *The Role of the Supreme Court in a Democratic Society—Judicial Activism or Restraint?*, 54 CORNELL L. REV. 1, 18 (1968).

53. Brown, *Busing and the Search for Equal Educational Opportunity*, 1 J. LAW & ED. 251, 266 (1972).

54. *See* Gomperts v. Chase, 404 U.S. 1237 (1971). *See also* Hobson v. Hansen, 269 F. Supp. 401 (1967), *aff'd sub nom.* Smuck v. Hobson, 408 F.2d 175 (1969).

55. 404 U.S. at 1240-41. The *Plessy* doctrine, according to Justice Douglas, might require a plan under which white as well as black students are required to use the inferior high school unless inequalities in the black school were removed through upgrading. *Id. But see* Cumming v. Richmond County Bd. of Educ., 175 U.S. 528 (1899), where the court rejected black petitioners' contention that the "separate but equal" standard required the closing of a white high school until a black high school closed by the school board was reopened. *Id.* at 544.

Lower courts during the *Plessy* era were no more willing than the Supreme Court to degrade the quality of white schools in order to improve black schools, particularly when the board claimed financial problems limited its ability to equalize school facilities. *See* Leflar & Davis, *Segregation in the Public Schools—1953*, 67 HARV. L. REV. 377, 395-96 & n.67 (1954).

But it was the "separate but equal" standard that led to desegregation of graduate schools in several pre-*Brown* cases, where the alternative, according to the Court, could never be made "equal." Sweatt v. Painter, 339 U.S. 629 (1950); McLaurin v. Oklahoma State Regents, 339 U.S. 637 (1950); Sipuel v. Board of Regents, 332 U.S. 631 (1948), Missouri *ex rel.* Gaines v. Canada, 305 U.S. 337 (1938). Even during the "all deliberate speed era" of *Brown v. Board of Educ.*, courts frequently ordered immediate desegregation where serious inequalities in facilities existed. *See, e.g.*, Rogers v. Paul, 382 U.S. 198 (1965).

has been held to deny an equal educational opportunity to children from Spanish-speaking homes.[56] Rejecting school board contentions that the failure to provide bilingual-bicultural programs did not constitute racially-motivated discrimination barred by the fourteenth amendment, the district court, noting the low achievement levels in predominantly Mexican-American schools, ordered the school board to reassess and enlarge its program directed to the specialized needs of its Spanish-speaking students.[57] The Supreme Court, moreover, has reflected a similar view regarding a school system's failure to provide English language instruction to students of Chinese ancestry who speak no English.[58] A unanimous Court held that the refusal to provide language instruction denied the Chinese children a meaningful opportunity to participate in the public educational program in violation of Title VI of the Civil Rights Act of 1964 and the HEW regulations.[59] It would seem only a short step to extend judicial recognition of the special educational needs of Mexican and Chinese children who do not speak English to that of black children whose preschool contact with standard English may be so minimal as to also constitute an educational barrier.[60]

While educationally-oriented relief is considered appropriate as part of a court-ordered desegregation plan, there is no reason why courts should not hold that it is absolutely essential in situations like Delta County where desegregation is not "feasible or reasonable." Relief of this character would

---

56. Serna v. Portales Municipal Schools, 351 F. Supp. 1279 (D.N. Mex. 1972), *aff'd on other grounds* (Title VI rather than fourteenth amendment), 499 F.2d 1147 (10th Cir. 1974); *cf.* Hobson v. Hansen, 269 F. Supp. 401 (1967), *aff'd sub nom.* Smuck v. Hobson, 408 F.2d 175 (1969).

57. 351 F. Supp. at 1282-83. *Cf.* United States v. Texas Educ. Agency, 467 F.2d 848 (5th Cir. 1972); Cisneros v. Corpus Christi Independent School Dist., 467 F.2d 142 (5th Cir. 1972); Arvizu v. Waco Independent School Dist., 373 F. Supp. 1264 (W.D. Tex. 1973), *rev'd on other grounds*, 495 F.2d 499 (5th Cir. 1974); Rangel & Alcala, *Project Report: De Jure Segregation of Chicanos in Texas Schools*, 7 HARV. CIV. RIGHTS—CIV. LIB. L. REV. 307 (1972).

58. Lau v. Nichols, 414 U.S. 563 (1974).

59. Where inability to speak and understand the English language excludes national origin-minority group children from effective participation in the educational program offered by a school district, the district must take affirmative steps to rectify the language deficiency in order to open its instructional program to these students.

35 Fed. Reg. 11595.

60. J. DILLARD, BLACK ENGLISH: ITS HISTORY AND USAGE IN THE UNITED STATES (1972); M. COLE, J. GAY, J. GLICK, & D. SHARP, THE CULTURAL CONTEXT OF LEARNING AND THINKING: AN EXPLORATION IN EXPERIMENTAL ANTHROPOLOGY (1971); van Geel, *The Right to be Taught Standard English: Exploring the Implications of* Lau v. Nichols *for Black Americans*, 25 SYRACUSE L. REV. 863 (1974).

The Supreme Court's refusal (by five-to-four vote) to require equalization of school funding formulas in San Antonio Independent School Dist. v. Rodriguez, 411 U.S. 1 (1973), does not seriously impair the ability of black children to require educational facilities to respond to their special needs. The concept of equalizing school funding formulas is not inherently defective, Serrano v. Priest, 5 Cal. 3d 584, 487 P.2d 1241, 96 Cal. Rptr. 601 (1971), but such contentions may be better raised in litigation designed to show that unequal school funding, whether intradistrict or interdistrict, adversely affects the school's ability to respond effectively to its obligation to remedy the effects of past discrimination.

cover equalization of physical plant, teacher quality, and curriculum. But real equality and educational effectiveness demand that public schools be responsive and responsible to those they serve.

Courts must recognize that groups long denied participation in school policy-making, and ill-equipped to monitor their children's educational progress, must have at least the judicial support and protection that have made current levels of desegregation possible. Perhaps paradoxically, separate schools which, through the implementation of alternative remedies, first become (in the educational sense) quality schools, may stand a better chance of eventually becoming integrated schools as well.[61]

At least one district court has recognized the necessity and possible value of alternative remedies.[62] Approving a school board's authority to both establish and later disestablish a community control experiment, the court indicated that a school system could experiment "to see how the effectiveness of the educational structure may be improved." And therefore, it could "not be prevented from ending one experiment and trying others, if the action is taken in good faith, without discriminatory intent or result."[63]

b. *School board representation* is an important element of an equal educational opportunity. Understandably, the Delta County board's settlement plan did not include representation of the black community on its five-person school board. Furthermore, since members are elected on an "at-large" basis, it will be quite difficult for the black community to elect a representative who will assert their special interests and needs.[64] But the argument can be made that *Brown* requires such representation or, at least, bars election processes which serve as discriminatory barriers to fair representation.

The Supreme Court has required that electoral districts be apportioned so as to equalize the value of each citizen's vote.[65] The principles of equal representation have also been applied to elected school trustees.[66] The Court

---

61. *See* K. CLARK, A POSSIBLE REALITY: A DESIGN FOR THE ATTAINMENT OF HIGH ACADEMIC ACHIEVEMENT FOR INNER-CITY STUDENTS (1972). This alternative remedy to integration for past discriminatory school policies, if vigorously enforced by the courts, might avoid the dire situation contained in Justice Douglas' warning that the court's rulings in *San Antonio Independent School Dist.* and *Milliken v. Bradley*, will return the problems of blacks and the society to the "separate but unequal" period. 418 U.S. at 759.

62. *See* Oliver v. Donovan, 293 F. Supp. 958 (E.D.N.Y. 1968).

63. *Id.* at 972. Thus the court held that there was no constitutional right to community controlled schools. Unlike segregation, which was "inherently unconstitutional," and called for the only alternative, desegregation, even if the court found "centralization" to be unconstitutional, "decentralization is [not] the only constitutional alternative." *Id.* at 968. The litigation involved the black community's futile effort to prevent the ending of New York City's Ocean Hill-Brownsville local control school experiment and illustrates that meaningful black participation in school policy-making can result in as much white resistance—from teacher's unions, school suppliers, and the like—as does school integration. *See* CONFRONTATION AT OCEAN HILL-BROWNSVILLE (M. Berube & M. Gittell eds. 1969).

64. *See* Owens v. School Comm. of Boston, 304 F. Supp. 1327 (D. Mass. 1969).

65. Reynolds v. Sims, 377 U.S. 533 (1964).

66. Hadley v. Junior College Dist., 397 U.S. 50 (1970).

has long recognized that at-large districts operate "to minimize or cancel out the voting strength of racial or political elements of the voting population,"[67] and has warned that a multi-member district would be found unconstitutional as invidiously discriminatory if it could be shown that it operated "designedly or otherwise . . . under the circumstances of a particular case . . . to minimize or cancel out the voting strength of racial or political elements of the voting population."[68]

Multimember districts in Dallas and Bexar Counties in Texas have been voided on a record that included proof of: a long history of official racial discrimination in Texas, particularly in voting; specific provisions of Texas primaries that disadvantage minority candidates; the total domination of the Democratic Party in selecting candidates for the legislature from Dallas County; the fact that only two blacks have been selected by the party and elected to the legislature since reconstruction days; and the fact that the party did not need black votes to win, and consequently did not "exhibit good-faith concern for the political and other needs and aspirations of the black community."[69]

In Delta County no blacks have ever been elected to the school board, and the board's long-term refusal to comply with *Brown* reflects an antipathy to black concerns that justifies a legal challenge to the present election system, either under the pending school desegregation litigation or in a separate suit.[70] The record of long-term evasion of existing law already established in the school desegregation litigation should enable the black com-

---

67. Dusch v. Davis, 387 U.S. 112, 117 (1967).

68. Fortson v. Dorsey, 379 U.S. 433, 439 (1965). *See* White v. Regester, 412 U.S. 755 (1973); Whitcomb v. Chavis, 403 U.S. 124 (1971).

69. White v. Regester, 412 U.S. at 766-67. The Court found the black community was "generally not permitted to enter into the political process in a *reliable and meaningful* manner." 412 U.S. at 767 (emphasis added). This decision's potential is discussed in Comment, *Reapportionment and Minority Politics*, 6 COLUM. HUMAN RIGHTS L. REV. 107 (1974).

See also Seals v. Quarterly Counts Court of Madison County, Tenn., 496 F.2d 76 (6th Cir. 1974); Zimmer v. McKeithen, 485 F.2d 1297 (5th Cir. 1973); Beer v. United States, 374 F. Supp. 363 (D.D.C. 1974); Yelverton v. Driggers, 370 F. Supp. 612 (M.D. Ala. 1974); Moore v. Leflore County Bd. of Election Comm'rs, 361 F. Supp. 603 (N.D. Miss. 1972).

70. A number of suits have been filed challenging the validity of school boards elected on a multi-member basis. *See, e.g.*, Calderon v. Waco Independent School Dist., Civil No. W-74-CA-21 (D. Tex. Apr. 16, 1974); LULAC v. Corpus Christi Independent School Dist., Civil No. CA-74-C-95 (S.D. Tex. Aug. 14, 1974); Mendoza v. Hafley, Civil No. 74-51 (D. Ariz. Mar. 28, 1974).

Each of these suits was filed on behalf of Chicano plaintiffs by lawyers with the Mexican-American Legal Defense Fund. Mexican-American civil rights groups have been far more sensitive than those serving blacks to the importance of giving priority to educational components in relief sought for past discrimination in public schools. *See, e.g.*, Serna v. Portales Municipal Schools, 499 F.2d 1147 (10th Cir. 1974).

But black civil rights groups have not opposed such suits, either. *See, e.g.*, Jolley v. McDonough, Civil No. CA-75-812-T (D. Mass. Mar. 4, 1975), a challenge to the at-large election procedure of the Boston School Committee.

munity to succeed with this issue where black plaintiffs in Boston failed.[71]

c. *Community control* as an addition to desegregation, or as a substitute when desegregation is not available, is a worthy aim and, at least within the black community, an uncontroversial one;[72] but serious legal and political problems are created by the suggestion that control over black schools by black parents can serve as an alternative to the desegregation to which they are entitled under post-*Brown* standards.

There are some blacks—although a minority—who reject school integration as worthless educationally and dangerous politically.[73] Others, including many civil rights leaders, believe that *Brown* intended school *integration*, and no other remedy is conceivable.[74] A majority, however, probably share the

---

71. Owens v. School Comm. of Boston, 304 F. Supp. 1327 (D. Mass. 1969). Black plaintiffs sought only a few weeks before a school board election and without an evidentiary hearing, to enjoin the at-large election of a five-person Boston School Committee. The court, in denying plaintiffs' motion, held that a school system is not constitutionally compelled to adopt a district system in order to better the minority group's chances of securing representation of their particular interests. *Id.* at 1330.

Black voters have had more success in striking down discriminatory electoral schemes in the South where the long history of racial segregation and discrimination ease the difficulty of meeting the heavy burden of showing that the scheme was intended to discriminate against black voters. *Compare* Whitcomb v. Chavis, 403 U.S. 124 (1971), *with* White v. Regester 412 U.S. 755 (1973).

Even if the at-large system is struck down, election officials may attempt to gerrymander the single member districts so as to make black voters a minority in each such district. *See* 5 HARV. CIV. RIGHTS—CIV. LIB. L. REV. 472 (1970).

In districts where school boards are appointed, the principles interpreting *Brown* to require desegregation of school faculties, Rogers v. Paul, 382 U.S. 198 (1965); United States v. Montgomery County Bd. of Educ., 395 U.S. 225 (1969), should be broadened to include effective representation of minority interests on the school board. Whatever the entitlement of blacks to representation under general equal protection principles, *cf.* Mayor of Philadelphia v. Educational Equality League, 415 U.S. 605 (1974); Pettway v. American Cast Iron Pipe Co., 494 F.2d 211 (5th Cir. 1974); Ferrell v. Oklahoma, 339 F. Supp. 73 (W.D. Okla. 1972), this remedy is essential where a school system is ordered to eliminate the effects of past racial discrimination.

72. *But see, e.g.*, critical comments made by Dr. Kenneth B. Clark, originally a strong proponent of the school decentralization movement. N.Y. Times, May 8, 1972, at 1, col. 3. *See also* Alberbach & Walker, *Citizen Desires, Policy Outcomes, and Community Control*, 8 URBAN AFFAIRS Q. 55, 64 (1972) (in general, black residents of Detroit more opposed to community control than whites); Sussman & Speck, *Community Participation in Schools: The Boston Case*, 7 URBAN ED. 341, 343 (1973) (84 per cent of black parents interviewed preferred traditional forms of parent involvement—*e.g.*, PTA, talking individually with teachers).

73. At the March 1972 National Black Political Convention in Gary, Indiana, CORE director Roy Innis authored a resolution that, as adopted, condemned both busing and school integration as a "bankrupt, suicidal method . . . based on the false notion that black children are unable to learn unless they are in the same setting as white children." N.Y. Times, Mar. 13, 1972, at 30, col. 4.

74. Typical is NAACP Executive Director Roy Wilken's comment: "We have suffered too many heartaches and shed too much blood in fighting the evil of racial segregation to return . . . to the lonely and dispiriting confines of its demeaning prison." *Voices of the Elder Statesmen*, SATURDAY REVIEW, June 21, 1969, at 70. And in 1974, NAACP General Counsel Nathaniel R. Jones criticized the Atlanta Compromise as follows: "The Atlanta Compromise of 1973 would have left 83 schools more than 90 percent black. It was a trade-off of pupil desegregation for ad-

view of the well-known black educator, Dr. Benjamin E. Mays, who favors continuing to work for school integration, but who recognizes the barrier to this goal posed by white flight:[75]

> Black people must not resign themselves to the pessimistic view that a non-integrated school cannot provide Black children with an excellent educational setting. Instead, Black people, while working to implement *Brown*, should recognize that integration alone does not provide a quality education, and that much of the substance of quality education can be provided to Black children in the interim.

In at least two cases—Atlanta and Forth Worth—district courts have approved plans that gave black parents a larger measure of control over school policy-making in exchange for less integration than would otherwise have been ordered. In Atlanta, school litigation was protracted more than a decade through innumerable court orders and several appeals.[76] A group of plaintiffs, discouraged by the prospect of achieving meaningful desegregation in a district which was becoming increasingly all-black,[77] worked out a compromise plan with the Atlanta School Board calling for full faculty and staff desegregation and limited pupil desegregation.[78] In exchange, the board promised to hire a number of blacks in administrative positions, including a black superintendent of schools.[79] In approving the plan, the court was undoubtedly influenced by petitions favoring its adoption signed by "[s]everal thousand of the plaintiff class."[80] However, some of the plain-

---

ministrative jobs, which would have, if the NAACP had not taken decisive action, doomed the Association's commitment to desegregation." Jones, Brown—*20 Years Later*, 81 THE CRISIS 152, 154 (May 1974).

75. Mays, Comment: *Atlanta—Living With* Brown *Twenty Years Later*, 3 BLACK L.J. 184, 191-92 (1974). On the surface, this view departs more in emphasis than principle from NAACP policy. A staff member of that group reports "The 1969 NAACP Annual Convention gave its blessing to the concept of community control with the caveat that it must aid in advancing desegregation and quality education while fulfilling its basic aim of providing parents with a greater voice in running their schools." Watson, *The Detroit School Challenge*, 81 THE CRISIS 188, 189 (June-July 1974). But on closer inspection, it becomes apparent that the NAACP caveat swallows up the concept. Black children may or may not get a better education if they are bused to the suburbs, but it is highly unlikely that their parents will have more than a token input into policy decisions at the "receiving schools."

76. *See* Mays, *supra* note 75 for a review of the history of the Atlanta school litigation.

77. In 1952 32 per cent of Atlanta's public school enrollment was black; by 1974 the figure was more than 82 per cent. *Id.* at 185-86.

78. *See* Calhoun v. Cook, 362 F. Supp. 1249 (N.D. Ga. 1973). The district court found that the plan, which provided that no school would contain less than 30 per cent blacks (or less than 20 per cent in already integrated "stablized" schools) was reasonable "considering the small percentage of white children (21%) now remaining in the system . . . ." *Id.* at 1251 & n.7.

79. The court pointed out that it "could not on its own order any hiring or firing except on the basis of merit. . . . Only by settlement could specific jobs be designated as 'black' or 'white,' even for initial appointment." 362 F. Supp. at 1251 n.6. *Cf.* Porcelli v. Titus, 431 F.2d 1254 (3d Cir. 1970), approving the Newark, New Jersey, school board's decision to appoint blacks as principals over some white applicants on the promotion list in order to better integrate administrative staffs and upgrade the public schools.

80. 362 F. Supp. at 1251 n. 5.

tiffs disagreed, termed the compromise a "sell out,"[81] and appealed. The appeal was burdened by a number of procedural issues concerning the lack of notice and the refusal of the district court to grant hearings on the compromise plan. This enabled the Fifth Circuit Court of Appeals to remand the case to the district court without deciding the merits of the settlement agreement.[82]

In Fort Worth, Texas, a district court approved continuance of a predominantly black high school and middle school located in a black neighborhood on a finding that black parents wanted to maintain a community school in which "the self concept of the blacks would be enhanced by giving them an opportunity to show their pride in their race and what they could do if given an opportunity."[83] In approving the plan which—in addition to the regular school program—would also provide educational and vocational programs for adults, the court found nothing unconstitutional about the concept where it comes at the plaintiffs' request. As did the court in Atlanta, this court cited no cases to support its conclusions, stating only that "it is beyond [our] comprehension to presume that the blacks are being denied equal rights with other races when they know what their rights are and they are getting something they requested."[84]

The Atlanta and Forth Worth settlement decisions are valuable as examples of arrangements deemed reasonable alternatives to full desegregation. In each case the plan was either supported or not strongly opposed by representative numbers of the class.

Somewhat similar issues were posed in *Newburg Area Council v. Board of Education of Jefferson County, Kentucky.*[85] Relying on its decision in the Detroit

---

81. Trillin, *U.S. Journal: Atlanta Settlement*, NEW YORKER 101, 103 (Mar. 17, 1973).

82. Calhoun v. Cook, 487 F.2d 680 (5th Cir. 1973). Significantly, the court—consisting of two liberals on school desegregation, Wisdom and Thornberry, and one conservative, Clark—permitted the district-court-approved settlement plan to take effect for the 1973-74 school year, pending further hearings on the plan. *Id.* at 683-84.

83. Flax v. Potts, Civil No. 4205 at 21 (N.D. Tex. Aug. 23, 1973). The court's statements in this unpublished opinion that Dunbar High School and Dunbar Middle School could be combined into the "Dunbar Complex," and that while "the schools will be desegregated," the "makeup of the neighborhood . . . [is such] that the attendance will be predominately black"—must be seen in the context of the entire plan adopted by the court in that case which effectively desegregated more than one hundred schools in the Fort Worth system. One of the attorneys for the plaintiff, Norman J. Chachkin, has stated that the case was not appealed by the plaintiffs in view of the success that the litigation had achieved with respect to the rest of the school system. Statement made at The Courts, Social Science, and School Desegregation Conference, Hilton Head Island, S.C., Aug. 20, 1974, on file at *Law and Contemporary Problems* office. *See also* note 84 *infra*.

84. Flax v. Potts, Civil No. 4205 at 21 (N.D. Tex. Aug. 23, 1973). Norman J. Chachkin, a Legal Defense Fund attorney, denied that plaintiffs had offered the compromise nor agreed to it; rather, the idea originated with the school board without approval of the plaintiffs. Statement made at The Courts, Social Science, and School Desegregation Conference, Hilton Head Island, S.C., Aug. 20, 1974, on file at *Law and Contemporary Problems* office.

85. 510 F.2d 1358 (6th Cir. 1974).

school case,[86] the Sixth Circuit Court of Appeals had ordered the Louisville City School District (50 percent black) and the surrounding Jefferson County School District (4 percent black) to desegregate their schools "[b]y whatever means the district court deems appropriate in the exercise of its equity powers . . . ."[87] When the Supreme Court set strict standards for metropolitan desegregation plans in *Milliken*, it also remanded the Louisville case to the Sixth Circuit[88] where the Louisville board argued: (1) that residential patterns and not an unwillingness to desegregate have caused racial isolation in its schools; (2) that a simple desegregation order will increase the already rapid rate of "white flight"; and, (3) that it is willing to merge with the predominantly white Jefferson County system, but only providing it could preserve the parental influence on policy-making and educational program that has enabled their elementary-level children in the lower grades to read on the national level. Forty percent of the pupils are from poverty-level families; 80 per cent of those families are black.[89]

The Louisville system attributes its educational gains to an "innovative superintendent" and to a program of shared decision-making power under which each of the fifty schools has a separate board, composed of patrons and educators, which participates in staff and curriculum selection and financial allocation. The local boards, according to the Louisville brief, "have been viable and their decisions responsible."[90] Community hostility toward particular schools has been reduced. But a simple merger, it is feared, will result in subordination of the poverty-level interests of Louisville's pupils in favor of the predominantly middle class white interests of Jefferson County. Nevertheless, upon remand of the case by the Supreme Court, the Sixth Circuit found the Louisville situation different from that in *Milliken*, concluding that the problem in *Milliken* was that the remedy "was broader than the constitutional violation" but that in this case "the situation presented is that of two districts in the same county of the state being equally guilty in failing to eliminate all vestiges of segregation . . . ." Accordingly, the Sixth Circuit noted that the district court's order could include an interdistrict remedy.[91]

Community-control plans have not received much judicial recognition, in part because relief of this type seldom has been sought in a school deseg-

---

86. Bradley v. Milliken, 484 F.2d 215 (6th Cir. 1973).

87. Newburg Area Council v. Board of Educ. of Jefferson County, 489 F.2d 925, 932 (1973).

88. Haycraft v. Board of Educ. of Louisville, 510 F.2d 1358 (6th Cir. 1974) (consolidated with Newburg Area Council v. Board of Educ. of Jefferson County).

89. Supplemental Brief of Board of Education of Louisville at 6-9, Haycraft v. Board of Educ. of Louisville, Civil No. 73-1408 (6th Cir. Dec. 11, 1974).

90. *Id.* at 28-29.

91. Haycraft v. Board of Educ. of Louisville, 510 F.2d 1358, 1361 (6th Cir. 1974).

School Board Attorney Triplett had advised the author that the Louisville Board was willing to merge unconditionally with the Jefferson County systemn but feared the educational

regation case.[92] However, the Congress of Racial Equality (CORE) has intervened with somewhat similar arguments in a number of school cases.[93] In *Swann*, for example, CORE argued that integration was not the only method of eliminating segregation in the system and that the establishment of two nondiscriminatory and nonracially exclusive unitary school districts to replace the former segregated system would be an appropriate means of implementing the edict of *Brown.*[94] Under the now-invalidated dual school system, CORE said, one white board of education maintained control over two school systems characterized by racial exclusivity and arbitrarily imposed without choice or consent in a manner that: (1) stigmatized blacks, (2) excluded them from any meaningful participation in policy-making, and (3) systematically denied them equal school resources.[95]

Furthermore, CORE pointed out that school integration usually perpetuates the worst aspects of segregation. Therefore, it suggested that dual school-district lines be drawn to serve "communities of educational interest": Each student would be permitted to attend schools in either district; each district would elect its own school board and set its own school policy. Given these criteria, CORE argued, there is no constitutional requirement of racial dispersal in these unitary systems.[96] An inflexible requirement of racial dispersal, CORE contended, can be educationally destructive of "the desire of local Black communities to develop their own means of achieving the constitutionally mandated ends."[97]

At first glance, the CORE argument, ignored by the Supreme Court in the *Swann* decision, would seem attractive to the majority in *Milliken v. Brad-*

---

consequences of that merger. Moreover, he reported that the Jefferson County system opposed merger. Telephone conversation with Mr. Henry A. Triplett, Louisville School Board Attorney, November 22, 1974.

92. *See* Oliver v. Donovan, 293 F. Supp. 958 (E.D.N.Y. 1968) for an unsuccessful attempt by black plaintiffs to urge that community control was an appropriate remedy for a violation of their thirteenth and fourteenth amendment rights.

93. *See, e.g.*, brief for CORE as Amicus Curiae, Swann v. Charlotte-Mecklenburg Bd. of Educ., 402 U.S. 1 (1971); Application for Intervention by CORE, Calhoun v. Cook, 362 F. Supp. 1249 (N.D. Ga. 1973) (considered by the court on an amicus basis).

94. Brief for CORE as Amicus Curiae at 8-10, Swann v. Charlotte-Mecklenburg Bd. of Educ., 402 U.S. 1 (1971).

95. *Id.*

96. *Id.* at 11-14.

97. *Id.* at 22. This position is also set out in CORE, *A Proposal for Community School Districts*, in THE GREAT SCHOOL BUS CONTROVERSY 311 (N. Mills ed. 1973).

CORE arguments are distinguishable from the seemingly similar positions taken by antibusing writers. *See, e.g.*, Glazer, *Is Busing Necessary?*, 53 COMMENTARY 39 (Mar. 1972). These writers recognize that large-scale busing and consolidation of school districts

> makes impossible one kind of organization that a democratic society may wish to choose for its schools: the kind of organization in which the schools are the expression of a geographically defined community of small scale and regulated in accordance with the democratically expressed views of that community.

Id. at 47. But they ignore the legal and political problems of how minority communities are to obtain control over policy-making and budgetary processes.

ley[98] which rejected the metropolitan school desegregation remedy approved by the lower courts because, among other things, such a plan would be destructive of the long tradition of local control and autonomy in American public school education.[99] It would also tend to support the argument of the circuit court judge who condemned what he considered excessive busing required to comply with desegregation standards in Memphis "merely because a child's skin is white or black . . . ," and who warned that:[100]

> [t]he elimination of neighborhood schools necessarily interferes with the interest and participation by parents in the operation of the schools through parent-teachers' associations, interferes with activities of children out of school, and interferes with their privilege of association, and it deprives them of walk-in schools. In can even lower the quality of education.

But it is doubtful if even these opponents of busing to achieve desegregation would accept the CORE alternative of two, perhaps overlapping, school districts which, in all likelihood, would be distinguishable by race.[101]

The CORE argument that racial dispersal may not be educationally sound or legally required is not without merit and might receive more serious judicial attention if the relief sought focused more on the legitimate interest of parental participation than on the politically threatening and constitu-

---

98. 418 U.S. 717 (1974).

99. *Id.* at 741-42. Also see Justice Powell's opinion (concurring in part and dissenting in part) in *Keyes*, expressing concern that large-scale or long distance transportation of students disrupts public education, and ignores the practical and educational benefits achieved when children attend community schools near home. 413 U.S. at 238-52. *See also* San Antonio Independent School Dist. v. Rodriguez, 411 U.S. 1, 50 (1973).

On the other hand, the *Milliken* Court's reaffirmation of the *Swann* standards as the means for remedying intradistrict, de jure segregation, 418 U.S. at 744-45, raises some question as to the legal fate of an Atlanta-type settlement. But the question of alternative remedies was not, unfortunately, before the Court in *Milliken.*

100. Judge Weick dissenting in Northcross v. Board of Educ. of Memphis City Schools, 466 F.2d 890, 898 (6th Cir. 1972). Subsequently, the court (including Judge Weick) affirmed —in a *per curiam* opinion—approval of a plan for Memphis that left nineteen all-black or predominantly black schools, including some that were all-black at the inception of the litigation in 1960. It did not affect any all-white schools. Northcross v. Board of Educ. of Memphis City Schools, 489 F.2d 15 (6th Cir. 1973), *cert. denied*, 416 U.S. 962 (1974).

101. The district court that approved the Atlanta compromise rejected CORE's motion to intervene on the ground "that the relief sought by that group [CORE] would be unconstitutional, *i.e.*, it would recreate a dual school system." Calhoun v. Cook, 487 F.2d 680, 682 (1973). However, it did consider the CORE views on an amicus basis. Calhoun v. Cook, 362 F. Supp. 1249, 1250 n. 2. On appeal the Fifth Circuit ruled the denial of CORE's intervention effort was improper at least partly because "further proceedings may have demonstrated that CORE would be entitled to some but not all of the relief it sought in a manner that would have kept its position from being patently unconstitutional." 487 F.2d at 683.

The Fifth Circuit has evolved a specific intervention procedure for use in school desegregation cases. It requires intervenors to set out in their petitions "the precise issues . . . [they] sought to present. . . . The district court could then determine whether these matters had been previously raised and resolved and/or whether the issues . . . were currently known to the court and parties in the initial suit. . . . If the court felt that the new group had a significant claim which it could best represent, intervention would be allowed." Hines v. Rapides Parish School Bd., 479 F.2d 762, 765 (5th Cir. 1973).

tionally questionable goal of racially identifiable school districts. Nevertheless, there is ample evidence available which indicates that many desegregation orders are destructive of precisely those elements which are essential to the effective functioning of the educational process[102] and that black schools can be educationally effective.[103] Even without a more detailed doctrinal argument, courts grown weary of enforcing busing orders favored by increasingly few might be amenable to Justice Powell's exhortation that the goal sought and often overlooked "is the best possible educational opportunity for all children" and that "[c]ommunities deserve the freedom and the incentive to turn their attention and energies to this goal of quality education, free from protracted and debilitating battles over court-ordered student transportation."[104]

Earlier, in his concurring-in-part, dissenting-in-part opinion in *Keyes*, Justice Powell had criticized the majority's requirement that, in order to establish "a prima facie case of unlawful segregative design," petitioners in a northern school desegregation case need only show "intentionally segregative school board actions in a meaningful portion of a school system."[105] Instead, he argued for an affirmative equal-protection right to an integrated education wherever public schools are segregated to a substantial degree and wherever school boards are substantially responsible.[106] Should such a standard be adopted, proof of school board obligation would be easier to show because Justice Powell's criteria would effectively abolish the de jure/de facto distinction.[107] Even so, the Powell formula would require school boards to take only "reasonable" steps to eliminate segregation, which would not include requiring school authorities to undertake "widespread student

---

102. *See* notes 132-34 *infra*. This proof would not be offered to reverse *Brown*, Stell v. Savannah-Chatham County Bd. of Educ., 318 F.2d 425, 427 (5th Cir. 1963), but to broaden the scope of relief available under *Brown* to include plans where parental involvement rather than integration is given priority. 318 F.2d at 427-28.

103. N.Y. STATE OFFICE OF EDUCATION, PERFORMANCE REVIEW—SCHOOL FACTORS INFLUENCING READING ACHIEVEMENTS: A CASE STUDY OF TWO INNER CITY SCHOOLS (1974); G. WEBER, INNER-CITY CHILDREN CAN BE TAUGHT TO READ: FOUR SUCCESSFUL SCHOOLS (Council for Basic Educ. Occasional Paper No. 18, 1971); Meyers, *Schools: Morgan's Tentative Revolution*, 2 CITY 6 (Nov.-Dec. 1968); *Black Schools That Work*, NEWSWEEK, Jan. 1, 1973, at 47; D. BELL, *supra* note 5, at 579-81; Fantini, *Participation, Decentralization, Community Control, and Quality Education*, 71 THE TEACHERS COLLEGE RECORD 93 (1969).

104. Keyes v. School Dist. No. 1, 413 U.S. 189, 253 (1973).

105. 413 U.S. at 208.

106. 413 U.S. at 224-27.

107. 413 U.S. at 232. In a separate opinion Justice Douglas agreed with Justice Powell on this point. 413 U.S. at 214-17.

Legal scholars have recommended abolition of these distinctions for a decade. *See* Dimond, *School Segregation in the North: There is But One Constitution*, 7 HARV. CIV. RIGHTS—CIV. LIB. L. REV. 1 (1972); Fiss, *Racial Imbalance in the Public Schools: The Constitutional Concepts*, 78 HARV. L. REV. 564 (1965); Goodman, *De Facto Segregation: A Constitutional and Empirical Analysis*, 60 CALIF. L. REV. 275 (1972); Wright, *Public School Desegregation: Legal Remedies for De Facto Segregation*, 40 N.Y.U.L. REV. 285 (1965).

transportation solely for the sake of maximizing integration."[108] Assuming that he did not wish to create a basically empty right (he did recognize the difficulty of racially balancing the larger urban areas of the country),[109] Justice Powell's approach must be read to encompass acceptance of those school plans which recognize the residential realities and propose educationally-viable, judicially monitored alternatives by which the equal protection right created by pre-existent segregation may be approached even though the integration aspect of it may not immediately be achieved.

The legal and educational value of alternative schemes has been recognized by Dr. Kenneth Clark, a committed school integrationist, who provided much of the social science data cited in the first *Brown* decision.[110] Reviewing the patterns of institutionalized residential segregation which characterize the nation's large metropolitan areas, Dr. Clark stated:[111]

> Given the fact that public schools, so far, reflect the racial populations of cities, the goal of attaining high quality education through the democratic process of realistic and administratively feasible forms of desegregation appears to be, at least temporarily, abandoned and is being replaced by the need to concentrate on raising the quality of education without regard to the present racial composition of a city's public schools. This educational imperative must be met, for the present generation of students in the public schools of our cities is not expendable. If we continue to frustrate these students educationally, they will be, in fact, the ingredients of the "social dynamite" which threatens the stability of our cities, our economy, and the democratic form of government. It is conceivable, also, that a present emphasis on raising the quality of education for these children will eventually facilitate rather than block the continued struggle for a non-racial organization of the public schools in the United States.

Several commentators who have discussed the problem of alternative remedies to school integration have suggested arguments that might help close the gap between Justice Powell's affirmative equal protection right and the educationally sound, constitutionally cognizable and presently available remedy urged by Dr. Clark.[112] The discussions properly focus on the basic elements of the *Brown* decision seen by one writer as "integration, uncoerced association, and racially equal educational outcomes."[113] But the assumption in *Brown* that racial isolation causes racially different outcomes and that racial integration will

---

108. 413 U.S. at 240.

109. 413 U.S. at 242 n. 21.

110. 347 U.S. 483, 494 n. 11.

111. K. Clark, *supra* note 61, at 54. Significantly, Dr. Clark recognizes, albeit almost reluctantly, the value of improving the reputation for quality of "black schools" in order to "facilitate" his goal of truly integrated schools in this country. *See also* text at notes 125-27 *infra.*

112. *See, e.g.*, Brown, *Busing and the Search for Equal Educational Opportunity*, 1 J. Law & Ed. 251 (1972); Canby, *'Northern' School Segregation: Minority Rights to Integrate and Separate*, 1971 Law & Social Order 489; Kirp, *Community Control, Public Policy, and the Limits of Law*, 68 Mich. L. Rev. 1355 (1970); Comment, *Alternative Schools for Minority Students: The Constitution, the Civil Rights Act and the Berkeley Experiment*, 61 Calif. L. Rev. 858 (1973).

113. Kirp, *supra* note 112, at 1362. *See also* Canby, *supra* note 112, at 510-11.

yield racially identical results has been refuted by social science evidence.[114] An alternative remedy, sought by a substantial percentage of the discriminated class, should be judicially cognizable, particularly in those cases where integration is not "feasible." Such alternative plans would not contravene Supreme Court strictures on freedom-of-choice plans which result in racially-identifiable schools,[115] especially if minority parents who would prefer to have their children attend predominantly white schools are permitted to do so.[116]

Judicial approval of a community control plan, as an interim alternative to integration, does not raise the equal protection issues presented by efforts to make community control a constitutional right.[117] School systems which wish to correct for racial imbalance even in the absence of a constitutional requirement to do so,[118] may also adopt community-approved, interim, alternative remedies.

Reviewing the integration alternatives available to Delta County's black community, the equalization of school facilities and, possibly, school board representation may be sought through litigation. But the school board has offered more than equalization of facilities: it has promised to permit the Bledsoe School parents to select their next principal and to provide that person with wide authority in personnel selection, curriculum, and teaching approach. The details of this offer must be carefully drafted; they would include funding guarantees, the principal selection process, the mechanism for ongoing parental involvement, a process for monitoring pupil performance and teacher responsiveness, and, of course, the question of minority representation on the school board. It is essential that all aspects of the plan be judicially approved and supervised.

Assuming the board would agree to all these conditions—as it might in order to avoid integration of Davis School when South Bridge is rebuilt—the question of the constitutional validity of a permanent settlement, as in Atlanta, would almost certainly be raised. Realization of the points set forth

---

114. For a summary of the findings of various studies, see Goodman, *supra* note 107, at 400-35 & nn. 356-465.

115. Green v. County School Bd., 391 U.S. 430, 439-42 (1968).

116. Kirp, *supra* note 112, at 1369-70.

117. Kirp, *supra* note 112, at 1374-84. But even if the remedial nature of the alternative to integration is ignored, there is ample basis for arguing that such alternatives meet even a strict scrutiny standard although they tend to give state sanction to racially identifiable schools. *See* Alternative Schools for Minority Students: The Constitution, the Civil Rights Act and the Berkeley Experiment, *supra* note 112.

Even proponents concede that community control does not guarantee educational quality, and although it has been promising where tried, the experience is far from problem-free. *See* M. ZIMET, DECENTRALIZATION: A CASE STUDY OF THE 1969 DECENTRALIZATION LAW IN NEW YORK CITY (1973); CONFRONTATION AT OCEAN HILL-BROWNSVILLE (M. Berube & M. Gittell eds. 1969); Cohen, *The Price of Community Control*, 48 COMMENTARY 23 (July 1969).

118. *See* Offermann v. Nitkowski, 378 F.2d 22 (2d Cir. 1967); Tometz v. Board of Educ., 39 Ill. 2d 593, 237 N.E.2d 498 (1968); Balsbaugh v. Rowland, 447 Pa. 423, 290 A.2d 85 (1972); State *ex rel.* Citizens Against Mandatory Busing v. Brooks, 80 Wash. 2d 121, 492 P.2d 536 (1972).

above would support an argument that the settlement plan is consistent with *Brown*.

These arguments will have greater impact if the board can be convinced to incorporate a review period, of five to ten years, after which it would automatically return to the courts for further consideration of the integration remedy. In support of this arrangement, its advocates could argue that: while *Brown* requires school desegregation, the courts gave whites fifteen years of "all deliberate speed" to get ready for racially-mixed schools;[119] most of this time was squandered in evasive tactics that further damaged black children. Now that desegregation has been ordered, many black parents recognize the need for a period during which they can choose schools where the priority is overcoming the dual image that black children cannot learn and that black schools are poor schools. Even if no educational benefit to black children occurs during the period, the principals of *Brown* are not affected; social science evidence has failed to reveal *any* educational strategy that is certain to equalize educational outcomes. By limiting the settlement plan, blacks also explicitly preserve their all-important right to attend schools with whites.

III

The *Brown* Decision Revisited

Whether Delta County, or other blacks, should seek a settlement plan of the type described will depend on many factors which are unique to each individual community; but some general considerations should assist parents in reaching conclusions endemic to conditions in their area.

Although the *Brown* decision purported to give blacks the right to attend school with whites, it actually provides blacks with the means to achieve educational equality in black schools.[120] The power inherent in the right to school desegregation has been frequently worth more than the educational value of exercising that right. This apparent paradox conforms perfectly with a societal pattern in which minority rights are granted or withheld by the majority according to which action will serve majority interests best. Blacks were the gratuitous beneficiaries when the northern states abolished slavery in the post-Revolutionary War period because slavery was not eco-

119. Brown v. Board of Educ., 349 U.S. at 301.

120. Certainly *Brown* comprised associational, as well as educational, components. But having judicially condoned the continued existence of "one-race" schools in a desegregated school system, Swann v. Charlotte-Mecklenburg Bd. of Educ., 402 U.S. at 25-27; Northcross v. Board of Educ. of Memphis City Schools, 489 F.2d 15 (6th Cir. 1973), *cert. denied*, 416 U.S. 962 (1974), and seemingly having consigned substantial numbers of inner-city black students to permanent assignment in all-black schools, Milliken v. Bradley, 418 U.S. 717 (1974), it is too late to argue the imperative in *Brown* of having black children actually attend school with whites.

nomically feasible and provided unwanted competition with white labor.[121] Southern slavery was prohibited by issuance of the Emancipation Proclamation less because it was morally reprehensible, than because such action was compelled by the need to disrupt the Confederate work force and the desire to win European support.[122] It is possible that history will show that the *Brown* decision also served the interests of white Americans more than black Americans.[123]

The multiple motivations that abolished slavery did not prevent blacks from obtaining their freedom; similarly, the progress made under *Brown* has been great, despite its ambivalent origins. But, further progress in the school area requires at least the basic recognition that there may be a distinction between what is offered and what can be obtained.

In accomplishing this cognitive process, some basic facts must be accepted:

a. *White opposition to school desegregation* is increasing. This is hardly a secret.[124] Most whites have never been enthusiastic about sending their children to school with more than a few blacks. The *Brown* decision won sympathy for the plight of black children, but it did not alter the steadfast opposition of white parents to enroll their children in predominately black schools. For all the reasons that a racist society could muster, most black schools were inferior to their white counterparts. But, in the course of arguing the need to admit black children to white schools, integrationists painted a far worse picture of the situation than even some pre-*Brown* black schools and their products deserved.[125] The appeals to white sympathy concerning the plight of black children gained support for desegregation in general, but increased the determination of white parents not to involve themselves and their children in what was presented as the only remedy.[126] As one writer put it:[127]

---

121. *See* A. ZILVERSMIT, THE FIRST EMANCIPATION: THE ABOLITION OF SLAVERY IN THE NORTH (1967).

122. *See* J. FRANKLIN, THE EMANCIPATION PROCLAMATION (1963); Dillard, *The Emancipation Proclamation on the Perspective of Time*, 23 LAW IN TRANSITION 95 (1963).

123. *See* Steel, *A Critic's View of the Warren Court—Nine Men in Black Who Think White*, N.Y. TIMES, Oct. 13, 1968 (Magazine), at 56.

124. Dissenting in *Milliken v. Bradley*, Justice Marshall expressed the fear that the Court's refusal to affirm a metropolitan area remedy "is more a reflection of a perceived public mood that we have gone far enough in enforcing the Constitution's guarantee of equal justice than it is the product of neutral principles of law." 418 U.S. at 814.

125. *See* Sowell, *Black Excellence—the Case of Dunbar High School*, 35 PUB. INTEREST 3 (Spring 1974).

126. In one survey, two-thirds of those questioned approved of desegregated public schools in principle, but 69 per cent opposed busing as a means of achieving desegregation. *What the Gallup Poll Discovered About Busing*, NEWSWEEK, Mar. 13, 1972, at 24. There is every reason to believe that the opposition has increased substantially in the period since that poll was taken.

127. L. FEIN, THE ECOLOGY OF THE PUBLIC SCHOOLS: AN INQUIRY INTO COMMUNITY CONTROL 6 (1971).

> In effect, the liberal community, both black and white, was caught up in a wrenching dilemma. The only way, it appeared, to move a sluggish nation towards massive amelioration of the Negro condition was to show how terrifyingly debilitating were the effects of discrimination and bigotry. The more lurid the detail, the more guilt it would evoke, and the more guilt, the more readiness to act. Yet the same lurid detail that did, in the event, prompt large-scale federal programs, also reinforced white convictions that Negroes were undesirable objects of interaction.

The social scientists did not help matters. In an effort to prove the educational value of desegregation, studies were published which seemed to show that black pupil performance improved when they were placed in white schools.[128] The corollary to this interpretation was: " 'when you mix Negroes with Negroes, you get stupidity.' "[129] Later studies were inconclusive, tending to show, according to Ronald Edmonds, Harvard's Urban Studies Center Director, that "under court-ordered integration, some Black pupils do better, some Black pupils do about the same and some Black pupils do worse."[130] Faced with such inconclusive data and, already concerned about the enforcibility of long-distance busing orders, all but the most committed federal judges paused and almost beseechingly looked for help.[131]

b. *Integration strategies remain inflexible* despite the unimpressive reports of the educational effectiveness of integration, despite the increasing white opposition as school integration standards designed for southern rural areas are applied to large urban areas, and, most important of all, despite indications that black parents in large numbers have lost faith in the basic strategy of school desegregation litigation, *i.e.*, to get the same quality of education white children are receiving, you must enroll black children in the same schools as white children.

The key to the disenchantment of black parents can be found in the desegregation orders themselves. In an effort to make school desegregation

---

128. *See, e.g.*, J. Coleman, Equality of Educational Opportunity 29 (1966); U.S. Commission on Civil Rights, Racial Isolation in the Public Schools (1967).

129. L. Fein, *supra* note 127, at 9.

130. Edmonds, *Advocating Inequity: A Critique of the Civil Rights Attorney in Class Action Desegregation Suits*, 3 Black L.J. 176, 177 (1974). *See also* Lines, *Race and Learning: A Perspective on the Research*, 11 Inequality in Ed. 26 (Mar. 1972).

131. In an unpublished order subsequent to Morgan v. Hennigan, 379 F. Supp. 410 (D. Mass. 1974), requiring the Boston School Committee to file a desegregation plan for 1975, Judge Garrity, after setting out detailed instructions for a plan that shall provide for the greatest possible degree of actual desegregation of all grades in all parts of the city, gave all parties and other interested community groups until Jan. 20, 1975, to submit to the court alternative plans to all or any portion of the defendants' student desegregation plan.

As Professor Bickel has observed:

> [C]ourts confronted with racial isolation in a school district that is doing precious little on its own to attack its [educational] problems will order busing because there is not much else that a court can do that will have an impact.

Bickel, *Education in a Democracy: The Legal and Practical Problems of School Busing*, 3 Human Rights 53, 59-60 (1973).

as palatable for whites as possible, courts have permitted school boards to close black schools, often over the vigorous protests of the black communities they served,[132] and authorized "one-way" busing in which black children do most or all of the bus riding while whites continue to attend schools in their nieghborhoods.[133] Black teachers and administrators, the largest black professional class, have been decimated by the desegregation process despite herculean efforts by civil rights attorneys to protect their jobs.[134] Even the percentages of black students assigned to white schools are determined less by the percentage of black students in the school district than by the number of blacks white parents will tolerate before withdrawing their children.[135]

---

132. *See* Allen v. Asheville City Bd. of Educ., 434 F.2d 902 (4th Cir. 1970); Norwalk CORE v. Norwalk Bd. of Educ., 423 F.2d 121 (2d Cir. 1970). Courts have said they will refuse to approve the closing of black schools based solely on school officials' fear that whites will not attend them. *See, e.g.*, Bell v. West Point Municipal Separate School Dist., 446 F.2d 1362 (5th Cir. 1971). But usually, closings are justified by school boards—and upheld by courts—where there are "non-racial reasons" for such closings. *See* Ellis v. Board of Pub. Instruction, 465 F.2d 878 (5th Cir. 1972), *cert. denied*, 410 U.S. 966 (1973); Mims v. Duval County School Bd., 447, F.2d 1330 (5th Cir. 1971); Carr v. Montgomery County Bd. of Educ., 429 F.2d 382 (5th Cir. 1970).

133. *See* Davis v. Board of School Comm'rs of Mobile County, 483 F.2d 1017 (5th Cir. 1973); Norwalk CORE v. Norwalk Bd. of Educ., 423 F.2d 121 (2d Cir. 1970); Parris v. School Comm. of Medford, Mass., 305 F. Supp. 356 (D. Mass. 1969).

134. The courts have developed standards for protecting the positions of black faculty during the desegregation process, *see, e.g.*, Cornist v. Richland Parish School Bd., 495 F.2d 189 (5th Cir. 1974); Smith v. Concordia Parish School Bd., 493 F.2d 8 (5th Cir. 1974); Davis v. School Dist. of Pontiac, Inc., 487 F.2d 890 (6th Cir. 1973); Singleton v. Jackson Municipal Separate School Dist., 419 F.2d 1211 (5th Cir. 1969).

But, after desegregation is completed, a wider range of criteria supporting dismissals or refusals to rehire are condoned by the courts. *See, e.g.*, Thompson v. Madison County Board of Educ., 496 F.2d 682 (5th Cir. 1974); Lee v. Macon County Bd. of Educ., 482 F.2d 1253 (5th Cir. 1973); Pickens v. Okolona Municipal Separate School Dist., 380 F. Supp. 1036 (N.D. Miss. 1974); George v. Davis, 365 F. Supp. 446 (M.D. La. 1973); United States v. Coffeeville Consolidated School Dist., 365 F. Supp. 990 (N.D. Miss. 1973).

135. Professor Thomas Pettigrew of Harvard has urged a racial mixture of 30 per cent black to 70 per cent white pupils so as to achieve a high correlation between race and socioeconomic class, thereby maximizing educational achievement. He also suggested that such a ratio would not precipitate middle class flight. Beckett v. School Bd. of Norfolk, 308 F. Supp. 1274, 1290-91 (E.D. Va. 1969). The district court agreed and approved a plan with this balance in some schools, but because of the high percentage of blacks in the system, 76 per cent of the elementary students would remain in one-race schools. Brewer v. School Bd. of Norfolk, 434 F.2d 408, 411 (4th Cir. 1970). Finding that the plan failed to establish a unitary school system, the Fourth Circuit reversed and remanded to the district court. 434 F.2d at 412.

In a subsequent school case in which the Pettigrew thesis was revived, Judge Sobeloff—in a separate concurring opinion—attacked it as "invidious, . . . a resurrection of the axiom of black inferiority, . . . and no less than a return to the spirit of *Dred Scott*." Brunson v. Board of Trustees of School Bd. No. 1, 429 F.2d 820, 826 (4th Cir. 1970). Undeterred by the threat of white flight, Judge Sobeloff stated that school desegregation "is not founded upon the concept that white children are a precious resource which should be fairly apportioned. . . . [S]chool segregation is forbidden simply because its perpetuation is a living insult to the black children and immeasurably taints the education they receive." *Id.*

Regrettably, treating white flight (and white opposition generally) as legally irrelevant serves the cause of logical debate better than it does the realities of actually desegregating schools.

Sensitivity to the concern of white parents for the quality of the desegregated school is, of necessity, acute. It is no surprise then that school policies regarding the use of standardized achievement test scores for assignment to tracks or special classes,[136] curriculum decisions, and disciplinary policies[137] seem designed to insure a high priority for the needs of white students.[138] If black students must go to court simply to secure the right to

---

See, e.g., Craven, *The Impact of Social Science Evidence on the Judge: A Personal Comment*, 39 LAW & CONTEMP. PROB. no. 1, at 150 (1975).

136. The courts have generally held that when a formerly dual, segregated school system has just recently been, or is in the process of being, dismantled, pupil assignment by standardized test scores is prohibited when the intended and actual result is the perpetuation of the dual system through segregation within the system, Lemon v. Bossier Parish School Bd., 444 F.2d 1400 (5th Cir. 1971), within individual schools, Moses v. Washington Parish School Bd., 456 F.2d 1285 (5th Cir.), *cert. denied*, 409 U.S. 1013 (1972), within the individual classrooms, Acree v. County Bd. of Educ., 458 F.2d 486 (5th Cir.), *cert. denied*, 409 U.S. 1006 (1972), or with each student by faculty evaluation of past grades, McNeal v. Tate County School Dist., 508 F.2d 1017 (5th Cir. 1975).

Even when there is no overt discriminatory intent, the racial bias inherent in standardized tests should render their use as suspect in education cases as they now are in employment discrimination litigation. Griggs v. Duke Power Co., 401 U.S. 424 (1971). The problems are discussed in Kagan, *The I.Q. Puzzle: What Are We Measuring?*, 14 INEQUALITY IN ED. 5 (July 1973). *See also* Larry P. v. Riles, 343 F. Supp. 1306 (N.D. Cal. 1972), *aff'd*, 502 F.2d 963 (9th Cir. 1974) (placing black students in classes for the educable mentally retarded on the basis of I.Q. test scores); Hobson v. Hansen, 269 F. Supp. 401 (D.D.C. 1967), *aff'd sub nom.* Smuck v. Hobson, 408 F.2d 175 (D.C. Cir. 1969) (standard aptitude tests are biased against black and other low-income students).

137. *See* CHILDREN'S DEFENSE FUND OF THE WASHINGTON RESEARCH PROJECT, INC., CHILDREN OUT OF SCHOOL IN AMERICA 117-50 (1974).

In Hawkins v. Coleman, 376 F. Supp. 1330 (N.D. Tex. 1974), for example, the superintendent of the Dallas school system conceded that the disproportionate number of black students who received suspensions was because "we are a White controlled institution, institutional racism, racism among individuals." *Id.* at 1336. An expert witness for plaintiffs testified: "[i]nstitutional racism exists . . . when the standard operating procedures of an institution are prejudiced against, derogatory to, or unresponsive to the needs of a particular racial group." *Id.* The court accepted this testimony, but stated that "[n]o court can decree a change in attitude," and urged "everyone involved to accentuate the positive while at the same time eliminating the negative effects of 'white institutional racism.' " 376 F. Supp. at 1338. The court then directed the Dallas Independent School District (DISD) "to review its present program and to put into effect an affirmative program aimed at materially lessening 'white institutional racism' in the DISD." *Id.*

138. Kenneth Haskins, recalling his experience in an integrated school, said decisions were generally made to satisfy whites as though "the purpose of integration was to benefit the black children, and really the white community was doing them a favor, by allowing this to happen." Statement of Mr. Kenneth W. Haskins, *Hearings on Quality and Control of Public Schools Before the Senate Select Comm. on Equal Educ. Opportunity*, 92d Cong., 1st Sess., pt. 13, at 5873 (1971).

Professor Charles Hamilton describes an experience in which a white teacher of a desegregated class, comprised of middle class white children and lower-class blacks from a public housing project, led a discussion of winter vacations, for which many of the white children would soon be departing. According to Professor Hamilton:

> The discussion from the white students was spirited and full of exciting accounts of flight plans, hotel reservations, Florida beaches and play areas. The black students sat silently. When a visiting black parent, who had observed the session, spoke to the teacher afterwards, the teacher was quite elated over the lively discussion and enthusiasm of the students. The parent, however, complained that that session was pre-

participate in extracurricular activities[139] or to terminate the use of a racially insulting school song or cheer,[140] it is not hard to imagine the level of the priority accorded their academic needs in all too many "integrated" classrooms.

This type of damage is precisely what *Brown* intended to eliminate in the coerced segregated setting. It is a measure of the virulence of racism that the problem still persists in some schools restructured to eliminate its effects; the failure to recognize it further decreases the chances that thousands of black students will experience any benefit from the *Brown* decision during their school years, while increasing the very real risk that continued rigid pressure solely for school integration will seriously erode the progress already made, not only in schools, but in other important areas of civil rights as well.

Professor Charles Hamilton several years ago warned that "[i]t is absolutely crucial to understand that the society cannot continue to write reports accurately describing the failure of the educational institutions vis-a-vis black people without ultimately taking into account the impact those truths will have on black Americans."[141] But the predominant litigation strategy today in school desegregation suits is to advocate "all out" integration and to categorically oppose predominantly black schools—a philosophy which "has brought us to the advent of metropolitan desegregation without sufficient regard having been given to the probable instructional consequences of such a move for those Black children most numerously affected."[142] This is attributable in part to the fact that those who generally handle school desegregation litigation do not always have the ongoing close community contact with members of the class they represent which is required to ensure continuing sensitivity to client interests. As a result, the emphasis has been

---

cisely the kind of insensitive education to which she felt the black students should not be exposed. The teacher was puzzled and hurt; she saw or heard nothing wrong or offensive in the discussion at all. The parent explained that the black children were totally excluded because their parents could not afford to take them on expensive vacations. Their sense of inferiority was reinforced, and they were made to feel that watching television and running the halls of the housing project during the week while their parents worked could not match the glamour and thrills of a week's vacation in the Florida sun. The teacher explained that she was unaware of the race of those students who did and did not participate. This episode, to the parent, was an example not of the admirable trait of color-blindness but of the insensitivity of the educational system to the needs of the black children, and it was further evidence of the dubious benefits of integration on both racial and class bases.

Hamilton, *The Nationalist vs. The Integrationist*, in THE GREAT SCHOOL BUS CONTROVERSY 297, 308 (N. Mills ed. 1973).

139. LAWYERS REVIEW COMM. TO STUDY THE DEPT. OF JUSTICE, A REPORT 43 & n. 81 (1972)

140. *Cf.* Melton v. Young, 465 F.2d 1332 (6th Cir. 1972); Smith v. St. Tammany Parish School Bd., 448 F.2d 414 (5th Cir. 1971); Caldwell v. Craighead, 432 F.2d 213 (6th Cir. 1970), *cert. denied*, 402 U.S. 953 (1971).

141. Hamilton, *Race and Education: A Search for Legitimacy*, 38 HARV. ED. REV. 669, 671 (1968).

142. Edmonds, *supra* note 130, at 179.

on total desegregation, even when white flight is certain to void the victory of any meaning. Generally, no consideration is given to settlement, although such action might better serve the interests of the disadvantaged class.[143]

For example, in the Boston School case[144] the court, having found the school committee responsible for blatant and overt racial discrimination, granted the only relief sought—racial balance—even though this required the busing of hundreds of poor black children to blue collar white areas where, if anything, the schools were educationally inferior to those from which the black students came.[145] The violent response of the white Bostonians was indefensible, but predictable, given their conviction that black students will deteriorate already inferior schools and their knowledge that the well-to-do suburbs are exempt from the problems they face.[146]

It is difficult not to give wholehearted support to even the most unfortunate school desegregation order intended to obtain compliance with *Brown.* But in Boston and in many other school systems, poor white as well as black parents have been provided public schools that are far less than they should be. The black parents are able to translate the inadequacies of their schools into constitutional terms, for which remedies are available. To insist that courts can only remedy these constitutional violations by mixing black children with the most disadvantaged whites in poor schools reflects a poverty of innovation foreign to equity and is potentially disastrous to hopes for an integrated society.

Conclusion

Chief Justice Earl Warren, in trying to formulate a constitutional basis for the contention that segregated schools were legally invalid, wrote:[147]

> In approaching this problem, we cannot turn the clock back to 1868 when the [fourteenth] Amendment was adopted, or even to 1896 when *Plessy v. Ferguson* was written. We must consider public education in the

143. Bell, *supra* note 49, at 278. *See also* Justice Harlan's dissent in NAACP v. Button, 371 U.S. 415, 461-63 (1962).

144. Morgan v. Hennigan, 379 F. Supp. 410 (D. Mass. 1974).

145. The two white high schools to which black students were assigned under the court order graduated a total of 865 students in the 1973 class. Only 173 (22 per cent) entered four year colleges. The two black high schools to which white students were assigned graduated 261 students during the same period, 74 of whom (28 per cent) entered four-year colleges. The state average is 32 per cent, and the city's two "elite" high schools (admission by tests and grades) sent 97.7 per cent of their graduates on to four-year colleges. Massachusetts Department of Education, Distribution of High School Graduates (1973).

Both white high schools are overcrowded. The black schools are underutilized. South Boston High (no black students in 1971-72) was overenrolled by 676 students. Girls High (now Roxbury High, with 91.7 per cent black enrollment) was underenrolled by 532 places in the same year. Morgan v. Hennigan, 379 F. Supp. at 426.

146. Milliken v. Bradley, 418 U.S. 717 (1974).

147. Brown v. Board of Educ., 347 U.S. at 492-93.

> light of its full development and its present place in American life throughout the Nation. Only in this way can it be determined if segregation in public schools deprives these plaintiffs of the equal protection of the laws.

Similarly, black people cannot expect to find in the *Brown* precedent a full and complete answer to problems that twenty years ago either did not exist in their present form or were not recognizable without the hard-earned contemporary understanding that societal racism can disadvantage black children as effectively (although more subtly) in integrated as in segregated schools. With that knowledge and with the experience gained over the last two decades, effective arguments can be made in the courts and through the political process to gain those public school rights which the *Brown* decision categorized as an "equal educational opportunity." In this effort, flexibility of approach is crucial. The principles of *Plessy v. Ferguson* as well as *Brown v. Board of Education* can be used effectively. No approach should be discarded, and few should be universally embraced. The guiding principle must be that black leadership in Delta County, as elsewhere, must listen carefully to what black parents want from schools for their children and then design strategies that utilize constitutional rights and political leverage to achieve these educational goals.

Sincerely,

Derrick A. Bell, Jr.

SUSPENSION AND EXPULSION OF BLACK STUDENTS FROM THE PUBLIC SCHOOLS: ACADEMIC CAPITAL PUNISHMENT AND THE CONSTITUTION

MARK G. YUDOF*

INTRODUCTION

The relationship between law and mathematics has been described as a "romance" which "has been for the most part a one-sided affair."[1] Mathematicians historically have toyed with the idea of bringing their discipline to bear on social problems and their resolution, but lawyers and judges have proved to be a recalcitrant lot. Many lawyers apparently chose law school to escape those mysteries of all mysteries, mathematics and science. But, alas, our escape has proven to be an illusion. At every turn we are besieged with preference contours, choice sets, random samples, and statistical probabilities.[2] While many of us remain xenophobic to the core, greeting with hostility each new incursion into the world of "plausibility," "commonsense" and "humanistic" thought,[3] frankness commands the admission that the affair has become serious. The one-sided romance has developed into a marriage of convenience, or, reflecting more recent conjugal innovations, a willingness to share the same quarters without the formalities of ceremony and family reception.[4]

Nowhere has the impact of this new relationship been more severely felt than with respect to the developing law of racial discrimination.[5] It

---

* Professor of Law, University of Texas at Austin. I wish to express my appreciation to Professor David Kirp for his thoughtful comments on an earlier version of this article.

1. *See* Finkelstein, *The Application of Statistical Decision Theory to the Jury Discrimination Cases,* 80 HARV. L. REV. 338 (1966).

2. *See generally* Tribe, *Trial by Mathematics: Precision and Ritual in the Legal Process,* 84 HARV. L. REV. 1329 (1971).

3. *But see* note 5 *infra.*

4. Professor Tribe, while noting the "rapidly growing interest in the conjunction of mathematics and the trial process," has grave misgivings about the marriage of the two:

> The literature of legal praise for the progeny of such a wedding has been little short of lyrical. Surely the time has come for someone to suggest that the union would be more dangerous than fruitful.

Tribe, *supra* note 2, at 1393.

5. *See* Bogen & Falcon, *The Use of Racial Statistics in Fair Housing Cases,* 34 MD. L. REV. 59 (1974); Dimond, *School Segregation in the North: There is But one Constitution,* 7 HARV. CIV. RIGHTS-CIV. LIB. L. REV. 1 (1972); Fiss, *A Theory of Fair Employment Laws,* 38 U. CHI, L. REV. 235, 268-70 (1971); Fessler & Haar, *Beyond the Wrong Side of the Tracks: Municipal Services in the Interstices of Procedure,* 6 HARV. CIV. RIGHTS-CIV. LIB. L. REV. 441 (1971); Finkelstein, *supra* note 1.

used to be easy to identify race-conscious public policies; for usually state officials were quite willing to articulate their racial biases and specifically incorporate them into state laws. But in an age where civility commands verbal racial neutrality and where so much progress has been made toward racial justice, proof of discrimination is more complex. Now everything seems to turn on the significance of numbers. Has a school system failed to comply with its obligation to dismantle the dual school system because there are still some one race schools in the district or because the relative percentages of blacks and whites in the school district are not reflected in each public school?[6] Has an employer engaged in racial discrimination because he employs few blacks?[7] Are colleges and graduate schools compelled or permitted to adopt affirmative action plans to increase minority enrollments because minorities are underrepresented in the student population?[8] Is the process by which school board members are selected suspect if few blacks are appointed to the nominating panel?[9] In each case, the question is not whether there is disproportional representation between racial groups—there surely is: the question is what logical conclusion should be drawn from that fact.

The law has dealt with statistical evidence bearing on racial discrimination in an inconsistent manner.[10] Judges tell us in jury discrimination cases that "figures speak and when they do, Courts listen."[11] The statistical showing that a county has a ten per cent black population and yet not a single black has served on a federal or state jury is sufficient to constitutionally damn the method of selecting jurors.[12] On the other hand, Justice Rehnquist assured us in a welfare case arising under the Equal Protection Clause that courts must be wary of such "naked statistical argument"; for if such statistics suffice to demonstrate discrimination or to shift the burden of persuasion

---

6. *See* Swann v. Charlotte-Mecklenburg Bd. of Educ., 402 U.S. 1 (1971). *See also* Wright v. City of Emporia, 407 U.S. 451 (1972). *See generally* Kalven, *The Supreme Court, 1970 Term—Foreword: Even When a Nation is at War,* 85 HARV. L. REV. 3, 78 (1971).

7. *See, e.g.,* Griggs v. Duke Power Co., 401 U.S. 424 (1971); Boston Chapter N.A.A.C.P. v. Beecher, 504 F.2d 1017 (1st Cir. 1974); The Vulcan Soc'y v. Civil Serv. Comm'n, 490 F.2d 387 (2d Cir. 1973); Chance v. Board of Examiners, 330 F. Supp. 203 (S.D.N.Y. 1971), *aff'd,* 458 F.2d 1167 (2d Cir. 1972); Note, *Business Necessity Under Title VII of the Civil Rights Act of 1964: A No-Alternative Approach,* 84 YALE L.J. 98 (1974).

8. *See* DeFunis v. Odegaard, 82 Wash. 2d 11, 507 P.2d 1169 (1973), *vacated,* 416 U.S. 312 (1974) (per curiam). *See generally* Kirp & Yudof, *DeFunis and Beyond,* 6 CHANGE no. 9, at 22 (1974); Ely, *The Constitutionality of Reverse Racial Discrimination,* 41 U. CHI. L. REV. 723 (1974); O'Neil, *Preferential Admissions: Equalizing the Access of Minority Groups to Higher Education,* 80 YALE L.J. 699 (1971); Graglia, *Special Admission of the "Culturally Deprived" to Law School,* 119 U. PA. L. REV. 351 (1970); Askin, *The Case for Compensatory Treatment,* 24 RUTGERS L. REV. 65 (1969).

9. *See* Mayor of Phila. v. Educational Equality League, 415 U.S. 605 (1974).

10. This rather ad hoc approach toward probabilistic proof is apparent in many areas of the law. *See* Tribe, *supra* note 2, at 1343-44.

11. Brooks v. Beto, 366 F.2d 1, 9 (5th Cir. 1966).

12. *Id.*

to the state, it "would render suspect each difference in treatment among the grant classes, however lacking in racial motivation and however otherwise rational the treatment might be."[13] In that case the Texas legislature had disfavored classes of welfare recipients in which the proportions of blacks and Mexican-Americans were highest. Yet a court of appeals recently held unconstitutional a method of allocating municipal services which, although ostensibly on the basis of need for the service, resulted in unequal services between blacks and whites.[14] Even in the absence of proof of a discriminatory motive, the court required the defendants to satisfy a heavy burden to justify such inequalities.

Perhaps the principle underlying these cases is not so difficult to discern. What the courts may be saying is that a statistical showing of inequalities between the races in the enjoyment of public benefits is always relevant to the disposition of the case. It is sufficient in itself, however, only where the disproportionality is of such a magnitude as to make any nonracial explanation implausible or where, despite some lesser showing, there appears to be no rational, racially neutral explanation for the pattern of allocations. Thus the issue will turn on the character of the benefits, and statements with respect to the probative impact of the statistical evidence are simply conclusionary labels attached after the court has considered the likelihood of nonracial explanations for the state's classificatory scheme.

This standard reflects three related judgments. First, nearly every governmental activity may fall unequally on racial and economic groups within the society. Public transportation may be more beneficial to low-income minorities than to middle-income whites, just as more whites may utilize public golf and tennis courts. There are questions of need and taste which must be taken into account, and it is unthinkable that the courts should mechanically require equal enjoyment by racial groups with respect to all government programs. Equal access on the basis of relevant and racially neutral criteria will suffice. Second, as Justice Powell has artfully stated, there are cases "in which it cannot be assumed that all citizens are fungible for purposes of determining whether members of a particular class have been unlawfully excluded."[15] In the context of jury selection, it may well be the case that most citizens are fungible. The standards for selection are not so rigorous that a large group of individuals is likely to be found to be incompetent to serve.

---

13. Jefferson v. Hackney, 406 U.S. 535, 548 (1972).

14. Hawkins v. Town of Shaw, 437 F.2d 1286 (5th Cir. 1971), *aff'd en banc,* 461 F.2d 1171 (5th Cir. 1972). *See also* United Farmworkers of Fla. Housing Project, Inc. v. City of Delray Beach, 493 F.2d 799 (5th Cir. 1974). *See generally* Fessler & Haar, *supra* note 5; Lineberry, *Mandating Urban Equality: The Distribution of Municipal Public Services,* 53 TEX. L. REV. 26 (1974); Note, *Equalization of Municipal Services: The Economics of* Serrano *and* Shaw, 82 YALE L.J. 89 (1972).

15. Mayor of Phila. v. Educational Equality League, 415 U.S. 605, 620 (1974). *See also* Carter v. Jury Comm'n of Greene County, 396 U.S. 320 (1970); James v. Wallace, 386 F. Supp. 815 (M.D. Ala. 1974).

Moreover, government is not allocating a scarce resource, and thus there is little need to draw distinctions on the basis of need, ability, or willingness to pay for the service. On the other hand, the selection process for administrative agencies involves wholly different considerations since there is a scarcity of opportunities and since personal characteristics play a large role in the selection process. Under such circumstances, a "naked" statistical presentation of lack of black representation will not carry the day in the absence of other indicators of racial discrimination. Finally, if there are racially innocent reasons which explain the apparent disproportionality in treatment, judicial intervention is an invitation to engage in reverse discrimination against whites. Neutral criteria must be distorted to ensure an absolute equality of outcomes by racial group.[16]

The use of statistical evidence, either with respect to the initial finding of a violation of law or the adoption of a remedy, is particularly problematic in the context of racial discrimination suits involving primary and secondary public schools. There is ample evidence that black students disproportionately suffer the burdens of public schooling while not sharing in its benefits in proportion to their numbers. Blacks, as a class, consistently do less well on standardized tests than whites.[17] They are overrepresented in the lower ability groups in schools which track their students.[18] Their drop-out rate (or push-out rate, as some critics assert) is much higher than that for whites.[19] In some urban areas, they attend the oldest schools and are exposed to the least experienced teachers.[20] In Texas, for example, the poorest school districts, offering the least adequate educational programs, tend to have large concentrations of black and chicano students.[21]

There may be some question as to whether the glass is half full or half empty, whether progress has been slow or dramatic, whether rising expectations have focused our attention on less consequential inequalities.[22] But surely there can be no resistance to the fact of inequality. The problem is what significance should be attached to these numbers? Should we infer that there is an absence of equal opportunity? That racism is at work, and that our institutions have failed? Or should the blame be cast on the black

---

16. Fiss, *The Fate of an Idea Whose Time Has Come: Antidiscrimination Law in the Second Decade After* Brown v. Board of Educ., 41 U. CHI. L. REV. 742, 763 (1974).

17. U.S. OFFICE OF EDUCATION, DEP'T OF HEALTH, EDUCATION, AND WELFARE, STUDY OF THE ACHIEVEMENT OF OUR NATION'S STUDENTS 27 (1973); C. JENCKS, INEQUALITY 81 (1972).

18. *See* D. KIRP & M. YUDOF, EDUCATIONAL POLICY AND THE LAW 657-73 (1974) [hereinafter cited as EDUCATIONAL POLICY AND THE LAW]; Kirp, *Schools as Sorters: The Constitutional and Policy Implications of Student Classification,* 121 U. PA. L. REV. 705 (1973).

19. *See* C. JENCKS, *supra* note 17; CHILDREN'S DEFENSE FUND OF THE WASHINGTON RESEARCH PROJECT, INC., CHILDREN OUT OF SCHOOL IN AMERICA ch. 2 (1974) [hereinafter cited as CHILDREN OUT OF SCHOOL].

20. *See, e.g.,* Hobson v. Hansen, 269 F. Supp. 401 (D.D.C. 1967), *aff'd en banc sub nom.* Smuck v. Hobson, 408 F.2d 175 (D.C. Cir. 1969).

21. San Antonio Independent School Dist. v. Rodriguez, 411 U.S. 1, 15 n.38 (1973).

22. *See generally* Glazer, *The Limits of Social Policy, in* COMMENTARY 52 (Sept. 1971).

students themselves for being incapable or unwilling to seize the opportunities afforded them? Does not the allocation of such blame to blacks contain the seeds of a new racism, grounded in genetic or cultural fatalism? Ultimately, we must ask: What can we say about the fairness of the processes by which rewards and punishments are distributed in the public schools by virtue of the existence of inequalities in the outcomes of those processes?[23] There are those who would urge that fairness, defined in terms of need, motivation, and competence, must be discarded in favor of a system of measured equality of outcomes between racial groups.[24] But, despite a recent intellectual push in that direction,[25] there appears to be no societal consensus to abandon the liberal concept of distributive justice.[26]

The probative value of statistical evidence of inequalities between the races in the public schools is at the heart of the dilemma posed by the subject of this article, the suspension and expulsion of black students from recently desegregated elementary and secondary schools. The fact is that in many desegregated school systems blacks are excluded from the schools far more often than whites.[27] The phenomenon is largely limited to secondary schools since roughly ninety per cent of all suspensions are imposed on children between the ages of twelve and seventeen.[28] Many of those who are suspended once find themselves suspended again and again. Even where a black youngster is not permanently expelled, suspension may lead to the decision by the student, in a sense voluntary but against the background of his prior difficulties with school authorities, to drop out of school.[29] Inevitably, the existence of this phenomenon has led to a search to identify the causes of black exclusion,[30] and just as inevitably, the matter has wound its way to the federal courts for resolution.[31]

---

23. *See generally* C. JENCKS, *supra* note 17.

24. *Id.* at 8-11. *See generally* Yudof, *Equal Educational Opportunity and the Courts,* 51 TEX. L. REV. 411, 420-22 (1973).

25. *See* J. RAWLS, A THEORY OF JUSTICE (1971). *But see* Simson, *Another View of Rawls's Theory of Justice,* 23 EMORY L.J. 473, 491 (1974).

26. *See* Nisbet, *The Pursuit of Equality*, 35 PUB. INTEREST 103 (Spring 1974); Bell, *On Meritocracy and Equality*, 29 PUB. INTEREST 29 (Fall 1972).

27. *See, e.g.,* SOUTHERN REGIONAL COUNCIL AND THE ROBERT F. KENNEDY MEMORIAL, THE STUDENT PUSHOUT: VICTIM OF CONTINUED RESISTANCE TO DESEGREGATION 6 (1974) [hereinafter cited as STUDENT PUSHOUT REPORT]; CHILDREN OUT OF SCHOOL ch. 2.

28. CHILDREN OUT OF SCHOOL 126.

29. *Cf.* Madera v. Board of Educ., 267 F. Supp. 356, 371 (S.D.N.Y. 1967), *rev'd on other grounds*, 386 F.2d 778 (2d Cir. 1967).

30. *See* STUDENT PUSHOUT REPORT 17-22; CHILDREN OUT OF SCHOOL.

31. *See* United States v. Wilcox County Bd. of Educ., 494 F.2d 575 (5th Cir. 1974); Floyd v. Trice, 490 F.2d 1154 (8th Cir. 1974); Hawkins v. Coleman, 376 F. Supp. 1330 (N.D. Tex. 1974); Rhyne v. Childs, 359 F. Supp. 1058 (N.D. Fla. 1973), *aff'd sub nom.* Sweet v. Childs, 507 F.2d 675 (5th Cir. 1975); Dunlap v. Charlotte-Mecklenburg Bd. of Educ., 367 F. Supp. 666 (W.D.N.C. 1973); Tillman v. Dade County School Bd., 327 F. Supp. 930 (S.D. Fla. 1971). *See generally* McClung, *The Problem of the Due Process Exclusion: Do Schools Have a Continuing Responsibility to Educate Children With Behavior Problems?*, 3 J. LAW & EDUC. 491 (1974).

The competing theories often advanced to explain black exclusions are volatile and less than complimentary to the actors. As David Hume sagely noted, cause and effect relations are generally established on the basis of experience and not reason. But our experiences, our perceptions of the world and views as to what is plausible, are so different. The civil rights advocate who has witnessed racial discrimination in a myriad of circumstances, who recalls George Wallace at the schoolhouse door, and who has viewed with alarm the increasing sophistication with which racism is practiced, believes that black students, once again, are the victims of racial discrimination. The first step was state-imposed separation of the races; the latest manifestation of the segregationist philosophy is state-imposed exclusion of many black students from formally integrated schools. The process of exclusion is no more benign than the process of student assignment by neighborhood.[32] For the black student, removed from his community and placed early in a white dominated world, exclusion is one more example of institutional and personal hostility toward his race. He perceives a lack of evenhandedness in the application of school rules and punishments, and an inability on the part of white adults and students to understand the ways in which blacks interact with each other. They are puzzled that conduct which they view as perfectly normal is perceived as threatening and detrimental to order and learning by school officials.[33] They often respond by not cooperating: " 'No way I'm going to do things the Man's way.' "[34] For white students, blacks may appear to be the less serious students, isolated from the "mainstream," who occasionally threaten or intimidate them. Extortion of money and other conduct deemed threatening is commonplace, and they view school officials as protecting their safety. The experienced white administrators and teachers—however understanding they may try to be of the institutional and structural factors within schools and the black community which may explain the behavior of black youngsters—indicate that there is a minority among black students who are troublemakers. These troublemakers engage in actions which are seen as physically threatening and disruptive of authority relationships within the school. In their view, black overrepresentation among those suspended or expelled is simply incident to the fair administration of essential school rules designed to safeguard the integrity of the teaching and learning environment.[35]

While the evidence supporting the various theories is sketchy at best, it seems likely that the causes of black exclusion are complex and interrelated, and that the application of any single theory exaggerates and distorts

---

32. *See* STUDENT PUSHOUT REPORT 19-22.
33. *Id.* at 12-16.
34. Elsner, *A Problem at Evanston High*, The Wall Street Journal, April 16, 1974, at 22, col. 4.
35. *See, e.g.*, Colen, *Black Pupils' Suspensions Up in County*, The Washington Post, Sept. 29, 1974, at A-1, col. 1.

reality. But the significance of the simplification of causes of black suspension and expulsion is this: the factual reasons for the phenomenon have been thought to be dispositive with respect to the assignment of legal responsibility and ultimately the formulation of remedies. If racism is the moving cause, then there is a violation of the fourteenth amendment. If the misconduct of black students is the moving cause, then no action for redress will lie. This approach is troublesome. First, by casting the problem in terms of a dichotomy of blame, litigants compel the courts to brand either school officials or black students as lawless. Individual responsibility becomes paramount when institutional factors, inherent in schools and in the desegregation process, may be more decisive. There is growing evidence that the structure of schooling is more important to the success of integration than the simple mixing of bodies.[36] Moreover, the courts, and justifiably so, may be reluctant to brand a whole school system and its staff and teachers as racist, preferring instead to perceive exclusion as incidental to the enforcement of necessary rules. Second, while proportionately, minorities suffer from the exclusion penalty more than whites, suspension and expulsion are not confined to any single segment of the school population. There are many whites, and particularly, one suspects, poor whites, whose educational careers are ruined by the imposition of such sanctions.

The false dialectic of racism versus blacks as uneducable ruffians also misses the real problem. Students often are suspended and expelled for trivial violations of the hidden curriculum; that is, the rules with respect to obedience to authority, adherence to time schedules, silence, and the like.[37] The penalty often is excessively punitive in light of the infraction. Whatever the merits of existing patterns of school governance and institutional rules, the fact is that school authorities often deal with relatively minor infractions with the heavy-handed sanction of exclusion. In addition, even where the offense significantly disrupts the school or endangers life and property, the official response is simply to give up on the child. The truth is that many school systems have not learned to deal with behavior problems, and their only response is the age-old one: banishment from the institution. Many children, indeed, may not belong in regular classes, but this does not mean that they may be denied any state-provided education. School systems must learn to deal more flexibly with student behavior problems: they must be more institutionally adaptive, and thus more considerate of the educational interests of their charges. Exclusion solves problems for

---

36. *See, e.g.*, Cohen, *Modifying the Effects of Social Structure,* 16 Am. Behavioral Scientist 861 (1973); Cohen & Roper, *Modification of Interracial Interaction Disability: An Application of Status Characteristic Theory,* 37 Am. Soc. Rev. 643 (1972).

37. Student Pushout Report 12; Children Out of School 120. *See generally* P. Jackson, Life in Classrooms (1968); H. Kohl, 36 Children (1967); C. Silberman, Crisis in the Classroom ch. 4 (1970).

teachers and administrators but only at the expense of those who look to the school as a mechanism for social and economic advancement. This is all the more problematic when it occurs in a desegregation context, thwarting the very expectations which are central to the integrationist ethic.

The basic premise of this article then is that school authorities should be held accountable for the educational welfare of their students. They should be responsible for educating them, and this means that exclusion from a school should be an extraordinary remedy employed only when other sanctions are unavailing or when the safety of persons and property demands. Even under these circumstances, school systems are obliged to provide the child with some reasonable level of educational services. Placement in vocational programs, home tutoring, and the like may be in order. This conclusion is not dependent on the allocation of blame among administrators, teachers, and students; rather, it proceeds from the assumption that public educators bear responsibility for students even if the source of difficulty is not of their own making. Nor does it require the passing of judgment on the rightness of school rules and the debate over the cultural biases of the modern public school. The focus is on the magnitude of the punishments imposed on students.

With this as a background, Part I of the article provides a more detailed examination of the many reasons for black exclusion, concluding that the search for blame is not likely to be fruitful and avoids consideration of the impact of suspension and exclusion on children. Part II examines the constitutional and policy framework for addressing black exclusion, suggesting the lines of legal analysis which might support a limitation on the power to exclude.

I
THE FACTS OF BLACK EXCLUSION: UNANSWERED QUESTIONS AND TENTATIVE THEORIES

The exclusion of black students from the public schools has only recently undergone intensive public scrutiny, and it is only in the last two years that researchers have begun the process of data collection to determine the extent of the problem.[38] This apparent insensitivity is a function of a number of legal, political, and educational factors. Most prominent among them is the hallowed position traditionally occupied by the public educational enterprise in American society; historically, schools were insulated from the type of public oversight regularly afforded other institutions. The "great school legend," the bundle of unproven assumptions about the efficacy of

---

38. *See* Statement of Peter E. Holmes, Director, Office of Civil Rights, Department of Health, Education, and Welfare, in *Hearings on H.R. 6265 Before the Subcommittee on Equal Opportunities of the House Committee on Education and Labor,* 93d Cong., 2d Sess., 747 (1974).

public schooling and its relation to the good life, had placed it on a pedestal with only occasional sniping by the dissatisfied.[39] Schooling decisions were for "professionals" and "politicization" of the process must be resisted.[40] Since the *Brown* decision[41] in 1954 and the *Coleman Report*[42] and other investigations of the effectiveness of schools[43] in the last decade, the imperviousness of public schooling to criticism has crumbled. That schools were long on promise and short on performance was suddenly revealed.[44] Legal and political efforts, first directed against system-wide segregation and funding inequalities, inevitably turned to what occurs within individual schools. Ability grouping,[45] bilingual education,[46] special education,[47] and now student exclusion[48] have become targets for reform and litigation. This trend was sharply reinforced by the Supreme Court's landmark decision in

---

39. *See* C. Greer, The Great School Legend (1972).

40. *See generally* R. Callahan, Education and the Cult of Efficiency (1962).

41. Brown v. Board of Educ., 347 U.S. 483 (1954).

42. J. Coleman, Equality of Educational Opportunity (1966).

43. *See, e.g.*, On Equality of Educational Opportunity (F. Mosteller & D. Moynihan eds. 1972); Rand Corporation, How Effective is Schooling (1972); J. Guthrie, G. Kleindorfer, H. Levin, & R. Stout, Schools and Inequality (1971).

44. *See* J. Coleman, *supra* note 42; J. Guthrie, G. Kleindorfer, H. Levin, & R. Stout, *supra* note 43; The Solution as Part of the Problem (C. Greer ed. 1973); C. Greer, *supra* note 39; C. Silberman, *supra* note 37.

45. *See* McNeal v. Tate County School Dist., 508 F.2d 1017 (5th Cir. 1975); Hobson v. Hansen, 269 F. Supp. 401 (D.D.C. 1967), *aff'd en banc sub nom.* Smuck v. Hobson, 408 F.2d 175 (D.C. Cir. 1969). *See generally* Kirp, *supra* note 18; Sorgen, *Testing and Tracking in Public Schools,* 24 Hast. L.J. 1129 (1973); Note, *Legal Implications of the Use of Standardized Ability Tests in Employment and Education,* 68 Colum. L. Rev. 691 (1968).

46. *See* Lau v. Nichols, 414 U.S. 563 (1974); Serna v. Portales Municipal Schools, 499 F.2d 1147 (10th Cir. 1974). *See generally* T. Anderson & M. Boyer, Bilingual Schooling in the United States (1970); Johnson, *The Constitutional Right of Bilingual Children to an Equal Educational Opportunity,* 47 S. Cal. L. Rev. 943 (1974); Sugarman & Widess, *Equal Protection for Non-English Speaking School Children:* Lau v. Nichols, 62 Calif. L. Rev. 157 (1974); Grubb, *Breaking the Language Barrier: The Right to Bilingual Education,* 9 Harv. Civ. Rights-Civ. Lib. L. Rev. 52 (1974); Montoya, *Bilingual-Bicultural Education: Making Equal Educational Opportunities Available to Natural Origin Minority Students*, 61 Geo. L.J. 991 (1973); Kobrick, *A Model Act Providing for Transitional Bilingual Education Programs in Public Schools*, 9 Harv. J. Legis. 260 (1972).

47. *See* Nickerson v. Thomson, 504 F.2d 813 (7th Cir. 1974); Larry P. v. Riles, 343 F. Supp. 1306 (N.D. Cal. 1972); McMillan v. Board of Educ., 430 F.2d 1145 (2d Cir. 1970). *See generally* Kirp, *supra* note 18; Sorgen, *supra* note 45; Herr, *Retarded Children and the Law: Enforcing the Constitutional Rights of the Mentally Retarded*, 23 Syr. L. Rev. 995 (1972); Note, *The Right to Education for Mentally Retarded Children*, 43 U.Mo.K.C.L. Rev. 79 (1974).

48. *See* Mills v. Board of Educ., 348 F. Supp. 866 (D.D.C. 1972); Pennsylvania Ass'n for Retarded Children v. Commonwealth, 334 F. Supp. 1257 (E.D. Pa. 1971), 343 F. Supp. 279 (E.D. Pa. 1972) (consent order); Hosier v. Evans, 314 F. Supp. 316 (D.V.I. 1970); Knight v. Board of Educ., 48 F.R.D. 115 (E.D.N.Y. 1969). *See generally* Van Geel, *Does the Constitution Establish a Right to an Education,* 82 School Rev. 293 (1974); Herr, *supra* note 47; Dimond, *The Constitutional Right to Education: The Quiet Revolution,* 2 Hast. L.J. 1087 (1973); J. Regal, R. Elliot, H. Grossman, & W. Morse, The Systematic Exclusion of Children From School (1971). The extent that due process protections must accompany a suspension or expulsion decision has also received extensive judicial treatment. *See, e.g.*, Goss v. Lopez, 419 U.S. 565 (1975).

Tinker v. Des Moines Independent Community School District[49] in 1969 in which it was held that federal courts were empowered to overturn school discipline decisions for constitutional infirmity. It has further been accelerated by the realization that the physical mixing of bodies is merely the beginning of the desegregation process, and that many changes in the school environment must occur if the humanistic aims of school desegregation are to be realized.

Interest in the black exclusion problem has been manifested by a number of studies recently undertaken by several private civil rights groups,[50] which in provocative and groundbreaking reports, have catalogued the dimensions of the problem with Nader-like zeal.[51] The essential conclusion of these studies of black exclusion is that black students in public schools are suspended or expelled in numbers more than twice their proportion of the school population. Exclusion from schooling, like academic success, is not randomly distributed between identifiable racial groups. Figures from specific school districts abundantly support this assertion. For example, blacks make up twenty-eight per cent of the high school population and thirty-five per cent of the junior high school population in Little Rock, Arkansas, and yet nearly two-thirds of those suspended are black.[52] Similar findings are reported for New Orleans, Columbus (Georgia), Charlotte-Mecklenburg County, St. Petersburg, and other recently desegregated southern school systems.[53] The dubious distinction award for the most black exclusions, however, must go to the Dallas Independent School District, where, in a recent year, officials suspended more than six thousand minority youngsters or nearly ten per cent of the black school population.[54] These

---

49. 393 U.S. 503 (1969). *See generally* EDUCATIONAL POLICY AND THE LAW 134-90; Denno, *Mary Beth Tinker Takes the Constitution to School,* 38 FORDHAM L. REV. 35 (1969); Goldstein, *Reflections on Developing Trends in the Law of Student Rights,* 118 U. PA. L. REV. 612 (1970); Nahmod, *Beyond* Tinker*: The High School as an Educational Public Forum,* 5 HARV. CIV. RIGHTS-CIV. LIB. L. REV. 278 (1970).

50. See, for example, STUDENT PUSHOUT REPORT AND CHILDREN OUT OF SCHOOL. These studies largely rely upon data collected by the Office of Civil Rights (OCR) of the Department of Health, Education, and Welfare in the fall of 1973. As part of its National School Survey of Public Elementary and Secondary Schools, OCR surveyed almost 3,000 school districts, accounting for over 50 per cent of the total enrollment in American public schools and about 90 per cent of all minority students. Brief for Children's Defense Fund of the Washington Research Project, Inc. and The American Friends Service Committee as Amici Curiae at 20, Goss v. Lopez, 419 U.S. 565 (1975). School districts were asked to reveal the total number of students suspended and expelled during the academic year, the cumulative number of suspension days out of school, and the racial and ethnic breakdowns of those figures. While the OCR has not completed its analysis of this data or issued any report, the private groups have relied upon its data to buttress their conclusion that blacks have been the victims of institutional and personal racism in their treatment by school authorities.

51. *See* note 50 *supra*. *See also* S. Browning, Racially Discriminatory Suspensions in the Akron Public Schools: A Tentative Analysis, Oct. 2, 1974 (unpublished memorandum at Lawyers Committee for Civil Rights Under Law, Washington, D.C.).

52. STUDENT PUSHOUT REPORT 2.

53. STUDENT PUSHOUT REPORT 2-6. *See generally* CHILDREN OUT OF SCHOOL 124-34.

54. STUDENT PUSHOUT REPORT 4; *see* Hawkins v. Coleman, 376 F. Supp. 1330 (N.D. Tex. 1974).

statistics exclude expulsions, a category w ich presumably would have swelled the totals even higher. There are also many examples from the North, from school districts which are in various stages of desegregation.[55] For example, the Lawyers' Committee for Civil Rights found that in Akron, Ohio, more than two-thirds of all schools reporting admitted that "their percentage of minority students suspended is greater than the percentage of white students suspended."[56]

Apart from the crude statistics on the scope of the exclusion problem within school districts, what do we know about the incidence and process of exclusion? Precious little. We know that blacks are suspended more repeatedly than whites, if not longer.[57] We know that, at least in some school districts, black students fall victim to exclusion more often than other racial and ethnic minorities.[58] Finally, there appears to be a general pattern which reveals that the problem is of a greater magnitude in small cities and rural areas than in populous urban areas.[59] There are, however, as Dallas and New Orleans exemplify, notable exceptions to this generalization. What we do not know, or what is known only on the basis of anecdotes which may or may not evidence more universal patterns, is far greater. The disproportionate exclusion of black students from the public schools is far from a universal phenomenon,[60] and there are great unexplained variations between school districts and indeed from school to school within school districts.[61] What accounts for these differences? Is it the attitudes of school officials? Are there variations in the characteristics of the black population between different geographic areas? Are there institutional factors which vary? What kinds of behavior by black students trigger the application of severe, exclusionary penalties? The raw statistics on exclusion of black students, standing alone, tell us very little about the reasons for their high rate of exclusion, and clearly are not determinative with respect to the existence of discrimination.[62]

There are a number of factors which would appear capable of explaining school expulsions and suspensions of black students. The most obvious of these is the educational philosophy and imagination of school administrators and teachers. Banishment, over the years, has been a controversial if typical manner of dealing with behavior problems in the schools. School systems recently have explored other means of dealing with assertedly dis-

---

55. CHILDREN OUT OF SCHOOL 124-34; S. Browning, *supra* note 51.

56. S. Browning, *supra* note 51, at 1.

57. CHILDREN OUT OF SCHOOL 132.

58. *See* STUDENT PUSHOUT REPORT 4.

59. *Id.* at 6.

60. *Id.* at 11; CHILDREN OUT OF SCHOOL 130.

61. *See, e.g.*, Hawkins v. Coleman, 376 F. Supp. 1330, 1334 (N.D. Tex. 1974).

62. *See* Statement of Peter E. Holmes, *supra* note 38, at 5-6; STUDENT PUSHOUT REPORT 10; CHILDREN OUT OF SCHOOL 149-50.

obedient students. Special classes or schools, isolation for a temporary period of time, corporal punishment, referrals to police authorities, deprivation of privileges, more schooling (detentions): all of these are alternative means of handling disciplinary problems which school officials employ.[63]

While doubtless many of these approaches do not generate universal enthusiasm—some within-school punishments may be more injurious and stigmatizing than suspension—it seems reasonable to believe that there is great diversity among superintendents, principals, and teachers with respect to their willingness to utilize particular punishments. "Law and order" is just as much a topic of debate among educators as in the public at large. In addition, there are probably variations in resources available—for example, special facilities and teaching skills—to individual schools and school districts, and thus some administrators may have the luxury, which others do not have, of considering other options. Thus, one way to account for the variations in exclusion practices is to focus on the increasing diversification of punishment and remedial approaches to student misbehavior.

Second, there may be more racial prejudice in some school districts than in others. Possibly such prejudice is more rampant in rural areas, thereby accounting for one of the few pieces of hard evidence in the studies. Administrators and teachers in some areas may feel public pressure to deal firmly and decisively with black students and to exclude them at the first sign of trouble. Possibly these areas attract and retain teachers who are less sympathetic to black youngsters. The context may also be important. In a district in the throes of desegregation, intemperate decisions, which would be rejected in calmer times, may be reached.[64] The history of interracial cooperation, or lack of it, within the community may be decisive. Moreover, as in any professional group, there are likely to be at least a few "bad apples" within school districts, teachers and principals who are racially prejudiced against blacks. This may account for the fact that within high exclusion districts, usually only a few schools, with student bodies which appear to be virtually indistinguishable from others, are responsible for the bulk of school exclusions. By its very nature, personal racial prejudice of this sort is difficult to prove since rarely will school officials admit of its existence, and there are always superficially neutral reasons which may be proferred to explain exclusions. In addition, as in many areas of debate over race policy, it may be difficult to disentangle a "law and order" philosophy of school punishments from a less defensible policy of racial discrimination.

Third, the behavioral characteristics of black students in different areas may not be uniform, and this would also help to explain the variations in exclusion rates. There may be differences between urban black children,

---

63. *See generally* S. GOLDSTEIN, LAW AND PUBLIC EDUCATION ch. 7 (1974).
64. *See* STUDENT PUSHOUT REPORT 10.

living in ghetto neighborhoods, and rural black children, with respect to their attitudes toward school authorities and their white peers. Some black populations are more affluent than others. Blacks bused from their neighborhoods and brought to a strange, middle-class environment may react with hostility. Both social dislocation and crimes of violence are more common among ghettoized blacks, and there is no reason to believe that the public schools are insulated from these social facts of life.[65]

Finally, and this is the most critical point, perceptions vary as to what constitutes behavior sufficiently threatening to the order of the school to trigger the application of severe sanctions.[66] To be sure, there are many black suspensions and expulsions for fighting, threatening white students, possession of dangerous weapons, and using or selling dangerous drugs or alcohol. There is little disagreement about the need for discipline in such cases—including removal from the school building. But I suspect that the vast majority of blacks excluded have not engaged in such behavior. Rather, they are more often suspended for smoking, habitual tardiness, speaking back to teachers, truancy, noisiness, and the like.[67] In short, they have assertedly engaged in institutionally inappropriate behavior, disregarding the "hidden curriculum" or values underlying institutional public schooling. When a black student or parent refers to "institutional racism," he is making reference to these institutional rules. He is arguing, in effect, that the institution has an obligation to alter its rules to make them less arbitrary and more consistent with the behavior patterns among blacks. An institution which consciously applies rules which systematically disfavor blacks is a "racist institution." On the other hand, when a white student or parent argues for the need for discipline, he is implicitly sanctioning the system of institutional rules, and maintaining that black children must learn to adapt to that system.

This theory of black exclusion is plausible, but the evidence supporting it is sketchy and anecdotal. It appears to have particular force as an explanation of exclusion in recently desegregated school systems. While we do not have statistically accurate measures of the rate of exclusion in all black schools before integration took hold, it seems likely that it is not so much that black behavior has changed radically as it is that reactions of school officials in desegregated schools, including the rigidity of application of rules and the choice of punishments, have changed. The black student is bused from his formerly all black, neighborhood school, and finds himself in a predominantly white, middle-class environment. Lacking friends in the white com-

65. *See generally* G. LEVY, GHETTO SCHOOL (1970).

66. *See* Statement of Peter E. Holmes, *supra* note 38, at 8; J. REGAL, R. ELLIOT, H. GROSSMAN, & W. MORSE, THE SYSTEMATIC EXCLUSION OF CHILDREN FROM SCHOOL 14 (1971). *See generally* McClung, *supra* note 31, at 517-18.

67. *See* STUDENT PUSHOUT REPORT 12; CHILDREN OUT OF SCHOOL 120. *See generally* Dixwell Legal Rights Foundation, *Report on School Suspensions in New Haven*, in S. GOLDSTEIN, LAW AND PUBLIC EDUCATION 445 (1974).

munity, the black students tend to stick together and build their own sub-culture within the school. One foundation of their sub-culture is their attitude toward authority:[68]

> Whites may be more accustomed to an authoritarian atmosphere . . . . When a white student is told by a teacher to do something, he is accustomed to doing it without asking why, while the black pupil often challenged the teacher's authority and got in trouble for it.

They also may view with disdain the careful scheduling and attention to time which is so much a part of public education:[69]

> "When desegregation first occurred at the secondary level . . . blacks were put into a predominantly white setting where there were entirely different attitudes toward schedules, promptness and so on. The segregated schools which black students had been attending were not as oriented toward time schedules. . . . Tardiness was a major violation.
>
> "The black students got the idea that the regulations had been instituted to persecute blacks. It took a couple of years for them to realize that the rules had existed before and for them to adapt to the stricter regulations."

If the failure to adhere to institutional rules relating to respect for authority and timeliness is the primary cause of black exclusions, then we can gain a number of additional insights into the process. At the heart of the problem lies the controversy, which has plagued thinkers since Plato, of the appropriate role of the state in socializing children to values endorsed by those who control education. The problem is inherently cultural. As Professor Bowles and others have pointed out, socialization to such values as the need for decorum, delayed gratification, obedience to authority, and punctuality are closely related to the demands that an industrialized society makes on its citizens in the work force.[70] Black children are subjected, like white children, to a system of rewards and punishments which furthers these values of the industrial society. While, as some have charged, the traditional values of institutional schooling may be more rigidly enforced in black or integrated schools than in white, middle class schools,[71] variation seems more likely at the fringes of the hidden curriculum—open classrooms, flexible curricula, and more class discussion. It seems implausible that core institutional guidelines relating to decorum, obedience, and punctuality vary all that significantly.

---

68. STUDENT PUSHOUT REPORT 20.

69. *Id.* at 18.

70. Bowles, *Understanding Unequal Economic Opportunity*, 63 AM. ECON. REV. 346 (1973). *See also* Behn, Carnoy, Carter, Crain, & Levin, *School is Bad; Work is Worse*, 83 SCHOOL REV. 49 (1974); Bowles, *Unequal Education and the Reproduction of the Social Division of Labor*, in SCHOOLING IN A CORPORATE SOCIETY 36 (M. Carnoy ed. 1972); Gintis, *Education, Technology, and the Characteristics of Worker Productivity*, 61 AM. ECON. REV. 266 (1971); Gintis, *Toward a Political Economy of Education: A Radical Critique of Ivan Illich's Deschooling Society*, in AFTER DESCHOOLING, WHAT? 29 (A. Gartner, C. Greer, & F. Riessman eds. 1973).

71. Behn, Carnoy, Carter, Crain, & Levin, *supra* note 70, at 57.

The exclusion problem also reminds us, if we needed reminding, that socialization in the public schools is accomplished as much or more through patterns of institutional governance as it is by what is directly taught in the classroom.[72] It is noteworthy that blacks, like whites, are more frequently punished for violations of the so-called hidden curriculum than they are for academic failure. Furthermore, exclusion brings forth the whole debate about appropriate pedogogy in the public schools. At least since the time of Dewey[73] and Counts,[74] educators have argued over the degree of order necessary to accomplish educational objectives. Most teachers and school administrators, in effect, have taken the position that a high degree of order, obedience, and punctuality is necessary to further learning. Others, including the John Holts and George Dennisons of the world, would argue that public schools are too rigid and highly structured to maximize learning.[75] At present, controversy over black exclusion is simply another level at which this debate is continued.

Black exclusion also may be less of a race than a poverty problem. The types of anti-institutional behavior ascribed to blacks is commonly ascribed to many low income groups.[76] The data thus far accumulated are not broken down into income categories. This would indicate, once again, that social science has failed to disentangle the variables of race and wealth. This insight is critical since it indicates that legal rules and remedies geared exclusively to racial disparities may well miss the mark since poor whites are as much victimized by suspension and expulsion as blacks. Even more significantly, it may illuminate the reasons why a disproportionate number of blacks fall victim to institutional rules in schools. Poverty is more prevalent among blacks, and the culture of the poor, emanating from the need to survive despite tremendous deprivations, may be inconsistent with the culture of schools:[77]

> [S]ome poor children withdraw from school simply because they are poor; they are too hungry in the morning to make their way to school or they cannot keep up with their schoolwork because they must travel so far with

---

72. *See, e.g.*, S. Sarason, The Culture of the School and the Problem of Change (1971); Bowles & Gintis, *IQ in the Class Structure*, 3 Social Policy 65 (1972); Raskin, *The Channeling Colony*, in Schooling in a Corporate Society 23 (M. Carnoy ed. 1972); Jackson, *Student's World*, 66 Elem. School J. 345 (1966). *See also* note 37 *supra*.

73. *See* J. Dewey, Democracy and Education (1916).

74. *See* G. Counts, The American Road to Culture (1930).

75. *See, e.g.*, G. Dennison, The Lives of Children (1969): E. Friedenberg, Coming of Age in America (1965); P. Goodman, The Community of Scholars and Compulsory Miseducation (1966); J. Holt, The Underachieving School (1969); C. Silberman, Crisis in the Classroom (1970).

76. Children Out of School 134-35.

77. Cottle, *Dying a Different Sort of Death: The Exclusion of Children From School*, 83 School Rev. 145, 148 (1974). *See generally* Children Out of School 78-89. I prefer this formulation of the problem to the more stigmatizing and obfuscating phrase "behaviorally handicapped." *See* McClung, *supra* note 31, at 511-15.

> inadequate transportation. They are lucky to make it to school one or two days a week. These are children who work inside as well as outside their homes.
>
> . . . Many poor children who do not hold jobs, who do have enough food, and who sleep well enough at night nevertheless cannot face the environment of school because they are ashamed of what we would call their "station in life." They dread being seen in the same shoes or dresses day after day. They fear the moment . . . when a well-meaning teacher may ask them about their background, their parents and grandparents, their home, their neighborhood . . . .

As is so often the case, the public schools mirror the problems of the larger community, neither isolating the students from those problems nor measurably aiding in their resolution.

Finally, all of these observations indicate that the problem of black exclusion from the public schools is complex, and that approaches premised on simplistic notions of personal or institutional racism are just that—simplistic. I venture to guess that if all the racist teachers and principals in the nation were magically removed from their positions of public trust, exclusion would still be very much with us—and it would still disproportionately affect blacks. Similarly, simply labeling the public schools as racist institutions does a grave injustice; for it fails to analyze the legitimacy of the socialization process, and the values inherent in that process, in the public schools. Unequal results do not necessarily reflect unfair rules and procedures.

Where does all this lead us? What is an appropriate response? By rejecting the theory that black exclusion is a manifestation of racial discrimination, we seem to have traveled from the barely manageable conundrums posed by *Brown* and its progeny to the unspeakable intellectual horrors of value transmission and the allocation of power between child, family, and state. The neglected web of *Pierce*[78] and *Meyer*[79] and *Farrington*[80] need be revisited, as well as *Yoder*[81] and *Barnette.*[82] I have no doubt that these issues deserve careful attention; for legal scholars have for too long overlooked the role of the state as a communicator, a communicator with vast power to influence behavior, attitudes, and ultimately political decisions. This is particularly acute in the public schools, given the captive audience status and immaturity of the students. But candor requires the admission that the nature of the socialization process in relation to black exclusion is such as to make it an unlikely judicial avenue for reaching the latter. The values which are not honored and which trigger exclusion emanate from the nature of

---

78. Pierce v. Society of Sisters, 268 U.S. 510 (1925). *See generally* EDUCATIONAL POLICY AND THE LAW 1-10.

79. Meyer v. Nebraska, 262 U.S. 390 (1923).

80. Farrington v. Tokushige, 273 U.S. 284 (1927).

81. Wisconsin v. Yoder, 406 U.S. 205 (1972).

82. West Virginia State Bd. of Educ. v. Barnette, 319 U.S. 624 (1943). *See* Note, *Freedom and Public Education: The Need for New Standards,* 50 NOTRE DAME LAWYER 530 (1975).

the institutional environment of the modern public school: the need to educate large numbers of students in a specialized institution, which is operated in hierarchical fashion by a professional bureaucracy.[83] More importantly, if these institutional values are to be destroyed, then either the institutions must be destroyed, or they must be so reconstructed that they bear little resemblance to what today we describe as a public school. While certainly some accomodation between competing value systems is possible, this more far-reaching result is unlikely. Specialized educational institutions, operated by government, appear to be a near universal fact of life in modern nations. They will not soon disappear in any society dedicated to technological development, industrialization, and the specialization of labor.[84] The demise of traditional, mediating institutions as vehicles for transmitting culture and skills, the necessity to delegate responsibility for education to a fraction of all adults, and the need to communicate so much, so quickly, all argue against a return to non-institutional educational systems. As C. Wright Mills has noted, the means of communication "have paralleled in range and efficiency the other institutions of greater scale that make up the modern society of masses."[85]

In the present context, it is also difficult to imagine an agency less willing or able to undertake a program of structural reform of the public schools than the courts. Whatever their ability, largely untested, to scrutinize direct indoctrination in the classroom, it would appear far more difficult to order substantial changes in patterns of institutional governance to obliterate objectional values. Moreover, as products of the public schools themselves, it appears unlikely that judges would seriously challenge the institutional values underlying public schooling. And if they seriously undertook such an analysis, they might well approve the transmission of values so closely related to the needs of industrial society.

II

Policy and Constitutional Framework

A. Policy

If the black exclusion problem is not a manifestation of racial discrimination, as that phrase is typically understood, the whole panoply of legal doc-

83. *See* Green, *Schools as Communities*, 39 Harv. Ed. Rev. 221 (1969). *See generally* C. Silberman, *supra* note 37; W. Waller, The Sociology of Teaching (1965).

84. *See, e.g.*, I. Illich, Deschooling Society (1971); P. Coombs, The World Educational Crisis: A Systems Analysis (1968); J. Vaizey, Education for Tomorrow (1966); Green, *supra* note 83; Bowles, *Understanding Unequal Economic Opportunity*, 63 Am. Econ. Rev. 346 (1973); Bowles, *Education and Socialist Man in Cuba*, in Schooling in a Corporate Society 272 (M. Carnoy ed. 1972).

85. Mills, *Mass Society and Liberal Education*, in Power, Politics, and People: The Collected Essays of C. Wright Mills 353, 361 (I. Horowitz ed. 1963).

trines associated with racial classifications is not applicable. The substantive rules which lead to exclusion in disproportionate numbers by race appear to have a racially neutral justification and purpose. While those substantive rules may be subject to attack as seeking to bring an unconstitutional orthodoxy to the public schools, everything we know about education in the modern industrial state argues against such a conclusion. In weighing the difficulties of accomplishing mass educational objectives against the incidental losses to individual decision-making wrought by institutionalized learning, the choice in favor of the latter is virtually inescapable. But there is a third level at which the problem of black suspension and expulsion may be approached. Even if school rules are nondiscriminatory and are sufficiently related to the educational process, we may appropriately inquire as to the gravity of the punishments imposed and the nexus between violations and those punishments.

While the courts often eschew reliance on notions of the reasonableness of punishments either absolutely or in relation to the wrongs committed, this is, at bottom, the issue presented by black exclusion. Black students, whose only offense, at best, may be a failure to adhere to the school schedule or to obey instructions promptly and respectfully, find themselves completely banished from the state's educational system. This is the age-old response of total and semi-total institutions which have not learned to deal with even the most minor threats to the institution. It is akin to a dishonorable discharge from the armed services or isolation of inmates in prisons. For a student who is consistently late to class or truant, it is bizarre to visit the penalty of complete exclusion upon him.[86] A student's failure to attend all classes results in a state-imposed requirement that he attend none. From the institution's perspective, however, there is great gain in ridding itself of a troublemaker who will not comply with the rules, who is perceived as a threat to authority, and who may set an example for others to deviate from the institutional ground rules.

Lurking behind the proposition that exclusion is often an inappropriate punishment lies two suppositions which may distinguish this situation from others in which the gravity of the punishment is challenged. First, the state has an obligation to provide an education to all children where it has chosen to establish a primary and secondary educational system and to make it freely available.[87] The state has assumed responsibility for the education of the young, and whatever the causes of exclusion of blacks, the state should not be permitted to shirk that responsibility. To be sure, as the Supreme Court has recently reminded us,[88] there may be no obligation to provide equal

86. *See* Dixwell Legal Rights Foundation, *supra* note 67.

87. *See* Van Geel, *supra* note 48; Dimond, *supra* note 48. *See, e.g.*, Mills v. Board of Educ., 348 F. Supp. 866 (D.D.C. 1972); Hosier v. Evans, 314 F. Supp. 316 (D.V.I. 1970).

88. San Antonio Independent School Dist. v. Rodriguez, 411 U.S. 1 (1973).

services or dollars or an equal educational opportunity defined in input or output terms.[89] Regular classes in the public schools may not be appropriate for youngsters with behavioral problems just as they may not be appropriate for retarded or hyperkinetic children. Within a wide range of discretion, the state may make educational decisions for its charges, concluding that special schools, vocational training, home instruction, or other nontraditional forms of learning are required. But it may not completely give up on those that it has obliged itself to educate.[90] All children are capable of learning, whether it be particular mechanical skills, higher mathematics, or simply sewing and cooking, and such learning may be of inestimable value in their adult lives.[91] Thus institutional concerns may dictate the nature of the educational setting in which learning takes place, but it may not compel the abandonment of all educational efforts. This is particularly true in the case of the poor and minorities since rarely will they be able to afford private alternatives to public schooling. Moreover, exclusion simply does not remedy or even address the problems which may underlie the child's asserted misbehavior:[92]

> Yet instead of giving children with problems the special attention they need, schools try to give them no attention at all. . . .
>
> Some children misbehave in school because they have emotional or psychological problems. Others cannot see or hear properly and may never have had the situation corrected medically. Still others may have learning disabilities. . . .

There is, of course, nothing inevitable about the universality and compulsoriness of public education. The state, out of a concern for efficiency, might well decide to educate only limited numbers of children or to exclude those who in one fashion or another later prove difficult or expensive to educate. Alternatively, it might decide not to educate its children at all, leaving schooling to the private sector, and employing its scarce resources for assertedly more worthy endeavors such as welfare or police protection. My assumption, however, is that government, reflecting the views of most citizens, has already decided in its laws, budgets, and public pronouncements to treat education as a "merit" good:[93]

---

89. *But see* J. Coons, W. Clune, & S. Sugarman, Private Wealth and Public Education (1970); Kirp, *The Poor, the Schools, and Equal Protection*, 38 Harv. Ed. Rev. 635 (1968); Horowitz, *Unseparate But Unequal—The Emerging Fourteenth Amendment Issue in Public School Education,* 13 U.C.L.A.L. Rev. 1147 (1966); Yudof, *supra* note 24.

90. Children Out of School 135-39. *See* Dimond, *supra* note 48; Kirp, *supra* note 18.

91. Yudof, *supra* note 24, at 474 n. 326 and authorities cited therein.

92. Children Out of School 136; McClung, *supra* note 31, at 507.

93. Calabresi & Melamed, *Property Rules, Liability Rules, and Inalienability: One View of the Cathedral,* 85 Harv. L. Rev. 1089, 1100 (1972). For discussions of state intervention to secure the satisfaction of "just wants" and of other phrases describing essentially the same concept, see Baker, *Utility and Rights: Two Justifications for State Action Increasing Equality,* 84 Yale L.J. 39 (1974); Michelman, *Foreword: On Protecting the Poor Through the Fourteenth Amendment,* 83 Harv. L. Rev. 7 (1969).

> If the choice of entitlements affects wealth distribution generally, it also affects the chances that people will obtain what have sometimes been called merit goods. Whenever a society wishes to maximize the chances that individuals will have at least a minimum endowment of certain particular goods—education, clothes, bodily integrity—the society is likely to begin by giving the individuals an entitlement to them. If the society deems such an endowment to be essential regardless of individual desires, it will, of course, make the entitlement inalienable.

Each child is entitled to an education at public expense, and that entitlement is inalienable and not normally a subject for bargain or exchange although currently school authorities have the power to extinguish that entitlement. The government might have chosen otherwise, but in fact it has not. The reasons for so treating education are numerous. First, it may be feared that the failure to provide an education may result in significant externalities.[94] An uneducated person may be more likely to commit crimes or become a welfare recipient, and thus the personal decision of a parent or child (or the decision of school authorities) may adversely affect third persons who have no role in the decision-making. Second, we may fear that parents, educators, and children will make inefficient decisions in the short run, responding to particular stresses and exigencies, and that universal and compulsory education comports more with what a rational individual would choose over the long run. This argument is what Calabresi describes as the "self paternalism" justification for forbidding the sale of merit goods.[95] Third, government may simply "bite the bullet" and decide that, because of its superior informational position or otherwise, individuals and society would be better off with a universal and compulsory education system from which no or few individuals were excluded. This is a straightforward argument for paternalism.[96]

The first three arguments for treating education as a merit good are essentially utilitarian in nature. Their premise is that such treatment will maximize the aggregate satisfaction of educational wants by correcting for inadequacies in market mechanisms which produce inefficiencies in the allocation of educational services. The last argument is rather different in character, proceeding from the assumption of a theory of right.[97] The state may afford certain rights to individuals even if satisfaction in the aggregate is reduced:[98]

> A right, in the sense Dworkin uses it, is a claim which the government would be wrong to override if the government's only grounds were that

94. *Cf.* Calabresi & Melamed, *supra* note 93, at 1111.

95. *Id.* at 1113.

96. *See id.* at 1113-14.

97. This distinction between utility and rights is developed in Baker, *supra* note 93. *See also* Dworkin, *Taking Rights Seriously,* in IS LAW DEAD? 168 (E. Rostow ed. 1971).

98. Baker, *supra* note 93, at 48. *See also* J. RAWLS, A THEORY OF JUSTICE (1971); Dworkin, *supra* note 97.

> overriding the right would increase the well-being of the community as a whole. Thus, a right is a claim to have a certain need satisfied even if having this need satisfied causes a decrease in total or average utility.

In the case of education, a right to satisfaction of educational wants may emanate from a sense of obligation on society's part,[99] or, put somewhat differently, the treatment of education as a merit good may be a response to a concern for the redistribution of wealth:[100]

> Whether an entitlement may be sold or not often affects directly who is richer and who is poorer. . . . Favoring the specific group that has benefited may or may not have been the reason for the prohibition on bargaining. What is important is that, regardless of the reason for barring a contract, a group did gain from the prohibition.

The assumption then may be that the poor, due to their inability to afford private schools, their lack of information, or other factors, will be deprived of the benefits of an education unless the state creates a positive entitlement to it. Since they are entitled to such benefits under theories of distributive justice, education must be treated as a merit good. Moreover, the just distribution of education services may also be an efficient distribution, particularly if it is assumed that there are declining marginal utilities or that personal utility is partially dependent on the well-being of others.[101]

If it is assumed that education is a merit good, defined as a utilitarian concept, the question, in the present context, must be whether or not school exclusion policies are likely to maximize its consumption. One such argument, treated below, is that temporary exclusion is more likely than other measures to increase the desire of the affected individuals to remain in school over the long run. There is little evidence to support such a supposition. A second argument is that the loss of the entitlement to education on the part of some students is more than offset by the educational gains to other students who no longer need tolerate interference with their education. Assuming that those who are denied their entitlement are in fact the same class of persons who significantly interfere with the education of others, in most cases it may be possible to prevent the interference without denying the entitlement. The rejoinder is that this may be quite expensive. At one level this may be no more than a recapitulation of the debate over whether education should be a merit good. As long as society adheres to the merit good approach to education, these added costs must be endured. Of course, government might respond by reducing the level of resources devoted to the class of children now in school and shifting those resources to the class of children now excluded. This would raise profound, if currently unanswer-

---

99. Baker, *supra* note 93, at 55.
100. Calabresi & Melamed, *supra* note 93, at 1114.
101. *Id.* at 44-46.

able, questions as to which course of action would maximize the overall consumption of public and private education.

If the treatment of education as a merit good rests on the notion that individuals are entitled to some minimum level of satisfaction of their educational needs, then the implications for school exclusion policies are obvious —if somewhat tautological. School children may not be temporarily or permanently denied a public education even if such a course of action lowers the aggregate satisfaction of educational wants. But equally as important, given the fact that we do not possess definitive data allowing us to compare the efficiency of the exclusionary and nonexclusionary alternatives, and given the plausibility of the assumption that the distributive justice approach will yield efficient results, I believe that a public policy choice against exclusionary practices is entirely defensible.

The second supposition underlying the analysis is that there is a significant relationship between assertedly temporary school suspension and expulsion decisions and permanent exclusion from the public schools.[102] Suspensions may range from only a few days to five or six weeks, and often expulsions, by their own terms, are not permanent, keeping the child out of school only for the remainder of the semester in which the offense took place. But the reality of the situation is far different from the limited nature of the punishment appearing on the surface. Many school districts do not allow a child to continue to receive his assignments for the period that he is excluded from the school building, nor is there an opportunity to take examinations at home. The student returns to school weeks behind his peers, and must make a tremendous personal effort to keep up with his present work while attempting to make up for lost work. For the student who, by virtue of his exclusion, may have demonstrated his failure to adjust to the demands of the public school, and who may not be a particularly serious student in the first instance, this burden may be virtually impossible to carry. He gets further and further behind in his work, and ultimately may drop out of school altogether. While this may be officially characterized as a "voluntary" decision, the reality is that it was the initial exclusion decision which triggered the "voluntary" decision to discontinue public schooling.[103] Absence from the school environment may produce further estrangement from the institution. In the absence of parental and peer pressure to remain in school, the student may learn that he enjoys being out of school and that it is not worth the "hassle" to return. If he returns even temporarily, he may be so hostile and alienated that he acts out his aggressions. This, in turn, may lead to additional suspension and expulsion decisions.

102. STUDENT PUSHOUT REPORT 8; CHILDREN OUT OF SCHOOL 119.

103. *See, e.g.*, Madera v. Board of Educ., 667 F. Supp. 356, 369 (S.D.N.Y. 1967), *rev'd on other grounds*, 386 F.2d 778 (2d Cir. 1967).

The point then is that individual suspension and expulsion decisions, however temporary, may effectively terminate the educational careers of those affected, thereby reducing their opportunity to enter college and obtain high status and high income employment. Even where this is not the case, exclusion is likely to affect academic performance as the student is required to double his workload on his return. And finally, exclusions are noted on the student's permanent school record, and this may independently affect his educational and employment opportunities.[104] All of this suggests that suspension and expulsion should be exceptional punishments meted out only where there are serious violations of school rules, and where there is significant danger of violence, destruction of school property, or disorder. Even in those circumstances, special services should be made available to the child for the period that he is out of school, and other alternatives—counseling, placement in special classes or schools, vocational programs in private industry—should be explored before the ultimate sanction is employed.[105] It is noteworthy in this regard that there appears to be little disparity between blacks and whites in terms of the level of educational expenditures while they remain in primary and secondary schools, but the overrepresentation of blacks among dropouts and pushouts leads to a lower lifetime state expenditure on blacks and whites.[106]

B. The Judicial Response: The Racial Discrimination Approach

Thus far, while black exclusion has lurked beneath the surface in many first and fourteenth amendment controversies in desegregating school districts,[107] there have only been a few cases in which the issue has been directly confronted.[108] In these relatively few decisions the federal courts have not been willing to allow the desegregation train to carry the extra baggage of student discipline problems. Unlike teacher and administrator dismissals[109] and intraschool ability grouping policies,[110] federal courts have tended to

---

104. *See generally* CHILDREN OUT OF SCHOOL 135-36.

105. *See generally* CHILDREN OUT OF SCHOOL 10, 147-48; R.E. PHAY & J. CUMMINGS, STUDENT SUSPENSIONS AND EXPULSIONS 7-8 (1970); McClung, *supra* note 31, at 520-26; *cf.* Carrington, *Civilizing University Discipline,* 69 MICH. L. REV. 393 (1971).

106. C. JENCKS, INEQUALITY 26-27 (1972).

107. *See, e.g.*, Lopez v. Williams, 372 F. Supp. 1279 (S.D. Ohio 1973), *aff'd sub nom.* Goss v. Lopez, 419 U.S. 565 (1975); Dunn v. Tyler Independent School Dist., 460 F.2d 137 (5th Cir. (1972).

108. Boykins v. Fairfield Bd. of Educ., 492 F.2d 697 (5th Cir. 1974); Hawkins v. Coleman, 376 F. Supp. 1330 (N.D. Tex. 1974); Rhyne v. Childs, 359 F. Supp. 1085 (N.D. Fla. 1973), *aff'd sub nom.* Sweet v. Childs, 507 F.2d 675 (5th Cir. 1975); Tillman v. Dade County School Bd., 327 F. Supp. 930 (S.D. Fla. 1971).

109. *See, e.g.,* Sparks v. Griffin, 460 F.2d 433 (5th Cir. 1972); Moore v. Board of Educ., 448 F.2d 709 (8th Cir. 1971). *Compare* Armstead v. Starksville Municipal Separate School Dist., 325 F. Supp. 560 (N.D. Miss. 1971), *with* United States v. Chesterfield County School Dist., 484 F.2d 70 (4th Cir. 1973).

110. *See, e.g.,* McNeal v. Tate County School Dist., 508 F.2d 1017 (5th Cir. 1975); Lemon

distinguish between present school disciplinary policies and the need to remedy past de jure discrimination practices: they have been unwilling to reverse exclusion decisions by simply invoking the remedial discretion of federal courts. Nonetheless, the courts have tended to focus exclusively and improperly, I believe, on allegations of racial discrimination.[111] The result is a great confusion of legal doctrine, a bit of dishonesty with the facts, and the lack of a remedy even where black plaintiffs prevail.

The earliest case in which the disproportionate exclusion of blacks was challenged is *Tillman v. Dade County School Board.*[112] In that case, the evidence showed that fighting had broken out between black and white youngsters at the South Dade High School. While in the court's view the evidence failed to reveal whether blacks or whites were initially responsible for the disruption and destruction of school property, all but six of the ninety-three students suspended were black. Many of those suspensions were lifted, leaving one white student and forty-seven black students out of school for ten or more days. School authorities explained this discrepancy by noting that their overriding concern had been to separate the black and white students. To this end, the police had moved in and pushed the white students off the campus, while containing the black students within the school building. As a result, defendants argued that only the black students were easily subject to identification and apprehension for misconduct. The court accepted the position of the defendants, attributing the disproportionality in exclusion to this "fortuitous circumstance."[113]

> While it is true that when figures speak courts listen, . . . it is apparent from a review of all the evidence in this case that the figures alone do not tell the whole story and consequently are not determinative of this issue.
>
> . . . .
>
> . . . The fact that Blacks were apprehended and many more Blacks than Whites suspended was nothing more than a fortuitous circumstance, a result of their physical location.

The court did not inquire as to why the decision was made to isolate black students rather than white students on the campus or as to the feasibility of identifying white students before they had departed from the campus. There appeared to be sufficient evidence of absence from regular classes (pictures were taken) to justify the suspension of each black student, and the court refused to take the matter further.

---

v. Bossier Parish School Bd., 444 F.2d 1400 (5th Cir. 1971); United States v. Sunflower County School Dist., 430 F.2d 839 (5th Cir. 1970). *See generally* Yudof, *supra* note 24, at 451; Kirp, *supra* note 18, at 763; Punke, *Competence as a Basis of Student Assignment,* 32 ALA. LAW 24 (1971).

111. *See, e.g.,* Floyd v. Trice, 490 F.2d 1154 (8th Cir. 1974); Hawkins v. Coleman, 376 F. Supp. 1330 (N.D. Tex. 1974); Rhyne v. Childs, 359 F. Supp. 1085 (N.D. Fla. 1973), *aff'd sub nom.* Sweet v. Childs, 507 F.2d 675 (5th Cir. 1975). *But see* Boykins v. Fairfield Bd. of Educ., 492 F.2d 697, 702 (5th Cir. 1974). *See generally* McClung, *supra* note 31, at 507-08.

112. 327 F. Supp. 930 (S.D. Fla. 1971).

113. *Id.* at 932.

Tillman was followed by *Rhyne v. Childs,*[114] which arose in Jackson County, Florida. The facts of that case were complex, and evidenced the deep social dislocations associated with school desegregation in an atmosphere of racial hostility. On January 3, 1972, black and white students at the Marianna High School engaged in a "general melee," and school officials were compelled to send the students home and cancel classes. School officials were threatened with bodily harm, and a number of students were armed with make-shift weapons. Three days later further disorders broke out, resulting in a temporary boycott by black students. While school authorities, and apparently the judge, did not attribute the disorders to any particular racial group, almost all of those disciplined were black. The plaintiffs, permanently excluded black students, introduced evidence of this disparity of treatment "in order to establish an overall scheme or pattern of racial discrimination."[115] The court held that the plaintiffs had not been denied their constitutional rights.

The court found that the plaintiffs threatened physical harm to school officials, and had shown disrespect toward them. Plaintiff Pittman, apparently among the many black students who had left the school campus on January 6, was temporarily suspended and then permanently expelled because "[h]is attitude at [a conference with school officials] was one of non-cooperation and non-participation."[116] Finding that there was evidence to support each of these disciplinary actions, the court then addressed itself to the allegation that there was a pattern of racial discrimination in these and other disciplinary actions:[117]

> The Court has considered the evidence, which standing alone, would constitute impressive, if not persuasive, statistics. But this allegation of discrimination must be viewed in light [sic] of all the testimony adduced, particularly that of five county school administrators whose testimony disclosed that this statistical disparity of suspensions of blacks vis-a-vis that of whites resulted in the main from the decision of black students to forego corporal punishment when a breach of discipline occurred and elect instead to be suspended from their classes. By the same token the record is not devoid of instances where defendants have expelled or suspended white students for similar breaches of discipline.

The court then upheld the specific expulsion decisions challenged in the litigation, and by inference the overall disciplinary policies and procedures of the school district.

---

114. 359 F. Supp. 1085 (N.D. Fla. 1973).

115. *Id.* at 1090.

116. *Id.* at 1089.

117. *Id.* at 1090. The court of appeals, in affirming the lower court, dealt even more cryptically with the racial discrimination argument:

> On appeal, appellants again contend that the disciplinary actions which befell them . . . were parts of a larger pattern of racial discrimination that pervaded the Jackson County School system. The gist of the argument is to make out a mathematical

The *Rhyne* decision is unsatisfying on a number of grounds as the court attempts to grapple with legal and factual issues that appear beyond its grasp. The court never specifies the number of white students who were suspended as a result of the outbursts, and only in the most sketchy terms refers to the fact that overall, black students are suspended or expelled more often than white students. When pushed for an explanation, the court carefully points out that black students, when given the choice of corporal punishment or exclusion, usually pick the latter. But why should this explanation suffice? How many black students, as compared with white students, allegedly commit infractions which lead to this choice of punishments? Do the data on white students show that the number receiving corporal punishment is roughly in proportion to the white percentage of the school population? Why do blacks choose exclusion more often than whites? Might it be because school officials urge them to make this choice? Because school officials beat black children more vigorously than white children? Because black children are so alienated by the school environment that they seize any opportunity to escape? Because black parents are able to put less pressure than white parents on school officials to avoid the imposition of more severe penalties? Furthermore, one must assume that corporal punishment is an alternative only to short-term suspensions, yet all of the named plaintiffs in the suit had been permanently expelled. If there is a disparity in expulsions and long-term suspensions as well as in short-term suspensions (the court never informs us), the corporal punishment/exclusion choice argument would not suffice as an explanation.

The *Rhyne* court, understandably, confuses the individual claims of the named plaintiffs with the allegation that there is an overall pattern of racial discrimination in the county's disciplinary policies. The court first concludes that there is substantial evidence in the record to justify each of the expulsions under attack. There is no evidence of racist behavior on the part of individual teachers and administrators. It then turns to the allegation of a pattern of discrimination as if it were a completely separate claim. Yet, obviously the plaintiffs, at a minimum, are asserting that there were white students who had engaged in similar behavior who were not punished, or at least not as severely, and that regardless of their individual culpability, their expulsions should be set aside. The court does not perceive the relationship between these claims. The reason for this may be that it is difficult for the court to accept the proposition that the infractions of the plaintiffs should

---

> equal protection argument: more black students had been disciplined than whites, hence, a violation of the equal protection clause. The answer to the argument is that it lacks a factual foundation. There was no showing of arbitrary suspensions or expulsions of black students nor of a failure to suspend or expel white students for similar conduct.

Sweet v. Childs, 507 F.2d 675, 680-81 (5th Cir. 1975).

be forgiven, simply because there are others who have committed wrongs who have not been punished, or because blacks on other occasions may have been punished unfairly. The problem smacks of the issues associated with prosecutorial discretion in criminal law, and the unwillingness of courts to overturn convictions where all those allegedly guilty have not been charged and convicted.

A second reason for the court's hesitancy is that a ruling favorable to plaintiffs might require it to review each disciplinary action of school authorities in the future to make sure that black students were not treated in a discriminatory fashion. Given the factual complexities of school discipline and the degree of judicial intrusion that would be required, the court was less than enthusiastic. Finally, the adoption of the plaintiffs' argument would label the school system of Jackson County as racist, and whatever the truth of the matter, the court may have been reluctant to attach such a stigmatizing and all-encompassing label to the administrators and teachers in that system. Thus, irrespective of the statistical showing of disproportionality, the court was perfectly willing to adopt the spurious corporal punishment argument to avoid this result. Simultaneously, it refused to place the blame for the outbursts on the black students, retreating to an examination of the conduct of each of the named plaintiffs in the litigation.

Despite its hostility to the plaintiffs' racial discrimination arguments, the court's opinion reveals a number of the dilemmas underlying black exclusion. The case arises in the context of violent confrontations between black and white students and school officials, and yet not a single plaintiff was expressly expelled for his part in those disorders. Instead, the plaintiff students were accused of refusing to yield to authority, of disrespect for school officials, of unauthorized absence from the campus, and of holding attitudes of non-cooperation and non-participation. In a number of instances, expulsion was grounded not only on these specific acts, but also on past acts of disobedience. To be sure, a number of the plaintiffs had engaged in physically threatening behavior, but the gist of the cases against them was their failure to abide by the institutional rules relating to scheduling, decorum, and respect for authority.[118] This reinforces the theory that an effective attack on black exclusion from the perspective of "institutional racism" would require an assault on the "hidden curriculum" of public schools.

While the court was unwilling to undertake such a task, it was willing to weigh the gravity of the plaintiffs' infractions against the magnitude of

118. Indeed, the court dismissed the claims of four of the plaintiffs for failure to answer interrogatories propounded by the school district pursuant to Rule 37(d) of the Federal Rules of Civil Procedure. 359 F. Supp. at 1088 n.1. These plaintiffs also were not available at the hearing in the case to answer defendants' questions, as counsel admitted "that he has been unable to communicate with [them]." *Id.* Thus their claims were dismissed largely because they failed to respect the court's authority, rules, and time schedules.

their punishment. Inexplicably, and without extended discussion or citation to authority, the court took it upon itself to reduce the penalties imposed on the plaintiffs from permanent expulsion to exclusion until the end of the school year, arguing that the former is too harsh under the circumstances:[119]

> It is this Court's view that expulsion was warranted; however, the severity of the punishment meted out by the defendant school board does not appear commensurate with the severity of the acts committed and this Court is of the view that the expulsions should not be made permanent but that they be lifted after the present school year terminates.

Thus for the court, the issue is one of making the punishment fit the crime, rather than one of scrutinizing the substantive rules which lead to disciplinary actions. In my view this is appropriate. What is lacking is a satisfactory legal theory to allow the court to reach this result, and a greater sensitivity to the injury done by exclusion. Permanent exclusion is too harsh, but what of temporary exclusion? The court never considers requiring school authorities to explore alternative placements for the expelled students or to provide make-up educational services to them while they are officially banished from the high school building. Despite the fact that a number of the plaintiffs could not be found by their own counsel,[120] the court does not comprehend the fact that even expulsion for the remainder of the semester may lead to a permanent severing of ties with the institution. Moreover, the court makes no effort to communicate to school authorities the necessity of limiting long-term suspension and expulsion to only the most serious violations of school rules, implicitly leaving them free to apply any exclusion sanction short of permanent expulsion.

The only successful constitutional assault on black exclusion, viewed as an instance of racial discrimination, occurred in *Hawkins v. Coleman,*[121] decided by Judge Sarah Hughes in June of 1974. Until the summer of 1971, the Dallas Independent School District continued to operate a dual school system, and after that date, pursuant to court order, students were reassigned in order to achieve a unitary school system.[122] Black students were transferred from schools in which they were in the majority to those in which they were in the minority. In the wake of this desegregation program, massive numbers of black students were suspended,[123] and plaintiffs, representing the class of black students attending majority white schools, contended that disciplinary rules were applied in a racially discriminatory manner. In order

---

119. 359 F. Supp. at 1095. The court of appeals did not disturb this aspect of the lower court's order, but simply described it in a footnote, failing to offer any legal reasoning to support the reduction in punishment. Sweet v. Childs, 507 F.2d 675, 678 n. 5 (5th Cir. 1975).

120. *See* note 118 *supra.*

121. 376 F. Supp. 1330 (N.D. Tex. 1974).

122. *See* Tasby v. Estes, 342 F. Supp. 945 (N.D. Tex. 1971).

123. *See* note 50 *supra.*

to demonstrate such discrimination, plaintiffs introduced statistical evidence showing that 60.5 per cent of all students suspended in 1972-73 were black, whereas blacks constituted only 38.7 per cent of the total enrollment. For the fall semester of 1973, the figures on suspension were virtually identical. In addition, as if to meet the argument made by the court in the *Rhyne* case, plaintiffs proved that over the same period of time, more blacks than whites were corporally punished.[124] For both corporal punishment and suspension, disparities between the races were greater within majority white schools than in the system as a whole—although there were significant differences between majority white schools in this respect. For example, in the Woodrow Wilson High School blacks constituted less than 14 per cent of the enrollment and yet accounted for more than 83 per cent of the three to ten day suspensions. In contrast, there were six junior and senior high schools, with black populations of from 1 per cent to 39.2 per cent, that did not impose a single three to ten day suspension during the fall of 1973.[125]

The court then proceeded to examine the reasons for the overrepresentation of blacks among suspended students. The court found that fully 60 per cent of all suspensions were for non-violent infractions such as truancy, class cutting, and disrespect for teachers.[126] From this data and the raw statistics on the incidence of suspension between whites and blacks, experts drew the conclusion that the disciplinary policies of the Dallas Independent School District (DISD) were infected with "institutional racism":[127]

> [T]he DISD fit [sic] into an existing national pattern of race discrimination in that the DISD is a "white controlled institution" with "institutional racism" existing in the operation of its discipline procedures. . . . "Institutional racism" exists . . . when the standard operating procedures of an institution are prejudiced against, derogatory to, or unresponsive to the needs of a particular racial group. . . .
>
> Because of the existence of racism . . . black students will become more frustrated as the institution continues to refuse to respond to their needs and ambitions. This frustration will be reflected either in increased passivity or increased hostility. Such hostilities will result in increased "suspendable behavior" . . . . Moreover . . . in a school district in which there is institutional racism toward the Blacks conduct by black students that would not be "unusual" or "offensive" in a black environment becomes to many teachers "disruptive" or "suspendable conduct." To teachers unfamiliar with Blacks, this conduct, that is non-violent and characteristic of the black race, stands out and becomes thereby subject to selective persecution.

The piece de resistance of the testimony, however, was given by Dr. Nolan Estes, Superintendent of the Dallas school system. When asked to explain

124. Hawkins v. Coleman, 376 F. Supp. 1330, 1333 (N.D. Tex. 1974). For a general discussion of recent corporal punishment cases, see Note, *Corporal Punishment*, 53 Tex. L. Rev. 395 (1975).

125. 376 F. Supp. at 1334.

126. 376 F. Supp. at 1335.

127. 376 F. Supp. at 1336.

the high rate of suspension, Dr. Estes, apparently to the amazement of all concerned, replied, " 'Well, we are a White controlled institution, institutional racism, racism among individuals.' "[128] In the absence of testimony rebutting Dr. Estes' statement and the statements of the two other experts called in the case, the court concluded that "institutional racism" was indeed responsible for the disproportionality between the races in rates of suspension and that the school district was constitutionally required to take steps to overcome it. To this end, Judge Hughes issued the following order:[129]

> While not attempting to dictate the details of an affirmative program this Court does direct the DISD to review its present program and to put into effect an affirmative program aimed at materially lessening "white institutional racism" in the DISD.

Hawkins, like *Rhyne,* is consistent with the theory that black exclusion is largely a product of the institutional rules, relating to decorum, respect for authority, and timeliness. In addition, the disparities in suspension rates between majority white schools may indicate some measure of personal racism on the part of teachers and principals, in some schools, variations in the socioeconomic composition of the student bodies between schools, or a diversity of attitudes with respect to the wisdom of employing exclusion sanctions. However, the court's simplistic conclusion, based upon the testimony of expert witnesses, that institutional racism permeates the Dallas school system must be taken with a grain of salt. The experts, adopting an attitude of cultural fatalism and superiority, seem to assume that black students are incapable of complying with the "hidden curriculum" and that it necessarily follows that the cultural characteristics of blacks are to be preferred to the cultural characteristics demanded by the Dallas public schools. Neither of these positions is necessarily correct. Indeed, while there may well be experts on the characteristics of black people—although I observe no unanimity among those experts—I am dubious that there are experts who can inform the courts as to whether one set of cultural values is superior to another set. Furthermore, this approach ignores the possibility of value accomodation in the public schools, preferring instead the all or nothing cultural choice. Were it not for the admission of racism by the chief administrative official of the school system, one wonders whether the court would have been so willing to find a pattern of institutional racism. This admission largely obviated the need to examine racially neutral pedagogical and institutional reasons which would explain the statistics on black exclusion.

But the most intriguing aspect of *Hawkins* is the remedy ordered by the court. Once it is determined that institutional as opposed to personal racism is the culprit, where does this leave the court and the parties in terms of a

128. *Id.*
129. 376 F. Supp. at 1338.

remedy? Does it mean that blacks may no longer be suspended, while whites may be suspended? Should quotas be set, with black suspensions not to exceed a predetermined number? Are these remedies appropriate even where the evidence clearly demonstrates that individual black youngsters have engaged in "suspendable" behavior? The court opted, in the most hortatory tone, to order the school district to do and think "right." And yet, as the court readily admitted:[130]

> No court can decree a change in attitude. That is something within the individual. Put briefly, there must be a real effort on the part of everyone involved to accentuate the positive while at the same time eliminating the negative effects of "white institutional racism."

If the court had more carefully analyzed the problem, it might just as well have admitted the necessity to completely restructure the schooling environment to eliminate the institutional rules which blacks most often violate. While I would be the last to take the position that there is no value in symbolic decrees which cannot be easily translated into specific actions by public officials,[131] the court, in effect, admitted its powerlessness to address the black exclusion problem when the legal arguments are cast in terms of institutional racism. Whatever the merits of that argument, and I am dubious, it does not lend itself to a meaningful remediation of the asserted injury.

In the absence of proof of individual racial bias, a more meaningful approach would have been to compel the school district to limit the number and types of infractions for which suspension would lie and to institute a program of alternative placement or out-of-school services to those suspended. Many schools in the Dallas system have demonstrated their ability to maintain order, and presumably educate, without relying substantially upon an exclusion sanction. This would have had the effect of ameliorating a great portion of the injury suffered by plaintiffs and their class, and simultaneously, of extending that remedy to many white children who also suffer from exclusion.

C. Nonracial Approaches to Exclusion: *Rodriguez* and Beyond

The translation of the proposition that exclusion of public school students is an inappropriate sanction for violations of school rules into constitutional law is not without its difficulties. Lower court judges have occasionally made this point,[132] but the general attitude has been that the severity of the

---

130. *Id.*

131. *See* Yudof, *supra* note 24, at 414-16. *But see* Kurland, *Equal Educational Opportunity: The Limits of Constitutional Jurisprudence Undefined,* 35 U. Chi. L. Rev. 583, 598-600 (1968).

132. *See, e.g.*, Boykins v. Fairfield Bd. of Educ., 492 F.2d 697, 702 (5th Cir. 1974) (Godbold, J., dissenting); Lee v. Macon County Bd. of Educ. 490 F.2d 458, 460 n. 3 (5th Cir. 1974) (dicta); Cook v. Edwards, 341 F. Supp. 307, 311 (D.N.H. 1972); *cf.* Strickland v. Inlow, 485 F.2d 186 (8th Cir. 1973), *vacated and remanded sub nom.* Wood v. Strickland, 95 S. Ct. 992 (1975).

punishment, except as it relates to the necessity for and nature of a due process hearing,[133] is a legislative and administrative matter.[134] This is consistent with traditional judicial attitudes toward the imposition of punishment in the criminal law context.[135]

The judicial attitude toward review of punishments appears to emanate from concepts of the appropriate role of the judiciary in such matters. What is excessive either absolutely, or under the circumstances, is by its very nature a subjective determination, wholly lacking in precision. Where lines must be drawn by someone, and where it is difficult to articulate standards under which to test that line drawing, the tendency is to affirm the determinations of legislative and administrative authorities. Judicial review of the infraction-punishment nexus smacks of substantive due process since it contemplates substitution of the court's judgment for that of more representative branches of government. This is particularly true where the applicable test is likely to be of the "shocks the conscience" variety.[136] This is all the more the case in a civil rather than criminal context, where the textual constitutional arguments are weaker (the eighth amendment does not apply) and the disability is often less serious.

Of course, all of us can find school exclusion cases where the courts have demonstrated a picayune concern for procedure and technicality where, at bottom, they were appalled by the severity of the punishment. While substantive due process attacks on exclusion are rare,[137] given the Court's hostility

---

133. *See, e.g.*, Goss v. Lopez, 419 U.S. 565 (1975); Hagopian v. Knowlton, 470 F.2d 201 (2d Cir. 1972); Banks v. Board of Pub. Instruction, 450 F.2d 1103 (5th Cir. 1971); Madera v. Board of Educ., 386 F.2d 778 (2d Cir. 1967). *See generally* Buss, *Procedural Due Process for School Discipline: Probing the Constitutional Outline*, 119 U. PA. L. REV. 545 (1971).

134. *See, e.g.*, Boykins v. Fairfield Bd. of Educ., 492 F.2d 697 (5th Cir. 1974); Ferguson v. Thomas, 430 F.2d 852 (5th Cir. 1970); *cf.* Wood v. Strickland, 420 U.S. 308 (1975).

135. *See* United States v. Cleveland, 503 F.2d 1067, 1071 (9th Cir. 1974); Packer, *Making the Punishment Fit the Crime*, 77 HARV. L. REV. 1071 (1964). To take an extreme example from criminal law, witness the inability of the justices of the Supreme Court to agree on a common approach toward the constitutionality of the death penalty under the eighth amendment. Furman v. Georgia, 408 U.S. 238 (1972). If four of the justices cannot be persuaded to overturn death sentences, the case for overturning school exclusions, a non-criminal penalty to which the eighth amendment does not apply, would appear hopeless. But note that the severe penalty imposed by the state in that case was occasioned by the commission of the most heinous crimes, rape and murder. If "Shuffling Sam," found guilty of loitering and disorderly conduct, Thompson v. Louisville, 362 U.S. 199 (1960), had been sentenced to death, the justices would have had little difficulty with the constitutionality of the punishment. *Cf.* Ralph v. Warden Maryland Penitentiary, 438 F.2d 786 (4th Cir. 1970). Indeed, there are a handful of cases which appear to be pushing the criminal law in this direction. *See, e.g.*, Trop v. Dulles, 356 U.S. 86 (1958); *In re Lynch*, 8 Cal. 3d 410, 503 P.2d 921, 105 Cal. Rptr. 217 (1972); Ralph v. Warden Maryland Penitentiary, 438 F.2d 786 (4th Cir. 1970); Robinson v. California, 370 U.S. 660 (1962) (dicta); Weems v. United States, 217 U.S. 349 (1910) (plurality opinion). *See generally* Packer *supra*. But this is hardly dispositive of school exclusions.

136. *See* note 137 *infra*.

137. *See, e.g.*, Jenkins v. Louisiana State Bd. of Educ., 506 F.2d 992, 1001-02 (5th Cir. 1975) ("no evidence" to justify suspension); Boykins v. Fairfield Bd. of Educ., 492 F.2d 697 (5th Cir. 1974); Strickland v. Inlow, 485 F.2d 186 (8th Cir. 1973), *vacated and remanded sub nom.*

to that mode of judicial analysis, judicial intervention generally occurs in first amendment school cases only where the sanction of suspension or expulsion is employed.[138] But it should be noted that the equal protection clause may also serve this function. If a punishment is unduly harsh, authorities may hesitate to make it generally applicable, straining to limit it to a particular class which they view as deserving of opprobrium. This in turn invites an equal protection challenge which may leave authorities with the Hobson's choice of abolishing the punishment or limiting its application in a more defensible, narrower fashion. While it is the classification which demands judicial scrutiny, the invalidation of the classification influences the choice and use of sanctions. In addition, the nature of the punishment itself may be decisive. If the punishment deprives the plaintiff of the enjoyment of highly significant privileges—what has been called a "fundamental interest"—the courts may impose a burden of justification on the state which invariably it cannot carry.[139] In such cases, the judicial message is clear: punishments of this sort are disfavored.

With respect to exclusion, the relevant classification is between those permitted to continue attending public schools or otherwise receive an education at public expense, and those who are not. The courts must be persuaded that the designation of these students for exclusion, who have committed relatively minor violations of the hidden cirriculum or who, having committed more serious offenses, have been denied out-of-school public educational services, is not a reasonable classification. Under the traditional

---

Wood v. Strickland, 95 S. Ct. 992 (1975); Cook v. Edwards, 341 F. Supp. 307, 311 (D.N.H. 1972). *See generally* McClung, *supra* note 31. Judge Godbold of the Fifth Circuit has argued forcefully for a due process limitation on the power of boards of education to exclude students for minor infractions of school rules:

> [The court hopes that the parties will settle their dispute] without the necessity of . . . repairing again to the federal courthouse for a judicial decision of whether there is such disparity between the offenses and the penalty that the commands of the fourteenth amendment have not been met.

Lee v. Macon County Bd. of Educ., 490 F.2d 458, 460 (5th Cir. 1974) (dicta).

> Such a case can, of course, arise. Clearly, for example, a school board could not constitutionally expel forever a pupil who had committed no offense other than being five minutes tardy one time. . . .
>
> . . . .
>
> . . . [This does] not license federal judges to review and revise school board disciplinary actions at will. Application is limited to the rare cases where there is shocking disparity between offense and penalty.

Id. at 460 n. 3. *See also* Boykins v. Fairfield Bd. of Educ., 492 F.2d 697, 702 (5th Cir. 1974) (Godbold, J., dissenting); Paine v. Board of Regents of University of Texas Sys., 355 F. Supp. 199 (W.D. Tex. 1972). Anderson v. Independent School Dist. No. 281, Civil No. 42043 (Dist. Ct. Minn., Feb. 18, 1969), *appeal dismissed as moot*, 289 Minn. 515, 176 N.W.2d 640 (1970); unreported injunctive order cited in S. GOLDSTEIN, *supra* note 63, at 439.

138. *See* Eisner v. Stamford Bd. of Educ., 440 F.2d 803 (2d Cir. 1971). *See generally* EDUCATIONAL POLICY AND THE LAW 139-74, 190-97.

139. *See generally* Goodpaster, *The Constitution and Fundamental Rights,* 15 ARIZ. L. REV. 479 (1973); Gunther, *The Supreme Court, 1971 Term—Foreword: In Search of Evolving Doctrine on a Changing Court: A Model for a Newer Equal Protection,* 86 HARV. L. REV. 1 (1972).

rational basis test, this result is unlikely. To the extent that a relatively loose tie between the state's interest in maintaining order in the public schools and the exclusion device will suffice, and this is the conclusion that the attachment of the rational basis test label would portend, the courts cannot be expected to overturn exclusion practices. Even out-of-school services may not be ordered on the ground that preservation of the public fisc is a sufficient state interest. To the extent that the courts recognize the importance of the continuation of the public educational experience to the student, the courts, whatever their conclusionary labels, will require a closer nexus between this extraordinary action and the state's educational objectives. If, as is clearly the case, most infractions can be punished and deterred by lesser sanctions, the courts may require education authorities to resort to these alternatives. Even where exclusion from regular schools or classes is justified, the courts may affirm the right of students to some nontraditional, publicly funded, form of education.

Without belaboring the well discussed variations in equal protection standards,[140] the success of exclusion litigation will depend on the willingness of courts to treat education, at least in this context, as a substantial personal interest which, in the ad hoc process of weighing competing interests, requires the state to stop short of termination for violation of school rules. For nearly twenty years after *Brown v. Board of Education*,[141] there was a widespread belief among commentators that education was such an interest. Almost invariably, scholarship in the law and education field began with the famous litany from *Brown:* "Education is perhaps the most important function of state and local governments . . . ."[142] This became less an assertion of fact, for surely at that level there could be no dispute, than an invocation of the constitutional deity of a "fundamental interest." In 1973, however, the Supreme Court rejected the wisdom of the earlier prophets. Fearing an avalanche of litigation relating to non-education public services, the Court held that education was not a fundamental interest triggering a higher degree of judicial scrutiny.[143] While admitting its relationship to voting and the exercise of first amendment rights, the Court barely left the door ajar:[144]

> Even if it were conceded that some identifiable quantum of education is a constitutionally protected prerequisite to the meaningful exercise of either right, we have no indication that the present levels of educational expenditures in Texas provide an education that falls short. . . . [N]o charge

---

140. *See* note 139 *supra*.

141. 347 U.S. 483 (1954).

142. *Id.* at 493. *See generally* J. COONS, W. CLUNE, & S. SUGARMAN, *supra* note 89.

143. San Antonio Independent School Dist. v. Rodriguez, 411 U.S. 1 (1973). *See generally* Yudof, *supra* note 24, at 500; Comment, San Antonio Independent School Dist. v. Rodriguez: *A Retreat From Equal Protection*, 22 CLEV. ST. L. REV. 585 (1973).

144. Id. at 36-37.

> fairly could be made that the system fails to provide each child with an opportunity to acquire the basic minimal skills necessary for the enjoyment of the rights of speech and of full participation in the political process.

In the absence of a racial classification and given the Court's extraordinary requirements for the establishment of a wealth classification, analysis of the school exclusion problem from an equal protection perspective must begin with a charitable reading of this dictum.

In *Rodriguez,* the plaintiffs asserted that Texas school financing laws created an unconstitutional discrimination between children living in property-poor districts and those living in more affluent districts. By relying on the local ad valorem property tax, and in the absence of state equalization, rich districts were able to offer a high cost education at low tax rates. Conversely, in poor districts, exorbitant tax rates yielded a second class public education. Both with respect to the class of plaintiffs, alleged to be personally poor, and the nature of the deprivation, the Court held that a relative denial of educational opportunities did not constitute a violation of the equal protection clause.[145] The clear inference, supported by few explicit statements, was that a complete denial of all educational opportunities might well constitute a denial of constitutional rights. If this is the case, then the argument in the present context must be that suspension and expulsion constitute such a denial, and thus are constitutionally impermissible.[146]

With respect to permanent exclusion, the applicability of the *Rodriguez* caveat is clear; a student permanently banished from the public schools, and not offered a public education outside of the school building, has been denied all opportunity to obtain an education. For those unable to afford a private education, this is unavoidable. For those expelled for a full semester or remainder of a semester, or suspended for days or weeks, the applicability of the *Rodriguez* caveat is less clear. The problem is both semantic and practical. The denial of an education is absolute for the period of time that the sanction remains in effect, but it is only partial or relative in comparison to the eight to twelve years that most students attend public elementary and secondary schools. There is a practical problem in that it is unrealistic to treat a one-day suspension as the equivalent of a full semester's expulsion. In terms of the injury done to the student, which is likely to be relatively trivial in a short-term suspension, and the weight of the state's interest, which may

---

145. *Id.* at 55.

146. Private citizens, law making bodies, and the media all bend their efforts toward encouraging children to complete their high school educations and to avoid becoming dropouts and burdens to society. In the twenty years since Brown v. Board of Education . . . this country has committed itself to a policy against state-imposed public school segregation. It is not lesser but more stringent state action to bar a child forever from public school, with the result that he secures no education at all.

Lee v. Macon County Bd. of Educ., 490 F.2d 458, 461 (5th Cir. 1974). *See generally* McClung, *supra* note 31.

be great where a short cooling off period may avoid future turmoil, a distinction is justified.[147] While there can be no precise line between a relative and absolute denial, and between an exclusion with significantly injurious consequences and one without, I would suggest a functional approach. Where the exclusion is of such a duration as to make the child fall significantly behind in his work or so as to otherwise jeopardize his continued attendance at public school, he has been denied equal protection of the laws unless there is no feasible alternative to removal from the school and other placements have been explored. My own sense is that generally this threshold point is reached when a student is suspended for two or more weeks, although on occasion, a shorter exclusion may have dire consequences.[148] Such an equal protection approach has been successfully employed by retarded,[149] truant,[150] pregnant,[151] emotionally disturbed,[152] and alien children[153] to attack exclusion decisions.[154] Most of these cases were decided before *Rodriguez*, but there does not appear to be a great ground swell to reverse them.[155] The case most directly on point is *Mills v. Board of Education*,[156] brought on behalf of an estimated 22,000 "exceptional" school children who were excluded from the public schools of the District of Columbia. The category of "exceptional" children included not only the mentally retarded, the physically handicapped, and the hyperkinetic, but, more generally, all of those children with "behavioral problems," regardless of the causes. The court, operating in the golden days before *Rodriguez*, reasoned that if a denial of an *equal* educational opportunity were constitutionally infirm, there could be no doubt about *complete* exclusion:[157]

> In *Hobson v. Hansen*, [269 F. Supp. 401 (D.D.C. 1967)], Judge Wright found that denying poor public school children educational opportunities equal to that available to more affluent public school children was violative of the [Constitution] . . . . *A fortiori*, the defendants' conduct here, denying plaintiffs and their class not just an equal publicly supported education but all publicly supported education while providing such education to other children, is violative of the [Constitution].

---

147. *See* Goss v. Lopez, 419 U.S. 565, 584 (1975) (Powell, J., dissenting).

148. Shanley v. Northeast Independent School Dist., 462 F.2d 960, 967 n.4 (5th Cir. 1972).

149. Pennsylvania Ass'n for Retarded Children v. Commonwealth, 334 F. Supp. 1257, 343 F. Supp. 279 (E.D. Pa. 1971) (consent order). *See* Kirp, *supra* note 18, at 747-48; Herr, *supra* note 47.

150. Knight v. Board of Educ., 48 F.R.D. 115 (E.D.N.Y. 1969).

151. *See, e.g.*, Ordway v. Hargraves, 323 F. Supp. 1155 (D. Mass. 1971). *See generally* Comment, *Marriage, Pregnancy, and the Right to Go to School*, 50 TEX. L. REV. 1196 (1972).

152. Mills v. Board of Educ., 348 F. Supp. 866 (D.D.C. 1972).

153. Hosier v. Evans, 314 F. Supp. 316 (D.V.I. 1970).

154. *See generally* Dimond, *supra* note 48; Kirp, *supra* note 18; McClung, *supra* note 31; Van Geel, *supra* note 48.

155. *See* McClung, *supra* note 31; Van Geel, *supra* note 48.

156. 348 F. Supp. 866 (D.D.C. 1972).

157. *Id.* at 875.

Despite its reliance on a poverty classification and on *Hobson,* the *Mills* decision is defensible today on the ground that a school system may not classify a group of youngsters for complete exclusion from the public educational system. The court recognized that not all children should be assigned to regular classes and that children with extraordinary needs and problems might require special attention. It ordered[158]

> That no child eligible for a publicly supported education in the District of Columbia public schools shall be excluded from a regular public school assignment by a rule, policy, or practice of the board of education of the District of Columbia or its agents unless such child is provided (a) adequate alternative educational services suited to the child's needs, which may include special education or tuition grants, and (b) a constitutionally adequate prior hearing and periodic review of the child's status, progress, and the adequacy of any educational alternative.

The court further held that the asserted insufficiency of funds did not excuse exclusion, for the school district had a constitutional obligation to divide its funds equitably so as to assure that no child was completely denied all public educational opportunities. In other words, and this may give rise to litigation in the future, if the district did not have the financial wherewithal to meet the needs of all of its students, it must reduce its per pupil expenditures and could not refuse to educate particular classes of children.[159]

Conclusion

A legal approach premised on the unconstitutionality of a denial of all educational opportunity offers the greatest hope of undoing the injury occasioned by the disproportionate exclusion of black students from public elementary and secondary schools. While it is tempting to try to make the black exclusion problem fit the mold of racial discrimination, that approach misconceives the true nature of that problem, distorts reality, and, most important, does not yield a workable remedy.

Perhaps there are costs in failing to treat black exclusion as an aspect of racial discrimination. With Koestler's Rubashov, we may fear that revolutionaries and reformers who "think through other people's minds," who identify with others, and "who understand and forgive," cannot "find a motive to act."[160] It is easier to arouse emotions and persuade to action, at least among the sympathetic, where there is racism, whether personal or institutional. But, in the long run, this approach will be counterproductive. Rather the responsibility for educating our young, both black and white, should be placed where it belongs, on the educational systems of the nation.

---

158. *Id.* at 878. *See generally* Kirp, Buss, & Kuriloff, *Legal Reform of Special Education: Empirical Studies and Procedural Proposals,* 62 CALIF. L. REV. 40 (1974).
159. *See* Yudof, *supra* note 24, at 474-75; Kirp, *supra* note 18, at 782.
160. A. KOESTLER, DARKNESS AT NOON 23 (1955).

When the right of every child to a public education is recognized, there will no longer be a black exclusion problem. But this is merely the beginning and not the end of the matter; for the ultimate goal must remain the successful implementation of educational programs for minority children. This, in turn, is dependent not only on their mere physical presence in public schools, but also on the development of new structures and pedagogical strategies adequate to the task.

ON THE FUTURE IMPLEMENTATION OF SCHOOL DESEGREGATION: SOME CONSIDERATIONS

WILLIS D. HAWLEY*
RAY C. RIST†

INTRODUCTION

When public officials act so as to maintain or increase racial separation in schools, they are denying students equal protection of the laws. But the greater difficulty is not in determining that the Constitution has been violated, but in devising a remedy accessible and acceptable to both the courts and policy makers. The situation is further complicated when school segregation is not directly attributable to actions of public officials, but comes about because of segregated housing.

The remedies for school segregation seemed readily apparent, so long as we believed that racial segregation, regardless of its cause, resulted in harm to those segregated and that desegregation would diminish or eradicate such harm. The present mood is one of less certainty. There is growing doubt that the hopes many have had for the outcomes of school desegregation can be fully achieved. This is particularly true for those who have looked to desegregation to overcome the persistent academic disparities between the average performance of white students and that of minority students. Desegregation does not appear to be the panacea many hoped it would be.

This uncertainty has led to an apparent increase of the ranks of those who argue that the time has come for the courts and policy makers to weigh the advantages of school desegregation against the costs.[1] Heretofore, the emphasis has been strongly on the benefits which were to accrue, while the costs of such social change have received only minimal attention, or have been ignored altogether. There is now a growing recognition that the costs as well as benefits must be calculated and that a range of values for both whites and nonwhites must be considered in the equation, if school desegregation is to occur in a

---

* Associate Director, Institute for Policy Sciences and Public Affairs and Associate Professor of Policy Sciences and Political Science, Duke University.

† Head, Desegregation Studies Unit, National Institute of Education, Department of Health, Education, and Welfare.

The authors, in preparing this paper, have relied heavily on the work of Elizabeth Cohen, Edgar Epps, and Meyer Weinberg published in this present issue of *Law and Contemporary Problems*. The second author wishes to note that the comments and conclusions in this article are solely his own and no endorsement or support from the National Institute of Education and the Department of Health, Education and Welfare is intended or should be inferred.

1. *Cf.* Fiss, *The Jurisprudence of Busing*, 39 LAW & CONTEMP. PROB. no. 1, at 194 (1975).

manner that recognizes the integrity of the students and the need for sound educational programs.

If we are to achieve any of the several objectives that school desegregation is meant to achieve, we will have to abandon the simplistic notion—now largely discredited by available evidence—that the mixing of races *in itself* will invariably have positive educational and social consequences. While this argument may seem obvious to those who have been involved in the desegregation controversy, its implications are not well understood. For to accept this argument means that in many situations, conventional court orders which result only in achieving greater racial balance by reassigning pupils will not be enough, even if coupled with such admonitions as the need for retraining of teachers and school administrators and for the provision of special programs during periods of transition. Moreover, if we accept the notion that the consequences of school desegregation must be considered in each case, not only will the job of the courts be complicated, but we will have to consider such broader issues—forced upon us by recent evidence—as the impact of school desegregation on the racial composition of cities.[2]

We are not suggesting that the presumption in favor of desegregated schools should not persist or that legal findings of segregation should not be cause for new public policies or a continuation of legal action. But we would not stop there. We argue that establishing the existence of segregated schools would trigger certain inquiries to determine what combination of strategies would be *most likely* to achieve a set of specified social and educational objectives. We argue that policies which foster desegregation without taking into account how local contexts shape the likelihood that alternative strategies will maximize the benefits minorities will receive, *have the effect of denying equal educational opportunity*. The issue is not whether actions by public officials which maintain or foster racial segregation in the schools should be tolerated. Such actions are clearly unconstitutional and are no longer debatable. Similarly, the issue whether we should, as a matter of national commitment and public policy, move toward the goal of integrated classrooms is no longer debatable. Rather, the issue is how the goal of increasing integration can best be attained.

I

ACHIEVING THE GOALS OF DESEGREGATION

Before one can develop a strategy for maximizing the probability that school desegregation will have positive consequences for children, one must be explicit about the goals one wants to achieve. If the goal is desegregation per se then the strategy is relatively simple—secure a reasonably proportional dis-

2. *See* Farley, *Racial Integration in the Public Schools, 1967-1972: Assessing the Effect of Governmental Policy*, 8 SOCIOLOGICAL FOCUS 1 (1975).

tribution of whites and nonwhites in each of the district's schools. But few of us really favor school desegregation for its own sake. Rather, we desire desegregation because of the impact we believe it has on children. It is important to judge desegregation as one would judge any other social policy: whether and to what extent it achieves certain valued ends. These values, of course, may be instrumental, symbolic, or they may be "first order" principles such as equal protection of the laws. Seeing school desegregation as a process rather than as an outcome with its own justification has important implications for the way we proceed to determine the criteria which govern the assignment of students to schools. Thus, for example, "racial balance" alone would seldom be a sufficient factor on which to base a desegregation plan.

We seek here to identify some considerations that would increase the probabilities that certain specified educational and social objectives will be achieved through desegregation. This article is not a definitive summary of the empirical evidence on the effects of desegregation but it does draw heavily from the research literature in an effort to encourage more flexibility and imagination among those who integrate the schools, whether they be judges, lawyers, school officials, or consultants charged with drawing up desegregation plans.

Those who turn to social science literature for information on the consequences of desegregation are faced with numerous problems including: considerable controversy over appropriate methodologies and levels of analysis; varying definitions of critical variables such as "desegregation" and "student achievement"; and contradictory conclusions which frequently are not harmonious with or are overstatements of the empirical evidence.[3] But perhaps the most important problem is that theories of cause and effect often do not underlie the analyses, and the data collected are seldom utilized to test or formulate such theories.[4] Thus, in this article, our basic analysis will be in the context of the theoretical assumptions which underlie the idea that desegregation can lead to the attainment of certain goals.[5]

The goals to which the advocates of desegregation aspire are of four general types:

(1) improvements in self-esteem, aspirations and other personality related dispositions of minority children;
(2) improvements in academic achievement;

3. As one federal district court judge has said, "much of the current research replies to precise policy based questions with the ambiguity of a Delphic oracle . . . ." Hart v. Community School Bd., 383 F. Supp. 699, 744 (E.D.N.Y. 1974).

4. For one effort to develop a comprehensive theory of the effects of school desegregation that could guide future research, see RAND CORPORATION, DESIGN FOR A NATIONAL LONGITUDINAL STUDY OF SCHOOL DESEGREGATION (1974).

5. We are dealing here with what Alvin Gouldner, in a slightly different context, has termed the "domain assumptions" which undergird a theoretical formulation but which are frequently left implicit. *See generally*, A. GOULDNER, THE COMING CRISIS OF WESTERN SOCIOLOGY (1970).

(3) reduction in interracial hostility and the elimination of racial intolerance; and
(4) increased access to educational resources and to post-education opportunities.

This article examines both the theory and the research concerning each of these goals and how they might be secured.

A. Psychological Consequences of School Desegregation

In *Brown v. Board of Education*, which in 1954 outlawed segregation in the public schools, the Supreme Court, speaking unanimously through Chief Justice Earl Warren, focused attention on the psychological impact of racial separation:[6]

> To separate [Negroes] from others of similar age and qualifications solely because of their race generates a feeling of inferiority as to their status in the community that may affect their hearts and minds in a way unlikely ever to be undone.

The social science evidence which the Court cited in support of this contention[7] was not strong but it seemed to make intuitive sense, especially when one considered the history of treatment of blacks by whites and the reasons schools were legally segregated by race in the first place. Whatever validity the stigma theory had in the 1950's, the events of the last two decades could be seen as undermining its logic. With segregation of all types now outlawed, the civil rights movement launched, and the racial pride of minorities enhanced through the actions of minority organizations, the argument that school desegregation is necessary to reduce psychological damage to blacks, which appears to some to be a quasi-racist position itself.

A number of researchers have sought to verify the "psychological damage" theory. However, this research is plagued with all of the problems that attend most research on desegregation—such as inadequate controls, inadequate definitions, and inadequate specification of conditions that characterize the learning environment. And the problems of drawing generalizations from this research are compounded by the multiplicity of measures researchers have used to assess the attitudes and personality characteristics of children and by the fact that most of these measures have not been validated.

When all of the available research is considered, two conclusions can be made:[8]

---

6. Brown v. Board of Educ., 347 U.S. 483, 494 (1954).
7. 347 U.S. at 494-95 n. 11.
8. For reviews of the research upon which these generalizations are founded, see N. ST. JOHN, SCHOOL DESEGREGATION OUTCOMES FOR CHILDREN (1975); Epps, *The Impact of School Desegregation on Aspirations, Self-Concepts and Other Aspects of Personality*, 39 LAW & CONTEMP. PROB. no. 2, at 300 (1975).

(1) blacks do not have lower self-esteem or aspirations than whites, when socioeconomic status is controlled; and
(2) when desegregation has been found to affect either self-esteem or aspirations, the effects are mixed at best.

The negative consequences of desegregation for self-esteem and sense of anxiety about school seem most likely to occur when minorities are placed in overwhelmingly white classrooms where competition for grades is intense and the racial minority is, at the time of desegregation, performing substantially below the classroom average. As might be expected, the effects of these conditions are likely to be greatest among older children.

The supportive role of teachers and the organization of the classroom appear to be significant factors both in minimizing invidious comparisons by whites of the lower performance of less well prepared classmates, and in providing a sense of achievement in terms of the base from which each individual student must work.[9] And the role of the principal in fostering pro-integration behavior by teachers has been found to be of significant importance.[10]

Thus in order to make an argument for using school desegregation to enhance the self-esteem and aspirations of minorities, one or more of three concomitant outcomes would be necessary:

(1) Improved academic achievement,
(2) improved race relations,
(3) increased opportunities to utilize one's talents both inside and outside of school settings.

It follows then that improvements in self-image may be seen as the products of the attainment of other objectives of school desegregation. Of course, students with self-confidence and with high aspirations are more likely to achieve at higher levels and to be less defensive in social relationships. But racial mixing in itself seems to hold little promise of directly increasing self-esteem and other aspects of psychological development.

B. The Effect of Desegregation on Academic Achievement

If increases in academic achievement can lead to increased self-confidence which in turn can lead to higher achievement, can desegregation increase the academic achievement of minorities? There is good reason to believe that (1) in most cases where nonwhites are in the minority, the academic performance of whites is unaffected by desegregation and (2) the performance of blacks—in

9. *Cf.* R. RIST, BLACK KIDS, WHITE REALITIES: A STUDY OF SCHOOL INTEGRATION (forthcoming 1975).

10. Narot, *Teacher Prejudice and Teacher Behavior in Desegregated Schools,* in 2 NATIONAL OPINION RESEARCH CENTER, SOUTHERN SCHOOLS: AN EVALUATION OF THE EFFECTS OF THE EMERGENCY SCHOOL ASSISTANCE PROGRAM AND OF SCHOOL DESEGREGATION (1973) [hereinafter cited as SOUTHERN SCHOOLS]; Orfield, *How to Make Desegregation Work: The Adaptation of Schools to Their Newly-Integrated Student Bodies*, 39 LAW & CONTEMP. PROB. no. 2, at 314, 322-24 (1975).

most cases—is not *negatively* affected by desegregation. However, evidence concerning the positive effects of desegregation on minority achievement is mixed and inconclusive.[11] There is some agreement among scholars who have done large-scale studies of the impact of desegregation that nonwhites—or at least blacks—do best academically in integrated settings where they are neither in the substantial majority nor in a minority of less than 10 to 20 per cent of the student body.[12]

In general, the studies show that black children going to school in majority white settings do better than black children in segregated schools. But the reasons for this finding are not clear. There is a considerable amount of research that shows that family background is a good predictor of student performance in school and that such surrogates for background as socioeconomic class account for substantially more of the variance in student performance than either race or the racial mix of the school or classroom. It is possible, indeed likely, that where desegregation involved voluntary enrollment by blacks in predominantly white schools, the positive effects resulting from desegregation are largely due to the mixing of students from different backgrounds. Some researchers have tried to "control" for family background in their analyses, but the control measures most commonly used—such as socioeconomic class—are only gross measures of those student experiences at home which are relevant to their attitudes, behavior, and capacity in school.

Given these problems in obtaining a definitive answer from the research on the effects of desegregation on achievement, it is necessary to examine the theoretical assumptions which might underlie the notion that a cause-effect relationship exists between desegregation (or integration) and educational attainment. It is sometimes inferred that blacks will do better when they attend school with whites because the latter act as role models. That individual blacks should emulate individual whites only because they are white seems unlikely. Blacks who are low achievers may use high achieving whites as models but two conditions must first be met: (1) racial hostility must be low, and (2) the dominant norms of the school or, more importantly, the classroom must be supportive of attitudes and behavior which encourage academic achievement. If these two conditions are necessary for the role model thesis to work, then that thesis needs reformulation.

An alternative theoretical assumption is that the achievement levels of blacks will increase following desegregation because the group norms in predominantly white schools are more supportive of higher achievement than those in predominantly black schools. But the difficulty with this premise is that

---

11. *See* N. ST. JOHN, *supra* note 8, at 36, 119.

12. The most recent study to report the finding is Jencks & Brown, *The Effects of Desegregation on Student Achievement: Some New Evidence From the Equality of Educational Opportunity Survey*, 48 SOCIOLOGY OF ED. 126 (1975).

it rests on the untenable proposition that skin color itself predicts the value placed on achievement.

A third and perhaps more intuitively believable hypothesis is that differences in family background, rather than the race of students, account for any variations that might be found in the emphasis placed by blacks and whites on achievement in school. In other words, families differ in the degree to which they stress the importance of working hard in school and in their capacity to provide reinforcement at home in the form of time, educational background, and resources. This "backup" capacity is related to a family's socioeconomic position. Wealth, occupation, and prior education all tend to be associated with a commitment to high academic performance. Thus the idea that minority children benefit from attending desegregated schools because their peers have values reinforcing cognitive learning is more an argument for social class integration than for racial integration.[13] The peer-group-norm hypothesis is most credible when desegregation occurs at the classroom level where the norms will be most unambiguous and enforceable.

Given that the racial minorities in the United States are disproportionately poor, racial desegregation can often result in increasing the socioeconomic heterogeneity of schools. Nevertheless, insofar as one expects to increase the achievement of minorities because of the peer group norms existing in desegregated schools, attention to racial mix is an imperfect and inadequate strategy. While racial minorities may often be low-income, so may the whites with whom they are integrated.

A fourth explanation for the increases in the academic achievement of minority students that are hypothesized as resulting from desegregation is the stigma theory discussed previously. Segregation, the argument goes, leads to low self-confidence and low aspirations. Yet as we noted earlier, the evidence that segregation leads to low self-esteem and feelings of hopelessness is at best inconclusive and is probably more supportive of the argument that differences in aspirations and self-esteem between blacks and whites are negligible, when social class is controlled. The evidence is also inconclusive with respect to desegregation and its impact on aspirations and self-esteem.

Blacks and other nonwhites might perform better in desegregated schools, a fifth explanation goes, because teachers in such schools expect more academically; that is, the norms found in the classroom are reinforced by the teacher demanding high performance. Why teacher expectations for blacks are higher in predominantly white schools than in predominantly black ones, if indeed they are, is not clear. Logic suggests that to the extent this phenomenon is true it should have little to do with race itself, although there is no question that

---

13. A substantial body of literature supports this theory. *See* U.S. COMMISSION ON CIVIL RIGHTS, RACIAL ISOLATION IN THE PUBLIC SCHOOLS (1967); N. ST. JOHN, *supra* note 8; J. COLEMAN, EQUALITY OF EDUCATIONAL OPPORTUNITY (1966); C. JENCKS, INEQUALITY (1972).

teacher expectations often play an important role in the achievement levels attained by children, particularly with younger children.[14]

A final hypothesis concerning the relationship between higher academic performance minorities and school desegregation is that predominantly white schools tend to have better facilities, greater resources, and—perhaps because they can pay more—better teachers. The *Coleman Report* has thrown some doubt on the importance of school facilities and per capita expenditures to improved student performance.[15] Other studies, however, show that the level of school resources is an important factor in raising achievement levels.[16] In any case, equity in school resources is not necessarily related to racial composition. Thus if desegregation is to be justified because it makes the resources money can buy more accessible to minorities, evidence that this will occur should be part of the criteria employed in drawing desegregation plans.

The foregoing examination of theoretical assumptions as to why, if at all, racial desegregation should lead to improved academic performance of nonwhite children suggests that desegregation plans should go beyond the criterion of black-white ratios and move to other considerations.[17] Among those considerations, the following appear most salient:

(1) The socioeconomic status of the majority of students in a school and within classrooms after desegregation;[18]

(2) the amount of school resources in those schools to which minorities are moved compared to the resources available in schools which are predominantly nonwhite;

(3) the extent to which explicit or tacit racism by teachers in desegregating schools can be mitigated;[19] and

(4) the extent to which racial tolerance can be maximized and racial stereotypes among classmates can be eliminated.

C. The Effect of School Desegregation on Race Relations

We have argued that good race relations in schools are likely to promote academic achievement. Since racial tolerance reduces the likelihood of defensiveness and invidious comparisons across racial lines, it seems likely that desegregation will contribute to the development of strong egos and positive

---

14. *Cf.* Rist, *Student Social Class and Teacher Expectations: The Self Fulfilling Prophecy in Ghetto Education*, 40 HARV. ED. REV. 411 (1970).

15. J. COLEMAN, *supra* note 13, at 312-16.

16. J. GUTHRIE, G. KLEINDORFER, H. LEVIN & R. STOUT, SCHOOLS AND INEQUALITY (1971). *See also* 1 SOUTHERN SCHOOLS 99.

17. *See* N. ST. JOHN, *supra* note 8, at 36-38; Jencks & Brown, *supra* note 12, at 137-40. *Contra*, 2 SOUTHERN SCHOOLS 80.

18. Other measures of family background and family disposition toward learning are needed, but social class is the most readily determined and widely agreed upon surrogate at the present.

19. Orfield, *supra* note 10.

attitudes toward school. But does school desegregation lead to improved race relations and, if so, why?

As with other areas of research on the effects of school desegregation, the evidence here is inconsistent and mixed. And since most of the research has been carried out without any firm hypotheses or theory on which to ground the research design, it is difficult to eliminate the ambiguity of the research findings.[20] Indeed, researchers seem to differ as to what a positive finding is. For example, is preference for friends of one's own race—especially with regard to the minority students—a sign of racial pride or of interracial hostility? Identity with one's own race does not necessarily lead to intolerance of other races, but not enough studies give us the kinds of data needed to uncover the interrelation of these two sets of attitudes.

Perhaps the most serious shortcoming of studies dealing with the effects of desegregation on race relations is that very few of them involve longitudinal research.[21] Attitudes toward persons of another race, especially where older children are involved, on theoretical grounds would be expected to reflect the values and attitudes of their families and their neighborhood peers. To expect that desegregation would have a considerable short-run impact in altering negative racial dispositions is unrealistic. Thus, in a very important sense, we have not yet really begun to test the effects that mixing the races in school might have on racial attitudes.

Nevertheless, the current research findings, as ambiguous as they are, should not be totally dismissed, as there is the possibility that the data now available can provide guidelines to enhance the probability that desegregation will lead to greater racial understanding. Differences in methodology and research design do not completely account for the variations among the studies in the findings.[22] If this is so, we need to search the data for evidence that the conditions under which racial mixing occurred in the schools studied might account for the apparent confusion. It is essential, however, that any conclusions one might draw from this approach—however tentative one claims them to be—make theoretical sense.

We believe that the available evidence does allow one to say that in the short run the mixing of races by itself is, at best, likely to have no positive effect on racial attitudes of either whites or nonwhites, and that the results may be more negative than positive.[23] This latter case is especially true in communities where

---

20. For a detailed attack on the theoretical character of research in this field, see Cohen, *The Effects of Desegregation on Race Relations*, 39 LAW & CONTEMP. PROB. no. 2, at 271 (1975).

21. Longitudinal studies are those which include at least two sets of data gathered over a period of time. Generally what is being measured is the change in a particular characteristic or phenomenon over time. Cross-sectional studies, on the other hand, are those based on data collected at one point in time. Relationships are static between people or groups or whatever is being studied at that point in time.

22. N. ST. JOHN, *supra* note 8, at 71-80.

23. Such are the findings of the recent controversial study by David Armor. Armor, *The Evi-*

desegregation is unpopular and contested by a substantial segment of the community. On the other hand, the data, when coupled with a theoretical understanding of the process by which prejudice and stereotypes are reduced, do allow one to specify some conditions which will increase the likelihood that desegregation will result in better race relations.

A dominant theoretical formulation of the conditions which foster the breakdown of prejudice and racial stereotypes was first formulated by Gordon Allport.[24] This perspective, as elaborated by scholars such as Thomas Pettigrew[25] and Elizabeth Cohen,[26] holds that the chances that school desegregation will improve race relations are greatest when the following conditions exist: (1) contact continues over a period of time, (2) the parties involved are of "equal status" and share common goals, and (3) racial interaction is approved and supported by those whom both races accept as authoritative. Let us examine each of these briefly.

1. *Continuous Long Run Contact*

The period of time necessary for school desegregation to "take" is not ascertainable from existing research. However, much of the research suggests that an increase in interracial understanding is more often the product of desegregation when young rather than middle school or high school children are involved. Moreover, the importance of classroom desegregation which fosters interracial interaction—what some prefer to consider "real integration"—is given additional support by this condition of Allport's theory. A recent major study of southern schools also shows that the longer students attend integrated schools the more positive they are toward other races.[27] This evidence suggests that to anticipate overnight improvement in race relations as a result of racial mixing in schools is unreasonable.

---

dence on Busing, 28 PUB. INTEREST 90 (Summer 1972). Though Armor's study of busing conflicts with other research, and though it has been subject to considerable criticism, it is not difficult to believe the conclusions he reaches with respect to the alienation and intolerance of whites that minority children attending overwhelmingly white schools feel. In the cities studied, nonwhites were bused—often fairly long distances—to schools where teachers and principals had little experience with nonwhite or poor children and where programs did not take into account differences in formal background. Moreover, these nonwhite children often returned home after school in the suburbs to fight their way back into neighborhood peer groups in which most children attended the same schools in central cities where nonwhites tended to possess racial self-consciousness and to advocate aggressive political action in the pursuit of the interests of minorities. This situation dramatizes the potential danger of so-called "token integration" in which small numbers of nonwhite students in a sense "represent" their race in white schools. But it also indicates that a finding that token integration has failed, especially in the kinds of situations Armor studied, is hardly a fair test of the probable effectiveness of desegregation in the long run.

24. G. ALLPORT, THE NATURE OF PREJUDICE (1954).

25. T. PETTIGREW, RACIALLY SEPARATE OR TOGETHER (1971).

26. Cohen, *supra* note 20.

27. 1 SOUTHERN SCHOOLS 53.

2. *Equal Status Cooperative Contact*

Scholars differ on what "equal status" entails. Present research findings do support the notion that desegregation most often results in improved race relations when it involves students of similar social class background. Ability grouping which results in resegregation within the school or classroom would certainly not promote the reduction of racial stereotypes, but then neither would conditions which force students who are less well prepared to compete with those who achieve at a substantially higher level. The impact of ability grouping is a complicated matter and seems to depend on the age and differences in achievement levels of the children involved. There is considerable agreement that ability grouping among elementary children is dysfunctional both in terms of achievement and improving race relations.[28] But as children get older, peers become more salient to their identity and the gap in achievement levels tends to widen. Then ability grouping in certain courses, especially when it involves the self-selection of students, may reduce anxiety among low achievers and foster more favorable interracial attitudes.[29] When correlations between race and achievement levels mean that interracial contact is minimized by ability grouping in certain high school classes, interracial contact will necessarily need to be encouraged in other classes and in other settings before school desegregation can result in improved racial attitudes.

Some educators believe that schools that are competitive and teacher-centered are not good environments in which to foster racial understanding. They urge schools to deemphasize such visible incentives as grades, to increase the use of individualized and multi-aged instructional strategies, and to seek out ways to promote positive interaction among children of different races. The latter goal is based on the recognition that if students have different strengths, conditions of "equal status" will occur when reciprocal dependencies between races on a variety of activities that are valued by the teacher and by other students are developed.[30] On the other hand, if teachers respond to the initial classroom disorder that often accompanies the introduction of children with different habits and expectations to new settings by employing more traditional and discipline oriented methods of instruction and classroom management, the possibilities of improving race relations may be greatly diminished.[31]

3. *Support From Authority*

There is every reason to believe that a crucial variable affecting the impact of desegregation on race relations is the role played by teachers and adminis-

---

28. Orfield, *supra* note 10, at 326.
29. *Id.* at 326-27. *See also* 1 SOUTHERN SCHOOLS 62, 83.
30. *See* Cohen, *supra* note 20, at 278-81.
31. *Cf.* N. St. John & R. Lewis, Children's Interracial Friendships: An Exploration of the Contact Hypothesis, 1973 (unpublished paper at the University of Massachusetts); R. RIST, *supra* note 9.

trators. Where teachers and school officials aggressively seek to improve race relations, establish norms, and deal with problems so as to create an environment that at the least discourages the expression of racial hostility, and at best creates a spirit of commitment to interracial harmony, the impact on race relations is substantial. As St. John has noted:[32]

> Administrative sanction is probably the most important precondition of prejudice-reducing contact in schools. If central office staff is determined that integration shall be complete, the status of all children made equal, and racial competition avoided, the other necessary ingredients of healthy biracial schools probably will follow.

Likewise, in his assessment of the desegregation programs in a number of California schools, Wirt has observed:[33]

> [That] principals appear in about every desegregating system who make a difference to the education of minorities, who bring all constituencies into their planning and implementation, and who produce an educational environment that literally bubbles with the excitement of learning.

D. Equal Access to School Resources and Opportunities for Post-School Success

We have already noted that the process of desegregation does not appear to have any necessary relationship to changes in the quality of school facilities and personnel that children of either race are likely to experience. Therefore, if the objective for desegregating schools is to assure equality of access to facilities, programs, and quality teachers, it is an inefficient tool. In other words, more direct approaches to achieve redistribution of resources are available and these are more feasible politically.

To a substantial extent, the notion that life chances—the probability that one will achieve one's definition of the good life—are enhanced by school desegregation depends on the accuracy of the assumed cause and effect relationships we've already discussed and that these things—academic achievement, psychological benefits, and the reduction of prejudice—lead to success after graduation.

Henry Levin, among others, has argued that the impact schools can have on life chances has been overstated.[34] It is difficult, however, to imagine that minorities would not have a greater chance of achieving their personal objectives if desegregation resulted in a reduction of racial prejudice on the part of

---

32. N. ST. JOHN, *supra* note 8, at 98.

33. F. Wirt, Contemporary School Turbulence and Administrative Authority 24, 1974 (paper presented to Northwestern University Conference on Problems in the Governance of the Learning Community). *See also* Orfield, *supra* note 10, at 322.

34. Levin, *Education, Life Chances and the Courts: The Role of Social Science Evidence*, 39 LAW & CONTEMP. PROB. no. 2, at 217 (1975). Perhaps the best known and most controversial discussion of this issue is in C. JENCKS, *supra* note 13.

whites, an increase in the achievement levels of nonwhites, and a greater understanding by nonwhites of the values of whites. The important questions are whether schools can do these things and under what conditions they can best be achieved.

Conclusion

The issue of school desegregation is likely to be with us for years to come. Despite substantial desegregation in southern and border states in recent years, more than half of black children still attend school in majority black schools. In the North and West less than 30 per cent of black children attend majority white schools.[35] Similarly in states where there is a sizable Hispano-American school population, less than half of these students attend majority white schools—and the proportion who do so is generally declining.[36] That so much of the task of desegregation lies before us, coupled with the growing realization that the desegregation of schools to date has not fulfilled the expectations many have had, suggests it is time for a reconsideration of the basic and underlying assumptions influencing the present approaches.[37]

Such a period of reevaluation is necessary if the desegregation process is to proceed in such a manner as to maximize the probabilities that the ultimate goals of this major systemic effort at social change will be achieved. While most people sympathetic to these goals will have little quarrel with our admonition in principle, the implications may be less widely accepted. Our reconsideration of existing research suggests that when a school district is legally found to be in violation of the fourteenth amendment to the Constitution, the remedy will have to be strongly situation-specific. Thus, it might include only partial desegregation, the preservation of some one-race schools, different strategies to be adopted in different parts of the district, and the implementation of experimental programs in some schools.

Having said this, it is well to recognize that a position advocating specific solutions to local situations generates the potential for another form of controversy—that of the "fairness" of one city's treatment versus another. In short, it raises the issue of distributive justice.[38] If the resolution of the school segregation situation in Atlanta is vastly different from that in Boston, or Indianapolis from Denver, doubts as to the fairness of courts or school ad-

---

35. Actual percentages in 1972 of blacks attending schools where more than 50 per cent of the students are white are: 46.3 in the South, 31.8 in the border states, and 28.3 in the North and West. U.S. Commission on Civil Rights, Twenty Years After Brown: Equality of Educational Opportunity 49 (1975).

36. *Id.* at 52.

37. For an excellent discussion of this point, see Cohen, *Segregation, Desegregation, and* Brown, 12 Society no. 1, at 34 (1974).

38. *Cf.* J. Rawls, A Theory of Justice (1971).

ministrators begin to arise. If Atlanta is allowed to retain several all-black schools, why must Boston eliminate each and every one of theirs? The moral force of the law exists only so long as those to whom it applies believe that they have been justly treated. When they come to believe they have not, the willingness to obey diminishes. There is the inverse situation as well, where one group can come to believe that it has "gotten away with something" others have not. Thus, when white parents in Atlanta become smug because they do not have to bus their own children as do the parents in Boston, the moral position of the law is undermined.

It is the authors' position that in formulating desegregation plans, greater attention should be given to meeting the educational and social needs of a particular community. The courts are beginning to move in this direction, as demonstrated by the development of a separate remedial plan by those intervening on behalf of Hispano Americans in the Denver case. This plan was accepted by the district court as appropriate to the specific problems of the Denver school district.[39]

Of course, more complex and differentiated strategies for achieving school desegregation will not obviate the need for busing. It seems important that the myth that busing is harmful to children be dispelled. The available evidence provides no reason to believe that busing itself—within limits broader than those contemplated by almost all desegregation planners—has negative consequences for children regardless of their race.[40]

While this article has discussed what desegregated schools might accomplish, it is well to remember that "a school case, like a vehicle, can carry only a limited amount of baggage."[41] Schools do not live in a vacuum apart from the rest of society or its institutions. This leads then to the further question of whether policy makers should become involved in other arenas as well to enhance the possibilities for the success of school desegregation. This would entail the development of various strategies, including litigation to assure that there is access to job opportunities, to "open housing," and to other forms of nondiscriminatory treatment over which the schools themselves have no control, but which can affect the pattern of residential segregation and hence school segregation. After *Milliken v. Bradley*,[42] school integration may be impossible to achieve in many of our largest cities unless there is a concomitant move to providing minorities with greater access to housing and jobs in the suburbs.

The manner in which to proceed with school desegregation is surely not a no-win situation. There continue to be options for courts and policy makers

39. Keyes v. School Dist. No. 1, 380 F. Supp. 673, 695-96 (D.C. Colo. 1974).

40. *Cf.* Weinberg, *The Relationship Between School Desegregation and Academic Achievement: A Review of the Research*, 39 LAW & CONTEMP. PROB. no. 2, at 240 (1975).

41. Bradley v. School Bd. of the City of Richmond, 462 F.2d 1058, 1066 (4th Cir. 1972).

42. 418 U.S. 717 (1974).

alike. Likewise, there are a variety of alternative educational philosophies and practices which are being employed as responses to the realities of desegregation. But amid these contingencies and multiple sets of assumptions as to what is to be done, there remains the imperative of a better understanding of the social and educational processes of desegregation. As we believe is apparent from this present volume, there are some dimensions of the issue where we can speak with some certainty and confidence, but there remain others where we have barely begun to understand the complexities and nuances involved.

THE COURTS, SOCIAL SCIENCE, AND SCHOOL DESEGREGATION

Hilton Head Island, South Carolina
August 20, 1974

CONFERENCE ATTENDEES

Carlos M. Alcala, Interim Director of Educational Litigation, Mexican-American Legal Defense and Educational Fund; co-author, *Project Report: De Jure Segregation of Chicanos in Texas Schools*, 7 HARV. CIV. RIGHTS—CIV. LIB. L. REV. 307 (1972); J.D. Harvard Law School.

Marguerite R. Barnett, Assistant Professor of Politics & Public Affairs, Princeton University; co-editor, POLITICAL & ECONOMIC STRATEGIES FOR BLACK PEOPLE IN THE COMING DECADES; Ph.D. in Political Science, University of Chicago.

Derrick A. Bell, Professor of Law, Harvard University; author, RACE, RACISM AND AMERICAN LAW (1973); formerly Director of Western Center on Law and Poverty; special assistant to the Secretary of the Department of Health, Education, and Welfare; attorney, the NAACP Legal Defense and Education Fund, Inc.; attorney, the United States Department of Justice. LL.B. University of Pittsburgh School of Law.

Norman J. Chachkin, Staff Attorney, NAACP Legal Defense and Educational Fund, Inc.; co-author, *Metropolitan School Desegregation: Evolving Law*, 10 INTEGRATED ED. 13 (1972); formerly in private practice in Arkansas; LL.B. New York University Law School.

Elizabeth G. Cohen, Professor, School of Education and Department of Sociology, Stanford University; Director of the Environment for the Teaching Program at Stanford School of Education; author, A NEW APPROACH TO APPLIED RESEARCH: RACE AND EDUCATION (1970) and of numerous articles on interracial interaction and on the effects of teacher behavior and classroom characteristics on children; Ph.D. in Sociology, Harvard University.

James P. Comer, Associate Professor of Psychiatry and Associate Dean for Student Affairs, Yale University School of Medicine; Chairman, American Psychiatric Association Committee of Black Psychiatrists; author, BEYOND BLACK AND WHITE (1972); author of other articles and books on child development, racism, mental health, and inner city schools; formerly staff member of National Institute of Mental Health; M.D. Howard University; M.A. in Public Health, University of Michigan.

Robert Crain, The Rand Corporation; Director of Emergency School Assistance Program Study, SOUTHERN SCHOOLS: AN EVALUATION OF THE EFFECTS OF THE EMERGENCY SCHOOL ASSISTANCE PROGRAM AND OF SCHOOL DESEGREGATION; co-author, POLITICAL STRATEGIES IN NORTHERN SCHOOL DESEGREGATION (1973); DISCRIMINATION, PERSONALITY, AND SOCIAL ACHIEVEMENT (1972); formerly with Center for Metropolitan Studies, John Hopkins University.

Ronald R. Edmonds, Director, Center for Urban Studies, Harvard University Graduate School of Education; author, with others, of *A Black Response to Christopher Jencks' Inequality and Certain Other Issues*, 43 HARV. ED. REV. 76 (1973); author of other articles on school desegregation; formerly Assistant Superintendent of the Michigan Department of Public Instruction; Human Relations Director of the Ann Arbor Public Schools; Certificate of Advanced Study, Career Program, Harvard Graduate School of Education.

Edgar G. Epps, Marshall Field IV Professor of Urban Education, University of Chicago; co-author, BLACK CONSCIOUSNESS, IDENTITY AND ACHIEVEMENT: A STUDY OF BLACK COLLEGE STUDENTS (forthcoming); author, FAMILY AND ACHIEVEMENT: A STUDY OF THE RELATION OF FAMILY BACKGROUND TO ACHIEVEMENT ORIENTATION AND PERFORMANCE AMONG URBAN NEGRO HIGH SCHOOL STUDENTS (1969); editor of BLACK STUDENTS IN WHITE SCHOOLS (1972), RACE RELATIONS: CURRENT PERSPECTIVES (1973), and of CULTURAL PLURALISM 1974; past Associate Editor of the *American Sociological Review*; formerly Director of the Division of Behavioral Science Research, Professor of Sociology, and Chairman of the Division of Social Sciences at Tuskegee Institute; Professor, Department of Psychology and the Survey Research Center, University of Michigan; Professor of Sociology, Florida A & M University; Ph.D. in Sociology, Washington State University.

Reynolds Farley, Associate Professor and Chairman of the Department of Sociology and Associate Director, Population Studies Center, University of Michigan; author of numerous articles on demographic studies bearing on racial issues, two of his most recent appearing in *American Sociological Review* and the *American Journal of Sociology*; formerly Assistant Professor of Sociology, Duke University; Ph.D. in Sociology, University of Chicago.

Owen M. Fiss, Professor of Law, Yale University; author, *School Desegregation: The Uncertain Path of the Law*, 4 PHILOSOPHY OF PUB. AFFAIRS 3 (1974), *The Charlotte-Mecklenburg Case—Its Significance for Northern Desegregation*, 38 U. CHI. L. REV. 697 (1971); *Racial Imbalance in the Public Schools: The Constitutional Concepts*, 78 HARV. L. REV. 564 (1965); formerly Professor of Law, University of Chicago; Special Assistant to the Assistant Attorney General, Civil Rights Division, United States Department of Justice; law clerk to Associate Justice William J. Brennan, Jr., United States Supreme Court; law clerk to Thurgood Marshall, then United States Circuit Judge, U.S. Court of Appeals for the Second Circuit; LL.B. Harvard Law School.

Gordon Foster, Professor of Education, Graduate School of Education and Director of the Florida School Desegregation Consulting Center, University of Miami; author of articles on desegregation in *The Urban Review* and *Harvard Educational Review*; conducted desegregation plan studies in 17 states and 20 Florida school districts, master plan studies for 20 school districts in Pennsylvania; member of Desegregation Panel requested by the Federal District Court to prepare a comprehensive plan for metropolitan Detroit; formerly held faculty appointments at Miami University and Ohio State University; Director of Southwestern Ohio Educational Research Council and Central Office Research

Associate for the Cincinnati Schools; taught secondary schools; Ph.D. in Education Administration, Ohio State University.

F. Chris Garcia, Associate Professor of Political Science, University of New Mexico; author, POLITICAL SOCIALIZATION OF CHICANO CHILDREN: A COMPARATIVE STUDY WITH ANGLOS IN CALIFORNIA SCHOOLS (1973); LA CAUSA POLITICA: A CHICANO POLITICS READER (1974); *Orientations of Mexican American and Anglo Children Toward the U.S. Political Community*, 53 SOCIAL SCI. Q. 814 (1973); editor, CHICANO POLITICS: READINGS (1973); and author of other articles on political influences, political participation, and the political socialization of Mexican-American children; previous teaching appointments at California State University at Fullerton, Indiana University, and University of California at Davis; Ph.D. in Political Science, University of California at Davis.

Willis D. Hawley, Associate Professor, Department of Policy Sciences and Political Science, and Associate Director, Institute of Policy Sciences and Public Affairs, Duke University; author, NONPARTISAN ELECTIONS AND THE CASE FOR PARTY POLITICS (1973); BLACKS AND METROPOLITAN GOVERNANCE: THE STAKES OF REFORM (1972); editor, IMPROVING THE QUALITY OF URBAN MANAGEMENT (1974), THE SEARCH FOR COMMUNITY POWER (1968); previously taught at Yale University; former assistant city manager; research associate at the Institute of Governmental Studies of University of California at Berkeley; assistant to the Vice President of the University of California; Ph.D. in Political Science, University of California at Berkeley.

Nathaniel R. Jones, General Counsel, National Association for the Advancement of Colored People; formerly practicing attorney in Ohio; Deputy General Counsel of the President's Commission on Civil Disorders; Assistant United States attorney for the Northern District of Ohio; co-chairman of the National Civilian-Military Task Force on Military Justice; LL.B. Youngstown University.

Brian Landsberg, Chief, Education Section, Civil Rights Division, Justice Department.

Betsy Levin, Associate Professor of Law, Duke University; editor, FUTURE DIRECTIONS FOR SCHOOL FINANCE REFORM (1974); author, *Recent Developments in the Law of Equal Educational Opportunity*, 4 J. LAW & ED. 411 (1975); *Alternatives to the Present System of Financing Schools: Their Problems and Prospects*, 61 GEO. L.J. 879 (1973); co-author, THE FINANCING OF SCHOOLS IN ILLINOIS (1973), THE HIGH COST OF EDUCATION IN THE CITIES: AN ANALYSIS OF THE PURCHASING POWER OF THE EDUCATIONAL DOLLAR (1973), THE POLITICAL LIMITS TO EDUCATION FINANCE REFORM (1973), SCHOOLS AND TAXES IN NORTH CAROLINA (1973), PAYING FOR PUBLIC SCHOOLS: ISSUES OF SCHOOL FINANCE IN CALIFORNIA (1972), PUBLIC SCHOOL FINANCE: PRESENT DISPARITIES AND FISCAL ALTERNATIVES (1972); former teaching positions at Georgetown University Law Center and Yale Law School; Director of Education Studies, The Urban Institute; Special Assistant and White House Fellow to Hon. Arthur J. Goldberg; law clerk to Simon E. Sobeloff, U.S. Circuit Judge for the Court of Appeals for the Fourth Circuit; LL.B. Yale Law School.

Henry M. Levin, Associate Professor, School of Education and Department of Economics, Stanford University; author, *Vouchers and Social Equity*, 5 CHANGE no. 8, at 29 (1973), *The Costs to the Nation of Inadequate Education*, a report for Senate Select Committee on Equal Educational Opportunity, monograph on educational vouchers (in preparation); editor (and co-author of chapter) of COMMUNITY CONTROL OF SCHOOLS (1970); joint author, SCHOOLS AND INEQUALITY (1971); author of numerous other articles on educational finance; vice president of the American Educational Research Association; former Research Associate in Social Economics, The Brookings Institution, Associate Research Scientist in the Graduate School of Public Administration at New York University; Ph.D. in Economics, Rutgers University.

Constantine C. Menges, Deputy Assistant Secretary for Education, Department of Health, Education, and Welfare; author of articles on the evaluation of federal education programs; other positions in HEW; staff member, The Rand Corporation; former assistant professor of political science at University of Wisconsin; staff of the Institute of War and Peace Studies, Columbia University, and the Hudson Institute.

Jane R. Mercer, Associate Professor of Sociology, University of California at Riverside; author, LABELLING THE MENTALLY RETARDED: CLINICAL AND SOCIAL SYSTEMS PERSPECTIVES ON MENTAL RETARDATION (1973); joint author, *Racial/Ethnic Segregation and Desegregation in American Public Education*, 73 NAT'L SOCIAL STUD. YRBK. pt. 2, at 274 (1974); author, *Policy Statement on Assessment Procedures and the Rights of Children*, 44 HARV. ED. REV. 125 (1974), *IQ: The Lethal Label*, 38 ED. DIGEST 17 (1973), *Sociocultural Factors in Labeling Mental Retardates*, 48 PEABODY J. ED. 188 (1970); author of numerous other articles on factors contributing to adjustment and achievement in racially desegregated schools and evaluations of desegregated education; Associate Editor of *Sociology of Education* and Consulting Editor for the *American Journal of Mental Deficiency*; Ph.D. in Sociology, University of Southern California.

Gary Orfield, Research Associate, The Brookings Institution, 1972-73 Scholar-in-Residence, U.S. Commission on Civil Rights; author, THE RECONSTRUCTION OF SOUTHERN EDUCATION: THE SCHOOLS AND THE 1964 CIVIL RIGHTS ACT (1969), CONGRESSIONAL POWER: CONGRESS AND SOCIAL CHANGE (1975), *Federal Policy, Local Power, and Metropolitan Segregation*, 89 POL. SCI. Q. 777 (1974-75), *School Integration and its Academic Critics*, 5 CIVIL RIGHTS DIGEST 2 (Summer 1973); formerly held teaching positions at the University of Virginia and Princeton University; Ph.D. in Political Science, University of Chicago.

Thomas F. Pettigrew, Professor of Social Psychology and Sociology, Harvard University; author or co-author of seven books on race relations, including RACIALLY SEPARATE OR TOGETHER (1971) and A PROFILE OF THE NEGRO AMERICAN (1964); other books in press or preparation, including SOCIAL PSYCHOLOGY AND AMERICAN RACE RELATIONS; author of many articles on race relations and education; former president of the Society for the Psychological Study of Social Problems, and Associate Editor of the *American Sociological Review*; member of the 1967 White House Task Force on Education; Ph.D. Social Psychology, Harvard University.

Frank T. Read, Dean, University of Tulsa Law School; co-author, LET THEM BE JUDGED: THE JUDICIAL INTEGRATION OF THE DEEP SOUTH (forthcoming), former Professor of Law and Associate Dean, Duke University; J.D. Duke Law School.

Sanford J. Rosen, Legal Director, Mexican-American Legal Defense and Educational Fund; author, *The Law and Racial Discrimination in Employment*, 53 CALIF. L. REV. 729 (1965), *Equalizing Access to Legal Education: Special Programs for Law Students Not Admissible by Ordinary Criteria*, 1970 U. TOLEDO L. REV. 321; former Assistant Legal Director, ACLU; Professor of Law, University of Maryland Law School; law clerk to Simon E. Sobeloff, U.S. Circuit Judge, U.S. Court of Appeals for the Fourth Circuit; LL.B. Yale Law School.

Joshua L. Smith, Program Officer, The Ford Foundation; author, FREE SCHOOLS: PANDORA'S BOX?; co-editor, REMOVING BARRIERS TO HUMANENESS IN THE HIGH SCHOOLS (1971); former Executive Secretary of the Citizens Advisory Committee on Racial Equality in Education (in Pittsburgh), high school administrator, and public school teacher; Ed.D. Harvard Graduate School of Education.

William L. Taylor, Director, Center for National Policy Review and Adjunct Professor of Law, Catholic University School of Law; author, HANGING TOGETHER: EQUALITY IN AN URBAN NATION (1971), *Federal Civil Rights Laws: Can They Be Made to Work?*, 39 GEO. WASH. L. REV. 971 (1971), *Legal Battle for Metropolitanism*, 81 SCHOOL REV. 331 (1975), *The Supreme Court and Urban Reality: A Tactical Analysis of* Milliken v. Bradley, 21 WAYNE L. REV. 751 (1975), *The Justice Department and Race Relations*, 12 INTEGRATED ED. no. 2, at 5 (1974), *Law as a Catalyst for Change: The Mississippi Experience*, 50 N.C.L. REV. 1038 (1972), and many other articles on civil rights, school desegregation, and busing; former Director of the U.S. Commission on Civil Rights; Secretary of the Sub-Cabinet Group on Civil Rights; Staff Attorney for the NAACP Legal Defense and Educational Fund, Inc.; LL.B. Yale Law School.

Meyer Weinberg, Professor of History, City Colleges of Chicago, and Lecturer, School of Education, Northwestern University; Editor, *Integrated Education*; currently preparing third edition of DESEGREGATION RESEARCH: AN APPRAISAL, and second edition of a bibliography on EDUCATION OF THE MINORITY CHILD; numerous other articles and books on school desegregation; M.A. University of Chicago.

Frederick M. Wirt, Director, Policy Sciences Graduate Program at University of Maryland, Baltimore County; co-author, THE POLITICAL WEB OF AMERICAN SCHOOLS (1972), THE POLITICS OF SOUTHERN EQUALITY: LAW AND SOCIAL CHANGE IN A MISSISSIPPI COUNTY (1971); co-editor, SCHOOL DESEGREGATION IN THE NORTH: THE CHALLENGE AND EXPERIENCE (1968), THE SEARCH FOR COMMUNITY POWER (2d ed. 1974); joint author, ON THE CITY'S RIM: POLITICS AND POLICY IN SUBURBIA (1972); editor of a series of books on public education; former Director of the Institute for School Desegregation Problems at Berkeley; Research Political Scientist, Institute of Governmental Studies and Lecturer, School of Education, University of California at Berkeley; former member of faculty, Denison University; Ph.D. in Political Science, Ohio State University.

Hon. John M. Wisdom, United States Circuit Judge, United States Court of Appeals for the Fifth Circuit since his appointment by President Eisenhower in 1957; formerly partner in Wisdom, Stone, Pigman & Benjamin; LL.B. Tulane University.

Mark G. Yudof, Professor of Law, University of Texas; co-author, EDUCATIONAL POLICY AND THE LAW (1974), *Serrano in the Political Arena*, 2 YALE REV. LAW & SOCIAL ACTION 143 (1971), Rodriguez v. San Antonio Independent School District: *Gathering the Ayes of Texas—The Politics of School Finance Reform*, 38 LAW & CONTEMP. PROB. 383 (1974); author, *Property Tax in Texas under State and Federal Law*, 51 TEXAS L. REV. 885 (1973), *Equal Educational Opportunity and the Courts*, 51 TEXAS L. REV. 411 (1973), *Indian Education: Federal Funds for Public Schools*, 7 INEQUALITY IN ED. 20 (1972); former Research Associate and Senior Staff Attorney, Center for Law and Education, Harvard University; Lecturer, Harvard School of Education; law clerk to Robert A. Ainsworth, Jr., U.S. Circuit Judge, Court of Appeals for the Fifth Circuit; LL.B. University of Pennsylvania Law School.